CHESS:

THEORY AND PRACTICE

CHESS:

THEORY AND PRACTICE.

CONTAINING

THE LAWS AND HISTORY OF THE GAME,

TOGETHER WITH

AN ANALYSIS OF THE OPENINGS, AND A TREATISE

ON END GAMES.

HOWARD STAUNTON.

EDITED BY

ROBERT B. WORMALD.

GYAN

Published by

Gyan Publishing House
5, Ansari Road
Daryaganj, New Delhi-110002
Phone: 011-47034999, 9811692060
E-mail: books@gyanbooks.com

Distribution Network
gyanbooks.com
India, USA, Canada, UK, Australia, France

ISBN : 978-81-212-9550-5 (PB)
First Published, 1876

2nd Impression 2023

Printed at: Gyan Press, Delhi.

CHESS: THEORY AND PRACTICE
Author: HOWARD STAUNTON, EDITED BY ROBERT B. WORMALD

CHESS:

THEORY AND PRACTICE.

CONTAINING

THE LAWS AND HISTORY OF THE GAME,

TOGETHER WITH

AN ANALYSIS OF THE OPENINGS, AND A TREATISE ON END GAMES.

BY THE LATE

HOWARD STAUNTON.

EDITED BY

ROBERT B. WORMALD.

1876.

IT WAS THE AUTHOR'S WISH TO INSCRIBE

THIS LITTLE VOLUME, TO

HIS FAITHFUL FRIEND,

J. RIMINGTON WILSON, Esq.

PREFACE.

In preparing the manuscript of this little work for the press, I have been guided by one leading consideration.

It has been my main object to make neither alterations nor additions, except when absolutely necessary, but to give the book to the reader, as nearly as possible, as it left the late Mr. Staunton's hands.

Its shortcomings, I feel sure, will be pardoned, when it is remembered that it never had the advantage of the talented author's revision.

R. B. W.

CONTENTS.

BOOK III.

SOME ACCOUNT

OF THE

ORIGIN AND HISTORY OF THE GAME OF CHESS.

It has now been proved, beyond the possibility of question, by the admirable researches of Dr. Duncan Forbes, that the original authors of the Chess-board and its arcana were the Hindoos. All the best modern writers upon the subject agree in admitting this conclusion, though some may still assert for the traditional claims of other nations more validity than they justly merit.

Previously to the inquiries of Dr. Forbes, writers on Chess gave us a wide choice as to the seat of its invention. The Persians, the Greeks, the Egyptians, the Chinese, the Hindoos, the Arabians, the Araucanians, the Jews, the Scythians, the Babylonians—nay, even the Irish and the Welsh, were indifferently credited with the possible contrivance of the art. In many of these cases the choice was sufficiently absurd as to the period when Chess was first played; but Chess authors had no definite idea except that the game was of very remote antiquity. Such tribes as the Scythians, the Irish, and the Welsh were in a state of rude barbarism; and existing literature shows that neither the classical nations nor those with which they were intimately associated had any acquaintance with the game. The Romans and the Greeks had their *ludus latrunculorum*, variously designated, but its loftiest pretension was to belong to the same class of sedentary sport as backgammon. Reasoning simply by exclusion, we should have ample ground for saying that the game could not have originated among the Western nations. The writings of classical authors are quite decisive on this point, for they would certainly not have failed to notice or describe it, had it been practised within the sphere of their observation.

All obscurity has, however, been dispelled by Dr. Forbes. Following up the labours of Sir William Jones and others, that writer has discovered in Hindoo literature, dating three thousand years before the Christian epoch, the description of a game which manifestly represents, in a primitive form, the modern game of Chess. This is not an occasion for entering into a discussion as to Brahminical documents. It is sufficient to say that they were for ages concealed from the knowledge of all except members of the caste to whose keeping they were confided. It was not until the latter part of the last century that, through the exertions and influence of Warren Hastings, European inquirers obtained access to the mine of ancient knowledge and tradition thus stored up. But now any scholar who is so inclined may make himself thoroughly conversant with the habits, diversions, romances, and poetical effusions of the early Hindoos.

According to the Brahmins, Chess was invented in the second age of the world by the wife of Ravan, King of Lanka (the capital of Ceylon), in order to amuse him with a kind of image of war while his chief city was closely besieged by an enemy. Similarly, the Chinese annals tell us that an inventive Mandarin, two thousand years ago, while on a military expedition that severely tried the endurance of his soldiers, devised the game of Chess as an exercise which would at once amuse and inspire them with martial ardour.

I need hardly repeat the story of Palamedes, who is related to have done, at the siege of Troy, as the Mandarin did in China; nor need I remark that it is wholly impossible for Chess either to have originated in the manner assumed, or to have been accepted off-hand by a camp of uneducated soldiery.

Dismissing these fables as creations of the fancy, we come to the true history of the game. This may be divided into three epochs. The first is that of the ancient Hindoo game, called *Chaturanga*, presently to be described, which carries us back to the most ancient period of Hindoo literature, and comes down to the fifteenth century of our era. The second epoch extends to the sixteenth century of our era, up to which date the moves and powers of the Chess-men remained principally as in the Chaturanga, though the men were ranked in two armies instead of four, and two of the Kings were transformed into Queens. In the third, or modern epoch, the moves of the Queen and of the Bishop have been greatly extended, and the privilege of Castling has been introduced. The game has therefore undergone a gradual improvement as players have brought to bear upon it their ingenuity and experience. In the early Hindoo game, termed Chaturanga, the board was constructed as it now is, of sixty-four squares, but the game was played by four persons, each having a differently-coloured little army, composed of a King, a Bishop, a Knight and a Rook (to use modern nomenclature), and four Pawns, as shown in the following diagram :—

BLACK.

YELLOW.

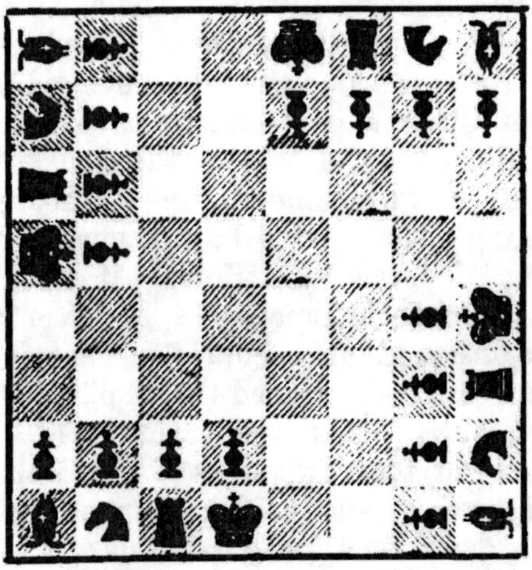

RED.

GREEN.

In this primitive game the two opposite players were allied as partners. The name of it, *Chaturanga*, signified four parts—*chatur*, "four," and *anga*, "a member," or component part. As the game was an imitation of war, so the men were endowed with such military qualities as Hindoo warfare would naturally suggest. The Piece stationed next the King was the Elephant—an important auxiliary in Indian warfare—the Horse, which occupied the adjoining square, represented the cavalry, while the Piece in the corner was the Ship—typifying the vessels which fought on the Ganges and other great rivers of the country—and the four Pawns were the infantry. The names of the Pieces—chosen in accordance with these attributes—have, in some measure, survived even to the present day. Our word *Rook*, for example, is no doubt the *Roka*, or Ship of the Hindoos; for by no other supposition can a meaning be ascribed to it. The powers of the ancient Pieces differed materially from those now in use. The Knight and Rook moved as they do at present, their privileges having remained undisturbed for a period of five thousand years. The King could move one square in all directions, as he can still, time having since given him and deprived him of one move similar to that of the Knight, and allowed him the right of Castling. The Bishop moved on diagonal rows of squares, as in the present day, but only to the third square from the one on which he stood at the time of being played. The move and power of the Pawn were then the same as now, except that the right of advancing two squares on the first move did not exist.

The game of Chaturanga seems to have been played by the throw of dice, for the text of the Sanskrit "Purana" reads—"If, on throwing the die, the number should turn up five, the King or one of the Pawns must move; if four, the Elephant; if three, the Horse; if two, the Ship." This element of chance imparted a spirit of gambling to the game, and instances are recorded in the primæval annals of India, where princes sacrificed the whole of their domains at the Chess-board. The die, however, was afterwards discarded, probably at the instigation of the Brahmans, whose notions of decorum would have prohibited indulging in a pastime which rested on a gambling basis.

I cannot attempt in a brief sketch like this to explain the details of a game conducted on the principles of Chaturanga. Those who are disposed to make themselves masters of this abstruse topic must be referred to the work, already mentioned, of Dr. Forbes. In this, many of the difficulties which puzzled earlier writers have been cleared away, but some still appear to be insurmountable.

The next form of the game met with in history is the *Shatranj* of the Arabs and Persians. This term is nothing more nor less than the Hindoo Chaturanga rendered conformable to the Arabic idiom. Sir William Jones is of opinion that the same word is the parent of the Italian *scacci*, the French *échecs*, the German *Schach*, and the English *chess*, *check*, and *exchequer*. Dr. Forbes, however, contends that these words are derived from the Arabic *Shah*, a King. Be this point determined as it may, there can be no question that the Hindoo game was at some unrecorded period (probably after the Sanscrit became a dead language) converted by the Hindoos themselves into the form which it presented when first introduced by them to the Arabs. An inspection of the foregoing diagram (page 3), will show how readily the Chaturanga resolves itself into this shape. Two of the sets of forces being combined into one army, the only essential change necessary is that one of each of the two Kings be shorn of regal prerogatives and turned into an officer. This transformation being naturally made, the Piece was designated by the Hindoos a *Mantri*, and by the Arabs a *Farzin*, each term signifying "monitor" or "counsellor." One of the previously allied Kings became the "right-hand man" of the other, and held a chief place in the forces by which royalty was surrounded. The Rook and the Bishop exchanged places, retaining their power and range, and the transformation from Chaturanga to Shatranj was complete.

The best and earliest account of this game is that given by the Bagdad poet, Firdausi, a manuscript of whose writings in the British Museum, transcribed A.D. 1486, is the one chiefly followed by Dr. Forbes.

This author relates that "once upon a time" an ambassador came from the Sovereign of Hind (or Hindostan) to the Persian monarch, Kisra Naushirawan, bearing costly presents, and, above all, a magnificent chess-board. The ambassador presented a letter also, which stated that if Naushirawan could in seven days discover the principles and practice of the game, the Hindoo monarch would pay him tribute, but, if he failed to do so, tribute would be demanded on the other side. From this difficulty the King of Persia, it is alleged, was delivered by the miraculous acuteness of his chief counsellor, who, by the mere inspection of the board and men, discovered the moves and powers of the forces. As these are entirely conventional, this is, of course, impossible, but the anecdote is valuable, as showing that modern Chess was originally brought from India, and as affording an interesting account of the structure of the game and the moves of the men.

The Arabs and Persians have given their own version also of the first introduction of the Shatranj into India. A manuscript in the possession of the Asiatic Society, apparently of about the date A.D. 1400 (as it gives eighteen Chess problems, which occurred in the play of Ali Shatranji, the Philidor of the Court of Timur), ascribes the origin of the game to a Greek sage named Hermes. The writer says that it was brought into Hindostan by Alexander the Great, with whom and his officers it was a favourite recreation, but was specially introduced into practice by a native Prince named Sassa. This Sassa is represented to have been a man of great parts, and to have recommended Chess to three sovereign rulers as a consolation at periods of distress. The three stories are evidently variations only of one legend, that probably being of a wholly imaginary character. The tale comes to us embellished with an addendum which bears a striking family resemblance to anecdotes of a more recent date, and shows that arithmetical puzzles were not unknown to the ancients. It is related that when Sassa had taught the game to one of the monarchs he was offered his own choice of a reward, and he then requested the seemingly modest one of a grain of corn placed on the first square of the board, two on the second, four on the third, and so on, doubling the number each time until every square was covered. The quantity of corn thus reckoned he would be satisfied with for his guerdon. The King, smiling at his moderation, readily granted his demand; but when the measure of corn came to be computed it was found to be more than the whole kingdom could raise in a year. It was no part of Sassa's intention to take advantage of the King's ignorance in the matter. He simply put his request in the f rm adopted to show how easily monarchs may be induced to promise more than they can spare. Arithmeticians have computed that the number of grains required to satisfy

Sassa's request would suffice to cover the whole earth, land and water, eight grains deep.

Though the Arabic and Persian authors were in a mist as to the original invention of Chess, and could only tell that the game came to their country from India, they were much more specific when treating on the game itself. There can be no doubt that, in the times with which we have been familiarised by those marvellous fictions, the "Arabian Nights' Entertainments," and for some centuries following, Chess was ardently studied and skilfully played in the land of the Caliphs. Dr. Forbes has given the particulars of four manuscripts relating to this subject in public libraries in London. The first, an Arabic MS.—the others are Persian—enumerates five classes into which players are divided, and gives a variety of examples of openings and end-games. The second contains a treatise on the openings and on end-games, together with some curiosities, such as the feat of the Knight in occupying each one of the sixty-four squares of the board in the same number of moves; directions for playing without seeing the Chess-board, and a collection of game-endings, with their solutions, represented on diagrams. The third is a kind of Encyclopædia, with a concise treatise on Chess among its contents. It is entitled "Treasures of the Sciences." The fourth authority recited by Dr. Forbes gives an account of "Timur's Great Game," of the invention of Chess in India, of the relative value of the Chess-men, of the gradations of odds in play and of drawn games. It contains besides, sixty-four diagrams of interesting positions unaccompanied with solutions. The best of the end-games are by Khwaja Ali Shatranji, most of them being the result of actual play. The rest profess to have been originated by the Caliph Mutasim Billah and other illustrious players. The author pretends to be a great proficient himself, though the work appears to contain nothing of his own production. In the preface he announces that he is about to explain the openings—which he declares to be "the very root and foundation of good play"—the conduct of games when they have been opened; stratagems by which the game can be won or drawn in situations where it appears desperate; the value of the Chess-forces, "without knowing which you cannot be a player;" the grades of odds; positions which lead to a drawn game, with the Knight's puzzle and an exposition of the Pieces which draw the game against certain other Pieces, "so that you may not uselessly prolong a contest in such circumstances."

Before concluding the description of these interesting works, which from their precision and comprehensiveness, might have been written in the present day, it should be said that, as with many other things in early times, Chess among the Asiatics had its typical as well as actual qualities. The following is from the "Treasures of the Sciences:"—"In India they test a person's fitness for the duties of mayor or minister by making two people play chess in his presence. If he looks on, and speaks not a word, they put confidence in him; but if he indulges in remarks on the moves, and gives advice to the players, he is considered to be deficient in discretion, and unsuited to the office." A similar instance of turning the game to account may be read in the "History of the Goths, Swedes, and Vandals," by Olaus Magnus, where illustrious northmen are represented as selecting suitable husbands for their daughters by means of Chess and Tables.

Some account here of the game itself, as expounded by the Arab and Persian writers, will probably be interesting. But in order that the reader may be able to follow the description, it is needful that he be exactly acquainted with the moves and powers then exercised by the chessmen. This knowledge can perhaps best be conveyed in the shape of two Arab problems. The first, the most ancient Chess problem on record, was composed by Mutasim Billah, Caliph of Bagdad from A.D. 833 to 842. He was the third son and third successor of the famous Haroun-al-Raschid, himself a good player, as was each of his family circle. The second was constructed by Khwaja Ali Shatranji, a great Chess authority, as his cognomen imports, and a man who was in high favour with Timur, at whose court he often resided, and with whom he frequently played. When analysing these positions, the student must bear in mind that the Queen could formerly only move or capture on one of the four squares adjoining her own, and that only *diagonally*, so that she commanded none but squares of the colour on which she stood. He must recollect also that a Bishop formerly could move and attack only the square next but one to that on which he stood, in a *diagonal* line, but he attacked or protected the square, notwithstanding a man stood on the intervening square; and in moving to, or capturing on the square, he leapt over the next diagonal square.

Problem by the Caliph Mutasim Billah.

BLACK.

WHITE.

White to move and checkmate on the ninth move.

Solution.

WHITE.	BLACK.
1. Q. R. takes Kt. (ch.)	1. Kt. takes R.
2. R. to Q. B's 8th (ch.)	2. K. to Q. R's 2nd.*
3. Kt. to Q. Kt.'s 5th (ch.)	3. K. must take Kt.
4. R. to Q. B's 6th (ch.)	4. K. must take Kt.
5. K. B. to Q's 7th (ch.)	5. K. to Q. Kt.'s 5th.
6. R. to Q. Kt.'s 6th (ch.)	6. K. to Q. B's 4th.
7. R. to Q. Kt.'s 5th (ch.)	7. K. to Q's 5th.
8. P. to K's 3rd (ch.)	8. K. to Q's 6th.
9. B. to K. B's 5th, giving checkmate.	

* Had he taken the Rook with the Bishop, as he could have done, by leaping the Bishop over the Knight, he would have been checkmated by the White Knights in two moves.

Problem by Ali Shatranji.

BLACK.

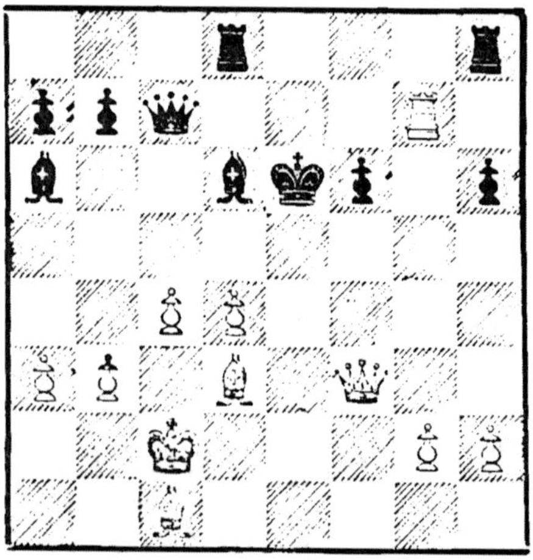

WHITE.

White to play and checkmate in eight moves.

Solution.

WHITE.	BLACK.
1. P. checks.	1. K. to K's 4th.
2. R. to K's 7th (ch.)	2. K. to K. B's 5th.*
3. R. to K's 4th (ch.)	3. K. to Kt.'s 4th.
4. R. to Kt.'s 4th (ch.)	4. K. to R's 4th.
5. R. to Kt.'s 7th.	5. P. to K. B's 4th (*best*).
6. B. takes K. B's P.	6. K. to R's 5th.
7. Q. to Kt.'s 4th.	7. Anything.
8. Kt. P. gives checkmate.	

Any player—after mastering the moves and powers of the Chess-men—who will take the trouble of playing over these two end-games will acquire a competent acquaintance with the game as it was conducted prior to the modifications introduced by the great European masters. As no actually played games have been handed down to us in Arab literature, it is fortunate that positions of this kind have been

* If to Q's 5th, he is mated on the 5th move.

preserved, for they afford a clear insight into the form and course of ancient Chess.

Considering that the Pawns could only advance one square on their first move, and that the Queen and Bishop had such restricted scope, the commencement of the ancient game must have been wearisomely slow. To obviate this disadvantage, good players adopted the expedient of playing eight or ten moves at once on each side, and that was termed, making their battle array.

A point to be noticed in this early game is that, as the Queens were originally placed on opposite coloured squares (all the Pieces stood as they do now), they could never attack or capture each other, for their diagonal move required the one always to traverse White squares and the other Black. Hence the line found in a Latin poem on Chess of the twelfth century:—

"Nam Regina non valebit impedire alteram."

A close examination of the board will reveal also that their peculiar action gave the Bishops a diocese of eight squares each, no one of them falling within the range of another Bishop. The accompanying diagram exhibits this feature of the two Kings' Bishops.

BLACK.

WHITE.

With respect to the Pawns, the Arab game allowed of their conversion, when they had reached the eighth square, into the Farzin, or Queen only, which was, next to the Bishop, the least powerful Piece of the Chess army. This was a deviation from the Chaturanga of the Hindoos. There might, however, be as many Queened Pawns as could be acquired, and in several of the Oriental manuscripts there are end-games presenting two or three Farzins on either side.

The Arabs made no distinction of colour in the squares of their Chess-board, as was, indeed, and is quite needless for the game, though the differences now observed are serviceable in point of convenience, and not undeserving consideration as a matter of ornament.

The players of this race we find to have been divided into five classes:—The givers of odds; those who received only a Pawn; those who received the Queen; those who accepted the Knight; and those who took the Rook. They had among them a number of nice distinctions as to the various odds of which the game is susceptible, but these are not of much present interest. The author of the fourth manuscript mentioned above, says of the extreme allowance, "To give any odds beyond the Rook can apply only to women, children, and tyros." Nevertheless it appears that there were strong-minded women in those days as well as in these. A very elegant problem illustrates the following pretty well-known anecdote:—Two Persian princes were playing at Chess, and the one who had the White men offered his favourite wife, Dilaram, as his stake upon the game. The contest had nearly reached its end, when the player who had risked the lady on the issue was threatened with checkmate next move unless he could find some remedy. As he hesitated in the agony of despair, Dilaram, who had eagerly watched the combat from behind the screen of gauze which separated male from female in Eastern households, cried out, Sacrifice, O prince, your Rooks, and save Dilaram; forward with your Bishop and your Pawn, and with the Knight deal death! The position which illustrates this favourite story is still known throughout the East as—

DILARAM'S MATE.

BLACK.

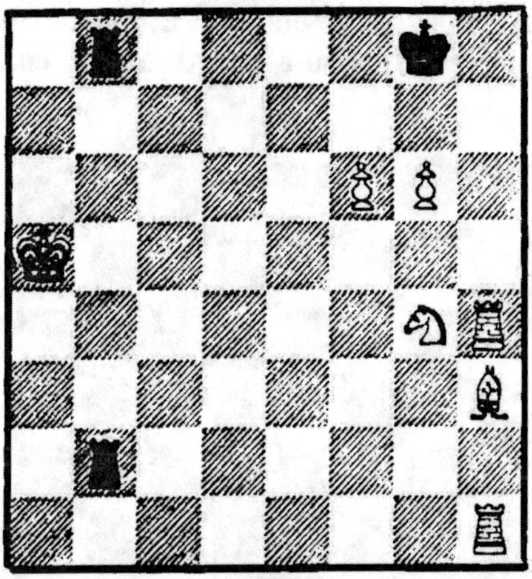

WHITE.

White to play and checkmate in six moves.

SOLUTION.

WHITE.	BLACK.
1. R. to K. R's 8th (ch.)	1. K. takes R.
2. B. to B's 5th (disg. ch.)	2. R. to K. R's 7th.
3. R. takes R. (ch.)	3. K. to Kt.'s sq.
4. R. to K. R's 8th (ch.)	4. K. takes R.
5. P. to K. Kt.'s 7th (ch.)	5. K. to Kt.'s sq.
6. Kt. to K. R's 6th.	

Checkmate.

The Arabs had three modes of winning the game. The first was by giving checkmate; the second by stalemate; and the third, when one player had any of his men remaining and had captured the whole of his adversary's. They devoted much attention to end-games or problems, and proverbially described a man's general moral disposition by a term implying excellence or the reverse in that branch of the art. As an example of their proficiency I append one more position, which is noteworthy as having been passed off as the composition both of Damiano and Stamma, though it is ound in one of the Eastern manuscripts which have already been mentioned. The problem has an additional interest from its exclusion of all the men formerly having moves which are no longer adopted in European play. It also presents two armies of equal strength and in equal peril.

BLACK.

WHITE.

White to play and checkmate in three moves.

SOLUTION.

WHITE.	BLACK.
1. Kt. to Kt.'s 5th (ch.)	1. R. takes Kt.
2. R. to K. B's 6th (ch.)	2. K. takes R.
3. R. to Q's 6th.	

Checkmate.

A number of other subtle positions might be given from Arabic and Persian sources; but as they generally involve many moves, they are what modern players would think dull, though they are all the more profound and far-seen.

Before concluding this short sketch of Oriental Chess, it should be stated that there is no reason to suspect that the Arabs or Persians gave the King any move except to the squares adjoining that on which he stood. The Knight's move, which he was subsequently allowed to take once, and the operation of *Castling*, in its diverse forms, were therefore of European introduction.

The actual date of the introduction of Chess into Persia was about the middle of the sixth century, two thousand five hundred years subsequent to the Sanskrit records of the game. From Persia it soon spread in other directions. About half a century later the game was known both to the Arabs and the Byzantines. It was forbidden to his followers by Mohammed on account of the image form into which the Chess-men were carved, and on this prohibition a question of some historical interest depends. The words of Mohammed were, "O, true believers, surely wine and lots, and *images*, and divining arrows are an abomination of the works of Satan; therefore avoid ye them that ye may prosper."

This admonition, though directed against games of chance, was held by Moslem writers to have no application to Chess other than to the figures into which the men were framed. Hence it followed that some of the sects made it a rule to play with Pieces rudely distinguished from each other, though some, holding more liberal ideas, retained the use of the carved Monarch, Elephant, Horseman, Charioteer, and Foot-soldier. Since the modern nations of Europe have, until a very recent period, employed Pieces without any animal or human device, this anecdote greatly strengthens the probability that the game found its way to Spain, Italy, and France through Arab channels. As with the decimal system of arithmetic, the elements of algebra, and the rudiments of trigonometry, all of which they also derived from India, the Arabs cultivated Chess in a masterly manner. Under the celebrated Caliphs of Bagdad the game flourished to a degree almost unexampled.

Pope has done something towards propagating the belief that Chess was played by the ancient Greeks. In his translation of the Odyssey there occur the lines :—

> "On hides of beeves, before the palace gate,
> (Sad spoils of luxury) the suitors sate.
> With rival arts and ardour in their mien,
> At Chess they vie to captivate the queen."

It is well ascertained now that the classical pastimes had no affinity with Chess. The elaborate paper of the late

Herbert Coleridge is quite decisive upon this point. When we find, then, that true Chess was known in the lower Empire, and that it bore the name of *Zatrikion*, which was not a Greek word, but a modification of *Chatrang*, the Persian rendering of the Hindoo *Chaturanga*, we understand clearly that the Byzantine players were indebted to the Persians for the game. That this was the case we have, in addition to other evidence, the testimony of Anna Comnena, who, telling that her father, the Emperor Alexis, was accustomed to play Chess, expressly says, "This game had then been brought into use among the Byzantines from the Assyrians."

A sign that Chess had taken firm root among these people at an early period, and was familiar enough to be interwoven with their ordinary feelings and expressions is furnished by a correspondence, said to have taken place, A.D. 802, between the Byzantine Emperor Nicephorus and Haroun-al-Raschid, wherein the former expressed himself in the phraseology of Chess.

The celebrated set of Chess-men presented to Charlemagne are on good grounds believed to have been the gift of the Empress Irene, who reigned from A.D. 797 to 802.

These Pieces, from an inscription known to have been carved by an Arab named Yusuf (or Joseph), at Nakuli, were probably made at Byzantium, as the figures present the costume of that place at the corresponding period. They are remarkable as constituting the first known instance of the "Counsellor" of the early Asiatics being converted into a Queen, and it is conjectured that Irene had this transformation effected from a desire to suggest that a Queen was the legitimate associate of a King in all his serious affairs. A marriage had before been projected between these sovereigns (as a means of reuniting the Empire of the East with that of the West), but the project fell through. The anecdote is of importance in Chess literature as offering some kind of explanation of the change which has taken place in the name of what has become the chief Piece on the board. "Be this as it may," says Dr. Forbes, "the terms Ferzin and Regina, the former adopted from the Saracens, and the latter from Charlemagne's imperial Chess-board, came to be used as synonomous for some centuries afterwards." Much that is interesting might be said if there were space in this sketch to say it, on the present condition of the game in Abyssinia, Syria, Arabia, Egypt, Persia, Hindostan, the islands of the Pacific, China, and other parts of Asia. It must suffice to state that in places where European traffic has prevailed, Chess is played chiefly in the modern way, while in those which are remote from such influence the mediæval type still exists. The Bishop may yet be seen moving only to the third square and springing over an intervening Man in Abyssinia and some other localities, but the march of civilisation, of tourists, and of armies, has destroyed this usage elsewhere.

Among the various deviations from the regular structure of the game indulged in by Eastern players, to one only need reference be made here. This is the "Great Chess" of Timur, or Tamerlane, the barbaric head of the Court at Samarkand, the conqueror of Persia, India, and Egypt, the plunderer of Bagdad, Delhi, and Cairo, and still better known as the captor of Bajazet. This hero invaded and overran India in the year 1393, at which time the game was played in high perfection at his Court. The courtier and biographer of Timur says of him that he was "devoted to the game of Chess, because he thereby whetted his intellect, but he possessed too lofty a mind to content himself by playing at the ordinary game." He accordingly engaged in the "Great Chess," which was played on a board containing 110 squares—eleven from right to left, and ten from top to bottom. A full description of this "improvement" on the game has been preserved, but few modern players would care to study it. It is said to have been Timur's custom whenever he subdued a city or region to inquire of the vanquished whether they had among them any good players; and if so, these were sent for to the royal presence, and were invited to play with the "Asylum of the Universe." Whether they won or lost, they were uniformly treated with condescension and courtesy, and sent back with substantial marks of bounty. Timur's fourth son was named *Shah-rukh** from

* Very erroneous notions have been entertained as to the meaning of the *Shah-rukh*, which has been mistakenly described as a check of the King by an adverse Rook. Dr. Forbes has settled the question by presenting a problem from an Oriental manuscript, in which

the circumstance that the Tartar potentate was playing at Chess and in the act of delivering the *coup* so denominated when he was informed of the prince's birth. A city founded by Timur owed its name to the same coincidence. It is recounted, too, that the great conqueror was playing at Chess when Bajazet was brought into his tent a prisoner.

There is reason to believe that Chess extended to Russia at a much later period than to the other nations of Europe. This is inferred from a peculiarity in the names of the men. They are translated into Russian words of the same signification as the names which the Pieces bore in primæval times. Thus the Bishop is still called an Elephant, and the Rook a Ship. Other countries have adopted designations really meaning the same thing, but in their case the Oriental words themselves have been imported without any regard to sense. Since the Russians have shown in their nomenclature a true knowledge of what the terms implied, it is assumed that they derived the game, at an early period, from an Asiatic source, and did not obtain it second-hand.

The introduction of Chess into Western Europe is no doubt ascribable to the conquest of Spain by the Saracens. This event occurred in the year A.D. 713. The Ommiade Caliphs soon established at Cordova a court which fully equalled, if it did not surpass, that maintained at Bagdad. We have seen the game of Chess flourishing at the one, and there can be little doubt as to its having been cultivated at the other.

Through the same instrumentality the game may have been propagated to Sicily and the south of Italy, while it had already taken root at the capital of the Lower Roman Empire. Its progress through the rest of Europe is thus explained in a perspicuous and reasonable manner.

When we read stories of Chess at the time of Athelstane

---

the "forking" of the King and the Rook is described as *Shah-rukh*. The *coup* was of far more importance in the mediæval Chess than in ours, because of the greater value of the Rook. It had, in fact, almost as decisive an influence upon the result of a game as the like "fork" to Queen and King would have now. The *Shah-rukh* could be effected either with a Pawn, a Knight, a Bishop, or the Queen; but the term seems to have been more strictly applied to the operation when performed by the Knight.

and Edgar (A.D. 925 to 975) in England, and in France at the time of Pepin and Charlemagne (A.D. 752 to 814), we need resort to no strained theories in order to account for the phenomenon. The game was manifestly transferred, through Constantinople or through Cordova, to the courts of those sovereigns.

The magnificent Chess-men deposited in the treasury of the Abbey of St. Denis by Charlemagne have already been noticed. Early Chess-figures have also been exhumed in England. In 1841, and again in 1857, a discovery of the kind was made at Warrington, the Pieces found being, in the judgment of the late Sir Frederic Madden, of the tenth century.

Others, now deposited in the British Museum, were found in one of the Hebrides, in the year 1831. These are pronounced to be of the eleventh century. Charlemagne's set prove their origin by being inscribed with the name of an Asiatic carver. The English specimens may have been of northern construction; but, if so, they were, in all probability, fashioned after Oriental models.

A book might be filled with the legends, romances, and historical anecdotes which testify to the popularity of Chess in the nations of Europe, from the time of the Moslem settlement in Spain, but that kind of matter does not fall within the scope of the present treatise. Suffice it to say that the game was frequently practised in polite circles, and was the subject of abundant reference and moralising. What we much desire, but cannot find, is some history of the game itself during the period of nearly eight hundred years, from the date of its introduction to the time of Cessolis, Vicent, Lucena, and Damiano. Throughout this long period, Europeans appear to have made only a plaything of the game—that is to say, no treatise was written upon it, and no player succeeded in rendering himself famous. But a like observation is applicable to any other branch of the liberal arts, and the game of Chess may truly be said to have run side by side, on the revival of learning, with any of the studies which marked the dawn of culture, whether in literature or science, among the nations of modern Europe.

A point of prime interest to cultivated Chess-players is the date and motive of the conversion of the Asiatic game to its present form. How and when, by whose suggestion, and by whose authority did the Bishop acquire the power of ranging over the whole of his diagonal, while losing that of leaping over an intervening Piece? When and why did the Queen become transformed from one of the feeblest to the most potential of all the Chess Pieces? When and why did the King acquire the prerogative of Castling, and lose the privilege once during the game, of moving like a Knight?

The exact history of these changes—so important in themselves—is hidden in the gloom of the dark ages. All we know is that, about A.D. 1500, both the ancient and the modern form of the game prevailed in some parts of Europe at the same time. There is no one, however, to tell us either the name, or the date, or the country of the player who was bold and inventive enough to develop those modifications on which the spirit of the modern game depends.

Awaiting any fresh discoveries, we must content ourselves with giving a brief notice of the celebrated players and writers to whom we are indebted for what we know of the history as well as the theory and practice of the game. In performing this task we begin with the masters whose distinction was earned ages before the game was chronicled in modern languages. The reader will bear in mind that Chess was known in India, and accurately described in Sanskrit writing five thousand years ago: that the game was introduced from India into Persia about the middle of our sixth century; that the Persian method of play, still practised in some parts of the East, was then propagated to all parts of the civilised world, and remained in operation everywhere till the end of the fifteenth century, at which date the modern system commenced.

One of the earliest treatises on Chess known was written by Abul Abbas, a physician at Bagdad, A.D. 899. Among early Easterns may be named Al Sali, a writer on the game and the most famous player of the East,—a veritable Philidor, who died at Basra, A.D. 946; Adoli-al-Rumi, who also composed a work on the game; Laala, another author; Ali Satranji, the Chess hero of Timur's Court (about A.D. 1400); and Ducas, a Byzantine historian (A.D. 1402).

CESSOLIS.—This author, a Dominican friar, wrote a fanciful book on Chess, highly valuable still from the insight it affords us of the moves and powers of the Chess-men at the time when its author lived. The work, printed in Florence, 1493, was translated and printed in London by Caxton, 1494.

VICENT (1495).—This Spanish writer published a work—the first really practical one on Chess of European authorship—containing a hundred positions; but it is so rare that no living person is known to have seen a copy of it.

LUCENA (1497) was also a Spaniard, who wrote a treatise on the game, containing several openings, and one hundred and fifty end-games, or problems on diagrams. Among his openings are some now familiar to us by the names of succeeding authors, such as *Damiano's Gambit*, and the *opening of Ruy Lopez*. Lucena's work appears to mark the date of the transition from Persian Chess to the modern form of play, for some of his problems are constructed on the principle of the old game and some on that of the new; and he advises students to learn both the ancient practice and that which he denominates, from the increased power of the Queen—*La Dama*.

DAMIANO (1512).—This author was a Portuguese apothecary. His work, "Libro da imparare Giocare a Scachi," was for a long time an authority on the game. It comprised a fair collection of openings and problems, chiefly taken from Lucena.

RUY LOPEZ (1561).—The treatise of Ruy Lopez, a Spanish author, was much in advance of any which preceded it; and it may still be consulted with profit and amusement.

GIANUTIO (1597).—A writer whose work embraced what had already been published by Damiano and Lopez, with many instructive additions. He invented what is called the *Two Knights' Defence*, and is diffuse upon the regulations for play. His rules, however, are very ambiguous, marking a transition period in the game. Sometimes in his openings the King retains the old privilege of leaping once during the game as a Knight; at others the King Castles, either to the corner square or to that of the Bishop. Giannutio was one of the old authors to whom Philidor was under obligations in his treatises on the game.

SALVIO (1604 to 1634).—A Doctor of Law at Naples. In the book of this writer we have the first description of the *Salvio Gambit*, as well as of the *Muzio Gambit*, though neither was of his own invention. The former he derived from some Portuguese work now unknown. The latter was communicated to him by Muzio, a good player of the day, who had seen it adopted between two other players. The work of Salvio contains games, with and without odds given, and many problems. His rules for playing allow of Castling, when the King has not been checked, in the manner of the "free rochade." In one case he permits the King to leap without combination with a Rook. The Pawn, on reaching his eighth square, he requires to become a Queen, and no other Piece.

POLERIO (1610).—In the sixteenth century the Spaniards were esteemed the best players, as might be expected from the Saracenic origin of the European game. About 1575, however, two celebrated Italian players, Paolo Boi, or Bove, and Leonardo, surnamed Il Puttino, "The Infant," visited several places, in company with Giulio Cesare Polerio, and achieved so many victories by their fine play that the palm began to be adjudged to their countrymen. Very few of their games were recorded, but there has been discovered an anonymous manuscript work containing, it is said, games by Polerio and others. An abstract has been given of it in the *Palamede*, *Illustrated London News*, and *Berlin Schach-Zeitung*.

SELENUS (1616).—The author of the work passing by this name was Augustus, Duke of Brunswick-Luneberg. It contains an account of the village of Ströbeck, famous for the Chess proclivities of the inhabitants.

CARRERA (1617).—Don Pietro Carrera was a Syracusan priest, born 1571, died 1647. His work is principally constructed on those of previous writers. It contains various openings of even games, with some examples of odds, methods of winning and drawing in different positions; problems; and an explanation of the art of playing without seeing the board.

GRECO (1619).—Born in Calabria 1600, and known as the "Calabrese." Gioachino Greco was a celebrated Chess genius. He visited Paris, where he was said to have won 5,000 scudi (or crowns) by the game, and afterwards went over to England. His short but brilliant career terminated in 1634, His work attained great celebrity, but the games, though frequently admirable, are sparkling rather than sound.

FRA ANTONIO (1647).—A Portuguese friar, Antonio Das

Neves, wrote a work on Chess, which appeared after his death, in 1647. The first books on the game appeared in the Peninsula, and there Chess literature first decayed. Sc far as is known, the work of Antonio was the last published either in Spain or in Portugal. It was a compilation merely from preceding authors.

Treatise of Lausanne (1698).—The latter half of the seventeenth century and the beginning of the eighteenth were particularly barren of Chess publications. There appeared, as the only one of the period, in 1698, a work entitled "Traité du jeu royal des échecs, par B. A. D. R. G. S., à Lausanne, par David Gentil." The author gives evidence in his games of having been a strong player, but his matter is principally derived from Lopez and Greco.

Bertin (1735).—Captain Joseph Bertin published at London, in 1735, a small octavo volume of seventy-eight positions, entitled "The noble Game of Chess, containing rules and instructions for the use of those who have already a little knowledge of this game." It contains ordinary openings and problems. Its principal feature is, however, the game now known as the *Cunningham Gambit.*

Stamma (1737—45).—Philip Stamma, of Aleppo, published at Paris, in 1737, a volume containing one hundred ingenious and subtle end-games. He was the first to mention the plan of numbering and lettering the squares, still used in Germany. His second work (in English), containing an addition of seventy-four openings (including the *Cunningham Gambit*), was published at London in 1745, when Stamma had become Interpreter of the Oriental Languages to His Britannic Majesty.

Philidor (1749—77).—François André Danican Philidor was born at Dreux, in France, 1726. His grandfather was a musician at the Court of Louis XIII., and at the age of six years Philidor was admitted into the choir of the Chapel Royal at Versailles. He devoted himself to music as a profession, and wrote twenty-five operas, which were performed with success, though said to have contained many plagiarisms. His chief fame was acquired at the game of Chess, at which he vanquished all the players of his day, some even without seeing the board. In this variety of the game he played three games simultaneously, to the prodigious amazement of his contemporaries, who were not acquainted with the more difficult feats of the Arab practitioners centuries before. Philidor first left France for Holland on a musical tour with a professional company. He then crossed over to England, where he principally resided. The St. James's Chess Club of that day allowed him a salary for attending and playing at the meetings. His work, which has gone through numerous editions, was first published in the French language at London, in 1749. Another edition was issued by the author in 1777. The following is his own description of the great object he had in view:—"My principal aim is to introduce a novelty which no one understands or is perhaps capable of mastering. It is that of properly playing the pawns. They form the real spirit of Chess. It is they alone which constitute the attack and the defence, and it is on their good or bad management that depends the gain or loss of the game." Philidor's Chess-writings were by no means up to the level of his fame as a Chess-player. Ponziani, a good judge, pronounces his *King's and Queen's Gambits* equally faulty, and adds that the Paris Club declared his work "more suggestive than correct, many of his assertions being contradicted by experience." Independent of theoretical considerations, it is unquestionable that this celebrated player was one of the greatest masters of the game who have appeared in modern days. Philidor died at London in 1795.

Del-Rio (1750).—Ercole Del-Rio, an Italian, published his "Practical Observations on the Game of Chess" in 1750, under the name of "An Anonymous Modenese." He subsequently published a second edition with notes. His work contained positions, problems, and games. Like Philidor, he devoted himself chiefly to the manœuvres of the centre pawns, and neglected the more spirited operations which arise from advancing the superior Pieces. The principle of the "free rochade" pervades the whole of his exposition.

Lolli (1763).—Giambatista Lolli, another Modenese, published at Bologna, in 1763, his theoretical and practical treatise on the game at the above date. This work, like those of other celebrated Italian authors, though otherwise of great excellence, is rendered to some extent useless to the modern student by the peculiar mode of Castling which it adopts throughout the play.

Cozio (1766).—We are now in the "classical days" of Chess literature. Works on the game were published in quick succession by the players of Italy. That of Count Carlo Cozio appeared at Turin in 1766. It professed to give new ideas both of attack and defence; but though highly meritorious, it is singularly deficient in theoretical explanations, and is indebted for much of its matter to previous writers.

Ponziani (1769).—The third great Modenese author, Domenico Canonico Ponziani, an advocate, first published his celebrated work anonymously at Modena in 1769. This work has been reprinted many times. It is divided into three parts. The first contains the laws of the game, with a criticism on the great writers of the time. In the second are well-arranged games at the Knight's and Bishop's opening, together with most of the varieties of *King's and Queen's Gambit*. The third part gives a remarkably interesting collection of end-games and problems.

French Amateurs (1775).—A treatise on the game was published in 1775 by a Society of Amateurs belonging to the club which met at the old Café de la Régence, pulled down in 1855. The notation adopted was that of letters and figures, originally proposed by Stamma. The work has been several times translated and re-edited.

Stein (1789).—Born at Forbach, in Alsace, Elias Stein was a professor of chess at the Hague, where he first published, in French, his well-known essay on the game and its military associations. He was considered so fine a player that his pupil, Mauvillon, said no one was held to be master of the game who had not had the benefit of his instruction. His work was well adapted for beginners, but not quite up to the standard of those who pursued the higher branches of the practice.

Van Nievelt (1792).—A Flemish General, Count Zuylen Van Nievelt, published at this date, in French, a work on Chess, "with plates illustrating the moves, and a chess-board with pieces of a new design." Some part of it had a political signification, and the whole is curious and interesting.

Allgaier (1795).—Johann Allgaier, an Austrian, born in Swabia, was one of the greatest masters the game of Chess has produced. His work, originally published at Vienna in

1795, and reprinted five times during his life, as well as frequently since, presented the first instance of games being arranged in a tabular form. His matter was in great measure taken from Philidor, Lolli, and Ponziani, but was given with brilliant variations of his own. He introduced the variety of the *King's Gambit* which is so well known by the name of its author.

PRATT (1799).—Peter Pratt, the English editor of Philidor, wrote himself two works on the game; one, entitled "The Theory of Chess," 1799; the other, "Studies of Chess," 1803. The latter, containing the analysis of Philidor, has been reprinted a great many times.

KOCH (1801—13—28—34).—The two German authors of this name were father and son. The elder, a priest of Magdeburg, published the games of Selenus, Philidor, Greco, the Amateurs, and Stamma. In a subsequently issued second part he gave the games of Allgaier. He also wrote an elementary treatise on the game (1828). The former work was republished in 1813 and 1814, and with additions by the son, in 1834.

SARRATT (1808—21).—We now come to the era of English chess authorship. Mr. J. H. Sarratt, professor of chess, London, who ranked as the strongest player of his day, published not only his own two treatises on the game, but useful, though incomplete, translations of Damiano, Lopez, Salvio, Gianutio, and Selenus.

COCHRANE (1822).—Mr. John Cochrane, known to all players by his brilliant and daring style, published at London, in 1822, "A Treatise on the Game of Chess, containing the games at odds from the 'Traité des Amateurs,' the games of the celebrated Anonymous Modenese (Ercole Del-Rio), a variety of games actually played, and a catalogue of writers on Chess." This writer had played in his earlier days with Deschappelles and De la Bourdonnais. A great number of his games have been published in the *Chess Player's Chronicle* and other works. Indeed, no collection of games would be complete without examples of his bold and subtle genius. He was the inventor of an interesting variation of the attack in the *Scotch Gambit*.

LEWIS (1817, *et seq.*)—Himself an admirable player, Mr. W. Lewis published numerous works on Chess, including editions of Stamma, Carrera, and Greco, and several of the games played between De la Bourdonnais and MacDonnell.

De la Bourdonnais (1833).—Among French players the successor to Philidor was Deschappelles. His successor was Louis Charles de la Bourdonnais, who, born in 1795, the year of Philidor's death, died in London in 1840, after a most distinguished career. He was regarded as the strongest player of the day. Against the celebrated MacDonnell he is said to have played eighty-five games, of which he won forty-six, his opponent twenty-six, and thirteen were drawn. He published a text-book of the game under the title of "Traité sur le Jeu des Echecs." He also took part in the first publication of "Le Palamède," afterwards resumed by St. Amant and others. He was buried at Kensal Green, where his distinguished antagonist, MacDonnell, had been carried to his grave, five years before, at the age of thirty-seven.

MacDonnell.—Alexander MacDonnell, an Irish player of the very foremost rank, wrote nothing on Chess himself, but a collection of his admirable games was published after his death by Mr. Greenwood Walker, and specimens of them are to be found in every modern work on the game.

Alexandre (1837).—The "Encyclopædia of Chess," published by this French writer in 1837, has the distinction of being the most voluminous work upon the game at present extant. It has also numerous other merits, being a lexicon of Chess literature down to the date of its publication. As a companion to the "Encyclopædia," Alexandre published, in 1846, a collection of two thousand ancient and modern problems.

We have now exhausted the historic period, and brought the narrative down to contemporary days. Of modern players and writers we need do little more than mention the names, though it is to their talent and industry that the game owes many of its most interesting features, as well as its full scientific development. Among the players of France we may notice Kiezeritsky, St. Amand, De Rivière, La Roche, Basterot, Préti, and Journoud. Germany has produced a great number of illustrious masters, such as Bilguer, Der Laza, Anderssen, Kling, Horwitz, Lowenthal, Harrwitz, Kolisch, Falkbeer, Lange, Bledow, Neumann, Zukertort, Paulsen, and Steinitz, several of them having, like Stamma,

Philidor, and De la Bourdonnais, found a home in England. Among English players and authors, the names of Fraser, Perigal, Pulling, Daniels, Walker, Captain Evans, Boden, Bird, De Vere, Owen, Brien, Wormald, Wayte, Ranken, Barnes, Blackburne, Wisker, Thorold, Mackenzie, are known to every reader. The United States of America have contributed Morphy, Stanley, Elson, and others. Jaenisch, Petroff, Schoumoff, and the Princes Ouroussoff, well sustain the reputation of Russia; while Calvi, Dubois, and Bonetti, in Italy, testify that the game is ardently and skilfully cultivated in other parts of the European continent. Among modern players in India—of whom there are many good ones, though their names have not become familiar—we may mention Ghulam Kassim, who published, in 1829, an analysis of the Muzio Gambit.

By the labours principally of Bilguer and Der Laza in Germany, of Jaenisch in Russia, and of Préti in France, the game has been reduced to a systematic plan, and has been set forth in plain and comprehensive text-books, with all the variations of play fully explained, and illustrations derived from the games of the most accomplished masters. Thanks to the services of these writers, the modern student can, in a short time, make himself thoroughly acquainted with every form and point of the game, and can see by the practical examples they furnish, clear demonstration of the force of every rule laid down.

Chess Nomenclature.

Considerable light is thrown on the history of Chess by the names of the Pieces and of the game itself. The words *Chess* and *Check* are derived either from the Sanskrit *Chatur*, or from the Persian *Shah*, a King, probably from the latter. Both are exotic in every European tongue. The name of the Rook is still more convincing. In European languages it means nothing but a Chess Piece, but its Sanskrit signification was a ship, and with that sense it has been retained for fifty centuries without any suspicion of its derivation being entertained till within one century of the present time. From the Italians converting the word into *Rocco*, which resembles *Rocca*, a rock or fortress, the terms castle and tower have also come to be used; but, at least in England, players seem in practice instinctively to cling to the genuine term, Rook. The Asiatic name of the Bishop also deserves notice, though it is only now to be traced in the Latin races of Europe. The Persian name of the Piece was *Pil*, an Elephant, its original type. The Arabs, having no P, called it *Fil*, or, with the definite article, *al*, as in Al-Koran, Al-kohol, Al-chymy, &c., *Al-Fil*. Hence the Latin and Italian *Alfieres*, *Alfiere*, *Alfino*, and *Aufin*. In France, the name is retained, without its prefix, in *Fou*, from *Fol*, and *Fil*. The word Bishop, used only in England, cannot be easily traced out. It may be mentioned, as a suggestion for inquirers, that in Italian, though *Rocca* signifies a fortress, *Rocco* means a Bishop's crozier. From some confusion in reference to these words, the English term Bishop may perhaps have originated. The Knight still retains in most countries its original name in a modern form. The Piece was called in Sanskrit, *Asca;* in Persian, *Asp;* and in Arabic, *Faras*, all denoting a horse. The Sanscrit for Pawn was *Podāta*, *Pādati*, or *Vātika*, a pedestrian, or foot-soldier; the Persian was *Piyāda*, of the same meaning; and the Arabic, *Baidak*, used only to denote a Chess Piece. In Europe, the Pawn was first known as *Pedes* and *Pedester*, words which simply reproduce the Oriental prototype. The Queen, called in Persian, *Farz*, or *Firz*, meaning wise, learned, a counsellor, a minister, or a general, became Latinised in Europe into *Farzia*, or *Fercia*. Hence, some contend, spring the words *Fierce*, *Fierge*, *Vierge*, *Dama*, *Donna*, *Dame*, and ultimately Queen, but this point has not been definitively proved.

Finally, we have to notice the term check-mate. In Persian the expression was *Shāh-mānd*, signifying a King, "driven to his last resource." In Arabic, it became *Shāh-māt*; and who can doubt that the modern substitute, check-mate, otherwise so utterly without meaning, is simply a repetition of that compound word? It seems perfectly clear that the Eastern derivation of the phraseology of the game, here very briefly noted, with the retention of the meanings originally ascribed to the Pieces by their Sanskrit inventors, point absolutely to the rise and propagation of Chess as described in the earlier portion of this sketch.

BOOK I.

CHAPTER I.

THE CHESS-BOARD AND CHESS-MEN.—POWERS AND MOVEMENTS OF THE LATTER.—RECOMMENDATIONS TO A BEGINNER.—SIMPLE CHECKMATES.

THE game of Chess is now played in most places of Europe and in America, on a board of sixty-four squares, by two

Diagram 1.*

BLACK.

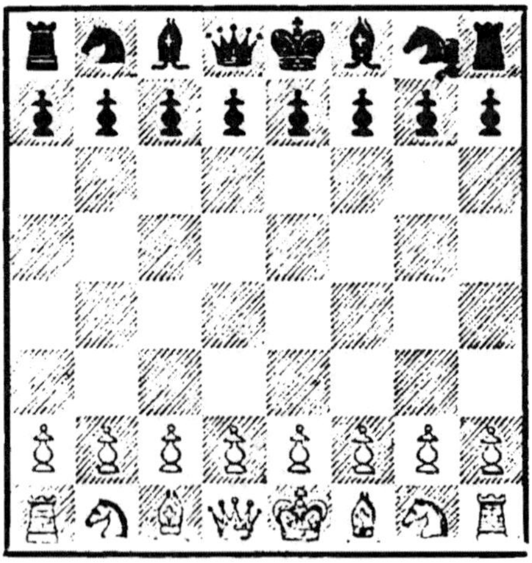

WHITE.

* The diagrams in this work are given that the reader may set the

parties, each of whom has a mimic army consisting of eight superior men, technically called "Pieces," and eight inferior ones, called "Pawns." The squares of the Chess-board are generally coloured White and Black alternately, and during the play must be so placed that each of the two contending parties has a white square on the right hand.

The preceding diagram shows the board and chess-men fitly arranged for the opening of the battle.

The men, for distinction sake, are of a different colour on the one side to those on the other, and in describing their movements it is customary to speak of the combatants as "White" and "Black." The eight superior "Pieces," or officers, on either side are:—

A King	♔	♚
A Queen	♕	♛
Two Rooks, or Castles (as they are called indifferently), ...	♖	♜
Two Bishops	♗	♝
Two Knights	♘	♞
And eight Pawns	♙	♟

The row of squares on which the superior men stand at the beginning of the combat is known as the "royal" line. The officers on the King's side are called the King's: viz., the *King's Bishop*, the *King's Knight*, the *King's Rook*; and those on the Queen's side are called the *Queen's Bishop*, *Queen's Knight*, and *Queen's Rook*. So the Pawns are also distinguished as King's or Queen's; the Pawn in front of the King being the *King's Pawn*, that in front of the King's Bishop being the *King's Bishop's Pawn*, that in front of the King's Knight being the *King's Knight's Pawn*, and that in

---

Chess-men according to them on his Chess-board. In each case, therefore, where a diagram is shown, the learner is requested to place the men in the same position on the board before reading farther.

front of the King's Rook the *King's Rook's Pawn.* In the same way the Pawns on the side of the Queen are called the *Queen's Pawn,* the *Queen's Bishop's Pawn,* the *Queen's Knight's Pawn,* and the *Queen's Rook's Pawn.*

Moves and Powers of the Chess-Men.

When the learner knows perfectly the titles of the men, and how to arrange them for combat, he must proceed to acquire a knowledge of their moves and powers.*

Moves of the Men.

♔ *The King.* ♚

The King can move to any square next to that on which he stands, provided such square is not defended by an adverse man. He can capture any one of the enemy's men which stands unprotected on any adjoining square to that he occupies, and, once in the game, he has the privilege of what is called "Castling," which enables him to move to a square next but one, in a lateral direction, to that he stands on. As it is a fundamental principle of the game that the King cannot be captured, he is not allowed to place himself on any square which is within the taking power of an adverse man, even if that power is inoperative in so far that the man is unable to move. Every other man can move directly *en*

---

* To render the present a complete guide to the game, it has been thought desirable not to omit the elementary instruction of which this chapter consists. A student, however, who has the opportunity, will save himself months of time, and an unspeakable amount of trouble, by inducing some one acquainted with the game to teach him the names, the movements, and the powers for capture and defence of the chess-men.

prise, as it is called, that is, so as to be taken by the enemy, when the interests of the game require it; but the King can never occupy a square or take a man while it is protected. He can make no move, in fact, which, if he were another Piece, would subject him to capture. The subjoined diagram will in some measure explain his movements :—

Diagram 2.

BLACK.

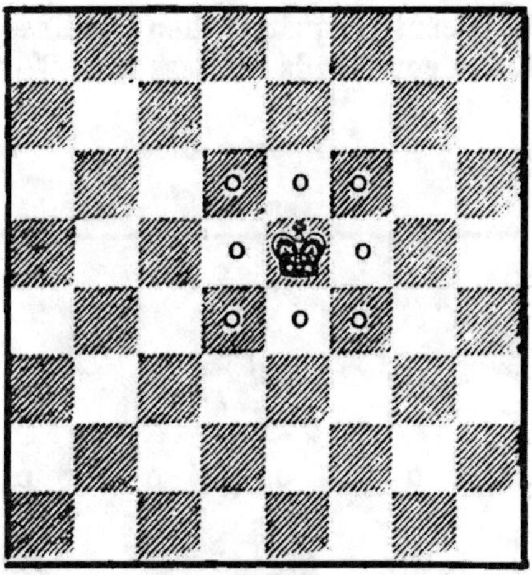

WHITE.

When placed in the middle of the board, *i. e.*, in any part where he has squares all round him, the King, it will be seen, can move to any one of eight squares for the purpose of defence or capture. But, as I have just said, he can occupy no square protected by the enemy, and he can capture no man which is guarded by a fellow-man. When at the sides of the board, or in the angles of it, his scope of action, like that of the other Pieces so circumstanced, is very much restricted.

The Queen.

The power and range of the Queen, though scarcely more than that of a Pawn in the ancient game of Chess, are in the modern one considerably greater than those of any other Piece. The Queen's movement, in fact, combines the moves of the Rook and Bishop, as she can march straight or obliquely from where she stands to the extremity of the board, provided the intervening squares are not occupied.

This is clearly shown on the annexed diagram, where it is seen that from a centre square, when her lines of march are unobstructed, she commands not less than 27 squares.

Diagram 3.

BLACK.

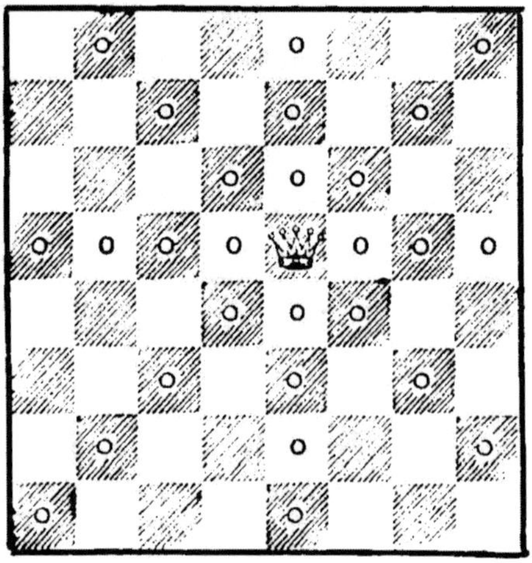

WHITE.

The Rook, or *Castle.*

This important officer ranks next in power to the Queen. His march, as shown in the following diagram, is in a straight line only, forwards, backwards, or sideways. He has a power also, once in the game, of moving in combination with the King, which will be explained under the operation of "Castling."

Diagram 4.

BLACK.

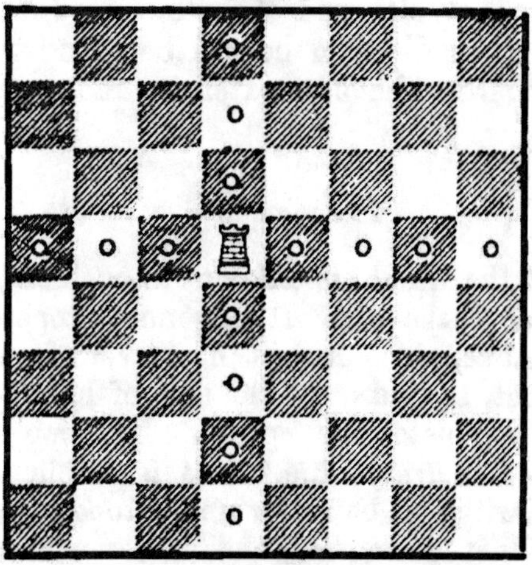

WHITE.

The Bishop.

The Bishop marches diagonally forwards or backwards to the extent of the board. He always, therefore, moves on

Diagram 5.

BLACK.

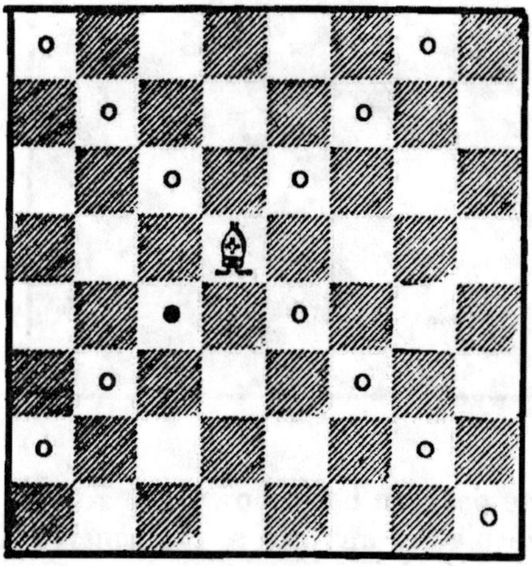

WHITE.

squares of the same colour as those on which he stands when the men are first set up for play, and each player has one Bishop moving on White and the other on Black squares. From the preceding diagram he will be found when in the middle of the board to have an extensive range over it.

The Knight.

The move of the Knight is different altogether from that of any of the other Chess-men. It may more properly be called a leap than a move, since he has the power of vaulting over any man in front, behind or at the side of him, to reach the square which completes his spring. His leap carries him over one square in a *straight line* to one in an oblique direction. But this peculiarity will be better understood by an attentive study of the annexed diagram, and very much more readily by the tuition of some chess-playing acquaintance:—

Diagram 6.

BLACK.

WHITE.

Placed in the position here shown, the Knight would have the power of leaping to any one of the squares, 1, 2, 3, 4, 5, 6, 7, 8, and of capturing any man of the enemy standing on that square, and this notwithstanding his being apparently hemmed in by the adverse forces. Any other man so surrounded, either with his own or with the adversary's soldiers, would be immovable till one of them were moved in a way to afford him a passage, but the Knight has the privilege of vaulting over their heads.

♙ *The Pawn.* ♟

The march of the Pawn reaches no farther than to the next square directly in front, excepting at his *first* move, when he may step to the square next but one in front of that where he stands, if that and the intervening square be unoccupied. But if an adverse Pawn commands the first square over which he steps, the opposing Pawn has the option of taking him as he passes, just as if he had made but one step. This will be illustrated by a diagram presently. There is another exception to the straightforward march of the Pawn. He does not capture, as all the other men do, in the line of his ordinary movement, but he takes an enemy and defends a fellow-man *diagonally*. (See Diagram No. 12.) Although so restricted in his march and power of capture, the Pawn has a prerogative which at times renders him all-powerful. This is, that whenever he can force his way to the last square of the file on which he marches, he becomes invested with the rank and powers of any officer (except the King's) the player of him chooses. Owing to this peculiar privilege, it occasionally happens that one party in a game will have more than one Queen, and more than the normal number of Pieces on the board at once.*

The Capturing and Defending Powers of the Chess-Men.

All captures in Chess are effected by removing the captive man from the board, and placing his captor on the square

* On this subject, the promotion of the victorious Pawn, I take the liberty of referring the student to vol. i. p. 28, of M. C. F. Jaenisch's valuable treatise, the *Analyse Nouvelle des Ouvertures du Jeu des Echecs*, and to my book called *Chess Praxis*, p. 41.

where the former stood ;—the only exception being when a Pawn takes *en passant* (see pp. 43, 44). And all the men capture in the direction that they move, except, as before mentioned, the Pawn.

POWER OF THE KING FOR CAPTURE AND DEFENCE.

Diagram 7.

BLACK.

WHITE.

The White King is here surrounded by enemies. It will be observed, however, that he is not attacked by any one of them. That is to say, he does not stand in the line of capture of any of them, and if the player had any other course more advantageous to his game, he need not cause his King to move. Supposing it necessary for him to move, it is evident he can only do so by capturing one of the men and placing himself on the square of the captive. But as I mentioned previously, a King can never go into a position, where, if he were another man, he could be taken. Any other man, circumstanced as the King now is, could offer himself to be sacrificed by taking any one of the *defended* men around him. The King can take only an unprotected enemy. We see, then, he can capture 1, 2, 3, 6, or 8, because they are undefended; but he cannot touch 4, or 5, or 7, because 4 is protected by one Knight, 5 by the other, and 7 by both. The student will learn, on looking forward to Diagram No. 12, that the Pawns 4 and 5 would be safe from capture by the King, even were the Knights away, since they are for the moment defended by their fellow Pawn 2; and 7 is defended by 4 and 5. Bear always in mind, that in Chess a man can make but one move, or one capture at a time. When he has made his move it becomes the turn of the other side to move. Having seen the power of the King for offence, we have to note his power for defence. As a rule, on whatever square a Chess-man can capture an enemy, he can, to the extent of his powers, protect a fellow-warrior. Supposing in Diagram No. 2 the White King were encompassed by men of his own army, no undefended man of the other side could capture one of them without the danger of being taken by the King in return.

POWER OF THE QUEEN FOR CAPTURE AND DEFENCE.

Diagram 8.

BLACK.

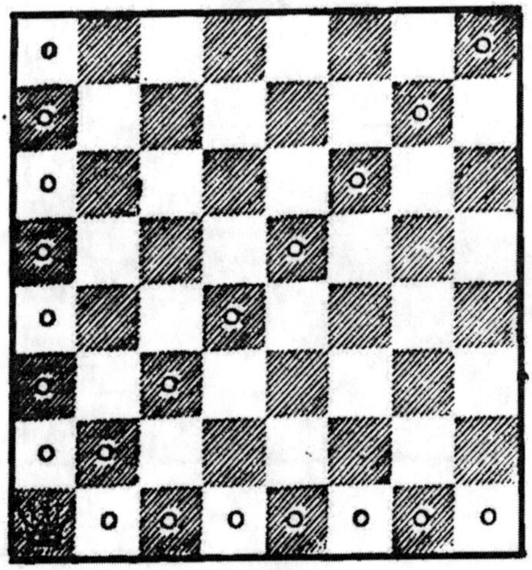

WHITE.

In Diagram No. 8 it is seen that the Queen, when placed in the centre of the board, without any impediment to her march, can move to any one of twenty-seven squares. In the position given here, from an angle of the board, she has a range of twenty-one squares. Her power for capture and defence is as her march. Placed as above, she can take any adverse man (always excepting the King) from any one of the dotted squares, provided no man intervene between her and the prize; and she can prevent any man of her own side being taken, except at the risk of the captor, from any one of the same squares, if her action is not impeded by intervening men. But her power alone, like that of every other man, great as it appears, is oftentimes enormously enhanced by the support of another Piece or a Pawn, and indeed can only be appreciated by practical experience.

Power of the Rook (or Castle) for Capture and Defence.

Diagram 9.

BLACK.

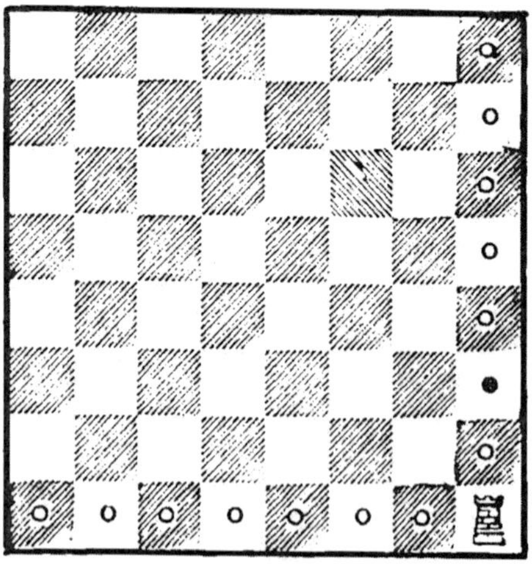

WHITE.

In the centre of the board, we see, by Diagram No. 4, that the range of the Rook is considerable. He has then the command, when the dotted squares are clear, of 14 squares, exclusive of the one he stands on. He is the only Piece whose importance is not seriously diminished at the angles of the board. In the diagram above he is seen to have as many empty squares to range over as he has in

Diagram No. 4. His power of capture and defence is as his power of movement.

Power of the Bishop for Capture and Defence.

Diagram 10.

BLACK.

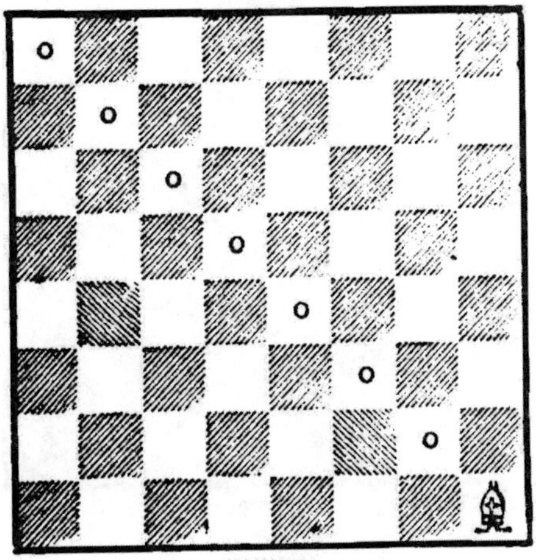

WHITE.

In Diagram No. 5 the Bishop is so posted as to show his fullest scope. Here he is purposely placed in a position of diminished range. In the former, he can move to any one of thirteen squares, if the intermediate ones are empty; and he can capture an enemy, or defend a fellow-soldier, on any one of them under the same conditions. In the present situation he has the same power only over seven squares.

Power of the Knight for Capture and Defence.

Diagram No. 6 exhibits the Knight in a situation to exert his utmost efficacy. He would there defend any fellow-man standing on the numbered squares, or capture an adverse man so standing. His capability of capture and defence, then, like the other superior men, is as his movement. When placed in a corner square as in Diagram No. 11, his efficiency is more seriously restricted than that of any other

Piece, for he can only move to, and consequently capture on and defend the two squares marked.

Diagram 11.

BLACK.

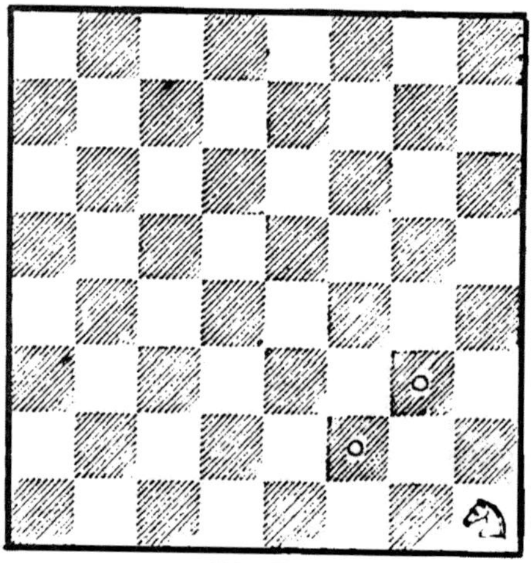

WHITE.

POWER OF THE PAWN FOR CAPTURE AND DEFENCE.

Diagram 12.

BLACK.

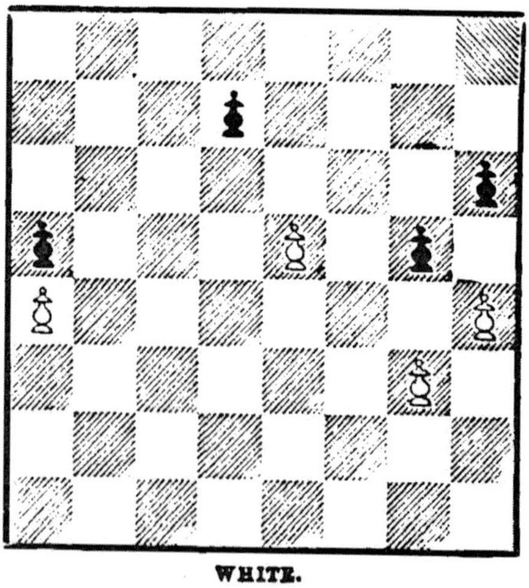

WHITE.

The Pawn, it has been explained, can march but one step *directly forward*, except on his first move, and he is the only man of the Chess army that makes a capture and defends a fellow out of his ordinary line of march. It should be added that he is the only man, too, who *cannot retreat*. The King, the Queen, a Rook, a Bishop, and a Knight, can move forward, and backward, and sideward; the Pawn can move but in one direction, which is right ahead. In the foregoing diagram the learner will see on the left-hand side of the board a White and a Black Pawn, each of which has advanced two steps. In this situation, as neither can go out of the file on which he stands, unless by taking an adverse man, they mutually block the way for each other, and can go no farther. On the right-hand side of the board, each party has two Pawns, one of which Pawns has been advanced two steps, the other only one. In this position, whichever player had the move could cause his Pawn to capture the other Pawn; but as the hinder Pawn *defends the former one*, the capturing Pawn in either case could be taken in return. To make this plain, suppose it to be White's turn to play (by "White" is always meant the player who has the white-coloured army), and that he thinks his best move is to capture his opponent's Pawn. Well, he takes the foremost of Black's two Pawns off the board, and places his own foremost Pawn on the square thus left empty. Now suppose Black considers it his best course to take White's Pawn, he does just as White did. He takes the White Pawn off the board and places his own Pawn on the vacant square. This operation would be simply an exchange of Pawns. Looking now to the middle of the field, we find that White has a Pawn advanced as far as the fifth square of his file, while Black has one which has not yet moved. Supposing Black has to move, and considers it best to play this Pawn, he has the choice, *it being the first move of the Pawn*, to advance it one step or two steps. If he advance it one step, it stands within the capturing capacity of the White Pawn, and White can, if he please, capture it, *i.e.*, take it off the board, and place his own Pawn on the vacant square. This is plain enough; but the strange thing is that White can do just the same, if he chooses, should Black elect to throw the Pawn forward *two steps*. He can arrest the Pawn in its passage and take it in the manner just described, precisely as though it had been moved only one square or step, placing his own Pawn on the square the other passed over. This is technically called "taking *en passant*." *

* This peculiar privilege of the Pawn at his first move is of great antiquity. How far back it dates has not been satisfactorily determined, but we find it described by Cessolis, a writer on Chess of the thirteenth century:—"All the Pawns have the right of moving to the third square from that they first occupy, as if they felt secure while within the limits of their own kingdom (that is the half of the board assigned to each player); but when they are beyond these limits, they must be content to move only one square, and must always go straightforward and never retrace their steps." It will be observed that Cessolis says nothing of their liability to being taken *en passant*. The reason of this is, that in Italy, from the earliest time till now, the rules of the game have allowed the Pawn free passage.

CHAPTER II.

NOTATION OF THE MOVES.

WHEN the learner has acquired a competent knowledge of the moves and powers of the Chess-men, it will be well for him to learn how to express them. In the first instance, he may content himself to do this by the system of Chess notation used in England,* which is as follows:—

Diagram 18.

BLACK.

Q. R's sq. Q. R's 8th.	Q. Kt's sq. Q. Kt's 8th.	Q. B's sq. Q. B's 8th.	Q's sq. Q's 8th.	K's sq. K's 8th.	K. B's sq. K. B's 8th.	K. Kt's sq. K. Kt's 8th.	K. R's sq. K. R's 8th.
Q. R's 2nd. Q. R's 7th.	Q. Kt's 2nd. Q. Kt's 7th.	Q. B's 2nd. Q. B's 7th.	Q's 2nd. Q's 7th.	K's 2nd. K's 7th.	K. B's 2nd. K. B's 7th.	K. Kt's 2nd. K. Kt's 7th.	K. R's 2nd. K. R's 7th.
Q. R's 3rd. Q. R's 6th.	Q. Kt's 3rd. Q. Kt's 6th.	Q. B's 3rd. Q. B's 6th .	Q's 3rd. Q's 6th.	K's 3rd. K's 6th.	K. B's 3rd. K. B's 6th.	K. Kt's 3rd. K. Kt's 6th.	K. R's 3rd. K. R's 6th.
Q. R's 4th. Q. R's 5th.	Q. Kt's 4th. Q. Kt's 5th.	Q. B's 4th. Q. B's 5th.	Q's 4th. Q's 5th.	K's 4th. K's 5th.	K. B's 4th. K. B's 5th.	K. Kt's 4th. K. Kt's 5th.	K. R's 4th. K. R's 5th.
Q. R's 5th. Q. R's 4th.	Q. Kt's 5th. Q. Kt's 4th.	Q. B's 5th. Q. B's 4th.	Q's 5th. Q's 4th.	K's 5th. K's 4th.	K. B's 5th. K. B's 4th.	K. Kt's 5th. K. Kt's 4th.	K. R's 5th. K. R's 4th.
Q. R's 6th. Q. R's 3rd.	Q. Kt's 6th. Q. Kt's 3rd.	Q. B's 6th. Q. B's 3rd.	Q's 6th. Q's 3rd.	K's 6th. K's 3rd	K. B's 6th. K. B's 3rd.	K. Kt's 6th. K. Kt's 3rd.	K. R's 6th. K. R's 3rd.
Q. R's 7th. Q. R's 2nd.	Q. Kt's 7th. Q. Kt's 2nd.	Q. B's 7th. Q. B's 2nd.	Q's 7th. Q's 2nd.	K's 7th. K's 2nd.	K. B's 7th. K. B's 2nd.	K. Kt's 7th. K. Kt's 2nd.	K. R's 7th. K. R's 2nd.
Q. R's 8th. Q. R's sq.	Q. Kt's 8th. Q. Kt's sq.	Q. B's 8th. Q. B's sq.	Q's 8th. Q's sq.	K's 8th. K's sq.	K. B's 8th. K. B's sq.	K. Kt's 8th. K. Kt's sq.	K. R's 8th. K. R's sq.

WHITE.

---

* For an account of the systems adopted in France and Germany, see "Chess Praxis," p. 63.

Comparing the above with Diagram No. 1, it will be seen that the eight squares of the first *rank* (that nearest the players on either side) are named each after the Piece which occupies it when the little armies are first marshalled in battle array. Thus the square on which the King stands is called the *King's square*, that on which the Queen stands the *Queen's square*, and so on with the other Pieces. The *files* likewise, that is the row of squares reaching from the top to the bottom of the Chess-board, are designated by the particular Piece which occupies the first square. Take the King's file as an example. Here the square on which the King stands at starting takes the name of the Piece on it, and is known as the King's square.* The next square forward on the same file is called the King's second square; the next, the King's third; and so on to the King's eighth.

As the same mode of describing the squares is adopted by both parties, White's *first* rank of squares is Black's *eighth*, and *vice versâ*. This is one of the faults of the modern notation, and it was not found in the notation used in England but a few years back. By that system the board was represented as a divided territory, one half of which belonged to White and the other half to Black. White, for example, was supposed to possess all the field so far as the fourth square inclusive, before all his men, and Black the same. If a White man were advanced to what we now should call the "White King's seventh," it would then have been said to be at *Black King's second*. It is to be regretted that this mode of notation has fallen into desuetude.

A little reflection and practice will render the present method of English notation, cumbrous though it is, sufficiently familiar to the reader. But, we repeat our advice to him, to take a few lessons on the names, moves, and powers of the Chess-men, and on the mode of describing them,

* Properly speaking, each square on the *first rank* should be designated as "First," as "K's Rook's *first* square," &c.; but it is customary to use the word "square" only in this case, and to omit it and give the number of the square instead when the squares of other ranks are mentioned. Thus in playing a Knight to K. B's 3rd square, we describe the move as merely Kt. to K. B's 3rd; but if the Knight were played to K. B's 1st square or K's 1st square, the move would be described as Kt. to K. B's square, or Kt. to K's square.

from some Chess-player. A good practice, after getting thus far, is to clear the board and then place on it a single Piece, moving it in every direction in which it can go until the beginner is master of its movements. As an example, place the White Queen on her square, then play her to her eighth, then to King's Rook's eighth, then to Queen's Rook's eighth, then to King's Rook's square, then to Queen's Rook's square, and then to her own square again. This little exercise will afford the student some conception of the immense command the Queen has over the board. He will do well then to take one of the Rooks, and practise with that only for a time. The same with the other Pieces, and lastly with a Pawn. After acquiring a thorough understanding of the movements of the men in their single capacity, he should begin to manœuvre them in combination with each other, for which purpose some easy positions will be given directly.

The foregoing exemplification of the modern English Chess notation invites attention to some of the abbreviations adopted in this treatise, for the purpose of saving space. Heretofore, when the King has been mentioned, or the Queen, or any of their movements described, this has been done at length. Henceforth the men and their actions will be generally abbreviated thus :—

K.	will indicate	King.
Q.	,,	Queen.
R.	,,	Rook.
B.	,,	Bishop.
Kt.	,,	Knight.
P.	,,	Pawn.
sq.	,,	square.
adv.	,,	adversary's.
ch.	,,	check.
dis. ch.	,,	discovered, or discovering check.
doub. ch.	,,	double check.

CHAPTER III.

TECHNICAL TERMS IN CHESS-PLAYING.

As tending to keep the student's interest alive, it will be a good thing for him here to direct his attention to some of the technical expressions used in play.

CHECK.

A word of warning given by one player to the other that he has attacked the adverse King. It being, as I have said, a fundamental principle of the game that the King can never be captured, whenever any direct attack is made upon him, the player whose King is so threatened must be warned of his danger by the exclamation "*check*." He is then obliged to do one of three things, namely: move his King out of the range of the attacking man, parry the danger by interposing a man between his King and the attacking man, or capture the checking man. When he can do no one of these three, he is checkmated, and the game is won by the adversary.

When the King is directly attacked by an adverse man, the move is called simply *check;* when the Piece or Pawn moved does not itself attack the King, but unmasks another which does, it is called a *discovered check;* and when both the man moved and the one unmasked attack the King, they are said to give *double check*. There is also a fourth description of *check*, known as *perpetual check*, which arises when one party has two or more squares on which he can attack (or check) the enemy King, and the other party can only parry one check by affording an opportunity for another. If the checking player choose to persist in the repetition of these checks, the game must be abandoned as a drawn battle.

It has already been remarked that a King can never move into check, that is, into a square commanded by an adverse man; it must be added here, that he must never remove any one of his men which screens him from check, unless to capture the attacking man; and when placed in check, he must, before making any other move, put himself out of check.

The following diagrams will help perhaps to make the above understood:—

CHECK.

Diagram 14.

BLACK.

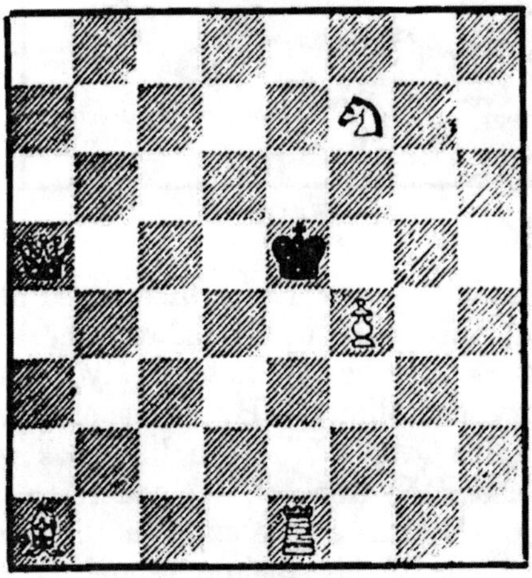

WHITE.

In this merely fanciful position, which could not occur in play, and is only given to show the attacking range of the men, the Black King is in check of one of each of the adverse army, Q., R., B., Kt., and P. Though so beset, he is not quite checkmated, since the attacking Pawn is undefended, and he can take it. Were that Pawn protected by a fellow-man, it would be a case of checkmate, and the game would be at an end.

Discovered Check.

Diagram 15.

BLACK.

WHITE.

In this diagram the power of a discovered check is well shown. White is in peril of immediate checkmate, but it being his turn to play he can not merely avert defeat but ensure a victory, as follows. He takes off the board the Black Pawn at his Q. B.'s 7th with his Rook, which is on that file, and places the Rook on the square vacated by the captured Pawn. By this act he exposes the Black King to the range or attack of his Bishop (standing on Q. Kt.'s 2nd), which is called *discovering check.* We see, further, that the Black King is so circumstanced that he can either move out of the range of the Bishop, or he can relieve himself from the attack by capturing the adverse Bishop. After making these moves,—that is, on White's part taking off the aforesaid Pawn with Rook, and on Black's part, either moving his King out of check or taking off the offending Bishop with the Black Rook,—the student must, I say, then look still further. He will presently see that by moving White's Rook—the Rook which took the Pawn—from Q. B.'s 7th to K. B.'s 7th he, on White's part, gives Black checkmate. This checkmate, which he will soon learn to comprehend, would be technically described thus :—

WHITE.	BLACK.
1. R. takes Q. B. P. (dis. ch.)	1. K. to K. B's 4th ; or R. takes B.
2. R. to K. B. 7th (checkmate).	

Double Check.

Diagram 16.

BLACK.

WHITE.

A double check is more powerful than any other. Here White, were it not his turn to move, must be inevitably checkmated. Having to play, he can by the double check, that is by the attack of his Rook and Knight on the adverse King, give checkmate at once.

WHITE.	BLACK.
Kt. to K. B. 5th (checkmate).	

Perpetual Check.

In this position White is in danger of being checkmated off-hand were it his adversary's turn to play. Having him-

Perpetual Check.

Diagram 17.

BLACK.

WHITE.

self the move, however, he is enabled to make a drawn game, by giving "perpetual check," thus:—

WHITE.	BLACK.
1. R. to K's 4th (ch.)	1. K. to Q. B's 4th.
2. R. to Q. B's 4th (ch.)	2. K. to Q's 3rd.
3. R. to Q. B's 6th (ch.)	3. K. to K's 4th.
4. R. to K's 6th (ch.)	4. K. to Q's 5th.
5. R. to K's 4th (ch.)	

And so on.

Stalemate.

Here White is so circumstanced that if he had no other Piece on the board than his King he would be "stalemated," because his King cannot move without going into check, which, as we have seen, is illegal. His policy, then, is to sacrifice the Rook, because if that be taken, it being then his turn to play, he will have no legal move left; and this he endeavours to effect thus:—

WHITE.	BLACK.
1. R. to Q. Kt.'s 8th (ch.)	1. K. to R's 2d.
2. R. to Q. Kt.'s 7th (ch.)	2. K. moves.

By keeping his Rook on the Q. Kt.'s file and checking the

STALEMATE.

Diagram 18.

BLACK.

WHITE.

adverse King every move, he places his opponent in the dilemma of being perpetually checked, or, by taking the Rook, of giving him, White, stalemate, in either case making a drawn game.

CHECKMATE.

Diagram 19.

BLACK.

WHITE.

This position is a capital exemplification of checkmate and other technicalities as well. The conditions are that if White is to play first (or *has the move*, as it is called), he is to checkmate in seven moves. Let us see the *modus operandi* by which White effects his object:—

WHITE.	BLACK.
1. Q. to Q's 5th (ch.) *	1. K. to R's sq. †
2. Kt. to K. B's 7th (ch.) ‡	2. K. to Kt's sq. §
3. Kt. takes R. (dis. ch.) ‖	3. K. to R's sq.
4. Kt. to K. B's 7th (ch.)	4. K. to Kt.'s sq.
5. Kt. to K. R's 6th ¶ (double ch.)	5. K. to R's sq. **

---

* This is a good example of *check*. The Queen is played to a square whereon she *attacks* the adverse King, and the player of the Queen must notify this by saying "*check*."

† As Black has no man which can interpose between the adverse Queen and his own King, and no man which can capture her, he is compelled to play the King out of check. To do this, he has the choice of two squares: the K. B's square, and the K. R's square. If he move the King to the former, White will reply by playing his Queen (which is guarded by the Kt.) to K. B's 7th, and give checkmate. Black therefore retreats his King to R's sq.

‡ Another example of check, and of what is termed a *fork* also, as the Kt. attacks both the *King* and *Rook*.

§ As the King can never remain in check, and Black has no power to take the Kt., he must move the King.

‖ Here we have a fine instance of *discovered check*. The moment before, White was in danger of losing his Queen, which is *pinned*, as it is called, by acting as the White King's defence against the enemy's Rook. White, however, is enabled to take off the Rook with his Kt., and as at the same time he leaves the King exposed to check from the Queen, he forces Black again to move his King.

¶ This beautiful composition now presents us with a case of *double check*, the Black King, it is clear, being within the capturing range of both the Queen and Knight. In such cases, the attacked King *must* move, as, if he could parry the check of one man, he would still remain under fire from the other.

** As in his previous moves, Black does not now play his King to B's sq., because White would at once give checkmate by moving his Queen (always guarded by the Kt.) to K. B's 7th sq.

WHITE.	BLACK.
6. Q. to K. Kt.'s 8th (ch.) *	6. R. takes Q. †
7. Kt. to K. B's 7th (checkmate). ‡	

Castling.

As previously observed, the King can move only to one or other of the squares immediately adjoining the square he stands on, except once in a game, when he is privileged to move, in conjunction with either of the Rooks, on to the third square laterally from that on which he stands at the beginning of a game, the Rook being at the same time placed on the square *over* which the King has moved. This compound movement is called *Castling*, and can be made only under the following restrictions:—

1st. The King must not be in check.

2nd. He must not have moved before in the game.

3rd. The Rook he Castles with must not have moved.

4th. The King must not pass over or on to any square at the time attacked by an adverse man.

5th. There must be no Piece either of his own army or of his adversary's between the King and the Rook he proposes to Castle with.

The following will show the method of Castling in general use:—

---

* This is a remarkably fine move. White could have gone on checking perpetually by playing the Kt., now to K. B's 7th (ch.), and then to K. R's 6th (double ch.), but that would only give him a *drawn game*. By this sacrifice of his Queen, however, he is enabled, as we shall see, to give a triumphant checkmate and win the game.

† A *forced move*, observe, for Black cannot take the Queen with his King, because that would be to place his King in check of the Kt., at the same time he cannot move his King out of the Queen's attacking power. Still he is not quite bereft of resource. To give this daring check, the Queen has placed herself within the capturing power of the Rook, and is taken.

‡ The succour is only momentary. By taking the Queen the Rook shuts up his King so effectually that the Kt. is now enabled to give the fatal *checkmate!* Black, you will find, can neither capture the checking Piece, nor ward off the check, nor escape by flight. The *Sheik* is dead! This instructive position is by an Italian writer, Lolli.

POSITION BEFORE CASTLING ON KING'S SIDE.

AFTER CASTLING ON KING'S SIDE.

POSITION BEFORE CASTLING ON QUEEN'S SIDE.

AFTER CASTLING ON QUEEN'S SIDE.

Such is the manner of Castling adopted in all parts of Europe, with the exception of Italy and Spain. In those countries players prefer the "Free Rochade," by which the King and Rook can be moved to any of the vacant squares occupied by or between them. (See "Chess Praxis," page 46.)

Consultation Game.

A game in which one or both the contending parties consist of two or more players, who consult upon the moves to be made.

Counter Attack

Is carrying the war into the adversary's territory, or attempting to repulse an attack on your forces by making one on those of your opponent.

Diagonal.

A row of squares of the same colour on the Chess-board, running from the top or bottom of the board to the sides.

Doubled Pawn.

When two Pawns of the same army are on one file, the front one is called a doubled Pawn.

Doubled Rooks.

When two Rooks of the same army are posted on the same file or on the same rank, with no man intervening, they are said to be doubled.

Drawn Game.

In addition to the cases previously mentioned where a game is drawn by *perpetual check*, or by *stale-mate*, a game may be drawn from neither party having sufficient force left to effect a checkmate, as a King and a Bishop only, or a King and two Knights, &c. A game may be drawn also where one side, although having sufficient force to win, does not know how to checkmate his opponent within the number of moves allowed in such games by Rule XIV. It is drawn also when both parties persist in repeating the same move, and usually when they are left with an equal force, as a King and Queen against a King and Queen, or a King and Rook against a King and Rook.

End-Game.

A situation of the forces towards the conclusion of a game.

En Passant.

To take *en passant* is to capture an adverse Pawn when it advances two steps at the first move. To do this the taking Pawn must always be at his fifth square. If then an enemy's Pawn on the next file is moved two squares, he can take it off in the same way as if it had been moved only one square. A Pawn can only be taken in passing by a Pawn; never by a Piece.

En Prise.

Any man in a situation to be captured by an enemy's man is said to be *en prise*, except the King, who, so attacked, is said to be "in check."

The Exchange.

If a player contrive to gain an enemy's Rook for one of his own Bishops or Knights, he is said to have *won the exchange*.

False Move.

A false move is playing a man to a square he cannot legally go to; as a Knight like a Rook, or a Bishop like a Knight. To Castle when the King is in check, or to Castle him into a check, or when he has previously been moved, would be a false move. A false move, in short, is an illegal move.

Fool's Mate.

A childish checkmate, which sometimes is given to a novice, by the second player. Place the men in order of battle, and then make the following moves:—

White.	Black.
1. P. to K. Kt's 4th.	1. P. to K's. 4th.
2. P. to K. B's 4th.	2. Q. to K. R's 5th.

giving checkmate.

Scholar's Mate.

Another childish checkmate, effected thus:—

WHITE.	BLACK.
1. P. to K's 4th.	1. P. to K's 4th.
2. B. to Q. B's 4th.	2. B. to Q. B's 4th.
3. Q. to K. R's 5th.	3. P. to Q's 3rd.
4. Q. takes K. B. P.	

giving checkmate.

Forced Move.

A move which the player is compelled to make; as when he has only one way of moving his King out of check, or, has otherwise no legal move at command.

Forced Game.

When a player is in such a position, that all the moves he can make lead to his certain defeat, his opponent is said to have a "forced game," or a "forced won game."

To Fork.

To fork, correctly speaking, is to attack two of an opponent's men at one time with a Pawn. As an example, suppose White has a Pawn on his K's third square, and Black has a Kt. standing on his K. B's 4th, and a Rook standing on his Q.'s 4th. If White now advance the Pawn to K's 4th, he "forks" the two Pieces. The term is frequently applied, however, to an attack with a Piece as well as with a Pawn, on any two of the adverse Pieces at the same time.

Gambit.

A Gambit is an opening in which one of the players sacrifices a Pawn for the purpose of rapidly developing his own forces and confusing the forces of his adversary. For example, place the men in order, then move as follows:—

WHITE.	BLACK.
1. P. to K's 4th.	1. P. to K's 4th.
2. P. to K. B's 4th.	2. P. takes P.

Here the Pawn thrown forward by White at his second move is called the *Gambit Pawn*. If it be taken, the opening is called a *Gambit;* if it be refused, the opening is called a *Gambit declined*.

To Interpose.

When the King or any other superior Piece is attacked, and a man is played between it and the offensive Piece, the man is said to be *interposed*.

J'adoube.

An expression, meaning "I adjust," or "replace," which, or its equivalent, must be used by a player before he touches a man to rectify its position.

Open File.

A row of squares from one end of the board to the other which has no man on it is termed an *open file*. So a blank row of squares from one side of the board to the other is called an *open rank*.

Open Game.

A game is called an *open game* when both players begin by advancing the King's Pawn to K's 4th square, or the Queen's Pawn to Q's 4th square.

Opposition

This expression involves a variety of manœuvres much too difficult for a beginner to grasp. The following is a simple form of the opposition:—

Diagram 20.

BLACK.

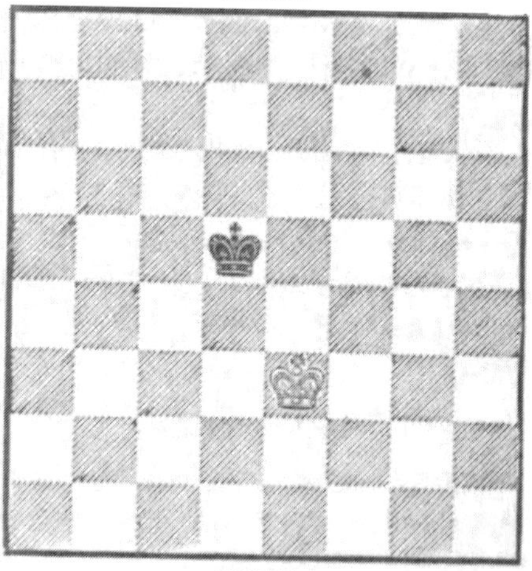

WHITE.

Here suppose it were absolutely essential for Black to cross over into White's territory, *i.e.*, to White's fourth rank, he could do so at once, were it his turn to play, by moving his King to Q. B's 5th. But if it were White's move, he could effectually prevent the Black King from ever moving beyond his own fourth rank, by playing his King *facing* the *Black King*, with one square intervening every time. On the other hand, supposing White desirous of marching beyond his 4th rank, he could do so by moving his King to B's 4th, were it his turn to play; but if

Black had the move, he would *get the opposition* by playing his King to K's 4th, and for ever prevent the White King from advancing.

Isolated Pawn.

Any Pawn which is alone, without the protection of a fellow-Pawn, is said to be *isolated*.

Passed Pawn.

A Pawn which cannot be impeded in its forward march by any adverse Pawn, either on the same file or on the file to the right or left of it, is termed a *Passed Pawn*.

Pion Coiffé, or Marked Pawn.

When one player undertakes the difficult task of checkmating his opponent with a particular Pawn, this Pawn has a ring or cap placed on it for distinction sake, and is called *Pion Coiffé*, or *Marked Pawn*.

Party.

A corruption or translation of the French *partie*, often now employed instead of the word "game."

Player, First and Second.

The person at a game of Chess who by lot or by agreement has the first move is called the first player: he who moves second is termed the second player.

Queening a Pawn.

When a player manages to push one of his Pawns through all the opposing obstacles to any square on the eighth rank, such Pawn, we have seen, assumes the name and privileges of any superior Piece (except a King) which the player chooses; and this is called *Queening* a Pawn.

CHAPTER IV.

RELATIVE WORTH OF THE CHESS-MEN.

THE KING.

As the King can neither be exchanged nor captured, his relative value as compared with the other forces is inestimable.

THE QUEEN.

The *average* value of the Queen is reckoned to be equivalent to two Rooks and a Pawn. When the board is tolerably clear, *i.e.*, when most of the forces have been captured, she is often not so valuable as two Rooks.

A ROOK.

A Rook is estimated to be worth a Bishop and two Pawns, or a Knight and two Pawns—two Rooks to be of about equal value with two Knights and a Bishop, or two Bishops and a Knight.

A BISHOP AND A KNIGHT.

These Pieces are generally thought to be of about the same value, though some authorities prefer the former.

A PAWN.

A Pawn stands lowest in the Chess army, and is usually reckoned at about one-third the value of a Bishop or of a Knight.

CHAPTER V.

GENERAL RULES AND RECOMMENDATIONS FOR A LEARNER.

1. Before beginning a game, be particularly careful that the men on both sides are properly arranged for battle.

2. Accustom yourself to play indifferently either with the White or the Black men.

3. Play invariably according to the strict rules of the game; neither recalling a move yourself nor permitting your opponent to recall one.

4. Never play many games at a sitting.

5. As nothing can conduce so much to your improvement in Chess as playing with adversaries more skilful than yourself, never lose an opportunity of doing so by the silly pride of not accepting odds.

6. Learn to play slowly—

> "Other graces
> Will follow in their proper places."

7. Exhibit no impatience when your adversary plays slowly, but consider his tardiness as a compliment to your skill.

8. Scrupulously avoid the evil habit of hovering with your hand over the board when it is your turn to play. It is a habit which will annoy your opponent, and is therefore ungentlemanly, and one which is sure to beget on your own part a feeble, vacillating style of play that must be fatal to the attainment of excellence.

Lastly. Whenever your game is hopeless, resign it at once, and with a good grace; and although the loss of it may discompose you, do not allow your discomposure to be visible.

THE KING.—Beware of playing your King early in the game, but rather Castle him as soon as you can, and generally with his own Rook. Be careful when you have so Castled, not to permit an adverse Kt. to gain undisturbed possession of your K's Bishop's 4th square; and never, without due consideration, be tempted to advance the Knight's and Rook's Pawns on the side you have Castled. When your King is checked, it is better generally to interpose a man that attacks the checking Piece, than one which only covers the King.

Avoid, as a rule, exposing your King to the danger of a *discovered check.*

Do not be tempted to check the adverse King uselessly; but when by checking you can force him to move, and *thus prevent his Castling*, it is often to be done advantageously.

Always keep in mind that, however perilous it may be to bring the King into action while the forces are unthinned by capture, yet when the superior Pieces are changed off, he should be brought immediately into play for the purpose of supporting your own Pawns and harassing your opponent's.

In end-games, where the surviving forces on either side are mainly the King and Pawns, the result is usually dependent on the rapidity and skill with which this then important Piece is manœuvred.

THE QUEEN.—It is not advisable to play the Queen, any more than the King, into the field very early in the fray. When so exposed, she is liable to attack from inferior foes, and if she escape from them it is often at the cost of many moves. Besides, her power is so much greater when she is sustained by other Pieces, that it is seldom good play to send her into action unsupported.

As a rule, be cautious of playing her in front of your King, and never employ her to protect or to attack, when you can do the same as effectually with a subordinate.

THE ROOK.—A Rook (or Castle) has not much scope for action at the opening of a game, but as the battle proceeds he becomes a valuable, and towards its end, an all-important adjuvant. Thus one of the strongest motives for a good player to bring out his other men speedily, is that his Rooks may come into operation.

When the game is fairly developed, it is generally a good

plan to take command of an *open file* by planting a Rook at one end of it; and, when possession is thus obtained, if your adversary attempt to dislodge you by playing one of his Rooks on to the same file, you should defend your occupying Rook with the other, rather than exchange Rooks or give up the position. It is generally good policy, too, to get both Rooks on to the same file. This is technically called doubling the Rooks. When thus posted one before the other on the same files, where they mutually sustain each other, two Rooks are often stronger than a Queen.

THE BISHOP.—As most games are opened by the players moving their K's Pawn to K's 4th sq., which enables each King's Bishop to be planted directly on the Q. B's 4th, attacking the adversary's weakest point, the K. B's Pawn, the K's Bishop is considered slightly superior to the Queen's.

It is very rarely advisable to play your K's Bishop to Q's 3rd before your Q's Pawn has been moved, and as a rule it is not good to play the Q's Pawn to Q's 3rd before moving the K's Bishop to Q. B's 4th, or Q. Kt.'s 5th, as you thereby afford him only the K's 2nd to go to.

Towards the end of a game, when you have to depend on the strength of your Pawns, it is often well to exchange off the enemy's Bishops, because they can offer more impediment to the progress of your Pawns than either the Rooks or the Knights. You must not, however, indiscriminately change your Bishops for Knights, or Knights for Bishops. And remember that, as the game approaches an end, two Bishops are generally stronger than two Knights, and that one Knight is usually stronger than one Bishop. When the field of action has become pretty well cleared of combatants, and you remain with a Bishop and two or more Pawns, place your Pawns, as soon as you can conveniently, on squares of a different colour to those on which your Bishop moves, as he can then prevent the adverse King from penetrating to the midst of them. When, however, you have an inferiority of force, and the game is against you, it is generally safer to keep your Pawns on squares which can be protected by the Bishop.

THE KNIGHT.—The best post for the K's Kt. at the outset of a game is at his K's B's 3rd. It at once attacks the adverse K's Pawn, if that has been played to K's 4th, and effectually prevents the opposing Queen from co-operating at K. R's 5th with the K's Bishop in an attack upon your K. B's Pawn. The Q's Kt. may generally be played advantageously to Q. B's 3rd at the beginning of a game, and often the more so when the Q. B's Pawn has been advanced two steps.

As the individual strength of the Castles is greatly enhanced when they act together, so the power of the Knights is much increased when one protects the other. Remember that a Knight with three or four Pawns, in an end-game, is somewhat superior to a Bishop with three or four Pawns, because he can command successfully squares of two colours, while a Bishop commands only squares of the colour of his diagonals.

THE PAWN.—Philidor's hackneyed saying, *Les Pions sont l'âme du jeu*, is in some degree true, though he appears to have exaggerated their importance in comparison with that of the superior Pieces. They are the least powerful soldiers of the exchequer, but each carries in his knapsack the baton of a Marshal, by his right to the highest promotion when once he has penetrated to the adverse royal line. It is advisable generally so to play your Pawns that they shall facilitate the development of your own Pieces, and retard the development of the enemy's. Most players, therefore, strive to occupy the centre squares of the board with their King's and Queen's Pawn. But it is dangerous to advance two Pawns abreast to the fourth rank until you are able to support them there with other men. As a rule, if you have thrown two Pawns forward to the fourth rank, and one of them be attacked by an enemy's Pawn, it is better to advance the threatened Pawn than to capture the attacker. Nevertheless, you must be careful not to advance your Pawns too far without adequate support. In the earlier stages of a game Pawns are safer and stronger when at the fourth rank than further on.

In an *open game*, it is not generally prudent to move the K. Kt.'s Pawn or Q. Kt.'s Pawn early in the fight, but you may often do so very advantageously in a *close* game. As the K. B's Pawn is the most vulnerable point, always have an especial eye to that, until by Castling on the King's side you have given it the protection of a Rook as well as the

King. After Castling, whether on the K's or Q's side, be wary of advancing the Kt's or Q. B's Pawn in front of your King, and be especially careful not to advance it two steps without good reason. Do not press your Pawns far forward on either side until you see on which your opponent Castles.

A doubled Pawn is often a weak Pawn, but not invariably. A Pawn doubled on a Rook's file, for instance, is generally useless; but the K's Bishop's Pawn, that has doubled on the K's file, sometimes strengthens the centre and opens the battery of your Rook upon the K's B's file.

A passed Pawn is very advantageous when adequately supported by another Pawn; but when isolated it is often lost. A Pawn being of less value than a Piece, it is generally better to defend with the former; and as no man can interpose between the attack of a Pawn, he can frequently check the King as serviceably as any superior Piece could.

In a cordon diagonal of Pawns you should preserve the topmost one, and never forget that Pawns united are very strong; when separated, very weak. Finally, remember that two Pawns, the hind one supporting the other, are safe against a King, and that at the end of a battle, when you have Pawns, or even a Pawn, against a Bishop or Knight, you may win in many cases, but that your opponent can scarcely ever do so.

CHAPTER VI.

SIMPLE CHECKMATES.

BEFORE proceeding to the examination of the *openings*, which involve the combined operations of all the forces, the learner will do well to devote some days to positions where the manœuvres of three or four of the men only are exhibited. He may begin with a few of the simplest checkmates.

TO CHECKMATE WITH THE KING AND QUEEN.

Diagram 21.

BLACK.

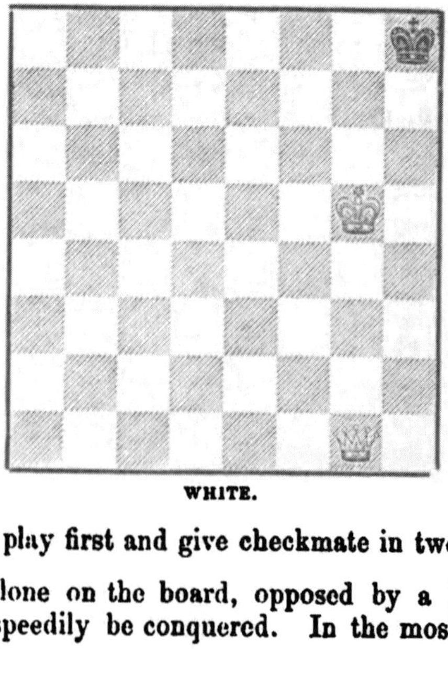

WHITE.

White to play first and give checkmate in two moves.

A King alone on the board, opposed by a King and a Queen, can speedily be conquered. In the most favourable position for defence he can be checkmated in nine moves. When he is confined to one of the extreme bands of the board, as in the situation before us, his defeat is much more expeditious. Before proceeding to work this modest little problem, it will familiarise you * with the chess notation if you describe the position of the men in writing. They stand thus :—

WHITE.	BLACK.
K. at K. Kt.'s 5th.	K. at K. R's sq.
Q. at K. Kt.'s sq.	

Here, having been told that the speediest way of effecting checkmate is to confine the adverse King to the outer band of the chess-board, you will naturally move your King so that the Queen, having command of the *open file*, shall prevent his escape. But even in a position like this, where White is certain of immediate victory if he play correctly, a want of care may rob him of the prize. For example, an experienced player would see at a glance that by moving his Queen to K. B's 6th, he will force the adverse King to go to K. R's 2nd (the only square open to him), and then by playing his Queen to K. Kt.'s 7th, he checkmates him. A tyro, however, having an eye only to imprisoning the King, would think it equally good to play his own King to K. R's 6th instead of to K. B's 6th, and would be surprised to find he had suffered his opponent to escape with a drawn game, having placed his King in the situation of *stalemate*. (*See* Diagram 18.)

The true solution, then, you see, is—

WHITE.	BLACK.
1. K. to K. B's 6th.	1. K. to K. R's 2nd.
2. Q. to K. Kt.'s 7th.	

Checkmate.

Play this over until you thoroughly understand the rationale of the moves, and then take another easy checkmate of the same description in Diagram 22.

Your first thought, probably, here, remembering the example just given, will be to play your Queen on to the

---

* I will suppose myself to be addressing the player of the *White* men.

Diagram 22.

BLACK.

WHITE.

White to play first and give checkmate in two moves.

Q. Kt.'s file, to prevent the enemy's King from escaping into the open. And that would be a very sure way to checkmate him shortly. But on looking attentively at the board you will find that you can much more speedily shut him up this time by playing your Queen across to the K. R's 6th square, since that gives him only a single square to move to. Having thus driven him face to face with your King, you march your Queen across the board from K. R's 6th to Q. R's 6th, and exclaim "Checkmate!" Write out for practice the technical solution, thus :—

WHITE.	BLACK.
1. Q. to K. R's 6th.	1. K. to Q. R's 5th.
2. Q. to Q. R's 6th.	

Checkmate.

The next position is also easy, but care must be taken to avoid placing the adverse King in a position of stalemate.

The conditions here are that White, whose turn it is to move, shall checkmate his opponent in three moves.

Diagram 23.

BLACK.

WHITE.

White to play and checkmate in three moves.

To effect this, play your Queen first to K. Kt.'s 7th. This move confines the Black King to the extreme line of the board at once. It may strike you that by playing your King to Q. B's 7th, you would still more restrict the action of the adverse King. This is true; and here is the danger to be guarded against by the player who has the winning force. You would so confine him by that move that no unassailed square would be left open to him, and he would consequently be stalemated.

Your move of Q. to K. Kt.'s 7th compels Black to move his King to Q's sq.; play your Queen then to K. B's 7th, and he must carry his King to Q. B's sq. Whereupon you move the Queen to Q. B's 7th, administering checkmate. As before, you will do well to write out this easy solution, *secundum artem*:—

WHITE.	BLACK.
1. Q. to K. Kt.'s 7th.	1. K. to Q's sq.
2. Q. to K. B's 7th.	2. K. to Q. B's sq.
3. Q. to Q. B's 7th.	

Checkmate.

One more example of checkmate with King and Queen

against an unprotected King must suffice for the moment. In this the Black King, instead of being on an extreme band of any of the four sides, stands in the open field, and before he can be checkmated by the King and Queen must be forced to an outer line.

Diagram 24.

BLACK.

WHITE.

White, having to play, gives checkmate in nine moves.

If left to yourself to checkmate in this position, you would probably take more moves than the rules of Chess allow in cases of that description, and you would thus only make a drawn game. You will find, however, that with the best moves on your part in attack and the best moves on Black's side in defence, checkmate cannot be averted beyond the 9th move. Here I give the solution in its technical form :—

WHITE.	BLACK.
1. Q. to K. Kt.'s 6th.	

Observe the confining power of this move.

	1. K. to K. B's 5th.

Black is not compelled to play his King to this square, but it is the best he can occupy to defer his fate.

2. K. to Q. Kt.'s 2nd.

It is impossible for a King and Queen to effect checkmate when only themselves and the despoiled King are left, unless they co-operate.

2\. K. to K's 4th.

Black's object is to maintain his King as long as possible in the open field, where he knows the King and Queen alone cannot checkmate him.

3\. K. to Q. B's 3d. 3. K. to K. B's 5th.

He will soon be dispossessed of these two squares, you will find.

4\. K. to Q's 4th.

Note that he is already excluded from one of them, and note further that, so terribly constrictive is the power of a King and Queen when they near the hapless monarch, he has only a single square at this moment of which he can take possession.

4\. K. to K. B's 6th.

5\. Q. to K. Kt.'s 5th. 5. K. to K. B's 7th.

Black has a choice of two squares here, and rightly takes the one by which he can protract his fall. If he play his King to K's 7th, you plant your Queen at once on K. Kt.'s 2nd, giving check, and, forcing him back on the extreme rank, checkmate him a move sooner than you can now.

6\. Q. to K. Kt.'s 4th. 6. K. to K's 8th.

If he move the King to K. B's 8th, you reply with King to your K's 3rd, and checkmate next move.

This is very obvious, but before going farther you should perfectly understand the mode of action.

7\. K. to K's 3rd.

You now threaten to give checkmate in two places, namely, by playing the Queen to K's 2nd, or to K. Kt's sq., either of which moves places the poor King *in check*, without leaving him a square to flee to. But it is not your turn to play, so for the moment he escapes by moving

7\. K. to K. B's 8th.

8\. Q. to K. Kt.'s 5th.

Note this move. It is what Chess-players technically call *a coup de repos*, and is made to compel Black to go back to a square facing the White King, and then be checkmated. You will find that the same end can be obtained by your *retreating* the Queen still farther down the same file; but mark, also, there is the same pitfall here as in the situations you have seen previously. If instead of retreating the Queen you were to advance her a square nearer the Black King, that is to your K. Kt.'s 3rd, you would throw away all your previous labour, letting Black off with a drawn game.

8. K. to K's 8th.
9. Q. to K. Kt.'s sq. Checkmate.

TO CHECKMATE WITH THE KING AND ROOK.

To give checkmate to the King with a King and a Rook is not quite so easy as the foregoing mates; but it is easy enough, and in the most favourable situations for the defence it can be effected in sixteen moves.

Diagram 25.

BLACK.

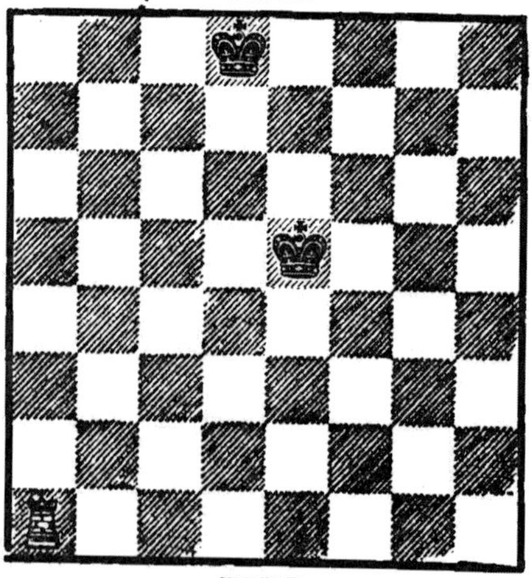

WHITE.

White playing first, gives checkmate in six moves.

As in the case of the King and Queen against the King, checkmate with the King and Rook against the King can only be given when the doomed monarch is on an extreme line of the board, unless he should be hemmed in by other men, which of course changes all the conditions.

In the diagram before us, the King, being already on a last line of the field, has but a short shrift. White's first step must be to keep him there. For that purpose he will play his Rook to Q. R's 7th. Place the position on your Chess-board and play thus:—

WHITE.	BLACK.
1. R. to Q. R's 7th.	1. K. to K's sq.

This is Black's best move to protract the checkmate. For the result of his playing the King to Q. B's sq., see (A).

2. K. to Q's 6th.	2. K. to K. B's sq.

By this time you will understand that if he move the King to Q's sq., you have the desired position of the two Kings *vis-à-vis*, with only one square between them, and you at once checkmate him.

3. K. to K's 6th.

The best move, because Black dare not return his King to K's square, opposite your King, as I have explained.

	3. K. to K. Kt.'s sq.
4. K. to K. B's 6th.	4. K. to K. R's sq.
5. K. to K. Kt.'s 6th.	

Black has now no option; he must face your King with his.

6. R. to Q. R's 8th.

Checkmating him.

(A.)

1. R. to Q. R's 7th.	1. K. to Q. B's sq.
2. K. to Q's 6th.	2. K. to Q. Kt.'s sq.

As he now attacks your Rook, you must lose a move to take that Piece out of danger, but of course you keep it on the penultimate line of squares.

3. R. to Q. B's 7th.

Here the Rook, while protected by your King, still more restricts the liberty of Black's King.

	3. K. to Q. R's sq.
4. K. to Q. B's 6th.	4. K. to Q. Kt.'s sq.
5. K. to Q. Kt.'s 6th.	5. K. to Q. R's sq.
6. R. to Q. B's 8th.	

Checkmate.*

In the next position, an example of the same kind of checkmate, the attacked King has more freedom, and his defeat is proportionally retarded.

Diagram 26.

BLACK.

WHITE.

Black to play and White to checkmate in 15 moves.

In this situation, it is the turn of Black to play, and he protracts his defeat for 15 moves.†

* The solution here is longer than it need be in actual play; but I wished the student to understand that, as a general rule, when the adverse King is on a last line, the proper course is to keep him there, by playing the Rook as above directed. In this particular instance, White can, by moving his King to Q's 6th at the outset, give checkmate in *three* moves.

† The position is one by the famous Italian writer on Chess, Ponziani. He thought Black could defer the checkmate for eighteen

M. Adam's solution, which you must work out on the Chess-board, is this:—

BLACK.	WHITE.
1. K. to Q's 5th.	

You must take for granted that the moves on each side are the best which can be made—on Black's part to delay the checkmate, on White's to hasten it—as an explanation why each player did not move otherwise than he did would take up more space than can be spared.

	1. R. to Q. R's 5th.

This, you will observe, cuts the Black King off at one blow from half the field of battle.

2. K. to Q. B's 5th.	

For the result of his moving the King to K's 5th, which would be equally efficacious, see A.

	2. K. to Kt.'s 2nd.
3. K. to Q. Kt.'s 5th.	

The consequences of the King being played to Q's 5th again are seen under B.

	3. R. to K. R's 5th.
4. K. to Q. B's 5th.	

If the King be moved to the next rank, White would for ever cut him off the rank he now moves on, by playing the Rook to K. R's 4th.

	4. K. to B's 3rd.
5. K. to Q's 5th.	5. R. to K. Kt.'s 5th.
6. K. to Q's 6th.	

If he had showed his King to Q. B's 5th, White would have followed with K. to K's 3rd, and have driven the adverse King more expeditiously to an extreme line of squares.

---

moves. A French amateur, M. Adam, who devoted great attention to Chess end-games, found out, however, that White could win in three moves less.

	6. R. to K. Kt.'s 4th.
7. K. to Q's 7th.	7. R. to Q's 4th (ch.)
8. K. to Q. B's 6th.	8. K. to K's 3rd.
9. K. to Q. B's 7th.	9. R. to Q. B's 4th (ch.)
10. K. to Q. Kt.'s 6th.	10. K. to Q's 3rd.
11. K. to Q. Kt's 7th.	11. R. to Q. Kt.'s 4th (ch.)
12. K. to Q. R's 6th (ch.)	12. K. to Q. B's 3rd.
13. K. to Q. R's 7th.	13. K. to Q. B's 2nd.
14. K. to Q. R's 6th.	

You, of course, see that if the Black were moved to the only other square he could be played to, White would checkmate him at once.

	14. R. to Q. B's 4th.

Now observe, we have a similar disposition of the forces, at the side of the board, which you have seen at the end of it in previous mates; that is, of the Black King being so placed that he has no move but to face the White King, with only a square between them.

15. K. to Q. R's 7th.	15. R. to Q. R's 4th. giving checkmate.

(A)

BLACK.	WHITE.
1. K. to Q's 5th.	1. R. to Q. R's 5th.
2. K. to K's 5th.	

In the solution above, you remember Black moved his King to Q. B's 5th.

	2. R. to K. R's 5th.
3. K. to K. B's 5th.	3. K. to K. Kt.'s 2nd.
4. K. to K. Kt.'s 5th.	

He might play the King with equal effect to K's 6th, on which you would again curtail his march by playing the Rook to K. R's 4th, and then proceed as above.

	4. R. to K's 5th.
5. K. to K. B's 5th.	5. R. to K's sq.

By this change in tactics, White will more speedily drive the King to any extremity of the board.

6. K. to K. Kt.'s 5th.	6. R. to K. B's sq.
7. K. to K. R's 5th.	7. K. to K. B's 3rd.
8. K. to K. Kt.'s 4th.	8. K. to Kt.'s 3rd.
9. K. to K. R's 4th.	9. K. to K. B's 4th.
10. K. to K. Kt.'s 3rd.	10. K. to K. Kt.'s 4th.
11. K. to K. R's 3rd.	11. K. to K. B's 5th.
12. K. to K. Kt.'s 2nd.	12. K. to K. Kt.'s 5th.
13. K. to K. R's 2nd.	13. K. to K. B's 6th.
14. K. to K. Kt.'s sq.	14. K. to K. Kt.'s 6th.
15. K. to K. R's sq.	15. R. to K. B's 8th.

giving checkmate.

(B)

BLACK.	WHITE.
1. K. to Q's 5th.	1. K. to Q. R's 5th.
2. K. to Q. B's 5th.	2. K. to K. Kt.'s 2nd.
3. K. to Q's 5th.	

In the first solution you will find Black here moved his King to Q. Kt.'s 5th.

	3. K. to K. B's 3rd.
4. K. to Q. B's 5th.	4. K. to K's 3rd.
5. K. to Q. Kt.'s 5th.	5. R. to K. R's 5th.
6. K. to Q. B's 5th.	6. R. to K. Kt.'s 5th.
7. K. to Q. B's 6th.	7. R. to K. Kt.'s 4th.
8. K. to Q. B's 7th.	8. R. to Q. B's 5th (ch.)
9. K. to Q. Kt.'s 6th.	9. K. to Q's 3rd.
10. K. to Q. Kt.'s 7th.	10. R. to Q. Kt.'s 4th (ch.)
11. K. to Q. R's 6th.	11. K. to Q. B's 3rd.
12. K. to Q. R's 7th (ch.)	12. R. to Q. R's 4th (ch.)
13. K. to Q. Kt.'s 8th.	13. R. to Q. R's 3rd.
14. K. to Q. B's 8th.	14. R. to Q. R's sq.

giving checkmate.

To Checkmate with the King and two Bishops.

The following diagram represents a very old, but a very excellent illustration of the way to checkmate with two Bishops. It is the invention of Ponziani. Place the men thus:—

Diagram 27.

BLACK.

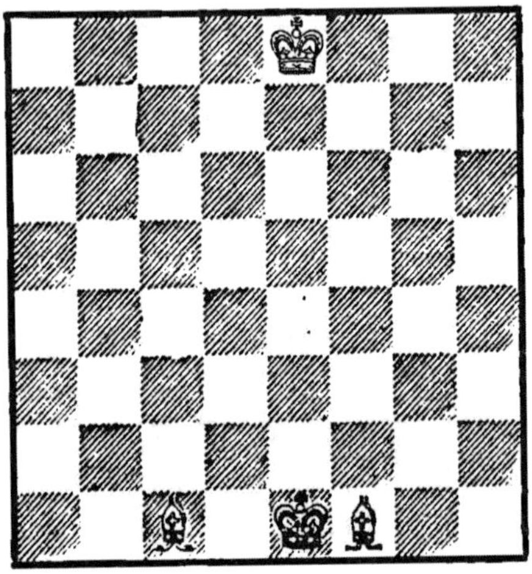

WHITE.

That is to say:—

WHITE.	BLACK.
K. at K's sq.	K. at K's sq.
B. at K. B's sq.	
B. at Q. B's sq.	

A single Bishop, like a single Knight, can never give checkmate with the aid of their King only, unless the adverse King is in some way hampered by his own men. The checkmate with two Bishops and a King is not, indeed, easy, and very few inexperienced players would be able to effect it within the number of moves prescribed by the laws for checkmating a despoiled King. The principle to be observed is to drive the adverse King into one of the corners of the board. Supposing you have the White men in the situation before us, you must, therefore, play your Bishops in such a way as to prevent the King being moved into the centre of the field. For example:—

WHITE.	BLACK.
1. B. to K. R's 3rd.	1. K. to Q's sq.
2. B. to K. B's 4th.	2. K. to K's 2nd.
3. K. to K's 2nd.	

Already the Bishops prevent the Black King crossing to the centre of the field, you have time, therefore, for playing your own King forward.

	3. K. to K. B's 3rd.
4. K. to K. B's 3rd.	4. K. to K's 2nd.
5. B. to K. B's 5th.	5. K. to K. B's 3rd.
6. K. to K. Kt.'s 4th.	6. K. to K's 2nd.

Black of course plays his King so as to avoid the corners of the board.

7. K. to K. Kt.'s 5th.	7. K. to Q's sq.
8. K. to K. B's 6th.	8. K. to K's sq.
9. B. to Q. B's 7th.	

Remark how every move now serves to circumscribe the action of the Black King.

	9. K. to K. B's sq.
10. B. to Q's 7th.	10. K. to K. Kt.'s sq.
11. K. to K. Kt.'s 6th.	11. K. to B's sq.
12. B. to Q's 6th (ch.)	12. K. to K. Kt.'s sq.
13. B. to K's 6th.	13. K. to R's sq.
14. B. to K's 5th.	

giving checkmate.

It has just been remarked that a single Knight with the aid of his King cannot effect checkmate unless the opposing King is impeded by his own men. Even two Knights cannot do so. But the accompanying diagram shows how one Knight may give checkmate if the adverse King is so hampered.

Set up the men thus:—

Diagram 28.

BLACK.

WHITE.

The position of the men, in writing, would be this:—

WHITE.	BLACK.
K. at Q. B's 2nd.	K. at Q. R's 7th.
Kt. at Q's 8th.	P. at Q. R's 6th,
	and Q. Kt.'s 3rd.

In this situation Black's Pawns are the cause of his defeat. But for them it would be impossible for the single Knight, or, indeed, two Knights, if he played correctly, to effect checkmate. As it is, the game can be very quickly won thus:—

WHITE.	BLACK.
1. Kt. to Q. B's 6th.	1. P. to Q. Kt.'s 4th.
2. Kt. to Q. Kt.'s 4th (ch.)	2. K. to Q. R's 8th.
3. K. to Q. B's sq.	3. P. to Q. R's 7th.

Observe that all Black's moves are compulsory.

4. Kt. to Q. B's 2nd.

Checkmate.

The examples before you, if played over repeatedly, may suffice to prepare you for the more complicated manœuvres it is now necessary for you to understand. Before attempting them, it will not be amiss for you to make yourself thoroughly acquainted with the Rules and Regulations appointed to govern Chess-playing at the present day.

Regulations for Playing.

Private Agreement.—Either at the commencement or in the course of a game, the players may mutually agree upon any deviation from the laws they think proper. But a player who has conceded an indulgence to his opponent has no right to demand a similar concession, unless it was specially stipulated to be reciprocal. Each player is bound by the laws of the game in all cases not provided for by distinct agreements to the contrary.

Rule I. Wrong Position on the Chess-board.—If during the progress of a game either player discovers that the chess-board has been improperly placed, he may insist on its being adjusted. The game to proceed from the point where the adjustment took place, as if no mistake in the position of the board had been made. (N.B. Lookers-on are privileged to inform the players of the chess-board being wrongly placed.)

II. Omission or Misplacement of the Chess-men.—If at any time in the course of a game it is found that the men were not properly placed, or that one or more of them were omitted at the beginning, the game in question must be annulled.

III. Right of Move and Choice of Colour.—The right of making the first move and (if either player require it) of choosing the colour of the men must be decided by lot. Each player then moves one man at a time, except in case of castling, or where odds of moves are given, or where his adversary has forfeited his move, alternately throughout the game. In any series of games between the same players at one sitting or in one match, each shall have the first move alternately in all the games whether won or drawn. But if a game is annulled, that is, not played out, the player who had the first move in that game shall move first in the next. When the players have each made one move in a game they must be considered to have chosen the men, and must retain them throughout the whole of a sitting or match, unless otherwise agreed by mutual arrangement.

IV. Commencing out of Turn.—If a player make the first move in a game when it is not his turn to do so, the game must be annulled and begun again, if the error is noticed by the adversary before he has made his fourth move. After four moves have been made on each side the game must proceed and be considered legal. If it occur in a match, the player deprived of the move must, when more games have to be played, take an additional first move in compensation.

V. Playing two Moves in Succession.—If in the course of a game a player move a man when it is not his turn to play, he must retract the last move, and, if his adversary chooses, after he himself has moved, must play the man wrongly moved, if it can be played legally. But the adversary can only enforce this penalty before touching a man in reply. If the error is discovered later it must be rectified by the *Giuoco a Monte*, without penalty. This rule applies only to complete moves, not to merely touching a man.

VI. Touch and Move.—A player must never touch any of the men except when it is his turn to play, and then only such man of his own as he intends to move, or such of his adversary's as he intends to take. A player who touches with his hand one of his own men when it is his turn to play, must move it if it can be legally moved, unless before touching it he say "*J'adoube*," or words to the same effect. And a player who touches one of his adversary's men (under the same conditions) must take it. If in either case the move cannot legally be made, the offender must move his King, and in the event of the King having no legal move he must play any other man legally movable that his adversary pleases. If a player, however, touches a man, in consequence of a false cry of "Check," or being checked and not apprised of it by his adversary, touches a man, he is not obliged to play it, or, having played it, may retract the move.

VII. Touching a Square with a Man.—A move is complete and irrevocable (provided it be a legal one) the moment the Piece or Pawn has quitted the player's hand, but as long as the hand remains on the man touched it may be played to any square it commands which the player has not touched with it during his deliberation on the move. But it must always be played to a different square from that it occupied previously to the move, and, if it has touched all the squares it commands, it must be played to any one of them the opponent elects.

VIII. False Moves.—If a player be guilty of a false move by playing a Piece or Pawn of his own to a square to which it cannot be legally moved, or capture an adverse man by a move which cannot legally be made, he must, at the choice of his adversary, either move his own or take the adverse man legally, forfeit his turn to move, or play any other man legally movable which his adversary may select. Castling, under circumstances forbidden in the fundamental laws, must be considered a false move in the meaning of this clause.

IX. Touching more than one Man.—If a player, when it is his turn to play, touch with his hand more than one of his own men (unless in castling), or of his adversary's, he must, when the men touched are his own, play any one of them legally movable that his opponent selects. When they are his adversary's, he must capture whichever of them his antagonist chooses, provided it can be legally taken. If, in such case, it happens that none of the men so touched can be moved or captured, then the offender must move his King, and, if the King cannot legally be moved, he must play any other Piece or Pawn legally movable that his opponent may name.

X. Enforcing Penalties. Giuoco a Monte.—A penalty can only be enforced before the adversary has touched a man in reply. If an illegality is discovered at any later period, the move on which it was committed, and all made subsequently, must be retracted, and the error corrected at the offending party's own option. If the source of a manifest illegality cannot be discovered, the game must be annulled. When the King is moved as a penalty, the player cannot castle on that move, and of course forfeits his right to castle during that game.

XI. Check.—A player must audibly say "Check" when he makes a move which puts the hostile King in check. The King must then be played out of check, on the move made in reply to that which gives it, either by being moved, by the capture of the checking man, or by the interposition of a man between the King and that which gives check. A player is not compelled to give check because he utters it, unless he has already touched a man which cannot move without giving check. But, if it is uttered and not given, the move on which it is uttered must be retracted and another made, if the adversary require it. If a player move his King into check; if he remove a man which covered his King and thereby place him in check; if, while his King is in check, he touch or move a man which does not cover the check; in either of these cases he has touched or moved a man in such a manner as to subject him to the penalties laid down in Section VI. If check is not uttered and the adversary makes a move which really covers the check, such move must stand, as it proves the check to have been observed.

XII. A KING REMAINING IN CHECK.—If the King of either player is placed in check, and the check is not announced or discovered until one or more moves have been made, all moves subsequently made must be retracted, and the player who ought to have announced the check must make some other move. If the check has been duly announced, but still not provided against, the moves must only be retracted as far as that of the King, which must be placed out of check in any manner its player chooses. If, however, the moves subsequent to the unannounced or uncovered check cannot be remembered, the game must be annulled. In this case, the player who moved first retains the first move for the next game.

XIII. J'ADOUBE.—When a player touches a man for the purpose of adjusting it, and not with the intention of moving it, he must, before touching it, say "*J'adoube*," or words to that effect. He will then have the right of moving any other man he thinks proper, notwithstanding his having touched the one in question. But this expression must not be used as an afterthought to prevent the necessity of moving a man already touched, nor must it be used to justify the touching of a man which does not require adjusting. If a player say "*J'adoube*" *after* touching a man, or before touching one which does not require adjusting, he is compelled to move or capture the man touched, as if *J'adoube* had not been said.

XIV. THE COUNTING FIFTY MOVES.—If at any period of

a game one player should persist in repeating a particular check, or series of checks, or the same line of play, his adversary can demand that the game shall be limited to fifty more moves on each side, and, if within that limit neither party win, the game must terminate as a drawn one. So also when a player has only a King remaining on the board, he may insist on the moves being counted from that moment, and, after fifty having been made on each side without result, the game must be considered drawn. This rule is applicable also in cases where one player has only a King and Queen, a King and Rook, and King and Bishop, or a King and Knight, against a superior or equal force. And whenever one player considers that one side can force the game, or that neither side can win it, he has the right of submitting the case to the umpire or bystanders, who shall decide whether it is one for the fifty-move counting.—N.B. But it does not apply to games wherein one party undertakes to mate with a particular man or on a particular square.

XV. Duration.—As a general principle, it is not expedient to limit the time of moving. But in matches of importance it may often be desirable to do so. In such case the best course appears to be the allotting a certain portion of time to each party for a certain number of moves, leaving him to expend his time at his discretion, and, in the event of his exceeding it, to impose a pecuniary fine for every instance of excess.*

XVI. Upsetting the Board.—Should the board be upset, and all or any of the men thrown off or out of position, they must be replaced, and the game must proceed in its regular course. And in case of a dispute respecting the replacing, the opinion of the player who did not upset the board shall always prevail over that of the player who did. Wilfully upsetting the board is equivalent to resigning the game.

XVII. Dropped Man.—If at any time it is discovered that a man has dropped off the board, and moves have been made during its absence, such moves shall be retracted and

---

* Though the time occupied in a move is not limited by law, a player must not purposely protract the game with the view of wearying or annoying his opponent.

the man restored. If the players cannot agree as to its restoration, the game must be annulled. A dropped man may be replaced on the board without saying "*J'adoube.*"

XVIII. Abandoning the Game.—If either player abandon the game, discontinue his moves, voluntarily resign, or refuse to abide by a decision of the umpire, he must be considered to have lost the game.

XIX. The Umpire or Bystanders.—The umpire shall have authority to decide any question whatever that may arise in the course of a game, but must never interfere except when appealed to by one of the players, unless a violation of the fundamental laws has taken place; and when appealed to he must always apply the laws as he finds them herein expressed, and neither assume the power of modifying them or deviating from them in particular cases, according to his own judgment. When a question is submitted to the umpire or to bystanders, by both players, their decision shall be final and binding upon both players. The term bystander comprises any impartial player of eminence who can be appealed to, absent or present.

Rules for Playing the Games at Odds.

I. In games where one player gives the odds of a piece, or "the exchange," or allows his opponent to count drawn games as won, or agrees to checkmate with a particular Piece or Pawn, or on a particular square, he has the right to choose the men and to move first, unless an arrangement to the contrary is agreed to between the combatants.

II. When the odds of Pawn and one move, or Pawn and more moves, are given, the Pawn given must be understood to be the King's Bishop's Pawn.

III. When a player gives the odds of his King's or Queen's Rook, he must not castle (or, more properly speaking, leap his King) on the side from whence he takes off the Rook, unless before commencing the game or match he stipulates to have the privilege of so doing.

IV. When a player undertakes to give checkmate with one of his Pawns, or with a particular Pawn, the said Pawn must not be converted into a Piece.

V. When a player accepts the odds of several moves, he

must not play any Piece or Pawn beyond the fourth square —*i.e.*, he must not cross the middle line of the board, before his adversary makes his first move. Such several moves are to be collectively considered as the first move of the player accepting the odds.

VI. In the odds of checkmating on a particular square, it must be the square occupied by the King mated, not by the man giving mate.

VII. The player who undertakes to win in a particular manner, and either draws the game or wins in some other manner, must be adjudged to be the loser.

In all other respects the play in games at odds must be governed by the regulations before laid down.

Rules for Playing the Game by Correspondence.

I. In playing a game by correspondence, the two parties should always agree beforehand in writing as to the persons who are to take part in the contest, as to the time and mode of transmitting the moves, as to the penalties to be inflicted for any breach of the contract, and as to the umpire or referee.

II. In a game of this description, a move once dispatched by the medium agreed on cannot be recalled. If a legal move, it must be abided by; and, if an illegal one, the party sending it will be subjected to the same penalty as for a false move played with an opponent *vis-à-vis*.

III. Neither party shall be obliged to send more than one move at a time, but, if either choose to send more, the moves so sent must be considered irrevocable if legal, and punishable in the manner before stated if unlawful.

IV. When several successive moves are sent at once, and one of them is found to be illegal, the sender must suffer the punishment for a false move, and the game then proceed from that point. The subsequent moves which were forwarded with the illegal one must, however, in that case be cancelled.

V. If a player send hypothetical moves—that is, moves on the assumption that his adversary will make certain others previously—they shall not be binding unless his adversary make the moves assumed.

VI. If a player send more than one move on the same turn to play, the adversary may select which he pleases.

VII. If either party in a game by correspondence accept the assistance of any player not originally engaged to take part in the contest, that party shall forfeit the game.

VIII. If a move bears more than one interpretation the player receiving it must announce, with his next move, which interpretation he adopts, or it must be interpreted according to the intention of the sender.

IX. A move not intelligibly described incurs the penalty of sending no move on the day appointed.

Rules for Playing the Games by Consultation.

I. The law of touch and move must be observed in these games.

II. Each party must be bound by the move communicated to the adversary, whether it be made on the adversary's board, in writing, or by word of mouth. If the move so communicated should prove to be different from that actually made on the party's own board, the latter must be altered to accord with the former.

III. If either party be detected in moving the men when it is not their turn to play, or in moving more than one man (except in castling) when it is their turn to play, they shall forfeit the game; unless they can show that the man was moved for the purpose of adjusting or replacing it.

IV. If either party have, accidentally or otherwise, removed a man from the board which has not been captured in the course of the game, and made certain moves under the impression that such man was no longer in play, the moves must stand, but the man may be replaced whenever the error is discovered.

V. If either party in a game by consultation permit a bystander to take part in the contest, that party shall forfeit the game.

CHAPTER VII.

PREPARATORY GAME.

Having acquired a competent knowledge of the move and power of each Chess-man, the student may proceed to the consideration of the openings; that is to say, to the most speedy and effective way of bringing his forces into action at the beginning of a game. As a preparation for this, I append an imaginary game, which will render many of the technical expressions before mentioned familiar to you, and give you a faint idea of the multifarious combinations of which the Chess-armies are capable. It is usual, though not at all necessary, in books on Chess to suppose the first player to have the *White* men. As this facilitates reference in the notes, I follow the custom; but a learner should accustom himself to play indifferently either with the White or with the Black men.

WHITE.	BLACK.
1. P. to K's 4th.	1 P. to K's 4th.

This is by far the most common mode of beginning a game, because the King's Pawn is the only one which, on being first moved, gives an outlet to two pieces in different directions.

2. B. to Q. B's 4th.	2. B. to Q. B's 4th.

These moves are also very common, and the opening so begun, you will remember, is known as the *King's Bishop's Opening*.

3. Q. to K. R's 5th.

This is a move inexperienced players are partial to, as it threatens to checkmate the opponent at once by taking the

K. B's Pawn with the Queen, and threatens also to win the K's Pawn. It is rarely good play, however, to bring the Queen into action at the outset of a game. In the present case, if Black defend himself properly, the attack, like most premature attacks in Chess, does not benefit White's game.

3. Q. to K's 2nd.

By this step Black for the moment protects both his K. B's Pawn and his K's Pawn.

4. Kt. to K. B's 3rd.

A natural move, as it again exposes Black's K's Pawn to the danger of capture.

4. P. to Q's 3rd.

Again, the reader will observe that Black secures his Pawn by the obvious course of bringing as many men to defend as there are men to attack it.

5. Kt. to K. Kt.'s 5th.

Another natural move, because it brings three Pieces to the attack of a point (the K. B's Pawn) which is protected only by two.

5. Kt. to K. R's 3rd.

Black makes the move which most young players would make here; he brings a third Piece to defend what three Pieces threaten. When more advanced in knowledge of Chess strategy, the learner will discover that, oftentimes, counter-attack is the best defence. In the case before us he will find it to be so, for Black can at least equalise the battle by attacking his adversary's Queen either with Kt. to K. B's 3rd or with P. to K. Kt.'s 3rd. (See the Analysis of this variation of the Opening farther on in the book.)

6. Kt. to Q. B's 3rd.

A good move. Threatening to attack the Queen, if not prevented, at Q's 5th, and dislodge her from her present post.

6. P. to Q. B's 3rd.

Black discerns the object of his adversary's last move, and guards against it.

7. Castles: (Moving the K. to K. Kt.'s sq. and the R. to K. B's sq.) — 7. Castles: (In the same manner).

As a general rule, young players should Castle early in the game. With their King secure, for the moment at least, from attack, they play with more self-possession, and are better enabled to develop their game.

8. P. to Q's 3rd. — 8. Kt. to Q's 2nd.

Black acts sagely here in not yielding to the temptation to attack the Queen at once by playing his Q's Bishop to K. Kt.'s 5th.

9. K. to K. R's sq.

This move must appear a very purposeless one to a novice, but it really is anything but useless. White wishes to strengthen his attack upon the opposing King's quarters by bringing more force to bear upon them. The best way to do this, he thinks, is to throw forward his K. B's Pawn, and by then taking the K's Pawn therewith, or by getting his own Pawn captured to open a road for his K's Rook to come into play. While his King stands on the Kt.'s sq. and the adverse Bishop attacks the K. B's Pawn, it is plain that Pawn cannot move, because in moving it will expose the King to check from the foresaid Bishop. White retreats his King, therefore, that he may be enabled, when it suits him, to throw forward the K. B's Pawn.

9. Kt. to K. B's 3rd.

Black now dislodges the Queen with much effect, and by bringing his other Knight to the defence renders his King, for the time, secure.

10. Q. to K. R's 4th. — 10. P. to Q's 4th.

Very well played; for if White does not take this Pawn with Pawn, his Bishop is driven back, and in a manner shut out, and the attack is virtually at an end, while if he does take it he affords Black an opportunity of making a serious onslaught with his K's Kt. on the Queen.

11. P. takes Q's P.

White prefers this—not foreseeing, perhaps, all the consequences—to retreating his Bishop.

11. Kt. to K. B's 4th.

This will be found a very difficult move for White to meet. It makes a direct attack upon the Queen, and forces her to move somewhere. But where can she move to? Every square but one, it will be seen, is attacked by the enemy's men. She has no retreat but to that one square.

12. Q. to K. R's 3rd. 12. Kt. to K's 6th.

A terrible move. It attacks White's Queen with the Bishop, and his Rook with the Knight.

13. Q. to K. R's 4th.

He appears to have no better move. He might, indeed, resort to a counter-attack by moving his foremost Pawn to Q's 6th, threatening the Black Queen, but in that case his opponent need not take the Pawn with his Queen, and so expose her to subsequent attack from one of the Knights; he could simply retreat her to her own square, where she would be as well posted as before, and in perfect safety.

13. Kt. takes R.

14. Kt. to K's 4th.

White has lost, not a Rook, but what is technically known as "the exchange;" that is, he has lost a Rook in exchange for a Piece of lesser weight, for the adverse Kt. cannot escape. In return for this loss he has an opportunity of resuming his attack upon his adversary's King; and this attack, unless opposed with care and skill, will prove very troublesome to Black.

14. P. to K. R's 3rd.

This saves him. A little consideration will show that any other move would have been fatal. If he had taken the Kt. with Kt., for example, White would at once have checkmated him by taking the K. R's Pawn with his Queen. So, if he had taken the Q's Pawn with Pawn, White would have checkmated him in two moves by merely taking the Knight with Knight checking, and then K. R.'s Pawn with Queen, checkmating.

15. P. to Q's 6th.

White defends himself very skilfully, observe, by thus maintaining an attack upon his foe, and this line of action is much better than simply retreating the threatened Knight.

15. B. takes P. at Q's 6th.

[This circumlocutory mode of expression is a grave necessity in the English system of notation. It is not often required, but occasionally, as in the present instance, it is indispensable to make the move clear to young players. Black plays with remarkable sagacity at this point, for if he had been induced by the hope of winning a Piece to capture the Knight, he would have lost the game. Why he would have done so is too instructive to be passed over. Suppose, therefore, he had played—

15. P. takes Kt.

Now, if White take the Queen with Pawn, Black can do the same, and he will have perhaps the best of the fight, but White will not play thus; he prefers—

16. Q's B. takes P.

And after that move Black cannot save the game, as even the tyro will discover after a few minutes' examination.]

16. Kt. to K. B's 3rd. 16. Kt. takes Kt.
17. Q. takes Kt. 17. K. to R's sq.

See the note to White's 9th move.

18. K. to Kt.'s sq.

White loses time here. His object of course is to capture the Knight; but the Knight cannot escape, and his attention should rather have been directed to prevent the threatened advance of Black's K. B's Pawn.

18. P. to K. B's 4th.

19. Q. to K's 2nd.

He would have done better in playing the Queen to K. R's 4th. As matters now stand, Black is very likely to release his Knight or gain another Piece in return for him.

19. P. to K's 5th.

20. Kt. to K. Kt.'s 5th.

The best move, for Black evidently cannot take the Knight without losing the game.

20. Kt. takes K. R's P.

Black has now contrived to free the Knight.

21. P. takes P. 21. P. takes P.
22. Q. to K. R's 5th.

Having lost a Rook, White cannot afford to take the Pawn with his Queen, and exchange Queens. He prefers rather to try and gain a Rook for his Knight.

22. Kt. to K. Kt.'s 5th.

Black has such a preponderance of material, and so good a position, that he need not object to the exchange his opponent seeks.

23. Q. to K. Kt.'s 6th.

He had better have carried out his first intention of checking with the Kt. at K. B's 7th.

23. B. to K. B's 4th.

Black might safely have taken the Knight with his K. R's Pawn, because his Knight is in a position to interpose at K. R's 3rd when the Queen gives check to K. R's 5th.

24. Q. to K. R's 5th.

White could still have gained the Rook for his Knight by giving check with his Knight, but in doing so he must have submitted to an exchange of Queens, which would have rendered the disparity of force between his and Black's army even greater than it now is.

24. P. to K. Kt.'s 3rd.

White is now precluded from the poor solace of obtaining the Rook for his Knight, and driven to a very disastrous retreat.

25. Q. to K. R's 4th. 25. B. to Q. B's 4th.

Black pushes his advantage with merciless persistency. By this step we see that he threatens to win the adverse Queen by taking the K. B's Pawn, and to avert this fatal blow, White must either move his Queen or interpose his Q's Bishop at K's 3rd—a choice of evils.

26. B. to K's 3rd.

This costs poor White two Pieces for one, but yet it was perhaps less fatally injurious than retreating his Queen.

26. B. takes B.

27. P. takes B. 27. Q. takes Kt.

White's game against any opponent of moderate Chess skill is past hope, but between inexperienced hands a game at Chess is never hopeless until checkmate is given.

28. Q. to K's sq.

Exchanging Queens is almost death to him; avoiding the exchange is almost as bad.

28. Kt. takes P.

He could have compelled the exchange of Queens by taking the K's Pawn at this moment with his Queen checking, but his position warrants his seeking for an advantage more decisive than even that.

29. Q. to Q. B's 3rd (ch.) 29. K. to R's 2nd.
30. Q. to Q's 2nd.

This move is less to the purpose than playing Bishop to K. B's sq., though that would only postpone the inevitable checkmate for a few more moves.

30. Q. R. to Q's sq.
31. Q. to K's 2nd. 31. B. to K. Kt.'s 5th.
32. Q. to K's sq. 32. Kt. takes K. Kt.'s P.

Far more decisive than taking the Bishop.

33. K. takes Kt. 33. B. to K. R's 6th. (*double check.*)

By this double check Black is enabled to deliver the *coup de grace* at once.

34. K. takes B. 34. R. to B's 6th (ch.).
35. K. to R's 2nd. 35. Q. to R's 4th (ch.).
36. K. to Kt.'s 2nd. 36. Q. to Kt.'s 5th (ch.).
37. K. to R's 2nd. 37. R. to R's 6th.

Checkmate.

BOOK II.

OPENINGS ON THE KING'S SIDE.

CHAPTER I.

THE KING'S BISHOP'S OPENING.

1. $\frac{\text{P. to K's 4th.}}{\text{P. to K's 4th.}}$ 2. $\frac{\text{B. to Q. B's 4th.}}{}$

GAME THE FIRST.

(LEWIS-GAME.)

WHITE.	BLACK.
1. P. to K's 4th.	1. P. to K's 4th.
2. B. to Q. B's 4th.	2. B. to Q. B's 4th.
3. P. to Q. B's 3rd.	

This opening, the favourite of Philidor, is first found in the work of Ruy Lopez, "Libro de la invencion liberal y arte del juigo del Axedres," &c., 1561. In pursuance of my wish to simplify the nomenclature of Chess, by giving to each *début* the name of some distinguished writer on or player of the game, I have thought it proper to call this opening by the name of a writer who appears to me to have done most towards developing its resources and bringing it into notice.

Upon the merits of Black's move, 2. $\frac{}{\text{B. to Q. B's 4th}}$ in comparison with those of 2. $\frac{}{\text{Kt. to K. B's 3rd}}$, which will be treated of farther on, opinions are divided, but the latter is undoubtedly more popular at the present day.

White's move, 3. $\frac{\text{P. to Q. B's 3rd}}{\quad}$, is styled the "classical" move. But although it has the advantage, as M. Preti observes, of preparing for the advance of P. to Q's 4th, and of affording an opening for the Queen to Q. Kt.'s 3rd, it is not so strong as 3. $\frac{\text{Kt. to K. B's 3rd}}{\quad}$, a move to be considered presently.

3. Kt. to K. B's 3rd.

A good move, though not better than 3. $\frac{\quad}{\text{P. to Q's 4th}}$, or 3. $\frac{\quad}{\text{Q. to K. Kt.'s 4th}}$, or 3. $\frac{\quad}{\text{Q. to K's 2nd}}$, which will be examined as Variations A. B. and C.

4. P. to Q's 4th. — 4. P. takes P.
5. P. to K's 5th.

If White prefer 5. $\frac{\text{P. takes P.}}{\quad}$, the natural continuation is 5. $\frac{\quad}{\text{B. to Q. Kt.'s 5th (ch.)}}$, 6. $\frac{\text{B. to Q's 2nd}}{\text{B. takes B. (ch.)}}$, 7. $\frac{\text{Kt. takes B.}}{\text{Kt. takes P.}}$, 8. $\frac{\text{Kt. takes Kt.}}{\text{P. to Q's 4th}}$, 9. $\frac{\text{B. to Q. Kt.'s 5th (ch.)}}{\text{P. to Q. B's 3rd}}$, 10. $\frac{\text{B. takes P. (ch.)}}{\text{Kt. takes B.}}$, 11. $\frac{\text{Kt. to Q. B's 3rd}}{\text{B. to K's 3rd}}$, and neither party can claim the superiority.

5. P. to Q's 4th.

If Black play here 5. $\frac{\quad}{\text{Q. to K's 2nd}}$, or 5. $\frac{\quad}{\text{Kt. to K's 5th}}$, he loses ground, *ex. gr.* 5. $\frac{\quad}{\text{Q. to K's 2nd}}$, 6. $\frac{\text{P. takes P.}}{\text{B. to Q. Kt.'s 5th (ch.)}}$, 7. $\frac{\text{K. to B's sq.}}{\text{Kt. to K's 5th}}$, 8. $\frac{\text{Q. to K. Kt.'s 4th}}{\text{P. to K. B's 4th}}$, 9. $\frac{\text{Q. to K. R's 5th (ch.)}}{\text{P. to Kt.'s 3rd}}$, 10. $\frac{\text{Q. to K. R's 6th}}{\text{P. to Q. B's 3rd}}$, 11. $\frac{\text{P. to K. B's 3rd}}{\text{P. to Q's 4th}}$, 12. $\frac{\text{B. to K's 2nd}}{\quad}$, with a winning advantage. Similarly, if 5. $\frac{\quad}{\text{Kt. to K's 5th}}$, 6. $\frac{\text{Q. to K's 2nd}}{\text{P. to Q's 4th}}$, 7. $\frac{\text{P. takes P. \textit{en passant}}}{\text{Castles}}$, 8. $\frac{\text{P. takes Q. B's P.}}{\text{Q. takes P}}$, 9. $\frac{\text{Q. takes Kt.}}{\quad}$, and again White has a winning game.

6. B. to Q. Kt.'s 5th (ch.)

White may also play 6. (B. to Q. Kt.'s 3rd / —), or 6. (P. takes Kt. / —), with the following result.

In the first place,—6. (B. to Q. Kt.'s 3rd / Kt. to K's 5th), 7. (P. takes P. / Q. to K. R's 5th), 8. (B. to K's 3rd / B. to Q. Kt.'s 5th (ch.)), 9. (K. to B's sq. / P. to Q. B's 3rd), 10. (P. to K. Kt.'s 3rd / B. to K. R's 6th (ch.)), 11. (Kt. takes B. / Q. takes Kt. (ch.)), 12. (K. to Kt.'s sq. / P. to K. R's 3rd), 13. (B. to Q. B's 2nd / —). White has a slight advantage.

In the second place,—6. (P. takes Kt. / P. takes B.) 7. (P. takes Kt.'s P. / R. to Kt.'s sq.). 8. (Q. to K. R's 5th / Q. to K's 2nd (ch.)), 9. (K. to Q's sq. / R. takes P.), 10. (Kt. to K. B's 3rd / Kt. to Q. B's 3rd), 11. (R. to K's sq. / B. to K's 3rd), 12. (R. takes B. / Q. takes R.), 13. (Q. takes B. / P. to Q. Kt.'s 3rd), 14. (Q. to Q. Kt.'s 5th / R. takes P.), 15. (P. takes P. / P. to Q. R's 3rd), with very little inequality.

To return to the original theme:—

	6. B. to Q's 2nd.
7. B. takes B.	7. K's Kt. takes B.
8. P. takes P.	8. B. to Q. Kt.'s 5th (ch.)
9. Kt. to Q. B's 3rd.	9. Castles.
10. K's Kt. to K's 2nd.	10. P. to Q. B's 4th.
11. P. takes P.	11. Kt. takes Q's B. P.
12. Castles.	12. B. takes Kt.
13. Kt. takes B.	13. P. to Q's 5th.
14. K. to K's 2nd.	14. Kt. to Q. B's 3rd.

An equal game.

Variations on Black's 3rd Move.

(A.)

3. P. to Q's 4th.

The extremely ingenious line of defence which this move inaugurates is due to the writer and player after whom I have named the opening.

4. B. takes P.

If White takes Pawn with Pawn, then follow 4. $\frac{}{\text{B. takes P. (ch.)}}$, 5. $\frac{\text{K. takes B.}}{\text{Q. to K. R's 5th (ch.)}}$, &c.

4. Kt. to K. B's 3rd.

Position after Black's 4th Move.

5. Q. to Q. Kt.'s 3rd.

Here White has the choice of three other moves, viz., 5. $\frac{}{\text{Q. to K. B's 3rd}}$, 5. $\frac{}{\text{Q. to Q. R's 4th (ch.)}}$, and 5. $\frac{}{\text{B. to Q's Kt. 3rd}}$, which, before proceeding farther, we will examine under the heads of *a*, *b*, and *c*.

(*a*.)

5. $\frac{\text{Q. to K. B's 3rd.}}{\text{Kt. takes B.}}$ (Black's best play is to capture the Bishop, for if he Castle, White may retreat the Bishop to Q. B's 4th, and then challenge an exchange of Queens at Q's 3rd.) 6. $\frac{\text{P. takes Kt.}}{\text{Castles}}$, 7. $\frac{\text{Kt. to K's 2nd}}{\text{P. to K. B's 4th}}$, 8. $\frac{\text{P. to Q's 4th}}{\text{P. takes P.}}$.

(This is better, I think, for Black than 8. $\frac{}{\text{P. to K's 5th}}$). 9. $\frac{\text{P. to Q. Kt.'s 4th}}{}$ (a move commended by M. Préti, instead of 9. $\frac{\text{Kt. takes P.}}{}$), 9. $\frac{}{\text{B. to Q. Kt.'s 3rd}}$, 10. $\frac{\text{P. to Q. B's 4th}}{\text{P. to Q. R's 3rd}}$, 11. $\frac{\text{P. to Q. B's 5th}}{\text{B. to Q. R's 2nd}}$, 12. $\frac{\text{Kt. takes P.}}{}$

White has the superior position.

(*b*.)

5. $\frac{\text{Q. to Q. R's 4th (ch.)}}{\text{P. to Q. B's 3rd}}$, 6. $\frac{\text{B. takes B's P. (ch.)}}{\text{K. to B's sq. (best)}}$, 7. $\frac{\text{Q. to Q. Kt.'s 3rd}}{\text{Kt. takes P.}}$, 8. $\frac{\text{Kt. to K. B's 3rd}}{\text{Kt. takes B's P.}}$, 9. $\frac{\text{Castles}}{\text{Kt. to Q's 6th (ch.)}}$, 10. $\frac{\text{K. to Q's sq.}}{\text{Q. to K. R's 3rd}}$, and Black has the better game.

(c.)

5. $\frac{\text{B. to Q. Kt.'s 3rd}}{\text{Kt. takes P.}}$, 6. $\frac{\text{Q. to K's 2nd}}{\text{Kt. takes B's P.}}$. (This is better than 6. $\frac{\quad}{\text{Q. to K. R's 5th}}$, which can be met efficiently by 7. $\frac{\text{Kt. to B's 3rd}}{\quad}$, and better also than 6. $\frac{\quad}{\text{B. takes P. (ch.)}}$), 7. $\frac{\text{Q. takes P. (ch.)}}{\text{Q. to K's 2nd}}$, 8. $\frac{\text{Q. takes Q. (ch.)}}{\text{K. takes Q.}}$, 9. $\frac{\text{P. to Q's 4th}}{\text{B. takes P.}}$, 10. $\frac{\text{P. takes B.}}{\text{Kt. takes R.}}$, where Black comes off with a game quite as good as his opponent's.

To return to the original theme,

5. Kt. takes B.

This capture is now preferred to Castling, which leads to the following:—5. $\frac{\quad}{\text{Castles}}$, 6. $\frac{\text{Kt. to K. B's 3rd}}{\text{Kt. takes B.}}$, 7. $\frac{\text{Q. takes Kt.}}{\text{Q. takes Q.}}$, 8. $\frac{\text{P. takes Q.}}{\text{P. to K's 5th}}$, the game being about equal.

At the 6th move of this last variation some instructive combinations arise from White taking the Q. Kt.'s Pawn, in place of playing 6. $\frac{\text{Kt. to K. B's 3rd}}{\quad}$; for example:—

6. $\frac{\text{B. takes Q. Kt.'s P.}}{\text{B. takes B.}}$, 7. $\frac{\text{Q. takes B.}}{\text{Q. to Q's 6th}}$, 8. $\frac{\text{Q. takes R.}}{\text{Q. to Q. R's 3rd}}$, 9. $\frac{\text{P. to Q's 4th}}{\text{Q. Kt. to Q's 2nd}}$, 10. $\frac{\text{Q. takes R. (ch.)}}{\text{B. takes Q.}}$, 11. $\frac{\text{P. to K. B's 3rd}}{\text{P. takes Q's P.}}$, 12. $\frac{\text{P. takes P.}}{\text{Q. to Q's 6th}}$, and White has an inferior game to Black's.

6. Q. takes Kt.	6. Q. takes Q.
7. P. takes Q.	7. B. to K. B's 4th.
8. Kt. to K. B's 3rd.	8. P. to K. B's 3rd.
9. Castles.	9. B. to Q's 6th.
10. R. to K's sq.	10. Castles.
11. P. to Q. Kt.'s 3rd.	11. P. to K's 5th.
12. Kt. to K. R's 4th.	12. P. to K. B's 4th.

Here, although White has a Pawn more than his adversary, yet the latter's position is quite an equivalent.

(B.)

3. Q. to K. Kt.'s 4th.

This is the defence against 3. $\frac{\text{P. to Q. B's 3rd}}{}$, which we find advocated by the celebrated Italian authors, Del Rio, Lolli, and Ponziani, and in modern days by the not less distinguished théoricen, M. Jaenisch.

4. Q. to K. B's 3rd.

The move recommended by Del Rio. Some writers, however, prefer playing 4. $\frac{\text{K. to B's sq.}}{}$, or 4. $\frac{\text{P. to K. Kt.'s 3rd}}{}$; and it will be well perhaps before proceeding farther to dispose of those moves. Suppose, then, 4. $\frac{\text{K. to B's sq.}}{\text{Q. to K's 2nd}}$, 5. $\frac{\text{P. to Q's 4th}}{\text{B. to Q. Kt.'s 3rd}}$, 6. $\frac{\text{Kt. to K. B's 3rd}}{\text{P. to Q's 3rd}}$, Black has the better game.

Then let us consider, 4. $\frac{\text{P. to K. Kt.'s 3rd}}{}$. This move is objected to because of the possibility of Black establishing his Q's B. at K. R's 6th, and preventing White's Castling, and it certainly presents that disadvantage. On the other hand, it gives White time, and thus enables him to develop his game very effectually.

4. Q. to K. Kt.'s 3rd.

If he bring out his K's Kt. at this moment he is liable to lose the advantage of his present position: *ex. gr.*— 4. $\frac{}{\text{Kt. to K. B's 3rd}}$, 5. $\frac{\text{Kt. to K's 2nd}}{\text{Q. to K. Kt.'s 3rd}}$, 6. $\frac{\text{P. to Q's 4th}}{\text{P. takes P.}}$, 7. $\frac{\text{P. takes P.}}{\text{B. to Q. Kt.'s 5th (ch.)}}$, 8. $\frac{\text{B. to Q's 2nd}}{\text{B. takes B. (ch.)}}$, 9. $\frac{\text{Q's Kt. takes B.}}{\text{P. to Q's 3rd}}$, 10. $\frac{\text{P. to K. R's 3rd}}{}$, and White has the superior position.

5. Kt. to K's 2nd. 5. Kt. to Q. B's 3rd.

Instead of so playing, Black may move 5. $\frac{}{\text{P. to Q's 3rd}}$, or 5. $\frac{}{\text{Kt. to Kt.'s 3rd}}$.

In the first place, suppose, 5. $\frac{}{\text{P. to Q's 3rd}}$ 6. $\frac{\text{P. to Q's 4th}}{\text{B. to Q. Kt.'s 3rd}}$,

7. $\frac{\text{P. takes P.}}{\text{P. takes P.}}$, 8. $\frac{\text{Kt. to K. Kt.'s 3rd}}{\text{Kt. to K. B's 3rd}}$, 9. $\frac{\text{P. to K. R's 3rd}}{}$, equal game.

In the second place,—5. $\frac{}{\text{Kt. to K. B's 3rd}}$, 6. $\frac{\text{P. to Q's 4th}}{\text{P. takes P.}}$, 7. $\frac{\text{P. to K's 5th}}{\text{Kt. to K's 5th}}$, 8. $\frac{\text{P. takes P.}}{\text{B. to Q. Kt.'s 5th (ch.)}}$, 9. $\frac{\text{Kt. to Q. B's 3rd}}{}$, and White has the game in his favour.

6. P. to Q's 3rd.	6. P. to Q's 3rd.
7. B. to K's 3rd.	7. B. to Kt.'s 3rd.
8. Kt. to Q's 2nd.	8. K's Kt. to K's 2nd.

The game is about equal.

(C.)

3. Q. to K's 2nd.

4. Kt. to K. B's 3rd.

If White play 4. $\frac{\text{P. to Q's 4th}}{}$, then follow 4. $\frac{}{\text{P. takes P.}}$, 5. $\frac{\text{P. takes P.}}{\text{Q. takes P. (ch.)}}$, 6. $\frac{\text{K's Kt. to K's 2nd}}{\text{B. to Q. Kt.'s 5th (ch.)}}$, (if 6. $\frac{}{\text{Q. takes Kt.'s P.}}$, White plays 7. $\frac{\text{Kt. to Kt.'s 3rd}}{}$,) 7. $\frac{\text{B. to Q's 2nd}}{\text{B. takes B. (ch.)}}$, 8. $\frac{\text{Q's Kt. takes B.}}{\text{Q. to K's 2nd (best)}}$, 9. $\frac{\text{Castles}}{\text{K. to K. B's 3rd}}$, and Black has at least as good a game as White.

4. P. to Q's 3rd.

Black may play also 4. $\frac{}{\text{Kt. to Q. B's 3rd}}$, which produces a position of the *Giuoco Piano* that will be examined hereafter. He may play, too, 4. $\frac{}{\text{Kt. to K. B's 3rd}}$, of which the probable continuation is, 5. $\frac{\text{P. to Q's 4th}}{\text{P. takes P.}}$, 6. $\frac{\text{Castles}}{\text{P. takes P.}}$, 7. $\frac{\text{Q. Kt. takes P.}}{\text{P. to Q's 3rd}}$, 8. $\frac{\text{P. to K's 5th}}{\text{P. takes P.}}$, 9. $\frac{\text{Kt. takes P.}}{\text{Castles}}$, 10. $\frac{\text{R. to K's sq.}}{\text{B. to K's 3rd}}$, 11. $\frac{\text{B. takes B.}}{\text{P. takes B.}}$, 12. $\frac{\text{Q. to Q. Kt.'s 3rd}}{\text{B. to Q. Kt.'s 3rd}}$, 13. $\frac{\text{Kt. to K. B's 3rd}}{}$, to White's advantage.

5. Castles.	5. B. to K's 3rd.

This is a better move than, 5. $\frac{}{\text{B. to K. Kt.'s 5th}}$, because then follow, 6. $\frac{\text{P. to Q's 4th}}{\text{B. to Q. Kt.'s 3rd (best)}}$, 7. $\frac{\text{P. to Q. R's 4th}}{\text{P. to Q. R's 4th}}$, 8. $\frac{\text{Kt. to Q. R's 3rd}}{\text{Kt. to K. B's 3rd}}$, 9. $\frac{\text{R. to K's sq.}}{\text{Q's Kt. to Q's 2nd}}$, 10. $\frac{\text{Kt. to Q. B's 2nd}}{\text{P. to K. R's 3rd}}$, 11. $\frac{\text{Kt. to K's 3rd}}{}$, which is very favourable to White.

6. Q. to Q. Kt.'s 3rd.	6. B. to Q. Kt.'s 3rd.
7. B. takes B.	7. Q. takes B.
8. Q. takes Q.	8. P. takes Q.
9. P. to Q's 4th.	9. P. takes P.
10. P. takes P.	10. Kt. to K. B's 3rd.

And the game is equal.

Game the Second.

WHITE.	BLACK.
1. P. to K's 4th.	1. P. to K's 4th.
2. B. to Q. B's 4th.	2. B. to Q. B's 4th.
3. Q. to K's 2nd.	

A move found first in the treatise by Lopez, and formerly a good deal practised, but which of late years is seldom adopted. The primary object the inventor of it had in view was to take the adversary's K. B's Pawn with the Bishop, and, if he captured the Piece, to check with the Queen at Q. B's 4th, and thus win a Bishop and Pawn in return, besides depriving the enemy of his Castling privilege. The secondary idea was to throw forward his Pawns on the King's wing, and Castle on the Queen's side.

	3. Kt. to Q. B's 3rd.

Black may also play 3. $\frac{}{\text{Q. to K's 2nd}}$, 3. $\frac{}{\text{P. to Q's 3rd}}$, and 3. $\frac{}{\text{Kt. to K. B's 3rd}}$; *ex. gr.*,

Firstly, 3. $\frac{}{\text{Q. to K's 2nd}}$, 4. $\frac{\text{P. to K. B's 4th}}{\text{Kt. to K. B's 3rd}}$, 5. $\frac{\text{Kt. to K. B's 3rd}}{\text{P. to Q's 3rd}}$, 6. $\frac{\text{Kt. to Q. B's 3rd}}{\text{P. to Q. B's 3rd}}$, 7. $\frac{\text{P. to Q's 3rd}}{\text{B. to K. Kt.'s 5th}}$, 8. $\frac{\text{P. to K. B's 5th}}{\text{Q. Kt. to Q's 2nd}}$, with an equal game.

Secondly, 3. $\frac{}{\text{P. to Q's 3rd}}$, 4. $\frac{\text{P. to K. B's 4th}}{\text{Kt. to K. B's 3rd}}$ (it is not well for Black to take the Knight, for if—4. $\frac{}{\text{B. takes Kt.}}$, 5. $\frac{\text{R. takes B.}}{\text{Kt. to K. B's 3rd}}$, 6. $\frac{\text{P. to Q's 3rd}}{\text{Q. to K's 2nd}}$, 7. $\frac{\text{Kt. to Q. B's 3rd}}{\text{Kt. to Q. B's 3rd}}$, 8. $\frac{\text{B. to K's 3rd}}{\text{P. takes P.}}$, 9. $\frac{\text{Q's B. takes P.}}{\text{Kt. to Q's 5th}}$, 10. $\frac{\text{Q. to K. B's 2nd}}{\text{Kt. to K's 3rd}}$, 11. $\frac{\text{P. to K. Kt.'s 4th}}{}$, and Black's position is inferior), 5. $\frac{\text{P. to Q's 3rd}}{\text{B. to K. Kt.'s 5th}}$, 6. $\frac{\text{Kt. to K. B's 3rd}}{\text{Q. to K's 2nd}}$, neither party has the advantage of the other.

Thirdly, 3. $\frac{}{\text{Kt. to K. B's 3rd}}$, 4. $\frac{\text{P. to K. B's 4th}}{\text{P. to Q's 4th}}$, 5. $\frac{\text{B. takes P.}}{}$, (5. $\frac{\text{P. takes P.}}{\text{P. to K's 5th}}$) 5. $\frac{}{\text{Kt. takes B.}}$, 6. $\frac{\text{P. takes Kt.}}{\text{Castles}}$, 7. $\frac{\text{P. takes P.}}{\text{Q. takes P.}}$, 8. $\frac{\text{Kt. to Q. B's 3rd}}{}$ (if 8. $\frac{\text{P. to Q. B's 3rd}}{\text{B. takes Kt.}}$) 8. $\frac{}{\text{Q. to Q's sq.}}$, 9. $\frac{\text{Kt. to K. B's 3rd}}{\text{B. to K. Kt.'s 5th}}$, 10. $\frac{\text{P. to Q's 3rd}}{\text{B. takes Kt.}}$, 11. $\frac{\text{Q. takes B.}}{\text{Kt. to Q. B's 3rd}}$, and, though minus a Pawn, Black has a superior position.

4. P. to Q. B's 3rd.

At first view it looks profitable for White to take the K. B's Pawn at this moment, but the following moves show this a *deceptio visus*:—4. $\frac{\text{B. takes B. P. (ch.)}}{\text{K. takes B.}}$, 5. $\frac{\text{Q. to Q. B's 4th (ch.)}}{\text{P. to Q's 4th}}$, 6. $\frac{\text{Q. takes B.}}{\text{P. takes K. P.}}$, 7. $\frac{\text{Q. to B's 4th (ch.)}}{\text{B. to K's 3rd}}$, 8. $\frac{\text{Q. takes P.}}{\text{Kt. to K. B's 3rd}}$. Black has lost a Pawn, but his position much more than compensates the loss.

4. Kt. to K. B's 3rd.

5. P. to K. B's 4th.

White will perhaps do better here to play 5. $\frac{\text{Kt. to K. B's 3rd}}{}$, and equalise the game.

5. B. takes Kt.

6. R. takes B. — 6. Castles.

7. P. to Q's 3rd. — 7. P. to Q's 4th.

8. B. takes P. — 8. Kt. takes B.

9. P. takes Kt.	9. P. takes K. B's P.
10. B. takes P.	10. R. to K's sq.
11. B. to K's 3rd.	11. Kt. to K's 4th.
12. P. to K. R's 3rd.	12. B. to K. B's 4th.
13. P. to Q's 4th.	13. B. to Q's 6th.

Winning a Piece next move by playing Kt. to Q. B's 5th.

Game the Third.

WHITE.	BLACK.
1. P. to K's 4th.	1. P. to K's 4th.
2. B. to Q. B's 4th.	2. B. to Q. B's 4th.
3. Q. to K. R's 5th.	

I remarked in the preliminary game, where this move occurs, that, as a rule, it is not prudent to play out the Queen at the beginning of a game. The present case is no exception to this salutary principle, since the utmost White can obtain against the best defence is a drawn battle.

3. Q. to K's 2nd.

Black may also play his Queen to K. B's 3rd, and ensure an equal game ;— 3. $\frac{\quad}{\text{Q. to K. B's 3rd}}$, 4. $\frac{\text{Kt. to K. B's 3rd}}{\text{P. to Q's 3rd}}$, 5. $\frac{\text{Kt. to Q. B's 3rd}}{\text{K. Kt. to K's 2nd}}$.

4. Kt. to K. B's 3rd.	4. P. to Q's 3rd.

If 4. $\frac{\quad}{\text{Kt. to K. B's 3rd}}$, 5. $\frac{\text{Q. takes K. P.}}{\text{B. takes B. P. (ch.)}}$, 6. $\frac{\text{K. to K's 2nd}}{\text{Q. takes Q.}}$, 7. $\frac{\text{Kt. takes Q.}}{\text{B. to Q. Kt.'s 3rd}}$, 8. $\frac{\text{B. takes B. P. (ch.)}}{\text{K. to K's 2nd}}$, 9. $\frac{\text{B. to Q. Kt.'s 3rd}}{\text{P. to Q's 3rd}}$, even game.

5. Kt. to K. Kt.'s 5th.	5. P. to K. Kt.'s 3rd.

If 5. $\frac{\quad}{\text{Kt. to K. B's 3rd}}$, 6. $\frac{\text{Q. takes B. P. (ch.)}}{\text{Q. takes Q.}}$, 7. $\frac{\text{B. takes Q. (ch.)}}{\text{K. to K's 2nd}}$, 8. $\frac{\text{B. to Q. B's 4th}}{\text{P. to K. R's 3rd}}$, 9. $\frac{\text{Kt. to K. B's 3rd}}{\text{Kt. takes P.}}$, 10. $\frac{\text{Castles}}{\text{K. to Q's sq.}}$, equal game.

6. B. takes B. P. (ch.)	6. Q. takes B.
7. Kt. takes Q.	7. P. takes Q.
8. Kt. takes R.	8. Kt. to K. B's 3rd.
9. P. to Q's 3rd.	9. B. to K's 3rd.

And Black has the advantage.

In the present game we may as well consider the effect of two other premature attacks of the Queen, namely, 3. $\frac{\text{Q. to K. Kt.'s 4th}}{}$, and 3. $\frac{\text{Q. to K. B's 3rd.}}{}$ In the first instance,—

3. Q. to K. Kt.'s 4th.

This move is not advantageous for White. It loses time, and places his Queen in a position of danger.

	3. Q. to K. B's 3rd.
4. Q. to K. Kt.'s 3rd.	

If White play 4. $\frac{\text{P. to Q's 4th}}{}$ the position is more decidedly in favour of the other side, the continuation being 4. $\frac{}{\text{B. takes P.}}$, 5. $\frac{\text{Kt. to K. B's 3rd}}{\text{Kt. to Q. B's 3rd}}$, 6. $\frac{\text{Q. to Kt.'s 3rd}}{\text{P. to Q's 3rd}}$, 7. $\frac{\text{B. to K. Kt.'s 5th}}{\text{Q. to Kt.'s 3rd}}$, 8. $\frac{\text{Q's Kt. to Q's 2nd}}{\text{P. to K. R's 3rd}}$, &c.

	4. P. to Q's 3rd.
5. Kt. to K. B's 3rd.	5. B. to K's 3rd.
6. B. takes B.	6. P. takes B.
7. Castles.	7. Kt. to K's 2nd.
8. P. to Q's 3rd.	8. Castles,

and White has no superiority.

In the second instance,—

3. Q. to K. B's 3rd.	3. Kt. to K. B's 3rd.
4. P. to K. Kt.'s 4th.	4. P. to Q's 4th.
5. B. takes Q's P.	5. Q's B. takes P
6. Q. to Q. Kt.'s 3rd.	6. Kt. takes B.
7. P. takes Kt.	7. B. to Q. Kt.'s 3rd.
8. Q. to K. Kt.'s 3rd.	8. Q. to K. B's 3rd.

Black has the better opening.

Game the Fourth. *

WHITE.	BLACK.
1. P. to K's 4th.	1. P. to K's 4th.
2. B. to Q. B's 4th.	2. B. to Q. B's 4th.
3. Kt. to K. B's 3rd.	

I prefer this move for the attack to 3. $\frac{\text{P. to Q. B's 3rd}}{}$, and believe it to be the best White has at command.

3. P. to Q's 3rd.

If Black play 3. $\frac{}{\text{Kt. to K. B's 3rd}}$ he compromises his game, for then follows,—4. $\frac{\text{Kt. takes P.}}{\text{Kt. takes P.}}$, 5. $\frac{\text{B. takes P. (ch.)}}{\text{K. to B's sq.}}$, 6. $\frac{\text{Q. to K. B's 3rd}}{\text{B. takes P. (ch.)}}$, 7. $\frac{\text{K. to K's 2nd}}{\text{P. to Q's 3rd}}$, 8. $\frac{\text{Q. takes Kt.}}{\text{P. takes Kt.}}$, 9. $\frac{\text{R. to B's sq.}}{}$, &c. If he play 3. $\frac{}{\text{Kt. to Q. B's 3rd}}$, the position is an ordinary one in the King's Knight's Opening, which will undergo examination hereafter.

4. P. to Q. B's 3rd.

White has two other moves deserving notice.

Firstly—4. $\frac{\text{P. to Q's 3rd}}{}$, runs on, 4. $\frac{}{\text{Kt. to K. B's 3rd}}$, 5. $\frac{\text{P. to Q. B's 3rd}}{\text{Q. to K's 2nd}}$, 6. $\frac{\text{P. to Q. Kt.'s 4th}}{\text{B. to Q. Kt.'s 3rd}}$, 7. $\frac{\text{P. to Q. R's 4th}}{\text{Kt. to K. Kt.'s 5th}}$, 8. $\frac{\text{Castles}}{\text{P. to Q. R's 3rd}}$, 9. $\frac{\text{P. to K. R's 3rd}}{\text{P. to K. R's 4th}}$, 10. $\frac{\text{Kt. to K. Kt.'s 5th}}{}$, and Black is at a disadvantage.

Secondly, 4. $\frac{\text{P. to Q's 4th}}{}$, may be continued thus:—

4. $\frac{}{\text{P. takes P.}}$ (This is better play than taking with Bishop).

5. $\frac{\text{P. to Q. B's 3rd}}{}$. (He may also take the Pawn with Knight, and the result will be an equal game); 5. $\frac{}{\text{P. takes P.}}$, 6. $\frac{\text{Kt. takes P.}}{\text{Kt. to Q. B's 3rd}}$, 7. $\frac{\text{Castles}}{\text{Kt. to K. B's 3rd}}$, 8. $\frac{\text{P. to K's 5th}}{}$, and although White has lost a Pawn, he has some compensating attack.

	4. Q. to K's 2nd. (A)
5. Castles.	5. Kt. to K. B's 3rd.
6. P. to Q's 4th.	6. B. to Q. Kt.'s 3rd.

This retreat of King's Bishop usually betokens weakness, I think. At any rate it loses time, and that in Chess usually produces weakness.

7. B. to K. Kt.'s 5th.	7. P. to Q. B's 3rd.
8. Q's Kt. to Q's 2nd.	8. P. to K. R's 3rd.
9. B. to K. R's 4th.	9. P. to K. Kt.'s 4th.
10. B. to K. Kt.'s 3rd.	10. B. to Q. B's 2nd.

White has more freedom, and at the same time less insecurity in his position, than Black has.

(A.)

Variation on Black's 4th move.

BLACK.

WHITE.

In this situation if, instead of playing his Queen to King's 2nd, Black move 4. $\frac{}{\text{P. to K. B's 4th}}$, White's best reply is 5. $\frac{\text{P. to Q's 4th}}{}$; if he move 4. $\frac{}{\text{B. to K. Kt's 5th}}$, the answer must be 5. $\frac{\text{Q. to Q. Kt.'s 3rd}}{}$; finally, if he move

4. $\frac{}{\text{Kt. to K. B's 3rd}}$, the game proceeds thus:—

	4. Kt. to K. B's 3rd.
5. P. to Q's 4th.	5. P. takes P.
6. P. takes P.	6. B. to Q. Kt.'s 5th (ch.)

(Better play than retreating the Bishop.)

7. B. to Q's 2nd.	7. B. takes B. (ch.)
8. Q. Kt. takes B.	8. P. to Q's 4th.

If 8. $\frac{}{\text{Kt. takes K. P.}}$, 9. $\frac{\text{B. takes K. B. P. (ch.)}}{}$, &c

If 8. $\frac{}{\text{Castles}}$, 9. $\frac{\text{B. to Q's 3rd}}{}$.

9. P. takes P.	9. Kt. takes P.
10. Q. to Q. Kt.'s 3rd.	10. P. to Q. B's 3rd.
11. Castles.	11. Castles.

And White only retains the move.

Game the Fifth.

WHITE.	BLACK.
1. P. to K's 4th.	1. P. to K's 4th.
2. B. to Q. B's 4th.	2. B. to Q. B's 4th.
3. P. to Q. Kt.'s 4th.	

This move, followed, if the offered Pawn be taken, by 4. $\frac{\text{P. to K. B's 4th}}{}$, is, I believe, an invention of Mr. M'Donnell, and was played by him against his renowned competitor, Labourdonnais. Unless correctly opposed it yields the first player a strong attack; but, properly met, it ends to the advantage of the second player, as we shall see.

	3. B. takes Kt.'s P.
4. P. to K. B's 4th.	

White may now form the game into an *Evans's Gambit* by playing 4. $\frac{\text{P. to Q. B's 3rd}}{}$, and 5. $\frac{\text{Kt. to K. B's 3rd}}{}$.

	4. P. to Q's 4th.

This, the best retort, was devised by Labourdonnais, and

has the effect of completely paralysing the attack. If Black play, instead of this fine move, 4. $\frac{\quad}{\text{P. takes P.}}$, White obtains an overpowering attack by 5. $\frac{\text{Kt. to K. B's 3rd}}{\text{Q. to K's 2nd}}$, 6. $\frac{\text{Q. to K's 2nd}}{\text{Kt. to K. B's 3rd}}$, 7. $\frac{\text{P. to K's 5th}}{\text{Kt. to K. R's 4th}}$, 8. $\frac{\text{P. to Q. B's 3rd}}{\text{B. to Q. R's 4th}}$, 9. $\frac{\text{P. to Q's 4th}}{\text{B. to Q. Kt.'s 3rd}}$, 10. $\frac{\text{P. to K. Kt.'s 4th}}{\text{P. takes P. \textit{en passant}}}$, 11. $\frac{\text{Kt. to K. Kt.'s 5th}}{\quad}$, &c.

5. P. takes P.

Taking with the Bishop is more disadvantageous even than taking with the Pawn: *ex. gr.* 5. $\frac{\text{B. takes P.}}{\text{P. to Q. B's 3rd}}$, 6. $\frac{\text{P. to Q. B's 3rd (best)}}{\text{P. takes B.}}$, 7. $\frac{\text{P. takes B.}}{\text{P. takes K. P.}}$, 8. $\frac{\text{P. takes P.}}{\text{Q. to Q's 5th}}$, 9. $\frac{\text{Q. to Q. B's 2nd}}{\text{B. to K. B's 4th}}$, &c.

	5. P. to K's 5th.
6. Kt. to K's 2nd.	6. Kt. to K. B's 3rd.
7. P. to Q. B's 3rd.	7. B. to Q. B's 4th.
8. P. to Q's 4th.	8. P. takes P, in passing.
9. Q. takes P.	9. Castles.
10. B. to Q. R's 3rd.	10. B. takes B.
11. Kt. takes B.	11. B. to K. Kt.'s 5th.
12. Castles.	12. B. takes Kt.
13. Q. takes B.	13. Kt. takes P.
14. Q. to K. B's 3rd.	14. P. to Q. B's 3rd.
15. Q. R. to Kt.'s sq.	15. Q. to K's 2nd.
16. B. takes Kt.	16. P. takes B.

Black has the advantage.

Game the Fifth.

WHITE.	BLACK.
1. P. to K's 4th.	1. P. to K's 4th.
2. B. to Q. B's 4th.	2. B. to Q. B's 4th.
3. P. to K. B's 4th.	

Besides this move, White has only one other feasible line of play which has not been examined, that is 3. $\frac{\text{P. to Q's 4th}}{\quad}$;

it is, however, very weak, and is usually continued thus :—

3. $\frac{\qquad}{\text{B. takes P. (best)}}$, 4. $\frac{\text{Kt. to K. B's 3rd}}{\text{Kt. to Q. B's 3rd}}$, 5. $\frac{\text{P. to Q. B's 3rd}}{\text{B. to Q. Kt.'s 3rd}}$, 6. $\frac{\text{Kt. to K. Kt.'s 5th}}{\text{Kt. to K. R's 3rd}}$, 7. $\frac{\text{Q. to K. R's 5th}}{\text{Q. to K. B's 3rd}}$, manifestly in favour of Black.

	3. B. takes Kt. (best).
4. Q. to K. R's 5th.	

If 4. $\frac{\text{R. takes B.}}{\qquad}$, then 4. $\frac{\qquad}{\text{Q. to K. R's 5th (ch.)}}$, 5. $\frac{\text{P. to K. Kt.'s 3rd}}{\text{Q. takes K. R. P.}}$, 6. $\frac{\text{K. to B's sq.}}{\qquad}$, &c.

	4. Q. to K's 2nd.
5. R. takes B.	5. Kt. to Q. B's 3rd.
6. P. to Q's 3rd.	6. Kt. to K. B's 3rd.
7. Q. to K's 2nd.	7. Kt. to Q's 5th.
8. Q. to Q's sq.	8. P. to Q's 4th.
9. P. to Q. B's 3rd.	9. Kt. to K. Kt.'s 5th.

(The combinations here well deserve attention from the student.)

10. P. to K. Kt.'s 3rd.	10. P. takes B.
11. P. takes Kt.	11. K. P. takes Q. P.
12. P. to K. R's 3rd.	12. Kt. to K. B's 3rd.
13. Q. to Q. R's 4th (ch.)	13. P. to Q. B's 3rd.
14. Q. takes Q. B. P.	14. B. takes K. R. P.
15. Q. takes Q. P.	15. R. to Q's sq.

And Black has an evident superiority of position.

CHAPTER II.

GAME THE FIRST.

King's Knight's Defence to the King's Bishop's Opening.

WHITE.	BLACK.
1. P. to K's 4th.	1. P. to K's 4th.
2. B. to Q. B's 4th.	2. Kt. to K. B's 3rd.

Black's second move is regarded by many authorities as the strongest defence possible to the King's Bishop's Game.

3. Kt. to K. B's 3rd.

White has now three other moves at his command, viz.,—

4. $\frac{\text{P. to Q's 4th}}{}$, 4. $\frac{\text{P. to K. B's 4th}}{}$, and 4. $\frac{\text{P. to Q's 3rd}}{}$,

each more or less worth notice, and which shall be examined under variations A, B, and C.

3. Kt. takes P. (best).

If Black play 3. Kt. to Q. B's 3rd, the position is the same as one in the "Bilguer" Game, which see.

4. P. to Q's 3rd.	4. Kt. to K. B's 3rd.
5. Kt. takes K's P.	5. P. to Q's 4th.

Even Game.

White can also play,—4. $\frac{\text{Q. to K's 2nd}}{}$, 4. $\frac{\text{Kt. takes P.}}{}$, and 4. $\frac{\text{Kt. to Q. B's 3rd}}{}$, which we may examine at once.

Firstly, 4. $\frac{\text{Q. to K's 2nd}}{\text{P. to Q's 4th}}$, 5. $\frac{\text{Kt. takes P.}}{\text{B. to Q. B's 4th (best)}}$, 6. $\frac{\text{Castles}}{\text{Castles}}$, (if 6. $\frac{\text{P. to Q's 3rd}}{\text{B. takes B's P (ch.)}}$, 7. $\frac{\text{K. to B's sq.}}{\text{B. to Q. Kt's 3rd.}}$,

8. $\frac{\text{B. to Q. Kt's 3rd}}{\text{Q. to K's 2nd}}$), 7. $\frac{\text{B. to Q. Kt.'s 3rd}}{\text{R. to K's sq.}}$, 8. $\frac{\text{P. to Q's 3rd}}{\text{Kt. takes K. B. P.}}$, Black has the advantage.

Secondly, 4. $\frac{\text{Kt. takes P.}}{\text{P. to Q's 4th}}$, 5. $\frac{\text{Q. to K's 2nd (best)}}{}$ (if 5. $\frac{\text{Kt. takes K. B. P.}}{\text{Q. to K's 2nd}}$, 6. $\frac{\text{Q. to K's 2nd}}{\text{Q. takes Kt.}}$, 7. $\frac{\text{B. takes P.}}{\text{Q. takes B.}}$, &c.), 5. $\frac{}{\text{B. to Q. B's 4th}}$, 6. $\frac{\text{Castles}}{}$, and we have the position examined in the previous variation.

Thirdly, 4. $\frac{\text{Kt. to Q. B's 3rd}}{\text{Kt. takes Kt.}}$. In my "Chess Praxis" (1860, p. 96) I spoke of this as the best move White can adopt. I am now disposed to prefer 4. $\frac{\text{P. to Q's 3rd}}{}$, though I still think White may play 4. $\frac{\text{Kt. to Q. B's 3rd}}{}$, without any disadvantage; (Instead of 4. $\frac{}{\text{Kt. takes Kt.}}$ Black may play 4. $\frac{}{\text{P. to Q's 4th}}$, leading to 5. $\frac{\text{B. takes P.}}{\text{Kt. to K. B's 3rd}}$, 6. $\frac{\text{B. to Q Kt.'s 3rd}}{\text{B. to Q's 3rd}}$, 7. $\frac{\text{P. to Q's 3rd}}{\text{Castles}}$, 8. $\frac{\text{P. to K. R's 3rd}}{\text{P. to K. R's 3rd}}$, 9. $\frac{\text{B. to K's 3rd}}{\text{Kt. to Q. B's 3rd}}$, but in that case White's position seems preferable.) 5. $\frac{\text{Q's P. takes Kt.}}{}$. Black has now two lines of defence, viz., 5. $\frac{}{\text{P. to Q. B's 3rd}}$, and 5. $\frac{}{\text{P. to K. B's 3rd}}$, the former of which leads to an even game, thus: 5. $\frac{}{\text{P. to Q. B's 3rd}}$, 6. $\frac{\text{Kt. takes K's P.}}{\text{P. to Q's 4th}}$, 7. $\frac{\text{Castles}}{\text{B. to Q's 3rd}}$. (If 7. $\frac{}{\text{P. takes B.}}$, 8. $\frac{\text{Q. takes Q. (ch.)}}{\text{K. takes Q.}}$, 9. $\frac{\text{Kt. takes B's P. (ch.)}}{\text{K. moves}}$, 10. $\frac{\text{Kt. takes R.}}{}$, and White will be able to extricate his Knight and then have the advantage.) 8. $\frac{\text{B. to Q's 3rd}}{\text{B. takes Kt.}}$, 9. $\frac{\text{R. to K's sq.}}{}$, &c., I prefer this defence to the other, which runs as follows, and abounds with pitfalls and difficulties for the second player:— 5. $\frac{}{\text{P. to K. B's 3rd}}$, 6. $\frac{\text{B. to K's 3rd}}{}$ (the move usually given is

6. $\frac{\text{Castles}}{\text{---}}$, the game then proceeding 6. $\frac{}{\text{Q. to K's 2nd}}$, 7. $\frac{\text{Kt. to K. R's 4th}}{\text{P. to K. Kt's 3rd}}$, to the profit of Black.). 6. $\frac{}{\text{Q. to K's 2nd}}$.

It is difficult to say which is the safest move for Black at this point. White threatens at once to take the K's Pawn, and, defend it as he may, Black is liable to a tantalizing and, in some cases, even dangerous attack. 7. $\frac{\text{Kt. to K. R's 4th}}{\text{P. to K. Kt's 3rd}}$ (If 7. $\frac{}{\text{P. to Q's 3rd}}$, then 8. $\frac{\text{Q. to K. R's 5th (ch.)}}{\text{K. to Q's sq. (best)}}$, and White has more than an equivalent in position for his lost Pawn), 8. $\frac{\text{Castles}}{\text{P. to Q's 3rd}}$, 9. $\frac{\text{P. to K. B's 4th}}{}$, White, to my mind, has quite as good a game as Black.

As this variation of 4. $\frac{\text{Kt. to Q. B's 3rd}}{}$ has excited a good deal of controversy, and may possibly lead to more, I append a diagram of the situation after White's 6th move, which is, I think, the crucial point in the variation. See also Pekoff's Defence, where the same position is brought about.

BLACK.

WHITE.

(A.)

3. P. to Q's 4th. 3. P. takes P.

Black's best move. If 3. $\frac{\quad}{\text{Kt. takes P.}}$, then follows 4. $\frac{\text{P. takes P.}}{\text{B. to Q. B's 4th}}$, 5. $\frac{\text{B. takes B's P. (ch.)}}{\text{K. to B's sq.}}$, 6. $\frac{\text{Q. to K. B's 3rd}}{\quad}$, with the better opening.

4. P. to K's 5th. | 4. P. to Q's 4th (best).
5. B. to Q. Kt's 3rd.

Taking the Knight with Pawn is inferior, but White may check with the Bishop at Q. Kt's 5th, to which Black's best reply is 5. $\frac{\quad}{\text{B. to Q's 2nd}}$.

5. Kt. to K's 5th.

6. Kt. to K's 2nd.

and Black can now play either 6. $\frac{\quad}{\text{P. to Q. B's 4th}}$, or 6. $\frac{\quad}{\text{B. to Q. B's 4th}}$, with a slightly superior game.

(B.)

3. P. to K. B's 4th. | 3. P. to Q's 4th.

Apparently Black's best move. If he play 3. $\frac{\quad}{\text{Kt. takes P.}}$, the continuation will probably be—4. $\frac{\text{Q. to K. B's 3rd}}{\text{P. to Q's 4th}}$, 5. $\frac{\text{P. takes P.}}{\quad}$, and White has the better position.

4. P. takes Q's P. | 4. P. takes P.
5. Q. to K's 2nd. (ch.) | 5. B. to K's 2nd.

Equal game.

(C.)

3. P. to Q's 3rd

The move 3. $\frac{\text{Kt. to Q. B's 3rd}}{\quad}$ leads also to a perfectly equal game, by 3. $\frac{\quad}{\text{B. to Q. B's 4th}}$, 4. $\frac{\text{P. to Q's 3rd}}{\text{Kt. to K. B's 3rd}}$.

3. B. to Q. B's 4th.

4. Kt. to K. B's 3rd.

White may have the gratification of making a fierce attack here by 4. $\frac{\text{P. to K. B's 4th}}{\text{P. to Q's 4th}}$, 5. $\frac{\text{B. takes P.}}{\text{Kt. takes B.}}$, 6. $\frac{\text{P. takes Kt.}}{\text{Q. takes P.}}$, 7. $\frac{\text{Kt. to K. B's 3rd}}{\text{P. takes P.}}$, 8. $\frac{\text{B. takes P.}}{\text{B. to Q. Kt's 3rd}}$. The game is about equal.

	4. P. to Q's 3rd.
5. P. to Q. B's 3rd.	5. Castles.
6. P. to Q. R's 4th.	6. P. to Q. R's 4th.
7. Castles.	7. B. to K's 3rd.
8. B. takes B.	8. P. takes B.
9. Q. to Q. Kt.'s 3rd.	9. Q. to Q. B's sq.

Equal game.

CHAPTER III.

GAME THE FIRST.

The Greco-Counter Gambit.

WHITE.	BLACK.
1. P. to K's 4th.	1. P. to K's 4th.
2. B. to Q. B's 4th.	2. P. to K. B's 4th.

This daring counter-move is attributed to the famous Calabrian player, Greco, and has received a good deal of attention from subsequent authorities. It is an endeavour to reverse the ordinary condition of Chess opening, which gives the power of attacking to the first player, and like all such endeavours, it is not very successful. White's best course in reply is not to take either the offered Pawn or Knight, but to play

3. P. to Q's 3rd.

The best reply; but he may also move 3. $\frac{\text{P. to Q's 4th}}{}$, 3. $\frac{\text{P. to Q. B's 3rd}}{}$, and 3. $\frac{\text{Kt. to K. B's 3rd}}{}$, which we can dispose of before proceeding farther.

Firstly, 3. $\frac{\text{P. to Q's 4th}}{}$, 3. $\frac{}{\text{P. takes Q's P. (best)}}$, 4. $\frac{\text{B. takes Kt. (best)}}{\text{R. takes B.}}$, 5. $\frac{\text{Q. takes P.}}{\text{Kt. to Q. B's 3rd}}$, (if 5. $\frac{}{\text{P. takes P.}}$, 6. $\frac{\text{Q. to Q's 5th}}{\text{R. to K. R's sq.}}$, 7. $\frac{\text{Q. to K. R's 5th (ch.)}}{\text{P. to Kt.'s 3rd}}$, 8. $\frac{\text{Q. to K's 5th (ch.)}}{}$, &c.) 6. $\frac{\text{Q. to Q's 5th}}{\text{Kt. to K's 2nd}}$, 7. $\frac{\text{Q. to Q's 3rd}}{\text{P. takes P.}}$, 8. $\frac{\text{Q. takes K's P.}}{\text{P. to K. Kt.'s 3rd}}$, equal game.

Secondly—3. $\frac{\text{P. to Q. B's 3rd}}{\text{Kt. to K. B's 3rd}}$, 4. $\frac{\text{P. to Q's. 4th}}{\text{Kt. takes K's P.}}$, 5. $\frac{\text{P. takes P.}}{\text{Kt. to Q. B's 3rd}}$, 6. $\frac{\text{Q. to Q's 5th}}{\text{Q. to K's 2nd}}$. The game is about as good for one as for the other.

Thirdly—3. $\frac{\text{Kt. to K. B's 3rd}}{\text{P. to Q. B's 3rd}}$, 4. $\frac{\text{P. to Q's 4th}}{\quad}$, White has some advantage.

3. Kt. to K. B's 3rd.

4. P. to K. B's 4th.

White may also play 4. $\frac{\text{Kt. to K. B's 3rd}}{\quad}$, and if Black answer with 4. $\frac{\quad}{\text{P. to Q. B's 3rd}}$, then 5. $\frac{\text{B. to K. Kt's 5th}}{\quad}$, &c.

4. P. takes K. B's P.

He may move here, 4. $\frac{\quad}{\text{P. to Q's 4th}}$, but not with any good result, as the game would go on,—5. $\frac{\text{P. takes Q's P.}}{\text{P. takes P.}}$, 6. $\frac{\text{Q. to K's 2nd (ch.)}}{\text{B. to K's 2nd}}$, 7. $\frac{\text{Kt. to Q. B's 3rd}}{\text{Q's Kt. to Q's 2nd}}$, 8. $\frac{\text{Q's B. takes P.}}{\text{Kt. to Q. Kt's 3rd}}$, 9. $\frac{\text{Castles}}{\quad}$. White has the superiority.

5. Q's B. takes P. — 5. P. takes P.

He can play, with no better effect though, 5. $\frac{\quad}{\text{P. to Q's 4th}}$, which would lead to 6. $\frac{\text{P. takes Q's P.}}{\text{Kt. takes P.}}$, 7. $\frac{\text{Q. to K's 2nd (ch.)}}{\text{B. to K's 2nd}}$, 8. $\frac{\text{Kt. to K. B's 3rd}}{\quad}$, &c.

6. P. takes P.	6. Q. to K's 2nd.
7. P. to K's 5th.	7. P. to Q's 3rd.
8. Q. to K's 2nd.	8. P. takes P.
9. B. takes P.	9. Kt. to Q. B's 3rd.
10. Kt. to K. B's 3rd.	White has the better opening.

We have now to examine the consequences of White's accepting the Gambit (*i.e.*, taking the proffered Pawn), or taking the King's Knight. We will do this in another game.

GAME THE SECOND.

WHITE.	BLACK.
1. P. to K's 4th.	1. P. to K's 4th.
2. B. to Q. B's 4th.	2. P. to K. B's 4th.
3. P. takes P.	

This capture is very inferior to any of the moves previously examined.

	3. Kt. to K. B's 3rd.

For the result of 3. $\frac{\text{B. takes Kt.}}{}$ (See VARIATION I.)

4. P. to Q's 4th.

White can now bring the game to a position of the *Cunningham Gambit*, the players being reversed, by playing 4. $\frac{\text{B. to K's 2nd}}{}$, or he can endeavour to maintain his Pawn by 4. $\frac{\text{P. to K. Kt.'s 4th}}{\text{P. to Q's 4th}}$, 5. $\frac{\text{B. to K's 2nd}}{\text{B. to Q. B's 4th}}$, 6. $\frac{\text{P. to Q's 3rd}}{\text{P. to K. R's 4th}}$, 7. $\frac{\text{P. to Kt.'s 5th}}{\text{Kt. to Kt.'s 5th}}$, 8. $\frac{\text{B. takes Kt.}}{\text{P. takes B.}}$, 9. $\frac{\text{Q. takes P.}}{\text{Castles}}$, 10. $\frac{\text{B. to K's 3rd}}{\text{Q's B. takes P.}}$, 11. $\frac{\text{Q. to K. Kt.'s 3rd}}{\text{P. to Q's 5th}}$, 12. $\frac{\text{B. to Q's 2nd}}{\text{P. to K's 5th}}$.

Black has the advantage.

	4. P. takes P.
5. Q. takes P.	5. P. to Q's 4th.
6. B. to Q's 3rd.	6. Kt. to Q. B's 3rd.
7. Q. to K's 3rd (ch.).	7. K. to B's 2nd.

Threatening to win immediately by checking with the King's Bishop and then moving the Rook to K's sq.

8. Kt. to K's 2nd.	8. B. to Q. Kt.'s 5th (ch.)
9. P. to Q. B's 3rd.	9. R. to K's sq.
10. Q. to K. Kt's 3rd.	10. B. to Q's 3rd.

Black has a freer game.

VARIATION I.

Beginning at White's 3rd move.

3. B. takes Kt.

This is a better move for White than taking the Pawn.

3. R. takes B.

4. Q. to K. R's 5th. (ch.)

I prefer here, 4. $\frac{\text{P. to Q's 4th}}{}$, in reply to which Black can play 4. $\frac{}{\text{Q. to K's 2nd}}$, and the game strikes me as being about equal.

If, instead of either of these moves, White play 4, $\frac{\text{P. takes P.}}{}$, the continuation is 4. $\frac{}{\text{P. to Q's 4th}}$, 5. $\frac{\text{P. to K. Kt's 4th}}{\text{P. to K. R's 4th}}$. (He may play with equal profit 5. $\frac{}{\text{Kt. to Q. B's 3rd}}$), 6. $\frac{\text{P. to K. R's 3rd}}{\text{P. takes P.}}$, 7. $\frac{\text{P. takes P.}}{\text{P. to K. Kt's 3rd}}$, 8. $\frac{\text{P. takes P.}}{\text{R. takes P.}}$, 9. $\frac{\text{P. to K. B's 3rd}}{\text{P. to K. 5th}}$. Both games are too much exposed, but Black has more command over the field. In this last variation, we should not pass unobserved that White, instead of playing 5. $\frac{\text{P. to K. Kt's 4th}}{}$, may give check with his Queen. In that case the probable continuation is 5. $\frac{\text{Q. to K. R's 5th (ch.)}}{\text{P. to Kt.'s 3rd}}$, 6. $\frac{\text{P. takes P.}}{\text{R. takes P.}}$, 7. $\frac{\text{Q. takes K. R's P.}}{}$. (Here White may move 7. $\frac{\text{Kt. to K. B's 3rd}}{}$, to which Black's best rejoinder is 7. $\frac{}{\text{Kt. to Q. B's 3rd}}$.)

7. $\frac{}{\text{Q. to K. B's 3rd}}$, 8. $\frac{\text{Q. takes Q. B's P.}}{\text{Kt. to Q. B's 3rd}}$ (if 8. $\frac{\text{Kt. to Q. B's 3rd}}{\text{R. takes P.}}$, 9. $\frac{\text{Q. to K. R's 5th (ch.)}}{\text{K. to Q's sq.}}$, 10. $\frac{\text{Q. to K's 2nd}}{\text{B. to Q. B's 4th}}$, Black for choice), 9. $\frac{\text{Q. to K. R's 7th}}{\text{Kt. to Q's 5th}}$ (he may play also 9. $\frac{}{\text{R. takes P.}}$, and

then proceed, 10. $\frac{\text{Q. to K. R's 5th (ch.)}}{\text{K. to Q's sq.}}$, 11. $\frac{\text{Q. to K's 2nd}}{\text{Kt. to Q's 5th}}$, &c.),

10. $\frac{\text{Kt. to Q. B's 3rd}}{\text{Kt. takes P. (ch.)}}$. Black has the better game.

	4. P. to K. Kt.'s 3rd.
5. Q. takes K. R's P.	5. R. to Kt.'s 2nd.
6. Q. to K. R's 8th.	6. Q. to K. Kt.'s 4th.
7. Q. to K. R's 3rd.	7. P. takes P.
8. Kt. to Q. B's 3rd.	8. Q. to K. B's 4th.
9. Q. to K's 3rd.	9. R. to B's 2nd.
10. Kt. to R's 3rd.	10. P. to Q's 4th.
11. Kt. takes P.	11. Kt. to Q. B's 3rd.
12. P. to Q's 3rd.	12. Kt. to Q's 5th.
13. Q. to Q's 2nd.	13. P. takes P.
14. P. takes P.	14. Kt. to K. B's 6th. (ch.)
15. P. takes Kt.	15. Q. takes B's P.
16. R. to K. Kt.'s sq.	16. B. takes Kt.
17. Kt. to Q. B's 3rd.	

If 17. $\frac{\text{Kt. to K's 3rd}}{\text{B. to Q. Kt's 5th}}$,

17. R. to Q's sq.

And Black should win.

CHAPTER IV.

Queen's Bishop's Pawn Deeence.

Game the First.

WHITE.	BLACK.
1. P. to K's 4th.	P. to K's 4th.
2. B. to Q. B's 4th.	P. to Q. B's 3rd.

The fault of this defence is that it affords the adversary too much time to develop his game. We find it first in Cozio's work, "Il Giuoco degli Scacchi," &c., &c., 1766, and it has been copiously treated of by the writers since his day.

3. Q. to K's 2nd.

(This is unanimously accepted by the chief authorities as White's best reply. Philidor, to be sure, commends 3. $\frac{\text{P. to Q's 4th}}{}$, but the advantage White obtains, if he obtain any, is certainly less pronounced, than that which follows on the move in the text.)

3. Kt. to K. B's 3rd.

4. P. to K. B's 4th.

(A good move for White, as it prevents his opponent establishing his Pawns in the centre, and keeps him on the defensive.)

4. P. to Q's 3rd.

(Perhaps Black's best resource, however unsatisfactory. If he play instead 4. $\frac{}{\text{P. takes P.}}$, then follow 5. $\frac{\text{P. to K's 5th}}{\text{Kt. to Q's 4th}}$, 6. $\frac{\text{P to Q's 4th}}{\text{B to K's 2nd}}$, 7. $\frac{\text{B. takes Kt.}}{\text{B. to K. R's 5th (ch.)}}$, 8. $\frac{\text{P. to Kt.'s 3rd}}{\text{P. takes P.}}$, 9. $\frac{\text{B. takes B's P. (ch.)}}{\text{K. takes B.}}$ 10. $\frac{\text{Q. to K. B's 3rd (ch.)}}{\text{K. to K's sq.}}$ 11. $\frac{\text{P. takes P.}}{\text{B. to K's 2nd.}}$, White has an indisputable advantage.

Again, if he play, 4. $\frac{\qquad}{\text{B. to Q. B's 4th}}$, the result is equally unpropitious, for then follows 5. $\frac{\text{P. takes P.}}{\text{B. takes Kt.}}$, 6. $\frac{\text{R takes B.}}{\text{P. to Q's 4th}}$, 7. $\frac{\text{P. takes P. in passing}}{\text{Castles}}$, 8. $\frac{\text{P. to K's 5th}}{\text{R. to K's sq.}}$, 9. $\frac{\text{P. to Q's 4th}}{\qquad}$, &c.)

5. P. takes P.	5. P. takes P.
6. Kt. to K. B's 3rd.	6. B. to Q's 3rd.

Black has seemingly no better move. If he play 6. $\frac{\qquad}{\text{B. to K. Kt.'s 5th}}$, the reply is 7. $\frac{\text{B. takes K. B. P. (ch.)}}{\text{K. takes B.}}$, 8. $\frac{\text{Kt. takes K. P. (ch.)}}{\qquad}$, and 9. $\frac{\text{Kt. takes B.}}{\qquad}$. So, if he play 6. $\frac{\qquad}{\text{Q. Kt. to Q's 2nd}}$, or 6. $\frac{\qquad}{\text{Q. to Q. B's 2nd}}$, then by 7. $\frac{\text{Kt. to Kt's 5th}}{\qquad}$, White gains a Pawn.

7. P. to Q's 4th.	7. P. takes P.
8. P. to K's 5th.	8. Castles.
9. Castles.	8. B. to Q. B's 4th.

Better than playing 9. $\frac{\qquad}{\text{R. to K's sq.}}$, because of 10. $\frac{\text{Kt. to Kt's 5th}}{\text{R. takes P.}}$, 11. $\frac{\text{Kt. takes B. P.}}{\text{R. takes Q.}}$, 12. $\frac{\text{Kt. takes Q. (dis. ch.)}}{\text{K. to R's sq.}}$, 13. $\frac{\text{B. takes R.}}{\qquad}$, and White has a winning position.

10. Q. to Q's 3rd.

(This prevents the advance of Black's Q's Pawn, and the terrible check by discovery from the Bishop.)

10. Kt. to Q's 4th.

10. $\frac{\qquad}{\text{Kt. to K. Kt's 5th}}$ would be very bad play on account of 11. $\frac{\text{Kt. to Kt.'s 5th}}{\qquad}$, 11. $\frac{\qquad}{\text{P. to K. Kt.'s 3rd}}$, 12. $\frac{\text{B. takes B. P. (ch.)}}{\qquad}$, &c.

11. Kt. to Kt.'s 5th.	11. P. to K. Kt.'s 3rd.
12. Kt. to K's 4th.	12. B. to K.'s 2nd.
13. B. takes Kt.	13. P. takes B.
14. Kt. to B's 6th (ch.)	14. B. takes Kt.
15. P. takes B.	

White has a winning advantage.

ILLUSTRATIVE GAMES.

GAME I.—Between Messrs. McDonnell and De Labourdonnais.

WHITE (Mr. McD.).	BLACK (Mr. De L.).
1. P. to K's 4th.	1. P. to K's 4th.
2. B. to Q. B's 4th.	2. B. to Q. B's 4th.
3. P. to Q. B's 3rd.	3. Q. to K's 2nd.
4. Kt. to K. B's 3rd.	4. P. to Q's 3rd.
5. Castles.	5. B. to Q. Kt.'s 3rd.
6. P. to Q's 4th.	6. Kt. to K. B's 3rd.
7. Kt. to Q. R's 3rd.	

(7 $\frac{\text{B. to K. Kt.'s 5th}}{\quad}$, appears to me a better move).

	7. B. to K. Kt's 5th.
8. Kt. to Q. B's 2nd.	8. Q's Kt. to Q's 2nd.

(Taking the K's Pawn would evidently have been unwise, because White could have replied with 9. $\frac{\text{B. to Q's 5th}}{\quad}$).

9. Q. to Q's 3rd.

(A remarkable error for such a player, in such a match, to make.)

	9. P. to Q's 4th.
10. P. takes P.	10. P. to K's 5th.
11. Q. to Q's 2nd.	11. P. takes Kt.
12. R. to K's sq.	12. Kt. to K's 5th.
13. Q. to K. B's 4th.	13. P. to K. B's 4th.
14. P. takes P.	14. P. to K. Kt.'s 4th.
15. Q. to K's 3rd.	15. Kt. to K's 4th.

(The learner will do well to note the resource of these two great masters in a position so complex and difficult as the present).

16. B. to Q. Kt.'s 5th (ch.)	16. P. to Q. B's 3rd.
17. P. takes B.	17. Kt. takes K. Kt.'s P.
18. Q. to K's 2nd.	18. P. takes B.

19. P. to K. B's 3rd.	19. Q. Kt. to K. B's 3rd.
20. P. takes Kt.	20. Kt. takes P.
21. Q. takes P. (ch.)	21. Q. to Q's 2nd.
22. Q. takes Q. (ch.)	22. K. takes Q.

(Mr. McDonnell seems now to have overcome the difficulties which his 9th move involved with wonderful success. It will be found, however, that his position is not so secure as it looks).

23. P. to Q. B's 4th.	23. Q. R. to K's sq.
24. P. to Q. B's 5th.	24. B. to Q's sq.
25. P. to Q's 6th.	25. P. to K. B's 5th.
26. P. to Q. Kt.'s 4th.	26. K. R. to B's sq.
27. R. to K. B's sq.	27. P. to K. R's 4th.
28. Kt. to Q. R's 3rd.	

(If 28. $\frac{\text{P. to K. R's 4th}}{}$, then probably would have followed

28. $\frac{}{\text{Kt. to Kt.'s 6th}}$, 29. $\frac{\text{R. to B's 2nd}}{\text{P. to K. Kt.'s 5th}}$, &c.)

	28. B. to K. B's 3rd.
29. B. to Q. Kt.'s 2nd.	29. P. to K. Kt.'s 5th.
30. Kt. to Q. B's 4th.	30. P. to K. B's 6th.
31. Kt. to K's 5th (ch.)	31. B. takes Kt.
32. P. takes B.	32. P. to K. R's 5th.
33. Q. R. to Q's sq.	33. P. to B's 7th (ch.)

(Mark how finely these Pawns are manœuvred).

34. K. to R's sq.	34. P. to K. R's 6th.

(The natural move is 34. $\frac{}{\text{P. to K. Kt.'s 6th}}$, but then followed 35. $\frac{\text{P. to K. R's 3rd}}{}$, and it is not easy to see a way out of the dead lock).

35. R. to Q's 3rd.	35. R. to K. Kt.'s sq.
36. P. to Kt.'s 5th.	36. P. to Kt.'s 6th.
37. P. takes P.	37. R. takes P.
38. R. to Q's 4th.	38. Q. R. to K. Kt's sq.
39. P. to K's 6th (ch.)	39. K. to Q's sq.
40. Q. R. to Q's sq.	40. P. to K. R's 7th.
41. P. to K's 7th (ch.)	41. K. to Q's 2nd.

42. P. to Q. B's 6th (ch.)	42. P. takes P.
43. P. takes P. (ch.)	43. K. takes Q. B. P.
44. P. to K's 8th ("Queens" checking).	

(How fine is all this! The study of a few such games is almost a liberal Chess education).

	44. R. takes Q.
45. K. takes P.	45. R. to K's 3rd.
46. R. to Q. B's sq. (ch.)	46. K. to Kt.'s 4th.
47. P. to Q. R's 4th (ch.)	47. K. to Kt.'s 5th.
48. B. to Q. B's 3rd (ch.)	

(He had no better move).

	48. R. takes B.
49. R. takes R.	49. K. takes R.
50. P. to Q's 7th.	50. R. to Q's 3rd.
51. K. to Kt.'s 2nd.	51. R. takes Q. P.
52. R. to Q. B's sq. (ch.)	52. K. to Q's 6th.
53. K. to B's sq.	

(If 53. $\frac{\text{R. to Q's sq. (ch.)}}{\text{K. to K's 7th (wins)}}$).

	53. K. to K's 6th.

And Mr. McDonnell resigned.

Game II.—Between Messrs. Walker and Daniels.

White (Mr. W.)	Black (Mr. D.)
1. P. to K's 4th.	1. P. to K's 4th.
2. B. to Q. B's. 4th.	2. B. to Q. B's 4th.
3. P. to Q. B's 3rd.	3. P. to Q's 4th.
4. B. takes P.	4. Kt. to K. B's 3rd.
5. Q. to Q. Kt.'s 3rd	5. Castles.
6. Kt. to K. B's 3rd.	6. P. to Q. B's 3rd.

(He ought to have taken the Bishop with his Knight).

7. B. takes B. P. (ch.)	7. R. takes B.
8. Kt. takes P.	8. Q. to K's 2nd.
9. Q. takes R. (ch.)	9. Q. takes Q.
10. Kt. takes Q.	10. K. takes Kt.
11. P. to Q's 4th.	11. B. to Q. Kt.'s 3rd.
12. P. to K. B's 3rd.	12. B. to K's 3rd.
13. B. to K's 3rd.	13. Kt. to Q. R's 3rd.

14. K. to B's 2nd.	14. Kt. to Q. B's 2nd.
15. Kt. to Q's 2nd.	15. P. to K. Kt.'s 3rd.
16. P. to K. Kt.'s 4th.	16. K. to Kt.'s 2nd.
17. P. to K. R's 4th.	17. R. to K's sq.
18. P. to K. R's 5th.	18. B. to K. B's 2nd.
19. P. takes P.	19. B. takes K. Kt.'s P.
20. Q. R. to K. Kt.'s sq.	20. Kt. to K's 3rd.
21. Kt. to Q. B's 4th.	21. B. to Q. B's 2nd.
22. P. to K's 5th.	22. Kt. to Q's 4th.
23. B. to K. R's 6th (ch.)	23. K. to B's 2nd.
24. K. to Kt.'s 3rd.	24. P. to Q. Kt.'s 4th.
25. Kt. to K's 3rd.	25. Kt. takes Kt.
26. B. takes Kt.	26. P. to Q. B's 4th.
27. P. to K. B's 4th.	27. P. takes Q. P.
28. P. takes P.	28. B. to Q's 6th.
29. P. to K. B's 5th.	

And Mr. Daniels resigned.

GAME III.—Between the Author and Mr. Cochrane.

WHITE (Mr. S.)	BLACK (Mr. C.)
1. P. to K's 4th.	1. P. to K's 4th.
2. B. to Q. B's 4th.	2. B. to Q. B's 4th.
3. P. to Q. B's 3rd.	3. P. to Q's 3rd.
4. P. to Q's 4th.	4. P. takes P.
5. P. takes P.	5. B. to Q. Kt.'s 3rd.
6. Kt. to Q. B's 3rd.	6. P. to K. R's 3rd.
7. B. to K's 3rd.	7. Kt. to K. B's 3rd.
8. P. to K. R's 3rd.	8. Q. to K's 2nd.
9. Q. to Q's 3rd.	9. Kt. to Q. B's 3rd.
10. P. to Q. R's 3rd.	10. Castles.
11. K. Kt. to K's 2nd.	11. B. to Q's 2nd.
12. Kt. to K. B's 4th.	

(This threatened to win the "exchange" by going to Kt.'s 6th; but as the object was sure to be seen by so acute an opponent as Mr. Cochrane, White would have done better in Castling on the King's side. The move in the text was premature, and, as we shall presently see, occasioned loss of time and its concomitants in Chess—retreat and break-up of position.)

	12. K. to R's sq.
13. P. to Q. Kt.'s 4th.	13. Q. R. to K's sq.
14. Castles, on K's side.	14. P. to K. Kt.'s 4th.

(A bold and good move.)

15. K. Kt. to K's 2nd.	15. Kt. takes K. P.
16. Kt. to Q's 5th.	16. Q. to Q's sq.
17. P. to K. B's 4th.	17. P. to Kt's 5th.
18. P. to K. B's 5th.	18. P. takes K. R. P.

(The rest of the game is fought by Mr. Cochrane with all the fire and brilliancy for which his play is celebrated.)

19. B. takes K. R. P.	19. P. takes Kt. P.
20. R. to K. B's 4th.	20. B. takes K. B. P.
21. B. takes R.	21. Kt. to K's 4th.
22. B. to K's 7th.	

(The only parry to Black's terrible move of Kt. to K's 4th, and this an ineffectual one.)

	22. R. takes B.
23. R. to K. R's 4th (ch.)	23. K. to Kt.'s 2nd.
24. Q. to K's 3rd.	24. R. to K's 3rd.
25. Kt. to K. Kt.'s 3rd.	25. Kt. takes Kt.
26. Q. takes K. Kt. (ch.)	26. R. to Kt.'s 3rd.
27. Q. to K. B's 4th.	27. Q. takes R.

(This was unavoidable. Nothing, in fact, but an error on Black's part could save White's game.)

28. Q. takes Q.	28. Kt. to B.'s 6th (ch.)
29. K. to B's 2nd.	29. Kt. takes Q.
30. Kt. takes B.	30. Q. R. P. takes Kt.
31. R. to K. Kt.'s sq.	31. B. to K's 5th.

And wins.

GAME IV.—Between the same opponents.

WHITE (Mr. C.)	BLACK (Mr. S.)
1. P. to K's 4th.	1. P. to K's 4th.
2. B. to Q. B's 4th.	2. B. to Q. B's 4th.
3. P. to Q. B's 3rd.	3. Q. to K's 2nd.
4. Kt. to K. B's 3rd.	4. Kt. to Q. B's 3rd.
5. Castles.	5. P. to Q's 3rd.

6. P. to K. R's 3rd.	6. P. to K. R's 3rd.
7. P. to Q's 4th.	7. B. to Q. Kt.'s 3rd.
8. P. to Q. R's 4th.	8. P. to Q. R's 4th.
9. P. to Q's 5th.	9. Kt. to Q's sq.

(This forced retreat of the Kt. is a drawback in Black's game which he has some trouble to overcome.)

10. B. to K's 3rd.	10. B. takes B.
11. P. takes B.	11. Kt. to K. B's 3rd.
12. Q. Kt. to Q's 2nd.	12. Castles.
13. Q. to K's sq.	13. B. to Q's 2nd.
14. Q. to K. R's 4th.	14. P. to Q. B's 3rd.
15. P. to K. Kt.'s 4th.	

(This appears, at first view, a very good move, but in reality it costs White one of his best Pawns.)

	15. P. takes Q. P.
16. P. takes P.	16. P. to K's 5th.
17. Kt. to Q's 4th.	17. Kt. takes Q. P.

(We now discover the miscalculation, or rather want of calculation, exhibited by White in throwing forward his K. Kt. Pawn.

18. Q. takes Q.	18. Kt. takes Q.

(The forces are equal, and Mr. Cochrane's pieces are better posted than those of his adversary, but his King is too much exposed.)

19. Kt. takes P.	19. P. to Q's 4th.
20. Kt. to Q. B's 5th.	20. B. takes K. Kt. P.
21. P. takes B.	21. P. takes B.
22. Kt. to Q's 7th.	22. R. to K's sq.
23. Kt. to Q. Kt.'s 5th.	23. Kt. to Q's 4th.

And Black wins.

GAME V.—Played between Mr. Horwitz and Dr. Bledow.

WHITE (Mr. H.)	BLACK (Dr. B.)
1. P. to K's 4th.	1. P. to K's 4th.
2. B. to Q. B's 4th.	2. B. to Q. B's 4th.
3. P. to Q. B's 3rd.	3. P. to Q's 4th.
4. B. takes P.	4. Kt. to K. B's 3rd.

5. Q. to Q. Kt.'s 3rd.	5. Castles.
6. B. takes Q. Kt. P.	6. B. takes B.
7. Q. takes B.	7. Q. to Q's 6th.
8. Q. takes Q. R.	8. P. to Q. B's 3rd.
9. Q. to Kt.'s 7th.	9. Q. takes K. P. (ch.)
10. K. to B's sq.	10. Q. to Q. B's 7th.
11. Kt. to K. B's 3rd	11. Q. takes B. (ch.)
12. Kt. to K's sq.	12. Kt. to K's 5th.
13. K. to K's 2nd.	13. R. to Q's sq.
14. P. to Q's 3rd.	14. Kt. takes K. B. P.
15. P. to Q's 4th.	15. P. takes P.
16. K. takes Kt.	16. P. takes P. (dis. ch.)
17. K. to B's sq.	17. R. to K's sq

And Black resigned.

GAME VI.—Between Messrs. De Labourdonnais and McDonnell.

WHITE (Mr. De L.)	BLACK (Mr. McD.)
1. P. to K's 4th.	1. P. to K's 4th.
2. B. to Q. B's 4th.	2. B. to Q. B's 4th.
3. Q. to K's 2nd.	3. Kt. to K. B's 3rd.
4. P. to Q's 3rd.	4. Kt. to Q. B's 3rd.
5. P. to Q. B's 3rd.	5. Kt. to K's 2nd.
6. P. to K. B's 4th	6. P. takes P.

(We have seen in the analysis of this opening that the second player does ill in taking the Gambit Pawn.)

7. P. to Q's 4th.	7. B. to Q. Kt.'s 3rd.
8. Q. B. takes P.	8. P. to Q's 3rd.
9. B. to Q's 3rd.	9. Kt. to K. Kt's 3rd.
10. B. to K's 3rd.	10. Castles.
11. P. to K. R.'s 3rd.	11. R. to K's sq.
12 Kt. to Q's 2nd.	12. Q. to K's 2nd
13. Castles.	13. P. to Q. B's 4th.
14. K. to Kt.'s sq.	14. P. takes P.
15. P. takes P.	15. P. to Q. R's 4th.
16. K. Kt. to B's 3rd.	16. B. to Q's 2nd.
17. P. to K. Kt.'s 4th.	17. P. to K. R's 3rd.
18. Q. R. to K. Kt.'s sq.	18. P. to Q. R's 5th.
19. P. to K. Kt.'s 5th.	19. P. takes P.

20. B. takes P.	20. P. to Q. R's 6th.
21. P. to Q. Kt.'s 3rd.	21. B. to Q. B's 3rd.
22. R. to K. Kt.'s 4th.	22. B. to Q. R's 4th.
23. P. to K. R's 4th.	23. B. takes Kt.
24. Kt. takes B.	24. R. to Q. R's 4th.
25. P. to K. R's 5th.	25. R. takes B.

(This part of the game is very cleverly played on both sides.)

26. R. takes R.	26. Kt. to K. B's 5th.
27. Q. to K. B's 3rd.	27. Kt. takes B.
28. P. to Q's 5th.	28. Kt. takes Q. P.
29. K. R. to Kt.'s sq.	

(The position is intensely interesting here. It seems hardly possible for either player to save his game.)

	29. Kt. to Q. B's 6th (ch.)
30. K. to R's sq.	30. B. takes K. P.
31. R. takes Kt. P. (ch.)	31. K. to R's sq.
32. Q. to K. Kt.'s 3rd.	32. B. to K. Kt.'s 3rd.
33. P. takes B.	33. Q. to K's 8th (ch.)
34. R. takes Q.	

[When a young player, and diligently studying these beautiful games, I was very much struck by this position, and suggested the following as a course of play by which I thought White could win the battle :—

34. Kt. to Q. Kt.'s sq.	34. Q. takes Q. (best).
35. R. to K. R's 7th (ch.)	

Great nicety of play is demanded in this remarkable position. If White take the Queen, he cannot possibly save the game.

	35. K. to Kt.'s sq.
36. P. takes P. (double ch.)	36. K. takes R.

Manifestly his best move.

37. R. to K. R's sq. (ch)	37. K. to Kt.'s 2nd.

Again, this is evidently his best line of action.

38. P. takes R., becoming a Queen, and White can win without much trouble.]

	34. R. takes R. (ch.)
35. Q. takes R.	35. Kt. takes Q.
36. R. to K. R's 7th (ch.)	36. K. to Kt.'s sq.
37. P. takes K. B. P. (ch.)	37. K. takes R.
38. P. to B's 8th, becoming a Queen.	38. Kt. to B's 7th, Checkmate.

GAME VII.—Between Messrs. McDonnell and De Labourdonnais.

WHITE (Mr. McD.)	BLACK (Mr. De L.)
1. P. to K's 4th.	1. P. to K's 4th.
2. B. to Q. B's 4th.	2. Kt. to K. B's 3rd.
3. P. to Q's 4th.	3. P. takes P.
4. P. to K's 5th.	4. Q. to K's 2nd.

(This is not now thought so favourable for the defence as 4. $\overline{\text{P. to Q's 4th.}}$).

5. Q. to K's 2nd.	5. Kt. to K. Kt.'s sq.

(Black's error in playing his Q. to K's 2nd entailed, we see, the loss of a move—a loss at such a moment, and in face of such an opponent as Mr. McDonnell, which could hardly be retrieved.)

6. Kt. to K. B's 3rd.	6. Kt. to Q. B's 3rd.
7. P. to Q. B's 3rd.	7. P. to Q's 3rd.
8. Q. B. P. takes P.	8. B. to K. Kt.'s 5th.
9. B. to Q. Kt.'s 5th.	9. P. to Q's 4th.
10. Kt. to Q. B's 3rd.	10. Q. to K's 3rd.
11. P. to K. R's 3rd.	11. B. takes Kt.
12. Q. takes B.	12. Castles.
13. B. takes Kt.	13. Q. takes B.
14. Q. takes K. B. P.	14. B. to Q. Kt.'s 5th.
15. B. to Q's 2nd.	15. Kt. to K's 2nd.
16. Castles (K's side)	16. Q. R. to K. B's sq.
17. Q. to K. R's 5th.	17. Kt. to K. B's 4th.
18. P. to Q. R's 3rd.	18. B. takes Kt.
19. P. takes B.	19. P. to K. Kt.'s 3rd.
20. Q. to Q's sq.	20. P. to K. R's 4th.
21. R. to Q. B's sq.	21. Q. to K's 3rd.
22. B. to K's sq.	

(Mainly to prevent the adverse Kt. being played to K. Kt.'s 6th after White had thrown forward his K. B's Pawn; but the move appears to me a weak one.)

	22. K. to Kt.'s sq.
23. P. to K. B's 4th.	23. P. to K. R's 5th.
24. R. to K. B's 3rd.	24. Q. R. to K. Kt.'s sq.
25. Q. to Q's 2nd.	25. R. to K. R's 2nd.
26. Q. to Q's 3rd.	26. K. R. to Kt.'s 2nd.
27. B. to Q's 2nd.	27. P. to Q. R's 3rd.
28. P. to Q. Kt.'s 4th.	28. Q. to Q. Kt.'s 3rd.

(This move might have been serviceable before Black advanced his Q. Kt.'s Pawn. It appears now to be a useless *coup de repos*.

29. B. to Q. B's 3rd.

(He should rather have played, I think, 29. $\frac{\text{R. to Q. B's 5th}}{}$.)

	29. Kt. to Kt.'s 6th.
30. P. to Q. R's 4th.	30. Kt. to K's 5th.
31. P. to Q. Kt.'s 5th.	31. P. to K. Kt.'s 4th.
32. P. to K. B's 5th.	32. P. to K. Kt.'s 5th.

(The battle now becomes exciting, and each party plays with care and skill.)

33. P. takes K. Kt.'s P.	33. R. takes P.
34. R. to Q. B's 2nd.	34. P. to K. R's 6th.
35. R. takes K. R. P.	35. R. to K. Kt.'s 6th.
36. R. takes R.	36. R. takes R.
37. P. to Q. R's 5th.	

(Well played, both this and the move following.)

37. Q. to K. R's 3rd.

(If Mr. De Labourdonnais had taken the Queen, he would have lost the game off-hand. Suppose, for example :—

37. $\frac{}{\text{R. takes Q.}}$, 38. $\frac{\text{P. takes Q.}}{\text{R. takes B.}}$ (if 38. $\frac{}{\text{Kt. takes B.}}$, 39. $\frac{\text{R. takes Kt.}}{\text{R. takes R.}}$, 40. $\frac{\text{P. to K. B's 6th}}{}$, and wins), 39. $\frac{\text{P. takes R.}}{\text{Kt. takes R.}}$, 40. $\frac{\text{P. to K. B's 6th.}}{}$, and wins.)

38. Q. B. to Q's 2nd.	38. Q. to K. R's 6th.
39. Q. to K. B's sq.	39. R. to K. Kt.'s sq.
40. P. to K. B's 6th.	40. Q. to K. R's 4th.
41. P. to K. B's 7th.	41. R. to K. B's sq.
42. P. to K's 6th.	42. Kt. to K. Kt.'s 6th.
43. Q. to K. B's 3rd.	43. Q. to K. R's 8th (ch.)
44. K. to B's 2nd.	44. Kt. to K's 5th (ch.)
45. K. to K's 2nd.	45. Q. to Q. Kt.'s 8th.

(Merely desperate. The game is irredeemable by any skill.)

46. P. to K's 7th.	46. Q. takes Q. Kt.'s P. (ch.)
47. Q. to Q's 3rd.	47. Kt. to K. Kt.s 6th (ch.)
48. K. to Q's sq.	

And Black wins; for if

	48. Q. takes Q.
49. P. takes R. "Queens" (ch.)	
	49. K. to R's 2nd.
50. Q. to Q. B's 5th. (ch.)	50. P. to Kt.'s 3rd.
51. Q. takes Q. B. P. (ch.)	51. K. to R's sq.
52. P. "Queens."	

Giving checkmate.

Game VIII.—Between Messrs. Boncourt and St. Amant.

Black (Mr. B.)	White (Mr. St. A.)
1. P. to K's 4th.	1. P. to K's 4th.
2. B. to Q. B's 4th.	2. Kt. to K. B's 3rd.
3. P. to Q's 3rd.	3. B. to Q. B's 4th.
4. Kt. to K. B's 3rd.	4. Kt. to Q. B's 3rd.
5. P. to Q. B's 3rd.	5. B. to Q. Kt.'s 3rd.
6. Castles.	6. Castles.
7. B. to K. Kt.'s 5th.	7. P. to Q's 3rd.
8. P. to Q. Kt.'s 4th.	8. B. to K's 3rd.
9. Q. Kt. to Q's 2nd.	9. P. to K. R's 3rd.
10. B. to K. R's 4th.	10. K. to R's 2nd.
11. P. to Q. R's 4th.	11. P. to Q. R's 3rd.
12. K. to R's sq.	12. R. to K. Kt.'s sq.
13. Q. to Q. B's 2nd.	

(Mr. Boncourt, from want of vigour in his opening, has suffered the attack to pass effectually into the hands of his adversary.)

	13. P. to K. Kt.'s 4th.
14. B. to K. Kt.'s 3rd.	14. P. to K. R's 4th.
15. P. to K. R's 3rd.	

(This looks very inefficient, compared with 15. $\frac{\text{P. to K. R's 4th.}}{}$, which, apparently, would have restored the initiative to Black.)

	15. P. to K. R's 5th.
16. B. to K. R's 2nd.	16. Kt. to K. R's 4th.
17. P. to Q's 4th.	17. P. to K. Kt.'s 5th.
18. B. takes B.	18. P. takes B.
19. P. takes K. Kt. P.	19. R. takes P.
20. P. takes P.	20. P. takes P.
21. Kt. to Q. B's 4th.	21. Kt. to K. Kt.'s 6th (ch.)

(Finely played.)

22. P. takes Kt.	22. P. takes P.
23. Q. R. to Q's sq.	23. Q. to K's 2nd.
24. P. to Q. Kt.'s 5th.	24. R. to K. R's 5th.
25. Kt. takes B.	

(He would obviously have been checkmated at once if he had taken the Rook.)

	25. R. takes B. (ch.)
26. K. to Kt.'s sq.	26. Q. to Q. B's 4th (ch.)
27. R. to K. B's 2nd.	27. P. takes Kt.
28. Kt. takes R.	28. P. takes P.
29. P. takes P.	29. R. to K. B's sq.
30. Kt. to K. B's 3rd.	30. Kt. to Q. R's 4th.
31. Q. to K's 2nd.	31. Kt. to Q. B's 5th.
32. Kt. to Kt.'s 5th (ch.)	

(This is of no avail; but the position does not afford a move that is of any.)

	32. K. to Kt.'s 3rd.
33. Kt. to K. B's 3rd.	33. R. to K. B's 5th.
34. R. to Q's 3rd.	34. P. takes R. (ch.)
35. Q. takes P.	35. Q. takes Q. (ch.)
36. K. takes Q.	36. R. takes P.

37. R. to Q's 7th.	37. R. to K. B's 5th.
38. R. takes Q. Kt.'s P	38. P. to K's 5th.
39. K. to Kt.'s 3rd.	39. P. takes Kt.

And Black resigned.

GAME IX.—Between Messrs. St. Amant and Perigal.

WHITE (Mr. St. A.)	BLACK (Mr. P.)
1. P. to K's 4th.	1. P. to K's 4th.
2. B. to Q. B's 4th.	2. B. to Q. B's 4th.
3. Q. to K. Kt.'s 4th.	3. Q. to K. B's 3rd.
4. P. to Q's 4th.	4. B. takes P.
5. Kt. to K. B's 3rd.	5. Kt. to Q. B's 3rd.
6. Q. to Kt.'s 3rd.	6. P. to K. R.'s 3rd.
7. P. to Q. B's 3rd.	7. B. to Q. Kt.'s 3rd.
8. P. to Q. Kt.'s 4th	8. P. to Q's 3rd.
9. P. to Q. R's 4th.	9. P. to Q. R's 4th.
10. P. to Q. Kt.'s 5th.	10. Kt. to Q's sq.
11. Castles.	11. K. Kt. to K's 2nd.
12. Kt. to Q. R's 3rd.	12. Kt. to K. Kt.'s 3rd.
13. Kt. to Q. B's 2nd.	13. B. to K's 3rd.
14. B. to Q's 3rd.	14. Castles.
15. K. to R's sq.	15. Kt. to K. B's 5th.
16. Kt. to K. Kt.'s sq.	16. Kt. takes B.
17. Q. takes Kt.	17. Q. to K's 2nd.
18. B. to K's 3rd.	18. P. to K. B's 4th.
19. B. takes B.	19. P. takes P.
20. Q. takes K. P.	20. P. takes B.
21. Kt. to K's 3rd.	21. R. to K. B's 5th.
22. Q. to Q's 3rd.	22. R. to Q. B's sq.
23. Kt. to Q's 5th.	23. B. takes Kt.
24. Q. takes B. (ch.)	24. Kt. to K. B's 2nd.
25. Q. R. to Q. B's sq.	25. R. takes Q. R. P.
26. Kt. to K. B's 3rd.	26. K. R. to Q. B's 5th.
27. Q. R. to K's sq.	27. Q. R. to Q. B's 4th.
28. Q. to Q's 2nd.	28. Q. R. takes Q. Kt. P.

(Mr. Perigal has contrived to pick up some valuable Pawns, but meanwhile he suffers his opponent to obtain a fine attacking situation.

29. Kt. to Q's 4th.	29. Q. R. to Q. B's 4th.
30. P. to K. B's 4th.	30. P. to K's 5th.
31. P. to K. B's 5th.	31. K. R. takes Q. B. P.
32. P. to K. B's 6th.	

(This part of the game is played by Mr. St. Amant with remarkable ability.)

	32. P. takes P.
33. Kt. to K. B's 5th.	33. Q. to K's 4th.
34. Q. to K's 2nd.	34. K. to B's sq.
35. Q. to K. Kt.'s 4th.	35. Q. to K's 3rd.
36. Q. to Kt.'s 7th (ch.)	36. K. to K's sq.
37. Q. to Kt.'s 8th (ch.)	37. K. to Q's 2nd.
38. Kt. to Kt.'s 7th.	38. Q. to K's 2nd.
39. R. takes K. B. P.	39. K. R. to Q. B's 8th.

(He would have been checkmated or have lost his Queen, incontinently, if he had captured the Rook.)

40. K. R. to K. B's sq.	40. R. takes R
41. R. takes R.	41. R. to Q. B's sq.
42. Q. to K. R's 7th.	42. K. to Q. B's 2nd.
43. R. takes K. P.	43. K. to Kt.'s sq.
44. P. to K. R's 3rd.	44. Kt. to Kt.'s 4th.
45. R. takes Q.	45. Kt. takes Q.
46. Kt. to K. B's 5th.	46. R. to B's 2nd.
47. R. to K's 8th (ch.)	47. K. to R's 2nd.
48. Kt. takes Q. P.	48. R. to Q's 2nd.
49. Kt. to B's 8th (ch.)	49. K. to R's 3rd.
50. R. to K's 6th.	50. R. to Q's 8th (ch.)
51. K. to R's 2nd.	51. R. to Q. Kt.'s 8th.
52. R. takes K. R. P.	52. P. to Q. R's 5th.
53. R. takes Kt.	

(The conclusion of this game is in the highest degree instructive, and very excellently played.)

	53. P. to Q. R's 6th.
54. Kt. to Q's 6th.	54. P. to Q. Kt.'s 4th.
55. R. to K. R's 8th.	55. P. to Kt.'s 5th.
56. R. to Q. R's 8th (ch.)	56. K. to Kt.'s 3rd.
57. P. to K. R's 4th.	57. R. to Q. B's 8th.

58. P. to R's 5th.	58. R. to Q. B's 3rd.
59. Kt. to K. B's 7th.	59. R. to K. B's 3rd.
60. P. to K. R's 6th.	

(Capitally played.)

	60. R. takes Kt.
61. P. to Kt.'s 4th.	61. K. to Kt.'s 4th.
62. P. to Kt.'s 5th.	62. R. to K. R's 2nd.
63. K. to Kt.'s 3rd.	63. K. to B's 5th.
64. K. to Kt.'s 4th.	64. P. to Kt.'s 4th.
65. K. to R's 5th.	65. P. to Kt.'s 6th.
66. P. to Kt.'s 6th.	66. R. to Q's 2nd.
67. P. to Kt.'s 7th.	67. R. to Q's 4th (ch.)
68. K. to Kt.'s 4th.	68. P. to Kt.'s 7th.
69. P. "Queens."	69. P. "Queens."
70. R. to Q. B's 8th (ch.)	70. K. to Q's 5th.
71. Q. to Kt.'s 7th (ch.)	

And in a few moves Mr. Perigal surrendered.

GAME X.—Between Mr. Anderssen and an Amateur.

WHITE (Amateur.)	BLACK (Mr. A.)
1. P. to K's 4th.	1. P. to K's 4th.
2. B. to Q. B's 4th.	2. P. to K. B's 4th.
3. P. takes P.	3. Kt. to K. B's 3rd.
4. P. to K. Kt.'s 4th.	4. P. to Q's 4th.
5. B. to Q. Kt.'s 3rd.	5. B. to Q. B's 4th.
6. P. to Q's 3rd.	6. P. to K. R's 4th.
7. P. to Kt.'s 5th.	7. Kt. to Kt.'s 5th.
8. Kt. to K. R's 3rd.	8. Q. B. takes P.
9. P. to K. B's 3rd.	9. Castles.

(This leads to an animated conclusion.)

10. Kt. to Q. B's 3rd.

(If he had taken the Kt., the consequences would have been very disastrous. *Ex. gr.*

10. P. takes Kt.	10. B. takes P.
11. Q. to Q's 2nd.	11. B. takes Kt.

And White's game is desperate.)

	10. P. to Q. B's 3rd.
11. Q. to K's 2nd.	11. Kt. to Q. R's 3rd.
12. P. to Q. R's 3rd.	

(He should have played his Bishop to Q's 2nd, with the view of Castling next move.)

	12. Kt. to Q. B's 2nd.
13. Kt. to Q's sq.	13. Q. to Q's 3rd.
14. K. Kt. to B's 2nd.	14. Kt. takes Kt.
15. Kt. takes Kt.	15. Kt. to K's 3rd.
16. P. to K. R's 4th.	16. Kt. to Q's 5th.
17. Q. to Q's sq.	17. P. to K's 5th.
18. Q. P. takes P.	18. Q. to K. Kt.'s 6th.
19. Q. to Q's 3rd.	19. B. takes K. P.
20. P. takes B.	20. Q. takes Kt. (ch.)
21. K. to Q's sq.	21. Kt. takes B.
22. Q. takes Kt.	22. R. to K. B's 6th.
23. Q. to Q. R's 4th.	23. Q. R. to K. B's sq.
24. P. takes Q. P.	

And Mr. Anderssen announced checkmate in six moves.

GAME XI.—Between Messrs. Walker and Daniels.

WHITE (Mr. D.)	BLACK (Mr. W.)
1. P. to K's 4th.	1. P. to K's 4th.
2. B. to Q. B's 4th.	2. B. to Q. B's 4th.
3. Q. to K's 2nd.	3. Kt. to K. B's 3rd.
4. P. to K. B's 4th.	4. Kt. to Q. B's 3rd.
5. Kt. to K. B's 3rd.	5. P. to Q's 3rd.
6. P. to Q. B's 3rd.	6. P. to Q. R's 4th.
7. P. to Q. R's 4th.	7. Castles.
8. Kt. to Q. R's 3rd.	

(He should have played 8. $\frac{\text{P. to Q's 3rd}}{}$. The move in the text loses precious time.)

	8. P. takes K. B. P.
9. P. to Q's 4th.	9. B. takes Q. Kt.
10. R. takes B.	10. Kt. takes K. P.
11. Castles.	11. P. to Q's 4th.

12. B. to Q's 3rd.	12. R. to K's sq.
13. Q. to Q. B's 2nd.	13. Q. to K. B's 3rd.
14. Kt. to Q's 2nd.	14. Kt. takes Q. P.

(Very well conceived.)

15. P. takes Kt.	15. Q. takes P. (ch.)
16. K. to R's sq.	16. Kt. to B's 7th (ch.)

(After this move, White's game appears to be irredeemable.)

17. R. takes Kt.

(Compulsory, because if he move 17. $\frac{\text{K. to R's sq.}}{\quad}$, then follow 17. $\frac{\quad}{\text{Kt. to K. R's 6th (doub. ch.)}}$, 18. $\frac{\text{K. to R's sq.}}{\text{Q. to Kt.'s 8th (ch.)}}$, 19. $\frac{\text{R. takes Q.}}{\text{Kt. to B's 7th.}}$, checkmate.)

	17. Q. takes R.
18. B. takes P. (ch.)	

(This is merely suicidal. He might have protracted, if not have averted, defeat by moving his Kt. to K. B's sq.)

	18. K. to R's sq.

And Mr. Daniels resigns.

Game XII.—Between Mr. Cochrane and a leading London Player.

White (Mr. ——.)	Black (Mr. C.)
1. P. to K's 4th.	1. P. to K's 4th.
2. B. to Q. B's 4th.	2. B. to Q. B's 4th.
3. P. to Q. B's 3rd.	3. Q. to K. Kt.'s 4th.
4. Q. to K. B's 3rd.	4. Kt. to K. B's 3rd.
5. Kt. to K's 2nd.	5. Q. to Kt.'s 3rd.
6. P. to Q's 4th.	6. P. takes P.
7. P. to K's 5th.	7. Kt. to Q. B's 3rd.

(This is eminently characteristic of Mr. Cochrane's daring genius.)

8. P. takes Kt.	8. Kt. to K's 4th.
9. Q. to Q's 5th.	9. P. to Q's 3rd.
10. P. takes Q. P.	10. P. to Q. B's 3rd.
11. P. takes Kt. P.	11. R. to K. Kt.'s sq.

(If he had taken the Pawn with his Queen, White would have extricated his Queen.)

12. Kt. to K. B's 4th.	12. Q. to Q. B's 7th.
13. Kt. to Q. R's 3rd.	13. B. to Q. Kt.'s 5th (ch.)
14. B. to Q's 2nd.	

(Or, checkmate on the move.)

	14. Q. takes B. (ch.)
15. K. to B's sq.	15. P. takes Q.

And Mr. Cochrane won the game.

GAME XIII.—Between Messrs. Schulten and Stanley.

WHITE (Mr. Schulten.)	BLACK (Mr. Stanley.)
1. P. to K's 4th.	1. P. to K's 4th.
2. B. to Q. B's 4th.	2. B. to Q. B's 4th.
3. P. to Q. B's 3rd.	3. Q. to K's 2nd.
4. Kt. to K. B's 3rd.	4. P. to Q's 3rd.
5. Castles.	5. Kt. to K. B's 3rd.
6. P. to Q's 4th.	6. B. to Q. Kt.'s 3rd.
7. B. to K. Kt.'s 5th.	7. P. to K. R's 3rd.
8. B. to K. R's 4th.	8. B. to K's 3rd.
9. Q. Kt. to Q's 2nd.	9. B. takes B.
10. Kt. takes B.	10. Q. Kt. to Q's 2nd.
11. P. to Q. R's 4th.	11. P. to Q. R's 4th.

("It is highly probable," Mr. Stanley remarks on the move, "that P. to Q. B's 3rd would have been better play."

12. Kt. takes B.	12. Kt. takes Kt.
13. Kt. to Q's 2nd.	

(Mr. Schulten plays throughout this game with remarkable judgment.)

	13. P. to K. Kt.'s 4th.

(This weakens Black's position; but he thought it indispensably necessary to prevent the advance of his opponent's K. B's Pawn.

14. B. to Kt.'s 3rd.	14. P. to K. R's 4th.
15. P. to K. R's 4th.)	

(Well played.)

	15. P. takes K. R. P.

(15. $\frac{\quad}{\text{Kt. to K. Kt.'s 5th}}$ looks preferable.)

16. B. takes K. R. P.	16. Q. to K's 3rd.

(A lost move. He had better have Castled on the Q's side at once.)

17. P. to Q's 5th.	17. Q. to K's 2nd.
18. P. to K. B's 4th.	18. Q. Kt. to Q's 2nd.
19. P. takes K. P.	19. P. takes P.
20. Q. to Q. Kt.'s 3rd.	

(A crushing blow. From this point Black's game is irretrievable, unless by an error on the other side.)

	20. Castles (Q's side.)
21. Q. to Kt.'s 5th.	

(An excellent stroke; quiet, but immensely potent.)

	21. P. to Q. Kt.'s 3rd.
22. Q. to B's 6th.	22. R. to K. R's 3rd.
23. Kt. to Q. B's 4th.	23. Q. R. to K. Kt.'s sq.

(Useless; but what could he do? If 23. $\frac{\quad}{\text{Q. to Q. B's 4th (ch.)}}$, then 24. $\frac{\text{K. to R's sq.}}{\quad}$, &c.)

24. P. to Q's 6th.	24. Q. to Q's sq.
25. R. takes Kt.	25. Kt. takes R.
26. Kt. takes P. (ch.)	26. K. moves.
27. Q. checkmates.	

GAME. XIV.—Between Mr. Paulsen and Chevalier St. Bon.

WHITE (Mr. P.)	BLACK (Chev. St. B.)
1. P. to K's 4th.	1. P. to K's 4th.
2. B. to Q. B's 4th.	2. P. to K. B's 4th.
3. P. to Q's 3rd	3. B. to Q. B's 4th.
4. B. takes Kt.	4. R. takes B.
5. Q. to K. R's 5th (ch.)	5. K. to B's sq.

6. Kt. to K. B's 3rd.	6. Q. to K. B's 3rd.
7. Kt. to Kt.'s 5th.	7. R. to K. R's sq.
8. Kt. takes R. P. (ch.)	8. R. takes Kt.
9. Q. takes R.	9. P. takes P.
10. Castles.	10. P. to Q's 4th.
11. Kt. to Q. B's 3rd.	11. B. to K's 3rd.
12. Q. to K. R's 8th (ch.)	12. K. to K's 2nd.
13. P. takes P.	13. P. to Q. B's 3rd.
14. P. takes P.	14. P. takes P.
15. B. to K's 3rd.	15. B. to Q's 3rd.
16. Q. R. to Q's sq.	16. Q. to K. B's 2nd.
17. P. to Q. Kt.'s 4th.	17. B. takes P.
18. Kt. to K's 4th.	18. Q. to K. B's sq.
19. Q. to K. R's 4th (ch.)	19. K. to Q's 2nd.
20. P. to K. B's 4th.	20. Kt. to Q. B's 3rd.
21. P. takes P.	21. Q. to K. R's sq.
22. Q. to K. Kt.'s 3rd.	

And Black resigns.

GAME XV.—Between Messrs. Falkbeer and Anderssen.

White (Mr. F.)	Black (Mr. A.)
1. P. to K's 4th.	1. P. to K's 4th.
2. B. to Q. B's 4th.	2. Kt. to K. B's 3rd.
3. P. to K. B's 4th.	3. P. to Q's 4th.
4. P. takes Q. P.	4. P. to K's 5th.
5. Kt. to Q. B's 3rd.	5. B. to Q. B's 4th.
6. P. to Q's 4th.	6. P. takes P. in passing.
7. P. takes P.	7. Castles.
8. P. to Q's 4th.	8. B. to Q. Kt.'s 3rd.
9. Kt. to K. B's 3rd.	9. P. to Q. B's 3rd.
10. Q. to Q. Kt.'s 3rd.	10. B. to K. Kt.'s 5th.

(The opening of the present game is played with great care, and is an instructive example of this form of the K's Bishop's game.)

11. Castles.

(11. $\frac{\text{B. to K's 3rd}}{\quad}$ would have been better.)

	11. B. takes Kt.
12. R. takes B.	12. B. takes P. (ch.)
13. K. to R's sq.	

(Here, again, he should have moved the Q's Bishop to K's 3rd.)

	13. B. takes Kt.
14. Q. takes B.	14. P. takes P.
15. B. to Q's 3rd.	15. Kt. to K's 5th.
16. Q. to Q. B's 2nd.	16. Kt. to Q. B's 3rd.
17. B. to K's 3rd.	17. R. to K's sq.
18. P. to Q. R's 3rd.	18. R. to Q. B's sq.
19. Q. to Q. R's 4th.	19. P. to Q's 5th.

(Mr. Anderssen now prosecutes his attack with merciless persistence.

20. B. to K. Kt.'s sq.	20. P. to Q. R's 3rd.
21. P. to Q. Kt.'s 4th.	21. Kt. to Q. R's 2nd.
22. Q. to Q's sq.	22. Q. to Q's 2nd.
23. R. to K. R's 3rd.	23. R. to Q. B's 6th.
24. Q. to K. R's 5th.	24. P. to K. R's 3rd.
25. R. to Q's sq.	25. Kt. to K. B's 3rd.
26. Q. to K. R's 4th.	26. Kt. to Q. Kt.'s 4th.
27. P. to Q. R's 4th.	27. Kt. to Q's 3rd.
28. B. takes Q. P.	28. Kt. to K. B's 4th.

(This is highly ingenious; for if White captures this Kt., Black takes the Queen's Bishop with Queen, and must win.)

29. B. takes R.	29. Kt. takes Q.
30. B. to K. R's 7th (ch.)	30. K. takes B.
31. R. takes Q.	31. Kt. takes R.
32. R. takes Kt.	32. R. to K's 6th.
33. R. to K. R's 3rd.	

(Compulsory; for if 33. $\frac{\text{B. to Q's 7th}}{\text{R. to K's 7th}}$, 34. $\frac{\text{B. to Q. B's 3rd}}{\text{R. to Q. B's 7th}}$, 34. $\frac{\text{B. to K's sq.}}{\text{R. to Q. B's 8th}}$.)

	33. R. takes R.
34. P. takes R.	34. Kt. to Q. Kt.'s 3rd.
35. P. to Q. R's 5th.	35. Kt. to Q's 4th.
36. B. to Q's 2nd.	36. K. to Kt.'s 3rd.

37. K. to Kt.'s 2nd.	37. K. to B's 4th.
38. K. to B's 3rd.	38. P. to K. R's 4th.
39. P. to K. R's 4th.	39. P. to K. B's 3rd.
40. P. to K. R's 3rd.	40. P. to K. Kt.'s 3rd.

White is obliged now to make a self-injuring move. The least directly harmful appears to be K. to Kt.'s 3rd. Whereupon Black moves his K's 5th, and forces the game in a few moves. Seeing all this, Mr. Falkbeer resigned.

BOOK III.

THE KING'S KNIGHT'S OPENING.

CHAPTER I.

PETROFF'S DEFENCE.

1. $\frac{\text{P. to K's 4th}}{\text{P. to K's 4th}}$, 2. $\frac{\text{Kt. to K. B's 3rd}}{\text{Kt. to K. B's 3rd}}$.

GAME THE FIRST.

3. $\frac{\text{Kt. takes P.}}{\text{P. to Q's 3rd}}$; 3. $\frac{\text{Kt. takes P.}}{}$; 3. $\frac{}{\text{Q. to K's 2nd}}$.

GAME THE SECOND.

3. $\frac{\text{P. to Q's 4th}}{\text{P. takes P.}}$; 3. $\frac{}{\text{Kt. takes P.}}$.

GAME THE THIRD.

3. $\frac{\text{B. to Q. B's 4th}}{}$

This defence, or rather counter-attack, is preferred by some excellent players before any other reply to 2. $\frac{\text{Kt. to K. B's 3rd}}{}$. The first notice of it occurs in the treatise by Lucena, from whom Damiano borrowed and slightly expanded it. Subsequent writers on Chess, as Lopez, Greco, Cozio, Ponziani, Lolli, down to Lewis and Walker, have treated it more or less copiously. Its real merits and shortcomings were never clearly ascertained, however, until Mr. Von Petroff, a distinguished Russian Chess-player, adopted it frequently in his games. This led his friend Von Jaenisch to analyze it thoroughly. As a result of his earliest examination, he pronounced it a sound defence. Afterwards, however, he published an exhaustive analysis of the move, and stated that the discovery of new combinations in the attack had somewhat qualified his previous opinions.

Game the First.

WHITE.	BLACK.
1. P. to K's 4th.	1. P. to K's 4th.
2. Kt. to K. B's 3rd.	2. Kt. to K. B's 3rd.
3. Kt. takes P.	

(This is the oldest and perhaps the best mode of continuing the attack. The result of 3. $\frac{\text{P. to Q's 4th}}{\quad}$, and 3. $\frac{\text{B. to Q. B's 4th}}{\quad}$, shall be shown in Games the Second and Third. That of 3. $\frac{\text{Kt. to Q. B's 3rd}}{\quad}$ may be conveniently demonstrated here. Suppose then :—3. $\frac{\text{Kt. to Q. B's 3rd}}{\text{B. to Q. Kt.'s 5th}}$, 4. $\frac{\text{Kt. takes P.}}{\text{B. takes Kt.}}$, 5. $\frac{\text{Q. P. takes B.}}{\text{P. to Q's 3rd}}$, 6. $\frac{\text{Kt. to K. B's 3rd}}{\text{Kt. takes P.}}$, 7. $\frac{\text{B. to Q's 3rd}}{\text{Kt. to K. B's 3rd}}$, 8. $\frac{\text{Castles}}{\text{Castles}}$, and White has only achieved an equal game.)

	3. P. to Q.'s 3rd.

(For the consequences of 3. $\frac{\quad}{\text{Kt. takes P.}}$ and 3. $\frac{\quad}{\text{Q. to K's 2nd}}$, see Variation A.)

4. Kt. to K. B's 3rd.

(Here Mr. Cochrane struck out a new and daring line of

assault, by taking the enemy's K. B's Pawn with his Knight. This sacrifice gives a fierce attack for the moment, undoubtedly, yet, if properly met, it does not at present appear to me equivalent to the piece it costs. For example:—

4. $\frac{\text{Kt. takes B's P.}}{\text{K. takes Kt.}}$, 5. $\frac{\text{B. to Q. B's 4th (ch.)}}{\text{P. to Q's 4th}}$. [If 5. $\frac{}{\text{B. to K's 3rd}}$, 6. $\frac{\text{B. takes B. (ch.)}}{\text{K. takes B.}}$, 7. $\frac{\text{P. to Q's 4th}}{}$, and White can maintain his attack.] 6. $\frac{\text{B. to Q. Kt.'s 3rd}}{}$. [If 6. $\frac{\text{P. takes P.}}{}$, then Black, I think, can rapidly disengage his forces, and become the assailant by 6. $\frac{}{\text{Q. to K's sq. (ch.)}}$, 7. $\frac{\text{Q. to K's 2nd or K. to B's sq.}}{\text{B. to Q's 3rd}}$.] 6. $\frac{}{\text{B. to K. Kt.'s 5th}}$, 7. $\frac{\text{P. to K. B's 3rd}}{\text{B. to K's 3rd}}$, 8. $\frac{\text{Kt. to Q. B's 3rd}}{\text{P. takes P.}}$, 9. $\frac{\text{B. takes B. (ch.)}}{\text{K. takes B.}}$, and White has only two Pawns to compensate him for his lost Knight.)

4. Kt. takes P.

5. P. to Q's 4th.

(If 5. $\frac{\text{Kt. to Q. B's 3rd}}{\text{Kt. takes Kt.}}$, 6. $\frac{\text{Q. P. takes Kt.}}{\text{B. to K's 2nd}}$, Black has nothing further to apprehend from the opening. If 5. $\frac{\text{Q. to K's 2nd}}{\text{Q. to K's 2nd}}$, 6. $\frac{\text{P. to Q's 3rd}}{\text{Kt. to K. B's 3rd}}$, 7. $\frac{\text{Q. takes Q. (ch.)}}{\text{B. takes Q.}}$, and the game is equal. Finally, if 5. $\frac{\text{P. to Q's 3rd}}{\text{Kt. to K. B's 3rd}}$, 6. $\frac{\text{P. to Q's 4th}}{\text{P. to Q's 4th}}$, 7. $\frac{\text{B. to Q's 3rd}}{\text{B. to Q's 3rd}}$, 8. $\frac{\text{Castles}}{\text{Castles}}$, 9. $\frac{\text{P. to Q. B's 4th}}{}$, the game is perfectly equal.*)

5. P. to Q's 4th.

6. B. to Q's 3rd. 6. B. to Q's 3rd.

---

* The position is identical with a leading variation of the French Game.—[ED.]

(Jaenisch commends also 6. $\frac{}{\text{B. to K's 2nd}}$, which appears to be a very safe move. The probable continuation is 7. $\frac{\text{Castles}}{\text{Kt. to Q. B's 3rd}}$, 8. $\frac{\text{P. to Q. B's 4th}}{\text{B. to K's 3rd}}$, the second player being at no disadvantage. He can nearly equalise the game too by 6. $\frac{}{\text{Kt. to Q. B's 3rd}}$, and 6. $\frac{}{\text{Kt. to K. B's 3rd}}$. In the latter case the continuation would be—7. $\frac{\text{Castles}}{\text{B. to K's 2nd}}$, 8. $\frac{\text{P. to Q. B's 4th}}{\text{P. takes P.}}$, 9. $\frac{\text{B. takes P.}}{\text{Castles}}$, 10. $\frac{\text{Kt. to K's 5th}}{\text{P. to Q. B's 3rd}}$, 11. $\frac{\text{Kt. to Q. B's 3rd}}{\text{Q's Kt. to Q's 2nd}}$. If then 6. $\frac{}{\text{Kt. to Q. B's 3rd}}$, 7. $\frac{\text{Castles}}{\text{B. to K's 2nd}}$, 8. $\frac{\text{P. to Q. B's 4th}}{\text{B. to K's 3rd}}$. But if 6. $\frac{}{\text{P. to Q. B's 4th}}$, 7. $\frac{\text{P. to Q. B's 4th}}{\text{P. takes Q's P.}}$, 8. $\frac{\text{Castles}}{\text{B. to Q. B's 4th}}$, 9. $\frac{\text{P. takes Q's P.}}{}$, White has an advantage.) *

7. Castles.	7. Castles.
8. P. to Q. B's 4th.	8. B. to K's 3rd.†
9. Q. to Q. B's 2nd.	

---

* The authors of the German *Handbuch* consider 6. $\frac{}{\text{Kt. to Q. B's 3rd}}$ to be stronger than 6. $\frac{}{\text{B. to Q's 3rd}}$ 6. $\frac{}{\text{B. to K's 2nd}}$ or 6. $\frac{}{\text{Kt. to K. B's 3rd}}$ and continue 6. $\frac{}{\text{Kt. to Q. B's 3rd}}$ 7. $\frac{\text{Castles}}{\text{B. to K's 2nd}}$ 8. $\frac{\text{P. to Q. B's 4th}}{\text{B. to K. Kt.'s 5th}}$ 9. $\frac{\text{Kt. to Q. B's 3rd}}{\text{Kt. takes Kt.}}$ 10. $\frac{\text{P. takes Kt.}}{\text{Castles}}$ 11. $\frac{\text{Q. to Q. Kt's 3rd}}{\text{Q's P. takes P.}}$ 12. $\frac{\text{Q. takes Kt.'s P.}}{\text{B. takes Kt.}}$ &c., the result being an even game.—[Ed.]

† Black's best move at this point is, I think, 8. $\frac{}{\text{Kt. to K. B's 3d.}}$ —[Ed.]

(By 9. $\frac{\text{Q. to Q. Kt.'s 3rd}}{\text{P. takes P.}}$, 10. $\frac{\text{B. takes P.}}{}$. [If 10. $\frac{\text{Q. takes Q. Kt.'s P.}}{\text{B. to Q's 4th}}$, and Black will have the superiority.] 10. $\frac{}{\text{B. takes B.}}$, 11. $\frac{\text{Q. takes B.}}{\text{P. to Q. B.'s 3rd}}$, 12. $\frac{\text{Kt. to Q. B's 3rd}}{\text{Kt. to K. B's 3rd}}$, 13. $\frac{\text{Q. to Q. Kt.'s 3rd}}{\text{Q. to Q. B's 2nd}}$, 14. $\frac{\text{B. to K. Kt.'s 5th}}{\text{Q's Kt. to Q's 2nd}}$, White only makes an equal game. So also by 9. $\frac{\text{R. to K's sq.}}{\text{R. to K's sq.}}$, 10. $\frac{\text{Q. to Q. Kt.'s 3rd}}{\text{P. takes P.}}$, 11. $\frac{\text{B. takes P.}}{\text{B. takes B.}}$, 12. $\frac{\text{Q. takes B.}}{\text{Kt to Q's 2nd}}$, the result is the same.)

	9. P. to K. B.'s 4th.
10. Q. to Q. Kt.'s 3rd.	10. P. takes P.
11. Q. takes Q. Kt.'s P.	11. P. to Q. B's 3rd.

(If 11. $\frac{}{\text{Kt. to Q's 2nd}}$, 12. $\frac{\text{B. takes Kt.}}{\text{R. to Q. Kt.'s sq.}}$, 13. $\frac{\text{Q. to Q. R's 6th}}{\text{R. to Q. Kt.'s 3rd}}$, 14. $\frac{\text{Q. to Q. R's 4th}}{\text{P. takes B.}}$, 15. $\frac{\text{Kt. to Kt.'s 5th}}{\text{B. to Q's 4th}}$, 16. $\frac{\text{Kt. to Q. B's 3rd}}{}$, with the superior position.)

12. B. takes Kt.

(Taking the Queen's Rook would be most unwise.)

	12. P. takes B.
13. Kt. to K. Kt.'s 5th.	13. B. to K. B's 4th.
14. Kt. to Q. B's 3rd.	14. Q. to Q's 2nd.

(If 14. $\frac{}{\text{B. to Q. B's sq.}}$ Black gains the adverse Queen, but at the cost of a Rook and two lesser pieces—more than she is worth.)

15. Q. takes Q.	15. Kt. takes Q.
16. K's Kt. takes K's P.	

White has the advantage.

VARIATION A, BEGINNING AT BLACK'S 3RD MOVE.

BLACK.

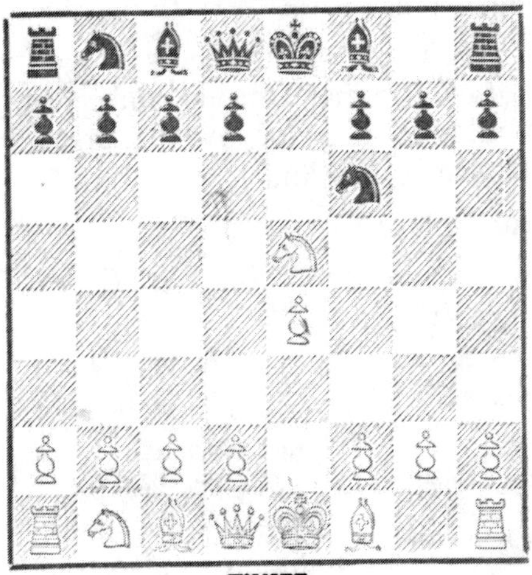

WHITE.

Position prior to Black's 3rd Move.

In the first place :—

	3. Kt. takes P

(An imprudent capture.)

4. Q. to K's 2nd.	4. Q. to K's 2nd.

(The retreat of the Knight would cost the Queen by 5. $\frac{\text{Kt. to Q. B's 6th (ch.)}}{}$.

5. Q. takes Kt.	5. P. to Q's 3rd.
6. P. to Q's 4th.	6. P. to K. B's 3rd.
7. P. to K. B's 4th.	7. Kt. to Q's 2nd.

(If 7. $\frac{}{\text{Q's P. takes Kt.}}$, 8. $\frac{\text{B's P. takes P.}}{\text{P. takes P.}}$, 9. $\frac{\text{Q. takes K's P.}}{}$, having won a Pawn.)

8. Kt. to Q. B's 3rd.	8. Q's P. takes Kt.

(It matters little whether Black takes the Knight with this or the Bishop's Pawn.)

9. Kt. to Q's 5th.	9. Q. to Q's 3rd.
10. Q's P. takes P.	10. P. takes P.
11. P. takes P.	11. Q. to Q. B's 3rd.
12. B. to Q. Kt.'s 5th.	12. Q. to K. Kt.'s 3rd.

(White can now obtain a decisive advantage by the commonplace course of exchanging Queens and taking the Queen's Bishop's Pawn, checking, or by the more refined one of playing his Queen to K's 2nd.)

In the second place :—

	3. Q. to K's 2nd.
4. P. to Q's 4th.	

(If 4. $\frac{\text{Kt. to K. B's 3rd}}{\text{Q. takes P. (ch.)}}$, 5. $\frac{\text{B. to K's 2nd}}{\text{B. to Q. B's 4th}}$, 6. $\frac{\text{Castles}}{\text{Castles}}$, 7. $\frac{\text{P. to Q's 4th}}{\text{B. to Q. Kt.'s 3rd}}$, 8. $\frac{\text{P. to Q. B's 4th}}{\text{P. to Q. B's 3rd}}$, 9. $\frac{\text{Kt. to Q. B's 3rd}}{\text{Q. to K.'s 2nd}}$, 10. $\frac{\text{B. to K. Kt.'s 5th}}{}$. White has also the freer disposed game.)

	4. P. to Q's 3rd.
5. Kt. to K. B's 3rd	5. Q. takes P. (ch.)
6. B. to K's 2nd	6. B. to K. B's 4th.
7. P. to Q. B's 4th.	7. B. to K's 2nd.
8. Castles.	8. Castles.
9. Kt. to Q. B's 3rd.	

Black's position is inferior.

Game the Second.

WHITE.	BLACK.
1. P. to K's 4th.	1. P. to K's 4th.
2. Kt. to K. B's 3rd.	2. Kt. to K. B's 3rd.
3. P. to Q's 4th.	

(This is not thought so good as 3. $\frac{\text{Kt. takes P.}}{}$, and it usually leads to less interesting games.)

	3. P. takes P.

(For the consequences of 3. $\frac{}{\text{Kt. takes P.}}$ see Variation A.)

4. P. to K's 5th.	4. Kt. to K's 5th.

(If Black play 4. $\frac{\qquad}{\text{Kt. to Q's 4th.}}$, then by 5. $\frac{\text{Q. takes P.}}{\qquad}$, White at once obtains an ascendancy; but the second player may nearly equalise the game by 4. $\frac{\qquad}{\text{Q. to K's 2nd}}$, 5. $\frac{\text{B. to K's 2nd}}{\text{Kt. to Kt.'s 5th}}$, 6. $\frac{\text{Q. takes P.}}{\text{P. to Q's 3rd}}$, 7. $\frac{\text{P. takes P.}}{\text{Q. takes P.}}$, 8. $\frac{\text{B. to K. B's 4th}}{\qquad}$.)

5. Kt. takes P.	5. P. to Q's 3rd.
6. P. takes P.	6. B. takes P.
7. B. to Q. B's 4th.	7. B. to Q. B's 4th.
8. B. to K's 3rd.	8. B. takes Kt.
9. Q. takes B.	9. Q. takes Q.
10. B. takes Q.	10. Castles.

And there is little superiority on White's side.

Variation, beginning at Black's 3rd Move.

(A.)

BLACK.

WHITE.

Position prior to Black's 3rd Move.

	3. Kt. takes P.
4. B. to Q's 3rd.	4. P. to Q's 4th.
5. P. takes P.	

(If 5. $\frac{\text{Kt. takes P.}}{\text{P. to Q. B's 4th.}}$, equal game.)

	5. Kt. to Q. B's 3d.
6. Castles.	

(If 6. $\frac{\text{B. to Q. Kt.'s 5th}}{\text{B. to Q. B's 4th}}$, 7. $\frac{\text{B. takes Kt. (ch.)}}{\text{P. takes B.}}$, 8. $\frac{\text{B. to K's 3rd}}{\text{P. to Q's 5th}}$, Black will have rather the better game.)

	6. B. to Q. B's 4th.
7. P. to Q. B's 4th.	7. B. to K's 3rd.
8. P. takes P.	8. Q. takes P.
9. B. takes Kt.	9. Q. takes B.
10. Kt. to Q. B's 3rd.	10. Q. to K. B's 4th.

An equal game.

Game the Third.

WHITE.	BLACK.
1. P. to K's 4th.	1. P. to K's 4th.
2. Kt. to K. B's 3rd.	2. Kt. to K. B's 3rd.
3. B. to Q. B's 4th.	

(We have now a position in the *Knight's Defence* to the *Bishop's Game*, which begins:—1. $\frac{\text{P. to K's 4th}}{\text{P. to K's 4th}}$, 2. $\frac{\text{B. to Q. B's 4th}}{\text{Kt. to K. B's 3rd}}$, 3. $\frac{\text{Kt. to K. B's 3rd.}}{}$)

	3. Kt. takes P. (best.)

(If 3. $\frac{}{\text{Kt. to Q. B's 3rd}}$, we arrive at the *Two Knights' Game*, which see.)

4. Q. to K's 2nd.

(If 4. $\frac{\text{Kt. to Q. B's 3rd}}{}$, we recur to a much controverted situation in this opening, for the result of which see Variation A.

If 4. $\frac{\text{Kt. takes P.}}{\text{Q. to K. Kt.'s 4th}}$, or 4. $\frac{}{\text{P. to Q's 4th}}$, Black has some advantage.)

	4. P. to Q's 4th.
5. Kt. takes P.	5. B. to Q. B's 4th.

(If 5. $\frac{}{\text{P. takes B.}}$, 6. $\frac{\text{Q. takes Kt.}}{\text{Q. to K's 2nd.}}$, 7. $\frac{\text{Kt. to Q. B's 3rd}}{}$, White's position is preferable. If 5. $\frac{}{\text{B. to K's 3rd}}$, 6. $\frac{\text{P. to Q's 3rd}}{\text{Kt. to Q. B's 4th}}$, 7. $\frac{\text{B. to Q. Kt.'s 3rd}}{}$. There is no choice between the positions.)

6. P. to Q's 3rd (best.)	6. P. takes B.

(For the effect of 6. $\frac{}{\text{B. takes P. (ch.)}}$, and 6. $\frac{}{\text{P. takes P.}}$, see Variation B.)

7. Q. takes Kt.	7. Castles.
8. Q. takes Q. B's P.	8. Q. to K's 2nd.
9. P. to K. B's 4th.	9. Kt. to Q. B's 3rd.
10. Q. to K's 4th.	10. R. to K's sq.

(This move, first given by me in the "Chess-Player's Handbook," is admitted to be stronger than 10. $\frac{}{\text{Kt. takes Kt.}}$, which was the line of play recommended in the German *Handbuch.*)

11. K. to. Q's sq.

(If 11. $\frac{\text{Kt. takes Kt}}{\text{Q. to K. R's 5th (ch.)}}$, and wins the Queen.)

	11. Q. to K. R's 5th.
12. P to K. Kt.'s 3rd.	

(If 12. $\frac{\text{Kt. to Q's 2nd}}{\text{Q. to K. R's 4th (ch.)}}$, 13. $\frac{\text{Q. Kt. to K. B's 3rd}}{\text{B. to K. Kt.'s 5th}}$, and Black has a manifest advantage.)

	12. Q. to K. R's 4th (ch.)
13. K. to Q's 2nd.	13. Kt. takes Kt.
14. P. takes Kt.	14. R. takes P.

And White is lost.

Variation, beginning at White's 4th Move.

(A.)

BLACK.

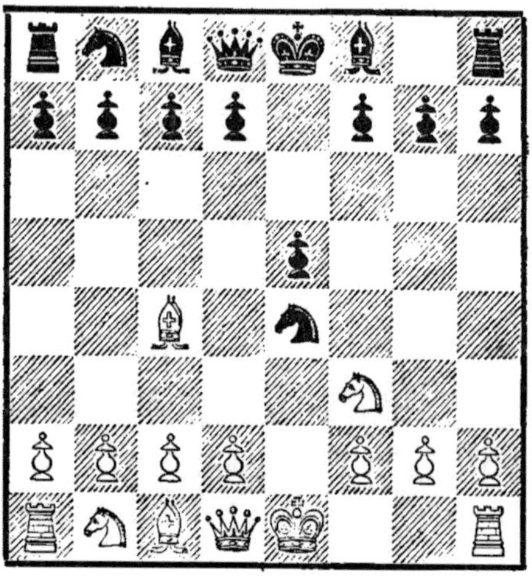

WHITE.

Position prior to White's 4th Move.

WHITE.	BLACK.
4. Kt. to Q. B's 3rd.	4. Kt. takes Kt.

(At one time I believed the attack obtained by White was so formidable, after this capture, that Black would do better to play 4. $\frac{\quad}{\text{Kt. to K. B's 3rd}}$, or 4. $\frac{\quad}{\text{P. to Q's 4th}}$. It has been clearly demonstrated, however, of late years, that the Knight may be taken without danger. If 4. $\frac{\quad}{\text{Kt. to K. B's 3rd}}$, 5. $\frac{\text{Kt. takes P.}}{\text{P. to Q's 4th}}$, 6. $\frac{\text{B. to Q. Kt.'s 3rd}}{\text{B. to Q's 3rd}}$, 7. $\frac{\text{P. to Q's 4th}}{\text{Castles}}$, the advantage on White's side is not of much weight. Again, if 4. $\frac{\quad}{\text{P. to Q's 4th}}$, 5. $\frac{\text{B. takes P.}}{\text{Kt. to K. B's 3rd}}$, 6. $\frac{\text{B. to Q. Kt's 3rd}}{\text{B. to Q's 3rd}}$, 7. $\frac{\text{P. to Q's 3rd}}{\text{Castles}}$, 8. $\frac{\text{P. to K. R's 3rd}}{\text{P. to K. R's 3rd}}$, 9. $\frac{\text{B. to K's 3rd}}{\text{Kt. to Q. B's 3rd}}$, the superiority of White's game is very trifling.)

5. Q's P. takes Kt. 5. P. to K. B's 3rd.

(If Black play 5. $\frac{}{\text{P. to Q. B's 3rd}}$, we have 6. $\frac{\text{Kt. takes P.}}{\text{P. to Q's 4th}}$, 7. $\frac{\text{B. to Q. Kt.'s 3rd, or B. to Q's 3rd}}{\text{B. to Q's 3rd}}$, and there is no superiority on either side.)

6. Castles.

(If 6. $\frac{\text{Kt. to K. R's 4th}}{\text{P to K. Kt.'s 3rd}}$, 7. $\frac{\text{Kt. to K. B's 5th}}{\text{P. to Q's 4th}}$, and the attack is paralyzed. It will not do, however, for Black to take the Knight here, or he will inevitably lose the game. For example: 7. $\frac{}{\text{P. takes Kt.}}$, 8. $\frac{\text{Q. to K. R's 5th (ch.)}}{\text{K. to K's 2nd}}$, 9. $\frac{\text{Q. to B's. 7th (ch.)}}{\text{K. to Q's 3rd.}}$, 10. $\frac{\text{Q. to K's 5th (ch.)}}{\text{K. to K's 2nd.}}$, 11. $\frac{\text{B. to K. Kt.'s 5th (best).}}{\text{Q. to K's sq.}}$ [Any other move is fatal to him.] 12. $\frac{\text{Q. takes K's P. (ch.)}}{\text{K. to Q's sq.}}$, 13. $\frac{\text{B. takes P. (ch.)}}{\text{B. to K's 2nd}}$, 14. $\frac{\text{B. takes R.}}{}$, and Black is lost. It may be added that if, instead of Castling at his 6th move, White play 6. $\frac{\text{Kt. takes P.}}{}$, Black must answer with 6. $\frac{}{\text{Q. to K's 2nd}}$, not with 6. $\frac{}{\text{P. takes Kt.}}$.)

6. Q. to K's 2nd.

(A move suggested by Mr. Brien, and which is better than 6. $\frac{}{\text{P. to Q's 3rd}}$, or 6. $\frac{}{\text{Kt. to Q. B's 3rd}}$, although either of those moves can be played without danger, I think. For instance, Firstly, 6. $\frac{}{\text{P. to Q's 3rd}}$. 7. $\frac{\text{Kt. to K. R's 4th}}{\text{Q. to K's 2nd}}$, 8. $\frac{\text{P. to K. B's 4th}}{\text{B. to K's 3rd}}$, 9. $\frac{\text{Q. to K. R's 5th (ch.)}}{\text{K. to Q's sq.}}$, and Black has a Pawn more, and no serious inferiority of situation. Secondly, 6. $\frac{}{\text{Kt. to Q. B's 3rd}}$, 7. $\frac{\text{Kt. to K. R's 4th}}{\text{Q. to K's 2nd}}$, 8. $\frac{\text{Kt. to K. B's 5th}}{\text{Q. to Q. B's 4th}}$, 9. $\frac{\text{B. to Q. Kt.'s 3rd}}{\text{P. to Q's 4th}}$,

10. B. to K's 3rd / Q. to Q. R's 4th. It appears to me that Black has nothing to fear.)

7. Kt. to K. R's 4th. 7. P. to K. Kt.'s 3rd.

And White's attack is exhausted.

Variation B, beginning at Black's 6th Move.

BLACK.

WHITE.

Position prior to Black's 6th Move.

In the first place :—

WHITE.	BLACK.
	6. B. takes P. (ch).
7. K. to Q's sq. (best.)	

(If 7. K. to B's sq. / B. to Q. Kt.'s 3rd, 8. B. to Q. Kt.'s 3rd / Q. to K's 2nd, 9. B. takes P. / Q. takes Kt., 10. Q. takes Kt. / Q. takes Q., 11. B. takes Q. / Castles., and Black has a better disposed game.)

	7. B. to Q. Kt.'s 3rd.
8. Kt. takes K. B's P.	8. B. to K. Kt.'s 5th.

(If 8. $\frac{\quad}{\text{K. takes Kt.}}$, Black will lose, by 9. $\frac{\text{Q. takes Kt.}}{\text{B. to K's 3rd}}$, 10. $\frac{\text{R. to K. B's sq. (ch.)}}{\text{K. to K's 2nd}}$, 11. $\frac{\text{B. to K. Kt.'s 5th (ch.)}}{\text{K. to Q's 2nd}}$, 12. $\frac{\text{B. takes P.}}{\text{Q. takes Q's B.}}$, 13. $\frac{\text{Q. takes B. (ch.)}}{\text{K. to Q's sq.}}$, 14. $\frac{\text{B. takes Q. Kt.'s P.}}{\quad}$,)

9. Kt. takes Q.	9. B. takes Q. (ch.)
10. K. takes B.	10. Kt. to K. B's 7th.
11. R. to K. B's sq.	11. P. takes B.
12. Kt. to K's 6th.	12. P. takes P. (ch.)
13. P. takes P.	13. K. to K's 2nd.
14. Kt. takes K. Kt.'s P.	14. R. to K. Kt.'s sq.
15. Kt. to K. B's 5th (ch).	15. K. to K's 3rd.
16. B. to K's 3rd.	

I prefer White's game.

In the second place:—

	6. Kt. takes B's P.
7. Kt. to Q. B's 6th (dis. ch.)	7. K. to Q's 2nd.
8. Kt. takes Q.	8. R. to K's sq.
9. Q. takes R. (ch.)	9. K. takes Q.
10. B. takes Q's P.	10. Kt. takes R.
11. Kt. takes K. B's P.	11. Kt. to K. B's 7th.
12. P. to K. R's 3rd.	

White has the superior position.

ILLUSTRATIVE GAMES.

GAME I.—Between Messrs. McKenzie and Hammond.

WHITE (Mr. M.)	BLACK (Mr. H.)
1. P. to K's 4th.	1. P. to K's 4th.
2. Kt. to K. B's 3rd.	2. Kt. to K. B's 3rd.
3. Kt. takes K's P.	3. P. to Q's 3rd.
4. Kt. to K. B's 3rd.	4. Kt. takes K's P.
5. P. to Q's 4th.	5. P. to Q's 4th.
6. B. to Q's 3rd.	6. B. to Q's 3rd.*

* Black might also play, as we have shown, 6. B. to K's 2nd, or 6. Kt. to Q. B's 3rd, at this point.

7. Castles.	7. Castles.
8. P. to Q. B's 4th.	8. P. to Q. B's 3rd.*
9. P. takes P.	9. P. takes P.
10. Kt. to Q. B's 3rd.	10. Kt. takes Kt.
11. P. takes Kt.	11. B. to K. Kt's 5th.
12. R. to Q. Kt. s sq.	12. Q. to Q. B's 2nd.
13. P. to K. R's 3rd.	13. B. to K. R's 4th.
14. B. takes R's P. (ch.)	14. K. takes B.†
15. Kt. to Kt.'s 5th (ch.)	15. K. to Kt.'s 3rd.
16. P. to K. Kt.'s 4th.	16. B. to K. B's 5th.
17. R. takes Q. Kt.'s P.‡	17. Q. takes R.
18. B. takes B.	18. R. to K. R's sq.
19. Q. to Q's 3rd (ch.)	19. K. to B's 3rd.
20. R. to K's sq.	20. B. to K. Kt.'s 3rd.
21. Kt. to R's 7th (ch.)	21. R. takes Kt.
22. P. mates.	

Game II.—Between Messrs. Lowenthal and Morphy.

White (Mr. L.)	Black (Mr. M.)
1. P. to K's 4th.	1. P. to K's 4th.
2. Kt. to K. B's 3rd.	2. Kt. to K. B's 3rd.
3. Kt. takes K. P.	3. P. to Q's 3rd.
4. Kt. to K. B's 3rd.	4. Kt. takes P.
5. P. to Q's 4th.	5. P. to Q's 4th.
6. B. to Q's 3rd.	6. B. to K's 2nd.
7. Castles.	7. Kt. to Q. B's 3rd.
8. P. to Q. B's 4th.	8. B. to K's 3rd.§
9. P. takes P.	9. B. takes P.
10. Kt. to Q. B's 3rd.	10. Kt. takes Kt.
11. P. takes Kt.	11. Castles.
12. B. to K. B's 4th.	12. B. to Q's 3rd.

* This is not a commendable move. His best reply is probably, 8. Kt. to K. B's 3rd.

† This capture is fatal. He ought to have submitted quietly to the loss of the Pawn, and retired the King to Rook's square.

‡ Well conceived. The terminating moves are played in Mr. McKenzie's best style.

§ This may be played with safety now that the King's Bishop is posted at King's 2nd.

13. B. takes B.	13. Q. takes B.
14. Kt. to Kt.'s 5th.	14. P. to K. B's 4th.
15. P. to Q. B's 4th.	15. B. takes K. Kt.'s P.*
16. K. takes B.	16. Q. to K. Kt.'s 3rd.
17. P. to K. B's 4th.	17. P. to K. R's 3rd.
18. P. to Q's 5th.	18. Kt. to Q's sq.
19. P. to K. R's 4th.	19. P. takes Kt.
20. R's P. takes P.	20. Kt. to K. B's 2nd.
21. Q. to K. B's 3rd.	21. Kt. to K. R's 3rd.
22. Q. to K. Kt.'s 3rd.	22. Kt. to K. B's 2nd.
23. P. to Q. B's 5th.	23. Q's R. to Q's sq.
24. B. to Q. B's 4th.	24. P. to Q. Kt.'s 4th.
25. B. to Q. Kt.'s 3rd.	25. P. to Q. R's 4th
26. Q. R. to K's sq.	26. K's R. to K's sq.
27. R. to K's 6th.†	27. R. takes R.
28. P. takes R.	28. K. to B's sq.
29. P. takes Kt.	29. P. to Q. R's 6th.
30. R. to Q's sq.	30. R. takes R.
31. B. takes R.	31. Q. to Q. B's 3rd (ch.)
32. B. to K. B's 3rd.	32. Q. takes P.
33. P. to K. Kt.'s 6th.	33. Q. to Q's 3rd.
34. Q. to K. Kt.'s 5th.	34. Q. to Q's 7th (ch.)
35. K. to R's 3rd.	35. Q. to Q's 6th.
36. Q. to K. R's 5th.	36. K. to K's 2nd.
37. Q. to R's 4th (ch.) ‡	37. K. to Q's 2nd.
38. K. to Kt.'s 3rd.	38. Q. to Q's 3rd.
39. Q. to K. R's 8th.§	39. Q. takes P. (ch.)
40. K. to B's 2nd.	40. Q. takes P.
41. P. to Q. R's 3rd.	41. Q. to K's 2nd.
42. K. to Kt.'s 3rd.	42. Q. to K's 8th (ch.)
43. K. to Kt.'s 2nd.	43. Q. to Q's 7th (ch.)
44. K. to Kt.'s 3rd.	44. Q. to K's 8th (ch.)

And draws by perpetual check.

---

* Seemingly the lesser of two evils. Had he played 15. B. to K. B's 2nd, White would have rejoined with 16. P. to Q's 5th.

† Well played, winning a piece by force.

‡ Hastily played. He might have won offhand by 37. P. to B's 8th, becoming a Queen, as the slightest examination will show.

§ An unaccountable blunder. After this Black ought to draw without difficulty.

Game III.—Between Messrs. Anderssen and Kolisch.

White (Mr. A.)	Black (Mr. K.)
1. P. to K's 4th.	1. P. to K's 4th.
2. Kt. to K. B's 3rd.	2. Kt. to K. B's 3rd.
3. Kt. takes K's P.	3. Q. to K's 2nd.*
4. Kt. to K. B's 3rd.	4. Q. takes K's P.
5. B. to K's 2nd.	5. B. to Q. B's 4th.
6. Castles.	6. Castles.
7. P. to Q's 4th.	7. B. to Q. Kt.'s 3rd.
8. P. to Q. B's 4th.	8. P. to Q. B's 3rd.
9. Kt. to Q. B's 3rd.	9. Q. to K's 2nd.
10. B. to K. Kt.'s 5th.	10. P. to K. R's 3rd.
11. B. to K. R's 4th.	11. P. to K. Kt.'s 4th.
12. B. to K. Kt.'s 3rd.	12. P. to Q's 4th.
13. Kt. to K's 5th.	13. Q's Kt. to Q's 2nd.
14. P. takes Q's P.	14. Kt. takes P.
15. Q's Kt. takes K's Kt.	15. P. takes Kt.
16. P. to K. B's 4th.†	16. P. takes P.
17. Kt. takes Kt.	17. P. takes B.
18. Kt. to B's 6th (ch.)	18. K. to Kt.'s 2nd.
19. Q. to Q's 3rd.	19. R. to K. R's sq.
20. B. to K. R's 5th.	20. B. to K's 3rd.
21. Q. takes P. (ch.)	21. K. to B's sq.
22. Q. to K's 5th.	22. Q. to Q. B's 2nd.
23. Q. to K's 3rd.	23. Q. to Q's 3rd.
24. R. to K. B's 4th.	24. Q's R. to Q. B's sq.
25. Q's R. to K. B's sq.	25. Q's R. to B's 2nd.
26. Q. to K. Kt.'s 3rd.	26. R. to Q. B's th.
27. Kt. to R's 7th (ch.)	27. K. to K's sq.
28. Q. to K. Kt.'s 7th.	

And wins.

Game IV.—Between Mr. Cochrane and the Brahmin Mohes-chunder Bonnerjee.

White (Mr. C.)	Black (M. B.)
1. P. to K's 4th.	1. P. to K's 4th.
2. Kt. to K. B's 3rd.	2. Kt. to K. B's 3rd.

* This, as we have shown, is not so strong as 3. P. to Q's 3rd.
† We now see the weakness of Black's 11th move.

3. Kt. takes K's P.	3. P. to Q's 3rd.
4. Kt. takes K. B's P.	4. K. takes Kt.
5. B. to Q. B's 4th (ch).	5. K. to K's sq.*
6. Castles.	6. P. to Q. B's 3rd.
7. B. to Q. Kt.'s 3rd.	7. Q's Kt. to R's 3rd.
8. P. to Q's 4th.	8. P. to K. Kt.'s 3rd.
9. P. to Q. B's 4th.	9. B. to K's 2nd.
10. Kt. to Q. B's 3rd.	10. Q. to Q's 2nd.
11. P. to K. R's 3rd.	11. P. to Q. Kt.'s 3rd.
12. P. to K. B's 4th.	12. Q's B. to Kt.'s 2nd.
13. B. to K's 3rd.	13. K. to Q's sq.
14. P. to Q. R's 4th.	14. Kt. to K. R's 4th.
15. Q. to K. B's 3rd.	15. R. to K. B's sq.
16. Q's R. to Q's sq.	16. Kt. to Q. Kt's 5th.
17. P. to K's 5th.	17. K. to Q. B's 2nd.
18. Q. to K. B's 2nd.	18. P. to Q. R's 3rd.
19. P. to Q's 5th.	19. Q's P. takes P.†
20. P. to Q's 6th (ch.)	20. B. takes P.
21. B. takes Q. Kt.'s P. (ch.)	21. K. to Q. Kt.'s sq.
22. P. to Q. B's 5th.	22. R. takes K. B's P.
23. R. takes B.	23. Q. takes R.
24. P. takes Q.	24. R. takes Q.
25. P. to Q's 7th.	25. R. to Q's 7th
26. R. to B's 8th (ch.)	

And wins.‡

---

* The best move we have seen is P. to Q's 4th.
† After this, Black has indeed a difficult game.
‡ The terminating moves are capitally played by Mr. Cochrane.

CHAPTER II.

THE GIUOCO PIANO.

1. $\frac{\text{P. to K's 4th}}{\text{P. to K's 4th}}$, 2. $\frac{\text{Kt. to K. B's 3rd}}{\text{Kt. to Q. B's 3rd}}$, 3. $\frac{\text{B. to Q. B's 4th}}{\text{B. to Q. B's 4th}}$.

GAME THE FIRST.

4. $\frac{\text{P. to Q. B's 3rd}}{\text{Kt. to K. B's 3rd}}$.

GAME THE SECOND.

4. $\frac{}{\text{P. to Q's 3rd}}$; 4. $\frac{}{\text{B. to Q. Kt.'s 3rd}}$; 4. $\frac{}{\text{Q. to K's 2nd}}$;

4. $\frac{}{\text{P. to K. B's 4th}}$.

GAME THE THIRD.

4. $\frac{\text{Castles}}{}$; 4. $\frac{\text{P. to Q's 3rd}}{}$; 4. $\frac{\text{P. to Q's 4th}}{}$.

GAME THE FOURTH.

5. $\frac{\text{P. to Q's 4th.}}{}$

GAME THE FIRST.

WHITE.	BLACK.
1. P. to K's 4th.	1. P. to K's 4th.
2. Kt. to K. B's 3rd.	2. Kt. to Q. B's 3rd.
3. B. to Q. B's 4th.	3. B. to Q. B's 4th.
4. P. to Q. B's 3rd.	

(The move most commonly played. White, however, may move without disadvantage 4. $\frac{\text{Castles.}}{}$, or 4. $\frac{\text{P. to Q's 3rd}}{}$, for the result of which see Games Third and Fourth.)

4. Kt. to K. B's 3rd.

(The consequences of 4. $\frac{}{\text{B. to Q. Kt.'s 3rd}}$, 4. $\frac{}{\text{P. to Q's 3rd}}$, 4. $\frac{}{\text{Q. to K's 2nd}}$, and 4. $\frac{}{\text{P. to K. B's 4th}}$, will be shown in Game the Second. We may as well dismiss the poor defence of Q. to K. B's 3rd at once. If, then, 4. $\frac{}{\text{Q. to K. B's 3rd}}$, 5. $\frac{\text{P. to Q's 4th}}{\text{B. to Q. Kt.'s 3rd}}$, 6. $\frac{\text{Castles}}{\text{P. to Q's 3rd}}$, 7. $\frac{\text{B. to K. Kt.'s 5th}}{\text{Q. to K. Kt.'s 3rd}}$, 8. $\frac{\text{P. takes P.}}{\text{P. takes P.}}$, 9. $\frac{\text{Kt. takes P.}}{\text{Q. takes B.}}$, 10. $\frac{\text{Kt. takes B's P.}}{\text{Q. to Q. B's 4th}}$, 11. $\frac{\text{B. to Q's 5th}}{}$. White has the best of the battle.)

5. P. to Q's 4th. 5. P. takes P.
6. P. to K's 5th.

(White can also play 6. $\frac{\text{P. takes P.}}{}$, the probable continuation then being 6. $\frac{\text{P. takes P.}}{\text{B. to Q. Kt.'s 5th (ch.)}}$, 7. $\frac{\text{B. to Q's 2nd}}{\text{B. takes B.}}$, 8. $\frac{\text{Q's Kt. takes B.}}{\text{P. to Q's 4th}}$, 9. $\frac{\text{P. takes P.}}{\text{K's Kt. takes P.}}$, 10. $\frac{\text{Q. to Q. Kt.'s 3rd}}{\text{Q's Kt. to K's 2nd}}$. [This is stronger than 10. $\frac{}{\text{Q's Kt. to R's 4th}}$.] 11. $\frac{\text{Castles}}{\text{Castles}}$, 12. $\frac{\text{K's R. to K's sq.}}{\text{P. to Q. B's 3rd}}$, and the game is, if anything, slightly in favour of White.)

6. P. to Q's 4th.

(If 6. $\frac{}{\text{Kt. to K's 5th}}$, 7. $\frac{\text{B. to Q's 5th}}{\text{Kt. takes K. B's P.}}$, 8. $\frac{\text{K. takes Kt.}}{\text{P. takes P. (dis. ch.)}}$, 9. $\frac{\text{K. to Kt.'s 3rd (best)}}{\text{P. takes P.}}$, 10. $\frac{\text{Q's B. takes P.}}{\text{Kt. to K's 2nd}}$, 11. $\frac{\text{Q. to Q. B's 2nd}}{\text{P. to Q's 3rd}}$. I prefer White's game. Instead of

11. $\frac{\text{Q. to Q. B's 2nd}}{\quad}$, he may play, without any danger, 11. $\frac{\text{P. to K. R's 3rd}}{\quad}$; or 11. $\frac{\text{B. to K's 4th}}{\quad}$, or, as Jaenisch recommends, 11. $\frac{\text{R. to K's sq.}}{\quad}$.)

7. B. to Q. Kt's 5th.	7. Kt. to K's 5th.
8. P. takes P.	8. B. to Q. Kt.'s 3rd.

(If 8. $\frac{\quad}{\text{B. to Q. Kt.'s 5th (ch.)}}$, 9. $\frac{\text{B. to Q's 2nd}}{\text{Kt. takes B.}}$, 10. $\frac{\text{Q. Kt. takes Kt.}}{\text{Castles}}$, 11. $\frac{\text{B. takes Kt.}}{\text{P. takes B.}}$, 12. $\frac{\text{Castles}}{\quad}$, to White's advantage.)

9. B. takes Kt. (ch.)	9. P. takes B.
10. Kt. to Q. B's 3rd.	10. P. to K. B's 4th.
11. P. takes P. in passing.	11. Q. takes P.
12. Kt. takes Kt.	12. P. takes Kt.
13. Kt. to K's 5th.	13. Castles.
14. Castles.	14. B. to Q. R's 3rd.
15. Kt. to Q's 7th.	15. Q. to Q's 3rd.

(If 15. $\frac{\quad}{\text{Q. takes Q's P.}}$, 16. $\frac{\text{Kt. takes R.}}{\text{B. takes R.}}$, 17. $\frac{\text{Q. takes Q.}}{\text{B. takes Q.}}$, 18. $\frac{\text{Kt. to K's 6th}}{\quad}$, with a winning superiority.)

16. Kt. takes B.	16. B's P. takes Kt.
17. R. to K's sq.	

This game is much about equal.

Game the Second.

WHITE.	BLACK.
1. P. to K's 4th.	1. P. to K's 4th.
2. Kt. to K. B's 3rd.	2. Kt. to Q. B's 3rd.
3. B. to Q. B's 4th.	3. B. to Q. B's 4th.
4. P. to Q. B's 3rd.	4. P. to Q's 3rd.

(This move may be adopted without danger. I prefer, however, 4. $\frac{\quad}{\text{Kt. to K. B's 3rd}}$. If, at this point, Black play 4. $\frac{\quad}{\text{B. to Q. Kt.'s 3rd}}$, the game is usually continued 5. $\frac{\text{P. to Q's 4th}}{\text{P. to Q's 3rd}}$,

6. $\frac{\text{P. takes P.}}{\text{P. takes P.}}$, 7. $\frac{\text{Q. takes Q. (ch.)}}{\text{K. takes Q.}}$, White has the better game.

For the effect of 4. $\frac{}{\text{Q. to K's 2nd}}$, and 4. $\frac{}{\text{P. to K. B's 4th}}$, see Variation A. and Variation B.)

5. P. to Q's 4th.	5. P. takes P.
6. P. takes P.	6. B. to Kt.'s 3rd.

(If 6. $\frac{}{\text{B. to Q. Kt.'s 5th (ch.)}}$, 7. $\frac{\text{K. to B's sq.}}{\text{B. to K. Kt.'s 5th}}$, 8. $\frac{\text{Q. to Q. R's 4th}}{\text{B. takes Kt.}}$, 9. $\frac{\text{P. takes B.}}{\text{Q. to Q's 2nd}}$, 10. $\frac{\text{B. to Q. Kt.'s 5th}}{\text{Castles}}$, 11. $\frac{\text{K. to Kt.'s 2nd}}{}$, White gains a piece.)

7. Kt. to Q. B's 3rd.	7. B. to K. Kt.'s 5th
8. B. to Q. Kt.'s 5th.	

White seems to have a better opened game.

Variation A, on Black's 4th Move.

BLACK.

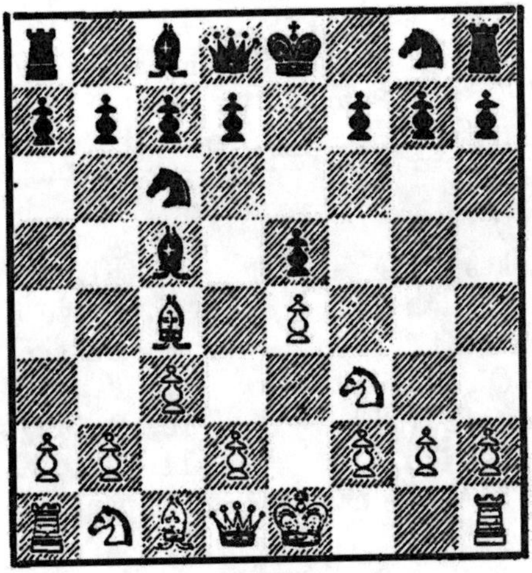

WHITE.

Position prior to Black's 4th Move.

	4. Q. to K's 2nd.
5. P. to Q's 4th.	5. B. to Q. Kt's 3rd.

(If 5. $\frac{\quad}{\text{P. takes P.}}$, 6. $\frac{\text{Castles}}{\text{Kt. to K's 4th}}$, 7. $\frac{\text{Kt. takes Kt.}}{\text{Q. takes Kt.}}$, 8. $\frac{\text{P. to K. B's 4th}}{\text{P. takes P. (dis. ch.)}}$, 9. $\frac{\text{K. to R's sq.}}{\text{P. takes Q. Kt.'s P.}}$, 10. $\frac{\text{P. takes Q.}}{\text{P. takes R.}}$ (Queening), 11. $\frac{\text{Q. to Q's 5th}}{\quad}$, winning easily.)

6. P. takes K's P.	6. Kt. takes P.
7. Kt. takes Kt.	7. Q. takes Kt.
8. Castles.	8. P. to Q's 3rd.
9. R. to K's sq.	9. B. to K's 3rd.

The game is considered pretty equal.

Variation B, on Black's 4th Move.

(*See preceding Diagram.*)

4. P. to K. B's 4th.

(A very hazardous line of defence.)

5. P. to Q's 4th.

(This is the correct reply, and, after it, play as Black may, he must have an inferior game.)

5. P. takes K's P.

(If 5. $\frac{\quad}{\text{P. takes Q's P.}}$, 6. $\frac{\text{Kt. to Kt.'s 5th}}{\text{P. to Q's 4th}}$, 7. $\frac{\text{B. takes P.}}{\text{P. takes K's P.}}$, 8. $\frac{\text{B. takes K's Kt.}}{\text{R. takes B.}}$, 9. $\frac{\text{Q. to K. R's 5th (ch.)}}{\text{P. to K. Kt.'s 3rd.}}$, 10. $\frac{\text{Q. takes R's P.}}{\text{Q. to Q's 4th}}$, 11. $\frac{\text{P. to Q. B's 4th}}{\text{Q. takes P.}}$, 12. $\frac{\text{Kt. to Q's 2nd}}{\quad}$, and White has the better Game.)

6. Kt. takes P.	6. Kt. takes Kt.
7. Q. to R's 5th (ch.)	7. Kt. to Kt.'s 3rd.
8. B. takes Kt.	8. R. takes B.
9. Q. to Q's 5th.	9. K. to B's sq.
10. Q. takes B. (ch.)	10. P. to Q's 3rd.
11. Q. to Q's 5th.	11. Q. to K's 2nd.

White has the better opening.

Game the Third.

WHITE.	BLACK.
1. P. to K's 4th.	1. P. to K's 4th.
2. Kt. to K. B's 3rd.	2. Kt. to Q. B's 3rd.
3. B. to Q. B's 4th.	3. B. to Q. B's 4th.
4. Castles.	

(Castling is thought to be less attacking for White than advancing the Q's Pawn. For 4. $\frac{\text{P. to Q's 3rd}}{}$, 4. $\frac{\text{P. to Q's 4th}}{}$, see Variation I.)

4. Kt. to K. B's 3rd.

(If 4. $\frac{}{\text{P. to Q's 3rd}}$, 5. $\frac{\text{P. to Q. B's 3rd}}{\text{Kt. to K. B's 3rd}}$, 6. $\frac{\text{P. to Q's 4th}}{\text{P. takes P.}}$, 7. $\frac{\text{P. takes P.}}{\text{B. to Q. Kt.'s 3rd}}$, 8. $\frac{\text{B. to K. Kt.'s 5th}}{\text{B. to K. Kt.'s 5th}}$, 9. $\frac{\text{P. to Q's 5th}}{\text{Kt. to K's 4th}}$, 10. $\frac{\text{Q. to Q. R's 4th (ch.)}}{\text{B. to Q's 2nd}}$, 11. $\frac{\text{Q. to Q. Kt.'s 3rd}}{}$. White has the freer game)

5. R. to K's sq.

(For 5. $\frac{\text{P. to Q's 4th}}{}$, see the Fourth Game.)

	5. Castles.
6. P. to Q. B's 3rd.	6. P. to Q's 3rd.
7. P. to Q's 4th.	7. B. to Q. Kt.'s 3rd.

There is no advantage on either side.

Variation I, beginning at White's 4th Move.

BLACK.

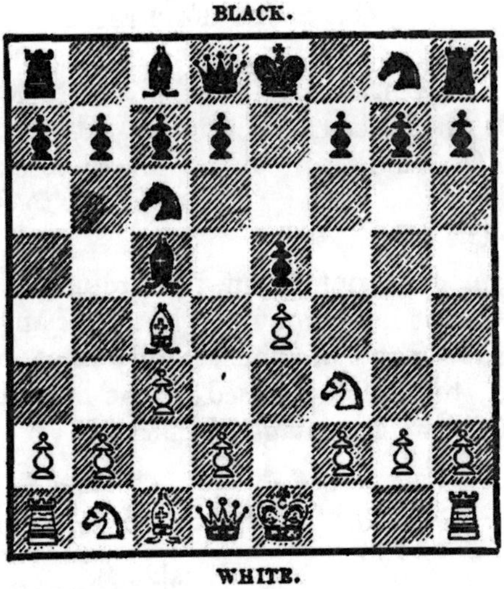

WHITE.

Position prior to White's 4th Move.

4. P. to Q's 3rd.

(If 4. $\frac{\text{P. to Q's 4th}}{\text{B. takes P. (best)}}$, 5. $\frac{\text{P. to Q. B's 3rd}}{\text{B. to Q. Kt.'s 3rd}}$, 6. $\frac{\text{Kt. to K. Kt.'s 5th}}{\text{Kt. to K. R's 3rd}}$, 7. $\frac{\text{Q. to K. R's 5th}}{\text{Castles.}}$, 8. $\frac{\text{P. to K. B's 4th}}{\text{P. takes P.}}$, 9. $\frac{\text{Q's B. takes P.}}{\text{P. to Q's 3rd}}$, 10. $\frac{\text{R. to K. B's sq.}}{\text{Q. to K's 2nd}}$, and White has no compensation for the lost Pawn.)

4. P. to Q's 3rd.

5. P. to Q. B's 3rd.

(If 5. $\frac{\text{Kt. to Kt.'s 5th}}{\text{Kt. to K. R's 3rd}}$, 6. $\frac{\text{Q. to K. R's 5th}}{\text{Castles}}$, and White's attack is over.)

5. Kt. to K. B's 3rd.

(If 5. $\frac{}{\text{B. to K. Kt.'s 5th}}$, 6. $\frac{\text{Q. to Q. Kt.'s 3rd}}{}$, and White has the advantage.)

6. P. to Q's 4th.	6. P. takes P.
7. P. takes P.	7. B. to Q. Kt.'s 3rd.
8. Kt. to Q. B's 3rd.	8. B. to K. Kt.'s 5th.
9. P. to Q's 5th.	9. Kt. to K's 4th.

I prefer White's position.

Game the Fourth.

WHITE.	BLACK.
1. P. to K's 4th.	1. P. to K's 4th.
2. Kt. to K. B's 3rd.	2. Kt. to Q. B's 3rd.
3. B. to Q. B's 4th.	3. B. to Q. B's 4th.
4. Castles.	4. Kt. to K. B's 3rd.
5. P. to Q's 4th.	

(This ingenious variation on the ordinary lines of attack in the present opening we owe to Mr. M. Lange. It gives a brilliant assault, and if not steadily met becomes very troublesome; but when opposed by the best defence it ends in a repulse, to the advantage of Black.)

5. P. takes P. (best.)

(If 5. $\frac{}{\text{Kt. takes Q. P.}}$, 6. $\frac{\text{Kt. takes P.}}{}$, White gets the best of the opening. If 5. $\frac{}{\text{B. takes P.}}$, 6. $\frac{\text{Kt. takes B.}}{\text{Kt. takes Kt.}}$. [If 6. $\frac{}{\text{P. takes Kt.}}$,

7. $\frac{\text{P. to K's 5th}}{\text{}}$.] 7. $\frac{\text{P. to K. B's 4th}}{\text{P. to Q's 3rd}}$, 8. $\frac{\text{P. takes P.}}{\text{P. takes P}}$, 9. $\frac{\text{B. to K. Kt's 5th}}{\text{Q. to K's 2nd}}$, and White can gain a Pawn in return for the one sacrificed, but Black will have a slight advantage in position.)*

6. P. to K's 5th.	6. P. to Q's 4th.
7. B. to Q. Kt.'s 5th.	

(For the result of 7. $\frac{\text{P. takes Kt.}}{\text{}}$, see Variation A.)

	7. Kt. to K's 5th.
8. Kt. takes P.	8. B. to Q's 2nd.
9. B. takes Kt.	9. B. takes B.
10. Kt. takes B.	10. P. takes Kt.

Black has a slight advantage.

Variation A, on White's 7th Move.

BLACK.

WHITE.

Position prior to White's 7th Move.

7. P. takes Kt.	7. P. takes B.
8. R. to K's sq. (ch.)	

* 5. $\frac{\text{}}{\text{B. takes P.}}$ is now considered preferable to 5. $\frac{\text{}}{\text{P. takes P.}}$ —[Ed.]

(If 8. $\frac{\text{P. takes P.}}{\text{R. to K. Kt.'s sq.}}$, 9. $\frac{\text{B. to K. Kt's 5th}}{\text{B. to K's 2nd}}$, 10. $\frac{\text{B. takes B.}}{\text{K. takes B.}}$,

11. $\frac{\text{R. to K's sq. (ch.)}}{\text{B. to K's 3rd}}$, Black has the preferable game.)

8. K. to B's sq.

(For the result of Black's playing 8. $\frac{}{\text{B. to K's 3rd}}$, see Variation B.)

9. P. takes P. (ch.)

(If 9. $\frac{\text{B. to K. Kt.'s 5th}}{\text{Q. to Q's 4th}}$, &c.)

9. K. takes P.

10. Kt. to K's 5th.

(If 10. $\frac{\text{Kt. to Kt.'s 5th}}{\text{R. to K's sq.}}$, 11. $\frac{\text{R. takes R.}}{\text{Q. takes R.}}$, 12. $\frac{\text{Kt. takes R's P.}}{\text{B. to K. B's 4th}}$.

[If 12. $\frac{}{\text{Kt. takes Kt.}}$, 13. $\frac{\text{Q. to K. R's 5th (ch.)}}{}$, drawn game by perpetual check.] 13. $\frac{\text{Kt. to Kt.'s 5th}}{\text{P. takes B's P.}}$, Black wins.)

10. R. to K's sq.*

---

* The authors of *Theorie und Praxis* give 10. $\frac{}{\text{Kt. takes Kt.}}$ as best for Black, and continue as under: 10. $\frac{}{\text{Kt. takes Kt.}}$, 11. $\frac{\text{R. takes Kt.}}{\text{B. to K's 2nd}}$ 12. $\frac{\text{R. to K's 4th}}{\text{P. to Q. B's 4th}}$, 13. $\frac{\text{Kt. to Q. R's 3rd}}{\text{B. to K's 3rd}}$, 14. $\frac{\text{K. to K. Kt.'s 4th (ch.)}}{\text{K. to B's sq.}}$ 15. $\frac{\text{B. to R's 6th (ch.)}}{\text{K. to K.s sq.}}$ 16. $\frac{\text{R. to K's 4th}}{\text{Q. to Q's 4th}}$ and Black is said to have the better game. The above variation is also given in the *Handbuch*. Mr. Wormald, in the *Chess Openings*, however, points out that White might obtain a better game by playing 12. $\frac{\text{Q. to R's 5th}}{}$ in reply to

(If 10. $\frac{}{\text{B. to K's 3rd}}$, 11. $\frac{\text{Q. to K. R's 5th}}{\text{B. to K. B's sq.}}$, 12. $\frac{\text{Kt. to Kt.'s 4th}}{\text{P. to K. R's 3rd}}$,

13. $\frac{\text{B. takes P. (ch.)}}{\text{K. to Kt.'s sq.}}$, 14. $\frac{\text{R. takes B.}}{}$, White must win.)

11. B. to K. R's 6th (ch.)	11. K. to Kt.'s sq.
12. Kt. takes Q. B's P.	12. B. to K's 3rd.

It is difficult to say which side has the advantage.

(If at Move 12 White play 12 $\frac{\text{Q. to K. B's 3rd}}{}$, the continuation is very pretty :—12. $\frac{}{\text{Kt. takes Kt.}}$, 13. $\frac{\text{R. takes Kt.}}{\text{R. takes R.}}$,

14. $\frac{\text{Q. to Kt.'s 3rd (ch.)}}{\text{Q. to K. Kt.'s 4th}}$, 15. $\frac{\text{Q. takes Q. (ch.)}}{\text{R. takes Q.}}$, 16. $\frac{\text{B. takes R.}}{\text{B. to K. B's 4th}}$,

and Black has an indisputable superiority.)

---

11. $\frac{}{\text{B. to K's 2nd}}$, and gives the following as the proper continuation :—

	10. Kt. takes Kt.
11. R. takes Kt.	11. B. to Q's 3rd (best)
12. R. to K. Kt.'s 5th (ch.)	12. K. to B's sq.
13. Q. to R's 5th.	13. Q. to K's 2nd.
14. K. to B's sq.	

14. $\frac{\text{B. to Q's 2nd}}{}$ would be obviously bad for White: as it would prevent the Queen's Knight being brought advantageously into play. If he play 14. $\frac{\text{Q. to K. R's 6th (ch.)}}{}$ then follow—14. $\frac{}{\text{K. to K's sq.}}$

15. $\frac{\text{K. to B's sq.}}{\text{Q. to K's 5th}}$ and Black has the better position.

	14. P. to Q's 6th.

And Black has a Pawn *plus*, with at least an equal position.—[Ed.]

Variation B, beginning at Black's 8th Move.

BLACK.

WHITE.

Position prior to Black's 8th Move.

	8. B. to K's 3rd.
9. Kt. to Kt.'s 5th.	9. Q. to Q's 4th.

(If 9. ——— / Q. takes P., 10. Q. to K. R's 5th / ———, and White has an advantage.)

10. Kt. to Q. B's 3rd.	10. Q. to K. B's 4th.
11. P. to K. Kt.'s 4th.	11. Q. to K. Kt.'s 3rd.

(If 11. ——— / Q. to B's 3rd, taking P., 12. Q's Kt. to Q's 5th / Q. to Q's sq., 13. R. takes B. (ch.) / P. takes R., 14. Kt. takes K.'s P. / Q. to Q's 3rd (best.), 15. B. to K. B's 4th / Kt. to K's 4th, [If 15. ——— / Q. to Q's 2nd, 16. Q's Kt. takes B's P. (ch.) / K. moves, 17. K's Kt. takes B. / ———, &c.] 16. Q. to K's 2nd / ———, and White has a winning game.)

12. Q's Kt. to K's 4th.

(If 12. $\frac{\text{Kt. takes B.}}{\text{P. takes Kt.}}$, 13. $\frac{\text{R. takes P. (ch.)}}{\text{K. to B's 2nd.}}$, 14. $\frac{\text{Kt. to Q's 5th}}{\text{B. to Q's 3rd}}$, Black has the advantage. So if 12. $\frac{\text{R. takes B. (ch.)}}{\text{P. takes R.}}$, 13. $\frac{\text{Kt. takes K's P.}}{\text{P. takes Q's Kt.}}$, 14. $\frac{\text{Q. to K's 2nd}}{\text{Kt. to K's 4th}}$, and play as White may, the game will be against him.)

	12. B. to Q. Kt.'s 3rd.
13. P. to K. B's 4th.	13. Castles on Q's side.
14. P. to K. B's 5th.	14. B. takes P.
15. P. takes B.	15. Q. to K. B's 4th, taking P.

Black has three Pawns for his lost piece, and a very attacking position.

ILLUSTRATIVE GAMES.

—GAME I.—Between Messrs. Lowenthal and Ralli.

WHITE (Mr. R.).	BLACK (Mr. L.)
1. P. to K's 4th.	1. P. to K's 4th.
2. Kt. to K. B's 3rd.	2. Kt. to Q. B's 3rd.
3. B. to Q. B's 4th.	3. B. to Q. B's 4th.
4. P. to Q. B's 3rd.	4. K's Kt. to B's 3rd.
5. P. to Q's 4th.	5. P. takes P.
6. P. to K's 5th.	6. P. to Q's 4th.
7. B. to Q. Kt.'s 5th.	7. Kt. to K's 5th.
8. B. takes Q's Kt. (ch.)	8. P. takes B.
9. P. takes P.	9. B. to Q. Kt.'s 3rd.
10. Kt. to Q. B's 3rd.	10. Castles.
11. Q's B. to K's 3rd.	11. P. to K. B's 4th.
12. Q. to Q. B's sq.*	12. B. to Q. R's 3rd.
13. Kt. to K. Kt.'s 5th.	13. P. to K. B's 5th.†
14. B. takes P.	14. R. takes B.
15. K's Kt. to K's 6th.	15. Kt. takes Q's Kt.‡

* Better to have Castled at once.

† From this point Mr. Lowenthal plays very skilfully.

‡ Beautifully played, and as sound as it is brilliant.

16. Q. takes R.*	16. Kt. to K's 7th.
17. Kt. takes Q.	17. Kt. takes Q.
18. Kt. takes Q. B's P.	18. B. to Q. Kt.'s 2nd.
19. Kt. to Q. Kt.'s 4th.	19. B. takes Q's P.
20. P. to K. Kt.'s 3rd.	20. Kt. to R's 6th.
21. P. to K. B's 4th.	21. B. takes Q. Kt.'s P.
22. Q's R. to Kt.'s sq.	22. P. to Q's 5th.
23. Q's R. takes B.	23. B. takes K's R.
24. Kt. to Q. R's 6th.	24. R. to Q. B's sq.
25. Kt. to B's 5th.	25. P. to K. Kt.'s 4th.
26. P. to K. B's 5th.	26. P. to K. Kt.'s 5th
27. R. to Q. Kt.'s 4th.	27. Kt. to K. Kt.'s 4th.
28. P. to K's 6th.	28. Kt. to K's 5th.
29. R. takes Q's P.	29. Kt. takes Kt.
30. R. takes P. (ch.)	30. K. to B's sq.
31. R. to Q. B's 4th.	31. Kt. to K's 5th.
32. P. to K. Kt.'s 4th.	32. B. to K. B's 6th.
33. P. to K. B's 6th.	33. R. to Q. Kt.'s sq.

And White resigned.

GAME II.—Between Messrs. Buckle aud Anderssen.

WHITE (Mr. B.)	BLACK (Mr. A.)
1. P. to K's 4th.	1. P. to K's 4th.
2. K's Kt. to B's 3rd.	2. Kt. to Q. B's 3rd.
3. B. to Q. B's 4th.	3. B. to Q. B's 4th.
4. P. to Q. B's 3rd.	4. K's Kt. to B's 3rd.
5. P. to Q's 4th.	5. P. takes P.
6. P. takes P.	6. B. to Q. Kt.'s 5th (ch.)
7. B. to Q's 2nd.	7. B. takes B.
8. Q's Kt. takes B.	8. P. to Q's 4th.

---

* He could not with safety have taken the Queen; *e.g.*:—

16. Kt. takes Q.	16. R. to K's 5th (ch.)
17. K. to Q's 2nd.	17. Kt. to K's 7th.
18. Q. to Q. Kt.'s sq. (best.)	18. R. takes Q's P.
19. K. to K's sq.	19. B. to R's 4th (ch.)
20. P. to Q. Kt.'s 4th.	20. R. takes Kt.'s P.

And wins.

9. P. takes P.	9. Kt. takes P.
10. Q. to Q. Kt.'s 3rd.	10. Q's Kt. to K's 2nd.
11. Castles.	11. Castles.
12. K's R. to K's sq.	12. K's Kt. to B's 5th.
13. K's R. to K's 4th.	13. Q's Kt. to K. Kt.'s 3rd.
14. Q's R. to K's sq.	14. Q. to K. B's 3rd.
15. K's Kt. to K's 5th.	15. Q. to K. Kt.'s 4th.*
16. B. takes K. B's P. (ch.)	16. K. to R's sq.
17. Kt. takes Kt. (ch.)	17. P. takes Kt.
18. Q. to K. Kt's 3rd.†	18. Q. takes Q.
19. K. R's P. takes Q.	19. R. takes B.
20. R. takes Kt.	20. K. to Kt.'s sq.‡
21. Q. R. to K's 8th (ch.)	

And wins.

GAME III. Between Messrs. Max Lange and Heineman.

WHITE (Mr. L.)	BLACK (Mr. H.)
1. P. to K's 4th.	1. P. to K's 4th.
2. K's Kt. to B's 3rd.	2. Q's Kt. to B's 3rd.
3. B. to Q. B's 4th.	3. B. to Q. B's 4th.
4. Castles.	4. K's Kt. to B's 3rd.
5. P. to Q's 4th.	5. K's B. takes P. §
6. Kt. takes B.	6. Kt. takes Kt.
7. P. to K. B's 4th.	7. Kt. to K's 3rd.
8. P. takes P.	8. Kt. to K. Kt.'s sq.
9. K's R. takes B's P.‖	9. K. takes R.
10. B. takes Kt. (ch.)	10. K. takes B.
11. Q. to Q's 5th (ch.)	11. K. to K's 2nd.
12. B. to K. Kt.'s 5th (ch.)	12. Kt. to K. B's 3rd.
13. Kt. to Q. B's 3rd.	13. K's R. to K. B's sq.
14. R. to K. B's sq.	14. P. to Q's 3rd.

* Black is bent on having a counter attack at all hazards.
† Well conceived.
‡ A slip, but it is of little importance, as the game was irretrievably gone.
§ Not so good, as we have seen, as P. takes P
‖ Well played.

15. P. takes Kt. (ch.)	15. P. takes P.
16. R. takes P.	16. R. takes R.
17. P. to K's 5th.	17. B. to K's 3rd.
18. B. takes R. (ch.)	18. K. to B's 2nd.
19. Q. to K. B's 3rd.	19. Q. to K. Kt.'s sq.
20. Kt. to K's 4th.	20. P. takes P.
21. B. to Q's 8th (dis. ch.)	

And wins.

CHAPTER III.

The Evans Gambit.

1. P. to K's 4th / P. to K's 4th, 2. Kt. to K. B's 3rd / Kt. to Q. B's 3rd, 3. B. to Q. B's 4th / B. to Q. B's 4th,

4. P. to Q. Kt.'s 4th / ———.

First to Third Games.

4. ——— / B. takes Kt.'s P., 5. P. to Q. B's 3rd / B. to Q. B's 4th.

Fourth and Fifth Games.

5. ——— / B. to Q. R's 4th; 5. ——— / B. to K's 2nd; 5. ——— / B. to Q's 3rd;

5. ——— / B. to K. B's sq.

Sixth and Seventh Games.

5. ——— / P. to Q's 4th; 5. ——— / B. to Q. Kt.'s 3rd.

Of all the openings of which Chess is susceptible, the *Evans Gambit* is the most interesting. Its combinations are more varied and more beautiful, the opportunities it affords for brilliant attack and scientific defence are more abundant than in any other *début* yet invented. In addition to these great recommendations, the *Evans Gambit* is considered by many of the best authorities to be an opening of perfect fairness to both sides, that is to say, the attack obtained by the sacrifice of the Gambit Pawn is worth no more than it costs. So that it remains a moot point to this moment whether the first or second player ought to win, supposing the best moves were adopted by each of them.

Game the First.

WHITE.	BLACK.
1. P. to K's 4th.	1. P. to K's 4th.
2. Kt. to K. B's 3rd.	2. Kt. to Q. B's 3rd.
3. B. to Q. B's 4th.	3. B. to Q. B's 4th.
4. P. to Q. Kt.'s 4th.	4. B. takes Kt.'s P.
5. P. to Q. B's 3rd.	5. B. to Q. B's 4th.

(For the result of Black's retiring his Bishop otherwise, see Game the Fifth.)

6. P. to Q's 4th.

(It is not quite a matter of indifference whether White play thus or Castle on his 6th move. For the latter see Game the Second.)

	6. P. takes P.
7. Castles.	7. P. to Q's 3rd.

(If Black takes the Pawn, the best reply is 8. $\frac{\text{P. to K's 5th}}{}$.)

8. P. takes P.	8. B. to Q. Kt.'s 3rd.

This phase of the opening is represented on the accompanying diagram, and is that into which the game commonly resolves itself after the 8th move of each side.

Ordinary Position of the Evans Gambit.

BLACK.

WHITE.

Position after the first eight moves on each side.

In this position there are several modes of pursuing the attack at White's command. The most important of these are

(1.) 9. $\frac{\text{P. to Q's 5th}}{}$, (4.) 9. $\frac{\text{P. to K. R's 3rd}}{}$,

(2.) 9. $\frac{\text{B. to Q. Kt's 2nd}}{}$, (5.) 9. $\frac{\text{B. to Q. R's 3rd}}{}$,

(3.) 9. $\frac{\text{Kt. to Q. B's 3rd}}{}$,

which we can examine in the order they are mentioned.

First Attack.

9. P. to Q's 5th.

This is the favourite move at the present day; but I am not satisfied that it is preferable either to 9. $\frac{\text{Kt. to Q. B's 3rd}}{}$, or to 9. $\frac{\text{B. to Q. Kt.'s 2nd}}{}$.

9. Kt. to Q. R's 4th.

The customary move; as some think, the best one. There are not wanting authorities, however, that think this relegation of the Knight to long inactivity an error, and prefer playing him to K's 2nd. (For the effect of that move and that of 9. $\frac{}{\text{Q. Kt. to K's 4th}}$, see Variation A.)

10. B. to Q. Kt.'s 2nd. 10. Kt. to K's 2nd.

(If Black, instead of this move, play 10. $\frac{}{\text{P. to K. B's 3rd}}$, the probable continuation is 11. $\frac{\text{B. to Q's 3rd}}{\text{Kt. to K's 2nd}}$, 12. $\frac{\text{Kt. to Q. B's 3rd}}{\text{Castles}}$, 13. $\frac{\text{Kt. to K's 2nd}}{}$, and White has a very commanding position. Again, if in lieu of 10. $\frac{}{\text{Kt. to K's 2nd}}$, Black play 10. $\frac{}{\text{Kt. to K. B's 3rd}}$, he comes off but badly, *ex. gr.* 11. $\frac{\text{B. to Q's 3rd}}{\text{B. to K. Kt.'s 5th}}$, 12. $\frac{\text{Kt. to Q. B's 3rd}}{\text{Castles}}$, 13. $\frac{\text{Kt. to K's 2nd}}{}$, with the better game, clearly.

11. B. to Q's 3rd.

(If White venture to take the undefended Pawn, it will cost him dear:—11. $\frac{\text{B. takes P.}}{\text{R. to K. Kt.'s sq.}}$, 12. $\frac{\text{B. to K. B's 6th}}{\text{Kt. takes B.}}$,

13. $\frac{\text{Q. to Q. R's 4th (ch.)}}{\text{Q. to Q's 2nd}}$, 14. $\frac{\text{Q. takes Kt.}}{\text{R. takes Kt.'s P. (ch.)}}$, and must lose.)

	11. Castles.
12. Kt. to Q. B's 3rd.	12. Kt. to K. Kt.'s 3

(If 12. $\frac{}{\text{P. to Q. B's 4th}}$, 13. $\frac{\text{P. to K's 5th}}{}$, with a fine position.)

13. Kt. to K's 2nd.	13. P. to Q. B's 4th.

(If Black play 13. $\frac{}{\text{P. to K. B's 3rd}}$, then follows 14. $\frac{\text{K's Kt. to Q's 4th}}{\text{P. to Q. B's 4th}}$, 15. $\frac{\text{Kt. to K. B's 5th}}{}$.)

14. Q. to Q's 2nd.	14. P. to K. B's 3rd.

An important precaution, as White threatens Kt. to K. Kt.'s 3rd, and B. takes K. Kt.'s P.

15. K. to K. R's sq.	15. B. to Q. B's 2nd.

I give a diagram here, the present being an important stage of the combat.

BLACK.

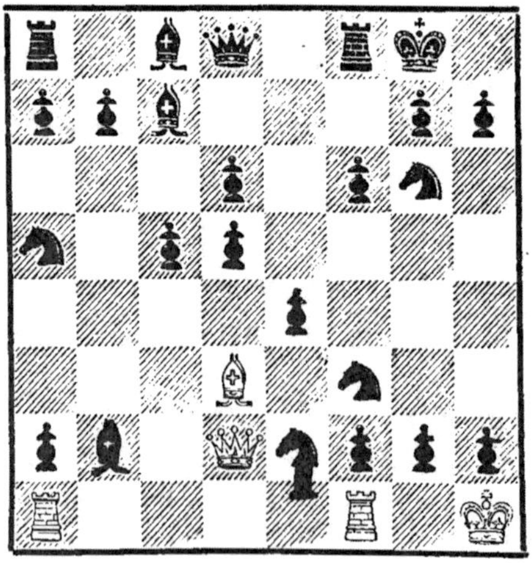

WHITE.

Position of the forces after the first 15 moves on each side.

16. Q. R. to Q. B's sq.

(If 16. $\frac{\text{Kt. to K. Kt.'s 3rd}}{\text{Kt. to K's 4th}}$, 17. $\frac{\text{Kt. takes Kt.}}{\text{Q's P. takes Kt.}}$, 18. $\frac{\text{Kt. to B's 5th}}{\text{B. takes Kt.}}$,

19. $\frac{\text{P. takes B.}}{\text{Q. to Q's 3rd}}$, 20. $\frac{\text{B. to K's 4th}}{\text{Kt. to Q. B's 5th}}$. White has no longer any attack.)

6. R. to Q. Kt.'s sq.

(A move first suggested, and that recently, by Mr. Neumann; P. to Q. R's 3rd was previously played.)

17. Kt. to K. Kt's 3rd.

And White appears to me to have more than an equivalent for the Gambit Pawn.*

Second Attack.

9. B. to Q. Kt.'s 2nd. 9. K's Kt. to K's 2nd.

(Black may also play 9. $\frac{}{\text{K. to Q. R's 4th}}$, and if White reply with 10. $\frac{\text{P. to Q's 5th}}{}$, we have the position examined under the head of "First Attack."

He may also reply to 9. $\frac{\text{B. to Q. Kt.'s 2nd}}{}$ with 9. $\frac{}{\text{Kt. to K. B's 3rd}}$, which is perhaps as good as anything. The continuation is—9. $\frac{}{\text{Kt. to K. B's 3rd}}$, 10. $\frac{\text{P. to Q's 5th}}{\text{Kt. to K's 2nd}}$, 11. $\frac{\text{B. takes Kt.}}{\text{P takes B.}}$, &c.)

---

* The result of recent experience hardly endorses Mr. Staunton's *dictum*. The correct continuation apparently is—

17. P. to Q. Kt.'s 4th (best).

18. Kt. to K. B's 5th.

This move has the sanction of the *Handbuch*, but it is questionable whether 18. Kt. to K's sq., or even 18. Kt. to K. Kt.'s sq., is not equally good.

18. P. to Q. B's 5th.

If 18. $\frac{}{\text{B. takes Kt.}}$, 19. $\frac{\text{P. takes B.}}{\text{Kt. to K's 4th}}$, 20. $\frac{\text{B. takes Kt.}}{\text{B's P. takes B.}}$, 21. $\frac{\text{Kt. to Kt.'s 5th}}{}$, &c.

19. B. to K's 2nd (best).	19. P. to Q. Kt.'s 5th.
20. B. to Q's 4th.	20. P. to B's 6th.
21. Q. to Q.'s sq. (best).	21. B. to Q. Kt.'s 3rd.
22. P. to Q. R's 3rd (best).	

And White has no superiority.—[Ed.]

10. Kt. to K. Kt.'s 5th.	10. P. to Q's 4th.
11. P. takes P.	11. Kt. to Q. R's 4th.
12. P. to Q's 6th.	12. Kt. takes B.
13. P. takes Kt.	13. Q. to Q's 4th.
14. Kt. to Q. B's 3rd.	14. Q. takes Kt.
15. Q. to Q. R's 4th (ch.)	15. P. to Q. B's 3rd.
16. Q. takes Kt.	16. B. to Q. R's 6th.

And Black has, I think, the better game.

Third Attack.

9. Kt. to Q. B's 3rd.

(This line of action, though not apparently so attacking as 9. P. to Q's 5th / —, is very solid and enduring.)

9. B. to K. Kt.'s 5th.

(Black has also the choice of 9. — / Kt. to K. B's 3rd, and 9. — / Kt. to Q. R's 4th, which shall be examined in Variations B and C.)

10. B. to Q. Kt.'s 5th.

(Mr. G. B. Fraser, of Dundee, proposed a variation of singular elegance and ingenuity at this point, beginning with 10. Q. to Q. R's 4th / — See Games Second and Third.)

10. B. to Q's 2nd.

(If he play 10. — / K. to B's sq., he paralyzes the attack for a time, but his game becomes miserably embarrassed.)

11. P. to K's 5th. 11. P. takes P.

(Here, if 11. — / K's Kt. to K's 2nd, then follows 12. B. to K. Kt's 5th / Castles, 13. Kt. to Q's 5th / Q. to K's sq., 14. Kt. to B's 6th (ch.) / P. takes Kt., 15. B. takes P. / —, and White should win.)

12. R. to K's sq.

Having a good attack and a well-disposed position.

VARIATION B, ON BLACK'S 9TH MOVE.

	9. Kt. to K. B's 3rd.
10. P. to K's 5th.	10. P. takes P.

(If 10. $\frac{\quad}{\text{P. to Q's 4th}}$, 11. $\frac{\text{P. takes Kt.}}{\text{P. takes B.}}$, 12. $\frac{\text{P. takes P.}}{\text{R. to K. Kt.'s sq.}}$, 13. $\frac{\text{R. to K's sq. (ch.)}}{\text{B. to K's 3rd}}$, 14. $\frac{\text{P. to Q's 5th}}{\quad}$, and White has a winning advantage.)

11. B. to Q. R's 3rd.	11. Kt. to Q. R's 4th.
12. R. to K's sq.	12. Kt. takes B.
13. Q. to Q. R's 4th (ch.)	13. P. to Q. B's 3rd.
14. Q. takes Kt.	14. B. to K's 3rd.
15. R. takes P.	15. Q. to Q's 2nd.
16. R. takes B. (ch.)	16. P. takes R.
17. Kt. to K's 5th.	

And White must win.

VARIATION C, ON BLACK'S 9TH MOVE.

	9. Kt. to Q. R's 4th.
10. Kt. to K. Kt.'s 5th	10. Kt. takes B.
11. Q. to Q. R's 4th (ch.)	11. Q. to Q's 2nd.

(If 11. $\frac{\quad}{\text{P. to Q. B's 3rd}}$, 12. $\frac{\text{Q. takes Kt.}}{\text{Q. to K's 2nd}}$, 13. $\frac{\text{P. to K. B's 4th}}{\text{P. to K. R's 3rd}}$, 14. $\frac{\text{Kt. to K. B's 3rd}}{\text{B. to K's 3rd}}$, 15. $\frac{\text{Q. to Q. R's 4th}}{\text{Kt. to K. B's 3rd}}$, 16. $\frac{\text{P. to K's 5th}}{\text{P. takes P.}}$, 17. $\frac{\text{B's P. takes P.}}{\text{Kt. to Q's 4th}}$, 18. $\frac{\text{Kt. to K's 4th}}{\quad}$, and White has more than compensation for the Gambit Pawn.)

12. Q. takes Kt.	12. P. to K. R's 3rd.
13. Kt. to K. B's 3rd.	13. Q. to Q. B's 3rd.
14. Q. to Q's 3rd.	14. B. to K. Kt.'s 5th.
15. P. to Q's 5th.	15. Q. to Q's 2nd.
16. Kt. to Q's 4th.	16. Kt. to K's 2nd.

I do not think White has an equivalent for the sacrificed Pawn.

Fourth Attack.

9. P. to K. R's 3rd.

A move frequently adopted by McDonnell, but which is now thought to retard the attack.

9. Kt. to K. B's 3rd.

(If 9. — / P. to K. R's 3rd, 10. Kt. to Q. B's 3rd / Kt. to K's 2nd, 11. B. to Q. Kt.'s 2nd / Castles, 12. Q's Kt. to K's 2nd / Kt. to K. K[illegible]d, equal game.)

10. B. to K. Kt.'s 5th.	10. P. to K. R's 3rd.
11. B. to K. R's 4th.	11. Kt. to K's 2nd.
12. B. takes Kt.	12. P. takes B.

Black is considered to have the better game.

Fifth Attack.

9. B. to Q. R's 3rd.	9. B. to K. Kt.'s 5th.
10. Q. to Q. Kt.'s 3rd.	

(If 10. B. to Q. Kt.'s 5th / B. takes Kt., 11. B. takes Kt. (ch.) / P. takes B., 12. Q. takes B. / B. takes Q. P., Black's game is preferable.)

	10. Kt. to Q. R's 4th.
11. B. takes P. (ch.)	11. K. to B's sq.
12. Q. to Q's 5th.	12. Kt. to K. B's 3rd.
13. Q. to K. Kt.'s 5th.	13. B. takes Kt.
14. P. to K's 5th.	14. K. takes B.
15. P. takes Kt.	15. Q. takes P.

White has an inferior situation.

Variation A.

Beginning at Black's 9th move, after 9. $\frac{\text{P. to Q's 5th.}}{}$

BLACK.

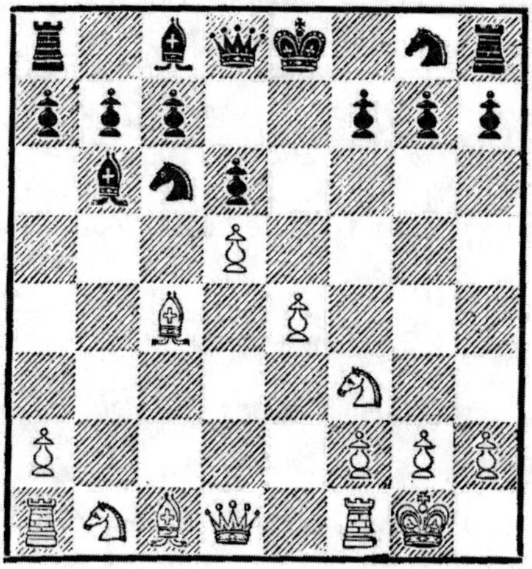

WHITE.

Position prior to Black's 9th Move.

	9. Q's Kt. to K's 2nd.
10. P. to K's 5th.	10. B. to K. Kt's 5th.

(If 10. $\frac{}{\text{Kt. to K. Kt.'s 3rd}}$, 11. $\frac{\text{P. to K's 6th}}{\text{P. takes P.}}$, 12. $\frac{\text{P. takes P.}}{\text{K. Kt. to K's 2nd}}$, 13. $\frac{\text{Kt. to K. Kt.'s 5th}}{\text{Castles}}$, 14. $\frac{\text{Kt. to Q. B's 3rd}}{}$, or, 14. $\frac{\text{Q. to R's 5th}}{}$, and White has a strong attack. If 10. $\frac{}{\text{Kt. to K. R's 3rd}}$, 11. $\frac{\text{Kt. to Q. B's 3rd}}{\text{Castles}}$, 12. $\frac{\text{B. takes Kt.}}{\text{P. takes B.}}$, 13. $\frac{\text{Kt. to K's 4th}}{\text{P. takes P.}}$, 14. $\frac{\text{Kt. to K. B's 6th (ch.)}}{\text{K. to R's sq.}}$, 15. $\frac{\text{Kt. takes K. P.}}{\text{Q. to Q's 3rd}}$, and I prefer Black's game. These moves, with the exception of Black's last move, occurred in a game between Anderssen and Steinitz.)

11. Q. to Q. R's 4th (ch.)	11. B. to Q's 2nd.
12. Q. to Q. Kt's 3rd.	12. Kt. to K. Kt.'s 3rd.
13. Kt. to Q. B's 3rd.	

With the better opening.

As we have said, Black can also move his attacked Knight to King's 4th at the 9th move of this Variation, but this is inferior to 9. $\frac{\quad}{\text{Kt. to Q. R's 4th}}$, or 9. $\frac{\quad}{\text{Kt. to K's 2nd}}$. For instance :—9. $\frac{\quad}{\text{Kt. to K's 4th}}$, 10. $\frac{\text{Kt. takes Kt.}}{\text{P. takes Kt.}}$, 11. $\frac{\text{Kt. to Q's 2nd}}{\text{Kt. to K's 2nd}}$, 12. $\frac{\text{B. to Q. R's 3rd}}{\quad}$, and White has a good attack.

Game the Second.

Mr. Fraser's Attack.

White.	Black.
1. P. to K's 4th.	1. P. to K's 4th.
2. Kt. to K. B's 3rd.	2. Kt. to Q. B's 3rd.
3. B. to Q. B's 4th.	3. B. to Q. B's 4th.
4. P. to Q. Kt.'s 4th.	4. B. takes Kt.'s P.
5. P. to Q. B's 3rd.	5. B. to Q. B's 4th.
6. P. to Q's 4th.	6. P. takes Q's P.
7. Castles.	7. P. to Q's 3rd.
8. P. takes P.	8. B. to Q. Kt.'s 3rd.
9. Kt. to Q. B's 3rd.	9. B. to K. Kt.'s 5th.
10. Q. to Q. R's 4th.	

I at one time thought this ingenious move of Mr. Fraser the best White could adopt; subsequent analysis of the combinations depending on it somewhat modified my estimation. My opinion now is, that the validity of Mr. Fraser's move depends upon the soundness of Mr. Mortimer's variation. If carried out as Mr. Fraser himself planned, the course of the attack breaks down. Supported by Mr. Mortimer's line of action, it was at one time considered almost irresistible, but this view has been qualified considerably by recent analysis.

10. B. to Q's 2nd.

This appears to be the best reply at Black's command.

(If 10. $\frac{}{\text{B. takes Kt.}}$, 11. $\frac{\text{P. to Q's 5th}}{\text{B. to K. Kt.'s 5th}}$, 12. $\frac{\text{P. takes Kt.}}{\text{P. takes P.}}$, 13. $\frac{\text{Q. takes P. (ch.)}}{\text{B. to Q's 2nd}}$, 14. $\frac{\text{Q. to Q's 5th}}{\text{B. to K's 3rd}}$, 15. $\frac{\text{B. to Q. Kt.'s 5th (ch)}}{\text{K. to B's sq.}}$, 16. $\frac{\text{Q. to Q's 3rd}}{\text{Kt. to K's 2nd}}$, 17. $\frac{\text{B. to K. Kt.'s 5th}}{}$, Black has not an enviable game.)

11. Q. to Q. Kt.'s 3rd.	11. Kt. to Q. R's 4th.
12. B. takes B's P. (ch.)	12. K. to B's sq.
13. Q. to Q's 5th.	

It is at this point the interesting variation of Mr. Mortimer begins with 13. $\frac{\text{Q. to Q. B's 2nd}}{}$, for which see the Third Game—the Fraser-Mortimer Variation.

	13. Kt. to K. B's 3rd.
14. Q. to K. Kt.'s 5th.	14. K. takes B.
15. P. to K's 5th.	15. Kt. to K. Kt.'s 5th.

(Black may also play 15. $\frac{}{\text{R. to K's sq.}}$, 16. $\frac{\text{P. takes Kt.}}{\text{Q. takes P.}}$, and have the better position.)

16. Q. to K. B's 4th (ch.)	16. K. to Kt.'s sq.
17. Kt. to K. Kt.'s 5th.	17. Kt. to K. B's 3rd (best).
18. P. to K's 6th.	18. B. to K's sq.
19. Kt. to Q's 5th.	19. Kt. to Q. B's 3rd.
20. R. to K's sq.	20. Kt. to K's 2nd.
21. Kt. to K. B's 7th.	21. Q's Kt. takes Kt.
22. Q. to K. B's 3rd.	22. Kt. takes Kt.
23. Q. takes Q's Kt.	23. Q. to K. B's 3rd.
24. Q. takes Kt.'s P.	24. R. to Q's sq.
25. P. to K's 7th.	25. B. takes Q's P.
26. B. to Q. Kt.'s 2nd.	26. B. takes B.
27. P. takes R. (Queening.)	27. Q. takes Q.
28. Q. takes B.	28. Kt. to K's 4th.

Black has the advantage.

GAME THE THIRD.

The Fraser-Mortimer Variation.

WHITE.	BLACK.
1. P. to K's 4th.	1. P. to K's 4th.
2. Kt. to K. B's 3rd.	2. Kt. to Q. B's 3rd.
3. B. to Q. B's 4th.	3. B. to Q. B's 4th.
4. P. to Q. Kt.'s 4th.	4. B. takes Kt.'s P.
5. P. to Q. B's 3rd.	5. B. to Q. B's 4th.
6. P. to Q's 4th.	6. P. takes P.
7. Castles.	7. P. to Q's 3rd.
8. P. takes P.	8. B. to Q. Kt.'s 3rd.
9. Kt. to Q. B's 3rd.	9. B. to K. Kt.'s 5th.
10. Q. to Q. R's 4th.	10. B. to Q's 2nd.
11. Q. to Q. Kt.'s 3rd.	11. Kt. to Q. R's 4th.
12. B. takes B's P. (ch.)	12. K. to B's sq.
13. Q. to Q. B's 2nd.	

This highly ingenious supplement to the Fraser Variation was suggested by Mr. Mortimer a few years back. It has not yet been perhaps sufficiently tested by analysis and practice for a decisive judgment to be pronounced on its merits, but it is undoubtedly a valuable and interesting addition to the many forms of attack which the Evans Gambit admits.

BLACK.

WHITE.

Position prior to Black's 14*th Move.*

13. K. takes B.

14. P. to K's 5th.

Black has two leading lines of defence. These are—

1. 14. $\frac{\quad}{\text{P. to K. R's 3rd}}$, 2. 14. $\frac{\quad}{\text{K. to B's sq.}}$. 14. $\frac{\quad}{\text{P. to K. Kt.'s 3rd}}$ is obviously bad on account of 15. P. to K's 6th (ch.)

In the first place :—

14. P. to K. R's 3rd.

15 P. to Q's 5th. 15. Kt. to K. B's 3rd.

This is thought by many authorities to be the best defence.

(If Black, instead of boldly offering the Knight in return for the piece he has gained, play—15. $\frac{\quad}{\text{B. to K. Kt.'s 5th}}$, he fares badly. For example,—16. $\frac{\text{P. to K's 6th (ch.)}}{\text{B. takes P. (best.)}}$, 17. $\frac{\text{P. takes B. (ch.)}}{\text{K. takes P.}}$, 18. $\frac{\text{Q. to K. Kt.'s 6th (ch.)}}{\text{Q. to K. B's 3rd (best.)}}$, 19. $\frac{\text{R. to K's sq. (ch.)}}{\text{K. to Q's 2nd}}$, 20. $\frac{\text{Q. to Kt.'s 4th (ch.)}}{\text{K. to Q's sq.}}$, 21. $\frac{\text{Kt. to Q's 5th}}{\text{Q. to B's 2nd}}$. He does not appear to have any better move. 22. $\frac{\text{B. to Kt.'s 5th (ch.)}}{\text{P. takes B.}}$, 23. $\frac{\text{Kt. takes P.}}{\text{Q. to Q's 2nd}}$. [If 23. $\frac{\quad}{\text{Q. to K. R's 4th}}$, White gives mate in five moves. If 23. $\frac{\quad}{\text{Q. takes Kt.}}$, Black loses his Queen.] 24. $\frac{\text{Kt. to K's 6th (ch.)}}{\text{K. to B's sq.}}$, 25. $\frac{\text{Kt. to K. B's 8th}}{\text{Kt. to K. B's 3rd}}$, 26. $\frac{\text{R. to K's 8th (ch.)}}{\quad}$, and White wins.)

16. P. to K's 6th (ch.)

This move is given by Mr. Mortimer as preferable to taking the Knight. In the latter case the following is a probable continuation:—16. $\frac{\text{P. takes Kt.}}{\text{Q. takes P.}}$, 17. $\frac{\text{Kt. to K's 4th}}{\text{B. to K. B's 4th}}$, 18. $\frac{\text{B. to Q. Kt.'s 2nd}}{\text{Q. to K. Kt.'s 3rd}}$. [If 18. $\frac{\quad}{\text{B. takes Kt.}}$, 19. $\frac{\text{Q. takes B.}}{\text{Q. takes B.}}$

20. $\frac{\text{Q. to K's 6th (ch.)}}{\text{K. to B's sq.}}$, 21. $\frac{\text{Kt. to K. R's 4th}}{}$, &c.] 19. $\frac{\text{Kt. to K. R's 4th}}{\text{B. takes Kt.}}$, 20. $\frac{\text{Kt. takes Q.}}{\text{B. takes Q.}}$, 21. $\frac{\text{Kt. takes R. (ch.)}}{\text{R. takes Kt.}}$, and White, I think, in spite of Mr. Mortimer, has the better game. Mr. Mortimer, however, does not follow out this variation so far as I do.)

	16. B. takes P. (best.) *
17. P. takes B. (ch.)	17. K. takes P.
18. Q. to K. Kt.'s 6th.	18. Q. to K. B's sq. (best.)
19. B. to K. Kt.'s 5th.	19. Kt. to Q. B's 3rd.

(If 19. $\frac{}{\text{P. takes B.}}$, 20. $\frac{\text{Kt. takes P. (ch.)}}{\text{K. to K's 2nd}}$, 21. $\frac{\text{Q. R. to K's sq. (ch.)}}{\text{K. to Q's 2nd}}$, 22. $\frac{\text{Q. to K. B's 5th}}{}$, and wins.)

20. Q. R. to K's sq. (ch.)	20. Kt. to K's 4th.

(If 20. $\frac{}{\text{K. to Q's 2nd}}$, 21. $\frac{\text{Q. to K. B's 5th (ch.)}}{}$.)

21. Kt. takes Kt.	21. P. takes Kt.
22. R. takes P. (ch.)	22. K. takes R. (best.)
23. R. to K's sq. (ch.)	

And White must win.

In the second place :—

	14. K. to B's sq. (best.)
15. R. to K's sq.	15. Kt. to Q. B's 3rd.

---

* The retreat of 16. K. to Kt.'s sq. is now generally preferred to this capture, *e. g.* :—

	16. K. to Kt.'s sq.
17. P. takes B.	17. Q. takes P
18. Kt. to K. R's 4th.	

If White play instead 18. $\frac{\text{P. to K. R's 3rd}}{}$, Black's reply is apparently 18. $\frac{}{\text{R. to K's sq.}}$

	18. P. to K. Kt.'s 4th.
19. Kt. to Kt.'s 6th.	19. R. to R's 2nd.
20. K. to R's sq.	20. R. to K's sq.

And Black is out of danger.—[Ed.]

This is given by Anderssen as best, and is unquestionably stronger than 15. $\frac{\quad}{\text{Q. to Q. B's sq.}}$, as recommended by Mr. Mortimer.

16. B. to K. Kt.'s 5th.

(If 16. $\frac{\text{P. to K's 6th}}{\text{B. to K's sq.}}$, 17. $\frac{\text{B. to K. Kt.'s 5th}}{\text{K's Kt. to K's 2nd}}$, 18. $\frac{\text{Kt. to Q's 5th}}{\text{K. to Kt.'s sq.}}$,

And Black should win.)

	16. Q. to K's sq.
17. P. to K's 6th.	

Better than 17. $\frac{\text{P. takes P.}}{\quad}$, to which Black replies with 17. $\frac{\quad}{\text{Q. to K. Kt.'s 3rd}}$, and will win.

	17. Q. to K. Kt.'s 3rd.
18. Q. takes Q.	18. P. takes Q.
19. P. takes B.	19. Kt. to K. B's 3rd.
20. P. to Q's 5th.	20. Kt. to K's 4th.
21. Kt. takes Kt.	21. P. takes Kt.

And Black has an obvious superiority.

Game the Fourth.

White.	Black.
1. P. to K's 4th.	1. P. to K's 4th.
2. Kt. to K. B's 3rd.	2. Kt. to Q. B's 3rd.
3. B. to Q. B's 4th.	3. B. to Q. B's 4th.
4. P. to Q. Kt.'s 4th.	4. B. takes Kt.'s P.
5. P. to Q. B's 3rd.	5. B. to Q. R's 4th.

(In one respect this move is certainly preferable to 5. $\frac{\quad}{\text{B. to Q. B's 4th}}$, which we have been examining, that is, it allows Black to adopt the defence of 6. $\frac{\quad}{\text{Kt. to K. B's 3rd}}$ more advantageously. On the other hand, when the Bishop retires to Q. R's 4th, White can more safely push the attack by $\frac{\text{Q. to Q. Kt.'s 3rd}}{\quad}$, as Black cannot reply with $\frac{\quad}{\text{Kt. to Q. R's 4th}}$, so that it is difficult to say which really should have the preference.)

6. P. to Q's 4th.

(This is considered more attacking than 6. $\frac{\text{Castles}}{}$, the result of which shall be shown in Variation I.)

6. P. takes P.

7. Castles. 7. P. to Q's 3rd.

(He may also play 7. $\frac{}{\text{Kt. to K. B's 3rd}}$, 7. $\frac{}{\text{P. to Q's 6th}}$, 7. $\frac{}{\text{B. to Q. Kt.'s 3rd}}$, and 7. $\frac{}{\text{P. takes P.}}$, for the result of which see Variations A, B, C, and D.)

8. Q. to Q. Kt.'s 3rd.

(If 8. $\frac{\text{P. takes P.}}{\text{B. to Q. Kt.'s 3rd}}$, we have the classic phase of the Gambit.)

8. Q. to K. B's 3rd.

(This is usually reckoned better for Black than any other move, but the German critics make a good case for the following defence: — 8. $\frac{}{\text{Q. to K's 2nd}}$, 9. $\frac{\text{P. to K's 5th}}{\text{P. takes P.}}$, 10. $\frac{\text{R. to K's sq.}}{\text{B. to Q's 2nd}}$, 11. $\frac{\text{B. to Q. R's 3rd.}}{\text{Q. to K. B's 3rd.}}$, 12. $\frac{\text{Kt. takes K's P.}}{\text{Castles, Q's side}}$, 13. $\frac{\text{Kt. takes P.}}{\text{P. takes P.}}$, 14. $\frac{\text{Kt. takes Q's R. (best.)}}{\text{Kt. takes Kt.}}$, 15. $\frac{\text{Q. to Q. B's 2nd}}{\text{Kt. to Q. B's 3rd}}$, &c.)

9. P. takes P.

(If 9. $\frac{\text{P. to K's 5th}}{\text{P. takes K's P.}}$, 10. $\frac{\text{R. to K's sq.}}{\text{B. to Q's 2nd}}$, 11. $\frac{\text{K. takes K's P.}}{\text{Kt. takes Kt.}}$, 12. $\frac{\text{P. to K. B's 4th}}{\text{K's Kt. to K's 2nd}}$, 13. $\frac{\text{P. takes Kt.}}{\text{Q. to K. Kt's 3rd}}$, 14. $\frac{\text{P. to K's 6th}}{\text{B. to Q. B's 3rd}}$, 15. $\frac{\text{P. takes P. (ch.)}}{\text{K. to Q's sq.}}$, Black has the better game.)

9. B. to Q. Kt.'s 3rd.

10. B. to Q. Kt.'s 5th.

(If 10. $\frac{\text{P. to K's 5th}}{\text{P. takes P.}}$, 11. $\frac{\text{P. takes P.}}{\text{Q. to K. Kt.'s 3rd}}$, 12. $\frac{\text{Kt. to K. Kt.'s 5th}}{\text{Kt. to Q's sq.}}$, and Black, though with a restrained position, maintains the advantage of a Pawn more.)

	10. B. to Q's 2nd.
11. P. to K's 5th.	11. P. takes P.
12. R. to K's sq.	12. K's Kt. to K's 2nd.
13. P. takes P.	13. Q. to K. Kt.'s 3rd.
14. B. to K. Kt.'s 5th.	

Again Black retains the advantage of a Pawn *plus*, but at the cost of a confined situation.

Variation I, beginning at White's 6th Move.

BLACK.

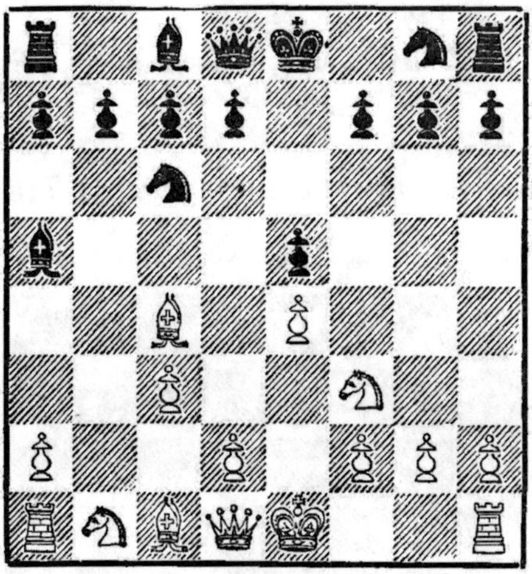

WHITE.

Position before White's 6th Move.

6. Castles.	6. Kt. to K. B's 3rd.

As I remarked before, Black can play this Knight out more effectively when his Bishop is at Q. R's 4th, than when it is at Q. B's 4th.

7. P. to Q's 4th.

(If 7. Kt. to K. Kt.'s 5th / Castles, 8. P. to K. B's 4th / P. to Q's 4th. [If 8. — / P. to K. R's 3rd, 9. Kt. takes K. B's P. / R. takes Kt., 10. B. takes R. (ch.) / Kt. takes B., 11. Q. to K. R's 5th (ch.) / —, and White wins. If 8. — / P. takes B's P., 9. P. to Q's 4th / P. to K. R's 3rd, 10. Q's B. takes P. / P. takes Kt., 11. Q's B. takes Kt.'s P. (ch.) / —, &c.] 9. P. takes Q's P. / Kt. takes P., 10. B. to Q. R's 3rd / Kt. takes K. B's P., 11. R. takes Kt. / Q. takes Kt., and Black has the best of the combat.)

	7. Castles.
8. P. takes K's P.	8. K's Kt. takes K's P.
9. Q. to Q's 3rd.	9. Kt. to Q. B's 4th.
10. Q. to Q's 5th.	10. Kt. to K's 3rd.
11. B. to Q. R's 3rd.	

And Black has a very constrained position.

Variation A, beginning at Black's 7th Move.

BLACK.

WHITE.

Position prior to Black's 7th Move.

7. Kt. to K. B's 3rd.

8. B. to Q. R's 3rd.

(White may also play without any disadvantage, 8. $\frac{\text{P. to K's 5th}}{\text{P. to Q's 4th}}$, 9. $\frac{\text{B. to Q. Kt.'s 5th}}{}$. [If 9. $\frac{\text{P. takes Kt.}}{\text{P. takes B.}}$, 10. $\frac{\text{P. takes Kt.'s P.}}{\text{R. to K. Kt.'s sq.}}$, 11. $\frac{\text{B. to K. Kt.'s 5th}}{\text{Q. to Q's 4th}}$, 12. $\frac{\text{Q's Kt. to Q's 2nd}}{\text{B. to K. B's 4th}}$, and Black will be safe in a few more moves.] 9. $\frac{}{\text{Kt. to K's 5th}}$, 10. $\frac{\text{P. takes P.}}{}$. [White can play also 10. $\frac{\text{Q. to Q. R's 4th}}{\text{Castles}}$, 11. $\frac{\text{B. takes Kt.}}{\text{P. takes Q. B's P.}}$, 12. $\frac{\text{Kt. takes B.}}{\text{Kt. takes Kt.}}$, 13. $\frac{\text{Q. to Q. B's 2nd}}{\text{P. takes B.}}$, but not advantageously. He may play, too, 10. $\frac{\text{B. to Q. R's 3rd}}{\text{B. to Q's 2nd}}$, 11. $\frac{\text{Q. to Q. Kt.'s 3rd}}{\text{Q. takes Q. B's P.}}$, 12. $\frac{\text{Kt. takes B.}}{\text{Kt. takes Kt.}}$, 13. $\frac{\text{B. takes Kt.}}{\text{P. takes P.}}$, 14. $\frac{\text{Kt. takes P.}}{\text{Kt. to K's 5th}}$, 15. $\frac{\text{P. to K. B's 3rd}}{\text{Kt. to Q's 7th}}$, 16. $\frac{\text{Q. to K. Kt.'s 3rd}}{}$, and have a strong attack.] 10. $\frac{}{\text{Castles}}$, 11. $\frac{\text{B. takes Kt.}}{\text{P. takes B.}}$, 12. $\frac{\text{Q. to Q. R's 4th}}{\text{B. to Q. Kt's 3rd}}$, 13. $\frac{\text{Q. takes P.}}{\text{B. to K. Kt.'s 5th}}$, 14. $\frac{\text{B. to Q. Kt.'s 2nd}}{\text{B. takes Kt.}}$, 15. $\frac{\text{P. takes B.}}{\text{Kt. to K. Kt.'s 4th}}$, 16. $\frac{\text{Kt. to Q's 2nd}}{\text{R. to K's sq.,}}$, and White has won back the Gambit Pawn, though at some cost of ground.

8. P. to Q's 3rd.

9. P. to K's 5th. 9. P. to Q's 4th.

(If 9. $\frac{}{\text{P. takes P.}}$, 10. $\frac{\text{Q. to Q. Kt.'s 3rd}}{\text{Q. to Q's 2nd}}$, 11. $\frac{\text{R. to K's sq.}}{}$, White should win. If 9. $\frac{}{\text{Kt. to K's 5th}}$, 10. $\frac{\text{K's P. takes P.}}{\text{Kt. to Q's 3rd, taking P.}}$. [If 10. $\frac{}{\text{Q. takes Q's P.}}$, 11. $\frac{\text{R. to K's sq.}}{\text{P. to Q's 4th}}$, 12. $\frac{\text{Kt. takes P.}}{}$, &c.] 11. $\frac{\text{R. to K's sq. (ch.)}}{\text{K. to B's sq. (best.)}}$, 12. $\frac{\text{Kt. takes Q's P.}}{}$, and White has the better game.)

10. B. to Q. Kt.'s 5th.	10. Kt. to K's 5th.
11. P. takes P.	11. B. to Q's 2nd.
12. Q. to Q. Kt.'s 3rd.	12. P. to Q. R's 3rd

(If 12. $\frac{\qquad}{\text{Kt. to K's 2nd}}$, 13. $\frac{\text{B. takes B. (ch.)}}{\text{Q. takes B.}}$. [If 13. $\frac{\qquad}{\text{K. takes B.}}$, 14. $\frac{\text{B. takes Kt.}}{\qquad}$, winning a piece.] 14. $\frac{\text{B. takes Kt.}}{\qquad}$, with the gain of a piece.)

13. B. to Q's 3rd.

With a good game.

Variation B, at Black's 7th Move.

(See Diagram.)

	7. P. to Q's 6th.
8. Q. to Q. Kt.'s 3rd.	8. Q. to K. B's 3rd.
9. P. to K's 5th.	9. Q. to K. Kt.'s 3rd.
10. R. to K's sq.	10. K's Kt. to K's 2nd.
11. B. to Q. R's 3rd.	

And Black has half his forces locked up

Variation C, at Black's 7th Move.

(See Diagram.)

	7. B. to Q. Kt.'s 3rd.
8. P. to K's 5th.	8. P. to Q's 4th.
9. P. takes P. (*en pass.*)	

And whether Black takes the Pawn with Pawn or Queen, he must have an inferior position.

Variation D, at Black's 7th Move.

	7. P. takes P.

(This capture, which was condemned by all the early writers on the Opening, has recently come into vogue in Germany, where it is known as the "Compromised Defence.")

8. Q. to Q. Kt.'s 3rd.

(The once favourite move of 8. $\frac{\text{P. to K's 5th}}{\qquad}$, Lange has shown to be of doubtful efficacy, because of 8. $\frac{}{\text{K's Kt. to K's 2nd}}$, 9. $\frac{\text{Kt. to K. Kt.'s 5th}}{\text{Q's Kt. takes P.}}$, 10. $\frac{\text{Kt. takes B's P.}}{\text{Kt. takes Kt.}}$, 11. $\frac{\text{B. takes Kt. (ch.)}}{\text{R. takes B.}}$, 12. $\frac{\text{Q. to K. R's 5th (ch.)}}{\text{P. to K. Kt.'s 3rd}}$, 13. $\frac{\text{Q. takes B}}{\text{P. to Q's 4th}}$, 14. $\frac{\text{Kt. takes P.}}{\text{B. to K's 3rd}}$, &c.)

	8. Q. to K. B's 3rd.
9. P. to K's 5th.	9. Q. to K. Kt.'s 3rd.
10. Q's Kt. takes P.	10. K's Kt. to K's 2nd.

(If 10. $\frac{}{\text{B. takes Kt.}}$, 11. $\frac{\text{Q. takes B.}}{\text{P. to Q. Kt.'s 3rd}}$, 12. $\frac{\text{P. to K's 6th}}{\text{B's P. takes P.}}$, 13. $\frac{\text{B. to Q. Kt.'s 5th}}{}$, and White has a good game.)

Continuing the text game after Black's 10th move of 10. $\frac{}{\text{K's Kt. to K's 2nd}}$, White has three ways of proceeding with his attack, namely,—11. $\frac{\text{Kt. to K's 2nd}}{}$, 11. $\frac{\text{R. to K's sq.}}{}$, and 11. $\frac{\text{B. to Q. R's 3rd}}{}$. Let us consider them seriatim. In the first place :—

BLACK.

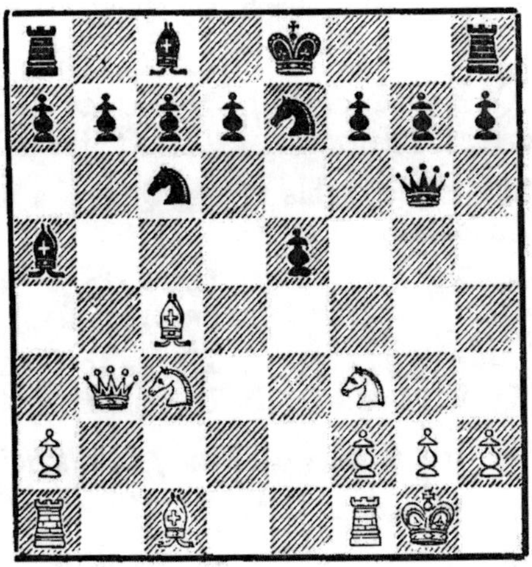

WHITE.

Position prior to White's 11th Move.

11. Kt. to K's 2nd. — 11. P. to Q. Kt.'s 4th.

This counter-gambit is the only means by which Black can maintain the superiority.

The *Neue Berliner Schachzeitung*, to which I owe the combinations in this particular variation, presents the following moves to demonstrate the superiority of Black's 11th move of $\frac{}{\text{P. to Q. Kt.'s 4th}}$, to the ordinary step of Castling:—11. $\frac{}{\text{Castles}}$, 12. $\frac{\text{B. to Q's 3rd}}{\text{Q. to K's 3rd}}$, 13. $\frac{\text{B. takes P. (ch.}}{\text{K. to R's sq.}}$, 14. $\frac{\text{Q. to Q. R's 4th}}{\text{P. to Q's 3rd}}$, 15. $\frac{\text{Kt. to K. B's 4th}}{}$. (If 15. $\frac{\text{Q. to K. R's 4th}}{\text{Q. to K. Kt.'s 5th}}$.) 15. $\frac{}{\text{Q. to Q's 2nd}}$, 16. $\frac{\text{P. to K's 6th}}{\text{P. takes P.}}$, 17. $\frac{\text{K's Kt. to K. Kt.'s 5th}}{\text{P. to K's 4th.}}$, 18. $\frac{\text{Q's Kt. to K's 6th}}{\text{R. to K. B's 3rd}}$, 19. $\frac{\text{Q. to K. R's 4th}}{\text{R. to K. R's 3rd}}$, 20. $\frac{\text{Kt. to K. B's 7th (ch.)}}{\text{K. takes B.}}$, 21. $\frac{\text{B. takes R.}}{}$, and White should win.

12. B. to Q's 3rd.

(If 12. $\frac{\text{B. takes Q. Kt.'s P.}}{\text{R. to Q. Kt.'s sq.}}$, 13. $\frac{\text{Q. to Q. R's 4th}}{\text{P. to Q. R's 3rd}}$, 14. $\frac{\text{B. takes Kt.}}{\text{Kt. takes B.}}$, 15. $\frac{\text{B. to Q. R's 3rd}}{\text{R. to Q. Kt.'s 4th}}$, and Black has some advantage.)

	12. Q. to K's 3rd.
13. Q. to Q. Kt.'s 2nd.	13. Kt. to K. Kt.'s 3rd.
14. Kt. to K. B's 4th.	14. Kt. takes Kt.

(This capture is preferable to 14. Q. to K's 2nd, as recommended by Anderssen.)

15. B. takes Kt.	15. P. to K. R's 3rd (best.)
16. Q's R. to B's sq.	16. P. to Q. R's 3rd.
17. K's R. to Q's sq.	17. B. to Q. Kt.'s 2nd.
18. Q. to Q. Kt.'s sq.	18. Q's R. to Q's sq.

And Black has won two Pawns, with a safe game.

In the second place :—

11. R. to K's sq. — 11. P. to Q. Kt.'s 4th.

(If 11. $\frac{}{\text{Castles}}$, 12. $\frac{\text{Kt. to K. R's 4th}}{\text{Q. to K. R's 4th}}$, 13. $\frac{\text{Q. to K's 4th}}{}$,

White has the better game. So, also, if 11. $\frac{\quad}{\text{B. takes Kt.}}$, 12. $\frac{\text{Q. takes B.}}{\text{Castles.}}$, 13. $\frac{\text{B. to Q's 3rd}}{\text{Q. to K. R's 4th}}$, 14. $\frac{\text{R. to K's 4th}}{\text{Kt. to K. Kt.'s 3rd}}$, 15. $\frac{\text{P. to K. Kt.'s 4th}}{\text{Q. to K. R's 6th}}$, 16. $\frac{\text{B. to K. B's sq.}}{\quad}$, White has the superiority.)

12. Kt. takes Q. Kt.'s P.

(If White take this Pawn with his Bishop, Black replies by 12. $\frac{\quad}{\text{R. to Q. Kt.'s sq.}}$, and wins a piece.)

	12. R. to Q. Kt.'s sq. (best.)
13. Kt. to K. R's 4th.	13. Q. to K. Kt.'s 5th.
14. Q. to Q. R's 4th.	

(If 14. $\frac{\text{B. takes P. (ch.)}}{\text{K. to Q's sq.}}$, &c.)

14. K. to Q's sq

(Black may apparently give up his Queen, secure of an equivalent, by 14. $\frac{\quad}{\text{B. takes R.}}$, 15. $\frac{\text{B. takes B's P. (ch.)}}{\text{K. takes B.}}$, 16. $\frac{\text{Q. takes Q.}}{\text{R. takes Kt.}}$.)

15. Kt. to K. B's 3rd.	15. B. takes R.
16. Kt. takes B.	16. P. to Q. R's 3rd.
17. Kt. to Q. R's 3rd.	17. R. to Q. Kt.'s 5th.
18. Q. to Q. B's 2nd.	18. Kt. takes P.

And Black has the better game.

In the third place :—

11. B. to Q. R's 3rd.	11. P. to Q. Kt.'s 4th.
12. Kt. takes P.	12. R. to Q. Kt.'s sq.
13. B. takes Kt.	

(If 13. $\frac{\text{Q. to Q. R's 4th}}{\text{P. to Q. R's 3rd}}$, 14. $\frac{\text{Kt. to Q's 4th}}{\text{Kt. takes Kt.}}$, 15. $\frac{\text{Kt. takes Kt.}}{\text{B. to Q. Kt.'s 2nd}}$, with a winning position.)

13. P. to Q. R's 3rd (best.)

(If 13. $\frac{}{\text{Kt. takes B.}}$, then 14. $\frac{\text{Q. to R's 3rd (ch.)}}{\text{B. to Q. Kt.'s 5th}}$, 15. $\frac{\text{Q. to K's 3rd}}{}$, &c.)

14. B. to Q. R's 3rd.	14. P. takes Kt.
15. B. to Q's 3rd.	15. Q. to K. R's 4th (best.)
16. B. to Q. Kt.'s 2nd.	16. Castles.

Black has a fine game, and a Pawn *plus*.

The above Variations are by Mr. Zukertort.

Game the Fifth.

1. P. to K's 4th.	1. P. to K's 4th.
2. Kt. to K. B's 3rd.	2. Kt. to Q. B's 3rd.
3. B. to Q. B's 4th.	3. B. to Q. B's 4th.
4. P. to Q. Kt.'s 4th.	4. B. takes Kt.'s P.
5. P. to Q. B's 3rd.	5. B. to K's 2nd.

(This retreat of the Bishop is generally condemned. It is not worse play, perhaps hardly such bad play, as retreating the Bishop to Q's 3rd. For example:—5. $\frac{}{\text{B. to Q's 3rd}}$, 6. $\frac{\text{Castles}}{\text{Q. to K's 2nd}}$, 7. $\frac{\text{P. to Q's 4th}}{\text{Kt. to K. B's 3rd}}$, 8. $\frac{\text{R. to K's sq.}}{\text{Castles}}$, 9. $\frac{\text{B. to K. Kt.'s 5th}}{}$, and Black's game is hopelessly restrained. Neither is it so bad as—5. $\frac{}{\text{B. to K. B's sq.}}$, which would still more confine Black's game.)

6. P. to Q's 4th.	6. P. takes P.
7. Q. to Q. Kt.'s 3rd.	7. Kt. to Q. R's 4th.
8. B. takes P. (ch.)	8. K. to B's sq.
9. Q. to Q. R's 4th.	

With much the better game.

Game the Sixth.

The Evans Gambit Declined.

WHITE.	BLACK.
1. P. to K's 4th.	1. P. to K's 4th.
2. Kt. to K. B's 3rd.	2. Kt. to Q. B's 3rd.

3. B. to Q. B's 4th.	3. B. to Q. B's 4th.
4. P. to Q. Kt.'s 4th.	4. P. to Q's 4th.

(This Counter-Gambit I consider the preferable way of avoiding the ordinary attack of the Evans Gambit. For the effect of 4. $\frac{}{\text{B. to Q. Kt.'s 3rd}}$, see Game the Seventh.)

5. P. takes P.

(White may also move his attacked Bishop to Q. Kt.'s 5th, but not to his benefit. For, suppose,—5. $\frac{\text{B. to Q. Kt.'s 5th}}{\text{P. takes K's P.}}$, 6. $\frac{\text{P. takes B.}}{\text{P. takes Kt.}}$, 7. $\frac{\text{Q. takes P.}}{\text{Kt. to K's 2nd}}$, and Black has much the better position. There is another move here for White, namely,—5. $\frac{\text{B. takes P.}}{}$, which merits more attention. This move is likely, I think, to lead to a drawn game. *Ex. gr.* :— 5. $\frac{\text{B. takes Q's P.}}{\text{Kt. takes P.}}$, 6. $\frac{\text{B. to Q. Kt.'s 3rd}}{}$. [If 6. $\frac{\text{B. takes K. B's P. (ch.)}}{\text{K. takes B.}}$, 7. $\frac{\text{Kt. takes P. (ch.)}}{\text{K. to B's sq.}}$, 8. $\frac{\text{Q. to K. B's 3rd (ch.)}}{\text{Q. to K. B's 3rd}}$, or 8. $\frac{\text{Q. to K. R's 5th}}{\text{Q. to K's 2nd}}$. and White has lost a piece for very little.] 6. $\frac{}{\text{Kt. to K. B.'s 3rd}}$, 7. $\frac{\text{Q. to K's 2nd}}{\text{Castles}}$, 8. $\frac{\text{Castles}}{\text{B. to K. Kt.'s 5th}}$, 9. $\frac{\text{B. to Q. Kt.'s 2nd}}{\text{Q. to K's 2nd *}}$, 10. $\frac{\text{P. to K. R's 3rd}}{}$. The game appears to be equal.)

	5. Kt. takes P.
6. P. to Q. B's 3rd.	

---

* This move of 9. $\frac{}{\text{Q. to K's 2nd}}$ is not quite so strong as 9. $\frac{}{\text{Kt. to Q. B's 3rd}}$. In the latter case the continuation would be 10. $\frac{\text{P. to K. R's 3rd}}{\text{B. takes Kt.}}$, 11. $\frac{\text{Q. takes B.}}{\text{Q. to K's 2nd}}$, and the game is almost even. —[Ed.]

(If White play 6. $\frac{\text{B. to Q. R's 3rd}}{\quad}$, the probable continuation is—6. $\frac{\quad}{\text{Q. to Q's 3rd}}$, 7. $\frac{\text{P. to Q. B's 3rd}}{\quad}$. [If 7. $\frac{\text{B. takes Kt.}}{\text{B. takes B.}}$, 8. $\frac{\text{P. to Q. B's 3rd}}{\text{B. to Q. B's 4th}}$, I would rather have Black's position.] 7. $\frac{\quad}{\text{Kt. takes Q's P.}}$. [If 7. $\frac{\quad}{\text{P. to K's 5th}}$, 8. $\frac{\text{P. takes Kt.}}{\text{P. takes Kt.}}$, 9. $\frac{\text{Castles}}{\quad}$, and White has the advantage.] 8. $\frac{\text{B. takes B.}}{\text{Q. takes B.}}$, 9. $\frac{\text{Q. to Q. Kt.'s 3rd}}{\text{K's Kt. to K. B's 3rd}}$, 10. $\frac{\text{Kt. takes P.}}{\text{Castles}}$. Even game.

White, however, has another move at command, namely,—6. $\frac{\text{Kt. takes P.}}{\quad}$, which shall be examined as Variation I.)

	6. Kt. takes Q's P.
7. Q. to Q. Kt.'s 3rd.	7. P. to Q. B's 3rd (best.)
8. Kt. takes P.	8. Q. to K. Kt.'s 4th.
9. Castles.	

The game is thought to be equal.

Variation I, beginning at White's 6th Move.

BLACK.

WHITE.

Position prior to White's 6th Move.

6. Kt. takes P.	6. Q. to K. Kt.'s 4th.

(This vigorous counter move is now thought to be the most conclusive reply to White if he captures the King's Pawn. For the effect of 6. $\frac{\quad}{\text{Kt. takes Q's P.}}$, refer to Variation A.)

7. P. to Q's 4th.

(Instead of this move White can play 7. $\frac{\text{Q. to K's 2nd}}{\quad}$, or 7. $\frac{\text{Castles}}{\quad}$, which shall be considered forthwith. In the first place, then, suppose 7. $\frac{\text{Q. to K's 2nd}}{\text{Kt. takes B's P. (ch.)}}$, 8. $\frac{\text{K. to Q's sq.}}{\text{Kt. to Q's 5th}}$, 9. $\frac{\text{Kt. to K. B's 3rd. (dis. ch.)}}{\text{Q. to K's 2nd}}$, 10. $\frac{\text{Q. takes Q. (ch.)}}{\text{Kt. takes Q.}}$, 11. $\frac{\text{Kt. takes Kt.}}{\text{B. takes Kt.}}$, 12. $\frac{\text{Kt. to Q. B's 3rd}}{\text{B. takes B's P.}}$. The game is evidently in Black's favour. In the second place,— 7. $\frac{\text{Castles}}{\text{B. to K. R's 6th}}$, 8. $\frac{\text{Q. to K. B's 3rd*}}{\text{Q. takes Kt.}}$, 9. $\frac{\text{P. to Q. B's 3rd}}{\text{B. to Q's 3rd}}$, the advantage is with Black.)

	7. Q. takes Kt.'s P.
8. Q. to K. B's 3rd	8. Q. takes Q.
9. Kt. takes Q.	9. Kt takes P. (ch.)
10. K. to Q's sq.	10. Kt. takes Q's P.

And Black has decidedly the better position.

---

* He may play, we believe, with more advantage, 8. $\frac{\text{P. to K. Kt.'s 3rd}}{\quad}$.—[Ed.]

Variation A, beginning at Black's 6th Move.

BLACK.

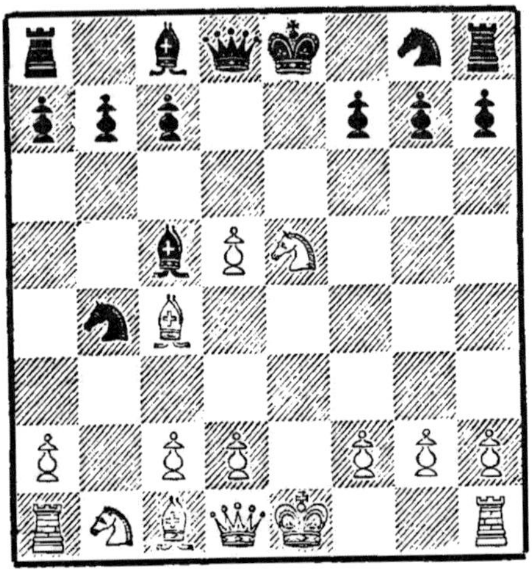

WHITE.

Position prior to Black's 6th Move.

	6. Kt. takes Q's P.
7. B. to Q. Kt.'s 5th (ch.)*	7. P. to Q. B's 3rd.
8. Kt. takes Q. B's P.	8. Q. to Q. Kt.'s 3rd.

(If 8. ——— / B. takes P. (ch.), 9. K. takes B. / Q. to Q. Kt.'s 3rd (ch.)

[If 9. ——— / Q. to K. R's 5th (ch.), 10. P. to K. Kt.'s 3rd / ———, &c.]

10. Kt. to Q's 4th (dis. ch.) / Kt. to Q's sq., 11. B. to Q. Kt.'s 2nd / ———, White has won a piece.)

9. Q. to K's 2nd (ch.)	9. K. to B's sq.

---

* The fifth edition of the German *Handbuch* gives the following:—

7. P. to Q's 4th.	7. B. to Q. Kt.'s 5th (ch.)
8. B. to Q's 2nd.	8. B. takes B. (ch.)
9. Kt. takes B.	9. B. to K's 3rd.

Even game.—[Ed.]

(If 9. $\frac{}{\text{B. to K's 3rd}}$, 10. $\frac{\text{Kt. to Q. Kt.'s 4th (dis. ch.)}}{\text{—}}$. If 9. $\frac{}{\text{K. to Q's 2nd}}$, 10. $\frac{\text{Kt. to Q. Kt.'s 4th (dis. ch.)}}{}$).

10. Kt. to Q. Kt.'s 4th	10. B. to K's 3rd.

(If 10. $\frac{}{\text{Q's Kt. to K's 2nd}}$, 11. $\frac{\text{Kt. to Q's 5th}}{}$, and Black has an inferior game. If 10. $\frac{}{\text{B. takes P. (ch.)}}$, 11. $\frac{\text{Q. takes B.}}{\text{Q. takes B.}}$, 12. $\frac{\text{Kt. takes Kt.}}{\text{Q. takes Kt.}}$, 13. $\frac{\text{B. to Q. R's 3rd (ch.)}}{\text{Kt. to K's 2nd.}}$, White can now Castle with an overwhelming attack.)

11. Kt. takes Kt.	11. B. takes Kt.
12. Castles.	12. Q. to K. Kt.'s 3rd.
13. P. to K. Kt.'s 3rd.	

The advantage is plainly on the White side.

Game the Seventh.

WHITE.	BLACK.
1. P. to K's 4th.	1. P. to K's 4th.
2. Kt. to K. B's 3rd.	2. Kt. to Q. B's 3rd.
3. B. to Q. B's 4th.	3. B. to Q. B's 4th.
4. P. to Q. Kt.'s 4th.	4. B. to Q. Kt.'s 3rd.
5. P. to Q. Kt.'s 5th.	

(White can also play 5. $\frac{\text{P. to Q. R's 4th}}{}$, as in Variation I.)

	5. Kt. to Q. R's 4th.
6. Kt. takes K's P.	6. Kt. to K. R's 3rd.

(It was formerly thought that Black's best move at this point was to play his Queen to K. B's 3rd. Analysis has shown, however, that the move in the text, though less attacking, is somewhat safer. For the consequences of 6. $\frac{}{\text{Q. to K. B's 3rd}}$, see Variation A.)

7. P. to Q's 4th.	7. P. to Q's 3rd.
8. B. takes K's Kt.	8. P. takes Kt.

(If 8. $\frac{}{\text{P. takes B.}}$, 9. $\frac{\text{Kt. takes K. B's P.}}{}$, &c.)

9. B. takes K. Kt.'s P.	9. R. to K. Kt.'s sq.

(If 9. $\frac{\quad}{\text{Q. takes Q.'s P.}}$, 10. $\frac{\text{Q. takes Q.}}{\text{B. takes Q.}}$, 11. $\frac{\text{B. takes R.}}{\text{B. takes R.}}$, 12. $\frac{\text{B. to Q's 3rd}}{\quad}$, White has an advantage.

10. B. takes B's P. (ch.)	10. K. takes B.
11. B. takes K's P.	11. Q. to K. Kt.'s 4th.

(If 11. $\frac{\quad}{\text{R. to K. Kt.'s 3rd}}$, 12. $\frac{\text{Q. to Q's 3rd}}{\quad}$, &c.)

12. Kt. to Q's 2nd.	12. Q. takes Kt.'s P.
13. Q. to K. R's 5th (ch.)	13. Q. to K. Kt.'s 3rd.
14. Q. to K. R's 4th.	14. P. to K. R's 3rd.
15. Castles (Q's side).	15. Q. to K. Kt.'s 4th.
16. Q. takes Q.	16. R. takes Q.
17. K's R. to K. Kt.'s sq.	

The superiority is with White.

VARIATION I, BEGINNING AT WHITE'S 5TH MOVE.

BLACK.

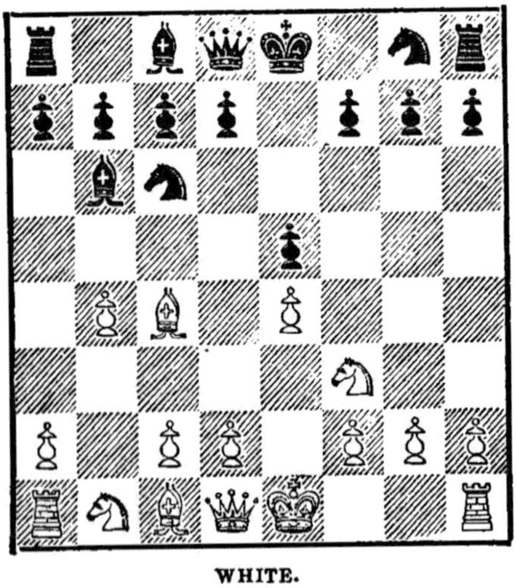

WHITE.

Position prior to White's 5th Move.

5. P. to Q. R's 4th. | 5. P. to Q. R's 3rd.

(If 5. $\frac{}{\text{P. to Q. R's 4th}}$, 6. $\frac{\text{P. to Q. Kt.'s 5th}}{\text{Kt. to Q's 5th}}$, 7. $\frac{\text{Kt. takes P.}}{\text{Q. to K. B's 3rd}}$, 8. $\frac{\text{Kt. to K. B's 3rd}}{\text{Kt. to K's 3rd}}$, 9. $\frac{\text{P. to K's 5th}}{}$, White has the advantage. If 5. $\frac{}{\text{Kt. takes Kt.'s P.}}$, 6. $\frac{\text{P. to K. R's 5th}}{\text{B. to Q. B's 4th}}$, 7. $\frac{\text{P. to Q. B's 3rd}}{\text{Kt. to Q. B's 3rd}}$, 8. $\frac{\text{Castles}}{}$, and again White has the better position.)

6. P. to Q. B's 3rd.

(White may also Castle at this point, or play 6. $\frac{\text{B. to Q. Kt.'s 2nd}}{\text{P. to Q's 3rd}}$, 7. $\frac{\text{P. to Q. Kt.'s 5th}}{\text{P. takes P.}}$, 8. $\frac{\text{P. takes P.}}{\text{R. takes R.}}$, 9. $\frac{\text{B. takes R.}}{\text{Q's Kt. to K's 2nd}}$, and Black has a good game.)

	6. P. to Q's 3rd.
7. Q. to Q. Kt.'s 3rd.	7. Q. to K's 2nd.
8. P. to Q's 3rd.	8. Kt. to K. B's 3rd.
9. B. to K. Kt.'s 5th.	9. P. to K. R's 3rd.

I prefer White's position.

Variation A, beginning at Black's 6th Move.

BLACK.

WHITE.

Position prior to Black's 6th Move.

6. Q. to K. B's 3rd.

(As I have said, this used to be considered a very strong move for the defence, but it is now considered inferior to 6. $\frac{}{\text{Kt. to K. R's 3rd}}$, which we have just examined.)

7. B. takes P. (ch.) — 7. K. to B's sq.

(If 7. $\frac{}{\text{K. to Q's sq.}}$, 8. $\frac{\text{P. to Q's 4th}}{\text{P. to Q's 3rd}}$, 9. $\frac{\text{B. takes Kt.}}{\text{R. takes B.}}$. [If 9. $\frac{}{\text{P. takes Kt.}}$, 10. $\frac{\text{P. takes K's P. (dis. ch.)}}{}$, &c.] 10. $\frac{\text{B. to K. Kt.'s 5th}}{\text{Q. takes 5th}}$, 11. $\frac{\text{Kt. to K. B's 7th (ch.)}}{}$, and White wins. So also if 7. $\frac{}{\text{K. to K's 2nd}}$, 8. $\frac{\text{P. to Q's 4th}}{\text{P. to Q's 3rd}}$, 9. $\frac{\text{B. to Q. R's 3rd}}{\text{Kt. to K. R's 3rd}}$, 10. $\frac{\text{B. to Q. Kt.'s 3rd}}{}$, White's game is preferable.)

8. P. to Q's 4th. — 8. P. to Q's 3rd.
9. B. takes Kt.

(This is stronger than playing Bishop to Q. R's 3rd. For example:—9. $\frac{\text{B. to Q. R's 3rd}}{\text{Kt. to K's 2nd}}$, 10. $\frac{\text{P. to K. B's 4th}}{\text{P. takes Kt.}}$, 11. $\frac{\text{Q's P. takes P.}}{\text{Q. takes B.}}$, 12. $\frac{\text{Q. to Q's 8th (ch.)}}{\text{Q. to K's sq.}}$, 13. $\frac{\text{B. takes Kt. (ch.)}}{\text{K. to B's 2nd}}$, 14. $\frac{\text{Q. takes Q. (ch.)}}{\text{Kt. takes Q.}}$, 15. $\frac{\text{B. to Q. Kt.'s 4th}}{}$; equal game.)

9. P. takes Kt.

(The German and French authorities pronounce this to be better than taking the Bishop, but it appears to me that Black would make a stronger fight by 9. $\frac{}{\text{R. takes B.}}$, 10. $\frac{\text{Kt. to K. B's 3rd}}{\text{B. to K. Kt.'s 5th}}$, &c., though the game in either case is against him.)

10. B. to Q's 5th. — 10. B. takes Q's P.

(If Black now play 10. $\frac{}{\text{P. to Q. B's 3rd}}$, White should not then move 11. $\frac{\text{P. to K. B's 4th}}{}$. His best answer appears to be 11. $\frac{\text{B. to Q. R's 3rd (ch.)}}{\text{K. to K's sq.}}$, 12. $\frac{\text{Castles}}{\text{P. takes B.}}$, 13. $\frac{\text{Kt. to Q. B's 3rd}}{}$ and White, in Pawns and position, has more than an equivalent for the piece he has given up.) *

11. P. to K. B's 4th.

(The force of this move is very remarkable. Black appears to have no satisfactory reply to it.)

11. B. takes Q's R.

(This is bad enough, but if 11. $\frac{}{\text{P. to K. Kt.'s 4th}}$, White answers with 12. $\frac{\text{Q. to Q's 2nd}}{}$, and has a winning advantage. If he play 11. $\frac{}{\text{P. takes P.}}$, then follows 12. $\frac{\text{Q's B. takes P.}}{}$, and 13. $\frac{\text{R. to K. B's sq.}}{}$, &c.)

12. P. takes K's P.

And now, whether Black play 12. $\frac{}{\text{Q. takes K's P.}}$, or 12. $\frac{}{\text{B. takes P.}}$, 12. $\frac{}{\text{Q. to K. Kt.'s 3rd}}$, or 12. $\frac{}{\text{Q. to K's 2nd}}$, he must have a bad game. In the first place, suppose,—
12. $\frac{}{\text{Q. takes K's P.}}$, 13. $\frac{\text{R. to K. B's sq. (ch.)}}{\text{K. to K's 2nd}}$, 14. $\frac{\text{B. to Q. R's 3rd (ch.)}}{}$,

---

* The continuation is,—13. $\frac{}{\text{B. takes Q's P.}}$, 14. $\frac{\text{Kt. takes Q's P.}}{\text{B's 2nd}}$, 15. $\frac{\text{B. to Q's 6th (best.)}}{\text{B. to Q. Kt.'s 3rd (best.)}}$, 16. $\frac{\text{B. takes K's P.}}{}$, and White has three Pawns for the piece he has sacrificed. Had Black at move 15 played $\frac{}{\text{B. takes R.}}$, White would have checked with Knight at B's 7, and then taken the Rook, regaining the piece with a winning position. Similarly had Black moved 15. $\frac{}{\text{Kt. to Q. B's 5th}}$, White would have won by 16. $\frac{\text{Kt. to B's 7th (ch.)}}{\text{K. to Q's sq.}}$, 17. $\frac{\text{B. takes P.}}{\text{Kt. takes B.}}$, 18. $\frac{\text{B. takes Q's P.}}{}$, &c. — [ED.]

&c. In the second place,—12. $\frac{\quad}{\text{B. takes P.}}$, 13. $\frac{\text{R. to K. B's sq.}}{\quad}$, winning the Queen. In the third place,—12. $\frac{\quad}{\text{Q. to K. Kt.'s 3rd}}$, 13. $\frac{\text{R. to K. B's sq. (ch.)}}{\text{K. to K's sq. (best.)}}$, 14. $\frac{\text{B. to K. B's 7th (ch.)}}{\quad}$, &c.; and in the fourth place,—12. $\frac{\quad}{\text{Q. to K's 2nd}}$, 13. $\frac{\text{B. to Q. R's 3rd}}{\text{B. to Q. B's 6th (ch.)}}$, 14. $\frac{\text{Kt. takes B.}}{\text{Q. takes B.}}$, 15. $\frac{\text{Castles (ch.)}}{\text{K. to K's sq.}}$, 16. $\frac{\text{B. to B's 7th (ch.)}}{\text{K. to K's 2nd}}$, 17. $\frac{\text{Kt. to Q's 5th (ch.)}}{\quad}$, and White in every case has a great advantage.

ILLUSTRATIVE GAMES.

Game I.—Between Messrs. Schallopp and Minkwitz.

White (Mr. S.)	Black (Mr. M.)
1. P. to K's 4th.	1. P. to K's 4th.
2. Kt. to K. B's 3rd.	2. Kt. to Q. B's 3rd.
3. B. to Q. B's 4th.	3. B. to Q. B's 4th.
4. P. to Q. Kt.'s 4th.	4. B. takes P.
5. P. to Q. B's 3rd.	5. B. to B's 4th.
6. P. to Q's 4th.	6. P. takes P.
7. Castles.	7. P. to Q's 3rd.
8. P. takes P.	8. B. to Q. Kt.'s 3rd.
9. P. to Q's 5th.	9. Kt. to Q. R's 4th.
10. B. to Q. Kt.'s 2nd.	10. Kt. to K's 2nd.
11. B. to Q's 3rd.	11. Castles.
12. Kt. to Q. B's 3rd.	12. Kt. to Kt.'s 3rd.
13. Kt. to K's 2nd.	13. P. to Q. B's 4th.
14. Q. to Q's 2nd.	14. P. to K. B's 3rd.*
15. K. to R's sq.	15. B. to Q. B's 2nd.
16. Q's R. to B's sq.	16. P. to Q. R's 3rd.†
17. Kt. to Kt.'s sq.	17. P. to Q. Kt.'s 4th.

* According to Anderssen, the proper time for this move is immediately after White has played Q. to Q's 2nd.

† Anderssen, Neumann, and others, condemn this move, and unanimously prefer R. to Q. Kt.'s sq.

18. P. to K. B's 4th.	18. B. to Q. Kt.'s 3rd.
19. Kt. to Kt.'s 3rd.	19. R. to Q. R's 2nd.
20. K's Kt. to K's 2nd.	20. R. to Q. B's 2nd.
21. P. to K. B's 5th.	21. Kt. to K's 4th.
22. Kt. to B's 4th.	22. Q's Kt. to B's 5th.*
23. B. takes Kt.	23. Kt. takes B.
24. R. takes Kt.	24. P. takes R.
25. B. to Q. B's 3rd.	25. R. to Kt.'s 2nd.
26. P. to K. R's 4th.	26. Q. to K's sq.
27. Kt. to K's 6th.	27. K's R. to B's 2nd.
28. Kt. to R's 5th.	28. B. to Q's sq.†
29. Q. to B's 4th.	29. B. takes Kt.
30. Q's P. takes B.	30. R. to B's sq.
31. Q. to B's 3rd.	31. R. to Q. Kt.'s 4th.
32. R. to Q's sq.	32. Q. to K's 2nd.
33. Q. to Kt.'s 3rd.	33. R. to Q. Kt.'s 3rd.
34. B. to R's 5th.	34. R. to Q. Kt.'s 2nd.
35. B. to Q's 2nd.	35. K. to R's sq.
36. Kt. to B's 4th.	36. Q. to Q. B's 2nd.
37. Kt. to K. Kt.'s 6th (ch.)	37. P. takes Kt.
38. P. takes P.	38. R. to K's sq.
39. B. to B's 4th.	39. P. to B's 6th.
40. Q. to Kt.'s 4th.	40. K. to Kt.'s sq.
41. Q. to R's 5th.	41. R. takes P.
42. Q. to R's 7th (ch.)	42. K. to B's sq.
43. Q. to R's 8th (ch.)	43. K. to K's 2nd.
44. Q. takes P. (ch.)	44. K. to K's sq.
45. Q. to R's 8th (ch.)	45. K. to Q's 2nd.
46. P. to Kt.'s 7th.	46. P. to B's 7th.
47. R. to Q. B's sq.	47. R. to K's sq.
48. Q. takes R. (ch.)	48. K. takes Q.
49. P. Queens (ch.)	49. K. to Q's 2nd.
50. P. to R's 5th.	50. R. to Kt.'s 8th.
51. P. to R's 6th.	51. Q. to R's 4th.
52. Q. to K. Kt.'s 4th (ch.)	52. K. to B's 3rd.
53. Q. to K's 2nd.	53. P. to B's 4th.

* Black should have played Kt. takes B., followed by P. to Q. B's 5th; but he had not apparently counted on the sacrifice of the exchange, which now becomes compulsory for White.

† Absolutely necessary for the defence of the King's Pawn.

54. Q. takes B's P	54. R. takes R. (ch.)
55. Q. takes R.	55. P. takes P.
56. Q. to R's sq.*	56. P. to B's 5th.
57. P. to K. Kt.'s 4th.	57. Q. to R's 6th.
58. Q. to K. B's sq.	58. Q. to Q. B's 6th.
59. P. to Kt.'s 5th.	59. P. to Q's 4th.
60. K. to R's 2nd.†	60. P. to K's 6th.

And the game was drawn.

GAME II.—Between Messrs Kolisch and Anderssen.

WHITE (Mr. K.)	BLACK (Mr. A.)
1. P. to K's 4th.	1. P. to K's 4th.
2. Kt. to K. B's 3rd.	2. Kt. to Q. B's 3rd.
3. B. to Q. B's 4th.	3. B. to Q. B's 4th.
4. P. to Q. Kt.'s 4th.	4. B. takes Kt.'s P.
5. P. to Q. B's 3rd.	5. B. to Q. B's 4th.
6. Castles.	6. P. to Q's 3rd.
7. P. to Q's 4th.	7. P. takes P.
8. P. takes P.	8. B. to Q. Kt.'s 3rd.
9. P. to Q's 5th.	9. Kt. to Q. R's 4th.
10. P. to K's 5th.	10. Kt. to K's 2nd.
11. R. to K's sq.‡	11. Kt. takes B.
12. Q. to Q. R's 4th (ch.)	12. Q. to Q's 2nd.§
13. Q. takes Kt.	13. Castles.
14. B. to K. Kt.'s 5th.	14. P. takes P.
15. Kt. takes P.	15. Q. to K. B's 4th.
16. B. to K. R's 4th.	16. Kt. to Kt.'s 3rd.
17. B. to K. Kt.'s 3rd.	17. B. takes K. B's P. (ch.)
18. B. takes B.	18. Kt. takes Kt.
19. Q. takes Q. B's P.	19. Kt. to Q's 6th.
20. R. to K. B's sq.	20. Kt. takes B.
21. R. takes Kt.	21. Q. takes Q's P.

* Better, we should have thought, to play Q. to Q's sq., or P. to K. Kt.'s 4th.

† By this move the first player throws away a well-earned victory. By playing P. to K. R's 7th, he must have won.

‡ The usual move is P. to K's 6th.

§ The best reply, we believe.

22. Kt. to Q. B's 3rd.	22. Q. to Q. B's 3rd.
23. Q. to K. Kt.'s 3rd.	23. B. to K's 3rd.
24. Q's R. to K's sq.	24. P. to K. B's 4th.
25. Kt. to K's 2nd.	25. B. takes Q. R's P.*
26. Kt. to Q's 4th.	26. Q. to Q. Kt.'s 3rd.
27. Q. to K. B's 4th.	27. Q's R. to K's sq.
28. R. takes R.	28. R. takes R.
29. P. to K. R's 3rd.	29. B. to K's 3rd.
30. K. to R's 2nd.	30. R. to Q's sq.
31. Kt. takes B's P.	31. B. takes Kt.
32. Q. takes B.	32. Q. to Q's 3rd (ch.)
33. K. to R's sq.	33. R. to K. B's sq.
34. Q. to Q. B's 2nd.	34. R. takes R.
35. Q. takes R.	35. Q. to Q. Kt.'s sq.
36. P. to K. R's 4th.	36. P. to Q. Kt.'s 4th.
37. Q. to Q. R's 2nd (ch.)	37. K. to R's sq.
38. P. to K. R's 5th.	38. P. to K. R's 3rd.
39. Q. to Q. Kt.'s 3rd.	39. P. to Q. Kt.'s 5th.
40. K. to Kt.'s sq.	40. P. to Q. R's 4th.
41. K. to B's 2nd.	41. Q. to Q. Kt.'s 4th.
42. Q. to K. B's 7th.	42. P. to Q. Kt.'s 6th.
43. Q. to B's 8th (ch.)	43. K. to R's 2nd.
44. Q. to K's 7th.	44. Q. to K. B's 4th (ch.)

And wins.

Game III.—Between Messrs. Hirschfield and Kolisch.

White (Mr. H.)	Black (Mr. K.)
1. P. to K's 4th.	1. P. to K's 4th.
2. Kt. to K. B's 3rd.	2. Kt. to Q. B's 3rd.
3. B. to Q. B's 4th.	3. B. to Q. B's 4th.
4. P. to Q. Kt.'s 4th.	4. B. takes Kt.'s P.
5. P. to Q. B's 3rd.	5. B. to B's 4th.
6. Castles.	6. P. to Q's 3rd.
7. P. to Q's 4th.	7. P. takes P.
8. P. takes P.	8. B. to Q. Kt.'s 3rd.
9. Kt. to Q. B's 3rd.	9. B. to K. Kt.'s 5th.

* Black has now secured two passed Pawns on the Queen's side, and his victory is merely a question of time.

10. B. to Q. Kt.'s 5th.	10. B. to Q's 2nd.
11. P. to K's 5th.	11. P. takes P.
12. P. to Q's 5th.	12. Q's Kt. to K's 2nd.
13. B. takes B. (ch.)	13. Q. takes B.
14. Kt. takes K's P.	14. Q. to K. B's 4th.
15. Q. to Q. R's 4th (ch.)	15. K. to Q's sq.*
16. B. to K. B's 4th.	16. Kt. to K. Kt.'s 3rd.
17. P. to K. Kt.'s 4th.†	17. Q. to Q. B's sq.
18. K's R. to K's sq.	18. Kt. takes Kt.
19. B. takes Kt.	19. P. to K. B's 3rd.
20. B. takes Q. B's P. (ch.)‡	20. K. takes B.
21. Kt. to Q. Kt.'s 5th (ch.)	21. K. to Q's sq.
22. Kt. to Q's 6th.	22. Q. to Q's 2nd.
23. R. to K's 8th (ch.)	23. Q. takes R.§
24. Q. takes Q. (ch.)	24. K. to Q. B's 2nd.
25. Kt. to Kt.'s 5th (mate.)	

GAME IV.—Between Messrs. Steinitz and Zukertort.

WHITE (Mr. S.)	BLACK (Mr. Z.)
1. P. to K's 4th.	1. P. to K's 4th.
2. K's Kt. to B's 3rd.	2. Kt. to Q. B's 3rd.
3. B. to Q. B's 4th.	3. B. to Q. B's 4th.
4. P. to Q. Kt.'s 4th.	4. B. takes P.
5. P. to Q. B's 3rd.	5. B. to R's 4th.
6. P. to Q's 4th.	6. P. takes P.
7. Castles.	7. P. takes P.
8. Q. to Q. Kt.'s 3rd.	8. Q. to K. B's 3rd.
9. B. to K. Kt.'s 5th. ‖	9. Q. to K. Kt.'s 3rd.
10. Kt. takes P.	10. B. takes Kt.
11. Q. takes B.	11. Kt. to K. B's 3rd.
12. B. to Q's 3rd.	12. Castles.
13. Q's R. to K's sq.	13. P. to Q. Kt.'s 4th.

* This is not a good move, but Black has anything but an enviable game.

† Very ingeniously played.

‡ Again an excellent stroke of play.

§ Had he moved K. to Q. B's 2nd, White would have rejoined with Kt. to Q. Kt.'s 5th (ch.)

‖ This is, we think, inferior to the customary move of P. to K's 5th.

14. P. to K's 5th.	14. Kt. to Q's 4th.
15. Q. to Q. B's 2nd.	15. Q. to K. R's 4th.
16. P. to Q. R's 3rd.	16. P. to K. R's 3rd.
17. B. to Q's 2nd.	17. K's Kt. to K's 2nd.*
18. R. to K's 4th.	18. Kt. to K. Kt.'s 3rd.†
19. K's R. to K's sq.	19. B. to Kt.'s 2nd.
20. P. to K. Kt.'s 4th.	20. Q. to R's 6th.
21. K's R. to K's 3rd.	21. P. to K. B's 4th.
22. P. takes P. (*en pass.*)	22. R. takes P.
23. B. to K. B's sq.	23. Q. takes Kt.
24. Q. to Q. Kt.'s 3rd.	24. P. to Q's 4th.
25. R. takes Q.	25. R. takes R.
26. R. takes R.	26. P. takes R.
27. Q. takes P.	27. K's Kt. to K's 4th.
28. P. to B's 4th.	28. Kt. to B's 5th.
29. Q. to K's 6th (ch.)	29. K. to R's sq.
30. B. to B's 3rd.	30. Q's Kt. to K's 4th.
31. B. takes Kt.	

And wins.

GAME V.—Between Messrs. Aummacher and Anderssen.

WHITE (Mr. Aum.)	BLACK (Mr. And.)
1. P. to K's 4th.	1. P. to K's 4th.
2. Kt. to K. B's 3rd.	2. Kt. to Q. B's 3rd.
3. B. to Q. B's 4th.	3. B. to Q. B's 4th.
4. P. to Q. Kt.'s 4th.	4. B. takes P.
5. P. to Q. B's 3rd.	5. B. to Q. R's 4th.
6. P. to Q's 4th.	6. P. takes P.
7. Castles.	7. P. takes P.
8. Q. to Q. Kt.'s 3rd.	8. Q. to K. B's 3rd.
9. P. to K's 5th.	9. Q. to K. Kt.'s 3rd.
0. Kt. takes P.	10. K's Kt. to K's 2nd.
1. Kt. to K's 2nd.	11. P. to Q. Kt.'s 4th.
2. B. takes Kt.'s P.	12. R. to Q. Kt.'s sq.

* It would have been much better to have played the other Knight to the square.

† By no means a commendable move. By playing P. to K. Kt.'s 4th the Queen would have had a chance of escaping.

13. Q. to R's 4th.	13. P. to Q. R s 3rd.
14. B. takes Kt.	14. Kt. takes B.
15. Kt. to K. B's 4th.	15. Q. to B's 4th.
16. B. to R's 3rd.	16. R. to Kt.'s 4th.*
17. Kt. to K's 2nd.	17. Kt. takes P.
18. K's Kt. to Q's 4th.	18. Q. to K's 5th.
19. Q. to Q's sq.	19. B. to Q. Kt.'s 2nd.
20. P. to K. B's 3rd.	20. Q. to K's 6th (ch.)
21. K. to R's sq.	21. R. to Q's 4th.
22. Q's R. to Kt.'s sq.	22. B. to Kt.'s 3rd.
23. B. to B's sq.	23. Q. to Q's 6th.
24. Q. takes Q.	24. Kt. takes Q.
25. B. to K's 3rd.	25. Castles.
26. Q's R. to Q's sq.	26. Kt. to K's 4th.
27. B. to K. Kt.'s sq.	27. Kt. to K's 3rd.
28. Kt. to K. Kt.'s 3rd.	28. R. to K. Kt.'s 4th.
29. K's Kt. to K's 2nd.	29. B. takes B.
30. Kt. takes B.	30. P. to Q's 3rd.
31. Kt. to R's 3rd.	31. Q's R. to R's 4th.
32. R. to K. B's 2nd.	32. P. to K. B's 4th.
33. P. to K. B's 4th.	33. Kt. to R's 5th.
34. Kt. to K. Kt.'s 5th.	34. R. to K's sq.
35. R. to Q. Kt.'s sq.	35. R. to Q. Kt.'s 4th.
36. R. to Q. B's sq.	36. Kt. takes Kt.'s P.
37. R. takes Kt.	37. R. to Q. Kt.'s 7th.†
38. R. to K. Kt.'s sq.‡	38. R. takes R.
39. R. takes R.	

And Black mates in two moves.

---

* Threatening to play Kt. to Kt.'s 5th next move.

† The whole of this game is a beautiful example of Mr. Anderssen's style.

‡ He might have prevented immediate finale by K's Kt. to K's 4th, but nothing could have averted ultimate defeat.

CHAPTER IV.

The Scotch Gambit.

$1. \frac{\text{P. to K's 4th}}{\text{P. to K's 4th}}, \quad 2. \frac{\text{Kt. to K. B's 3rd}}{\text{Kt. to Q. B's 3rd}}, \quad 3. \frac{\text{P. to Q's 4th}}{\cdot}.$

Game the First.

$3. \frac{\quad}{\text{Kt. takes P.}}, \quad 4. \frac{\text{Kt. takes Kt.}}{\text{Kt. takes P.}}.$

Game the Second.

$3. \frac{\quad}{\text{P. takes P}}, \quad 4. \frac{\quad}{\text{B. to Q. B's 4th}}.$

Game the Third.

$4. \frac{\text{B. to Q. B's 4th}}{\text{B. to Q. Kt.'s 5th (ch.)}}; \quad 4. \frac{\quad}{\text{P. to Q's 3rd}}; \quad 4. \frac{\quad}{\text{Q. to K. B's 3rd}};$

$4. \frac{\quad}{\text{Kt. to K. B's 3rd}}.$

Game the Fourth.

$4. \frac{\text{Kt. takes P.}}{\quad}.$

Game the Fifth.

$5. \frac{\text{Kt. to K. Kt.'s 5th}}{\quad}.$

This fine opening, which took its appellation of the Scotch Gambit from the fact of its having been brought into notice by the Match by correspondence between the London and Edinburgh Chess Clubs, wherein each side adopted it in one of their games, is a favourite method of commencing the game, and should be thoroughly mastered.

Game the First.

WHITE.	BLACK.
1. P. to K's 4th.	1. P. to K's 4th.
2. Kt. to K. B's 3rd.	2. Kt. to Q. B's 3rd.
3. P. to Q's 4th.	3. Kt. takes P.

The famous Italian master, Lolli, approves of this mode of capturing the Gambit Pawn, but most modern authorities prefer taking the Pawn with Pawn, as in Game the Second.

4. Kt. takes Kt.

White may also take the King's Pawn. for the result of which see Variation A.

	4. P. takes Kt.
5. Q. takes P.	5. Kt. to K's 2nd.

(If 5. $\frac{}{\text{Q. to K. B's 3rd}}$, White secures an advantage by 6. $\frac{\text{P. to K's 5th}}{\text{Q. to K. Kt.'s 3rd}}$, 7. $\frac{\text{Kt. to Q. B's 3rd}}{\text{Q. takes Q. B's P.}}$, 8. $\frac{\text{B. to Q's 3rd}}{}$, &c.)

6. B. to Q. B's 4th.	6. Kt. to Q. B's 3rd.
7. Q. to Q's 5th.	7. Q. to K. B's 3rd.
8. Castles.	8. B. to K's 2nd.

White has a slight advantage, the usual result of being a move in advance, but nothing more.

Variation A.

BLACK.

WHITE.

Position prior to White's 4th Move.

4. Kt. takes P. 4. Kt. to K's 3rd.

(A better move for him than B. to Q. B's 4th, *ex. gr*:—
4. $\frac{}{\text{B. to Q. B's 4th}}$, 5. $\frac{\text{B. to Q. B's 4th}}{\text{Kt. to K's 3rd}}$, 6. $\frac{\text{B. takes Kt.}}{\text{K. B's P. takes Kt.}}$,
7. $\frac{\text{Q. to K. R's 5th (ch.)}}{}$, &c.)

5. B. to Q. B's 4th.

I am inclined to think that White may obtain quite as good an opening for his men by the adoption of M. Laroche's move, P. to K. B's 4th. Witness the following series of moves dependent on it:—5. $\frac{\text{P. to K. B's 4th}}{\text{B. to Q. B's 4th}}$, 6. $\frac{\text{Kt. to K. B's 3rd}}{\text{Q. to K. B's 3rd}}$.
(If 6. $\frac{}{\text{P. to Q's 3rd}}$, 7. $\frac{\text{P. to K. B's 5th}}{}$.) 7. $\frac{\text{P. to K's 5th}}{\text{Q. to K. Kt.'s 3rd}}$,
8. $\frac{\text{Kt. to Q. B's 3rd}}{\text{B. to Q. Kt.'s 5th}}$, 9. $\frac{\text{B. to Q's 3rd}}{\text{Q. takes K's P.}}$, &c.

5. P. to Q. B's 3rd.

This is preferable to playing P. to Q's 3rd, or Kt. to K. B's 3rd; for if 5. $\frac{\qquad}{\text{P. to Q's 3rd}}$, then follows,—

6. $\frac{\text{B. to Q. Kt.'s 5th (ch.)}}{\text{P. to Q. B's 3rd}}$, 7. $\frac{\text{Kt. takes Q. B's P.}}{\text{P. takes Kt.}}$, 8. $\frac{\text{B. takes P. (ch.)}}{\text{B. to Q's 2nd}}$,

9. $\frac{\text{B. takes R.}}{\text{Q. takes B.}}$, 10. $\frac{\text{Kt. to Q. B's 3rd}}{\text{Kt. to K. B's 3rd}}$, 11. $\frac{\text{P. to K. B's 3rd}}{\qquad}$, and

Black's game is confined. So on the other hand, if

5. $\frac{\qquad}{\text{Kt. to K. B's 3rd}}$, 6. $\frac{\text{Castles}}{\text{P. to Q's 3rd}}$, 7. $\frac{\text{Kt. to K. Kt.'s 4th}}{\text{B. to K's 2nd}}$, and

Black's game is not well developed.

6. B. takes Kt.

Instead of this move, Mr. Cochrane has introduced the bold and ingenious innovation of taking the K. B's Pawn with the Knight. It may not be perfectly sound, but it demands great care in the defence, and leads to many interesting situations. According to the German *Handbuch*, the proper mode of meeting it is this:—6. $\frac{\text{Kt. takes K. B's P.}}{\text{K. takes Kt.}}$,

7. $\frac{\text{B. takes Kt. (ch.)}}{\text{K. takes B.}}$, 8. $\frac{\text{Castles}}{\text{P. to Q's 4th}}$, 9. $\frac{\text{R. to K's sq.}}{\text{K. to B's 2nd.}}$,

10. $\frac{\text{B. to K's 3rd}}{\text{B. to Q. Kt.'s 5th}}$, 11. $\frac{\text{P. to Q. B's 3rd}}{\text{B. to Q. R's 4th}}$, 12. $\frac{\text{B. to Q's 4th}}{\text{Kt. to K. B's 3rd}}$,

13. $\frac{\text{P. to K's 5th}}{\text{Kt. to K's 5th}}$, 14. $\frac{\text{P. to K. B's 3rd}}{\text{Kt. to K. Kt.'s 4th}}$, 15. $\frac{\text{P. to K. B's 4th}}{\text{Kt. to K's 5th}}$,

16. $\frac{\text{P. to K. B's 5th}}{\text{R. to K. B's sq.}}$, 17. $\frac{\text{P. to K's 6th (ch.)}}{\text{K. to Kt.'s sq.}}$, and Black has certainly the better game.

	6. Q. to Q. R's 4th (ch.)
7. Kt. to Q. B's 3rd.	7. Q. takes K's Kt.
8. B. to Q. Kt.'s 3rd.	8. B. to Q. B's 4th.
9. Castles.	

Neither party has any advantage over the other.

Game the Second.

WHITE.	BLACK.
1. P. to K's 4th.	1. P. to K's 4th.
2. Kt. to K. B's 3rd.	2. Kt. to Q. B's 3rd.
3. P. to Q's 4th.	3. P. takes P.
4. B. to Q. B's 4th.	

(For the result of White taking the Pawn at once with his Knight, see Game the Fourth.)

BLACK.

WHITE.

Position after White's 4th Move.

4. B. to Q. B's 4th.

Black can also play,—4. ——— B. to Q. Kt.'s 5th (ch.), or 4. ——— Kt. to K. B's 3rd; or 4. ——— P. to Q's 3rd, as in Game the Third, but the move above is generally preferred to either of the three.

5. Castles.

The important variation arising here, if White play his Kt. to K. Kt.'s 5th, forms the subject of Game the Fourth.

If in place of Castling White move 5. $\frac{\text{P. to Q. B's 3rd}}{\quad}$, as recommended in the *Handbuch*, the correct reply is—5. $\frac{\quad}{\text{Kt. to K. B's 3rd}}$, which converts the opening into a *Giuoco Piano*, which see.

5. P. to Q's 3rd.

(If 5. $\frac{\quad}{\text{Q. to K. B's 3rd}}$, White will have the best of the battle, by 6. $\frac{\text{P. to Q. B's 3rd}}{\text{P. to Q's 3rd}}$, 7. $\frac{\text{P. to Q. Kt.'s 4th}}{\text{B. to Q. Kt.'s 3rd}}$, 8. $\frac{\text{B. to Q. Kt.'s 2nd}}{\text{Kt. to K's 4th}}$, 9. $\frac{\text{Kt. takes Kt.}}{\text{P. takes Kt.}}$, 10. $\frac{\text{P. takes P.}}{\text{B. takes P.}}$, 11. $\frac{\text{B. takes B.}}{\text{P. takes B.}}$. White can now attack the Queen with his King's Pawn, and develop his forces speedily.)

BLACK.

WHITE.

Position prior to Black's 6th Move.

6. P. to Q. B's 3rd.

White may also move here, 6. $\frac{\text{P. to Q. Kt.'s 4th}}{\quad}$, or

6. $\frac{\text{Kt. to K. Kt.'s 5th}}{}$, the effect of which shall be shown at once. Firstly, then,—6. $\frac{\text{P. to Q. Kt.'s 4th}}{\text{B. takes P.}}$, 7. $\frac{\text{P. to Q. B's 3rd}}{\text{B. takes P.}}$, (If 7. $\frac{}{\text{P. takes P.}}$, 8. $\frac{\text{Q. to Q. Kt.'s 3rd}}{\text{Q. to K's 2nd}}$, 9. $\frac{\text{B. to Q. Kt.'s 5th}}{}$, with the better position.) 8. $\frac{\text{Q. to Q. Kt.'s 3rd}}{\text{Q. to K. B's 3rd}}$, 9. $\frac{\text{Kt. takes B.}}{\text{P. takes Kt.}}$, 10. $\frac{\text{R. to K's sq.}}{\text{K's Kt. to K's 2nd}}$, 11. $\frac{\text{P. to K's 5th}}{\text{Kt. takes K's P. (best.)}}$, 12. $\frac{\text{Kt. takes Kt.}}{\text{P. takes Kt.}}$, Black has the advantage.

Secondly,—6. $\frac{\text{Kt. to K. Kt.'s 5th}}{\text{Kt. to K. R's 3rd}}$. (If 6. $\frac{}{\text{Kt. to K.'s 4th}}$, 7. $\frac{\text{B. to Q. Kt.'s 3rd}}{\text{Kt. to K. R's 3rd}}$, 8. $\frac{\text{P. to K. B's 4th}}{\text{Q's Kt. to K. Kt.'s 5th}}$, 9. $\frac{\text{Q. to K's sq.}}{}$, White's position is superior to his opponent's.) 7. $\frac{\text{P. to K. B's 4th}}{\text{B. to K. Kt.'s 5th}}$. (This is preferable to 7. $\frac{}{\text{P. to Q's 6th (dis. ch.)}}$) 8. $\frac{\text{Kt. to K. B's 3rd}}{}$. (He has no better move, apparently; for if 8. $\frac{\text{Q. to Q's 3rd}}{}$, or 8. $\frac{\text{Q. to K's sq.}}{}$, Black gains a Rook for a Bishop by 8. $\frac{}{\text{B. to K's 7th}}$, and if 8. $\frac{\text{B. takes K. B's P. (ch.)}}{\text{K. to K's 2nd}}$, winning a piece.)

6. B. to K. Kt.'s 5th.

A move said to have been introduced by Mr. Suhle.

7. Q. to Q. Kt.'s 3rd.	7. B. takes Kt.
8. B. takes B's P. (ch.)	8. K. to B's sq.
9. B. takes Kt.	9. R. takes B.
10. P. takes B.	10. P. to K. Kt.'s 4th.
11. K. to R's sq.	11. Q. to K. B's 3rd.
12. P. to K. B's 4th.	12. Kt.'s P. takes P.
13. Q. takes Q. Kt.'s P.	13. Q. to K. Kt.'s 4th.

The above moves occurred in a game between Messrs. Anderssen and Suhle. Except that at Move 13, Mr. Anderssen (Black) played Q's R. to K's sq.

14. Q. takes R. (ch.) — 14. Kt. to Q's sq.
15. P. to K's 5th. — 15. P. to Q. B's 3rd.

And Black has a winning advantage.

GAME THE THIRD.

WHITE.	BLACK.
1. P. to K's 4th.	1. P. to K's 4th.
2. Kt. to K. B's 3rd.	2. Kt. to Q. B's 3rd.
3. P. to Q's 4th.	3. P. takes P.

BLACK.

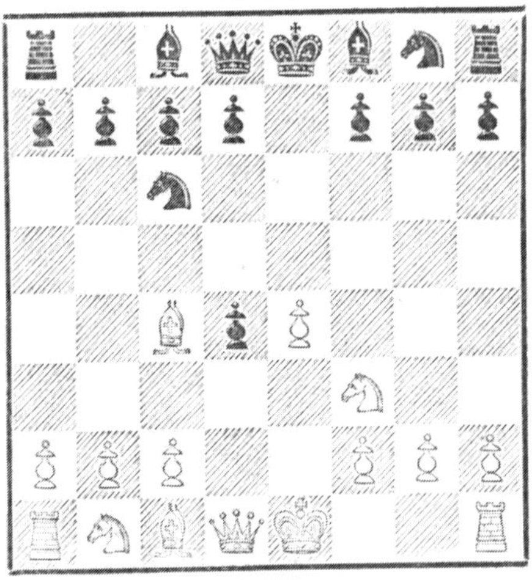

WHITE.

Position prior to Black's 4th Move.

4. B. to Q. B's 4th.	4. B. to Q. Kt.'s 5th (ch.)

(For the effect of 4. ——— / Kt. to K. B's 3rd, and 4. ——— / P. to Q's 3rd, and 4. ——— / Q. to K. B's 3rd, see Variation A.)

5. P. to Q. B's 3rd.	5. P. takes P.
6. Castles.	

Mr. Cochrane introduced the following line of play here :—

6. $\frac{\text{P. takes P.}}{\text{B. to Q. R's 4th}}$, 7. $\frac{\text{P. to K's 5th}}{\text{P. to Q's 4th}}$, 8. $\frac{\text{B. takes P.}}{\text{K's Kt. to K's 2nd}}$,
9. $\frac{\text{B. takes Kt. (ch.)}}{\text{Kt. takes B.}}$, the game is about equal.

6. P. to Q. B's 7th.

(If 6. $\frac{}{\text{P. takes P.}}$, White retakes with Bishop, and speedily obtains the better game.)

7. Q. takes Q. B's P.	7. P. to Q's 3rd.
8. P. to Q. R's 3rd.	8. B. to Q. R's 4th.
9. P. to Q. Kt.'s 4th.	9. B. to Q. Kt.'s 3rd (best).
10. B. to Q. Kt.'s 2nd.	10. Kt. to K. B's 3rd.

Equal game.

Variation A.

Position prior to Black's 4th Move.

In the first place:—

WHITE.	BLACK.
	4. Kt. to K. B's 3rd.
5. Kt. takes P.	5. Kt. takes P.

6. B. takes P. (ch.)	6. K. takes B.
7. Q. to K. R's 5th (ch.)	7. P. to Kt.'s 3rd.
8. Q. to Q's 5th (ch.)	8. K. to Kt.'s 2nd.
9. Kt. takes Kt.	9. Q. to K's sq.

There is little or no advantage on either side.

In the second place :—

	4. P. to Q's 3rd.
5. P. to Q. B's 3rd.	

(Preferable, I think, to Castling; for suppose,—5. $\frac{\text{Castles}}{\text{P. to Q's 3rd}}$, 6. $\frac{\text{P. to Q. B's 3rd}}{\text{B. to K. Kt.'s 5th}}$, and Black will have the better position.)

	5. Kt. to K. B's 3rd.
6. P. to K's 5th.	6. P. to Q's 4th.

And the position is one in the *Giuoco Piano*, without any superiority for either party.

In the third place :—

	4. Q. to K. B's 3rd.

A favourite defence with Mr. McDonnell, who adopted it, not always unsuccessfully, against his great compeer, Labourdonnais.

5. Castles.	5. P. to Q's 3rd.

(If 5. $\frac{}{\text{B. to Q. B's 4th}}$, 6. $\frac{\text{P. to K's 5th}}{\text{Q. to Kt.'s 3rd}}$, 7. $\frac{\text{R. to K's sq.}}{}$, threatening to win the Queen next move.)

6. P. to Q. B's 3rd.	6. P. to Q's 6th (best.)
7. Q. takes P.	7. Q. to Kt.'s 3rd.
8. B. to K. B's 4th.	8. B. to K's 2nd.
9. Q's Kt. to Q's 2nd.	9. Kt. to K. R's 3rd
10. Q's R. to K's sq.	10. Castles.
11. Kt. to Q's 4th.	11. Kt. to K's 4th.
12. B. takes Kt.	12. P. takes P.
13. K's Kt. to K. B's 3rd.	13. B. to Q's 3rd.

White's game has a little more freedom, but the advantage in this respect is trifling.

Game the Fourth.

WHITE.	BLACK.
1. P. to K's 4th.	1. P. to K's 4th.
2. Kt. to K. B's 3rd.	2. Kt. to Q. B's 3rd.
3. P. to Q's 4th.	3. P. takes P.
4. Kt. takes P.	

Black has now the choice of two lines of play, viz.:—

4. $\frac{\quad}{\text{Q. to K. R's 5th}}$, and 4. $\frac{\quad}{\text{B. to Q. B's 4th}}$.

In the first place:—

4. Q. to K. R's 5th.

He may also take Knight with Knight at once. The move in the text, however, is more insidious and attacking, and leads to some fine combinations.

5. Kt. to Q. Kt.'s 5th.

This remarkably ingenious reply to Black's counter-attack we owe to Mr. Horwitz. Before his introduction of this move, White's answer usually was—5. $\frac{\text{Q. to Q's 3rd}}{\quad}$, and the game proceeded:—5. $\frac{\text{Q. to Q's 3rd}}{\text{Kt. to K. B's 3rd}}$, 6. $\frac{\text{Kt. to Q's 2nd (best.)}}{\text{Kt. takes Kt.}}$. (If 6. $\frac{\quad}{\text{B. to Q. B's 4th}}$, 7. $\frac{\text{P. to K. Kt.'s 3rd}}{\quad}$.) 7. $\frac{\text{Q. takes Kt.}}{\text{P. to Q's 4th}}$, 8. $\frac{\text{P. to K. Kt.'s 3rd}}{\text{Q. to K. Kt.'s 5th}}$, 9. $\frac{\text{B. to K's 2nd}}{\text{Q. to Q's 2nd}}$, 10. $\frac{\text{P. to K's 5th}}{\quad}$, &c. Or if White replied with 5. $\frac{\text{Kt. to Q. B's 3rd}}{\quad}$, the game then proceeding,—5. $\frac{\quad}{\text{B. to Q. Kt.'s 5th}}$, 6. $\frac{\text{Q. to Q's 3rd}}{\text{B. takes Kt. (ch.)}}$, 7. $\frac{\text{P. takes B.}}{\text{Kt. to K. B's 3rd}}$, the advantage being still on the side of Black.*

---

* In addition to these moves, Mr. G. B. Fraser, of Dundee, has suggested the ingenious move of 5. $\frac{\text{Kt. to K. B's 3rd}}{\quad}$. In this case the best continuation is, apparently,—

	5. B. to Q. Kt.'s 5th (ch.)

Some of the German authorities recommend 5. $\frac{\quad}{\text{B. to Q. B's 4th}}$ as a good defence, I think erroneously: for example:—

5. $\frac{\quad}{\text{B. to Q. B's 4th}}$, 6. $\frac{\text{Q. to K. B's 3rd}}{\text{Kt. to Q's 5th}}$, 7. $\frac{\text{Kt. takes P. (ch.)}}{\text{K. to Q's sq.}}$, 8. $\frac{\text{Q. to K. B's 4th}}{\text{Kt. takes P. (ch.)}}$, 9. $\frac{\text{K. to Q's sq.}}{\text{Q. takes Q.}}$, 10. $\frac{\text{B. takes Q.}}{\quad}$, and certainly White has the advantage.

6. B. to Q's 2nd.	6. Q. takes K's P. (ch.)

It is worthy of remark that Black's last two moves cannot be safely transposed, although at first sight it would seem that they might be played indifferently; *e.g.*:—

5. $\frac{\quad}{\text{Q. takes K's P. (ch.)}}$, 6. $\frac{\text{B. to K's 3rd (best.)}}{\text{B. to Q. Kt.'s 5th (ch.)}}$, 7. $\frac{\text{Kt. to Q's 2nd}}{\quad}$, and White has the superiority. At one time some of the German writers gave 5. $\frac{\quad}{\text{Q. takes P. (ch.)}}$, followed by 6. $\frac{\quad}{\text{K. to Q's sq.}}$, but this is inferior.

7. B. to K's 2nd.	7. K. to Q's sq.
8. Castles.	8. B. takes B.
9. Kt. takes B.	9. Q. to K. B's 5th.

---

5. Kt. to K. B's 3rd.	5. Q. takes K's P. (ch.)
6. B. to K's 2nd.	6. B. to Q. Kt.'s 5th (ch.)

If he play 6. $\frac{\quad}{\text{B. to Q. B's 4th}}$, or 6. $\frac{\quad}{\text{P. to Q's 4th}}$, White replies with 7. $\frac{\text{Castles}}{\quad}$; and if 6. $\frac{\quad}{\text{Kt. to Q. Kt.'s 5th}}$, with 7. $\frac{\text{Kt. to Q. R's 3rd}}{\quad}$, &c.

7. P. to Q. B's 3rd.	7. B. to Q. B's 4th.

Better than 7. $\frac{\quad}{\text{B. to K's 2nd}}$ on account of 8. $\frac{\text{Castles}}{\quad}$, &c.

8. Castles.	8. K's Kt. to K's 2nd.
9. R. to K's sq.	

&c.—[Ed.]

This move, which first occurred in the game by correspondence between the clubs of London and Vienna, is stronger than the old line of play,—9. $\frac{\quad}{\text{Q. to K. R's 4th}}$.

10. P. to Q. B's 4th.

White has a good game, but Black is a Pawn ahead.

In the second place :—

	4. B. to Q. B's 4th.
5. B. to K's 3rd (best.)	5. Q. to K. B's 3rd (best.)
6. P. to Q. B's 3rd.	6. K's Kt. to K's 2nd.
7. B. to K's 2nd.	

White's best reply, we believe; but he may also play 7. B. to Q. B's 4th, and 7. P. to K. B's 4th, which we will briefly dispose of.

Firstly :—7. $\frac{\text{B. to Q. B's 4th}}{\text{Castles.}}$, 8. $\frac{\text{Castles}}{\text{Q's Kt. to K's 4th}}$, 9. $\frac{\text{B. to Q. Kt.'s 3rd}}{\text{P. to Q's 3rd}}$, even game.

Secondly :—7. $\frac{\text{P. to K. B's 4th}}{\text{Q. to K. Kt.'s 3rd (best.)}}$, 8. $\frac{\text{Q. to K. B's 3rd}}{\text{Kt. takes Kt.}}$, 9. $\frac{\text{P. takes Kt.}}{\text{B. to Q. Kt.'s 5th (ch.)}}$, 10. $\frac{\text{Kt. to Q. B's 3rd}}{\text{P. to Q's 4th}}$, 11. $\frac{\text{P. to K's 5th}}{\quad}$, and the game is about equal.

	7. P. to Q's 4th (best.)
8. B. to K. B's 3rd.	8. P. takes P.
9. B. takes P.	9. B. takes Kt. (best.)
10. P. takes B.	10. Castles.

Even game.

Game the Fifth.

WHITE.	BLACK.
1. P. to K's 4th.	1. P. to K's 4th.
2. Kt. to K. B's 3rd.	2. Kt. to Q. B's 3rd.
3. P. to Q's 4th.	3. P. takes P.
4. B. to Q. B's 4th.	4. B. to Q. B's 4th.
5. Kt. to K. Kt.'s 5th.	5. Kt. to K. R's 3rd.

If Black play Kt. to K's 4th, he loses more ground; *e.g.*:—

5. $\frac{\quad}{\text{Kt. to K's 4th}}$, 6. $\frac{\text{Kt. takes B's P.}}{\text{Kt. takes Kt.}}$, 7. $\frac{\text{B. takes Kt. (ch.)}}{\text{K. takes B.}}$,

8. $\frac{\text{Q. to K. R's 5th (ch.)}}{\text{P. to K. Kt.'s 3rd}}$, 9. $\frac{\text{Q. takes B.}}{\quad}$ &c.

6. Kt. takes B's P.

(For 6. $\frac{\text{Q. to K. R's 5th}}{\quad}$, see Variation A.)

6. Kt. takes. Kt.

7. B. takes Kt. (ch.) — 7. K. takes B.
8. Q. to K. R's 5th (ch.) — 8. P. to K. Kt.'s 3rd (ch.)
9. Q. takes B. — 9. P. to Q's 4th.

(If 9. $\frac{\quad}{\text{P. to Q's 3rd}}$, 10. $\frac{\text{Q. to Q. Kt.'s 5th}}{\text{R. to K's sq.}}$, 11. $\frac{\text{Castles}}{\text{R. takes P.}}$, 12. $\frac{\text{Q. to Q's 3rd}}{\quad}$. I should take Black's game for choice.)

10. Castles.

(If 10. $\frac{\text{Q. takes P. (ch.)}}{\text{Q. takes Q.}}$, 11. $\frac{\text{P. takes Q.}}{\text{R. to K's sq. (ch.)}}$, 12. $\frac{\text{K. to Q's sq.}}{\text{Kt. to Kt.'s 5th}}$, Black has the advantage.

Again, if 10. $\frac{\text{P. takes P.}}{\text{R. to K's sq. (ch.)}}$, 11. $\frac{\text{K. to Q's sq.}}{\text{Kt. to Kt.'s 4th}}$, 12. $\frac{\text{P. to Q. B's 4th}}{\text{Q. to K. R's 4th}}$, 13. $\frac{\text{Q. to Q. R's 3rd}}{\text{B. to K. Kt.'s 5th}}$, Black's position is superior to his adversary's.)

10. P. takes P.

11. P. to Q. B's 3rd.

This is the only way by which White can prevent his opponent maintaining the centre Pawns.

11. B. to K's 3rd.

Advancing the Queen's Pawn would evidently lose him the other Pawn, as White could give check at Q. B's 4th, and then take it.

12. P. takes P. — 12. Q. takes P.
13. Q. to Q. Kt.'s 5th.

It is not easy to determine which side has the advantage.

VARIATION A.

BLACK.

WHITE.

Position prior to White's 6th Move.

WHITE.	BLACK.
6. Q. to K. R's 5th.	

(This move—the invention of which is attributed, though erroneously, I believe, to Count Vitzhum—requires some nicety in answering.)

6. Q. to K's 2nd.

(If 6. $\frac{\text{————}}{\text{Q. to K. B's 3rd}}$, 7. $\frac{\text{P. to K. B's 4th}}{\text{P. to Q's 3rd}}$, 8. $\frac{\text{P. to K. R's 3rd}}{\text{Castles}}$. 9. $\frac{\text{Castles}}{\text{B. to K's 3rd}}$, 10. $\frac{\text{B. to Q's 3rd}}{\text{Q. to K. Kt.'s 3rd}}$, 11. $\frac{\text{Q. to K. R's 4th}}{\text{————}}$, White has a freer game.)

WHITE.	BLACK.
7. Castles.	7. P. to Q's 3rd.
8. P. to K. R's 3rd.	8. B. to Q's 2nd.
9. P. to K. B's 4th.	9. Castles (Q's side).

And Black has gained a Pawn without loss of situation.

ILLUSTRATIVE GAMES.

Game I.—Between Mr. Paulsen and an Amateur.

White (Mr. P.)	Black (Mr. —.)
1. P. to K's 4th.	1. P. to K's 4th.
2. Kt. to K. B's 3rd.	2. Kt. to Q. B's 3rd.
3. P. to Q's 4th.	3. P. takes P.
4. B. to Q. B's 4th.	4. B. to Q. Kt.'s 5th (ch.)
5. P. to Q. B's 3rd.	5. P. takes P.
6. Castles.	6. P. takes P.*
7. Q's B. takes P.	7. B. to K. B's sq.†
8. Kt. to Q. B's 3rd.	8. B. to K's 2nd.
9. Kt. to Q's 5th.	9. Kt. to K. B's 3rd.
10. Kt. to K. Kt.'s 5th.‡	10. Castles.
11. Kt. to K. B's 4th.	11. P. to Q's 3rd.§
12. B. takes Kt.	12. B. takes B.
13. Kt. takes K. R's P.	13. B. takes R.
14. Q. to K. R's 5th.	14. Kt. to K's 4th.
15. Kt. to K. Kt.'s 5th.	15. R. to K's sq.
16. Kt. takes K. B's P.	16. Kt. takes Kt.

And White mated in two moves.

Game II.—Between Messrs. Kolisch and Anderssen.

White (Mr. K.)	Black (Mr. A.)
1. P. to K's 4th.	1. P. to K's 4th.
2. Kt. to K. B's 3rd.	2. Kt. to Q. B's 3rd.
3. P. to Q's 4th.	3. P. takes P.

---

* This second capture is not to be commended.

† The best move at this point is, perhaps, 7. K. to B's sq., but in any case Black has a very embarrassed game.

‡ Well played.

§ Had he moved 11. P. to K. R's 3rd, the following is probable:—

	11. P. to K. R's 3rd.
12. Kt. takes B's P.	12. R. takes Kt.
13. B. takes R.	13. K. takes B.
14. P. to K's 5th.	

With a winning attack.

4. B. to Q. B's 4th.	4. B. to Q. B's 4th.
5. Castles.	5. P. to Q's 3rd.
6. P. to Q. B's 3rd.	6. B. to K. Kt.'s 5th.*
7. Q. to Q. Kt.'s 3rd.	7. B. takes Kt.
8. B. takes B's P. (ch.)	8. K. to B's sq.
9. B. takes Kt.	9. R. takes B.
10. P. takes B.	10. P. to K. Kt.'s 4th.†
11. Q. to Q's sq.	11. Q. to Q's 2nd.
12. P. to Q. Kt.'s 4th.	12. B. to Q. Kt.'s 3rd.
13. B. to Q. Kt.'s 2nd.	13. P. to Q's 6th.
14. Q. takes P.‡	14. Kt. to K's 4th.
15. Q. to K's 2nd.	15. Q. to K. R's 6th.
16. Kt. to Q's 2nd.	16. P. to K. Kt.'s 5th.

† Game III.—Between Messrs. Maczuski and Kolisch.

White (Mr. M.)	Black (Mr. K.)
1. P. to K's 4th.	1. P. to K's 4th.
2. Kt. to K. B's 3rd.	2. Kt. to Q. B's 3rd.
3. P. to Q's 4th.	3. P. takes P.
4. Kt. takes P.	4. Q. to K. R's 5th.
5. Kt. to Q. B's 3rd.	5. B. to Q. Kt.'s 5th.
6. Q. to Q's 3rd.	6. Kt. to K. B's 3rd.§
7. Kt. takes Q's Kt.	7. Q's P. takes Kt.
8. B. to Q's 2nd.	8. B. takes Kt.
9. B. takes B.	9. Kt. takes K's P.
10. Q. to Q's 4th.	10. Q. to K's 2nd.
11. Castles (Q's R.)	11. Q. to K. Kt.'s 4th (ch.)
12. P. to K. B's 4th.	12. Q. takes P. (ch.)
13. B. to Q's 2nd.	13. Q. to K. Kt.'s 5th.
14. Q. to Q's 8th (ch.)‖	14. K. takes Q.
15. B. to K. Kt.'s 5th (dis. ch.)	15. K. moves.
16. R. mates.	

---

* This move, the invention of Anderssen, is far superior to the old play of 6. Kt. to K. B's 3rd.

† The *coup juste*.

‡ He might have prolonged the game for a considerable time by 14. Kt. to Q's 2nd.

§ The correct move is 6. B. takes Kt.

‖ A piquant finish.

GAME IV.—Between Messrs. Macdonnell and Wisker.

WHITE (Mr. M.)	BLACK (Mr. W.)
1. P. to K's 4th.	1. P. to K's 4th.
2. Kt. to K. B's 3rd.	2. Kt. to Q. B's 3rd.
3. P. to Q's 4th.	3. P. takes P.
4. Kt. takes P.	4. Q. to K. R's 5th.
5. Kt. to Q. Kt.'s 5th.	5. B. to Q. Kt.'s 5th (ch.)
6. B. to Q's 2nd.	6. Q. takes K's P. (ch.)
7. B. to K's 2nd.	7. K. to Q's sq.
8. Castles.	8. B. takes B.
9. Kt. takes B.	9. Q. to K. B's 5th.*
10. P. to Q. R's 4th.†	10. P. to Q. R's 3rd.
11. P. to K. Kt.'s 3rd.	11. Q. to K. B's 3rd.
12. Kt. to Q. B's 3rd.	12. Kt. to K. R's 3rd.
13. R. to Q. Kt.'s sq.	13. R. to K's sq.
14. Q's Kt. to K's 4th.	14. Q. to K. B's 4th.
15. B. to Q's 3rd.‡	15. Kt. to K's 4th.
16. P. to K. B's 3rd.	16. Kt. takes B.
17. Q. takes Kt.	17. P. to Q's 3rd.
18. P. to Q. Kt.'s 4th.	18. P. to Q. Kt.'s 3rd
19. Q's R. to Q's sq.	19. R. to K's 3rd.
20. P. to K. Kt.'s 4th.	20. Q. to K. Kt.'s 3rd.
21. Kt. to Q's 5th.§	21. Kt. takes Kt.'s P.
22. K. to R's sq.	22. B. to Q. Kt.'s 2nd.‖
23. Kt. to K. B's 4th.	23. Q. takes Kt.
24. P. takes Q.	24. B. takes P. (ch.)
25. K. to Kt.'s sq.¶	25. B. takes Q.
26. Kt. takes R. (ch.)	26. P. takes Kt.
27. R. to B's 8th (ch.)	27. K. to K's 2nd.
28. R. takes R.	28. B. takes Q. B's P.

---

* A move first tried in the game by correspondence between London and Vienna, and superior, we think, to Q. to K. R's 4th.

† We prefer P. to Q. B's 4th.

‡ This Bishop ought to have been played to K. B's 3rd.

§ A slip which costs a Pawn.

‖ The commencement of a flashy combination which loses the game.

¶ The correct reply.

29. R. to Q. B's sq.	29. B. takes R's P.
30. R. takes P. (ch.)	30. K. to B's 3rd.
31. R. takes Q. R's P.	

And wins.

GAME V.—Between Messrs. Bourn and Charleton.

WHITE (Mr. B.)	BLACK (Mr. C.)
1. P. to K's 4th.	1. P. to K's 4th.
2. Kt. to K. B's 3rd.	2. Kt. to Q. B's 3rd.
3. P. to Q's 4th.	3. P. takes P.
4. Kt. takes P.	4. B. to Q. B's 4th.
5. B. to K's 3rd.	5. Q. to K. B's 3rd.
6. P. to Q. B's 3rd.	6. K's Kt. to K's 2nd.
7. B. to K's 2nd.*	7. P. to Q's 4th.
8. B. to K. B's 3rd.	8. P. takes P.
9. B. takes P.	9. Kt. to K's 4th.
10. P. to K. B's 4th.	10. B. to K's 3rd.†
11. Kt. takes B.	11. Q. takes Kt.
12. B. takes B.	12. Kt. to Q's 2nd.
13. Q. to Q. R's 4th.	13. P. to Q. Kt.'s 4th.
14. Q. to Q's 4th.	14. Kt. takes B.
15. Kt. to Q's 2nd.	15. Kt. to Q. R's 5th.
16. Castles (K's R.)	16. R. to Q's sq.
17. Q. to K. B's 2nd.	17. Kt. takes Q. Kt.'s P.
18. K's R. to K's sq.	18. Q. to Q. Kt.'s 3rd.
19. Q. takes Q.	19. B's P. takes Q.
20. Kt. to K. B's 3rd.	20. Kt. to Q's 6th.
21. B. takes Kt.	21. R. takes B.
22. Kt. to Q's 4th.	22. R. takes Kt.‡
23. P. takes R.	23. K. to Q's 2nd.
24. Q's R. to Q. Kt.'s sq.	24. P. to Q. R's 3rd.
25. P. to Q. R's 4th.§	25. Kt. to Q's 4th.

* If White play at this point 7. P. to K. B's 4th, Black rejoins with 7. Q. to K. Kt.'s 3rd.

† This combination, by which Black gives up a piece for the moment, is highly ingenious and original.

‡ We do not at all see the necessity of giving up the exchange.

§ The winning move, breaking up the adverse Pawns. Mr. Bourn has played the game with commendable care and correctness throughout.

26. P. takes P.	26. Kt. to Q. B's 6th.
27. P. takes P.	27. Kt. takes R.
28. R. takes Kt.	28. K. to B's 3rd.
29. K. to B's 2nd.	29. R. to Q. R's sq.
30. R. to Q. R's sq.	30. P. to Q. Kt.'s 4th.
31. K. to K's 3rd.	31. P. to K. B's 4th.
32. R. to Q. B's sq. (ch.)	32. K. to Kt.'s 3rd.
33. P. to Q's 5th.	33. K. takes P.
34. R. to Q. R's sq. (ch.)	34. K. to Kt.'s 2nd.
35. R. takes R.	35. K. takes R.
36. K. to Q's 4th.	36. K. to Kt.'s 2nd.
37. K. to B's 5th.	37. K. to B's 2nd.
38. K. takes P.	

And Black resigned.

GAME VI.—Between Messrs. De Vere and Duffy in consultation against Mr. Staunton.

WHITE (Mr. S.)	BLACK (Messrs. De V. and D.)
1. P. to K's 4th.	1. P. to K's 4th.
2. Kt. to K. B's 3rd.	2. Kt. to Q. B's 3rd.
3. P. to Q's 4th.	3. P. takes P.
4. B. to Q. B's 4th.	4. B. to Q. B's 4th.
5. Kt. to K. Kt.'s 5th.	5. Kt. to K. R's 3rd.
6. Kt. takes B's P.	6. Kt. takes Kt.
7. B. takes Kt. (ch.)	7. K. takes B.
8. Q. to K. R's 5th (ch.)	8. P. to K. Kt.'s 3rd.
9. Q. to Q's 5th (ch.)*	9. K. to Kt.'s 2nd.
10. Q. takes B.	10. R. to K's sq.†
11. P. to K. B's 3rd.	11. R. to K's 4th.
12. Q. to Q. R's 3rd.‡	12. Q. to R's 5th (ch.)
13. P. to K. Kt.'s 3rd.	13. R. takes P. (ch.)

* We greatly prefer capturing the Bishop at once to this check.

† This move was first introduced by Mr. Staunton in a game playd by him against Messrs. Wayte and Ranken in consultation. In the *partie* referred to, the allies Castled in reply, leaving the King's Pawn to be taken; but in the present case, Mr. Staunton, defending himself against his own move, attempts to protect the Pawn, not very successfully, by P. to K. B's 3rd.

‡ The usual move at this point is 12. Q. to Q. B's 4th.

14. K. to K. B's 2nd.	14. Q. to K. B's 3rd.
15. B. to K. Kt.'s 5th.	15. Q. takes B.*
16. P. takes R.	16. P. to Q's 3rd.
17. K. to Kt.'s 2nd.	17. Q. to K. Kt.'s 5th.
18. R. to K's sq.	18. Kt. to K's 4th.
19. Kt. to Q's 2nd.	19. Q. to K. R's 4th.
20. K. to R's sq.	20. B. to Q's 2nd.†
21. Q. to Q. Kt.'s 4th.	21. P. to Q. B's 4th.
22. Q. takes Q. Kt.'s P.	22. R. to K. B's sq.
23. R. to K. B's sq.	23. R. takes R. (ch.)
24. R. takes R.	24. Q. to K's 7th.
25. Q. to Q. Kt.'s 8th.	25. Kt. to K. B's 2nd.
26. Q. takes Q. R's P.	26. B. to K's 3rd.
27. Q. to K's 7th.	27. Q. to K. Kt.'s 5th.‡
28. Q. to K. B's 6th (ch.)	28. K. to Kt.'s sq.
29. P. to Q. R's 4th.	29. P. to Q's 4th.
30. Kt. to K. B's 3rd.	30. P. to K. R's 4th.
31. Kt. to K. Kt.'s 5th.	

And Black resigned.

GAME VII.—Played by correspondence between the Chess Clubs of Edinburgh and Dundee.

WHITE (Edinburgh).	BLACK (Dundee).
1. P. to K's 4th.	1. P. to K's 4th.
2. Kt. to K. B's 3rd.	2. Kt. to Q. B's 3rd.
3. P. to Q's 4th.	3. P. takes P.
4. B. to Q. B's 4th.	4. B. to Q. B's 4th.
5. Kt. to K. Kt.'s 5th.	5. Kt. to K. R's 3rd.
6. Castles.	6. P. to Q's 3rd.
7. P. to K. R's 3rd.	7. B. to Q's 2nd.
8. P. to Q. B's 3rd.	8. Q. to K. B's 3rd.
9. K. to R's sq.	9. Castles (Q's R.)
10. P. to K. B's 4th.	10. B. to K's sq.
11. P. to Q. Kt.'s 4th.	11. B. to Q. Kt.'s 3rd.

* Black now gives up the "exchange," but in return obtains a smart attack.

† This Bishop ought to have been played, we think, to K. R's 6th.

‡ Had they played B. to K. B's 4th, White would have answered with P. to K. Kt.'s 4th, winning a piece.

12. Q. to Q. Kt.'s 3rd.*	12. Kt. to K. Kt.'s 5th.
13. P. to Q. R's 4th.	13. P. to Q's 6th.
14. Kt. takes B's P.	14. Kt. to B's 7th (ch.)
15. K. to R's 2nd.	15. B. takes Kt.
16. B. takes B.	16. P. to Q's 4th.
17. P. takes P.	17. Kt. to Kt.'s 5th (ch.)
18. K. to Kt.'s 3rd.†	18. Q. takes B.
19. P. takes Kt.	19. P. to K. R's 4th.
20. P. to Q. R's 5th.	20. P. takes Kt.'s P.
21. Q. to Q's sq.‡	21. Kt. to K's 2nd.
22. P. to K. B's 5th.	22. Q. to K. B's 3rd.
23. P. to Q. B's 4th.	23. Kt. takes P. (ch.)

And White resigned.

---

* This is not a good move.

† The best reply.

‡ If P. takes B., Black replies with 21. Q. to K. R's 4th. The whole of the game is beautifully managed by the Dundee players.

CHAPTER V.

The Two Knights' Defence.

$$1.\ \frac{\text{P. to K's 4th}}{\text{P. to K's 4th}},\quad 2.\ \frac{\text{Kt. to K. B's 3rd}}{\text{Kt. to Q. B's 3rd}},\quad 3.\ \frac{\text{B. to Q. B's 4th}}{\text{Kt. to K. B's 3rd}}.$$

Game the First.

$$4.\ \frac{\text{Kt. to K. Kt.'s 5th}}{\text{- - - - - - - -}}$$

Game the Second.

$$4.\ \frac{\text{Kt. to Kt.'s 5th}}{\text{P. to Q's 4th}},\quad 5.\ \frac{\text{P. takes P.}}{\text{Kt. to Q. R's 4th}},\quad 6.\ \frac{\text{P. to Q's 3rd}}{\text{- - - - - -}}$$

Game the Third.

$$4.\ \frac{\text{P. to Q's 4th}}{\text{- - - - - -}};\quad 4.\ \frac{\text{Castles}}{\text{- - - -}};\quad 4.\ \frac{\text{Kt. to Q. B's 3rd}}{\text{- - - - - - -}};$$

$$4.\ \frac{\text{Q. to K's 2nd.}}{\text{- - - - - -}}$$

Game the Fourth.

$$4.\ \frac{\text{- - - - - -}}{\text{Kt. takes P.}}$$

The opening before us is of considerable antiquity, it being found in the treatise of Gianutio, 1597, by whom it is said to have been invented. It is an offshoot, but an extremely important one, from the *Giuoco Piano*, and deserves every consideration, since it enables the second player to avoid the attack of the *Evans-Gambit*, and, in the opinion of many authorities, to nullify the advantage of the first move.

Game the First.

WHITE.	BLACK.
1. P. to K's 4th.	1. P. to K's 4th.
2. Kt. to K. B's 3rd.	2. Kt. to Q. B's 3rd.
3. B. to Q. B's 4th.	3. Kt. to K. B's 3rd.

This gives the title to the opening. Black instead of bringing into the field a Bishop and a Knight, like his adversary, deploys his two Knights.

4. Kt. to K. Kt.'s 5th.

This is thought to be the strongest move for attack. The consequences of 4. $\frac{\text{P. to Q's 4th}}{\quad}$, 4. $\frac{\text{Castles}}{\quad}$, 4. $\frac{\text{Kt. to Q. B's 3rd}}{\quad}$, and 4. $\frac{\text{Q. to K's 2nd}}{\quad}$, shall be briefly shown in Game the Third.

4. P. to Q's 4th.

Black may also play 4. $\frac{\quad}{\text{Kt. takes P.}}$, for the result of which the reader is referred to Game the Fourth.

5. P. takes P.	5. Kt. to Q. R's 4th (best).

The customary course of defence, till of late years, was for Black to take the Pawn with his Knight, the game proceeding thus :—5. $\frac{\quad}{\text{Kt. takes P.}}$, 6. $\frac{\text{Kt. takes K. B's P.}}{\text{K. takes Kt.}}$, 7. $\frac{\text{Q. to K. B's 3rd (ch.)}}{\text{K. to K's 3rd}}$, 8. $\frac{\text{Kt. to Q. B's 3rd}}{\text{Q's Kt. to K's 2nd (best)}}$. (If 8. $\frac{\quad}{\text{Kt. to Q. Kt.'s 5th}}$, 9. $\frac{\text{Q. to K's 4th}}{\text{P. to Q. B's 3rd}}$, 10. $\frac{\text{P. to Q. R's 3rd}}{\quad}$, and White has the advantage.) 9. $\frac{\text{P. to Q's 4th}}{\text{P. to Q. B's 3rd}}$, 10. $\frac{\text{B. to K. Kt.'s 5th}}{\text{Q. to Q. R's 4th}}$. Black has not a good game, and he comes off still worse, it will be found, if he play 10. $\frac{\text{P. to Q. Kt.'s 4th}}{}$, 10. $\frac{\text{P. to K. R's 3rd}}{}$, or 10. $\frac{\text{K. to Q's 2nd}}{}$

6. B. to Q. Kt.'s 5th (ch.)

(For 6. $\frac{\text{P. to Q's 3rd}}{}$, see Game the Second.)

6. P. to Q. B's 3rd (best).

If 6. $\frac{}{\text{B. to Q's 2nd}}$, 7. $\frac{\text{Q. to K's 2nd}}{\text{B. to Q's 3rd}}$, 8. $\frac{\text{B. takes B. (ch.)}}{\text{Q. takes B.}}$, 9. $\frac{\text{P. to Q. B's 4th}}{}$, and White has seemingly the best of the battle.

7. P. takes P. — 7. P. takes P.

8. Q. to K. B's 3rd.

(For the result of 8. $\frac{\text{B. to K's 2nd}}{}$, see Variation A.)

He may also play 8. $\frac{\text{B. to Q. R's 4th}}{}$, which we will briefly examine,—8. $\frac{\text{B. to Q. R's 4th}}{\text{P. to K. R's 3rd}}$, 9. $\frac{\text{Kt. to K. B's 3rd}}{\text{P. to K's 5th}}$, 10. $\frac{\text{Q. to K's 2nd}}{\text{B. to Q. B's 4th}}$, 11. $\frac{\text{Castles}}{\text{Castles}}$, 12. $\frac{\text{Kt. to K's sq.}}{\text{Q. to Q. Kt.'s 3rd}}$, White has an unenviable position.

8. Q. to Q. Kt.'s 3rd.

Opinions differ as to whether this or 8. $\frac{}{\text{Q. to Q. B's 2nd}}$ is most to Black's profit. I prefer the move in the text. If 8. $\frac{}{\text{Q. to Q. B's 2nd}}$, 9. $\frac{\text{B. to Q. R's 4th}}{\text{B. to Q's 3rd}}$, 10. $\frac{\text{P. to Q's 3rd}}{\text{Castles}}$, 11. $\frac{\text{Castles}}{\text{P. to K. R's 3rd}}$, 12. $\frac{\text{Kt. to K's 4th}}{\text{Kt. takes Kt.}}$, and Black cannot claim to have any advantage, I think.

BLACK.

WHITE.

Position prior to White's 9th Move.

9. B. to Q. R's 4th.

If he play 9. B. to K's 2nd / ——, Black rejoins also with 9. —— / B. to K's 2nd.

	9. B. to K. Kt.'s 5th.
10. Q. to K. Kt.'s 3rd (best).	10. P. to K. R's 3rd.
11. Kt. to K. R's 3rd (best).	

If 11. Kt. to K. B's 3rd / Castles, 12. Kt. to Q. B's 3rd / P. to K's 5th, 13. Kt. to K's 5th / ——. (If 13. Q's Kt. takes P. / Q's R. to K's sq., 14. Kt. to K's 5th / B. to K. B's 4th, 15. P. to K. B's 3rd / Kt. to K. R's 4th, and Black's game is far preferable.) 13. —— / B. to Q's 3rd, 14. P. to K. R's 3rd / B. to K. B's 4th, and White must lose a piece.

	11. B. to Q's 3rd.
12. Castles (best)	12. Castles (Q's side.)
13. Kt. to Q. B's 3rd.	

If 13. P. to Q's 3rd / P. to K's 5th, 14. Q. to K's 3rd / Q. to Q. B's 2nd, 15. P. takes P. / B. takes P. (ch.),

16. $\frac{\text{K. to R's sq.}}{\text{B. to K's 4th}}$, 17. $\frac{\text{Kt. to Q. B's 3rd}}{\text{B. to Q's 5th}}$, 18. $\frac{\text{Q. to Q's 3rd}}{\text{K. to Kt.'s 2nd}}$, Black for choice. Again, if 13. $\frac{\text{Q. to K's 3rd}}{\text{Q. to Q. B's 2nd}}$, 14. $\frac{\text{P. to Q's 3rd}}{\text{Kt. to Q's 4th}}$, Black has the better position.

	13. P. to K's 5th.
14. Q. to K's 3rd.	14. Q. to Q. B's 2nd.
15. Kt. takes K's P.	15. B. takes P. (ch.)
16. K. to R's sq.	16. K's R. to K's sq.

And White must lose.

Variation A.

BLACK

WHITE.

Position after White's 8th Move.

8. B. to K's 2nd.

The German writers unanimously pronounce this retreat to be White's strongest line of play.

	8. P. to K. R's 3rd.
9. Kt. to K. B's 3rd.	9. P. to K's 5th.
10. Kt. to K's 5th.	10. Q. to Q's 5th.
11. Kt. to K. Kt.'s 4th.	

The best move according to the *Handbuch*. The authors of *Theorie und Praxis*, however, prefer 11. $\frac{\text{P. to K. B's 4th}}{}$, and continue—11. $\frac{\text{P. to K. B's 4th}}{\text{B. to Q. B's 4th}}$, 12. $\frac{\text{R. to K. B's sq.}}{\text{B. to Q's 3rd}}$, 13. $\frac{\text{P. to Q. B's 3rd}}{\text{Q. to Q. Kt.'s 3rd}}$, 14. $\frac{\text{Q. to Q. R's 4th}}{\text{B. to Q's 2nd}}$, 15. $\frac{\text{Kt. takes B.}}{\text{K. takes Kt.}}$, and White is said to have a slight advantage on account of his extra Pawn.

	11. B. takes Kt. (best).
12. B. takes B.	12. Kt. to Q. B's 5th.

The German authorities denounce 12. $\frac{}{\text{P. to K's 6th}}$, which would lead to the following:—12. $\frac{}{\text{P. to K's 6th}}$, 13. $\frac{\text{B. to K. B's 3rd}}{\text{P. takes P. (ch.)}}$, 14. $\frac{\text{K. to B's sq.}}{\text{Castles}}$, 15. $\frac{\text{Q. to K's 2nd}}{\text{B. to Q. B's 4th}}$, 16. $\frac{\text{P. to Q. B's 3rd}}{\text{Q. to Q. R's 5th}}$, 17. $\frac{\text{Q. to Q. R's 6th (ch.)}}{\text{K. to Kt.'s sq.}}$, 18. $\frac{\text{P. to Q's 4th}}{}$, &c. &c.

13. P. to Q. B's 3rd.	13. Q. to Q. Kt.'s 3rd.
14. B. to K's 2nd.	14. Kt. takes Kt.'s P.
15. B. takes Kt.	15. Q. takes B.
16. Q. to Q. Kt.'s 3rd.	16. R. to Q. Kt.'s sq.

And the game is dismissed as even.

Game the Second.

WHITE.	BLACK.
1. P. to K's 4th.	1. P. to K's 4th.
2. Kt. to K. B's 3rd.	2. Kt. to Q. B's 3rd.
3. B. to Q. B's 4th.	3. Kt. to K. B's 3rd.
4. Kt. to K. Kt.'s 5th.	4. P. to Q's 4th.
5. P. takes P.	5. Kt. to Q. R's 4th.

BLACK.

WHITE.

Position prior to White's 6th Move.

6. P. to Q's 3rd.

This move is not new, but it has been more in vogue of late years in consequence of its adoption by Mr. Morphy.

6. P. to K. R's 3rd.

If 6. $\frac{\text{}}{\text{B. to Q. B's 4th}}$, 7. $\frac{\text{Castles}}{\text{Castles}}$, 8. $\frac{\text{P. to Q. B's 3rd}}{\text{P. to K. R's 3rd}}$. (Black may also play—8. $\frac{\text{}}{\text{Kt. takes B.}}$, 9. $\frac{\text{P. takes Kt.}}{\text{B. to K. Kt.'s 5th}}$, advantageously.) 9. $\frac{\text{P. to Q. Kt.'s 4th}}{\text{R's P. takes Kt.}}$, 10. $\frac{\text{P. takes B.}}{\text{Kt. takes Q's P.}}$, 11. $\frac{\text{B. takes Kt.'s P.}}{\text{P. to K. B's 3rd}}$, 12. $\frac{\text{B. takes Kt. (ch.)}}{\text{Q. takes B.}}$. The game is about even.

7. Kt. to K. B's 3rd.	7. P. to K's 5th.
8. Q. to K's 2nd.	8. Kt. takes B.
9. P. takes Kt.	9. B. to Q. B's 4th (best).
10. P. to K. R's 3rd.	10. Castles.
11. Kt. to K. R's 2nd.	11. P. to Q. Kt.'s 4th.

A move proposed by Dr. Suhle, and which certainly appears to strengthen Black's game considerably.

12. P. takes P.

If 12. $\frac{\text{P. to Q. Kt.'s 3rd}}{\text{P. takes P.}}$, 13. $\frac{\text{P. takes P.}}{\text{B. to Q. R's 3rd}}$, 14. $\frac{\text{Kt. to Q. B's 3rd}}{\text{P. to Q. B's 3rd}}$, Black has the advantage. So also if 12. $\frac{\text{Kt. to Q. B's 3rd}}{\text{P. takes P.}}$, 13. $\frac{\text{Q. takes B's P.}}{\text{Q. to Q's 3rd}}$, White has an inferior game.

	12. Kt. takes Q's P.
13. Castles.	13. Q. to K's 2nd.

And Black has a finely attacking position.

Game the Third.

WHITE.	BLACK.
1. P. to K's 4th.	1. P. to K's 4th.
2. Kt. to K. B's 3rd.	2. Kt. to Q. B's 3rd.
3. B. to Q. B's 4th.	3. Kt. to K. B's 3rd.
4. P. to Q's 4th.	

We have seen from the preceding analysis that the promising and favourite attack begun by 4. $\frac{\text{Kt. to K. Kt.'s 5th}}{}$, appears to be successfully opposed by the defence of 4. $\frac{}{\text{P. to Q's 4th}}$, 5. $\frac{\text{P. takes P.}}{\text{Kt. to Q. R's 4th}}$. Some good authorities begin to doubt, therefore, whether White will not do better to abandon that attack, and in reply to Black's move of 3. $\frac{}{\text{Kt. to K. B's 3rd}}$, play 4. $\frac{\text{P. to Q's 4th}}{}$, or 4. $\frac{\text{Castles}}{}$, and equalise the game. (For the result of 4. $\frac{\text{Castles}}{}$, 4. $\frac{\text{Kt. to Q. B's 3rd}}{}$, and 4. $\frac{\text{Q. to K's 2nd}}{}$, see Variation A.)

	4. P. takes P.
5. P. to K's 5th.	

(If 5. Castles, Black's best reply is 5. Kt. takes K's P., and we have the position examined in Variation A.)

	5. P. to Q's 4th.
6. B. to Q. Kt.'s 5th.	6. Kt. to K's 5th.
7. Kt. takes P.	7. B. to Q's 2nd.
8. B. takes Kt.	8. P. takes B.
9. Castles.	9. B. to K's 2nd.
10. P. to Q. B's 4th.	10. Castles.

The game is equal.

Variation A.

BLACK.

WHITE.

Position prior to White's 4th Move.

4. Castles.

White, as we have before said, may likewise play 4. $\frac{\text{Kt. to Q. B's 3rd}}{}$ and 4. $\frac{\text{Q. to K's 2nd}}{}$. In the first place, suppose—4. $\frac{\text{Kt. to Q. B's 3rd}}{\text{B. to Q. Kt.'s 5th}}$, 5. $\frac{\text{Castles}}{\text{Castles}}$, 6. $\frac{\text{P. to Q's 3rd}}{\text{P. to Q's 3rd}}$, 7. $\frac{\text{B. to K. Kt.'s 5th}}{\text{B. takes Kt.}}$, 8. $\frac{\text{P. takes B.}}{\text{B. to K's 3rd}}$, Black's game is better developed. In the second place,—4. $\frac{\text{Q. to K's 2nd}}{\text{B. to Q. B's 4th}}$, 5. $\frac{\text{Kt. to K. Kt.'s 5th}}{\text{Kt. to Q's 5th}}$, 6. $\frac{\text{B. takes P. (ch.)}}{\text{K. to B's sq.}}$, 7. $\frac{\text{Q. to Q. B's 4th}}{\text{Q. to K's 2nd}}$, and again Black has the advantage.

4. Kt. takes K's P.

If 4. $\frac{\quad}{\text{B. to Q. B's 4th}}$, 5. $\frac{\text{P. to Q's 4th}}{\quad}$, and the advantage is with White.

5. P. to Q's 4th.	5. P. takes P.
6. R. to K's sq.	6. P. to Q's 4th.
7. B. takes P.	7. Q. takes B.
8. Kt. to Q. B's 3rd.	8. Q. to K. R's 4th.*
9. Kt. takes Kt.	9. B. to K's 2nd.

If 9. $\frac{\quad}{\text{B. to K's 3rd}}$, White rejoins with 10. $\frac{\text{B. to K. Kt.'s 5th}}{\quad}$, and the result is an even game.

10. B. to K. Kt.'s 5th.	10. B. to K. Kt.'s 5th.

And Black has the better game.

Game the Fourth.

WHITE.	BLACK.
1. P. to K's 4th.	1. P. to K's 4th.
2. Kt. to K. B's 3rd.	2. Kt. to Q. B's 3rd.
3. B. to Q. B's 4th.	3. Kt. to K. B's 3rd.
4. Kt. to K. Kt.'s 5th.	4. Kt. takes P.

This is not so good a line of defence as that before examined of 4. $\frac{\quad}{\text{P. to Q's 4th}}$, in every phase of which Black appears to

---

* Instead of this move Mr. Wayte has suggested 8. Q. to K. B's 5th, which is certainly stronger. The best continuation is apparently—

	8. Q. to Q. B's 5th.
9. Kt. takes Kt.	9. B. to K's 3rd.
10. B. to K. Kt.'s 5th.	10. B. to Q. Kt.'s 5th.
11. P. to Q. B's 3rd.	11. P. takes P.
12. P. takes P.	12. B. to R's 4th (best).

And Black has the superiority.—[Ed.]

have some advantage. Still the move in the text requires to be correctly met, or it will give White some trouble.

5. B. takes P. (ch.)

(For 5. Kt. takes B's P./———, see Variation I.)

	5. K. to K's 2nd.
6. P. to Q's 3rd.	6. Kt. to K. B's 3rd.

Black cannot take the Knight without losing his Queen for very inadequate compensation; and if he play 6. ———/Kt. to Q's 3rd, that equally costs his Queen by White moving 7. Kt. to K's 6th/———, &c.

7. B. to Kt.'s 3rd.	7. P. to Q's 4th.
8. P. to K. B's 4th.	8. B. to K. Kt.'s 5th.
9. Q. to Q's 2nd.	9. P. to K. R's 3rd.*
10. P. takes K's P.	10. Kt. takes P.
11. Q. to K's 3rd.	11. P. takes Kt.
12. Q. takes Kt. (ch.)	12. K. to B's 2nd.
13. Castles.	13. P. to Q. B's 3rd.
14. Q. takes Kt.'s P.	14. B. to Q's 3rd.

And although White has won a Pawn, I doubt if he have much advantage.

---

* Mr. Zukertort has pointed out that the correct move for Black at this point is 9. K. to Q's 2nd. The continuation is—

	9. K. to Q's 2nd.
10. Kt. to B's 7th.	

White may Castle with an even game.

	10. Q. to K's sq.
11. Kt. takes R.	11. P. takes P. (dis. ch.)
12. Kt. to B's sq.	12. Kt. to Q's 5th (best).
13. Kt. to B's 3rd.	13. B. to Q. B's 4th.

And Black has the advantage.—[Ed.]

Variation I.

BLACK.

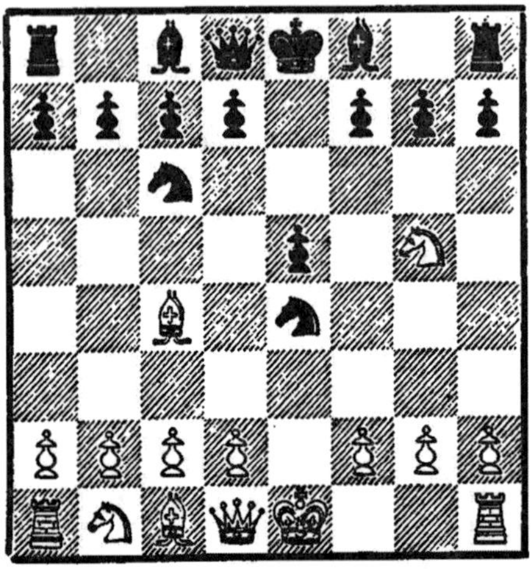

WHITE.

Position prior to White's 5th Move.

5. Kt. takes K. B's P.

I may note in passing here that if White take Knight with Knight, Black can play 5. $\frac{\qquad}{\text{P. to Q's 4th}}$, and have at least an equal game.

The move in the text has usually been decried on account of Black's reply of 5. $\frac{\qquad}{\text{Q. to K. R's 5th}}$, which was thought to be much against White. The Rev. W. Wayte, however, has clearly shown by the following Variation that the reply in question is not so formidable as it was imagined to be.

5. Q. to K. R's 5th.

6. Q. to K's 2nd.

This is the move proposed by Mr. Wayte. The game has generally been continued thus:—6. $\frac{\text{P. to K. Kt.'s 3rd}}{\text{Kt. takes Kt.'s P.}}$,

7. $\frac{\text{R. to K. Kt.'s sq.}}{\text{Q. to K's 5th (ch.)}}$, 8. $\frac{\text{B. to K's 2nd}}{\text{Q. takes B. (ch.)}}$, 9. $\frac{\text{Q. takes Q.}}{\text{Kt. takes Q.}}$,

10. $\frac{\text{K. takes Kt.}}{\text{K. takes Kt.}}$, leaving Black winner of a piece.

6. Kt. to Q's 5th.

If 6. $\frac{}{\text{B. to Q. B's 4th}}$, 7. $\frac{\text{P. to K. Kt.'s 3rd}}{\text{B. takes P. (ch.)}}$, 8. $\frac{\text{Q. takes B.}}{\text{Kt. takes Q.}}$,

9. $\frac{\text{P. takes Q.}}{\text{Kt. takes R.}}$, 10. $\frac{\text{Kt. takes R.}}{\text{Kt. to Q's 5th}}$, 11. $\frac{\text{Kt. to Q. R's 3rd}}{\text{P. to Q. B's 3rd}}$,

12. $\frac{\text{Kt. to K. B's 7th}}{\text{P. to Q's 4th}}$, 13. $\frac{\text{Kt. to Q's 6th (ch.)}}{\text{K. to Q's 2nd}}$, 14. $\frac{\text{Kt. takes B.}}{\text{R. takes Kt.}}$,

White has the better game.

7. P. to K. Kt.'s 3rd.	7. Kt. takes Q. (best.)
8. P. takes Q.	8. Kt. to Q's 5th.
9. Kt. takes R.	9. Kt. takes Q. B's P. (ch.)
10. K. to K's 2nd.	10. Kt. takes R.
11. Kt. to K. B's 7th.	11. Kt. to Q. B's 7th.
12. P. to K. B's 3rd.	12. Kt. to Q's 3rd.

This is much stronger than 12. Kt. to K. B's 3rd.

13. Kt. takes K's P.	13. Kt. takes B.
14. Kt. takes Kt.	14. P. to Q's 4th.

And Black has the advantage.

CHAPTER VI.

Staunton's Opening.

1. $\frac{\text{P. to K's 4th}}{\text{P. to K's 4th}}$, 2. $\frac{\text{Kt. to K. B's 3rd}}{\text{Kt. to Q. B's 3rd}}$, 3. $\frac{\text{P. to Q. B's 3rd}}{\quad}$.

Game the First.

3. $\frac{\quad}{\text{Kt. to K. B's 3rd}}$.

Game the Second.

3. $\frac{\quad}{\text{P. to Q's 4th}}$; 3. $\frac{\quad}{\text{P. to Q's 3rd}}$.

Game the Third.

3. $\frac{\quad}{\text{P. to K. B's 4th}}$.

This opening appears to have been little practised by the early players, and to have been little known to the modern ones until I drew attention to its merits some twenty-six years ago. It has since then been grudgingly admitted into favour, and in another quarter of a century it may possibly take the rank it deserves among our best *débuts*.

Game the First.

WHITE.	BLACK.
1. P. to K's 4th.	1. P. to K's 4th.
2. Kt. to K. B's 3rd.	2. Kt. to Q. B's 3rd.
3. P. to Q. B's 3rd.	3. Kt. to K. B's 3rd.

Many players look upon this as the best defence at Black's command, and I think it, at least, as good as any other.

The defence of 3. $\frac{\qquad}{\text{P. to Q's 4th}}$ will be examined in Game the Second, and 3. $\frac{\qquad}{\text{P. to K. B's 4th}}$, and 3. $\frac{\qquad}{\text{B. to Q. B's 4th}}$, will form the subjects of Games the Third and Fourth.

4. P. to Q's 4th. 4. P. to Q's 4th.

Instead of this counter-buff, Black can play 4. $\frac{\qquad}{\text{Kt. takes K's P.}}$, the result of which shall be considered in Variation A.

5. B. to Q. Kt.'s 5th.

If 5. $\frac{\text{P. takes K's P.}}{\text{Kt. takes K's P.}}$, 6. $\frac{\text{B. to Q's 3rd}}{\text{B. to K's 2nd}}$, and the game is pretty even.

5. Kt. takes K's P.

If 5. $\frac{\qquad}{\text{B. to Q's 2nd}}$, 6. $\frac{\text{P. takes Q's P.}}{\text{P. to K's 5th}}$, 7. $\frac{\text{B. takes Kt.}}{\text{P. takes B.}}$, 8. $\frac{\text{P. takes P.}}{\text{B. takes P.}}$, 9. $\frac{\text{Kt. to K's 5th}}{\qquad}$, and White is the gainer. If 5. $\frac{\qquad}{\text{P. takes Q's P.}}$, 6. $\frac{\text{P. to K's 5th}}{\text{Kt. to K's 5th}}$, 7. $\frac{\text{Kt. takes Q's P.}}{\text{B. to Q's 2nd}}$, 8. $\frac{\text{Q. to Q. Kt.'s 3rd}}{\text{Kt. takes Kt.}}$, 9. $\frac{\text{B. takes B. (ch.)}}{\text{Q. takes B.}}$, 10. $\frac{\text{P. takes Kt.}}{\text{Any Move.}}$, White has the advantage.

6. Kt. takes P. 6. B. to Q's 2nd.
7. Q. to Q. Kt.'s 3rd. 7. Kt. to K. B's 3rd.

Mr. Fraser, of Dundee, who has devoted much attention to this opening, considers 7. $\frac{\qquad}{\text{Kt. to K. B's 3rd}}$ to be Black's best move. If 7. $\frac{\qquad}{\text{Kt. to Q's 3rd}}$, 8. $\frac{\text{Kt. takes B.}}{\text{Q. takes Kt.}}$, 9. $\frac{\text{Q. takes Q's P.}}{\qquad}$, &c. If 7. $\frac{\qquad}{\text{Kt. takes Kt.}}$, 8. $\frac{\text{Q. takes P.}}{\text{Q. to K's 2nd}}$, 9. $\frac{\text{P. takes Kt.}}{\qquad}$, &c.

8. B. to K. Kt.'s 5th. 8. B. to K's 2nd.

If 8. $\frac{\qquad}{\text{P. to Q. R's 3rd}}$, 9. $\frac{\text{B. takes K's Kt.}}{\text{Kt.'s P. takes B.}}$, 10. $\frac{\text{B. takes Kt.}}{\text{B. takes B.}}$, 11. $\frac{\text{Kt. to Q's 3rd}}{\qquad}$, White has clearly an advantage.

9. B. takes K's Kt.	9. Kt.'s P. takes B.
10. B. takes Kt.	10. P. takes B.
11. Kt. to K. B's 3rd.	

And Black's doubled Pawns place him at some disadvantage.

Variation A, beginning at Black's 4th Move.

BLACK.

WHITE.

Position prior to Black's 4th Move.

4. Kt. takes K's P.

The move of 4. $\frac{\quad}{\text{P. to Q's 3rd}}$ may be summarily disposed of. It is manifestly inferior to either 4. $\frac{\quad}{\text{P. to Q's 4th}}$ or 4. $\frac{\quad}{\text{Kt. takes P.}}$ For suppose,—4. $\frac{\quad}{\text{P. to Q's 3rd}}$, 5. $\frac{\text{B. to K. Kt.'s 5th}}{\text{B. to K. Kt.'s 5th}}$, 6. $\frac{\text{Q's Kt. to Q's 2nd}}{\quad}$, and play as he can, Black has a badly developed game.

5. P. takes P.

The consequences of playing 5. $\frac{\text{P. to Q's 5th}}{}$ will be seen in Variation B.

5. B. to Q. B's 4th.

This is now thought by most authorities to be better play than 5. $\frac{}{\text{P. to Q's 4th}}$, but its superiority appears to me "not proven." Black certainly makes a good defence by the latter. For example,—5. $\frac{}{\text{P. to Q's 4th}}$, 6. $\frac{\text{B. to Q. Kt.'s 5th}}{\text{B. to Q. B's 4th}}$, 7. $\frac{\text{Kt. to Q's 4th}}{\text{Castles}}$, 8. $\frac{\text{B. takes Kt.}}{\text{P. takes B.}}$, and Black's position is in no respect inferior to his antagonist's.

6. B. to Q. B's 4th.

If, as Jaenisch recommends, 6. $\frac{\text{Q. to Q's 5th}}{\text{B. takes P. (ch.)}}$, 7. $\frac{\text{K. to K's 2nd}}{\text{P. to K. B's 4th}}$, 8. $\frac{\text{Q's Kt. to Q's 2nd}}{\text{Q's Kt. to K's 2nd}}$, and Black has the advantage.

6. Kt. takes K. B's P.

7. B. takes B's P. (ch.)

If 7. $\frac{\text{Q. to Q's 5th}}{\text{Q. to K's 2nd}}$, 8. $\frac{\text{R. to K. B's sq.}}{\text{Kt. to K. Kt.'s 5th}}$, and Black has a Pawn more.

	7. K. takes B.
8. Q. to Q's 5th (ch.)	8. K. to K's sq.

The move now recommended in the books is 9. $\frac{\text{R. to K. B's sq.}}{}$, the game then proceeding—

9. R. to K. B's sq.	9. Kt. to K's 2nd.
10. Q. to Q. B's 4th.	10. P. to Q's 4th.
11. P. takes P. (in passing.)	11. Q. takes P.
12. R. takes Kt.	12. B. takes R. (ch.)
13. K. takes B.	13. B. to K's 3rd.

And Black has the better game by far.

Variation B, beginning at White's 5th Move.

BLACK.

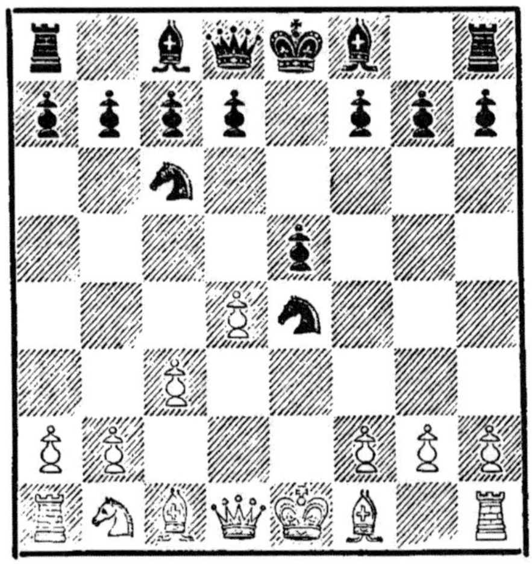

WHITE.

Position prior to White's 5th Move.

5. P. to Q's 5th. 5. B. to Q. B's 4th.

Playing the Bishop thus is a suggestion of Mr. Fraser, of Dundee, and it is generally accepted as preferable to retreating the Q's Kt. to Q. Kt.'s sq., or to K's 2nd, either of which gives Black a constrained position. *Ex. gr.*: 5. $\frac{}{\text{Kt. to Kt.'s sq.}}$, 6. $\frac{\text{B. to Q's 3rd}}{}$, &c., or 5. $\frac{}{\text{Kt. to K's 2nd}}$, 6. $\frac{\text{Kt. takes P.}}{\text{Kt. to K. Kt.'s 3rd}}$, 7. $\frac{\text{Kt. takes Kt.}}{\text{R's P. takes Kt.}}$, 8. $\frac{\text{B. to K's 2nd}}{\text{Kt. to K. B's 3rd}}$, and White has some advantage in position.

6. Q. to K's 2nd, or Var. C. 6. Kt. takes B's P.
7. P. takes Q's Kt. 7. Kt. takes R.
8. B. to K's 3rd. 8. B. to Q's 3rd (best).

Because if 8. $\frac{}{\text{B. takes B.}}$, 9. $\frac{\text{Q. takes B.}}{\text{Castles}}$, 10. $\frac{\text{P. takes Q's P.}}{\text{B. takes P.}}$, 11. $\frac{\text{P. to K. Kt.'s 3rd}}{}$, and Black cannot save his Knight.

9. Q's Kt. to Q's 2nd.

And I do not see how Black can extricate the Knight.

VARIATION C, BEGINNING AT WHITE'S 6TH MOVE.

BLACK.

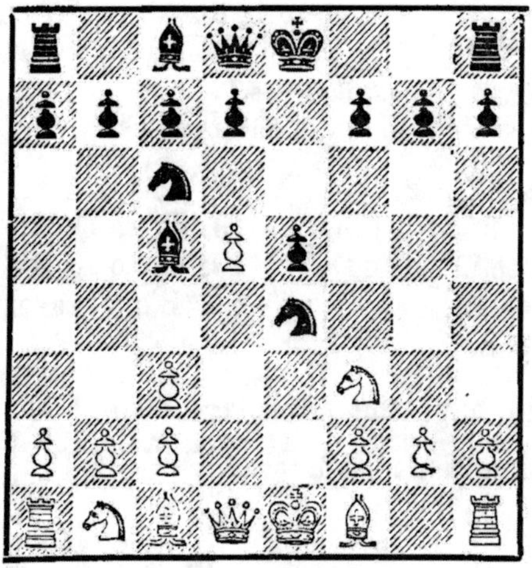

WHITE.

Position prior to White's 6th Move.

6. P. takes Kt.

This is White's best reply, but he has also two other feasible moves, viz., 6. $\frac{\text{Q. to Q. R's 4th}}{}$, and 6. $\frac{\text{B. to K's 3rd}}{}$.

In the first place,—6. $\frac{\text{Q. to Q. R's 4th}}{\text{Kt. takes K. B's P.}}$, 7. $\frac{\text{R. to K. Kt.'s sq.}}{\text{P. to K's 5th}}$, and there can no doubt of Black having the advantage.

In the second place,—6. $\frac{\text{B. to K's 3rd}}{\text{B. takes B.}}$, 7. $\frac{\text{P. takes B.}}{\text{Kt. to Q. Kt.'s sq.}}$, 8. $\frac{\text{B. to Q's 3rd}}{\text{Kt. to Q. B's 4th}}$, 9. $\frac{\text{Kt. takes P.}}{\text{Q. to K's 2nd}}$, 10. $\frac{\text{Kt. to Q. B's 4th}}{\text{P. to Q. Kt.'s 4th}}$, 11. $\frac{\text{K's Kt. to Q. R's 3rd}}{\text{Q. takes P. (ch.)}}$, and White has an inferior position.

6. B. takes B's P. (ch.)

(For the result of 6. $\frac{\quad}{\text{Kt. takes K. B's P.}}$, see Variation D.)

7. K. to K's 2nd.	7. P. to Q's 4th.

Black can also play—7. $\frac{\quad}{\text{Q. Kt.'s P. takes P.}}$, and, according to the German *Handbuch*, obtain an equal game by the following continuation :—8. $\frac{\text{Q. to Q. R's 4th}}{\text{P. to K. B's 4th}}$, 9. $\frac{\text{Q's Kt. to Q's 2nd}}{\text{Castles}}$, 10. $\frac{\text{Kt. takes Kt.}}{\text{P. takes Kt.}}$, 11. $\frac{\text{Q. takes K's P.}}{\text{P. to Q's 4th (best).}}$, &c.

8. P. takes Kt.'s P.	8. Q's B. takes P.
9. Q. to Q. R's 4th (ch.)	9. P. to Q. B's 3rd.
10. Q's Kt. to Q's 2nd.	10. P. to K. B's 4th (best).
11. Kt. takes Kt.	11. B's P. takes Kt.
12. K. takes B.	

White would have the advantage also, I believe, by the following line of action:—12. $\frac{\text{Kt. takes P.}}{\text{Q. to Q. Kt.'s 3rd}}$, 13. $\frac{\text{Kt. to Kt.'s 4th}}{\text{Cast. K's side}}$, 14. $\frac{\text{Q. to Q. Kt.'s 3rd}}{\text{B. to Q. B's sq.}}$, 15. $\frac{\text{P. to K. R's 3rd}}{\text{B. takes Kt. (ch.)}}$, 16. $\frac{\text{P. takes B.}}{\text{Q. to Q. B's 4th}}$, 17. $\frac{\text{K. to Q's sq.}}{\quad}$, &c.

12. Castles.

At one time I thought Black had somewhat the advantage here; but I am now disposed to agree with Mr. Wormald, that by continuing the game,—

13. B. to K's 3rd.	13. P. takes Kt.
14. P. to K. Kt.'s 3rd.	

The position is in favour of White.

VARIATION D, BEGINNING AT BLACK'S 6TH MOVE.

BLACK.

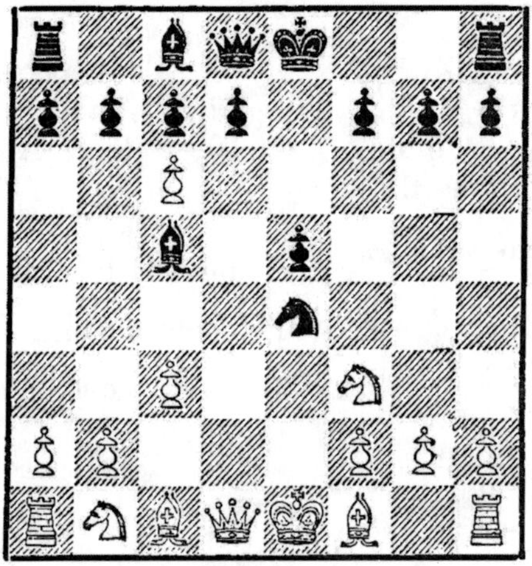

WHITE.

Position prior to Black's 6th Move.

	6. Kt. takes B's P.
7. Q. to Q's 5th.	7. B. to Q. Kt.'s 3rd.

This is now considered a better move for Black than either 7. $\frac{}{\text{P. to Q's 3rd}}$, or 7. $\frac{}{\text{Q. to K's 2nd}}$, which are usually continued thus:—

In the first place,—7. $\frac{}{\text{P. to Q's 3rd}}$, 8. $\frac{\text{P. takes P.}}{\text{Q's B. takes P.}}$, 9. $\frac{\text{Q. takes Q's B.}}{\text{Kt. takes R.}}$, 10. $\frac{\text{Q. to Q. B's 6th (ch.)}}{}$, and White has the advantage.

In the second place,—7. $\frac{}{\text{Q. to K's 2nd}}$, 8. $\frac{\text{P. takes P.}}{\text{B. takes P.}}$, 9. $\frac{\text{Q. takes Q's B.}}{\text{Castles}}$, 10. $\frac{\text{R. to Kt.'s sq.}}{\text{Q. to Q's 3rd}}$, 11. $\frac{\text{Q. to Kt.'s 3rd}}{\text{P. to K's 5th}}$, 12. $\frac{\text{Kt. to Q's 4th}}{\text{B. takes Kt.}}$, 13. $\frac{\text{P. takes B.}}{\text{Kt. to Q's 6th (ch.)}}$, 14. $\frac{\text{B. takes Kt.}}{\text{Q. takes Q's P.}}$,

15. $\frac{\text{K. to B's sq.}}{\text{P. takes B.}}$, 16. $\frac{\text{Kt. to Q's 2nd}}{\text{K's R. to K's sq.}}$, 17. $\frac{\text{Kt. to K. B's 3rd}}{\text{Q. to K's 5th}}$, 18. $\frac{\text{Q. to Q's sq.}}{\text{Q's R. to Kt.'s sq.}}$, 19. $\frac{\text{K. to B's 2nd}}{}$, and again White has the better game.

8. P. takes Q. Kt.'s P.	8. Q's B. takes P.
9. Q. takes B.	9. Kt. takes R.
10. B. to K. Kt.'s 5th.	10. P. to K. B's 3rd.
11. B. to K. R's 4th.	

If 11. $\frac{\text{Kt. takes P.}}{}$, Black should not take the Bishop at once, because in that case White could obtain a strong attack by 12. $\frac{\text{Q. to Q's 5th}}{}$. His safest move appears to be 11. $\frac{}{\text{P. to Q. B's 3rd}}$.

11. P. to K. Kt.'s 4th.

This move, the suggestion of Mr. Holloway, a member of the Bristol Chess Club, has been too hastily supposed to give Black the better game.

12. Q's Kt. to Q's 2nd.

White can obtain a specious attack at this critical moment by 12. $\frac{\text{Kt. takes Kt.'s P.}}{}$, or 12. $\frac{\text{B. to Q. B's 4th}}{}$, or 12. $\frac{\text{B. to K's 2nd}}{}$, but, if properly opposed, it is doubtful whether in any one of the three cases he could do more than make a drawn battle. (See Variation E.)

12. P. to Q. B's 3rd.

If 12. $\frac{}{\text{P. takes B.}}$, White will gain the superiority by 13. $\frac{\text{Kt. to K's 4th}}{}$.

13. Kt. to K's 4th.

If 13. $\frac{\text{Kt. to Q. B's 4th}}{}$, Black plays 13. $\frac{}{\text{R. to Q. Kt.'s sq.}}$, and can repulse the attack.

13. Castles.

If 13. $\frac{\text{}}{\text{R. to Q. Kt.'s sq.}}$, 14. $\frac{\text{Kt. takes P. (ch.)}}{\text{K. to K's 2nd (best).}}$, 15. $\frac{\text{Q. takes Q's P. (ch.)}}{\text{Q. takes Q.}}$, 16. $\frac{\text{Kt. takes Q.}}{\text{K. takes Kt. (best.)}}$, 17. $\frac{\text{Kt. takes Kt.'s P.}}{\text{}}$, and as Black's Knight cannot escape, White has the better game.

14. R. to Q's sq.

Far better than Castling.

	14. R. to Q. Kt.'s sq. (best.)
15. Q. takes Q's P.	15. Q. takes Q.
16. R. takes Q.	16. Q's R. to Q's sq.

If 16. $\frac{\text{}}{\text{P. takes B.}}$, 17. $\frac{\text{B. to Q. B's 4th (ch.)}}{\text{K. to R's sq.}}$, 18. $\frac{\text{Kt. to K. Kt.'s 5th}}{\text{}}$, and Black cannot possibly save the game.

17. B. to Q. B's 4th (ch.)	17. K. to R's sq.
18. Kt. takes K. B's P.	18. R. takes R.

If 18. $\frac{\text{}}{\text{R. takes Kt.}}$, 19. $\frac{\text{B. takes Kt.'s P.}}{\text{K's R. to K. B's sq. (best.)}}$, 20. $\frac{\text{B. takes Q's R.}}{\text{B. takes B.}}$, 21. $\frac{\text{Kt. takes K's P.}}{\text{}}$, &c. (If 20. $\frac{\text{}}{\text{R. takes B.}}$, 21. $\frac{\text{R. to K's 7th}}{\text{}}$, and White has much the better game.)

19. Kt. takes R.	19. R. to K. B's 4th.

If 19. $\frac{\text{}}{\text{R. takes Kt.}}$, 20. $\frac{\text{P. takes R.}}{\text{P. takes B.}}$, 21. $\frac{\text{Kt. takes B.}}{\text{P. takes Kt.}}$, 22. $\frac{\text{B. to K. B's sq.}}{\text{}}$, and White must win easily.

20. B. takes Kt.'s P.	20. P. to K's 5th.
21. B. to B's 6th (ch.)	21. R. takes B.
22. Kt. takes R.	22. P. takes K's Kt.
23. P. takes P.	23. Kt. to K. B's 7th.
24. B. to K. B's sq.	

White must win.

Since writing the foregoing Variations, which depend on Black's adopting the line of defence proposed by Mr. Holloway as best against White's move of 12. $\frac{\text{Q's Kt. to Q's 2nd}}{\text{}}$, it has occurred to me that Black may perhaps play 12. $\frac{}{\text{P. to Q's 4th}}$,

with more advantage than 12. $\frac{}{\text{P. to Q. B's 3rd}}$ appears to

yield. In that case, however, I believe White can get the better game by the following line of play among others, namely,—

	12. P. to Q's 4th.
13. B. to Q. Kt.'s 5th (ch.)	13. K. to K. B's sq.

Black can move his King also to K. B's 2nd, but if to K's 2nd, he loses at once, because White can take the K's Pawn with his Kt.

14. K. to K's 2nd.	14. P. takes B. (best.)
15. R. takes Kt.	

And White has, I think, an undoubted superiority.

VARIATION E, BEGINNING AT WHITE'S 12TH MOVE.

BLACK.

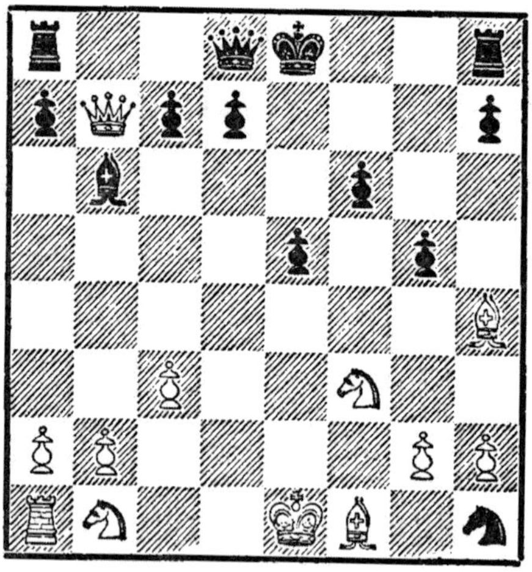

WHITE.

Position prior to White's 12th Move.

In the first place,—

12. Kt. takes Kt.'s P.	12. P. takes Kt.
13. Q. to K. B's 3rd.	

If 13. $\frac{\text{B. takes P.}}{}$, then follow 13. $\frac{}{\text{R. to Q. Kt.'s sq.}}$, 14. $\frac{\text{B. takes Q.}}{\text{R. takes Q.}}$, 15. $\frac{\text{B. to K. R's 4th}}{\text{R. to K. B's sq.}}$, Black has the advantage.

	13. P. takes B.

He may likewise play, but less efficaciously, 13. $\frac{}{\text{P. to Q. B's 3rd}}$, I think. For instance,—12. $\frac{}{\text{P. to Q. B's 3rd}}$, 13. $\frac{\text{Q. to R's 5th (ch.)}}{\text{K. to B's sq.}}$, 14. $\frac{\text{B. takes P.}}{\text{Q. to K's sq.}}$, 15. $\frac{\text{Q. to R's 6th (ch.)}}{\text{K. to B's 2nd (best).}}$, 16. $\frac{\text{B. to K's 2nd}}{\text{Q. to K. B's sq.}}$, 17. $\frac{\text{Q. to B's 6th (ch.)}}{\text{K. to Kt.'s sq.}}$, 18. $\frac{\text{Kt. to Q. R's 3rd}}{}$. The game is not far from equal.

14. B. to Q. B's 4th.	14. P. to Q's 4th.

This is almost forced, for if 14. $\frac{}{\text{R. to K. B's sq.}}$, 15. $\frac{\text{Q. to K. R's 5th (ch.)}}{}$, and Checkmate next move.

15. B. takes P.	15. R. to K. B's sq.

If 15. $\frac{}{\text{Q. to K. Kt.'s 4th}}$, 16. $\frac{\text{Q. to K. B's 7th (ch.)}}{\text{K. to Q's sq.}}$, 17. $\frac{\text{B. takes R.}}{\text{Q. to K's 6th (ch.)}}$, and Black will evidently win in a few moves.

16. Q. to R's 5th (ch.)	16. K. to K's 2nd.
17. Q. takes P. (ch.)	17. K. to Q's 3rd.

And White's attack is exhausted.

In the second place,—

12. B. to Q. B's 4th.	12. P. takes B.
13. Q. to Q's 5th.	13. R. to K. B's sq.

And Black has a good game.

In the third place,—

12. B. to K's 2nd.	12. P. takes B.
13. Kt. takes K's P.	13. P. takes Kt.
14. B. to K. R's 5th (ch.)	14. K. to K's 2nd.
15. Q. to K's 4th.	15. B. to K. B's 7th (ch.)
16. K. to K's 2nd.	16. P. to Q's 3rd.
17. Kt. to Q's 2nd.	17. Q. to K. B's sq.
18. R. takes Kt.	18. Q. to K. R's 3rd.

And Black has the advantage.

Game the Second.

WHITE.	BLACK.
1. P. to K's 4th.	1. P. to K's 4th.
2. Kt. to K. B's 3rd.	2. Kt. to Q. B's 3rd.
3. P. to Q. B's 3rd.	3. P. to Q's 4th.

If Black play 3. $\frac{}{\text{P. to Q's 3rd}}$, the probable continuation is —4. $\frac{\text{B. to Q. Kt.'s 5th}}{\text{B. to Q's 2nd}}$, 5. $\frac{\text{P. to Q's 4th}}{\text{Kt. to K. B's 3rd}}$, the game then being quite equal.

4. B. to Q. Kt.'s 5th.

White can likewise play his Queen to Q. R's 4th without disadvantage. *Ex. gr.*:—4. $\frac{\text{Q. to Q. R's 4th}}{\text{P. takes P.}}$. (If 4. $\frac{}{\text{Q. to Q's 3rd}}$, 5. $\frac{\text{P. to Q's 4th}}{\text{B. to Q's 2nd}}$, 6. $\frac{\text{B. to Q. Kt.'s 5th}}{\text{P. takes K's P.}}$, 7. $\frac{\text{P. takes P.}}{\text{Q. to K. Kt.'s 3rd}}$, and the game is about equal.) 5. $\frac{\text{Q. takes K's P.}}{\text{Kt. to K. B's 3rd}}$, 6. $\frac{\text{Q. to K's 3rd}}{\text{B. to Q's 3rd}}$, 7. $\frac{\text{B. to Q. Kt.'s 5th}}{\text{Castles}}$, the game being equal. Or 5. $\frac{\text{Kt. takes P.}}{\text{Q. to Q's 4th}}$, 6. $\frac{\text{Kt. takes Kt.}}{\text{P. takes Kt.}}$, 7. $\frac{\text{B. to Q. B's 4th}}{\text{Q. to Q's 2nd}}$, 8. $\frac{\text{Castles}}{\text{Kt. to K. B's 3rd}}$, and there is no advantage on either side.

	4. P. takes P.
5. Kt. takes P.	5. Q. to Q's 4th.

(If 5. $\frac{\qquad}{\text{Q. to K. Kt.'s 4th}}$, 6. $\frac{\text{Q. to Q. R's 4th}}{\qquad}$, &c.)

6. Q. to Q. R's 4th.	6. Kt. to K's 2nd.
7. P. to K. B's 4th.	7. P. takes P. in passing.
8. Kt. takes P.	8. P. to Q. R's 3rd.
9. B. to Q. B's 4th.	9. Q. to K's 5th (ch.)

(If 9. $\frac{\qquad}{\text{Q. to K. R's 4th}}$, 10. $\frac{\text{Castles}}{\qquad}$, &c.)

10. K. to B's 2nd.	10. B. to K's 3rd.
11. P. to Q's 3rd.	11. Q. to K. B's 4th.
12. R. to K's sq.	12. R. to Q's sq.

White appears to me to have a slight advantage.

Game the Third.

WHITE.	BLACK.
1. P. to K's 4th.	1. P. to K's 4th.
2. Kt. to K. B's 3rd.	2. Kt. to Q. B's 3rd.
3. P. to Q. B's 3rd.	3. P. to K. B's 4th.

This counter-gambit we owe to the inventive genius of Ponziani. It is a very ingenious conception, and leads to some fine combinations.

4. P. to Q's 4th.

The best move, I believe, but White can play, though not advantageously, 4. $\frac{\text{B. to Q. Kt.'s 5th}}{\text{P. takes P.}}$, 5. $\frac{\text{B. takes Kt.}}{\text{Q's P. takes B.}}$, 6. $\frac{\text{Kt. takes P.}}{\text{Q. to K. Kt.'s 4th}}$, and Black has the preferable game. Or he can play—4. $\frac{\text{P. takes P.}}{\text{P. to Q's 3rd}}$, 5. $\frac{\text{P. to K. Kt.'s 4th}}{\text{P. to K. R's 4th}}$, 6. $\frac{\text{Kt. to Kt.'s sq.}}{\text{P. takes P.}}$, 7. $\frac{\text{Q. takes P.}}{\text{K's Kt. to K's 2nd}}$, 8. $\frac{\text{B. to Q's 3rd}}{\text{P. to K. Kt.'s 3rd}}$, but again Black has the better position.

4. P. to Q's 3rd.

If 4. $\frac{\qquad}{\text{P. takes K's P.}}$, then follow—5. $\frac{\text{Kt. takes P.}}{\text{Kt. to K. B's 3rd}}$, 6. $\frac{\text{B. to Q. Kt.'s 5th}}{\text{P. to Q. R's 3rd}}$, 7. $\frac{\text{B. takes Kt.}}{\text{Q's P. takes B.}}$, 8. $\frac{\text{B. to K. Kt.'s 5th}}{\text{B. to Q's 3rd}}$,

9. $\frac{\text{Kt. to Q's 2nd}}{\text{B. to K. B's 4th}}$, 10. $\frac{\text{Q. to Q. Kt.'s 3rd}}{}$, and White has a winning advantage.

5. B. to Q. Kt.'s 5th.

If 5. $\frac{\text{P. takes K's P.}}{\text{K. B's P. takes P.}}$, 6. $\frac{\text{Kt. to Kt.'s 5th}}{\text{Kt. takes P.}}$, and the game is pretty equal.

	5. P. takes K's P.
6. Kt. takes P.	6. P. takes Kt.
7. B. takes Kt. (ch.)	7. P. takes B.
8. Q. to K. R's 5th (ch.)	8. K. to Q's 2nd.
9. Q. to K. B's 5th (ch.)	9. K. to K's 2nd.

The German *Handbuch* (1864) and the *Stratégie Raisonnée* (1867) pursue the variation by 9. $\frac{}{\text{K. to Q's 3rd}}$, 10. $\frac{\text{Q. takes P. (ch.)}}{}$, &c., remarking that if White play 10. $\frac{\text{P. takes P. (ch.)}}{}$, then follow 10. $\frac{}{\text{K. to K's 2nd}}$, 11. $\frac{\text{B. to Kt.'s 5th (ch.)}}{\text{K. to K's sq.}}$, 12. $\frac{\text{P. to K's 6th}}{\text{Kt. to K. B's 3rd}}$, and Black will win. But these authorities, strangely enough, both overlook the obvious fact that if White, instead of advancing his K's Pawn, play 12. $\frac{\text{Q. takes K's B. (ch.)}}{}$, he regains his piece, and has a winning game. It is evident, then, that Black's proper course is to avoid moving his King to Q's 3rd, and in that case I do not see that White can do more than make a drawn game by perpetually checking.

ILLUSTRATIVE GAMES.

Game I.—Between the Rev. W. Wayte and the Rev. C. E. Ranken.

White (Mr. W.)	Black (Mr. R.)
1. P. to K's 4th.	1. P. to K's 4th.
2. Kt. to K. B's 3rd.	2. Kt. to Q. B's 3rd.
3. P. to Q. B's 3rd.	3. Kt. to K. B's 3rd.
4. P. to Q's 4th.	4. P. to Q's 4th.

5. B. to Q. Kt.'s 5th.	5. K's Kt. takes P.
6. Kt. takes P.	6. B. to Q's 2nd.
7. Q. to Q. Kt.'s 3rd.*	7. Kt. takes Kt.
8. Q. takes Q's P.	8. Q. to K's 2nd.†
9. Q. takes Q. Kt.'s P.‡	9. B. takes B.
10. Q. takes R. (ch.)	10. K. to Q's 2nd.
11. P. takes Kt.§	11. Q. takes P.
12. B. to K's 3rd.	12. B. to Q. B's 4th.
13. Q. takes R.	13. Kt. takes K. B's P.
14. K. to Q's 2nd.	

And Black mated in three moves.

GAME II.—Between the Rev. W. Wayte and the Rev. C. E. Ranken.

WHITE (Mr. W.)	BLACK (Mr. R.)
1. P. to K's 4th.	1. P. to K's 4th.
2. Kt. to K. B's 3rd.	2. Kt. to Q. B's 3rd.
3. P. to Q. B's 3rd.	3. Kt. to K. B's 3rd.
4. P. to Q's 4th.	4. Kt. takes K's P.
5. P. to Q's 5th.	5. B. to Q. B's 4th.
6. P. takes Kt.	6. B. takes B's P. (ch.)
7. K. to K's 2nd.	7. P. to Q's 4th.
8. P. takes Q. Kt.'s P.	8. Q's B. takes P.
9. Q. to Q. R's 4th (ch.)	9. P. to Q. B's 3rd.
10. Q's Kt. to Q's 2nd.	10. P. to K. B's 4th
11. Kt. takes Kt.	11. K. B's P. takes Kt.
12. K. takes B.	12. Castles.
13. Q's B. to K's 3rd.	13. P. takes Kt.
14. P. to K. Kt.'s 3rd.	14. Q. to Q. B's sq.‖
15. B. to Q. B's 5th.	15. R. to K. R's 3rd.

* The best move, we believe.

† The correct reply; B. takes B. is very inferior.

‡ The best continuation is Q. takes K's Kt., to which Black rejoins with Kt. to B's 6th (ch.).

§ If he had taken the other Knight, he would have lost his Queen. The whole of this little game is beautifully played by Mr. Ranken.

‖ It is not easy to decide on Black's best move at this juncture. If he play Q. to Q's 3rd, the answer is—P. to Q. Kt.'s 4th; or if he move P. to Q. R's 4th, White replies with 15. Q's R. to Q's sq.

16. Q's R. to Q's sq.	16. P. to Q. R
17. Q's R. to Q's 2nd.	17. B. to Q. R
18. B takes B.	18. Q. takes B.
19. K s R. to K's sq.	19. P. to K's 5
20. P. to Q. R's 3rd.*	20. Q. to Q. B'
21. K. to Kt.'s sq.	21. Q. to K. R
22. P. to Q. Kt.'s 4th.	22. Q's R. to K
23. Q. takes Q. R's P.	23. P. to K. R'
24. Q. to Q. R's 6th.	24. P. to K. R'
25. Q. to K. B's sq.	25. Q. to K. Kt.'s 5th
26. Q. to K. B's 2nd.	26. R. to K. Kt.'s 3rd.
27. P. to Q. Kt.'s 5th.	27. R's P. takes P.
28. R's P. takes P.	28. R. to K. R's 3rd.
29. B. to K's 3rd.	29. R. to K. R's 6th.
30. B. to K. B's 4th.	30. Q. to K. R's 4th.
31. Q. to K. R's 2nd.‡	31. Q. takes Q.
32. Q's R. takes R.	32. Q. to K. Kt.'s 3rd.
33. P. to Q. Kt.'s 6th.	33. P. to K's 6th.§
34. K's R. takes P.	34. R. takes R.
35. B. takes R.	35. Q. takes P.
36. K. to R's sq.	36. Q. to K's 8th (ch.)
37. B. to K. Kt.'s sq.	37. Q. takes Q. B's P.

And wins.

GAME III.—Between the Rev. C. E. Ranken and the Rev. W. Wayte.

WHITE (Mr. R.)	BLACK (Mr. W.)
1. P. to K's 4th.	1. P. to K's 4th.
2. Kt. to K. B's 3rd.	2. Kt. to Q. B's 3rd.
3. P. to Q. B's 3rd.	3. Kt. to K. B's 3rd.
4 P. to Q's 4th.	4. Kt. takes K's P.
5. P. to Q's 5th.	5. B. to Q. B's 4th.
6. P. takes Kt.	6. B. takes K. B's P. (ch.)
7. K. to K's 2nd.	7. P. to Q's 4th.

* At this point, we believe, P. to Q. B's 4th would have given White the better game.

† From this point Black plays admirably, and every move tells.

‡ H nas clearly no other resource.

§ Quite conclusive.

8. Q. to Q. R's 4th.*	8. Castles.
9. P. takes P.	9. B. takes P.
10. Q's Kt. to Q's 2nd.	10. P. to K. B's 4th.†
11. Kt. takes Kt.	11. K. B's P. takes Kt.
12. K. takes B.	12. P. takes Kt.
13. P. to K. Kt.'s 3rd.	13. Q. to Q's 3rd.
14. B. to K. R's 3rd.	14. P. to Q. B's 4th.
15. K's R. to K's sq.	15. P. to Q's 5th.
16. P. takes P.	16. Q. B's P. takes P.
17. B. to Q's 2nd.	17. P. to K's 5th.
18. Q. to Q. B's 4th (ch.)	18. K. to R's sq.
19. Q's R. to Q's sq.	19. K's R. to Q's sq.‡
20. R. takes K's P.§	20. B. takes R.
21. B. to Q. B's 3rd.	21. Q. to K. R's 3rd.
22. Q's B. takes P.	22. Q. takes K's B.
23. B. takes K. Kt.'s P. (ch.)	23. K. takes B.
24. Q. to Q. B's 7th (ch.)	24. K. to Kt.'s 3rd.
25. R. to Q's 6th (ch.)	25. R. takes R.
26. Q. takes R. (ch.)	26. K. to B's 2nd.
27. Q. to Q. B's 7th (ch.)	27. K. to B's 3rd.
28. Q. to Q. B's 3rd.	28. K. to Kt.'s 3rd.

And White resigned.

GAME IV.—Between Herr Zukertort and Herr Munk.

WHITE (Herr M.)	BLACK (Herr Z.)
1. P. to K's 4th.	1. P. to K's 4th.
2. Kt. to K. B's 3rd.	2. Kt. to Q. B's 3rd.
3. P. to Q. B's 3rd.	3. P. to Q's 4th.
4. B. to Q. Kt.'s 5th.	4. P. takes P.
5. Kt. takes K's P.	5. Q. to Q's 4th.
6. Q. to Q. R's 4th.	6. Kt. to K's 2nd.
7. Kt. takes Kt.‖	7. Kt. takes Kt.

* Better, we should have thought, to take P. with P., and then check at Q. R's 4th.

† Very well played.

‡ Stronger, we believe, than playing P. to K's 6th.

§ This is almost compulsory.

‖ This move wins a Pawn, but it is decidedly inferior to P. to K. B's 4th.

8. Castles.	8. B. to Q's 3rd.
9. R. to K's sq.	9. Castles.
10. B. takes Kt.	10. P. takes B.
11. Q. takes K's P.	11. Q. to K. R's 4th.
12. P. to K. Kt.'s 3rd.	12. B. to K. Kt.'s 5th.
13. P. to Q's 4th.	13. B. to K. B's 6th.
14. Q. to Q's 3rd.*	14. Q's R. to K's sq.
15. B. to K's 3rd.	15. R. to K's 5th.
16. Kt. to Q's 2nd.†	

Black mates in three moves.

---

* Had he played 14. Q. to K. R's 4th, the second player would have equally replied with Q's R. to K's sq.

† If 16. Q. to K. B's sq., Black wins by R. to K. R's 5th, &c.

CHAPTER VII.

Knight's Game of Ruy Lopez.

1. $\frac{\text{P. to K's 4th}}{\text{P. to K's 4th}}$, 2. $\frac{\text{Kt. to K. B's 3rd}}{\text{Kt. to Q. B's 3rd}}$, 3. $\frac{\text{B. to Q. Kt.'s 5th}}{\quad}$.

Game the First.

3. $\frac{\quad}{\text{P. to Q. R's 3rd}}$.

Game the Second.

3. $\frac{\quad}{\text{Kt. to K. B's 3rd}}$.

Game the Third.

3. $\frac{\quad}{\text{B. to Q. B's 4th}}$; 3. $\frac{\quad}{\text{Q. to K. B's 3rd}}$.

Game the Fourth.

3. $\frac{\quad}{\text{Kt. to Q's 5th}}$; 3. $\frac{\quad}{\text{P. to K. B's 4th}}$; 3. $\frac{\quad}{\text{K's Kt. to K's 2nd}}$;

3. $\frac{\quad}{\text{B. to Q's 3rd}}$; 3. $\frac{\quad}{\text{P. to Q's 3rd}}$.

The attack obtainable by this ancient mode of opening the game was thought very highly of a few years ago. Recent analysis and practice have, however, shown that it is not so formidable as it appeared to be, and at the present moment there is a disposition to treat it, perhaps, too lightly.

Game the First.

WHITE.	BLACK.
1. P. to K's 4th.	1. P. to K's 4th.
2. Kt. to K. B's 3rd.	2. Kt. to Q. B's 3rd.
3. B. to Q. Kt.'s 5th.	3. P. to Q. R's 3rd.

According to some good authorities this move, a move given by Del Rio, is the best at Black's command. Others, including Von der Laza and Anderssen, maintain that 3. $\frac{\quad}{\text{Kt. to K. B's 3rd}}$ is quite as good, and that one or other may be played indifferently.

4. B. to Q. R's 4th (best).

If 4. $\frac{\text{B. takes Kt.}}{\text{Kt.'s P. takes B.}}$. (If 4. $\frac{\quad}{\text{Q's P. takes B.}}$, 5. $\frac{\text{Kt. takes P.}}{\text{Q. to Q's 5th}}$, 6. $\frac{\text{P. to K. B's 4th}}{\text{Q. takes K's P. (ch.)}}$, equal game.) 5. $\frac{\text{Kt. takes P.}}{\text{Q. to K's 2nd}}$, 6. $\frac{\text{P. to Q's 4th}}{\text{P. to Q's 3rd}}$, 7. $\frac{\text{Kt. to K. B's 3rd}}{\text{Q. takes P. (ch.)}}$, 8. $\frac{\text{B. to K's 3rd}}{\text{B. to K. Kt.'s 5th}}$, 9. $\frac{\text{Q's Kt. to Q's 2nd}}{\text{B. takes Kt.}}$, 10. $\frac{\text{Kt. takes Q.}}{\text{B. takes Q.}}$, 11. $\frac{\text{R. takes B.}}{\text{R. to Q. Kt.'s sq.}}$, equal game.

4. Kt. to K. B's 3rd.

5. P. to Q's 4th.

He may also Castle or play 5. $\frac{\text{P. to Q's 3rd}}{\quad}$ without disadvantage. (See Variations A and B.) If he play 5. $\frac{\text{Q. to K's 2nd}}{\quad}$, then follow—5. $\frac{\quad}{\text{P. to Q. Kt.'s 4th}}$, 6. $\frac{\text{B. to Q. Kt.'s 3rd}}{\text{B. to Q. B's 4th}}$, 7. $\frac{\text{P. to Q. R's 4th}}{\text{R to Q. Kt.'s sq.}}$, 8. $\frac{\text{P. takes P.}}{\text{P. takes P.}}$, 9. $\frac{\text{Kt. to Q. B's 3rd}}{\text{P. to Q. Kt.'s 5th}}$, 10. $\frac{\text{Kt. to Q's 5th}}{\text{Castles}}$. I rather prefer White's position.

5. P. takes P.

If 5. $\frac{\quad}{\text{Kt. takes K's P.}}$, 6. $\frac{\text{P. to Q's 5th}}{\text{Kt. to Q. B's 4th}}$, 7. $\frac{\text{B. to Kt.'s 3rd}}{\quad}$,

White has some slight superiority. Again, if 5. $\frac{\qquad}{\text{Kt. takes Q's P.}}$, 6. $\frac{\text{Kt. takes Kt.}}{\text{P. takes Kt.}}$, 7. $\frac{\text{P. to K's 5th}}{\text{Kt. to K's 5th}}$, 8. $\frac{\text{Q. takes P.}}{\qquad}$, White has the better game.

6. P. to K's 5th.	6. Kt. to K's 5th.
7. Castles.	

(If 7. $\frac{\text{Q. to K's 2nd}}{\text{Kt. to Q. B's 4th}}$, &c.)

	7. Kt. to Q. B's 4th.

Black can play 7. $\frac{\qquad}{\text{B. to K's 2nd}}$ here without danger.

8. B. takes Kt.	8. Q's P. takes B.
9. Kt. takes P.	9. Kt. to K's 3rd.
10. Kt. takes Kt.	10. B. takes Kt.
11. Q. to K's 2nd.	11. B. to Q. B's 4th.
12. Kt. to Q. B's 3rd.	12. Q. to K's 2nd.
13. Kt. to K's 4th.	13. P. to K. R's 3rd.

White has a somewhat freer game.

VARIATION A, ON WHITE'S 5TH MOVE.

BLACK.

WHITE.

Position prior to White's 5th Move.

5. Castles. | 5. B. to K's 2nd.

In my opinion this is quite as good as the now fashionable defence of 5. $\frac{}{\text{Kt. takes K's P.}}$. In the latter case the following continuation is usually given :—5. $\frac{}{\text{Kt. takes K's P.}}$, 6. $\frac{\text{P. to Q's 4th}}{\text{P. to Q. Kt.'s 4th}}$, 7. $\frac{\text{B. to Q. Kt.'s 3rd}}{\text{P. to Q's 4th (best).}}$, 8. $\frac{\text{P. takes P.}}{}$, and Black can now play 8. $\frac{}{\text{B. to K's 3rd}}$, or 8. $\frac{}{\text{Kt. to K's 2nd}}$, followed by 9. $\frac{}{\text{B. to Q. Kt.'s 2nd}}$, with an even game. This is true if White reply, as in the above Variation, to 5. $\frac{}{\text{Kt. takes K's P.}}$, with 6. $\frac{\text{P. to Q's 4th}}{}$, but if he play 6. $\frac{\text{R. to K's sq.}}{}$, he will, I think, obtain a slight advantage; *e. g.*—5. $\frac{}{\text{Kt. takes K's P.}}$, 6. $\frac{\text{R. to K's sq.}}{\text{Kt. to Q. B's 4th}}$, 7. $\frac{\text{B. takes Kt.}}{\text{Q's P. takes B.}}$, 8. $\frac{\text{Kt. takes P.}}{\text{B. to K's 2nd}}$, and White's position is somewhat preferable.

6. P. to Q's 4th.

If 6. $\frac{\text{Kt. to Q. B's 3rd}}{\text{P. to Q's 3rd}}$, 7. $\frac{\text{P. to Q's 4th}}{\text{P. to Q. Kt.'s 4th}}$, and the game is about equal.

	6. P. takes P.
7. P. to K's 5th.	7. Kt. to K's 5th.
8. B. takes Q's Kt.	8. Q's P. takes B.
9. Q. takes P.	9. B. to K. B's 4th.

There is very little difference in the two positions.

VARIATION B, ON WHITE'S 5TH MOVE.

(See preceding Diagram.)

5. P. to Q's 3rd. | 5. P. to Q. Kt.'s 4th.
6. B. to Q. Kt.'s 3rd | 6. B. to Q. B's 4th.

7. P. to Q. B's 3rd.	7. P. to Q's 3rd.
8. P. to Q's 4th.	8. B. to Q. Kt.'s 3rd.
9. P. takes P.	9. P. takes P.
10. Q. takes Q. (ch.)	10. Kt. takes Q.
11. Kt. takes P.	11. Kt. takes P.
12. B. to Q's 5th.	12. B. to Q. Kt.'s 2nd.

Equal game.

Game the Second.

WHITE.	BLACK.
1. P. to K's 4th.	1. P. to K's 4th.
2. Kt. to K. B's 3rd.	2. Kt. to Q. B's 3rd.
3. B. to Q. Kt.'s 5th.	3. Kt. to K. B's 3rd.
4. P. to Q's 3rd.	

Anderssen prefers this to any other move. For the consequences of 4. $\frac{\text{Castles}}{\quad}$, see Variation A. If 4. $\frac{\text{P. to Q's 4th}}{\text{Kt. takes Q's P.}}$, 5. $\frac{\text{Kt. takes Kt.}}{\text{P. takes Kt.}}$, 6. $\frac{\text{P. to K's 5th}}{\text{P. to Q. B's 3rd}}$, 7. $\frac{\text{Castles}}{\text{Kt. to Q's 4th}}$, 8. $\frac{\text{Q. takes P.}}{\text{Kt. to Q. B's 2nd}}$, 9. $\frac{\text{B. to Q. B's 4th}}{\text{P. to Q's 4th}}$, the game is about even.

	4. B. to Q. B's 4th.

If 4. $\frac{\quad}{\text{P. to Q's 3rd}}$, 5. $\frac{\text{B. takes Kt. (ch.)}}{\text{P. takes B.}}$, 6. $\frac{\text{P. to K. R's 3rd}}{\text{P. to K. Kt.'s 3rd}}$, 7. $\frac{\text{Kt. to Q. B's 3rd}}{\text{B. to K's 2nd}}$, 8. $\frac{\text{Castles}}{\text{Castles}}$, there is little difference in the positions.

5. P. to Q. B's 3rd.	5. Q. to K's 2nd.

If 5. $\frac{\quad}{\text{P. to Q's 3rd}}$, 6. $\frac{\text{P. to Q's 4th}}{\text{P. takes P.}}$, 7. $\frac{\text{P. takes P.}}{\text{B. to Q. Kt.'s 5th (ch.)}}$, 8. $\frac{\text{K. to B's sq.}}{\quad}$, with the better game.

6. Castles.	6. P. to Q. R's 3rd.

If 6. $\frac{\qquad}{\text{Castles}}$, 7. $\frac{\text{P. to Q's 4th}}{\text{B. to Q. Kt.'s 3rd}}$, 8. $\frac{\text{B. to K. Kt.'s 5th}}{\text{P. to Q's 3rd}}$, 9. $\frac{\text{P. to Q's 5th}}{\text{Kt. to Q's sq.}}$, Black has a very confined position.

7. B. takes Kt.	7. Q's P. takes B.
8. P. to Q's 4th.	8. B. to Q. Kt.'s 3rd.
9. Kt. takes K's P.	

The game is in White's favour, I think.

Variation A, on White's 4th Move.

BLACK.

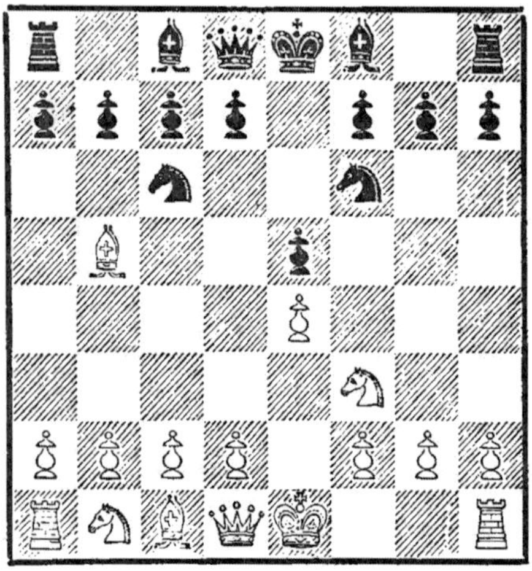

WHITE.

Position prior to White's 4th Move.

4. Castles.	4. Kt. takes P.

If 4. $\frac{\qquad}{\text{P. to Q. R's 3rd}}$, 5. $\frac{\text{B. to Q. R's 4th}}{\text{B. to K's 2nd}}$, 6. $\frac{\text{P. to Q's 4th}}{\text{P. takes P.}}$, 7. $\frac{\text{P. to K's 5th}}{\text{Kt. to K's 5th}}$, 8. $\frac{\text{R. to K's sq.}}{\text{Kt. to Q. B's 4th}}$, we have a position which

has already occurred. If 4. $\frac{}{\text{B. to K's 2nd}}$, 5. $\frac{\text{Kt. to Q. B's 3rd}}{\text{P. to Q's 3rd}}$, 6. $\frac{\text{P. to Q's 4th}}{\text{P. takes P.}}$, 7. $\frac{\text{Kt. takes P.}}{\text{B. to Q's 2nd}}$, 8. $\frac{\text{P. to K. B's 4th}}{\text{Kt. takes Kt.}}$, the game is considered equal.

5. R. to K's sq.	5. Kt. to Q's 3rd.

This is considered to be rather stronger than 5. Kt. to K. B's 3rd, which would be continued,—5. $\frac{}{\text{Kt. to K. B's 3rd}}$, 6. $\frac{\text{P. to Q's 4th}}{}$. (If 6. $\frac{\text{Kt. takes P.}}{\text{B. to K's 2nd (best)}}$.) 6. $\frac{}{\text{P. to K's 5th}}$, 7. $\frac{\text{P. to Q's 5th}}{\text{Kt. to K's 2nd}}$, 8. $\frac{\text{Kt. to K. Kt.'s 5th}}{}$, &c.

6. Kt. takes K's P.

He may also play 6. $\frac{\text{B. takes Kt.}}{}$.

	6. Kt. takes Kt.
7. R. takes Kt. (ch.)	7. B. to K's 2nd.
8. B. to Q. R's 4th.	8. Castles.
9. B. to Q. Kt.'s 3rd.	9. B. to K. B's 3rd.
10. R. to K's sq.	10. Kt. to K. B's 4th.

And the *Handbuch* declares it to be an even game.

GAME THE THIRD.

WHITE.	BLACK.
1. P. to K's 4th.	1. P. to K's 4th.
2. Kt. to K. B's 3rd.	2. Kt. to Q. B's 3rd.
3. B. to Q. Kt.'s 5th.	3. B. to Q. B's 4th.

This move was recommended by Calvi, but it affords White a good opportunity of establishing a strong centre with his Pawns.

4. P. to Q. B's 3rd.	4. K's Kt. to K's 2nd.

Black may also play 4. $\frac{}{\text{Q. to K's 2nd}}$, or 4. $\frac{}{\text{Q. to K. B's 3rd}}$, for which see Variations A and B. If 4. $\frac{}{\text{P. to Q's 3rd}}$, 5. $\frac{\text{P. to Q's 4th}}{\text{P. takes P.}}$, 6. $\frac{\text{P. takes P.}}{\text{B. to Kt.'s 5th (ch.)}}$, 7. $\frac{\text{K. to K's 2nd}}{\text{P. to Q's 4th}}$, 8. $\frac{\text{Q. to Q. R's 4th}}{\text{P. takes P.}}$, 9. $\frac{\text{B. takes Kt. (ch.)}}{\text{P. takes B.}}$, 10. $\frac{\text{Q. takes P. (ch.)}}{\text{B. to Q's 2nd}}$, 11. $\frac{\text{Q. takes K's P. (ch.)}}{}$, and White has the superiority. So if 4. $\frac{}{\text{Kt. to K. B's 3rd}}$, 5. $\frac{\text{Castles}}{\text{Castles}}$. (If 5. $\frac{}{\text{Kt. takes P.}}$, 6. $\frac{\text{P. to Q's 4th}}{\text{P. takes P.}}$, 7. $\frac{\text{R. to K's sq.}}{\text{P. to Q's 4th}}$, 8. $\frac{\text{P. takes P.}}{\text{B. to Q. Kt.'s 3rd}}$, 9. $\frac{\text{Kt. to K's 5th}}{\text{B. to Q's 2nd}}$, 10. $\frac{\text{Kt. takes B.}}{}$, with much the better game.) 6. $\frac{\text{P. to Q's 4th}}{\text{P. takes P.}}$, 7. $\frac{\text{P. takes P.}}{\text{B. to Q. Kt.'s 3rd}}$, 8. $\frac{\text{P. to K's 5th}}{\text{Kt. to K's sq.}}$, 9. $\frac{\text{P. to Q's 5th}}{\text{Kt. to K's 2nd}}$, Black's game is seriously restricted.

5. Castles.

If 5. $\frac{\text{P. to Q's 4th}}{\text{P. takes P.}}$, 6. $\frac{\text{P. takes P.}}{\text{B. to Kt.'s 5th (ch.)}}$, 7. $\frac{\text{Kt. to Q. B's 3rd}}{\text{P. to Q's 4th}}$, equal game.

5. Castles.

Black may play here 5. $\frac{}{\text{K. to K. Kt.'s 3rd}}$ without disadvantage.

6. P. to Q's 4th.	6. P. takes P.
7. P. takes P.	7. B. to Q. Kt.'s 3rd.
8. P. to Q's 5th.	8. Kt. to Q. Kt.'s sq.
9. P. to Q's 6th.	9. P. takes P.
10. B. to K. B's 4th.	10. B. to Q. B's 2nd.
11. Kt. to Q. B's 3rd.	11. P. to Q. R's 3rd.
12. B. to Q. B's 4th.	12. P. to Q. Kt.'s 4th.
13. B. to Q. Kt.'s 3rd.	

And White has the preferable position.

VARIATION A, ON BLACK'S 4TH MOVE.

BLACK.

WHITE.

Position prior to Black's 4th move.

	4. Q. to K's 2nd.
5. Castles.	5. P. to K. B's 3rd.

This gives Black a painfully constricted game; but if 5. $\frac{}{\text{Kt. to K. B's 3rd}}$, 6. $\frac{\text{P. to Q's 4th}}{\text{B. to Q. Kt.'s 3rd}}$, 7. $\frac{\text{B. to K. Kt.'s 5th}}{\text{P. to K. R's 3rd}}$, 8. $\frac{\text{B. takes Kt.}}{\text{P. takes B.}}$, 9. $\frac{\text{P. to Q's 4th}}{}$, Black has an equally bad position.

6. P. to Q's 4th.	6. B. to Q. Kt.'s 3rd.
7. Kt. to Q. R's 3rd.	7. Kt. to Q's sq.
8. Kt. to Q. B's 4th.	8. Kt. to K. B's 3rd.
9. Kt. to K's 3rd.	9. P. to Q. B's 3rd.
10. Kt. to K. B's 5th.	10. Q. to K. B's sq.

And White has very much the advantage.

Variation B, on Black's 4th Move.

(See preceding Diagram.)

4. Q. to K. B's 3rd.

A suggestion of Ponziani, the object of it being to prevent the formation of a centre by the adversary.

5. P. to Q's 4th.	5. P. takes P.

If 5. $\frac{\text{———}}{\text{B. to Q. Kt.'s 3rd}}$, 6. $\frac{\text{Castles}}{\text{K's Kt. to K's 2nd}}$, 7. $\frac{\text{B. to K. Kt.'s 5th}}{\text{Q. to Q's 3rd}}$, 8. $\frac{\text{B. takes Q's Kt.}}{\text{Q. takes B.}}$, 9. $\frac{\text{B. takes Kt.}}{\text{———}}$, gaining a Pawn, and having a superior position.

6. P. to K's 5th.	6. Q. to K. Kt.'s 3rd.
7. P. takes P.	7. B. to Kt.'s 5th (ch.)
8. B. to Q's 2nd.	8. B. takes B. (ch.)
9. Q's Kt. takes B.	9. Q. takes K. Kt.'s P.
10. R. to K. Kt.'s sq.	10. Q. to K. R's 6th.
11. R. takes P.	

And White has a fine game.

Game the Fourth.

WHITE.	BLACK.
1. P. to K's 4th.	1. P. to K's 4th.
2. Kt. to K. B's 3rd.	2. Kt. to Q. B's 3rd.
3. B. to Q. Kt.'s 5th.	3. Kt. to Q's 5th.

For the result of 3. $\frac{\text{———}}{\text{P. to K. B's 4th}}$, and 3. $\frac{\text{———}}{\text{Kt. to K's 2nd}}$, see Variations A and B. The consequences of 3. $\frac{\text{———}}{\text{B. to Q's 3rd}}$, and of 3. $\frac{\text{———}}{\text{P. to Q's 3rd}}$, may be shown at once.

In the first place,—3. $\frac{\text{———}}{\text{B. to Q's 3rd}}$, 4. $\frac{\text{P. to Q's 4th}}{\text{Q. to K's 2nd}}$, 5. $\frac{\text{Castles}}{\text{P. to Q. R's 3rd}}$, 6. $\frac{\text{B. to Q. R's 4th}}{\text{P. to Q. Kt.'s 4th}}$, 7. $\frac{\text{B. to Q. Kt.'s 3rd}}{\text{B. to K's 2nd}}$, 8. $\frac{\text{P. to Q's 5th}}{\text{———}}$, and White has a great advantage in position.

In the second place,—3. $\frac{\text{———}}{\text{P. to Q's 3rd}}$, 4. $\frac{\text{B. takes Kt. (ch.)}}{\text{P. takes B.}}$,

5. $\frac{\text{P. to Q's 4th}}{\text{P. takes P.}}$, 6. $\frac{\text{Q. takes P.}}{\text{P. to Q. B's 4th}}$, 7. $\frac{\text{Q. to Q's 3rd}}{\quad}$, and again White has a manifest advantage in the freedom of his men.

4. Kt. takes Kt.	4. P. takes Kt.
5. P. to Q's 3rd.	5. B. to Q. B's 4th.
6. Q. to K. R's 5th.	6. Q. to K's 2nd.
7. B. to K. Kt.'s 5th.	7. B. to Q. Kt.'s 5th (ch.)
8. P. to Q. B's 3rd.	8. P. takes P.
9. P. takes P.	

White may also play 9. $\frac{\text{B. takes Q.}}{\quad}$, in which case the following is a likely continuation :—9. $\frac{\quad}{\text{P. takes P. (dis. ch.)}}$, 10. $\frac{\text{B. takes B.}}{\text{P. takes Q. (Queens)}}$, 11. $\frac{\text{Q. to Q. B's 5th}}{\text{K. to K's 2nd}}$, and Black must lose.

	9. Q. to Q. B's 4th.
10. B. to Q. B's 4th.	10. P. to K. Kt.'s 3rd.
11. Q. to K. B's 3rd.	11. Q. takes Q's B.
12. Q. takes B's P. (ch.)	12. K. to Q's sq.
13. P. takes B.	

With a winning advantage.

Variation A, on Black's 3rd Move.

BLACK.

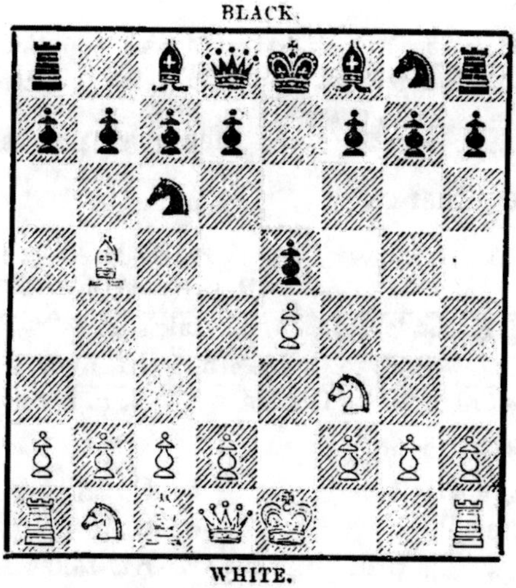

WHITE.

Position prior to Black's 3rd Move.

3. P. to K. B's 4th.

A counter attack proposed by Von Jaenisch.

4. Q. to K's 2nd.	4. P. takes P.

If 4. $\frac{}{\text{Q. to K's 2nd}}$, 5. $\frac{\text{Kt. to Q. B's 3rd}}{\text{P. to Q's 3rd}}$, 6. $\frac{\text{P. to Q's 4th}}{}$, and White has the better game.

5. B. takes Kt.	5. Q's P. takes B.
6. Q. takes P.	6. B. to Q's 3rd.
7. Kt. takes P.	7. Q. to K's 2nd.
8. P. to Q's 4th.	

And White has won a Pawn, with no sacrifice of situation.

Variation B, on Black's 3rd Move.

(See preceding Diagram.)

3. K's Kt. to K's 2nd.

The most ancient defence to the attack we are considering, of which there is any record, it being found in Lucena's treatise of 1495.

4. Castles.

If 4. $\frac{\text{P. to Q. B's 3rd}}{\text{P. to Q. R's 3rd}}$, 5. $\frac{\text{B. to Q. R's 4th}}{\text{P. to Q. Kt.'s 4th}}$, 6. $\frac{\text{B. to Q. Kt.'s 3rd}}{\text{P. to Q's 4th}}$, 7. $\frac{\text{P. takes P.}}{\text{Kt. takes P.}}$, 8. $\frac{\text{P. to Q's 4th}}{}$, there is not any marked superiority on either side.

4. P. to Q's 3rd.

If 4. $\frac{}{\text{Kt. to K. Kt.'s 3rd}}$, 5. $\frac{\text{P. to Q's 4th}}{\text{Kt. takes P.}}$, 6. $\frac{\text{Kt. takes Kt.}}{\text{P. takes Kt.}}$ 7. $\frac{\text{Q. takes P.}}{\text{P. to Q. B's 3rd}}$, 8. $\frac{\text{B. to Q. B's 4th}}{\text{P. to Q's 3rd}}$, 9. $\frac{\text{Kt. to Q. B's 3rd}}{\text{B. to K's 3rd}}$, White has a freer game.

5. P. to Q's 4th.	5. P. takes P.
6. Kt. takes P.	6. B. to Q's 2nd.
7. Kt. to Q. B's 3rd.	7. Kt. takes Kt.
8. Q. takes Kt.	8. B. takes B.

9. Kt. takes B.	9. Q. to Q's 2nd.
10. Q. to Q's 3rd.	10. Kt. to Q. B's 3rd.
11. P. to K. B's 4th.	11. B. to K's 2nd.
12. B. to Q's 2nd.	

I prefer White's game.

ILLUSTRATIVE GAMES.

GAME I.—Between Herr Max Lange and Major Fesca.

WHITE (Herr L.)	BLACK (Major F.)
1. P. to K's 4th.	1. P. to K's 4th.
2. Kt. to K. B's 3rd.	2. Kt. to Q. B's 3rd.
3. B. to Q. Kt.'s 5th.	3. Kt. to K. B's 3rd.
4. Castles.	4. Kt. takes P.
5. R. to K's sq.	5. Kt. to K. B's 3rd.*
6. P. to Q's 4th.	6. P. to K's 5th.
7. P. to Q's 5th.	7. Q's Kt. to K's 2nd.
8. Kt. to K. Kt.'s 5th.	8. P. to Q. B's 3rd.
9. P. to Q's 6th.	9. P. takes B.
10. Kt. takes K's P.	10. K's Kt. to Kt.'s sq.†
11. Q's Kt. to B's 3rd.	11. Q. to Q. R's 4th.
12. Kt. to Q's 5th.	12. K. to Q's sq.
13. B. to K. Kt.'s 5th.‡	13. P. to K. B's 3rd.
14. K's Kt. takes P.	14. P. takes Kt.
15. B. takes P.	15. Kt. takes B.
16. Kt. takes Kt.	16. P. to Q. Kt.'s 5th.
17. Q. to K's 2nd.	17. Q. to Q. B's 4th.
18. Q's R. to Q's sq.	18. P. to Q. Kt.'s 4th.
19. R. to Q's 5th.	19. Q. to Q. B's 5th.
20. Q. to K. R's 5th.	20. B. to K. Kt.'s 2nd.
21. Q. to K. B's 7th.	21. B. takes Kt.
22. Q. takes B.	22. R. to K's sq.
23. R. takes Kt.	

And wins.

---

* We rather prefer Kt. to Q's 3rd.
† The best reply.
‡ White plays the "high game" all through this attack.

GAME II.—Between Mr. R. B. Wormald and Mr. J. Wisker.

WHITE (Mr. Wormald).	BLACK (Mr. Wisker).
1. P. to K's 4th.	1. P. to K's 4th.
2. Kt. to K. B's 3rd.	2. Kt. to Q. B's 3rd.
3. B. to Q. Kt.'s 5th.	3. P. to Q. R's 3rd.
4. B. to Q. R's 4th.	4. Kt. to K. B's 3rd.
5. P. to Q's 4th.	5. P. takes P.
6. P. to K's 5th.	6. Kt. to K's 5th.
7. Castles.	7. B. to K's 2nd.
8. R. to K's sq.	8. Kt. to Q. B's 4th.
9. B. takes Kt.	9. Q's P. takes B.
10. Kt. takes P.	10. Castles.
11. Kt. to Q. B's 3rd	11. R. to K's sq.*
12. B. to K's 3rd.	12. Kt. to K's 3rd.
13. Kt. takes Kt.†	13. B. takes Kt.
14. Q. to K's 2nd.	14. P. to K. B's 4th.
15. Q's R. to Q's sq.	15. Q. to Q. B's sq.
16. P. to Q. R's 3rd.	16. P. to Q. Kt's 4th.
17. Q. to K. B's 3rd.	17. Q. to Q. Kt's 2nd.
18. Kt. to K's 2nd.	18. P. to K. Kt.'s 3rd.
19. Kt. to K. B's 4th.	19. B. to K. B's sq.
20. P. to K. R's 4th.	20. B. to Q. B's sq.
21. Q. to K. Kt.'s 3rd.	21. B. to K. Kt.'s 2nd.
22. Kt. takes P.	22. P. takes Kt.
23. Q. takes P.	23. B. to K's 3rd.
24. B. to K. R's 6th.‡	

And Black resigned.

GAME III.—Between Messrs. Wisker and Zukertort.

WHITE (Mr. W.)	BLACK (Mr. Z.)
1. P. to K's 4th.	1. P. to K's 4th.
2. Kt. to K. B's 3rd.	2. Kt. to Q. B's 3rd.
3. B. to Q. R's 5th.	3. P. to Q. R's 3rd.
4. B. to Q. R's 4th.	4. K's Kt. to B's 3rd.
5. Castles.	5. Kt. takes K's P.§

* We should have preferred Kt. to K's 3rd.

† If Kt. to K's 4th, Black would have replied with P. to Q. B's 4th.

‡ The whole of this game is beautifully played by White.

§ According to the latest German authorities this is stronger than

6. R. to K's sq.	6. Kt. to Q. B's 4th.
7. B. takes Kt.	7. Q's P. takes B.
8. P. to Q's 4th.	8. Kt. to K's 3rd.
9. Kt. takes K's P.*	9. B. to K's 2nd.
10. B. to K's 3rd.	10. Castles.
11. Kt. to Q. B's 3rd.	11. P. to K. B's 3rd.
12. Kt. to K. B's 3rd.	12. P. to K. B's 4th.
13. Q. to Q's 3rd.	13. P. to K. B's 5th.†
14. B. to Q's 2nd.	14. B. to Q's 3rd.
15. Kt. to K's 4th.	15. K. to R's sq.
16. P. to Q. B's 4th.	16. P. to Q. Kt.'s 4th.
17. P. to Q. Kt.'s 3rd	17. B. to Q. Kt.'s 2nd.
18. B. to B's 3rd.	18. Q. to Q's 2nd.
19. Q's R. to Q's sq.	19. Q. to K. B's 2nd.
20. Q. to K's 2nd.	20. K's R. to K's sq.
21. P. to Q. B's 5th.	21. B. to K's 2nd.
22. Kt. to K's 5th.	22. Q. to K. B's 4th.
23. R. to Q's 3rd.	23. Q's R. to K's sq.
24. P. to K. Kt.'s 4th.	24. Q. to K. B's sq.‡
25. R. to K. R's 3rd.	25. K. to Kt.'s sq.
26. Q. to Q's 3rd.	26. P. to K. Kt.'s 3rd.
27. P. to Q. Kt.'s 4th.	27. B. to K. B's 3rd.
28. Kt. to K. B's 3rd.	28. B. to Q. B's sq.
29. P. to Q's 5th.	29. B. to Kt.'s 2nd.
30. P. to Q's 6th.	30. P. takes P.
31. P takes P.	31. Kt. to Q. B's 2nd.
32. R. takes K. R's P.§	32. K. takes R.
33. K's Kt. to Kt.'s 5th (ch.)	33. K. to Kt.'s sq.
34. Q. to K. R's 3rd.	34. B. to K. R's 3rd.
35. Kt. to B's 6th (ch.)	35. Q. takes Kt.
36. R. takes R. (ch.)	36. Kt. takes R.
37. B. takes Q.	37. B. takes Kt.
38. B. takes B.	

And Black resigned.

---

5. B. to K's 2nd. This is true if White reply with 6. P. to Q's 4th; but if he play 6. R. to K's sq., as in the present game, we think the first player will obtain some advantage.

* White has already obtained the superior position.

† Not a good move.

‡ Had he taken the Pawn *en passant,* White would have replied with 25. R. to K. B's 3rd.

§ Leading to an elegant termination.

GAME IV.—Between Messrs. Campbell and Wormald.

WHITE (Mr. C.)	BLACK (Mr. W.)
1. P. to K's 4th.	1. P. to K's 4th.
2. Kt. to K. B's 3rd.	2. Kt. to Q. B's 3rd.
3. B. to Q. Kt.'s 5th.	3. P. to Q. R's 3rd.
4. B. to Q. R's 4th.	4. Kt. to K. B's 3rd.
5. Castles.	5. P. to Q. Kt.'s 4th.
6. B. to Q. Kt.'s 3rd.	6. B. to K's 2nd.
7. P. to Q's 4th.	7. Kt. takes K's P.
8. P. to Q's 5th.	8. Kt. to Q. R's 4th.
9. K's R. to K's sq.	9. Kt. takes B.*
10. R's P. takes Kt.	10. Kt. to K. B's 3rd.
11. Kt. takes K's P.	11. Castles.
12. P. to Q. B's 4th.	12. B. to Q. Kt.'s 2nd.
13. Kt. to Q. B's 3rd.	13. P. to Q's 3rd.
14. Kt. to K. B's 3rd.	14. P. to Q. Kt.'s 5th.
15. Kt. to K's 2nd.	15. Kt. to K's 5.
16. B. to K's 3rd.	16. B. to Q. B's sq.
17. Q's Kt. to Q's 4th.	17. B. to Q's 2nd.
18. B. to Q's 2nd.	18. Kt. takes B.
19. Q. takes Kt.	19. P. to Q. R's 4th.
20. R. to K's 2nd.	20. B. to K. B's 3rd.
21. Q's R. to Q's sq.	21. P. to K. R's 3rd.
22. P. to K. R's 3rd.	22. Q. to Q. Kt.'s sq.
23. Q. to Q's 3rd.	23. Q. to Q. B's sq.†
24. R. to Q. B's sq.	24. R. to K's sq.
25. R. takes R. (ch.)	25. Q. takes R.
26. R. to K's sq.	26. Q. to K. B's sq.
27. R. to Q. R's sq.	27. Q. to Q. Kt.'s sq.
28. Q. to K's 3rd.	28. Q. to Q. Kt.'s 3rd.
29. K. to B's sq.	29. R. to K's sq.
30. Q. to Q's 3rd.	

And the game was abandoned as drawn.‡

---

* By exchanging this Knight for the Bishop, Black is enabled to free his game considerably.

† All these moves are very carefully played.

‡ With proper play the game can have no other result.

GAME V.—Between Messrs. Duffy and Steinitz.

WHITE (Mr. D.)	BLACK (Mr. S.)
1. P. to K's 4th.	1. P. to K's 4th.
2. Kt. to K. B's 3rd.	2. Kt. to Q. B's 3rd.
3. B. to Q. Kt.'s 5th.	3. P. to K. B's 4th.
4. Castles.*	4. P. takes P.
5. B. takes Kt.	5. Kt.'s P. takes B.
6. Kt. takes P.	6. Kt. to K. B's 3rd.
7. P. to Q's 4th.	7. P. to Q's 3rd.
8. Kt. takes P.	8. Q. to Q's 2nd.
9. P. to Q's 5th.	9. B. to Kt.'s 2nd.
10. B. to K. Kt.'s 5th.†	10. Kt. takes P.
11. Q. takes Kt.	11. B. takes Kt.
12. Q. to Q's 4th.	12. Q. to K. B's 4th.
13. B. to K. R's 4th.	13. K. to Q's 2nd.
14. Kt. to Q. B's 4th.	14. R. to K's sq.
15. P. to Q. Kt.'s 4th.	15. Q. to K's 4th.
16. Q. to K's 3rd.	16. P. to K. Kt.'s 4th.
17. B. to Kt.'s 3rd.	17. Q. to K. B's 3rd.
18. Q's R. to Q's sq.	18. P. to K. R's 4th.
19. P. to Q. Kt.'s 5th.	19. R. to Q. R's sq.
20. Kt. to Q. R's 4th.	20. K. to B's sq.
21. Q. takes Q. R's P.	21. B. to K. Kt.'s 2nd.
22. Kt. to Kt.'s 6th (ch.)‡	22. P. takes Kt.
23. Q. takes P.	23. P. to R's 5th.
24. B. takes Q's P.	24. B. takes B.
25. R. takes B.	25. Q. to K's 2nd.
26. R. to Q. B's 6th.§	26. K. to Kt.'s sq.‖
27. P. to Q. R's 4th.	27. P. to K's 6th.
28. P. takes P.	28. Q. takes P (ch.)

---

* The move usually recommended at this point is 4. Q. to K's 2nd.

† The best reply, as he evidently cannot save the Pawn.

‡ Very ingenious, but the sacrifice of the piece was uncalled for. If we mistake not, he might have obtained a winning game by the more simple move of P. to Q. Kt.'s 6th. If Black reply with 22. P. to Q. B's 4th, White takes it with Knight, and if he play 22. P. to Q. B's 3rd, the answer is Kt. to Q. B's 5th.

§ Again very cleverly conceived, since if the Rook be taken, White would simply retake with Pawn, and win.

‖ Black's extra piece must now carry the day.

29. Q. takes Q.	29. R. takes Q.
30. R. to K. Kt.'s 6th.	30. R. to K's 4th.
31. R. to K. Kt.'s 7th.	31. R. to Q's sq.
32. P. to Q. B's 4th.	32. R. to Q's 7th.
33. P. to Q. R's 5th.	33. R. takes Kt.'s P. (ch.)

And wins.

GAME VI.—Between Herren Neumann and Schulten.

WHITE (Herr N.)	BLACK (Herr S.)
1. P. to K's 4th.	1. P. to K's 4th.
2. Kt. to K. B's 3rd.	2. Kt. to Q. B's 3rd.
3. B. to Q. Kt.'s 5th.	3. B. to Q. B's 4th.
4. P. to Q. B's 3rd.	4. K's Kt. to K's 2nd.
5. Castles.	5. Castles.
6. P. to Q's 4th.	6. P. takes P.
7. P. takes P.	7. B. to Q. Kt.'s 3rd.
8. P. to Q's 5th.	8. Kt. to Q. Kt.'s sq.
9. P. to Q's 6th.	9. Kt. to K. Kt.'s 3rd.*
10. P. to K's 5th.	10. Kt. to Q. B's 3rd.
11. R. to K's sq.	11. R. to K's sq.
12. B. to K. Kt.'s 5th.	12. P. to K. B's 3rd.
13. B. to Q. B's 4th (ch.)	13. K. to R's sq.
14. P. takes B's P.	14. R. takes R.
15. Q. takes R.	15. P. takes B's P.
16. Q. to K's 8th (ch.)	

And wins.

* This is inferior to the usual move of 9. P. takes P.

CHAPTER VIII.

Philidor's Defence.

1. $\frac{\text{P. to K's 4th}}{\text{P. to K's 4th}}$, 2. $\frac{\text{Kt. to K. B's 3rd}}{\text{P. to Q's 3rd}}$.

Game the First.

3. $\frac{\quad}{\text{P. takes P}}$.

Game the Second.

3. $\frac{\quad}{\text{P. to K. B's 4th}}$.

Game the Third.

3. $\frac{\text{B. to Q. B's 4th}}{\text{B. to K's 2nd}}$; 3. $\frac{\quad}{\text{P. to K. B's 4th}}$; 3. $\frac{\quad}{\text{P. to Q. B's 3rd}}$.

This defence, so warmly patronised by Philidor, has grown into favour of late years, owing to the dread many players have of facing the attack begun by 3. $\frac{\text{B. to Q. Kt.'s 5th}}{\quad}$. It is not, in my opinion, a commendable mode of play, because it restrains the action of Black's King's Bishop at a moment when his freedom is necessary to the development of Black's forces. As, however, many excellent authorities deem it a safe line of action, I have given a tolerably copious analysis of its many variations.

GAME THE FIRST.

WHITE.	BLACK.
1. P. to K's 4th.	1. P. to K's 4th.
2. Kt. to K. B's 3rd.	2. P. to Q's 3rd.*
3. P. to Q's 4th.	3. P. takes P.

Jaenisch pronounces this less vigorous than 3. $\frac{}{\text{Kt. to K. B's 3rd}}$, but there is really very little to choose between.

4. Q. takes P.

The consequences of 4. $\frac{\text{Kt. takes P}}{}$, which appears to me as good as the move in the text, shall be shown in Variation A.

4. B. to Q's 2nd.

Preferable, I think, to 4. $\frac{}{\text{Kt. to Q. B's 3rd}}$, and 4. $\frac{}{\text{Kt. to K. B's 3rd}}$. If, as Morphy recommends, 4. $\frac{}{\text{B. to K's 3rd}}$, Jaenisch replies 5. $\frac{\text{B. to K. Kt.'s 5th}}{\text{Q. to Q's 2nd}}$, 6. $\frac{\text{Q's Kt. to Q's 2nd}}{\text{Kt. to Q. B's 3rd}}$, 7. $\frac{\text{Q. to Q. B's 3rd}}{\text{P. to K. B's 3rd}}$, 8. $\frac{\text{B. to K. R's 4th}}{\text{Kt. to K's 4th}}$, 9. $\frac{\text{Kt. to Q's 4th}}{\text{Castles}}$, 10. $\frac{\text{P. to K. B's 4th}}{\text{Kt. to K. Kt.'s 5th}}$, 11. $\frac{\text{B. to K's 2nd}}{}$, and White has the advantage.

5. B. to K. Kt.'s 5th.

White can also play 5. $\frac{\text{B. to K. B's 4th}}{}$, followed by 5. $\frac{}{\text{Kt. to Q. B's 3rd}}$, 6. $\frac{\text{Q. to Q's 2nd}}{\text{B. to K's 2nd}}$, 7. $\frac{\text{Kt. to Q. B's 3rd}}{\text{Kt. to K. B's 3rd}}$,

---

* The defence of the King's Pawn by playing P. to Q's 3rd is inseparably associated with Philidor's name through the pains he took to establish its validity. It was known, however, two hundred years and more before Philidor was born, for it is mentioned in the early work on Chess of Lucena. There, divested of the cumbrous Spanish circumlocution of the original, the moves, in our notation, are—

1. P. to K's 4th.	1. P. to K's 4th.
2. Kt. to K. B's 3rd.	2. P. to Q's 3rd.
3. P. to Q. B's 3rd.	3. Kt. to K. B's 3rd.
4. P. to K. R's 3rd, &c.	

8. $\frac{\text{Castles}}{\text{Castles}}$, 9. $\frac{\text{B. to Q's 3rd}}{\text{P. to Q. R's 3rd}}$; another proof, Jaenisch thinks, of the inferiority of the defence 3. $\frac{}{\text{P. takes P.}}$, to 3. $\frac{}{\text{Kt. to K. B's 3rd}}$.

5. Kt. to Q. B's 3rd (best).

If 5. $\frac{}{\text{Kt. to K. B's 3rd}}$, 6. $\frac{\text{B. takes Kt.}}{\text{Q. takes B}}$, 7. $\frac{\text{Q. takes Q.}}{\text{P. takes Q.}}$, 8. $\frac{\text{Kt. to Q. B's 3rd}}{\text{P. to Q. B's 3rd}}$, 9. $\frac{\text{Castles}}{}$, and White has evidently the better game. The move 5. $\frac{}{\text{Kt. to K. B's 3rd}}$ has also the fault, as Jaenisch remarks, of provoking the attack of 6. $\frac{\text{P. to K's 5th}}{}$, which, against the best defence, 6. $\frac{}{\text{Kt. to Q. B's 3rd}}$, 7. $\frac{\text{Q. to K's 3rd}}{\text{P. takes P.}}$, 8. $\frac{\text{Kt. takes P.}}{\text{Q. to K's 2nd}}$, 9. $\frac{\text{B. takes Kt.}}{\text{P. takes B.}}$, 10. $\frac{\text{Kt. takes B.}}{\text{Q. takes Q. (ch.)}}$, 11. $\frac{\text{P. takes Q.}}{\text{K. takes Kt.}}$, 12. $\frac{\text{Kt. to Q. B's 3rd}}{}$, leaves White with a better developed position.

6. B. takes Q. (best.)	6. Kt. takes Q.
7. Kt. takes Kt.	7. K. takes B.

By taking with the Rook, Jaenisch says, Black exposes himself to some attacks which he now avoids. For example—

7. $\frac{}{\text{R. takes B.}}$, 8. $\frac{\text{Kt. to Q. B's 3rd}}{\text{Kt. to K. B's 3rd}}$, 9. $\frac{\text{B. to Q. B's 4th}}{\text{B. to K's 2nd}}$, 10. $\frac{\text{Castles (Q's side)}}{\text{Kt. to K. Kt.'s 5th}}$, 11. $\frac{\text{Kt. to Q's 5th (best)}}{\text{B. to Kt.'s 4th (ch.)}}$, 12. $\frac{\text{P. to K. B's 4th}}{\text{P. to Q. B's 3rd}}$, 13. $\frac{\text{P. takes B.}}{\text{P. takes Kt.}}$, 14. $\frac{\text{B. takes P.}}{\text{Kt. to K. B's 7th}}$, 15. $\frac{\text{B. takes B's P. (ch.)}}{\text{K. to K's 2nd}}$, 16. $\frac{\text{K's R. to B's sq.}}{\text{Kt. takes R.}}$, 17. $\frac{\text{K. takes Kt.}}{\text{K's R. to K. B's sq.}}$, &c.

This variation is given by Jaenisch, but it does not seem

to me to prove that 7. $\frac{\quad\quad}{\text{R. takes B.}}$ is any more objectionable than 7. $\frac{\quad\quad}{\text{K. takes B.}}$

8. B. to Q. B's 4th.	8. Kt. to K. R.'s 3rd.
9. Kt. to Q. B's 3rd.	9. B. to K's 2nd.
10. Kt. to Q's 5th.	10. R. to K's sq.
11. Castles (K's side).	11. P. to Q. B's 3rd.
12. Kt. takes B.	12. R. takes Kt.
13. K's R. to K's sq.	13. K. to Q. B's 2nd.

And Black has a well ordered, though defensive position.

Variation A.

BLACK.

WHITE.

Position prior to White's 4th Move.

4. Kt. takes P.	4. Kt. to K. B's 3rd.

A move recommended by Morphy and De Riviere. If 4. $\frac{\quad\quad}{\text{P. to Q's 4th}}$, 5. $\frac{\text{P. to K's 5th}}{\text{B. to Q. B's 4th}}$. (If 5. $\frac{\quad\quad}{\text{P. to Q. B's 4th}}$,

6. $\frac{\text{B. to Q. Kt.'s 5th (ch.)}}{\text{B. to Q's 2nd}}$, 7. $\frac{\text{P. to K's 6th}}{\text{B. takes B. (best)}}$, 8. $\frac{\text{P. takes P. (ch.)}}{\text{K. takes P.}}$, 9. $\frac{\text{Kt. takes B.}}{\text{Q. to K's sq. (ch.)}}$, and Black has little inferiority.) 6. $\frac{\text{Kt. to Q. B's 3rd}}{\text{B. to K's 2nd (best)}}$, 7. $\frac{\text{B. to K's 2nd}}{\text{Castles}}$, 8. $\frac{\text{Castles}}{}$. White's position is slightly preferable.

5. Kt. to Q. B's 3rd.	5. B. to K's 2nd.
6. B. to K's 2nd.	

He may also play 6. $\frac{\text{B. to Q's 3rd}}{}$, and 6. $\frac{\text{P. to K. B's 4th}}{}$, but the latter is inferior.

	6. Castles.
7. Castles.	7. P. to Q. B's 4th.
8. Kt. to K. B's 3rd.	8. Kt. to Q. B's 3rd.
9. B. to K. Kt.'s 5th.	

White's game is a little more free.

Game the Second.

White.	Black.
1. P. to K's 4th.	1. P. to K's 4th.
2. Kt. to K. B's 3rd.	2. P. to Q's 3rd.
3. P. to Q's 4th.	3. P. to K. B's 4th.

This counter-attack was the sheet-anchor of Philidor's system of defence in the present opening. Experience has proved, however, that it is not trustworthy.

4. P. takes K's P.

White may also play here with advantage 4. $\frac{\text{B. to Q. B's 4th}}{}$, to which Black's best reply is 4. $\frac{}{\text{Kt. to Q. B's 3rd}}$. The first player may also try 4. $\frac{\text{Kt. to Q. B's 3rd}}{}$, which Mr. Zukertort considers to be his best mode of play, but this conclusion is, I think, open to question.

	4. B's P. takes P.
5. Kt. to Kt.'s 5th.	5. P. to Q's 4th.
6. P. to K's 6th.	

A move first suggested, I believe, by Del Rio, in his article as the *Anonymous Modenese* impugning the soundness of Philidor's counter move, 3. $\frac{}{\text{P. to K. B's 4th}}$. Philidor at this point made White play 6. $\frac{\text{P. to K. B's 4th}}{}$, which affords Black an easy opportunity of developing his men. For example:—6. $\frac{\text{P. to K. B's 4th}}{\text{B. to Q. B's 4th}}$, 7. $\frac{\text{P. to Q. B's 4th}}{\text{P. to Q. B's 3rd}}$, 8. $\frac{\text{Kt. to Q. B's 3rd}}{\text{Kt. to K's 2nd}}$, 9. $\frac{\text{P. to K. R's 4th}}{\text{P. to K. R's 3rd}}$, 10. $\frac{\text{Kt. to K. R's 3rd}}{\text{Castles}}$, 11. $\frac{}{\text{B. to Q. Kt.'s 5th (ch.)}}$, 12. $\frac{\text{B. to Q's 2nd}}{\text{B. takes B. (ch.)}}$, 13. $\frac{\text{Q. takes B.}}{\text{P. to Q's 5th}}$, 14. $\frac{\text{Castles (Q's side)}}{\text{Kt. to K. B's 4th}}$, 15. $\frac{\text{P. to K. Kt.'s 4th}}{\text{Kt. to K. Kt.'s 6th}}$, 16. $\frac{\text{R. to K. Kt.'s sq.}}{\text{Q. takes K's P.}}$, 17. $\frac{\text{Q. to K. Kt.'s 2nd}}{\text{Kt. takes B.}}$, 18. $\frac{\text{Q's R. takes Kt.}}{}$, and Black has the better game.

6. Kt. to K. R's 3rd.

6. $\frac{}{\text{B. to Q. B's 4th}}$ is bad because of 7. $\frac{\text{Kt. takes K's P.}}{\text{P. takes Kt.}}$, 8. $\frac{\text{Q. to K. R's 5th (ch.)}}{\text{P. to K. Kt.'s 3rd}}$, 9. $\frac{\text{Q. takes B.}}{}$

7. Kt. to Q. B's 3rd.

The best move I believe. If 7. $\frac{\text{Kt. takes K. R's P.}}{\text{Q's B. takes P. (best)}}$, 8. $\frac{\text{Kt. takes B.}}{\text{K. takes Kt.}}$, 9. $\frac{\text{B. takes Kt.}}{\text{R. takes B.}}$, &c. If 7. $\frac{\text{Q. to R's 5th (ch.)}}{}$, then follows, 7. $\frac{}{\text{P. to K. Kt.'s 3rd}}$, 8. $\frac{\text{Q. to R's 3rd}}{\text{Q. to K. B's 3rd}}$, 9. $\frac{\text{P. to Q. B's 4th}}{}$, &c. Again, if 7. $\frac{\text{P. to Q. B's 4th}}{\text{B. to Q. Kt.'s 5th (ch.)}}$, 8. $\frac{\text{Kt. to Q. B's 3rd}}{\text{P. to P's 5th}}$, and Black in each case has no disadvantage. Finally, if 7. $\frac{\text{P. to K. B's 3rd}}{\text{P. to K's 6th (best)}}$, 8. $\frac{\text{B. takes P.}}{\text{B. to K's 2nd}}$, and Black has the better game.

7. P. to Q. B's 3rd.

If 7. $\frac{}{\text{B. to Q. B's 4th}}$, 8. $\frac{\text{Q. to K. R's 5th (ch.)}}{\text{K. to B's sq.}}$, 9. $\frac{\text{Kt. to B's 7th}}{}$, with a great superiority.

White	Black
8. K's Kt. takes K's P.	8. P. takes Kt.
9. Q. to K. R's 5th (ch.)	9. P. to K. Kt.'s 3rd.
10. Q. to K's 5th.	10. R. to K. Kt.'s sq.
11. B. takes Kt.	

(For 11. $\frac{\text{B. to K. Kt.'s 5th}}{}$, a move attributed to Löwenthal, see Variation A.)

	11. B. takes B.
12. R. to Q's sq.	12. Q. to K's 2nd.

If 12. $\frac{}{\text{Q. to K. Kt.'s 4th}}$, 13. $\frac{\text{Q. to Q. B's 7th}}{\text{Q's B. takes P.}}$, 14. $\frac{\text{Q. takes Kt.'s P.}}{\text{P. to K's 6th}}$, 15. $\frac{\text{P. to K. B's 3rd}}{\text{Q. to K's 2nd}}$, 16. $\frac{\text{Q. takes Q's R.}}{\text{K. to B's 2nd}}$, 17. $\frac{\text{R. to Q's 4th}}{}$, and White wins.

13. Kt. takes P.

The *Handbuch* avoids giving the variation depending on this move, although it appeared in the English Handbook as far back as 1847. It merely gives the bad move, 13. $\frac{\text{B. to Q. B's 4th}}{}$, which, of course, is followed by 13. $\frac{}{\text{B. to K. Kt.'s 2nd}}$, 14. $\frac{\text{Q. takes P.}}{\text{B. takes Kt. (ch.)}}$, and Black has the advantage.

	13. Q's B. takes P.

If 13. $\frac{}{\text{B. to K. Kt.'s 2nd}}$, 14. $\frac{\text{Kt. to Q's 6th (ch.)}}{}$, winning.

If 13. $\frac{}{\text{Q. takes P.}}$, 14. $\frac{\text{Q. to Q's 4th}}{\text{Q. to K's 2nd}}$, 15. $\frac{\text{B. to K's 2nd}}{}$, &c.

14. R. to Q's 6th.	14. B. to K. B's 4th.
15. Kt. to B's 6th (ch.)	15. K. to B's sq.
16. R. to Q's 8th (ch.)	16. K. to B's 2nd.

If 16. $\frac{}{\text{Q. takes R.}}$, 17. $\frac{\text{Kt. takes P. (ch.)}}{\text{K. to B's 2nd}}$, 18. $\frac{\text{B. to Q. B's 4th (ch.)}}{}$, &c.

17. B. to Q. B's 4th (ch.)	17. B. to K's 3rd.
18. Kt. takes R.	

And White must win.

Variation A.

BLACK.

WHITE.

Position prior to White's 11*th move.*

11. B. to K. Kt.'s 5th.

This move, though good, has been much overrated. At the best it gains a Pawn, and is decidedly inferior, I think, to taking the Knight.

11. Q. to Q's 3rd.

If 11. $\frac{\quad}{\text{Q. to Q. Kt.'s 3rd}}$, 12. $\frac{\text{Castles}}{\quad}$, and the attack speedily becomes irresistible. Again, if 11. $\frac{\quad}{\text{B. to K. Kt.'s 2nd}}$ 12. $\frac{\text{P. to K's 7th}}{\text{Q. to Kt.'s 3rd}}$, 13. $\frac{\text{Castles}}{\quad}$, and will win. If 12. $\frac{\quad}{\text{Q. to Q's 2nd}}$, 13. $\frac{\text{Q. to K. B's 4th}}{\quad}$, with an evident advantage. If 12. $\frac{\quad}{\text{Q. to Q.'s 5th}}$, 13. $\frac{\text{Q. to Q. B's 7th}}{\quad}$, with a decided superiority.

12. Q. takes Q.	12. B. takes Q.
13. Kt. takes P.	13. Kt. to B's 4th.
14. P. to K. Kt.'s 4th.	14. B. to K's 2nd.
15. P. takes Kt.	

And White has no very marked superiority.

Game the Third.

WHITE.	BLACK.
1. P. to K's 4th.	1. P. to K's 4th.
2. Kt. to K. B's 3rd.	2. P. to Q's 3rd.
3. B. to Q. B's 4th.	

According to some authorities this move, though less immediately attacking, is at least as serviceable for White in the end as 3. $\frac{\text{P. to Q's 4th}}{\qquad}$.

3. B. to K's 2nd.

A move attributed to Mr. Boden, and which the *Stratégie Raisonnée* speaks well of. (For the effect of 3. $\frac{\qquad}{\text{P. to K. B's 4th}}$, which Philidor sanctions, see Variation A.) If 3. $\frac{\qquad}{\text{P. to Q. B's 3rd}}$, 4. $\frac{\text{P. to Q's 4th}}{\text{P. to Q's 4th}}$, 5. $\frac{\text{K's P. takes P.}}{\text{P. to K's 5th}}$, 6. $\frac{\text{Kt. to K's 5th}}{\text{P. takes P.}}$, 7. $\frac{\text{B. to Q. Kt's 5th (ch.)}}{\text{B. to Q's 2nd}}$, 8. $\frac{\text{Q. to K. R's 5th}}{\text{P. to K. Kt.'s 3rd}}$, 9. $\frac{\text{Kt. takes Kt.'s P.}}{\text{B's P. takes Kt.}}$, 10. $\frac{\text{Q. to K's 5th (ch.)}}{\text{K. to B's 2nd}}$, 11. $\frac{\text{Q. takes Q's P. (ch.)}}{\text{K. to Kt.'s 2nd}}$, 12. $\frac{\text{Q. takes Q. Kt.'s P.}}{\qquad}$, and White has more than an equivalent for the piece given up. If 3. $\frac{\qquad}{\text{B. to K's 3rd}}$, 4. $\frac{\text{B. takes B.}}{\text{P. takes B.}}$, 5. $\frac{\text{P. to Q's 4th}}{\text{P. takes P.}}$, 6. $\frac{\text{P. to Q. B's 3rd}}{\text{Kt. to Q. B's 3rd}}$, 7. $\frac{\text{Q. to Q. Kt.'s 3rd}}{\text{Q. to Q. B's sq.}}$, 8. $\frac{\text{Kt. to K. Kt.'s 5th}}{\text{Kt. to Q's sq.}}$, White's position is certainly preferable. Finally, if Black play 3. $\frac{\qquad}{\text{Kt. to K. B's 3rd}}$, the likely continuation is 4. $\frac{\text{Kt. to K. Kt.'s 5th}}{\text{P. to Q's 4th}}$, 5. $\frac{\text{P. takes P.}}{\text{Kt. takes P.}}$, 6. $\frac{\text{Q. to K. B's 3rd}}{\text{Q. takes Kt.}}$, 7. $\frac{\text{B. takes Kt.}}{\text{---}}$, and White has still the superiority.

4. P. to Q's 4th.   4. P. takes P.
5. Kt. takes P.   5. Kt. to K. B's 3rd.
6. Kt. to Q. B's 3rd.   6. Castles.
7. K's Kt. to K's 2nd.

Black's forces have not the same freedom as White's have.

Variation A, beginning at Black's 3rd Move.

BLACK.

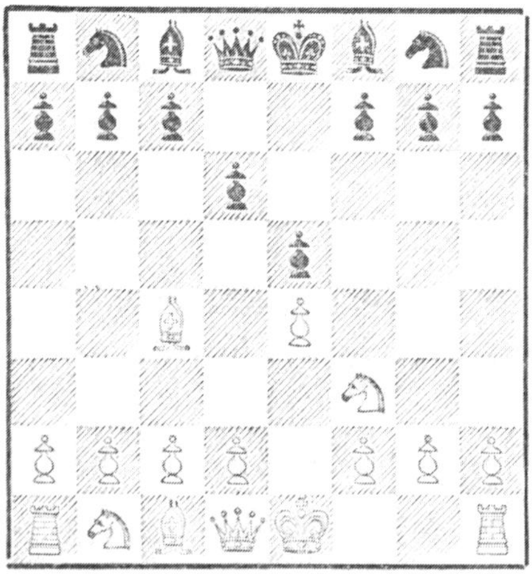

WHITE.

Position prior to Black's 3rd Move.

3. P. to K. B's 4th.

Notwithstanding Philidor's approval, this move, by general consent, has been condemned as uselessly hazardous.

4. P. to Q's 4th.   4. P. takes K's P.

If 4. $\frac{\text{---}}{\text{P. takes Q's P.}}$, 5. $\frac{\text{Kt. to K. Kt.'s 5th}}{\text{Kt. to K. R's 3rd}}$, 6. $\frac{\text{Castles}}{\text{Q. to K. B's 3rd}}$,

7. $\frac{\text{P. takes P.}}{\text{Q's B. takes P.}}$, 8. $\frac{\text{R. to K's sq. (ch.)}}{\text{K. to Q's 2nd}}$, 9. $\frac{\text{B. to K's 6th (ch.)}}{\text{B. takes B.}}$,

10. $\frac{\text{Kt. takes B.}}{\text{Kt. to Q. B's 3rd}}$, 11. $\frac{\text{B. takes Kt.}}{\text{P. takes B.}}$, 12. $\frac{\text{Q. to K. Kt.'s 4th}}{}$,

and White has a fine attack. Perhaps, however, Black's best course as his fourth move is to play Kt. to Q. B's 3rd.

5. Kt. takes K's P.	5. P. takes Kt.

If 5. $\frac{}{\text{P. to Q's 4th}}$, 6. $\frac{\text{Q. to K. R's 5th (ch.)}}{\text{P. to K. Kt.'s 3rd}}$, 7. $\frac{\text{Kt. takes P.}}{\text{Kt. to K. B's 3rd}}$,

8. $\frac{\text{Q. to K's 5th (ch.)}}{\text{B. to K's 2nd}}$, 9. $\frac{\text{Kt. takes B.}}{\text{Q. takes Kt.}}$, 10. $\frac{\text{B. to K. Kt.'s 5th}}{}$,

with a better game.

6. Q. to K. R's 5th (ch.)	6. K. to Q's 2nd (best).
7. Q. to K. B's 5th (ch.)	7. K. to Q. B's 3rd.
8. Q. to K's 5th, taking P.	

Better than taking the other Pawn, checking.

	8. P. to Q. R's 3rd.
9. P. to Q's 5th (ch.)	9. K. to Kt.'s 3rd.
10. B. to K's 3rd (ch.)	

And White has an evident advantage.

(c) ILLUSTRATIVE GAMES.

—Game I.—Between Messrs. Morphy and Harrwitz.

White (Mr. M.)	Black (Mr. H.)
1. P. to K's 4th.	1. P. to K's 4th.
2. Kt. to K. B's 3rd.	2. P. to Q's 3rd.
3. P. to Q's 4th.	3. P. takes P.
4. Q. takes P.	4. Kt. to Q. B's 3rd.
5. B. to Q. Kt.'s 5th.	5. B. to Q's 2nd.
6. B. takes Kt.	6. B. takes B.
7. B. to K. Kt.'s 5th.	7. P. to K. B's 3rd.*
8. B. to R's 4th.	8. Kt. to K. R's 3rd.

* Scarcely so effective, we think, as Kt. to K. B's 3rd.

9. Kt. to Q. B's 3rd.	9. Q. to Q's 2nd.
10. Castles (K's R.)	10. B. to K's 2nd.
11. Q's R. to Q's sq.	11. Castles (K's R.)
12. Q. to B's 4th (ch.)	12. R. to B's 2nd.
13. Kt. to Q's 4th.	13. Kt. to Kt.'s 5th.
14. P. to K. R's 3rd.	14. Kt. to K's 4th.
15. Q. to K's 2nd.	15. P. to K. Kt.'s 4th.
16. B. to K. Kt.'s 3rd.	16. R. to Kt.'s 2nd.
17. Kt. to B's 5th.	17. R. to Kt.'s 3rd.
18. P. to K. B's 4th.	18. P. takes B's P.
19. K's R. takes P.	19. K. to R's sq.
20. R. to K. R's 4th.	20. B. to B's sq.
21. B. takes Kt.	21. B's P. takes B.
22. Q's R. to K. B's sq.	22. Q. to K's 3rd.
23. Kt. to Q. Kt.'s 5th.	23. Q. to K. Kt.'s sq.
24. Q's R. to B's 2nd.*	24. P. to Q. R's 3rd.
25. Kt. takes Q. B's P.	25. Q's R. to B's sq.
26. Kt. to Q's 5th.	26. B. takes Kt.
27. P. takes B.	27. Q's R. to B's 2nd.
28. P. to Q. B's 4th.	28. B. to K's 2nd.
29. R. to R's 5th.	29. Q. to K's sq.
30. P. to Q. B's 5th.†	30. R. takes B's P.
31. K's R. takes P. (ch.)	31. K. takes R.
32. Q. to R's 5th (ch.)	32. K. to Kt.'s sq.
33. Kt. takes B. (ch.)	33. K. to Kt.'s 2nd.
34. Kt. to B's 5th (ch.)	34. K. to Kt.'s sq.
35. Kt. takes Q's P.	

And wins.

GAME II.—Between Messrs Brien and Wormald.

WHITE (Mr. B.)	BLACK (Mr. W.)
1. P. to K's 4th.	1. P. to K's 4th.
2. Kt. to K. B's 3rd.	2. P. to Q's 3rd.
3. P. to Q's 4th.	3. P. to K. B's 4th.
4. P. takes K.'s P.	4. B's P. takes P.
5. Kt. to Kt.'s 5th.	5. P. to Q's 4th.

---

* A necessary precaution preparatory to taking the Q. B's P.

† This wins, play as Black may.

6. P. to K.'s 6th.	6. Kt. to K. R's 3rd.
7. P. to K. B's 3rd.*	7. B. to Q. B's 4th.†
8. P. takes P.	8. Castles.
9. K's P. takes Q's P.	9. B. to B's 7th (ch.)
10. K. to K's 2nd.	10. B. to Q's 2nd.
11. P. takes B.	11. Q. to K's 2nd (ch.)
12. K. to Q's 3rd.	12. Q's Kt. takes P.
13. Q. to K's 2nd.	13. Kt. to B's 4th (ch.)
14. K. to Q. B's 4th.	14. P. to Q. Kt.'s 4th (ch.)
15. K. takes P.	15. R. to Kt.'s sq. (ch.)
16. K. to B's 4th.	16. R. to Kt's 5th (ch.)‡
17. K. takes R.	17. Kt. to Q's 6th (dis. ch.)

And wins.

GAME III.—In the following game Messrs. Staunton and Owen consulted against Messrs. Morphy and Barnes.

WHITE (Messrs. S. and O.)	BLACK (Messrs. M. and B.)
1. P. to K's 4th.	1. P. to K's 4th.
2. Kt. to K. B's 3rd.	2. P. to Q's 3rd.
3. P. to Q's 4th.	3. P. to K. B's 4th.
4. P. takes K's P.	4. B's P. takes P.
5. Kt. to Kt.'s 5th.	5. P. to Q's 4th.
6. P. to K's 6th.	6. Kt. to K. R's 3rd.
7. Kt. to Q. B's 3rd.	7. P. to Q. B's 3rd.
8. K's Kt. takes K's P.	8. P. takes Kt.
9. Q. to K. R's 5th (ch.)	9. P. to K. Kt.'s 3rd.
10. Q. to K's 5th.	10. R. to Kt.'s sq.
11. B. takes Kt.	11. B. takes B.
12. R. to Q's sq.	12. Q. to Kt.'s 4th.§
13. Q. to B's 7th.	13. B. takes P.
14. Q. takes Kt.'s P.	14. P. to K's 6th.

* This move was at one time in high favour with the German school, but it is very inferior to the accepted play of Kt. to Q. B's 3rd.

† The correct reply, as we have seen, is P. to K's 6th, but the move in the text is very strong.

‡ The game is finished off neatly enough.

§ The usual move at this point is Q. to K's 2nd. The move in the text, however, is noticed in Mr. Walker's "Art of Chess Play."

White	Black
15. P. to B's 3rd.	15. Q. to K's 2nd.
16. Q. takes R.	16. K. to B's 2nd.
17. Kt. to K's 4th.*	17. B. to K. B's 5th.
18. B. to K's 2nd.	18. K. to Kt.'s 2nd.
19. Castles.	19. Q. to Q. B's 2nd.
20. Kt. to B's 5th.	20. B. takes P. (ch.)
21. K. to R's sq.	21. B. to B's sq.†
22. R. to Q's 4th.	22. B. to Kt.'s 6th.
23. R. to K's 4th.	23. K. to R's sq.
24. R. to Q's sq.	24. Q. to K. Kt.'s 2nd.
25. R. to K. R's 4th.	25. B. takes R.
26. Q. takes Kt.	26. B. to R's 3rd.
27. Q. to R's 2nd.	27. B. takes B.
28. R. to Q's 7th.	28. Q. to R's 3rd.
29. Kt. to B's 4th.	29. B. to B's 5th.
30. Kt. to B's 6th.	30. P. to K's 7th.
31. R. to K's 7th.	31. Q. to B's 8th.
32. Q. to Kt.'s sq.	32. Q. takes Q. (ch.)
33. K. takes Q.	33. P. Queens,

And wins.

---

* Here White missed their way. They had simply to play Q's R. to Q's 4th, and the day was their own.

† The remainder of the game is very cleverly played by the Black allies.

CHAPTER IX.

GRECO-COUNTER GAMBIT IN THE KING'S KNIGHT'S GAME.

$$1. \frac{\text{P. to K's 4th}}{\text{P. to K's 4th}},\quad 2. \frac{\text{Kt. to K. B's 3rd}}{\text{P. to K. B's 4th}}.$$

GAME THE FIRST.

$$3. \frac{\text{Kt. takes P.}}{\quad}.$$

GAME THE SECOND.

$$3. \frac{\text{B. to Q. B's 4th}}{\quad}.$$

This mode of retorting the attack, though found in Damiano's treatise, appears to have been first analysed by the brilliant Calabrese. It leads to many striking combinations, and may be adopted successfully against a somewhat inferior opponent, but it cannot be commended as a trustworthy reply to 2. Kt. to K. B's 3rd.

GAME THE FIRST.

WHITE.	BLACK.
1. P. to K's 4th.	1. P. to K's 4th.
2. Kt. to K. B's 3rd.	2. P. to K. B's 4th.
3. Kt. takes P.	

This is reckoned White's strongest answer. He may without sustaining any damage, however, play 3. $\frac{\text{B. to Q. B's 4th}}{\quad}$, as in the next game. If he venture to take the Gambit Pawn he will certainly not profit by the capture, as a very slight examination will show.

3. Q. to K. B's 3rd.

Black may play, less satisfactorily, 8. $\frac{\qquad}{\text{Q. to K's 2nd}}$, the game then proceeding :—4. $\frac{\text{Q. to K. R's 5th (ch.)}}{\text{P. to Kt.'s 3rd}}$, 5. $\frac{\text{Kt. takes Kt.'s P.}}{\text{Q. takes K's P. (ch.)}}$, 6. $\frac{\text{B. to K's 2nd}}{\text{Kt. to K. B's 3rd}}$, 7. $\frac{\text{Q. to K. R's 3rd}}{\text{P. takes Kt.}}$, 8. $\frac{\text{Q. takes R.}}{\text{Q. takes Kt.'s P.}}$, 9. $\frac{\text{R. to K. B's sq.}}{\text{K. to B's 2nd}}$, and White has a better position.

4. P. to Q's 4th. 4. P. to Q's 3rd.

If 4. $\frac{\qquad}{\text{P. takes P.}}$, then 5. $\frac{\text{B. to Q. B's 4th}}{\text{P. to Q. B's 3rd (best)}}$, 6. $\frac{\text{B. to K. B's 7th (ch.)}}{\text{K. to K's 2nd}}$, 7. $\frac{\text{P. to K. R's 4th}}{\text{P. to K. R's 3rd}}$, 8. $\frac{\text{Q. to K. R's 5th}}{\text{K. to Q's 3rd}}$, 9. $\frac{\text{B. to K. Kt.'s 5th}}{\text{P. takes B.}}$, 10. $\frac{\text{Q. takes R.}}{\qquad}$, and White has the game in his hand.

5. Kt. to Q. B's 4th. 5. P. takes P.
6. Kt. to Q. B's 3rd. 6. P. to Q. B's 3rd.

The combinations springing from this move are sufficiently instructive to call for separate examination. They shall be examined as Variations A, B, and C.

7. Q's Kt. takes K's P. (best.) 7. Q. to K's 3rd.
8. Q. to K's 2nd. 8. P. to Q's 4th.
9. Q's Kt. to Q's 6th (ch.)

If 9. $\frac{\text{K's Kt. to Q's 6th (ch.)}}{\qquad}$, the result is not so unquestionably favourable for White, *e.g.* :—9. $\frac{\text{K's Kt. to Q's 6th (ch.)}}{\text{K. to Q's sq.}}$, 10. $\frac{\text{Kt. to K. Kt.'s 5th}}{\qquad}$. (If 10. $\frac{\text{B. to K. Kt.'s 5th (ch.)}}{\text{K. to B's 2nd}}$, &c.). 10. $\frac{\qquad}{\text{Q. takes Q. (ch.)}}$, 11. $\frac{\text{B. takes Q.}}{\text{B. takes Kt.}}$, 12. $\frac{\text{Kt. to B's 7th (ch.)}}{\text{K. to K's 2nd}}$, 13. $\frac{\text{Kt. takes R.}}{\text{B. to K's 3rd}}$, 14. $\frac{\text{B. to Q's 3rd}}{\text{Kt. to K. B's 3rd}}$, 15. $\frac{\text{B. to K. Kt.'s 5th}}{\text{Q's Kt. to Q's 2nd}}$, 16. $\frac{\text{Kt. to K. Kt.'s 6th (ch.)}}{\text{P. takes Kt.}}$, 17. $\frac{\text{B. takes P.}}{\qquad}$. Who has the advantage?

9. K. to Q's 2nd.

If 9. $\frac{\qquad}{\text{K. to Q's sq.}}$, the probable continuation is—
10. $\frac{\text{Kt. takes Kt.'s P. (ch.)}}{\text{K. to B's 2nd (best)}}$, 11. $\frac{\text{Q. takes Q.}}{\text{B. takes Q.}}$,
12. $\frac{\text{K's Kt. to Q. R's 4th}}{\text{K. to Kt.'s 3rd}}$, 13. $\frac{\text{B. to Q's 2nd}}{\text{Kt. to Q's 2nd}}$, 14. $\frac{\text{P. to Q. Kt.'s 4th}}{\qquad}$
and White has the masterdom.

10. Kt. to K. B's 7th.	10. Q's P. takes Kt.
11. Q. takes Q. (ch.)	11. K. takes Q.
12. B. takes P. (ch.)	12. K. to K's 2nd.
13. Kt. takes R.	13. B. to K's 3rd.
14. B. to Q's 3rd.	14. Kt. to K. B's 3rd.
15. B. to K. Kt.'s 5th.	15. P. to K. Kt.'s 3rd.

If 15. $\frac{\qquad}{\text{B. to K. Kt.'s sq.}}$, 16. $\frac{\text{Castles}}{\qquad}$, with the better position.

16. Kt. takes P. (ch.)	16. P. takes Kt.
17. B. takes P.	

And White has the preferable game.

Variation A, beginning at Black's 6th Move.

BLACK.

WHITE.

Position prior to Black's 6th Move.

	6. B. to K. B's 4th.
7. P. to K. Kt.'s 4th.	7. B. to Kt.'s 3rd.
8. B. to Kt.'s 2nd.	8. P. to Q. B's 3rd.
9. B. takes K's P.	9. B. takes B.
10. Kt. takes B.	10. Q. to K's 3rd.
11. Q. to K's 2nd.	11. P. to Q's 4th.
12. K's Kt. from B's 4th to Q's 6th (ch.)	

And White must win.

Mr. Petroff carries out this variation by 12. $\frac{\text{Kt. to K. B's 6th (ch.)}}{\text{K. to B's 2nd}}$, 13. $\frac{\text{Kt. to K's 5th (ch.)}}{\text{K. takes Kt.}}$, 14. $\frac{\text{B. to Kt.'s 5th (ch.)}}{\text{K. takes B.}}$, 15. $\frac{\text{Q. to K. B's 3rd}}{}$, and wins.

Variation B, on Black's 6th Move.

(*See the preceding Diagram.*)

	6. Kt. to K's 2nd.
7. P. to Q's 5th.	7. Q. to K. Kt.'s 3rd.
8. Q. to Q's 4th.	8. B. to K. B's 4th.
9. Kt. to K's 3rd.	

White must win a Pawn.

Variation C, on Black's 6th Move.

(*See the preceding Diagram.*)

	6. Q. to K. Kt.'s 3rd.
7. P. to K. B's 3rd.	

His best move I believe. If 7. $\frac{\text{Q. to K's 2nd}}{\text{Kt. to K. B's 3rd}}$. 8. $\frac{\text{P. to K. B's 3rd}}{\text{Kt. to Q. B's 3rd}}$, and the game is equal.

	7. Kt. to K. B's 3rd.
8. P. takes K's P.	8. Kt. takes P.
9. Q. to K's 2nd.	9. B. to K. B's 4th.
10. Kt. to Q's 2nd.	

And White will gain a Piece.

Game the Second.

WHITE.	BLACK.
1. P. to K's 4th.	1. P. to K's 4th.
2. Kt. to K. B's 3rd.	2. P. to K. B's 4th.
3. B. to Q. B's 4th.	3. P. takes P.

If Black play 3. $\frac{\quad}{\text{P. to Q's 3rd}}$, the proper answer is 4. $\frac{\text{P. to Q's 4th}}{\quad}$, which leads to a position in the *Philidor Defence* advantageous to White.

4. Kt. takes P. (best.)	4. Q. to K. Kt.'s 4th.
5. Kt. to K. B's 7th (best.)	

White may play 5. $\frac{\text{P. to Q's 4th}}{\quad}$, instead of 5. $\frac{\text{Kt. to K. B's 7th}}{\quad}$, and acquire a good position. Suppose :—5. $\frac{\text{P. to Q's 4th}}{\text{Q. takes K. Kt's P.}}$, 6. $\frac{\text{Q. to K. R's 5th (ch.)}}{\text{P. to K. Kt.'s 3rd}}$, 7. $\frac{\text{B. to B's 7th (ch.)}}{\text{K. to Q's sq.}}$, 8. $\frac{\text{Q. to K. Kt.'s 5th (ch.)}}{\text{Q. takes Q.}}$, 9. $\frac{\text{B. takes Q. (ch)}}{\text{B. to K's 2nd (best)}}$, 10. $\frac{\text{B. to Q. Kt.'s 3rd}}{\text{B. takes B.}}$, 11. $\frac{\text{Kt. to B's 7th (ch.)}}{\quad}$, &c.

	5. Q. takes Kt.'s P.
6. R. to K. B's sq.	6. P. to Q's 4th.
7. Kt. takes R.	7. P. takes B.
8. Q. to K. R's 5th (ch.)	8. P. to K. Kt.'s 3rd.
9. Q. takes K. R's P.	9. B. to K's 3rd.
10. Q. takes Kt.'s P. (ch.)	10. Q. takes Q.
11. Kt. takes Q.	

And White has a winning advantage.

ILLUSTRATIVE GAMES.

Game I.—Between Messrs. Mayet and Hanstein.

White (Mr. M.)	Black (Mr. H.)
1. P. to K's 4th.	1. P. to K's 4th.
2. Kt. to K. B's 3rd.	2. P. to K. B's 4th.

3. Kt. takes K's P.	3. Q. to K. B's 3rd.
4. P. to Q's 4th.	4. P. to Q's 3rd.
5. Kt. to Q. B's 4th.	5. P. takes P.
6. Kt. to Q. B's 3rd.	6. Kt. to K's 2nd.
7. P. to Q's 5th.	7. Q. to K. Kt.'s 3rd.
8. B. to K. B's 4th.*	8. B. to K. B's 4th.
9. P. to K. R's 3rd.	9. P. to K. R's 4th.
10. Q. to Q's 4th.	10. P. to Q. R's 3rd.
11. P. to Q. R's 4th.	11. Kt. to Q's 2nd.
12. Castles.	12. Kt. to K. B's 3rd.
13. B. takes Q's P.†	13. P. takes B.
14. Kt. takes Q's P. (ch.)	14. K. to Q's 2nd.
15. Kt. takes Q. Kt.'s P.	15. Kt. to Q. B's sq.
16. P. to Q's 6th.	16. K. to K's sq.
17. Q. to K's 5th (ch).	17. K. to Q's 2nd.
18. B. to Q. Kt.'s 5th (ch.)‡	18. P. takes B.
19. Q. takes Kt.'s P. (ch.)	19. K. to K's 3rd.
20. Kt. to Q's 8th.	

Mates.

GAME II.—Played by Messrs. Lowenthal and Medley in consultation, against Messrs. Morphy and Mongredien.

WHITE (Messrs. L. and M.)	BLACK (Messrs. M. and M.)
1. P. to K's 4th.	1. P. to K's 4th.
2. Kt. to K. B's 3rd.	2. P. to K. B's 4th.
3. B. to Q. B's 4th.	3. P. to Q's 3rd.
4. P. to Q's 4th.	4. Kt. to Q. B's 3rd.‖
5. P. takes K's P.§	5. Q's P. takes P.
6. Q. takes Q. (ch.)	6. Kt. takes Q.
7. Kt. takes K's P.	7. P. takes K's P.
8. B. to Q's 2nd.	8. B. to Q's 3rd.
9. B. to Q. B's 3rd.	9. Kt. to K. B's 3rd.
10. P. to K. R's 3rd.	10. B. to K's 3rd.

* As we have seen, 8. Q. to Q's 4th is the correct move.
† A strictly sound sacrifice. White has now a winning position.
‡ The mate is very neat.
§ Undoubtedly the best reply.
‖ We should have preferred Kt. to K. Kt.'s 5th.

11. Kt. to Q's 2nd.	11. Castles.
12. Castles (K's R.)	12. Kt. to Q's 4th.
13. B. takes Kt.	13. B. takes B.
14. Q's Kt. to Q. B's 4th.	14. P. to Q. Kt.'s 4th.
15. Kt. takes B.	15. P. takes Kt.
16. K's R. to Q's sq.	16. P. to K's 6th.
17. P. takes P.	17. B. takes K. Kt.'s P.
18. K. takes B.	18. P. takes Kt.
19. B. takes P.	19. Kt. to Q. B's 3rd.
20. B. to Q's 4th.*	20. Q's R. to K's sq.
21. R. to Q's 2nd.	21. R. to K's 3rd.
22. Q's R. to K's sq.	22. R. to K. Kt.'s 3rd (ch.)
23. K. to R's 2nd.	23. R. to K. B's 6th.
24. R. to K. Kt.'s 2nd.	24. Kt. takes B.
25. P. takes Kt.	25. R. to K. R's 3rd.
26. R. to K's 7th.	26. Q's R. takes P. (ch.)

And the game was abandoned as drawn.

---

* They ought to have retired the Bishop to K. B's 4th, in which case they would have been left with a pawn a head and a superior position.

CHAPTER X.

Centre Gambit.

$$1.\ \frac{\text{P. to K's 4th}}{\text{P. to K's 4th}},\ 2.\ \frac{\text{P. to Q's 4th}}{\text{P. takes P.}}.$$

This opening usually resolves into a form of the *Scotch Gambit.* It may be adopted without danger to either side, and it occasionally leads to positions of interest.

WHITE.	BLACK.
1. P. to K's 4th.	1. P. to K's 4th.
2. P. to Q's 4th.	2. P. takes P.

Black's best course is to accept the Gambit. Any other move loses him time and puts him at a disadvantage.

3. B. to Q. B's 4th.

(For the effect of $3.\ \frac{\text{Kt. to K. B's 3rd}}{\text{------}}$, see Variation A, and of $3.\ \frac{\text{P. to Q. B's 3rd}}{\quad}$, see Game the Second.)

3. Kt. to K. B's 3rd.

If $3.\ \frac{\quad}{\text{B. to Q. Kt.'s 5th (ch.)}},\ 4.\ \frac{\text{P. to Q. B's 3rd}}{\text{P. takes P.}},\ 5.\ \frac{\text{P. takes P.}}{\text{Q. to K. B's 3rd.}}$

White has now the choice of several lines of play. Firstly he can obtain a fine, but questionably sound, attack by taking the Bishop with Pawn, and sacrificing the exchange. Secondly he can play $6.\ \frac{\text{Q. to Q. Kt.'s 3rd}}{\quad}$, as recommended by the German *Handbuch;* and thirdly $6.\ \frac{\text{B. takes B's P. (ch.)}}{\text{------}}.$

4. P. to K's 5th.	4. P. to Q's 4th.
5. B. to Q. Kt.'s 3rd.	5. Kt. to K's 5th.
6. Kt. to K's 2nd.	6. P. to Q. B's 4th.
7. P. to K. B's 3rd.	7. Kt. to K. Kt.'s 4th.
8. Kt. to K. B's 4th.	8. P. to Q. B's 5th.
9. B. to Q. R's 4th (ch.)	9. Kt. to Q. B's 3rd.
10. B. takes Kt. (ch.)	10. P. takes B.
11. Q. takes P.	11. Kt. to K's 3rd.
12. Kt. takes Kt.	12. P. takes Kt.
13. Castles.	13. P. to Q. B's 4th.

White can now play his Queen to K. B's 2nd or to K. Kt.'s 4th, and the game is about equal.

Variation A, beginning at White's 3rd Move.

BLACK.

WHITE.

Position prior to White's 3rd Move.

WHITE.	BLACK.
1. P. to K's 4th.	1. P. to K's 4th.
2. P. to Q's 4th.	2. P. takes P.
3. Kt. to K. B's 3rd.	3. B. to Q. Kt.'s 5th (ch.)

Black may also resolve the opening into a *Scotch Gambit* by playing 3. Kt. to Q. B's 3rd.

4. B. to Q's 2nd.

If 4. $\frac{\text{P. to Q. B's 3rd}}{\text{P. takes P.}}$, 5. $\frac{\text{P. takes P.}}{\text{B. to Q. B's 4th}}$, 6. $\frac{\text{B. to Q. B's 4th}}{\text{P. to Q's 3rd}}$, and Black has at least as good a game as his opponent.

4. B. to Q. B's 4th.

He may equalise the game by 4. $\frac{\quad}{\text{Q. to K's 2nd}}$, 5. $\frac{\text{B to Q's 3rd}}{\text{Kt. to Q. B's 3rd}}$, 6. $\frac{\text{Castles}}{\text{B. takes B.}}$, 7. $\frac{\text{Q's Kt. takes B.}}{\text{P. to Q's 3rd}}$, 8. $\frac{\text{B. to Q. Kt.'s 5th}}{\text{B. to Q's 2nd}}$, 9. $\frac{\text{B. takes Kt.}}{\text{B. takes B.}}$, 10. $\frac{\text{Kt. takes P.}}{\text{Kt. to K. R's 3rd}}$, 11. $\frac{\text{Q. to K. R's 5th}}{\text{Castles, K's side}}$, 12. $\frac{\text{Q's R. to K's sq.}}{\text{B. to Q's 2nd}}$, &c.

5. B. to Q. B's 4th.	5. Kt. to Q. B's 3rd.
6. B. to K. B's 4th.	6. P. to Q's 3rd.
7. P. to Q. B's 3rd.	7. P. takes P.
8. Q's Kt. takes P.	8. B. to K's 3rd.
9. B. takes B.	9. P. takes B.
10. Q. to Q. Kt.'s 3rd.	10. Q. to Q. B's sq.
11. Kt. to K. Kt.'s 5th.	11. Kt. to Q's 5th.

Black's game is the better one.

Game the Second.

WHITE.	BLACK.
1. P. to K's 4th.	1. P. to K's 4th.
2. P. to Q's 4th.	2. P. takes P.
3. P. to Q. B's 3rd.	

The offer of a second Pawn in this opening is said to have been suggested by Dr. Lindehn, a Swedish player; but from the circumstance of its having been much practised by Mr. From of Denmark, the variation is commonly called the *Danish Gambit*. The conception is highly ingenious, but against the best defence the attack succumbs.

3. P. takes P.

It is best to take the Pawn. If 3. $\frac{\qquad}{\text{P. to Q's 4th}}$, 4. $\frac{\text{K's P. takes P.}}{\text{Q. takes P.}}$, 5. $\frac{\text{P. takes P.}}{\qquad}$, &c.

4. B. to Q. B's 4th.	4. P. takes P.
5. Q's B. takes P.	5. Kt. to K. B's 3rd.
6. P. to K's 5th.	6. B. to Q. Kt.'s 5th (ch.)
7. Kt. to Q. B's 3rd.*	7. Q. to K's 2nd.
8. K's Kt. to K's 2nd.	8. Kt. to K's 5th.

If 8. $\frac{\qquad}{\text{Q. takes P.}}$, 9. $\frac{\text{P. to K. B's 4th}}{\qquad}$, and White has the advantage.

9. Castles.	9. Kt. takes Kt.
10. Kt. takes Kt.	10. B. takes Kt.
11. B. takes B.	11. Castles.

And White has not attack enough to compensate for the two Pawns he has sacrificed.

ILLUSTRATIVE GAMES.

Game I.—Between Messrs. Wormald and Dalby.

White (Mr. W.)	Black (Mr. D.)
1. P. to K's 4th.	1. P. to K's 4th.
2. P. to Q's 4th.	2. P. takes P.
3. B. to Q. B's 4th.	3. B. to Kt.'s 5th (ch).
4. P. to Q. B's 3rd.	4. P. takes P.
5. P. takes P.	5. Q. to K. B's 3rd.

---

* In an analysis of the opening by Von der Laza, published in the *Schachzeitung*, White is made to play here 7. $\frac{\text{K. to B's sq.}}{\qquad}$, to which Black answers with 7. $\frac{\qquad}{\text{P. to Q's 4th}}$. Von der Laza then examines the consequences of White's three available replies, viz., 8. $\frac{\text{P. takes Kt.}}{\qquad}$; 8. $\frac{\text{Q. to R's 4th (ch.)}}{\qquad}$, and 8. $\frac{\text{B. to Q. Kt.'s 5th (ch.)}}{\qquad}$, all of which he shows should result in Black's favour.—[Ed.]

6. P. takes B.*	6. Q. takes R.
7. Q. to Q. Kt.'s 3rd.	7. Q. to K. B's 3rd.
8. Kt. to Q. B's 3rd.	8. P. to Q. B's 3rd.†
9. Kt. to K. B's 3rd.	9. P. to Q's 3rd.
10. P. to K's 5th.	10. P. takes P.
11. Kt. to K's 4th.	11. Q. to K. Kt.'s 3rd.
12. B. takes K. B's P. (ch.)	12. Resigns.

Game II.—Between Dr. Lindehn and Herr Soanberg.

White (Dr. L.)	Black (Herr S.)
1. P. to K's 4th.	1. P. to K's 4th.
2. P. to Q's 4th	2. P. takes P.
3. P. to Q. B's 3rd.	3. P. takes P.
4. B. to Q. B's 4th.	4. P. takes Kt.'s P.
5. Q's B. takes P.	5. B. to Q. Kt.'s 5th (ch.)
6. Kt. to Q's 2nd.	6. Q. to K. Kt.'s 4th.
7. Kt. to K. B's 3rd.	7. B. takes Kt. (ch.)
8. Kt. takes B.	8. Q. takes K. Kt.'s P.
9. K. to K's 2nd.	9. P. to Q's 3rd.
10. P. to K. R's 3rd.	10. B. takes K. R's P.
11. R. takes B.	11. Q. takes R.
12. Kt. to K. B's 3rd.	12. Q. to K. Kt.'s 5th.
13. B. takes B's P. (ch.)‡	13. K. takes B.
14. Q. to Q's 5th (ch.)	14. K. to K's 2nd.
15. R. to K. Kt.'s sq.	15. P. to Q. B's 3rd.
16. R. takes Q.	16. P. takes Q.
17. R. takes Kt.'s P. (ch.)	17. K. to K's sq.
18. R. takes Q. Kt.'s P.	18. P. takes P.
19. Kt. to Kt.'s 5th.	19. Kt. to K's 2nd.§
20. B. takes R.	20. P. to Q's 4th.
21. Kt. takes K. R's P.	21. Q's Kt. to Q. B's 3rd.
22. Kt. to K. Kt.'s 5th.	22. R. to Q. B's sq.
23. B. to K. B's 6th.	23. Kt. to K. B's 4th.

* The sacrifice of the exchange is perhaps not strictly sound, but it may be fairly ventured.

† He ought to have played Kt. to K's 2nd.

‡ All this is very ingenious.

§ Had he played Kt. to K. B's 3rd, White would have had a forced mate.

24. R. to K. R's 7th.	24. Q's Kt. to Q's 5th (ch).
25. K. to B's sq.	25. R. to B's 8th (ch.)
26. K. to Kt.'s 2nd.	26. Kt. to K's 7th.
27. R. takes Q. R's P.	27. R. to K. Kt.'s 8th (ch.)
28. K. to R's 2nd.	28. R. to K. B's 8th.
29. K. to Kt.'s 2nd.	29. R. to Q's 8th.
30. R. to R's 8th (ch.)	30. K. to Q's 2nd.
31. R. to Q's 8th (ch.)	31. K. to B's 3rd.
32. R. to B's 8th (ch.)	32. K. to Kt.'s 4th.
33. R. to B's 2nd.	33. Kt. to K. B's 5th (ch.)
34. K. to R's 2nd.	34. Kt. to Q's 3rd.
35. Kt. to K's 6th.	35. Kt. to K's sq.
36. R. to Q. B's 5th (ch.)	36. K. to R's 5th.
37. B. to Q. B's 3rd.*	

And wins.

---

* The terminating moves are very ingeniously played by Dr. Lindehn.

CHAPTER XI.

THE VIENNA OPENING.

$$1. \frac{\text{P. to K's 4th}}{\text{P. to K's 4th}},\ 2. \frac{\text{Kt. to Q. B's 3rd}}{\quad}.$$

GAME THE FIRST.

$$2. \frac{\quad}{\text{Kt. to Q. B's 3rd}}.$$

GAME THE SECOND.

$$2. \frac{\quad}{\text{Kt. to K. B's 3rd}}.$$

GAME THE THIRD.

$$2. \frac{\quad}{\text{B. to Q. B's 4th}}.$$

This opening, first introduced or, rather, first brought prominently into notice, by Mr. Hampe of Vienna, is a perfectly safe *début*. At one time it was thought that it tended to reverse the attitude of the combatants, the first player suffering his opponent to take the attack while he acts on the defensive; but this opinion has undergone a change, and there are few openings more popular at the present day.

GAME THE FIRST.

WHITE.	BLACK.
1. P. to K's 4th.	1. P. to K's 4th.
2. Kt. to Q. B's 3rd.	2. Kt. to Q. B's 3rd.

The question whether this or 2. $\frac{\quad}{\text{Kt. to K. B's 3rd}}$ is the better move for Black has not yet been settled. The result of 2. $\frac{\quad}{\text{Kt. to K. B's 3rd}}$ will be seen in the next game, and that of 2. $\frac{\quad}{\text{B. to Q. B's 4th}}$ in Game the Third.

In addition, however, to these two moves, Black may play 2. $\frac{\quad}{\text{P. to K. B's 4th}}$, or 2. $\frac{\quad}{\text{B. to Q. Kt.'s 5th}}$, which we can consider here. Suppose, then:—

Firstly.—2. $\frac{\quad}{\text{P. to K. B's 4th}}$, 3. $\frac{\text{P. takes P.}}{\text{Kt. to K. B's 3rd}}$, 4. $\frac{\text{P. to K. Kt.'s 4th}}{\quad}$, and we have a position of the *King's Knight's Gambit*; the second player attacking and the first defending; but with this distinction, that White has his Queen's Knight in the field, which gives him a striking advantage.

Secondly.—2. $\frac{\quad}{\text{B. to Q. Kt.'s 5th}}$, 3. $\frac{\text{P. to K. B's 4th}}{\text{P. takes P.*}}$, 4. $\frac{\text{Kt. to K. B's 3rd}}{\text{P. to K. Kt.'s 4th}}$, 5. $\frac{\text{B. to Q. B's 4th}}{\text{P. to K. Kt.'s 5th}}$, 6. $\frac{\text{Castles}}{\text{B. takes Kt.}}$, 7. $\frac{\text{Kt.'s P. takes B.}}{\text{P. takes Kt.}}$, 8. $\frac{\text{Q. takes P.}}{\text{Q. to K's 2nd}}$, 9. $\frac{\text{P. to Q's 4th}}{\text{P. to Q's 3rd}}$, 10. $\frac{\text{Q's B. takes P.}}{\text{B. to K's 3rd}}$, 11. $\frac{\text{P. to Q's 5th}}{\text{B. to Q's 2nd}}$, 12. $\frac{\text{P. to K's 5th}}{\quad}$, with a winning attack.

3. P. to K. B's 4th.

---

* The German *Handbuch* gives 3. $\frac{\quad}{\text{P. to Q's 3rd}}$, 4. $\frac{\text{K's Kt. to B's 3rd}}{\text{Kt. to K. B's 3rd}}$, 5. $\frac{\text{B. to Q. B's 4th}}{\text{P. to Q. B's 3rd}}$, and ultimately declares in favour of the second player, albeit the demonstration is scarcely satisfactory. In addition to 3. $\frac{\text{P. to K. B's 4th}}{\quad}$, as in the text, White may also play 3. $\frac{\text{Kt. to K. B's 3rd}}{\quad}$, or 3. $\frac{\text{B. to Q. B's 4th.}}{\quad}$—[ED.]

It is not yet settled whether this is White's best move, though none is so frequently adopted. In place of it he can play 3. $\frac{\text{Kt. to K. B's 3rd}}{}$, to which Black's best reply is generally considered to be 3. $\frac{}{\text{P. to K. Kt's 3rd.}}$

3. P. takes P.

4. Kt. to K. B's 3rd.

Instead of this move Mr. Steinitz has played with considerable success 4. $\frac{\text{P. to Q's 4th}}{}$, a novelty upon the merits of which there appears to be a difference of opinion among the best authorities. (See Variation A.)

	4. P. to K. Kt.'s 4th.
5. B. to Q. B's 4th.	5. B. to K. Kt.'s 2nd.
6. Castles.	6. P. to K. Kt.'s 5th.

Stronger, perhaps, than the move of the German *Hand-buch*, which is 6. $\frac{}{\text{P. to Q's 3rd}}$.

7. P. to Q's 3rd.

If 7. $\frac{\text{P. to Q's 4th}}{\text{P. takes Kt.}}$, 8. $\frac{\text{Q. takes P.}}{\text{B. takes P. (ch.)}}$, 9. $\frac{\text{K. to R's sq.}}{\text{Kt. to K's 4th}}$, 10. $\frac{\text{Q. takes P.}}{\text{Q. to K. B's 3rd}}$, 11. $\frac{\text{Kt. to Q's 5th}}{\text{Q. takes Q.}}$, 12. $\frac{\text{B. takes Q.}}{\text{Kt. takes B.}}$, 13. $\frac{\text{Kt. takes P. (ch.)}}{\text{K. to Q's sq.}}$, 14. $\frac{\text{Kt. takes R.}}{\text{B. to K's 4th}}$. Black has a winning superiority.

	7. P. takes Kt.
8. Q. takes P.	8. B. takes Kt.
9. P. takes B.	9. Q. to K. B's 3rd.
10. Q's B. takes P.	10. P. to Q's 3rd.

And Black has the better game. (See "The Chess Congress of 1862," p. 8.)

VARIATION A, BEGINNING AT WHITE'S 4TH MOVE.

BLACK.

WHITE.

Position prior to White's 4th Move.

4. P. to Q's 4th.

I have said that there is a conflict of opinion as to the soundness of this variation. My own opinion, formed upon the published analyses of it, and a careful examination, is against the validity of the move altogether: at the same time I admit its ingenuity.

	4. Q. to K. R's 5th (ch.)
5. K. to K's 2nd.	5. P. to Q's 4th.

If 5. $\frac{\quad}{\text{P. to Q's 3rd}}$, 6. $\frac{\text{Kt. to K. B's 3rd}}{\text{B. to K. Kt.'s 5th}}$, 7. $\frac{\text{Q's B. takes P}}{\text{Castles}}$

8. $\frac{\text{K. to K's 3rd}}{\text{Q. to K. R's 4th}}$, and White may defend himself; but his

King is painfully liable to attack. Again, if 5. $\frac{\quad}{\text{Q. to K. R's 4th (ch.)}}$,

6. $\frac{\text{Kt. to K. B's 3rd}}{\text{P. to K. Kt.'s 4th}}$, Black will have a very dangerous power of attack in a few more moves.

6. Kt. takes Q's P.

His best move probably. But he can play also 6. $\frac{\text{P. takes P.}}{}$, which shall be examined off-hand; *e.g.*, 6. $\frac{\text{P. takes P.}}{\text{B. to K. Kt.'s 5th (ch.)}}$, 7. $\frac{\text{Kt. to K. B's 3rd}}{\text{Castles}}$, 8. $\frac{\text{P. takes Kt.}}{\text{B. to Q. B's 4th}}$, 9. $\frac{\text{P. takes P. (ch.)}}{\text{K. to Kt.'s sq.}}$, 10. $\frac{\text{Kt. to Q. Kt.'s 5th (best)}}{\text{Kt. to K. B's 3rd}}$. In a game between Messrs. Steinitz and Zukertort, the former played here 11. $\frac{\text{K. to Q's 3rd}}{}$, to which the other replied with 11. $\frac{}{\text{Q. to R's 4th}}$, and the first player ultimately won. The German *Handbuch* continues:— 11. $\frac{\text{P. to Q. B's 3rd}}{\text{B. takes Kt. (ch.)}}$, 12. $\frac{\text{P. takes B.}}{\text{K's R. to K's sq. (ch.)}}$, 13. $\frac{\text{K. to Q's 3rd}}{\text{R. to K's 8th}}$, 14. $\frac{\text{Q. to Q. B's 2nd}}{\text{Q. to K. R's 4th}}$, 15. $\frac{\text{Q. to K. B's 2nd}}{}$, and the game is dismissed in White's favour.

	6. B. to K. Kt.'s 5th (ch.)
7. Kt. to K. B's 3rd.	7. Castles.
8. Q's B. takes P.	8. Kt. to K. B's 3rd.
9. B. to K. Kt.'s 3rd.	

If 9. $\frac{\text{K. to Q's 3rd}}{\text{R. takes Kt.}}$, 10. $\frac{\text{P. takes R.}}{\text{B. to K. B's 4th (ch.)}}$, 11. $\frac{\text{K. to K's 2nd}}{\text{Q. takes B.}}$, 12. $\frac{\text{P. takes Kt.}}{\text{B. to Q. Kt.'s 5th}}$, Black has a vastly superior game. If 9. $\frac{\text{Q. to Q's 3rd}}{\text{K's Kt. takes Kt.}}$, 10. $\frac{\text{P. takes Kt.}}{\text{R. takes P.}}$, 11. $\frac{\text{P. to Q. B's 3rd}}{\text{B. to Q. B's 4th}}$, and White has a bad position. Finally, if 9. $\frac{\text{B. takes Q. B's P.}}{\text{R. takes Kt.}}$, 10. $\frac{\text{P. takes R.}}{\text{K's Kt. takes P.}}$, 11. $\frac{\text{B. to K's 5th}}{\text{Kt. takes B.}}$, 12. $\frac{\text{P. takes Kt.}}{\text{B. to Q. B's 4th}}$, 13. $\frac{\text{Q. to K's sq.}}{\text{Kt. to B's 5th (ch.)}}$. With the superior game.

9. Q. to K. R's 3rd (best).

10. P. to Q. B's 4th (best).

If 10. $\frac{\text{Kt. takes Kt.}}{\text{Kt. takes Q's P. (ch.)}}$, 11. $\frac{\text{K. to B's 2nd}}{\text{Kt. takes Kt.}}$, &c. If 10. $\frac{\text{P. to Q. B's 3rd}}{\text{Kt. takes K's P.}}$, 11. $\frac{\text{B. to K. B's 4th}}{\text{P. to K. Kt.'s 4th}}$, 12. $\frac{\text{Q. to Q's 3rd}}{\text{Q. to K. Kt.'s 3rd}}$, Black has an inferior game.

10. Kt. takes K's P.

11. B. to K. B's 4th. 11. Q. to K's 3rd.

12. Kt. to K's 3rd. 12. Kt. takes P. (ch.)

Black must win.

Game the Second.

WHITE.	BLACK.
1. P. to K's 4th.	1. P. to K's 4th.
2. Kt. to Q. B's 3rd.	2. Kt. to K. B's 3rd.
3. P. to K. B's 4th.	

Instead of this move White may play without disadvantage—3. $\frac{\text{B. to Q. B's 4th}}{}$, or 3. $\frac{\text{Kt. to K. B's 3rd}}{}$, as in Variation A.

3. P. to Q's 4th.

4. P. takes Q's P.

If 4. $\frac{\text{P. takes K's P.}}{\text{Kt. takes K's P.}}$, 5. $\frac{\text{Kt. to K. B's 3rd}}{\text{B. to K. Kt.'s 5th (best)}}$, 6. $\frac{\text{P. to Q's 3rd}}{\text{Kt. takes Kt.}}$, 7. $\frac{\text{P. takes Kt.}}{\text{Kt. to Q. B's 3rd}}$, 8. $\frac{\text{P. to Q's 4th}}{\text{P. to K. B's 3rd}}$, White has at least an equal game. But if 4. $\frac{\text{P. to Q's 3rd}}{\text{P. takes K's P.}}$, 5. $\frac{\text{B's P. takes P.}}{\text{Kt. to Kt.'s 5th}}$, 6. $\frac{\text{P. to Q's 4th}}{\text{P. to K's 6th}}$, we have a position analogous to a well known one in *Philidor's Defence*, and Black has the superiority. In the *Philidor Defence* the position is reversed, White there having the attack which Black has here.

4. Kt. takes P.

If 4. $\overline{\text{P. to K's 5th}}$, the game becomes ultimately resolved into a well-known form of the *Gambit Declined*, in which the first player has a slight superiority.

5. Kt. takes Kt.	5. Q. takes Kt.
6. P. takes P.	6. Kt. to Q. B's 3rd.
7. Kt. to K. B's 3rd.	7. B. to K. Kt.'s 5th.
8. B. to K's 2nd.	8. Kt. takes P.

Black's position is slightly superior.

VARIATION A, BEGINNING AT WHITE'S 3RD MOVE.

BLACK.

WHITE.

Position prior to White's 3rd Move.

In the first place:—

3. B. to Q. B's 4th.	3. B. to Q. B's 4th (best).

If 3. $\overline{\text{Kt. takes P.}}$, 4. $\frac{\text{B. takes P. (ch.)}}{}$, &c.

4. Kt. to K. B's 3rd.

This is better than 4. $\frac{\text{P. to K. B's 4th}}{}$, or the tamer move of 4. $\frac{\text{P. to Q's 3rd.}}{}$

	4. P. to Q's 3rd.
5. P. to K. R's 3rd.	5. B. to K's 3rd.
6. B. to Q. Kt.'s 3rd.	6. Castles.
7. P. to Q's 3rd.	7. Q's Kt. to Q's 2nd.

An equal game.

In the second place :—

3. Kt. to K. B's 3rd.	3. B. to Q. Kt.'s 5th.

Black can also play, without disadvantage, 3. $\frac{}{\text{Kt. to Q. B's 3rd}}$; the probable continuation being 4. $\frac{\text{B. to Q. B's 4th}}{\text{B. to Q. Kt.'s 5th}}$, 5. $\frac{\text{Castles}}{\text{Castles}}$, 6. $\frac{\text{P. to Q's 3rd}}{\text{P. to Q's 3rd}}$, &c.

4. Kt. takes P. (best.)	4. Q. to K's 2nd.
5. P. to K. B's 4th	5. P. to Q's 3rd.
6. Kt. to K. B's 3rd.	6. B. takes Kt.
7. Q's P. takes B.	7. Kt. takes P.
8. B. to K's 2nd.	8. Castles.
9. Castles.	

Equal game.

Game the Third.

WHITE.	BLACK.
1. P. to K's 4th.	1. P. to K's 4th.
2. Kt. to Q. B's 3rd.	2. B. to Q. B's 4th.
3. P. to K. B's 4th.	3. P. to Q's 3rd.
4. Kt. to K. B's 3rd.	4. Kt. to K. B's 3rd.

If 4: $\frac{}{\text{Kt. to Q. B's 3rd}}$, 5. $\frac{\text{B. to Q. Kt.'s 5th}}{\text{B. to Q's 2nd}}$, 6. $\frac{\text{P. to Q's 3rd}}{\text{Kt. to K. B's 3rd}}$, &c.

5. B. to Q. B's 4th.

Equal game.

ILLUSTRATIVE GAMES.

Game I.—Between Herr Max Lange and An Amateur.

White (Herr Max L.)	Black (Mr. —).
1. P. to K's 4th.	1. P. to K's 4th.
2. Kt. to Q. B's 3rd.	2. B. to Q. B's 4th.
3. P. to K. B's 4th.	3. B. takes Kt.*
4. R. takes B.	4. P. takes P.
5. P. to Q's 4th.	5. Q. to R's 5th (ch.)
6. P. to K. Kt.'s 3rd.	6. P. takes P.
7. R. takes P.	7. Q. takes R's P.
8. Q. to K. B's 3rd.	8. P. to K. Kt.'s 3rd.
9. B. to Q. B's 4th.	9. P. to K. B's 3rd.
10. Kt. to Q's 5th.	10. K. to Q's sq.
11. B. to K. Kt.'s 5th.	11. P. to Q. B's 3rd.
12. B. takes P. (ch.)	12. K. to K's sq.
13. Kt. to Q. B's 7th (ch.)	13. K. to B's sq.
14. Q. to Q. R's 3rd (ch.)	

And wins.

Game II.—Between Messrs. Steinitz and Neumann.

White (Mr. S.)	Black (Mr. N.)
1. P. to K's 4th.	1. P. to K's 4th.
2. Kt. to Q. B's 3rd.	2. Kt. to K. B's 3rd.
3. P. to K. B's 4th.	3. P. to Q's 4th.
4. P. to Q's 3rd.	4. Q's P. takes P.
5. B's P. takes P.	5. Kt. to K. Kt.'s 5th.
6. Kt. takes P.†	6. Kt. takes K's P.
7. P. to Q's 4th.	7. Kt. to K. Kt.'s 3rd.
8. Kt. to K. B's 3rd.	8. Q. to K's 2nd.
9. B. to Q's 3rd.	9. P. to K. B's 4th.
10. B. to K. Kt.'s 5th.	10. Q. to K's 3rd.

* A bad move, from the effect of which Black never recovers. He ought to have played 3. P. to Q's 4th.

† White might also play 6. P. to Q's 4th at this point, converting the opening into a form of the Philidor Defence, with the position of the players reversed.

11. Castles.*	11. P. takes Kt.
12. B. takes P.	12. B. to Q's 3rd.
13. Kt. to K's 5th.	13. B. takes Kt.
14. P. takes B.	14. Kt. to Q's 2nd.
15. Q. to K. R's 5th.	15. Kt. to K. B's sq.
16. Q's R. to Q's sq.	16. B. to Q's 2nd.
17. P. to K. R's 3rd.	17. R. to K. Kt.'s sq.
18. K. to R's sq.	18. Q. to Q. Kt.'s 3rd.
19. P. to K's 6th.	19. B. takes P.
20. R. to Q's 2nd.	20. P. to Q. R's 4th.
21. P. to Q. Kt.'s 3rd.	21. P. to Q. R's 5th.
22. K's R. to Q's sq.	22. B. to Q's 2nd.
23. R. takes B.	

And Black resigned.

GAME III.—Between Messrs. Steinitz and Rosenthal.

WHITE (Mr. S.)	BLACK (Mr. R.)
1. P. to K's 4th.	1. P. to K's 4th.
2. Kt. to Q. B's 3rd.	2. Kt. to Q. B's 3rd.
3. P. to K. B's 4th.	3. P. takes P.
4. P. to Q's 4th.	4. Q. to R's 5th (ch.)
5. K. to K's 2nd.	5. P. to Q's 3rd.†
6. Kt. to K. B's 3rd.	6. B. to K. Kt.'s 5th.
7. B. takes P.	7. B. takes Kt. (ch.)
8. P. takes B.	8. Q. takes B.‡
9. Kt. to Q's 5th.	9. Q. to K. R's 3rd.
10. Kt. takes P. (ch.)	10. K. to Q's sq.
11. Kt. takes R.	11. K. to B's sq.
12. P. to Q's 5th.	12. Kt. to K. B's 3rd.
13. P. takes Kt.	13. P. to Q's 4th.
14. Q. to Q's 4th (ch.)	14. B. to Q's 3rd.
15. Q. takes Q. R's P.	15. Kt.'s P. takes P.
16. R. to K's sq.	16. R. to K's sq.
17. K. to Q's sq.	17. P. takes P.
18. R. takes P.	18. R. takes R.

* All this is very well played.

† The correct reply, as we have seen, is 5. P. to Q's 4th.

‡ Black "gains a loss" by this capture.

19. R. takes R.	19. Q. to B's 5th.
20. B. to K. R's 3rd.	20. K. to Q's sq.
21. R. to K. B's sq.	21. Q. takes K's P.
22. Q. to Q. Kt.'s 6th (ch.)	22. K. to K's sq.
23. R. to K.'s sq.*	

And wins.

---

* The whole of this game is very accurately played by Mr. Steinitz.

CHAPTER XII.

King's Bishop's Gambit.

$$1.\ \frac{\text{P. to K's 4th}}{\text{P. to K's 4th}},\ 2.\ \frac{\text{P. to K. B's 4th}}{\text{P. takes P.}},\ 3.\ \frac{\text{B. to Q. B's 4th}}{\qquad}.$$

Game the First.

$$3.\ \frac{\qquad}{\text{Q. to K. R's 5th (ch.)}}.$$

Game the Second.

$$3.\ \frac{\qquad}{\text{Kt. to K. B's 3rd}}.$$

Game the Third.

$$3.\ \frac{\qquad}{\text{P. to Q's 4th}}.$$

Game the Fourth.

$$3.\ \frac{\qquad}{\text{P. to K. B's 4th}}.$$

Game the Fifth.

$$3.\ \frac{\qquad}{\text{P. to Q. Kt.'s 4th}}.$$

Upon no opening in the game of Chess, not excepting even the famous Evans' Gambit, have analysts lavished so much labour as upon the King's Bishop's Gambit. But as in the commentaries upon some great classic the business of one annotator is to destroy the toil of his predecessor, so in Chess openings, every analyst endeavours to upset the conclusions arrived at before him. The result in the present instance is very perplexing. No one appears to have positively settled, even to his own satisfaction, whether this Gambit can be advantageously adopted by the first player. According to some authorities, the attack has the best of the fight; according to others, the superiority rests with the defence. The main cause of this uncertainty is the inconceivable variety of combinations to which the opening gives birth. A volume of considerable magnitude might be filled indeed with the variations springing from the first half-dozen moves. I will not pretend to clear up the difficulties of a subject so bewildering as this *début*. All I can hope to do in the compass of a few pages is to present a clear *résumé* of its numerous and complex ramifications, and assist the student to select the lines of play which appear the best.

Game the First.

WHITE.	BLACK.
1. P. to K's 4th.	1. P. to K's 4th.
2. P. to K. B's 4th.	2. P. takes P.
3. B. to Q. B's 4th.	3. Q. to K. R's 5th (ch.)

I give precedence to this line of defence, not as the best, for I cannot prove it to be so, and many excellent players now think it is not trustworthy. I place it first, because it is what is called the "classic defence," and leads to by far the most instructive and entertaining games of all the systems of defence of which the opening is susceptible.

4. K. to B's sq.	4. P. to K. Kt.'s 4th.

This advance of the K. Kt.'s Pawn is, or was, authorised by most of the leading writers on the openings. He may also play 4. $\frac{\qquad}{\text{Kt. to Q. B's 3rd}}$, or 4. $\frac{\qquad}{\text{Kt. to K. B's 3rd}}$, but neither move is quite satisfactory.

5. Kt. to Q. B's 3rd.

Probably the best move.

The consequences of 5. $\frac{\text{Kt. to K. B's 3rd}}{}$ shall be considered under Variation A. If 5. $\frac{\text{P. to Q's 4th}}{\text{B. to K. Kt.'s 2nd}}$, 6. $\frac{\text{Kt. to K. B's 3rd}}{}$. (If 6. $\frac{\text{Kt. to Q. B's 3rd}}{}$, we have the same position as in the text game.) 6. $\frac{}{\text{Q. to K. R's 4th}}$, 7. $\frac{\text{P. to K. R's 4th}}{\text{P. to Q's 3rd}}$, 8. $\frac{\text{Kt. to Q. B's 3rd}}{\text{P. to K. R's 3rd}}$, 9. $\frac{\text{P. to K's 5th}}{\text{Q's P. takes P.}}$, 10. $\frac{\text{Kt takes K's P.}}{}$. There is little to choose between the positions. If 5. $\frac{\text{P. to K. Kt.'s 3rd}}{\text{P. takes P.}}$, 6. $\frac{\text{Q. to K. B's 3rd}}{\text{P. to Kt.'s 7th (ch.)}}$, 7. $\frac{\text{K. takes P.}}{\text{Kt. to K. R's 3rd}}$, 8. $\frac{\text{P. to Q's 4th}}{\text{Kt. to Q. B's 3rd}}$, 9. $\frac{\text{P. to Q. B's 3rd}}{\text{B. to K's 2nd}}$, Black has the advantage.

5. B. to K. Kt.'s 2nd.

If 5. $\frac{}{\text{P. to Q. B's 3rd}}$, or 5. $\frac{}{\text{Kt. to K's 2nd}}$, White can take advantage of McDonnell's move (as in the text game) of 6. $\frac{\text{P. to K. Kt.'s 3rd}}{}$, 7. $\frac{\text{K. to Kt.'s 2nd}}{}$, fortified by Jaenisch's 7. $\frac{\text{Q. to K. B's 3rd}}{}$. For example, suppose 5. $\frac{}{\text{P. to Q. B's 3rd}}$, 6. $\frac{\text{P. to K. Kt.'s 3rd}}{\text{P. takes P.}}$, 7. $\frac{\text{Q. to K. B's 3rd}}{}$, with a powerful attack. So also if 5. $\frac{}{\text{Kt. to K's 2nd}}$, 6. $\frac{\text{P. to K. Kt.'s 3rd}}{\text{P. takes P.}}$, 7. $\frac{\text{Q. to K. B's 3rd}}{}$, and White has an excellent position of attack.

6. P. to K. Kt.'s 3rd.

The line of play adopted for White in this example of the opening is the same combination of the McDonnell manœuvre with Jaenisch's move, spoken of in the preceding note. This combination, though no novelty, it having been given in Jaenisch's *Analyse Nouvelle*, 1842-43, and in Walker's "Art of Chess Play," 1846, has never been appreciated until it was re-introduced by Mr. G. B. Fraser about three years ago. That gentleman has exhaustively analysed the combination, and in the opinion of many excellent players has proved it to be the best line of play which White can adopt.

Instead of the move in question, the customary line of play has been 6. $\frac{\text{P. to Q's 4th}}{}$, or 6. $\frac{\text{Kt. to K. B's 3rd}}{}$, which shall be the subjects of Variations B and C. I may note in passing that if White play 6. $\frac{\text{Kt. to Q. Kt.'s 5th}}{}$, the continuation 6. $\frac{}{\text{Kt. to Q. R's 3rd}}$, 7. $\frac{\text{P. to Q's 4th}}{\text{P. to Q's 3rd}}$, turns in Black's favour. So also if he play 6. $\frac{\text{Kt. to Q's 5th}}{}$, the game is advantageous to Black, by 6. $\frac{}{\text{K. to Q's sq.}}$, 7. $\frac{\text{P. to Q's 4th}}{\text{Kt. to K's 2nd}}$, in a few moves.

6. P. takes P. (best).

7. Q. to K. B's 3rd.

Appended is a diagram of this interesting position.

BLACK.

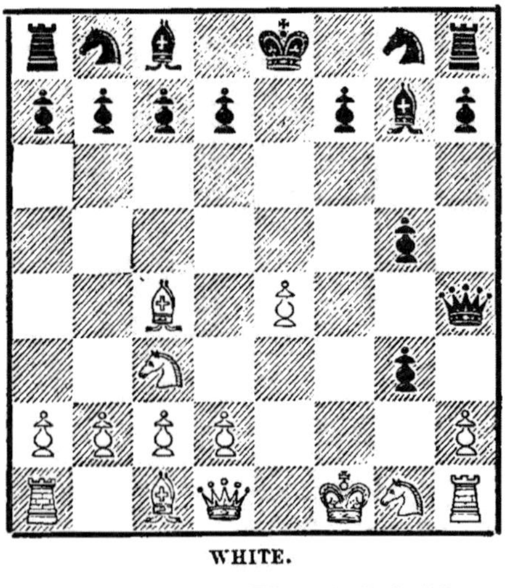

WHITE.

Position prior to White's 7th Move.

McDonnell's plan, after sacrificing the K. Kt.'s Pawn, was to play 7. $\frac{\text{K. to K. Kt.'s 2nd}}{\quad}$, an extremely ingenious one, but not so good as that of moving the Q. to K. B's 3rd, *e.g.* :—
7. $\frac{\text{K. to Kt.'s 2nd}}{\text{Q. to K. R's 3rd}}$, 8. $\frac{\text{P. takes P.}}{\text{Q. to K. Kt.'s 3rd}}$, 9. $\frac{\text{P. to Q's 4th}}{\text{Kt. to K's 2nd}}$, 10. $\frac{\text{Kt. to K. B's 3rd}}{\text{P. to K. R's 3rd}}$, 11. $\frac{\text{R. to K. B's sq.}}{\text{Castles.}}$. White has lost a pawn, and has no compensation in other respects

7. P. to K. Kt.'s 7th (ch.)

Presumably his best play.

If 7. $\frac{\quad}{\text{Q. to K. B's 5th}}$, 8. $\frac{\text{Kt. to Q's 5th}}{\quad}$ (a move first proposed by G. Walker, 1847), 8. $\frac{\quad}{\text{Q. takes Q. (ch.)}}$, 9. $\frac{\text{Kt. takes Q.}}{\text{K. to Q's sq.}}$, 10. $\frac{\text{Kt. takes Kt.'s P.}}{\quad}$, White has the better position.

If 7. $\frac{\quad}{\text{P. takes P.}}$, 8. $\frac{\text{Q. takes P. (ch.)}}{\text{K. to Q's sq.}}$, 9. $\frac{\text{P. to Q's 4th}}{\quad}$, White must win.

If 7. $\frac{\quad}{\text{P. to Q's 4th}}$, 8. $\frac{\text{R's P. takes P.}}{\text{Q. to K. Kt.'s 5th}}$, 9. $\frac{\text{Kt. takes Q's P.}}{\text{Q. to Q's 2nd.}}$, 10. $\frac{\text{Kt. to K's 2nd}}{\text{P. to Q. B's 3rd}}$, 11. $\frac{\text{Q's Kt. to B's 3rd}}{\text{P. to Q. Kt.'s 4th}}$, 12. $\frac{\text{B. to Q. Kt.'s 3rd}}{\text{P. to Q. Kt.'s 5th}}$, 13. $\frac{\text{Kt. to Q's sq.}}{\quad}$. Both Mr. Fraser and Mr. Wormald pronounce White's game to be much superior, but this, I think, is open to question.

If 7. $\frac{\quad}{\text{Kt. to K. B's 3rd}}$, 8. $\frac{\text{P. takes P.}}{\text{Q. to K. Kt.'s 5th}}$, 9. $\frac{\text{P. to Q's 4th}}{\text{Q. takes Q. (ch.)}}$, 10. $\frac{\text{Kt. takes Q.}}{\text{P. to K. Kt.'s 5th}}$, 11. $\frac{\text{Kt. to K. Kt.'s 5th}}{\text{Castles}}$, 12. $\frac{\text{P. to K's 5th}}{\quad}$. Black has a bad game.

8. K. takes P.	8. Kt. to K. R's 3rd.
9. Kt. to Q's 5th.	9. K. to Q's sq.
10. P. to Q's 4th.	10. P. to Q. B's 3rd.
11. Kt. to Q. B's 3rd.	11. P. to Q's 4th.

If 11. $\frac{\quad}{\text{B. takes P.}}$, 12. $\frac{\text{Q. to K. Kt.'s 3rd}}{\text{Q. takes Q.}}$, 13. $\frac{\text{P. takes Q.}}{\text{B. takes Kt.}}$,

14. $\frac{\text{R. takes Kt.}}{\text{B. to Kt.'s 2nd}}$, 15. $\frac{\text{B. takes P. (ch.)}}{}$, White has the advantage.

Again, if 11. $\frac{}{\text{P. to Q's 3rd}}$, 12. $\frac{\text{Q. to K. Kt.'s 3rd.}}{\text{Q. takes Q.}}$, 13. $\frac{\text{P. takes Q.}}{\text{P. to K. B's 3rd}}$, 14. $\frac{\text{Kt. to K. B's 3rd}}{\text{P. to K. Kt.'s 5th}}$, 15. $\frac{\text{Kt. to K's sq.}}{\text{Kt. to Kt.'s sq.}}$, White's game is the better one.

Finally, if 11. $\frac{}{\text{Q. to Kt.'s 5th (ch.)}}$, 12. $\frac{\text{Q. takes Q.}}{\text{Kt. takes Q.}}$, 13. $\frac{\text{P. to K. R's 3rd}}{\text{Kt. to K. R's 3rd}}$, 14. $\frac{\text{B. takes P. (ch.)}}{}$, and White is still in the ascendant.

12. Q. to K. Kt.'s 3rd.

This, Mr. Fraser rightly says, is stronger than taking Pawn with Pawn, or playing Bishop to Queen's 3rd.

White	Black
	12. Q. takes Q. (ch., best).
13. P. takes Q.	13. B. takes Q's P.

If 13. $\frac{}{\text{P. takes B.}}$, 14. $\frac{\text{B. takes P. (ch.)}}{\text{K. to B's 2nd}}$, 15. $\frac{\text{B. to B's 4th (ch.)}}{\text{K. to Kt.'s 3rd}}$, 16. $\frac{\text{B. takes K's Kt.}}{\text{B. takes Q's P.}}$, 17. $\frac{\text{Kt. to Q. R's 4th (ch.)}}{\text{K. to R's 3rd (best)}}$, 18. $\frac{\text{P. to Q. B's 3rd}}{}$, White regains the Gambit Pawn, and has the better position.

If 13. $\frac{}{\text{Kt. to Kt.'s 5th}}$, 14. $\frac{\text{P. takes P.}}{\text{B. takes P.}}$, 15. $\frac{\text{P. takes P.}}{\text{P. to K. B's 3rd}}$, 16. $\frac{\text{P. takes P.}}{\text{B. takes P. (ch.)}}$, 17. $\frac{\text{B. to Q's 5th}}{\text{Kt. to Q. B's 3rd}}$, 18. $\frac{\text{Kt. to Q. Kt.'s 5th}}{\text{B. to K's 4th}}$, 19. $\frac{\text{Kt. to K. B's 3rd}}{}$, Black has an inferior game.

White	Black
14. B. takes P. (ch.)	14. K. to B's 2nd (best).
15. B. to K. B's 4th (ch.)	15. K. to Kt.'s 3rd (best).
16. Kt. takes Q's P. (ch.)	16. P. takes Kt.
17. R. takes Kt. (ch.)	17. P. to K. B's 3rd.
18. B. takes Q's P.	

And White must win.*

* The reader desirous of perusing Mr. Fraser's variations on this interesting theme at large must consult the "Chess World," vol. iv., pp. 117, 262.

VARIATION A, BEGINNING AT WHITE'S 5TH MOVE.

BLACK.

WHITE.

Position prior to White's 5th move.

5. Kt to K. B's 3rd.

This move is not thought so good as 5. $\frac{\text{Kt. to Q. B's 3rd}}{}$, and if the combination we have lately been examining of 6. $\frac{\text{P. to K. Kt.'s 3rd}}{}$, 7. $\frac{\text{Q. to K. B's 3rd}}{}$, prove as favourable to White as Mr. Fraser declares it to be, that will be an additional reason for preferring 5. $\frac{\text{Kt. to Q. B's 3rd}}{}$.

5. Q. to K. R's 4th (best).

6. P. to K. R's 4th.

If 6. $\frac{\text{P. to Q's 4th}}{\text{B. to K. Kt.'s 2nd}}$, 7. $\frac{\text{P. to K. R's 4th}}{\text{P. to Q's 3rd}}$, 8. $\frac{\text{Kt. to Q. B's 3rd}}{\text{P. to K. R's 3rd}}$, 9. $\frac{\text{K. to B's 2nd}}{\text{Q. to K. Kt.'s 3rd}}$, 10. $\frac{\text{Kt. to Q's 5th}}{\text{K. to Q's sq.}}$, 11. $\frac{\text{Q. to Q's 3rd}}{\text{Kt. to K's 2nd}}$, 12. $\frac{\text{P. to K. R's 5th}}{\text{Q. to R's 2nd}}$, 13. $\frac{\text{Kt. takes Kt.}}{\text{K. takes Kt.}}$, and Black has a slight superiority.

6. B. to K. Kt.'s 2nd.

If 6. $\frac{}{\text{P. to Kt.'s 5th}}$, 7. $\frac{\text{Kt. to K's sq.}}{}$. If 6. $\frac{}{\text{P. to K. R's 3rd}}$, 7. $\frac{\text{Kt. to Q. B's 3rd}}{}$.

7. P. to Q's 4th.

Ponziani gives 7. $\frac{\text{R. to K. R's 2nd}}{}$, but the move is not good, because of 7. $\frac{}{\text{P. to K. Kt.'s 5th}}$, 8. $\frac{\text{Kt. to Kt.'s 5th}}{\text{Kt. to K. R's 3rd}}$, 9. $\frac{\text{P. to Q's 4th}}{\text{P. to Q's 4th}}$, 10. $\frac{\text{B. takes Q's P.}}{}$, &c. I may observe too that 7. $\frac{\text{K. to Kt.'s sq.}}{}$ is no better than Ponziani's move, because of 7. $\frac{}{\text{B. to Q's 5th (ch.)}}$, 8. $\frac{\text{K. to R's 2nd}}{\text{P. to K. Kt.'s 5th}}$, &c.

7. P. to K. R's 3rd.

Better than 7. $\frac{}{\text{P. to Q's 3rd}}$.

8. Kt. to Q. B's 3rd. 8. Kt. to K's 2nd.

If 8. $\frac{}{\text{P. to Q's 3rd}}$, White may play with advantage either 9. $\frac{\text{P. to K's 5th}}{}$, or 9. $\frac{\text{Kt. to Q's 5th}}{}$. In the first place, 8. $\frac{}{\text{P. to Q's 3rd}}$, 9. $\frac{\text{P. to K's 5th}}{\text{P. takes P.}}$, 10. $\frac{\text{Kt. to Q's 5th}}{\text{K. to Q's sq.}}$, 11. $\frac{\text{Q's P. takes P.}}{\text{B. to Q's 2nd}}$, 12. $\frac{\text{K. to Kt.'s sq.}}{\text{Q. to K. Kt.'s 3rd}}$, 13. $\frac{\text{P. takes P.}}{\text{P. takes P.}}$, 14. $\frac{\text{R. takes R.}}{\text{B. takes R.}}$, 15. $\frac{\text{K's Kt. takes P.}}{}$. (A fine stroke of play suggested by Petroff.) 15. $\frac{}{\text{Q. takes Kt.}}$, 16. $\frac{\text{Q's B. takes P.}}{\text{Q. to K. B's 4th (best)}}$, 17. $\frac{\text{P. to K's 6th}}{\text{P. takes P.}}$, 18. $\frac{\text{Kt. takes P.}}{\text{Q. to Q. B's 4th (ch.)}}$, 19. $\frac{\text{K. to R's sq.}}{\text{Q. takes B.}}$, 20. $\frac{\text{Q. to Q's 6th}}{\text{P. to K's 4th (best)}}$, 21. $\frac{\text{R. to Q's sq.}}{}$. (If 21. $\frac{\text{Kt. takes R.}}{\text{Q. takes B.}}$,

Black can draw the game.) 21. $\frac{\quad}{\text{P. takes B.}}$, 22. $\frac{\text{Kt. takes R.}}{\text{Kt. to K's 2nd}}$, 23. $\frac{\text{Q takes Q's Kt. (ch.)}}{\quad}$, &c. In the second place, 9. $\frac{\text{Kt. to Q's 5th}}{\text{K. to Q's sq.}}$, 10. $\frac{\text{P. to K's 5th}}{\quad}$, &c.

9. K. to Kt.'s sq.

If 9. $\frac{\text{P. to K's 5th}}{\text{P. to K. B's 3rd}}$, 10. $\frac{\text{B. to K's 2nd}}{\text{P. to K. Kt.'s 5th}}$, 11. $\frac{\text{Kt. to K. R's 2nd}}{\text{P. to K. B's 6th}}$, 12. $\frac{\text{K. Kt.'s P. takes P.}}{\text{P. takes K's P.}}$, 13. $\frac{\text{Q's P. takes P.}}{\text{P. takes P}}$, 14. $\frac{\text{Kt. takes P.}}{\text{B takes P.}}$, 15. $\frac{\text{Kt. to K. Kt.'s 5th}}{\text{R. to K. B's sq. (ch.)}}$, Black has an advantage.

	9. Q. to K. Kt.'s 3rd.
10. P. to K's 5th.	10. P. to K. B's 4th.

If 10. $\frac{\quad}{\text{P. to Q's 3rd}}$, 11. $\frac{\text{Kt. to Q's 5th}}{\quad}$, with a fine game.

11. P. takes P.	11. P. takes P.
12. R. takes R.	12. B. takes R.
13. P. tq K. Kt.'s 3rd.	13. Q's Kt. to B's 3rd (best).
14. P. takes P.	14. P. takes P. (dis. ch.)
15. K. to B's sq.	15. Q. to K. Kt.'s 6th.
16. Q. to K's 2nd.	

The game is about equal.

VARIATION B, BEGINNING AT WHITE'S 6TH MOVE.

BLACK.

WHITE.

Position prior to White's 6th Move.

6. P. to Q's 4th.	6. P. to Q's 3rd.
7. P. to K's 5th.	7. P. takes P.
8. Kt. to Q's 5th.	8. K. to Q's sq.

Black can play his Q's B. to K. Kt.'s 5th here effectively; *ex. gr.*: 8. —— / B. to K. Kt.'s 5th, 9. Kt. to K. B's 3rd / Q. to K. R's 4th, 10. Kt. takes P. (ch.) / K. to Q's sq., 11. Kt. takes R. / P. to K's 5th, 12. Q. to K's sq. / P. takes Kt., 13. Q. to Q. R's 5th (ch.) / P. to Q. Kt.'s 3rd, 14. Q. to Q's 5th (ch.) / Kt. to Q's 2nd, 15. B. to Q's 2nd / Kt. to K. B's 3rd, 16. Q. to Q. Kt.'s 7th / P. takes P. (ch.), 17. K. takes P. / Q. to R's 6th (ch.), 18. K. to B's 2nd / Kt. to K's 5th (ch.), 19. Q. takes K's Kt. / R. to K's sq., and Black has the advantage.

9. Kt. to K. B's 3rd.	9. Q. to R's 4th.
10. P. takes P.	10. B. to Q's 2nd.
11. B. to Q's 2nd.	

This clever move is the suggestion of Messrs. Stanley and Schulten. I give a diagram of the position to facilitate its study.

BLACK.

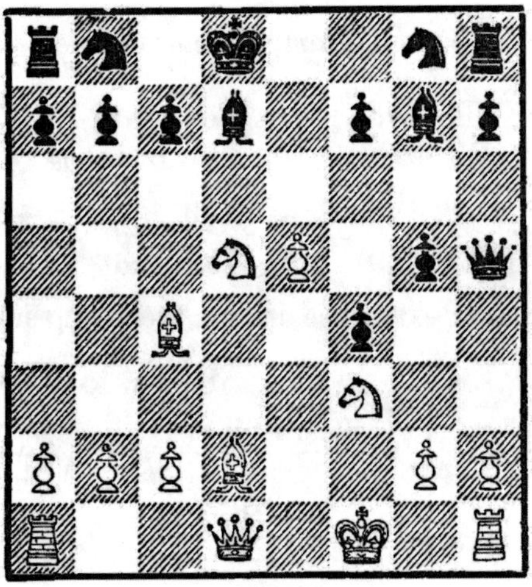

WHITE.

Position after White's 11*th Move.*

11. P. to Q. B's 3rd.

If 11. $\frac{\qquad}{\text{Kt. to Q. B's 3rd}}$, 12. $\frac{\text{B. to Q. B's 3rd}}{\text{K's Kt. to K's 2nd}}$, 13. $\frac{\text{Kt. takes Kt.}}{\text{Kt. takes Kt.}}$, 14. $\frac{\text{P. to K's 6th}}{\qquad}$, with a winning position.

So if 11. $\frac{\qquad}{\text{Kt. to K's 2nd}}$, 12. $\frac{\text{Kt. takes Kt.}}{\text{K. takes Kt.}}$, 13. $\frac{\text{B. to Q. Kt.'s 4th (ch.)}}{\text{K. to K.'s sq.}}$, 14. $\frac{\text{Q. to K's 2nd}}{\qquad}$, and White has a decisive advantage.

12. B. to Q. R's 5th (ch.)	12. P. to Q. Kt.'s 3rd.
13. B. to Q. B's 3rd.	13. Q. to K. Kt.'s 3rd.

14. Kt. to Q. Kt.'s 4th.	14. P. to K. Kt.'s 5th.
15. Kt. to Q's 4th.	15. P. to Q. R's 4th.
16. B. to Q's 3rd.	16. Q. to K. R's 4th.
17. Q's Kt. takes P. (ch.)	

And still the game is in White's favour.

Variation C, beginning at White's 6th Move.

(*See Diagram, Variation B.*)

6. Kt. to K. B's 3rd.	6. Q. to K. R's 4th.
7. P. to K. R's 4th.	7. B. takes Q's Kt.

If 7. $\frac{\quad}{\text{P. to K. R's 3rd}}$, 8. $\frac{\text{P. to Q's 4th}}{\text{P. to Q's 3rd}}$, 9. $\frac{\text{Kt. to Q's 5th}}{\text{K. to Q's sq.}}$ we have a position examined in the preceding note.

8. Q's P. takes B.	8. Kt. to Q. B's 3rd.

If 8. $\frac{\quad}{\text{Kt. to K's 2nd}}$, 9. $\frac{\text{K. to Kt.'s sq.}}{\quad}$. If 8. $\frac{\quad}{\text{Kt. to K. B's 3rd}}$, or 8. $\frac{\quad}{\text{Kt. to K. R's 3rd}}$, 9. $\frac{\text{Q. to Q's 4th}}{\quad}$.

9. B. to K's 2nd.	9. P. to K. Kt.'s 5th.
10. Kt. to Q's 4th.	

The game is about equal.

Game the Second.

WHITE.	BLACK.
1. P. to K's 4th.	1. P. to K's 4th.
2. P. to K. B's 4th.	2. P. takes P.
3. B. to Q. B's 4th.	3. Kt. to K. B's 3rd.

Jaenisch, I believe, regards this as a better line of defence than the "classical" course of 3. $\frac{\text{Q. to K. R's 5th (ch.)}}{\quad}$. There can be no doubt that it is a much safer one.

4. Kt. to Q. B's 3rd.

(For the result of 4. $\frac{\text{P. to Q's 3rd}}{\quad}$, which some good authorities prefer, see Variation A.)

If 4. $\frac{\text{Q. to K. B's 3rd}}{\text{Kt. to Q. B's 3rd}}$, 5. $\frac{\text{Q. takes P.}}{\text{B. to Q's 3rd}}$, 6. $\frac{\text{Q. to K. R's 4th}}{\text{Kt. to Q's 5th}}$, 7. $\frac{\text{B. to Q. Kt.'s 3rd}}{\text{P. to K. Kt.'s 4th}}$, 8. $\frac{\text{Q. takes Kt.'s P.}}{\text{R. to K. Kt.'s sq.}}$, Black has the better game. If 4. $\frac{\text{Q. to K's 2nd}}{\text{B. to Q. B's 4th}}$, 5. $\frac{\text{Kt. to K. B's 3rd}}{\text{Kt. to Q. B's 3rd}}$, 6. $\frac{\text{P. to Q. B's 3rd}}{\text{Castles}}$, 7. $\frac{\text{P. to Q's 4th}}{\text{P. to Q's 4th}}$, again Black has the advantage. If 4. $\frac{\text{P. to K's 5th}}{\text{P. to Q's 4th}}$, 5. $\frac{\text{B. to Q. Kt.'s 3rd}}{\text{Kt. to K's 5th}}$, 6. $\frac{\text{Kt. to K. B's 3rd}}{\text{B. to K. Kt.'s 5th}}$. (6. $\frac{\quad}{\text{Kt. to K. Kt.'s 5th}}$ is also a good move.) 7. $\frac{\text{Castles.}}{\text{Kt. to Q. B's 3rd}}$, 8. $\frac{\text{B. to Q. R's 4th (best)}}{\text{P. to K. Kt.'s 4th}}$, 9. $\frac{\text{B. takes Kt. (ch.)}}{\text{P. takes B.}}$, 10. $\frac{\text{P. to Q's 4th}}{\text{P. to Q. B's 4th}}$, 11. $\frac{\text{P. to Q. B's 3rd}}{\text{B. to K's 2nd}}$, 12. $\frac{\text{P. to Q. Kt.'s 4th}}{\text{P. takes Kt.'s P.}}$, 13. $\frac{\text{P. takes P.}}{\text{Castles}}$, with a good game, and a Pawn more than White has.

4. B. to Q. Kt.'s 5th.

4. $\frac{\quad}{\text{P. to Q's 4th}}$, and 4. $\frac{\quad}{\text{P. to Q. B's 3rd}}$, are inferior. Suppose 4. $\frac{\quad}{\text{P. to Q's 4th}}$, 5. $\frac{\text{Kt. takes P.}}{\text{B. to Q's 3rd}}$, 6. $\frac{\text{Kt. takes Kt. (ch.)}}{\text{Q. takes Kt.}}$, 7. $\frac{\text{P. to Q's 4th}}{\text{Q. to K. R's 5th (ch.)}}$, 8. $\frac{\text{K. to B's sq.}}{\quad}$, with an advantage. So if 4. $\frac{\quad}{\text{P. to Q. B's 3rd}}$, 5. $\frac{\text{Q. to K. B's 3rd}}{\text{P. to Q's 4th}}$, 6. $\frac{\text{P. takes P.}}{\text{B. to Q's 3rd}}$, 7. $\frac{\text{P. to Q's 3rd}}{\text{B. to K. Kt.'s 5th}}$, 8. $\frac{\text{Q. to K. B's 2nd}}{\text{Castles}}$, 9. $\frac{\text{B. takes P.}}{\quad}$, White has the superior game.

In addition, however, to 4. $\frac{\quad}{\text{B. to Q. Kt.'s 5th}}$, 4. $\frac{\quad}{\text{P. to Q's 4th}}$, and 4. $\frac{\quad}{\text{P. to Q. B's 3rd}}$, Black may play 4. $\frac{\quad}{\text{Kt. to Q. B's 3rd}}$, and apparently establish a safe defence; *e.g.*, 4. $\frac{\quad}{\text{Kt. to Q. B's 3rd}}$,

5. $\frac{\text{Kt. to X. B's 3rd}}{\text{B. to Q. Kt.'s 5th}}$, 6. $\frac{\text{Castles}}{\text{P. to Q's 3rd}}$, 7. $\frac{\text{Kt. to Q's 5th}}{\text{Castles}}$, and the game is about even.

5. P. to K's 5th.	5. P. to Q's 4th.
6. B. to Q. Kt.'s 5th (ch.)	6. P. to Q. B's 3rd (best).
7. P. takes Kt.	7. P. takes B.
8. Q. to K's 2nd (ch.)	8. B. to K's 3rd.
9. Q. takes P. (ch.)	9. Kt. to Q. B's 3rd.
10. Kt. to K. B's 3rd.	10. Q. takes P.
11. Q. takes Kt.'s P.	11. R. to Q. B's sq.
12. Kt. takes Q's P.	12. Q. to K. B's 4th.
13. Kt. to Q. B's 7th (ch.)	13. R. takes Kt.
14. Q. takes R.	14. Q. to K's 5th (ch.)
15. K. to Q's sq.	15. Castles.
16. P. to Q's 3rd.	16. Q. to K. Kt.'s 3rd.

Black is considered to have the advantage.

Variation A, beginning at White's 4th Move.

BLACK.

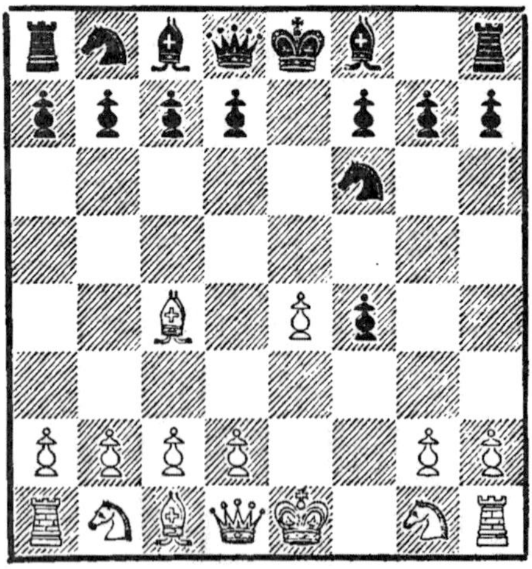

WHITE.

Position prior to White's 4th Move.

4. P. to Q's 3rd.	4. P. to Q's 4th.
5. P. takes P.	5. Kt. takes P.
6. Q. to K's 2nd (ch.)	6. B. to K's 3rd.
7. B. takes Kt.	7. Q. takes B.
8. B. takes P.	8. B. to Q. B's 4th.
9. Kt. to K. B's 3rd.	

If 9. $\frac{\text{B. takes Q. B's P.}}{\text{B. takes Kt.}}$, 10. $\frac{\text{R. takes B.}}{\text{Q. to Q. B's 4th}}$, &c., or 10. $\frac{\text{B. takes Q's Kt.}}{\text{B. to Q's 5th.}}$, &c.

	9. P. to Q. B's 3rd.

The game is about equal.

Game the Third.

WHITE.	BLACK.
1. P. to K's 4th.	1. P. to K's 4th.
2. P. to K. B's 4th.	2. P. takes P.
3. B. to Q. B's 4th.	3. P. to Q's 4th.

This move has risen in favour of late years, and, leading as it does to a very spirited contest, is likely to be still more popular.

4. B. takes P.

4. P. takes P. is obviously inferior.

Black has now the choice of two lines of play, viz., 4. $\frac{}{\text{Q. to R's 5th (ch.)}}$, and 4. $\frac{}{\text{Kt. to K. B's 3rd}}$, which we will examine in turn.

In the first place:—

	4. Q. to R's 5th (ch.)
5. K. to B's sq.	5. P. to K. Kt.'s 4th.
6. Kt. to Q. B's 3rd.	6. B. to K. Kt.'s 2nd.

If 6. $\frac{}{\text{Kt. to K's 2nd}}$, White speedily obtains an advantage; *e.g.*, 6. $\frac{}{\text{Kt. to K's 2nd}}$, $\frac{\text{P. to K. R's 4th}}{\text{P. to K. R's 3rd}}$, 8. $\frac{\text{Kt. to K. B's 3rd}}{\text{Q. to R's 4th}}$,

9. $\frac{\text{B. takes B's P. (ch.)}}{\text{Q. takes B. (best)}}$, 10. $\frac{\text{Kt. to K's 5th}}{\text{Q. to K. B's 3rd}}$, 11. $\frac{\text{Q. to R's 5th (ch.)}}{\text{K. to Q's sq.}}$, 12. $\frac{\text{Kt. to B's 7th}}{\text{K. to Q's 2nd}}$, 13. $\frac{\text{Kt. takes R.}}{\text{Q. takes Kt.}}$, 14. $\frac{\text{P. takes Kt.'s P.}}{\quad}$, with a winning position.

7. P. to Q's 4th.	7. Kt. to K's 2nd.
8. Kt. to K. B's 3rd.	8. Q. to K. R's 4th.
9. P. to K. R's 4th.	9. P. to K. R's 3rd.
10. K. to Kt.'s sq.	10. P. to K. Kt.'s 5th.
11. Kt. to K's 5th.	

This move is the invention of Mr. Zukertort, and is apparently White's best resource. If he play instead, 11. $\frac{\text{Kt. to K's sq.}}{\quad}$, Black speedily obtains the superior position by 11. $\frac{\quad}{\text{P. to K. B's 6th}}$.

	11. B. takes Kt.
12. P. takes B.	12. Kt. to Kt.'s 3rd.

Seemingly the best reply, but he may also play 12. $\frac{\quad}{\text{Q. takes K's P.}}$, or 12. $\frac{\quad}{\text{P. to K. B's 6th}}$, which may be briefly disposed of.

Firstly, 12. $\frac{\quad}{\text{Q. takes K's P.}}$, 13. $\frac{\text{Q. to K. B's sq.}}{\text{P. to B's 6th}}$, 14. $\frac{\text{P. takes P.}}{\text{Check.}}$, and Black draws by perpetual check.

Secondly, 12. $\frac{\quad}{\text{P. to B's 6th}}$, 13. $\frac{\text{P. to K. Kt.'s 3rd}}{\text{P. to Q. B's 3rd}}$, 14. $\frac{\text{B. to Q. Kt.'s 3rd}}{\text{B. to K's 3rd}}$, 15. $\frac{\text{Q. to Q's 6th}}{\quad}$, and White has somewhat the better game.

13. Q. to Q's 4th.	13. Kt. to Q. B's 3rd.
14. B. takes Kt. (ch.)	14. P. takes B.
15. Kt. to K's 2nd.	

And the game is about even.

In the second place :—

	4. Kt. to K. B's 3rd.
5. Kt. to Q. B's 3rd.	

Opinion is divided between this move and 5. $\frac{\text{Kt. to K. B's 3rd}}{\quad}$, for which see Variation A. Von der Laza gives 5. $\frac{\text{Q. to K's 2nd}}{\qquad}$ as the best, but he must have overlooked a variation in his analysis, that I proposed five-and-twenty years ago, and which appears to lessen the validity of the move considerably. (See Variation B.)

	5. B. to Q. Kt.'s 5th.
6. Kt. to K. B's 3rd.	

If 6. $\frac{\text{Kt. to K's 2nd}}{\text{P. to Q. B's 3rd.}}$, 7. $\frac{\text{B. to Q. B's 4th}}{\text{B. to K. Kt.'s 5th}}$, 8. $\frac{\text{P. to Q's 3rd}}{\text{Kt. to K. R's 4th}}$, 9. $\frac{\text{Castles}}{\qquad}$. Equal game.

	6. B. takes Q's Kt.
7. Q's P. takes B.	7. P. to Q. B's 3rd.
8. B. to Q. B's 4th.	8. Q. takes Q. (ch.)
9. K. takes Q.	9. Castles.
10. Q's B. takes P.	10. Kt. takes P.
11. R. to K's sq.	

The game is about equal.

Variation A, beginning at White's 5th Move.

BLACK.

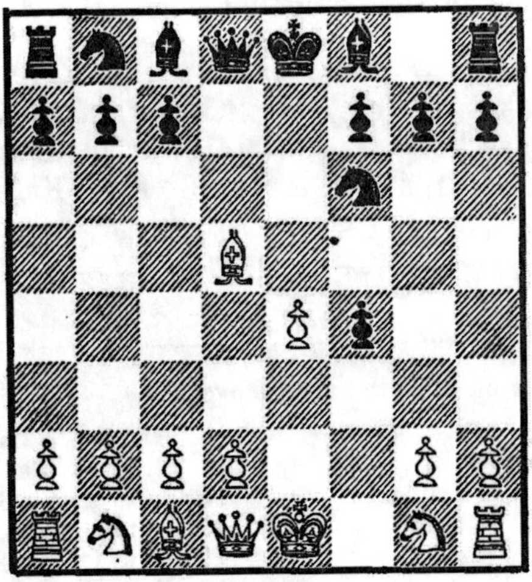

WHITE.

Position prior to White's 5th Move.

5. Kt. to K. B's 3rd.	5. Kt. takes B.
6. P. takes Kt.	6. Q. takes P.
7. Kt. to Q. B's 3rd.	7. Q. to K. R's 4th.
8. P. to Q's 4th.	8. B. to Q's 3rd.
9. Q. to K's 2nd (ch.)	9. K. to Q's sq.
10. Castles.	10. P. to K. Kt.'s 4th.
11. Q. to Q. Kt.'s 5th.	11. P. to K. B's 4th.
12. Q. to Q's 5th.	12. Kt. to Q. B's 3rd.
13. Kt. to K's 5th.	13. R. to K. B's sq.
14. B. to Q's 2nd.	

Up to this point the moves in the text are those of an interesting game, played by Messrs. Morphy, Walker, and Greenaway, consulting together against Messrs. Mongredien, Lowenthal, and Medley. It was abandoned as a remise after twenty moves owing to the lateness of the hour; the position then being slightly in favour of Black.* So far as I at present see, the opening tends to confirm the good opinion many players entertain of 5. $\frac{\text{Kt. to K. B's 3rd}}{}$. White has certainly no inferiority of position, and I am disposed to think by exchanging Knights would have a decided advantage. Let us suppose instead of 14. $\frac{\text{B. to Q's 2nd}}{}$, &c., as played in the foregoing game, the *début* were continued thus:—

14. Kt. takes Kt. (ch.)	14. P. takes Kt.
15. Q. takes P.	15. P. to K. B's 6th.
16. P. to K. Kt.'s 3rd.	16. P. to Kt.'s 5th.

If 16. $\frac{}{\text{Q. to K. R's 6th}}$, 17. $\frac{\text{B. takes P. (ch.)}}{}$, &c.

---

* The following were the after moves:—

14. B. to Q's 2nd.	14. Kt. to K's 2nd.
15. Q. to Q. B's 4th.	15. R. to K. B's 3rd.
16. Q's R. to K's sq.	16. P. to Q. B's 3rd.
17. Kt. to Q. R's 4th.	17. B. to Q's 2nd.
18. Kt. to Q. B's 5th.	18. B. to Q. B's sq.
19. R. to K. B's 3rd.	19. P. to K. Kt.'s 5th.
20. R. to Q. Kt.'s 3rd.	20. P. to Q. Kt.'s 3rd.

If 16. $\frac{}{\text{Q. to K. Kt.'s 5th}}$, 17. $\frac{\text{R. takes P.}}{}$, &c. If 16. $\frac{}{\text{P. to K. B's 5th}}$, 17. $\frac{\text{R. takes P.}}{}$. (17. $\frac{\text{Kt. to K's 4th}}{}$ would be bad, because of 17. $\frac{}{\text{P. to B's 7th (ch.)}}$, &c.) 17. $\frac{}{\text{P. to K. Kt.'s 5th}}$. (Black cannot safely play 17. $\frac{}{\text{P. takes P.}}$, on account of 18. $\frac{\text{R. takes R. (ch)}}{}$, by which White wins incontinently.) 18. $\frac{\text{R. takes P.}}{\text{R. takes R.}}$. (If 18. $\frac{}{\text{B. takes R.}}$, 19. $\frac{\text{B. takes B.}}{\text{R. takes P. (best)}}$, 20. $\frac{\text{P. takes R.}}{}$, and White has a winning superiority.) 19. $\frac{\text{B. takes R.}}{\text{B. takes B.}}$, 20. $\frac{\text{Q. takes R.}}{}$, and Black has a lost game.

Variation B, beginning at White's 5th move.

(See preceding Diagram.)

5. Q. to K's 2nd.	5. Kt. takes B.
6. P. takes Kt. (dis. ch.)	6. B. to K's 2nd.
7. Q. to K. B's 3rd.	7. B. to K. R's 5th (ch.)
8. P. to K. Kt.'s 3rd.	8. Castles.

This is the line of play I proposed. The *Handbuch* continues the opening by 8. $\frac{}{\text{P. takes P.}}$, 9. $\frac{\text{P. takes P.}}{\text{B. to Kt.'s 4th}}$, 10. $\frac{\text{Kt. to Q. B's 3rd}}{}$, and pronounces the game equal.

9. P. takes B.*

---

* Apparently an error. The correct continuation is 9. $\frac{\text{Kt. to K's 2nd}}{\text{R. to K's sq.}}$, 10. $\frac{\text{Kt. to Q. B's 3rd}}{\text{B. to K. B's 3rd}}$, 11. $\frac{\text{Kt. to K's 4th}}{}$, and the game is in White's favour.—[Ed.]

If 9. $\frac{\text{Q. takes P.}}{\text{Q. takes P.}}$, 10. $\frac{\text{Kt. to K. B's 3rd}}{\text{B. to K. Kt.'s 4th}}$, 11. $\frac{\text{Kt. to Q. B's 3rd}}{\text{Q. to Q. B's 3rd}}$, Black has a winning game.

	9. Q. takes P. (ch.)
10. Q. to K. B's 2nd.	10. R. to K's sq. (ch.)
11. Kt. to K's 2nd.	11. Q. to K. R's 4th.
12. Q's Kt. to B's 3rd.	12. P. to K. B's 6th.

Black must win.

Game the Fourth.

WHITE.	BLACK.
1. P. to K's 4th.	1. P. to K's 4th.
2. P. to K. B's 4th.	2. P. takes P.
3. B. to Q. B's 4th.	3. P. to K. B's 4th.

By many good players this, the favourite defence of Lopez, Gianutio, Salvio, and other old masters, is held to be preferable to all others. I cannot esteem it so highly. To me it appears scarcely so trustworthy as 3. $\frac{}{\text{P. to Q's 4th}}$, and certainly inferior to 3. $\frac{}{\text{Kt. to K. B's 3rd}}$.

4. Kt. to Q. B's 3rd.

In addition to this move, White can play, 4. $\frac{\text{Q. to K's 2nd}}{}$, for the consequences of which refer to Variation A, or 4. $\frac{\text{Kt. to K. R's 3rd.}}{}$, as in Variation B. The results of 4. $\frac{\text{B. takes Kt.}}{}$, 4. $\frac{\text{P. takes P.}}{}$, and 4. $\frac{\text{P. to Q's 3rd}}{}$, we can examine at once. In the first place, 4. $\frac{\text{B. takes Kt.}}{\text{Q. to K. R's 5th (ch.)}}$, 5. $\frac{\text{K. to B's sq.}}{\text{R. takes B.}}$, and the position seems to be in Black's favour. In the second place, 4. $\frac{\text{P. takes P.}}{\text{Q. to K. R's 5th (ch.)}}$, 5 $\frac{\text{K. to B's sq.}}{\text{P. to K. B's 6th}}$, 6. $\frac{\text{B. takes Kt.}}{}$. (I prefer playing here

6. $\frac{\text{B. to Q's 5th}}{\quad}$, although Black still appears to have the advantage.) 6. $\frac{\quad}{\text{P. takes P. (ch.)}}$, 7. $\frac{\text{K. takes P.}}{\text{Q. to K. Kt.'s 4th (ch.)}}$, and Black's position is assuredly preferable. In the third place, 4. $\frac{\text{P. to Q's 3rd}}{\text{Q. to K. R's 5th (ch.)}}$, 5. $\frac{\text{K. to B's sq.}}{\text{P. takes P}}$, 6. $\frac{\text{P. takes P.}}{\text{B. to Q B's 4th}}$, 7. $\frac{\text{Q. to K's 2nd}}{\text{P. to Q's 3rd}}$, and the superiority is on Black's side.

4. Q. to K. R's 5th (ch.)

If 4. $\frac{\quad}{\text{Kt. to K. B's 3rd}}$, 5. $\frac{\text{P. to K's 5th}}{\text{Kt. to Kt.'s 5th (best)}}$, 6. $\frac{\text{Kt. to K. B's 3rd}}{\text{P. to Q's 3rd}}$, 7. $\frac{\text{P. to Q's 4th}}{\text{P. takes P.}}$, 8. $\frac{\text{P. takes P.}}{\text{Q. takes Q. (ch.)}}$, 9. $\frac{\text{Kt. takes Q.}}{\text{Kt. to Q. B's 3rd}}$, 10. $\frac{\text{Q's B. takes P.}}{\quad}$, White appears to me to have a freer game.

5. K. to B's sq. — 5. P. takes P. (best).
6. Kt. takes P. — 6. P. to Q. B's 3rd.
7. Q. to K's 2nd. — 7. K. to Q's sq.
8. Kt. to K. B's 3rd.

If 8. $\frac{\text{B. takes Kt.}}{\text{R. takes B.}}$, 9. $\frac{\text{Kt. to K. B's 3rd}}{\text{Q. to K's 2nd}}$, 10. $\frac{\text{P. to Q's 4th}}{\quad}$. (If 10. $\frac{\text{P. to Q's 3rd}}{\text{P. to K. Kt.'s 4th}}$, &c.) 10. $\frac{\quad}{\text{P. to Q's 4th}}$, 11. $\frac{\text{Q's Kt. to K. Kt.'s 5th}}{\text{P. to K. R's 3rd}}$, 12. $\frac{\text{Q. takes Q. (ch.)}}{\text{B. takes Q.}}$, 13. $\frac{\text{Kt. to B's 7th (ch.)}}{\text{K. to K's sq.}}$, 14. $\frac{\text{Q's Kt. to K's 5th}}{\text{P. to K. Kt.'s 4th}}$, Black has a Pawn plus, and no inferiority of position.

8. Q. to K's 2nd.

9. P. to Q's 3rd.

This, I am aware, may not be critically sound, but it is novel, and in practical play would, I believe, prove better for White than the authorised course of 9. $\frac{\text{Q's Kt. to K. Kt.'s 5th}}{\quad}$. (For the result of the latter see Variation C.)

	9. P. to Q's 4th.
10. Q's B. takes P.	10. B. to K. Kt.'s 5th.

Apparently Black's best move.

If 10. $\frac{}{\text{P. takes Kt.}}$, 11. $\frac{\text{Kt. to Kt.'s 5th}}{\text{Kt. to K. R's 3rd}}$. (11. $\frac{}{\text{Q. to K. B's 3rd}}$ would be disastrous on account of 12. $\frac{\text{Kt. to B's 7th (ch.)}}{}$, &c.) 12. $\frac{\text{Kt. takes K's P.}}{\text{B. to K. Kt.'s 5th}}$, 13. $\frac{\text{Q. to K. B's 2nd}}{}$, threatening 14. $\frac{\text{B. to K. Kt.'s 5th}}{}$, 14. $\frac{\text{B. takes Q's Kt.}}{}$, and having, I think, the better game.

Again, if 10. $\frac{}{\text{P. takes B.}}$, 11. $\frac{\text{Q. to K. B's 2nd}}{\text{Kt. to Q's 2nd}}$, 12. $\frac{\text{R. to K's sq.}}{}$, Black has a very bad game.

11. Q. to Q's 2nd.	11. B. takes Kt.

If 11. $\frac{}{\text{P. takes Kt.}}$, 12. $\frac{\text{Kt. to Kt.'s 5th}}{\text{Kt. to K. R's 3rd}}$, 13. $\frac{\text{Kt. takes K's P.}}{}$, and once more White seems to have an equivalent for the piece sacrificed. So also if 11. $\frac{}{\text{P. takes B.}}$, 12. $\frac{\text{R. to K's sq.}}{\text{B. takes Kt.}}$, 13. $\frac{\text{P. takes B.}}{}$, White has a fine attack.

12. P. takes B.	12. P. takes B.

If 12. $\frac{}{\text{P. takes Kt.}}$, 13. $\frac{\text{B. takes K's Kt.}}{}$, equalising the forces, and having a better position.

13. R. to K's sq.

If 13. $\frac{\text{P. takes P. (dis. ch.)}}{\text{Q. to Q's 2nd}}$, 14. $\frac{\text{Q. to K's 3rd}}{}$ (threatening to win a piece by 15. $\frac{\text{B. takes Kt.}}{}$, and 16. $\frac{\text{Q. to K. B's 4th}}{}$), 14. $\frac{}{\text{Kt. to K. B's 3rd}}$. (If 14. $\frac{}{\text{Kt. to Q. R's 3rd}}$, 15. $\frac{\text{K. to K's 2nd}}{}$.

with a very powerful attack). 15. $\frac{\text{Kt. to K. Kt.'s 5th}}{\text{Kt. to Q. R's 3rd}}$, 16. $\frac{\text{K. to K's 2nd}}{\quad}$, and I believe White must win.

13. Q. to K. B's 2nd.

If 13. $\frac{\quad}{\text{Q. to Q's 2nd}}$, 14. $\frac{\text{B. takes Kt.}}{\text{R. takes B.}}$, 15. $\frac{\text{Q. to K. B's 4th}}{\quad}$, gaining a piece.

14. Kt. to K. Kt.'s 5th.

And Black must lose.

If he play 14. $\frac{\quad}{\text{Q. to Q's 4th}}$, then follows 15. $\frac{\text{R. to K's 5th}}{\quad}$, &c. If he play 14. $\frac{\quad}{\text{Q. to K. B's 4th}}$, 15. $\frac{\text{R. to K's 5th}}{\quad}$ again costs him a piece by 16. $\frac{\text{Kt. to K's 6th (ch.)}}{\quad}$, &c., after which his game is hopeless.

Variation A, beginning at White's 4th Move.

BLACK.

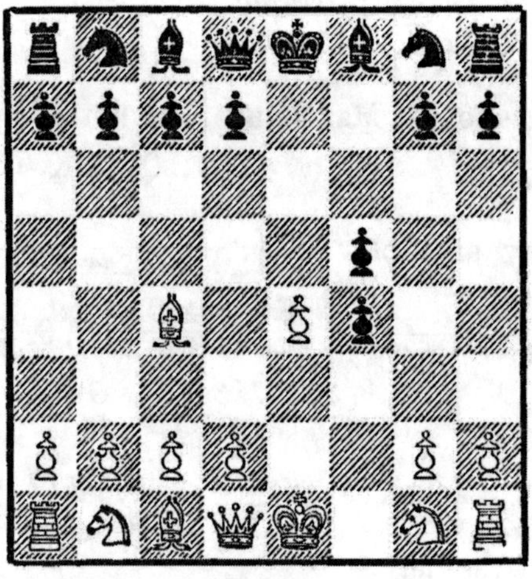

WHITE.

Position prior to White's 4th Move.

4. Q. to K's 2nd.	4. Q. to K. R's 5th (ch.)
5. K. to Q's sq.	5. P. takes P.
6. Q. takes P. (ch.)	6. B. to K's 2nd.

If 6. $\frac{\qquad}{\text{K. to Q's sq.}}$, 7. $\frac{\text{Kt. to K. B's 3rd}}{\text{P. to Q's 4th}}$, &c.

7. P. to Q's 4th.

If 7. $\frac{\text{B. takes Kt.}}{\text{R. takes B.}}$, 8. $\frac{\text{Kt. to K. B's 3rd}}{\text{Q. to K. B's 3rd}}$, 9. $\frac{\text{Kt. to Q. B's 3rd}}{\text{P. to Q. B's 3rd}}$, 10. $\frac{\text{P. to Q's 4th}}{\text{P. to Q's 4th}}$, 11. $\frac{\text{Q. takes B's P.}}{\text{Q. takes Q.}}$, 12. $\frac{\text{B. takes Q.}}{\text{B. to K. Kt.'s 5th}}$.

Equal game.

	7. Kt. to K. B's 3rd.
8. Q. takes K. B's P.	8. Q. takes Q.
9. B. takes Q.	9. P. to Q's 4th.
10. B. to Q's 3rd.	10. B. to K. Kt.'s 5th (ch.)
11. Kt. to K's 2nd.	11. Kt. to Q. B's 3rd.
12. P. to Q. B's 3rd.	

The game is equal.

VARIATION B, BEGINNING AT WHITE'S 4TH MOVE.

(See preceding Diagram.)

4. Kt. to K. R's 3rd.

A suggestion of Max Lange, but not a happy one.

4. Q. to K. R's 5th (ch.)

Black may also play 4. $\frac{\qquad}{\text{Q. to K's 2nd}}$ with advantage; *e. g.* :—4. $\frac{\qquad}{\text{Q. to K's 2nd}}$, 5. $\frac{\text{Kt. to Q. B's 3rd}}{\text{Kt. to K. B's 3rd}}$, 6. $\frac{\text{Kt. takes P.}}{\text{P. to Q. B's 3rd}}$, 7. $\frac{\text{P. to Q's 4th}}{\text{P. to Q's 4th}}$, 8. $\frac{\text{B. to Q. Kt.'s 3rd}}{\text{B's P. takes P.}}$, 9. $\frac{\text{Castles}}{\text{B. to K. Kt.'s 5th}}$, &c.

5. Kt. to B's 2nd.	5. P. takes P.
6. B. takes Kt.	6. R. takes B.
7. Q. to K's 2nd.	

He may also play 7. $\frac{\text{Kt. to Q. B's 3rd}}{\qquad}$.

	7. P. to Q's 4th.
8. P. to Q. B's 4th.	8. Kt. to Q. B's 3rd.
9. P. takes P.	9. Kt. to Q's 5th.
10. Q. takes P. (ch.)	10. Q. to K's 2nd.
11. Q. takes Q. (ch.)	11. B. takes Q.
12. K. to Q's sq.	12. B. to K. R's 5th.

Black has a decided superiority.

Variation C, beginning at White's 9th Move.

BLACK.

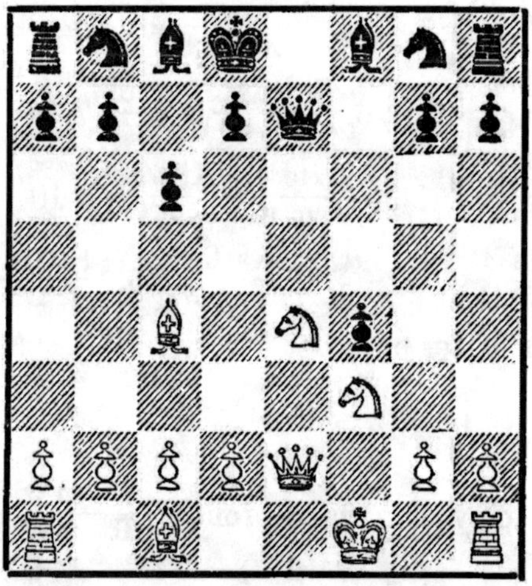

WHITE.

Position prior to White's 9th Move.

9. Q's Kt. to K. Kt.'s 5th	9. P. to Q's 4th.
10. Q. takes Q. (ch.)	10. K. takes Q.

And Black's game is the better one.

Game the Fifth.

WHITE.	BLACK.
1. P. to K's 4th.	1. P. to K's 4th.
2. P. to K. B's 4th.	2. P. takes P.
3. B. to Q. B's 4th.	3. P. to Q. Kt.'s 4th.

The present defensive move was suggested by Mr. Bryan, an American amateur, and underwent an exhaustive analysis by Kieseritzky. It is ingenious, but if properly met is not advantageous to Black.

4. B. takes Q. Kt.'s P. (best).

(For the result of 4. $\frac{\text{B. takes B's P. (ch.)}}{}$, and 4. $\frac{\text{B. to Q. Kt.'s 3rd}}{}$, see Variation A.)

	4. Q. to K. R's 5th (ch.)
5. K. to B's sq.	5. B. to Q. Kt.'s 2nd.

If 5. $\frac{}{\text{Kt. to K. B's 3rd}}$, 6. $\frac{\text{Kt. to K. B's 3rd}}{\text{Q. to K. R's 3rd}}$, 7. $\frac{\text{P. to Q's 3rd}}{\text{Kt. to K. R's 4th}}$, 8. $\frac{\text{Kt. to K. R's 4th}}{\text{P. to Kt.'s 3rd}}$, 9. $\frac{\text{P. to K. Kt.'s 4th}}{\text{B. to K.'s 2nd}}$, 10. $\frac{\text{P. takes Kt.}}{\text{B. takes Kt.}}$, 11. $\frac{\text{Q. to Kt.'s 4th}}{\text{Q. to Kt.'s 4th}}$, 12. $\frac{\text{Q. takes Q.}}{\text{B. takes Q.}}$, 13. $\frac{\text{Kt. to Q. B's 3rd}}{}$, White has the better position.

6. Kt. to K. B's 3rd.

White may play with equal profit 6. $\frac{\text{Kt. to Q. B's 3rd}}{\text{Kt. to Q. B's 3rd}}$. (If 6. $\frac{}{\text{B. to Q. Kt.'s 5th}}$, 7. $\frac{\text{P. to Q's 3rd}}{\text{B. takes Kt.}}$, 8. $\frac{\text{P. takes B.}}{\text{Kt. to K. B's 3rd}}$, 9. $\frac{\text{R. to Q. Kt.'s sq.}}{}$, with a good game.) 7. $\frac{\text{P. to Q's 4th}}{}$.

(If 7. $\frac{\text{Kt. to K. B's 3rd}}{}$, Black has the advantage by 7. $\frac{}{\text{Q. to K. R's 3rd}}$, 8. $\frac{\text{Kt. to Q's 5th}}{\text{Castles}}$, 9. $\frac{\text{P. to Q's 4th}}{\text{P. to Kt.'s 4th}}$, 10. $\frac{\text{P. to K. R's 4th}}{\text{P. to K. B's 3rd}}$, 11. $\frac{\text{P. to K's 5th}}{\text{P. takes R's P.}}$, 12. $\frac{\text{P. takes P.}}{\text{K's Kt. to K's 2nd}}$.) 7. $\frac{}{\text{Kt. to K. B's 3rd}}$, 8. $\frac{\text{P. to Q's 5th}}{\text{Kt. to K's 4th}}$, 9. $\frac{\text{Kt. to K. B's 3rd}}{\text{Kt. takes Kt.}}$, 10. $\frac{\text{Q. takes Kt.}}{\text{Kt. to K. R's 4th}}$, 11. $\frac{\text{P. to K. Kt.'s 4th}}{\text{P. takes P. in pass.}}$, 12. $\frac{\text{K. to Kt.'s 2nd}}{\text{B. to Q's 3rd}}$,

13. $\frac{\text{P. to K's 5th}}{\text{K's B. takes P.}}$, 14. $\frac{\text{B. takes P. (ch.)}}{\text{K. takes B.}}$ 15. $\frac{\text{Q. to K. B's 5th (ch.)}}{\text{K. to Q's 3rd}}$,

16. $\frac{\text{Kt. to K's 4th (ch.)}}{\text{K. takes P.}}$, White has the better game.

To resume the text game:—

	6. Q. to K. R's 4th.
7. B. to Q. B's 4th.	7. Kt. to K. B's 3rd.
8. Kt. to Q. B's 3rd.	8. B. to Q. Kt.'s 5th.
9. P. to Q's 3rd.	9. B. takes Kt.
10. P. takes B.	10. P. to K. Kt.'s 4th.
11. R. to Q. Kt.'s sq.	11. B. to Q. B's 3rd.
12. P. to K. R's 4th.	12. P. to K. R's 3rd.
13. K. to Kt.'s sq.	13. P. to Kt.'s 5th.
14. Kt. to Q's 4th.	14. Q. to K's 4th.
15. P. to Kt.'s 3rd.	15. P. to B's 6th.
16. B. to K. B's 4th.	

I prefer White's game.

Variation A, beginning at White's 4th Move.

BLACK.

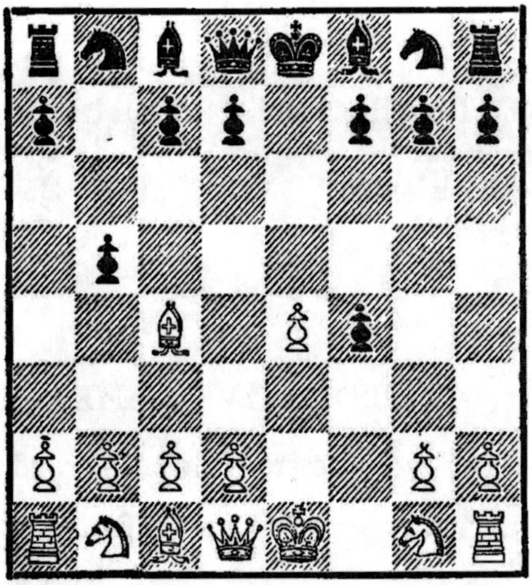

WHITE.

Position prior to White's 4th Move.

4. B. takes B's P. (ch.)

This sacrifice is not commendable. White certainly gains a superior piece in return for the Bishop, but his Queen becomes dangerously compromised.

	4. K. takes B.
5. Q. to K. R's 5th (ch.)	5. P. to K. Kt.'s 3rd.
6. Q. to Q's 5th (ch.)	6. K. to Kt.'s 2nd.
7. Q. takes R.	7. Kt. to Q. B's 3rd.
8. Kt. to Q. B's 3rd.	

If 8. $\frac{\text{P. to Q's 4th}}{\text{Q. to K. R's 5th (ch.)}}$, 9. $\frac{\text{K. to Q's sq.}}{\text{B. to Q. R's 3rd}}$, 10. $\frac{\text{P. to Q's 5th}}{\text{B. to Q. B's 4th}}$, Black's game for choice.

	8. Q. to K. R's 5th (ch.)
9. K. to Q's sq.	9. B. to Q. R's 3rd.
10. P. to Q. R's 4th.	10. P. to Q. Kt.'s 5th.
11. Kt. to Q's 5th.	11. B. to Q's 3rd.
12. P. to Q's 4th.	12. K's Kt. to K's 2nd.

Black has the advantage.

If instead of capturing either of the Pawns, White for his 4th move retired the Bishop, he loses ground. For example :—

4. B. to Q. Kt.'s 3rd.	4. P. to Q. R's 4th.
5. P. to Q. R's 4th.	5. Q. to K. R's 5th (ch.)
6. K. to B's sq.	6. P. to Q. Kt.'s 5th.
7. Kt. to K. B's 3rd.	7. B. to Q. R's 3rd (ch.)
8. P. to Q's 3rd.	8. Q. to K. B's 3rd.

Black's position is superior.

ILLUSTRATIVE GAMES.

GAME I.—Between Messrs. Lowenthal and Anderssen.

WHITE (Mr. L.)	BLACK (Mr. A.)
1. P. to K's 4th.	1. P. to K's 4th.
2. P. to K. B's 4th.	2. P. takes P.
3. B. to Q. B's 4th.	3. Q. to R's 5th (ch.)

4. K. to B's sq.	4. P. to K. Kt.'s 4th.
5. Kt. to Q. B's 3rd.	5. B. to K. Kt.'s 2nd.
6. P. to Q's 4th.	6. Kt. to K's 2nd.*
7. P. to K. Kt.'s 3rd.†	7. P. takes P.
8. K. to Kt.'s 2nd.	8. Q. to K. R's 3rd.
9. P. to K. R's 4th.	9. Q. to K. B's 3rd.
10. Q's B. to K's 3rd.	10. P. takes R's P.
11. Kt. to K. B's 3rd.	11. P. to R's 6th (ch.)
12. R. takes P.	12. P. to Q's 4th.
13. R. takes Kt.'s P.	13. P. takes K's B.
14. B. to K. Kt.'s 5th.	14. Q. to K's 3rd.
15. B. takes Kt.	15. K. takes B.
16. R. takes B.	16. Q. to R's 6th (ch.)
17. K. to B's 2nd.	17. B. to K. Kt.'s 5th.
18. Kt. to Q's 5th (ch.)	18. K. to B's sq.‡
19. R. takes B's P. (ch.)	19. K. takes R.
20. Kt. to K's 5th (ch.)	20. K. to B's sq.
21. Q. takes B.	21. Q. takes Q.
22. Kt. takes Q.	22. Kt. to Q. R's 3rd.
23. P. to K's 5th.	23. P. to Q. B's 3rd.
24. Kt. to K. B's 4th.	24. Kt. to Q. B's 2nd.
25. K. to B's 3rd.	25. K. to Kt.'s 2nd.§
26. R. to K. Kt.'s sq.	26. R. to K. B's sq.
27. Kt. to B's 6th (ch.)	27. K. to R's sq.
28. Kt. to Kt.'s 6th (ch.)	28. P. takes Kt.

And White mates in two moves.

Game II.—Between Messrs. Steinitz and Zukertort.

White (Mr. Z.)	Black (Mr. S.)
1. P. to K's 4th.	1. P. to K's 4th.
2. P. to K. B's 4th.	2. P. takes P.
3. P. to Q. B's 4th.	3. P. to Q's 4th.
4. B. takes P.	4. Q. to R's 5th (ch.)

* The usual move at this point is 6. P. to Q's 3rd, but the whole defence is now considered to be untenable.

† A good reply.

‡ Better to have retired the King to Q's sq.

§ Here we should have preferred K. to K's 2nd, with the object of playing Kt. to K's 3rd, on the following move.

5. K. to B's sq.	5. P. to K. Kt.'s 4th.
6. Kt. to Q. B's 3rd.	6. B. to K. Kt.'s 2nd.
7. P. to Q's 4th.	7. K's Kt. to K's 2nd.
8. Kt. to K. B's 3rd.	8. Q. to R's 4th.
9. P. to K. R's 4th.	9. P. to K. R's 3rd.
10. K. to Kt.'s sq.	10. P. to K. Kt.'s 5th.
11. Kt. to K's 5th.	11. B. takes Kt.
12. P. takes B.	12. Q. takes P.
13. Q. to K. B's sq.	13. P. to B's 6th.*
14. P. takes P.	14. Q. to K. Kt.'s 6th (ch.
15. Q. to Kt.'s 2nd.	15. Q. to K's 8th (ch.)

And draws by perpetual check.

GAME III.—Between Messrs. Gelbfechs and Rosenthal.

WHITE (Mr. G.)	BLACK (Mr. R.)
1. P. to K's 4th.	1. P. to K's 4th.
2. P. to K. B's 4th.	2. P. takes P.
3. B. to Q. B's 4th.	3. P. to Q's 4th.
4. B. takes P.	4. Q. to R's 5th (ch.)
5. K. to B's sq.	5. P. to K. Kt.'s 4th.
6. Kt. to Q. B's 3rd.	6. B. to Kt.'s 2nd.
7. Kt. to K. B's 3rd.	7. Q. to R's 4th.
8. P. to Q's 4th.	8. Kt. to K's 2nd.
9. P. to K. R's 4th.	9. P. to K. R's 3rd.
10. P. to K's 5th.	10. Kt. takes B.‡
11. Kt. takes Kt.	11. Kt. to R's 3rd.
12. Q. to K's 2nd.	12. P. to Q. B's 3rd.
13. Kt. to B's 6th (ch.)	13. B. takes Kt.
14. P. takes B. (dis. ch.)	14. B. to K's 3rd.
15. P. to Q's 5th.§	15. P. takes Q's P.
16. Q. to Kt.'s 5th (ch.)	16. K. to Q's sq.
17. Q. takes Kt.'s P.	17. Kt. to B's 2nd.

* The best play, insuring a draw. He would have gained nothing by checking with Queen at Q's 5th.

† We rather prefer 10. K. to Kt.'s sq., as in the previous game.

‡ This deviation is not to be commended. The correct move is 10. Kt. to Q. B's 3rd.

§ Well played. From this point White has a winning game.

18. B. to Q's 2nd.	18. R. to Q. B's sq.
19. Q. to Q. Kt.'s 4th.	19. R. to K's sq.
20. Q. to Q's 6th (ch.)	20. B. to Q's 2nd.
21. Kt. to K's 5th.	21. R. takes Kt.
22. Q. takes R.	22. Kt. to K's 3rd.
23. B. to R's 5th (ch.)	23. R. to B's 2nd.
24. Q. takes Q's P.	24. K. to K's sq.
25. B. takes R.	25. Kt. takes B.
26. Q. to Q's 6th.	26. B. to Kt.'s 4th (ch.)
27. K. to Kt.'s sq.	27. Q. to K's 7th.
28. K. to R's 2nd.	28. Q. to K's 6th.
29. K's R. to K's sq.	29. B. to K's 7th.
30. R. takes B.	30. Q. takes R.
31. Q. takes Kt.	31. Resigns.

GAME IV.—Between Messrs. Schulten and Kieseritzky.

WHITE (Mr. S.)	BLACK (Mr. K.)
1. P. to K's 4th.	1. P. to K's 4th.
2. P. to K. B's 4th.	2. P. takes P.
3. B. to Q. B's 4th.	3. Q. to R's 5th (ch.)
4. K. to B's sq.	4. P. to Q. Kt.'s 4th.
5. B. takes Kt.'s P.	5. Kt. to K. B's 3rd.
6. Kt. to Q. B's 3rd.	6. Kt. to K. Kt.'s 5th.
7. Kt. to K. R's 3rd.	7. Kt. to Q. B's 3rd.
8. Kt. to Q's 5th.*	8. Kt. to Q's 5th.
9. Kt. takes B's P. (ch.)	9. K. to Q's sq.
10. Kt. takes R.	10. P. to B's 6th.
11. P. to Q's 3rd.	11. P. to K. B's 3rd.
12. B. to Q. B's 4th.	12. P. to Q's 4th.
13. B. takes P.	13. B. to Q's 3rd.
14. Q. to K's sq.	14. P. takes P. (ch.)
15. K. takes P.	15. Q. takes Kt. (ch.)†
16. K. takes Q.	16. Kt. to K's 6th (dis. ch.)
17. K. to R's 4th.	17. Kt. to B's 6th (ch.)
18. K. to R's 5th.	18. B. mates.

* He might have played P. to Q's 4th.

† Very pretty and ingenious, leading to a beautiful termination.

GAME V.—Between Messrs. Lowenthal and Wayte.

WHITE (Mr. L.)	BLACK (Mr. W.)
1. P. to K's 4th.	1. P. to K's 4th.
2. P. to K. B's 4th.	2. P. takes P.
3. B. to Q. B's 4th.	3. Kt. to K. B's 3rd.
4. Q. to K's 2nd.*	4. B. to Q. B's 4th.
5. Kt. to K. B's 3rd.	5. Kt. to Q. B's 3rd.
6. P. to Q. B's 3rd.	6. Castles.
7. P. to Q's 4th.	7. P. to Q's 4th.
8. P. takes P.†	8. R. to K's sq.
9. Kt. to K's 5th.	9. Kt. takes Kt.
10. P. takes Kt.	10. B. to K. Kt.'s 5th.
11. Q. to Q. B's 2nd.‡	11. R. takes P. (ch.)
12. K. to B's sq.	12. Kt. takes P.
13. Kt. to Q. R's 3rd.	13. Kt. to K's 6th (ch.)
14. B. takes Kt.	14. P. takes B.
15. P. to Q. Kt.'s 4th.	15. R. to K. B's 4th (ch.)
16. K. to K's sq.	16. R. to K. B's 7th.
17. Q. to Q B's sq.	

And Black mates in two moves.

---

* By no means a bad move, though inferior, we think, to 4. Kt. to Q. B's 3rd.

† A fatal move. He ought to have taken Bishop with Pawn.

‡ Had he played 11. Q. to Q's 3rd, the Queen is evidently lost.

CHAPTER XIII.

THE KING'S GAMBIT.

$$1.\ \frac{\text{P. to K's 4th}}{\text{P. to K's 4th}},\ 2.\ \frac{\text{P. to K. B's 4th}}{}.$$

Under the general title of KING'S GAMBIT, it has been customary to include all the various *débuts* dependent on the moves above. The *Handbuch des Schachspiels* separates this cluster of openings into three classes. First, the games springing from what is known as the KING'S KNIGHT'S GAMBIT, beginning $1.\ \frac{\text{P. to K's 4th}}{\text{P. to K's 4th}},\ 2.\ \frac{\text{P. to K. B's 4th}}{\text{P. takes P.}},$ $3.\ \frac{\text{Kt. to K. B's 3rd}}{}.$ Second, those which arise from what is called the KING'S BISHOP'S GAMBIT, $1.\ \frac{\text{P. to K's 4th}}{\text{P. to K's 4th}},$ $2.\ \frac{\text{P. to K. B's 4th}}{\text{P. takes P.}},\ 3.\ \frac{\text{B. to Q. B's 4th}}{}.$ And third, irregular modifications of the parent opening, such as $1.\ \frac{\text{P. to K's 4th}}{\text{P. to K's 4th}},$ $2.\ \frac{\text{P. to K. B's 4th}}{\text{P. takes P.}},\ 3.\ \frac{\text{P. to K. R's 4th}}{};\ 3.\ \frac{\text{Q. to K. Kt.'s 4th}}{},$ &c. And those openings where the second player declines the gambit, such as $1.\ \frac{\text{P. to K's 4th}}{\text{P. to K's 4th}},\ 2.\ \frac{\text{P. to K. B's 4th}}{\text{P. to Q's 4th}};$ $2.\ \frac{}{\text{B. to Q. B's 4th}},$ &c. This classification is simple and perspicuous, and I shall proceed, therefore, to consider these groups of openings in the order just indicated.

1. $\frac{\text{P. to K's 4th}}{\text{P. to K's 4th}}$, 2. $\frac{\text{P. to K. B's 4th}}{\text{P. takes P.}}$, 3. $\frac{\text{Kt. to K. B's 3rd}}{\text{P. to K. Kt.'s 4th}}$,

4. $\frac{\text{B. to Q. B's 4th}}{}$.

4. $\frac{\text{P. to K. R's 4th}}{}$.

GRECO OR PHILIDOR'S GAMBIT.

Game the First.

WHITE.	BLACK.
1. P. to K's 4th.	1. P. to K's 4th.
2. P. to K. B's 4th.	2. P. takes P.
3. Kt. to K. B's 3rd.	3. P. to K. Kt.'s 4th.
4. B. to Q. B's 4th.	

This in the opinion of many authorities is the best line of attack, being the preliminary step to the beautiful openings familiar as the *Muzio Gambit*, the *Salvio Gambit*, and the fine *début* before us. It is not so impetuously aggressive as 4. $\frac{\text{P. to K. R's 4th}}{}$, but it is much less hazardous.

4. B. to K. Kt.'s 2nd.

Black has no safer move than this. The result of his playing 4. $\frac{}{\text{P. to K. Kt.'s 5th}}$ will be seen hereafter. If he play 4. $\frac{}{\text{P. to K. R's 3rd}}$, the continuation is likely to be 5. $\frac{\text{Kt. to K's 5th}}{\text{R. to K. R's 2nd}}$, 6. $\frac{\text{P. to Q's 4th}}{\text{P. to Q's 3rd}}$, 7. $\frac{\text{Kt. to Q's 3rd}}{}$, and White will be enabled to castle his King in safety and resume the attack. If he play 4. $\frac{}{\text{P. to Q's 3rd.}}$, he gives White time to improve his assault, and if 4. $\frac{}{\text{P. to K. B's 3rd}}$, the conclusive answer is 5. $\frac{\text{Kt. takes P.}}{}$, &c.

5. Castles.

White may play with almost equal effect, 5. $\frac{\text{P. to Q's 4th}}{\quad}$, as will be shown in Variation A. (For the result of 5. $\frac{\text{P. to K. R's 4th}}{\quad}$, see Game the Second.)

5. P. to Q's 3rd (best).

6. P. to Q's 4th.

If 6. $\frac{\text{P. to Q. B's 3rd}}{\text{P. to K. R's 3rd}}$, 7. $\frac{\text{Q. to Q. Kt.'s 3rd}}{\text{Q. to K's 2nd}}$, 8. $\frac{\text{P. to Q's 4th}}{\text{Kt. to Q. B's 3rd}}$, Black has little to apprehend.

6. P. to K. R's 3rd.

7. P. to Q. B's 3rd.

If 7. $\frac{\text{P. to K. Kt.'s 3rd}}{\text{P. to K. Kt.'s 5th}}$, 8. $\frac{\text{Q's B. takes P.}}{\text{P. takes Kt.}}$, 9. $\frac{\text{Q. takes P.}}{\text{B. takes P. (ch.)}}$, and Black can defend his gains.

7. Q. to K's 2nd.

A move having the high sanction of Von der Laza. Black, however, may play 7. $\frac{\quad}{\text{Kt. to Q. B's 3rd}}$, 7. $\frac{\quad}{\text{Kt. to Q's 2nd}}$, or 7. $\frac{\quad}{\text{Kt. to K's 2nd}}$. For instance, Firstly, 7. $\frac{\quad}{\text{Kt. to Q. B's 3rd}}$, 8. $\frac{\text{Q. to Q. Kt.'s 3rd}}{\text{Q. to K's 2nd}}$; or 7. $\frac{\quad}{\text{Kt. to Q. B's 3rd}}$, 8. $\frac{\text{Q. to Q. R's 4th}}{\text{K. to B's sq.}}$, and the game is about even. Secondly, 7. $\frac{\quad}{\text{Kt. to Q's 2nd}}$ (a move recommended by Von Jaenisch), 8. $\frac{\text{P. to K. Kt.'s 3rd}}{\text{Kt. to Q. Kt.'s 3rd}}$. (I prefer 8. $\frac{\quad}{\text{P. to K. Kt.'s 5th}}$.) 9. $\frac{\text{P. takes P.}}{\text{B. to K. R's 6th}}$, 10. $\frac{\text{R. to K. B's 2nd}}{\text{Kt. takes B.}}$, 11. $\frac{\text{Q. to Q. R's 4th (ch.)}}{\text{P. to Q. B's 3rd}}$, 12. $\frac{\text{Q. takes Kt.}}{\text{P. to K. Kt.'s 5th}}$, 13. $\frac{\text{Kt. to K's sq.}}{\text{Q. to K. R's 5th}}$, and the *Handbuch* thinks Black has the advantage. Thirdly, 7. $\frac{\quad}{\text{Kt. to K's 2nd}}$, 8. $\frac{\text{P. to K. Kt.'s 3rd}}{\text{P. to K. Kt.'s 5th}}$,

9. $\frac{\text{Kt. to K. R's 4th}}{\text{}}$. (White may also play 9. $\frac{\text{Q's B. takes P.}}{\text{}}$ without danger.) 9. $\frac{\text{}}{\text{P. to K. B's 6th}}$, 10. $\frac{\text{P. to K. R's 3rd}}{\text{P. to K. R's 4th}}$, 11. $\frac{\text{Kt. takes P.}}{\text{P. takes Kt.}}$, 12. $\frac{\text{Q. takes P.}}{\text{P. to K. B's 3rd *}}$, 13. $\frac{\text{P. to K's 4th}}{\text{P. to K. B's 4th}}$, 14. $\frac{\text{P. takes Q's B.}}{\text{P. takes P.}}$, 15. $\frac{\text{B. to K. Kt.'s 5th}}{\text{Kt. to K. B's 3rd}}$, and the game is pretty equal.

8. P. to K's 5th.

If 8. $\frac{\text{P. to K. Kt.'s 3rd}}{\text{P. to K. Kt.'s 5th}}$, 9. $\frac{\text{Q's B. takes P.}}{\text{P. takes Kt.}}$, 10. $\frac{\text{Q. takes P.}}{\text{Kt. to Q. B's 3rd}}$, 11. $\frac{\text{Q's Kt. to Q's 2nd}}{\text{B. to Q's 2nd}}$, 12. $\frac{\text{Q's R. to K's sq.}}{\text{Castles}}$, Black has at least as good a game as White.

	8. P. takes P.
9. Kt. takes P.	9. B. takes Kt.
10. R. to K's sq.	10. B. to K's 3rd.
11. B. takes B.	11. P. takes B.

And again Black is at no disadvantage.

---

* The *Handbuch* gives also 12. $\frac{\text{}}{\text{B. takes R's P.}}$, and continues, 13. $\frac{\text{Q. takes P. (ch.)}}{\text{K. to Q's 2nd}}$, 14. $\frac{\text{R. to B's 2nd}}{\text{Q. to K. B's sq.}}$, and should win. For this reason I prefer in the above variation 11. $\frac{\text{B. to K. Kt.'s 5th}}{\text{}}$, instead of taking Pawn with Kt.—[Ed.]

VARIATION A, BEGINNING AT WHITE'S 5TH MOVE.

BLACK.

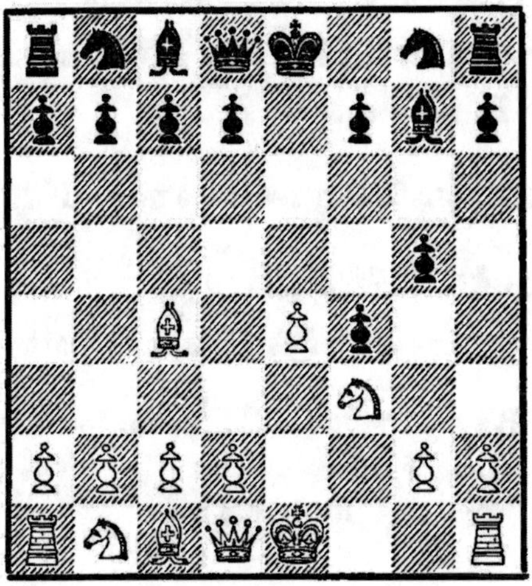

WHITE.

Position prior to White's 5th Move.

WHITE.	BLACK.
5. P. to Q's 4th.	5. P. to Q's 3rd.

This or 5. $\frac{\qquad}{\text{P. to K. R's 3rd}}$, seems to be the safest play for Black. If 5. $\frac{\qquad}{\text{P. to K. B's 4th}}$, 6. $\frac{\text{Kt. to K's 5th}}{\text{Kt. to K. B's 3rd}}$, and White has a strong attack. If 5. $\frac{\qquad}{\text{P. to K. Kt.'s 5th}}$, 6 $\frac{\text{Castles}}{\qquad}$ (or 6. $\frac{\text{Q's B. takes P.}}{\qquad}$, as suggested by Mr. W. Wayte), 6. $\frac{\qquad}{\text{P. takes Kt.}}$, 7. $\frac{\text{Q. takes P.}}{\text{B. takes P. (ch.)}}$, 8. $\frac{\text{K. to R's sq.}}{\text{P. to Q's 3rd (best)}}$, 9. $\frac{\text{Q's B. takes P.}}{\text{B. to K. B's 3rd}}$, 10. $\frac{\text{P. to K's 5th}}{\text{P. takes P.}}$, 11. $\frac{\text{B. takes K's P.}}{\text{Kt. to Q's 2nd}}$, 12. $\frac{\text{B. to Q. B's 3rd}}{\text{Q. to K's 2nd}}$, 13. $\frac{\text{R. to K's sq.}}{\text{B. to K's 4th}}$, 14. $\frac{\text{B. takes B.}}{\text{Kt. takes B.}}$,

15. $\frac{\text{Q. to K. R's 5th}}{\text{Kt. to K. B's 3rd}}$, 16. $\frac{\text{Q. takes Q's Kt.}}{}$, and White has the superior game.

6. P. to Q. B's 3rd. — 6. P. to K. Kt.'s 5th.

A favourable moment this for advancing the Pawn.

7. Kt. to K. Kt.'s sq.

White has no satisfactory resource now. If 7. $\frac{\text{Q's B. takes P.}}{\text{P. takes Kt.}}$, 8. $\frac{\text{Q. takes P.}}{\text{B. to K's 3rd}}$, &c. If 7. $\frac{\text{Q. to Q. Kt.'s 3rd}}{\text{P. takes Kt.}}$, 8. $\frac{\text{B. takes B's P. (ch.)}}{\text{K. to K's 2nd}}$, and Black will come out of the attack unscathed.

7. Q. to K. R's 5th (ch.)

8. K. to B's sq. — 8. B. to K. R's 3rd.

9. Q. to Q. Kt.'s 3rd.

If 9. $\frac{\text{Kt. to K's 2nd}}{\text{P. to K. B's 6th}}$, &c.

9. Q. to Q. R's 4th.

And White has an inferior position.

Game the Second.

WHITE.	BLACK.
1. P. to K's 4th.	1. P. to K's 4th.
2. P. to K. B's 4th.	2. P. takes P.
3. Kt. to K. B's 3rd.	3. P. to K. Kt.'s 4th.
4. B. to Q. B's 4th.	4. B. to K. Kt.'s 2nd.
5. P. to K. R's 4th.	5. P. to K. R's 3rd.

It is a matter of indifference whether Black play 5. $\frac{}{\text{P. to K. R's 3rd}}$, 6. $\frac{}{\text{P. to Q's 3rd}}$, or 5. $\frac{}{\text{P. to Q's 3rd}}$, 6. $\frac{}{\text{P. to K. R's 3rd}}$. If he play 5. $\frac{}{\text{P. to K. Kt.'s 5th}}$, then follows 6. $\frac{\text{Kt. to K. Kt.'s 5th}}{\text{Kt. to K. R's 3rd}}$, 7. $\frac{\text{P. to Q's 4th}}{\text{P. to K. B's 3rd}}$, 8. $\frac{\text{Q's B. takes P.}}{\text{P. takes Kt.}}$.

(If 8. $\frac{\text{}}{\text{P. to Q's 4th}}$, 9. $\frac{\text{B. takes Q's P.}}{\text{P. takes Kt.}}$, 10. $\frac{\text{P. takes P.}}{\text{Kt. to Kt.'s sq.}}$, 11. $\frac{\text{P. to Q. B's 3rd}}{\text{Kt. to K's 2nd}}$, 12. $\frac{\text{B. to Q. B's 4th}}{\text{}}$, &c.) 9. $\frac{\text{Q's B. takes P.}}{\text{B. to K. B's 3rd}}$, 10. $\frac{\text{B. takes Kt.}}{\text{}}$. (10. $\frac{\text{Q. to Q's 2nd}}{\text{}}$ is a strong move here.) 10. $\frac{\text{}}{\text{B. takes P. (ch.)}}$, 11. $\frac{\text{K. to Q's 2nd}}{\text{B. to K. Kt.'s 4th (ch.)}}$, 12. $\frac{\text{K. to Q's 3rd}}{\text{}}$. The game is considered to be equal.

6. P. to Q's 4th. | 6. P. to Q's 3rd.

This is superior to 7. $\frac{\text{}}{\text{P. to K. Kt.'s 5th}}$ because of 8. $\frac{\text{Q's B. takes P.}}{\text{P. takes Kt.}}$, 9. $\frac{\text{Q. takes P.}}{\text{}}$, &c.

7. P. to Q. B's 3rd.

The result of 7. $\frac{\text{Q. to Q's 3rd}}{\text{}}$ is shown in Variation A. That of 7. $\frac{\text{P. takes P.}}{\text{}}$ and 7. $\frac{\text{Kt. to Q. B's 3rd}}{\text{}}$ in Variations B and C.

7. P. to K. Kt.'s 5th.

Black's best move, I believe. If he play 7. $\frac{\text{}}{\text{Kt. to K. B's 3rd}}$, then follows 8. $\frac{\text{P. takes P.}}{\text{Kt. takes K's P.}}$, 9. $\frac{\text{Q. to K's 2nd}}{\text{Q. to K's 2nd}}$, 10. $\frac{\text{Q's B. takes P.}}{\text{P. takes P.}}$, 11. $\frac{\text{R. takes R. (ch.)}}{\text{B. takes R.}}$, and the game is equal. If 7. $\frac{\text{}}{\text{B. to K. Kt.'s 5th}}$, 8. $\frac{\text{Q. to Q. Kt.'s 3rd}}{\text{B. to K. R's 4th}}$, 9. $\frac{\text{P. takes P.}}{\text{P. takes P.}}$, 10. $\frac{\text{R. takes B.}}{\text{R. takes R.}}$, 11. $\frac{\text{B. takes B's P. (ch.)}}{\text{}}$, &c. If 7. $\frac{\text{}}{\text{Kt. to Q. B's 3rd}}$, 8. $\frac{\text{Q. to Q. Kt.'s 3rd}}{\text{Q. to K's 2nd}}$, 9. $\frac{\text{Castles}}{\text{}}$, with a good game.

8. Q's B. takes P.

If 8. $\frac{\text{Kt. to K. Kt.'s sq.}}{\text{Q. to K's 2nd}}$, 9. $\frac{\text{Q. to K's 2nd}}{\text{Kt. to K. B's 3rd}}$, 10. $\frac{\text{P. to K's 5th}}{\text{P. takes P.}}$, 11. $\frac{\text{P. takes P.}}{\text{Kt. to K. R's 4th}}$, Black has a fine position.

	8. P. takes Kt.
9. Q. takes P.	9. B. to K's 3rd.

If 9. $\frac{\rule{2em}{0pt}}{\text{Q. to K's 2nd}}$, 10. $\frac{\text{Kt. to Q's 2nd}}{\text{Kt. to Q. B's 3rd}}$, 11. $\frac{\text{Q. to K. Kt.'s 3rd}}{\text{P. to K. B's 3rd}}$, 12. $\frac{\text{Q. to Kt.'s 6th (ch.)}}{\text{K. to B's sq.}}$, 13. $\frac{\text{Castles}}{\rule{2em}{0pt}}$, with a position which more than compensates the loss of the Knight. If 9. $\frac{\rule{2em}{0pt}}{\text{Kt. to K. B's 3rd}}$, 10. $\frac{\text{Castles}}{\text{Kt. to Q. B's 3rd}}$, 11. $\frac{\text{P. to K's 5th}}{\text{P. takes P.}}$, 12. $\frac{\text{B. takes K's P.}}{\text{Kt. takes B.}}$, 13. $\frac{\text{P. takes Kt.}}{\rule{2em}{0pt}}$, and the advantage is again on White's side.

10. Kt. to Q's 2nd.	10. Kt. to K's 2nd.
11. P. to K. R's 5th.	11. B. takes B.
12. Kt. takes B.	12. P. to Q. Kt.'s 4th.

White has no equivalent for his lost Knight.

Variation A, beginning at White's 7th Move.

BLACK.

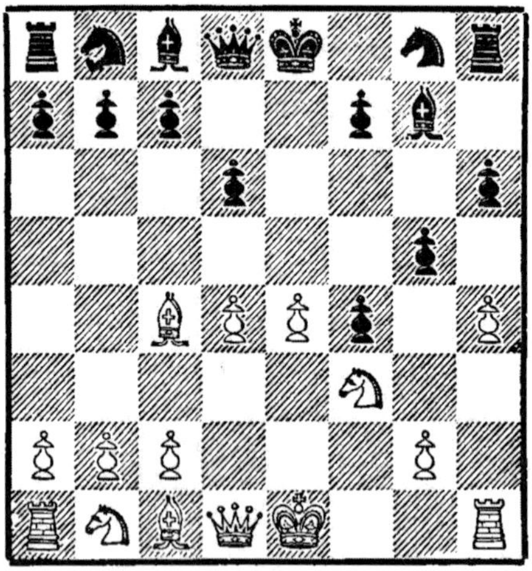

WHITE.

Position prior to White's 7th Move.

White	Black
7. Q. to Q's 3rd.	

A move proposed by Mr. Schultz, of Hanover, in 1858.

White	Black
	7. Kt. to Q. B's 3rd (best).
8. P. takes P.	8. P. takes P.
9. R. takes R.	9. B. takes R.
10. P. to K's 5th.	10. K. to B's sq.
11. Q. to K. R's 7th.	11. B. to K. Kt.'s 2nd.
12. Q. to K. R's 5th.	12. Kt. to K. R's 3rd.
13. P. to Q. B's 3rd.	

If 13. $\frac{\text{Kt. to K. Kt.'s 5th}}{\text{B. to K. Kt.'s 5th}}$.

13. P. to Q's 4th.

Black has the better game.

Variation B, beginning at White's 7th Move.

(See preceding Diagram.)

White	Black
7. P. takes P.	7. P. takes P.
8. R. takes R.	8. B. takes R.
9. Q. to Q's 3rd.	

This move, played by Kolisch against Anderssen in 1860, may have been suggested by the combination of Mr. Schultz which we have just examined.

9. Kt. to K. R's 3rd.

If 9. $\frac{\quad}{\text{P. to K. Kt.'s 5th}}$, 10. $\frac{\text{P. to K's 5th}}{\text{P. to Q's 4th}}$, 11. $\frac{\text{Q. to K. R's 7th}}{\text{K. to B's sq.}}$, 12. $\frac{\text{Q. takes B.}}{\text{P. takes Kt.}}$, 13. $\frac{\text{Q's B. takes P.}}{\text{P. takes K's B.}}$, 14. $\frac{\text{B. to K. R's 6th (ch.)}}{\text{K. to K's 2nd}}$, 15. $\frac{\text{B. to Kt.'s 5th (ch.)}}{\quad}$, and White has a winning superiority.

10. P. to K. Kt.'s 3rd.

If 10. $\frac{\text{P. to K's 5th}}{\text{B. to K. Kt.'s 5th}}$, &c. If 10. $\frac{\text{Kt to Q. B's 3rd}}{\text{P. to K. Kt.'s 5th}}$, 11. $\frac{\text{Q's B. takes P.}}{\text{P. takes Kt.}}$, 12. $\frac{\text{Castles}}{\text{Q. to K. R's 5th}}$, 13. $\frac{\text{Kt. to Q's 5th}}{\text{P. takes P.}}$,

Black has by far the better game.

	10. Q. to K's 2nd.

This move was adopted by Anderssen against Kolisch, but 10. $\frac{\quad}{\text{P. to Kt.'s 5th}}$ looks perhaps stronger.

11. Kt. to Q. B's 3rd.	11. P. to Q. B's 3rd.
12. P. takes P.	12. P. to K. Kt.'s 5th.
13. Kt. to K. Kt.'s 5th.	13. Kt. to Q's 2nd.

Black can win a Piece by 13. $\frac{\quad}{\text{P. to K. B's 3rd}}$, but the move in the text is sufficiently good.

14. P. to K's 5th.	14. Kt. to K. B's 3rd.
15. B. to K's 3rd.	15. P. to Q's 4th.
16. B. to Q. Kt.'s 3rd.	16. Kt. to K. B's 4th.
17. Castles.	17. Kt. to K. Kt.'s sq.

The game seems in Black's favour.

Variation C, beginning at White's 7th Move.

(See preceding Diagram.)

7. Kt. to Q. B's 3rd.	7. P. to K. Kt.'s 5th.
8. Kt. to K. Kt.'s sq.	

If 8. $\frac{\text{Q's B. takes P.}}{\text{P. takes Kt.}}$, 9. $\frac{\text{Q. takes P.}}{\text{B. takes Q's P.}}$, 10. $\frac{\text{Castles Q's side}}{\text{B. takes Kt.}}$, 11. $\frac{\text{B. to K's 5th}}{\text{R. to K. R's 2nd}}$, 12. $\frac{\text{Q. to K. Kt.'s 3rd}}{\quad}$. (If 12. $\frac{\text{B. takes B.}}{\text{P. to K. R's 4th}}$.) 12. $\frac{\quad}{\text{B. takes B.}}$, 13. $\frac{\text{Q. takes Kt. (ch.)}}{\text{K. to K's 2nd}}$, 14. $\frac{\text{Q. takes R.}}{\text{Q. to K. B's sq.}}$, 15. $\frac{\text{K's R. to K. B's sq.}}{\text{B. to K's 3rd}}$, White has not sufficient recompense for the sacrificed Piece.

	8. B. to K. B's 3rd.
9. Q's B. takes P.	9. B. takes P. (ch.)
10. P. to K. Kt.'s 3rd.	10. B. to K. Kt.'s 4th.
11. Q. to Q's 2nd.	11. B. takes B.

12. Q. takes B.	12. Q. to K. B's 3rd.
13. K's Kt. to K's 2nd.	13. Q. takes Q.
14. Kt. takes Q.	

The game is about even. White's free position being a fair set-off for the Gambit Pawn.

ILLUSTRATIVE GAMES.

GAME I.—Between Messrs. Thorold and Wayte.

WHITE (Mr. T.)	BLACK (Mr. W.)
1. P. to K's 4th.	1. P. to K's 4th.
2. P. to K. B's 4th.	2. P. takes P.
3. Kt. to K. B's 3rd.	3. P. to K.. Kt.'s 4th.
4. B. to Q. B's 4th.	4. B. to Kt.'s 2nd.
5. Castles.	5. P. to Q's 3rd.
6. P. to Q's 4th.	6. P. to K. R's 3rd.
7. P. to Q. B's 3rd.	7. P. to Q. B's 3rd.
8. Q. to Q. Kt.'s 3rd.	8. Q. to K's 2nd.
9. P. to K. Kt.'s 3rd.	9. P. to Kt.'s 5th.
10. Kt. to K. R's 4th.	10. P. to B's 6th.
11. B. to K. B's 4th.	11. P. to Q. Kt.'s 4th.
12. B. to Q's 3rd.	12. B. to K. B's 3rd.
13. Kt. to B's 5th.	13. B. takes Kt.
14. P. takes B.	14. P. to Q's 4th.
15. Kt. to Q's 2nd.	15. Q. to Q's 2nd.
16. K's R. to K's sq. (ch.)	16. Kt. to K's 2nd.
17. B. to K's 5th.*	17. B. takes B.
18. P. takes B.	18. Castles.
19. P. to K's 6th.	19. P. takes P.
20. R. takes P.	20. K. to Kt.'s 2nd.
21. Q's R. to K's sq.	21. P. to B's 7th (ch.)†
22. K. takes P.	22. Kt. takes P.
23. K. to Kt.'s 2nd.	23. Q. to K. B's 2nd.
24. Q's R. to K's 5th.‡	24. Kt. to Q's 2nd.

---

* All this part of the game is very skilfully played by White.
† His only resource to save the game.
‡ This looks threatening, but in reality it loses the exchange.

25. Q's R. takes Kt.*	25. Q. takes K's R.
26. Q. to B's 2nd.	26. R. takes R.
27. B. takes R.	27. Q. to K's 7th (ch).
28. K. to Kt.'s sq.	28. Kt. to K's 4th.

And White resigned.

GAME II.—Between Messrs. Skipworth and Ball.

WHITE (Mr. S.)	BLACK (Mr. B.)
1. P. to K's 4th.	1. P. to K's 4th.
2. P. to K. B's 4th.	2. P. takes P.
3. Kt. to K. B's 3rd.	3. P. to K. Kt.'s 4th
4. B. to Q. B's 4th.	4. B. to Kt.'s 2nd.
5. P. to Q's 4th.	5. P. to Q's 3rd.
6. Castles.	6. P. to K. R's 3rd.
7. P. to Q. B's 3rd.	7. Kt. to Q's 2nd.
8. Q. to Q. Kt.'s 3rd.	8. Q. to K's 2nd.
9. P. to K's 5th.	9. P. takes P.
10. Kt. takes P.	10. Kt. takes Kt.
11. P. takes Kt.	11. B. takes P.
12. B. takes K. B's P. (ch.)	12. K. to B's sq.
13. B. takes Kt.	13. R. takes B.
14. B. to K's 3rd.	14. K. to Kt.'s 2nd.
15. B. to K. B's 2nd.	15. P. to Q. B's 4th.
16. Kt. to Q's 2nd.	16. P. to Q. Kt.'s 3rd.
17. Kt. to K. B's 3rd.	17. R. to K's sq.
18. K's R. to K's sq.	18. Q. to Q. B's 2nd.
19. Kt. takes B.	19. R. takes Kt.
20. R. takes R.	20. Q. takes R.
21. R. to K's sq.	21. Q. to Q. B's 2nd.
22. Q. to Q. B's 4th.	22. Q. to K. B's 2nd.
23. Q. to K's 4th.	23. B. to Q. Kt.'s 2nd.
24. Q. to K's 7th.	24. R. to K. B's sq.
25. P. to Q. Kt.'s 4th.	25. P. takes P.
26. B. to Q's 4th (ch.)	26. K. to Kt.'s 3rd.

* If—

25. B. takes Kt.	25. Kt. takes R.
26. R. takes Kt.	26. Q. to K. R's 4th, and wins.

27. R. to K's 6th (ch.)	27. K. to R's 4th.
28. Q. to Q's 6th.	28. Q. to K. R's 2nd.
29. P. to K. R's 3rd.	29. R. to K. B's 2nd.
30. P. takes P.	30. Q. to Kt.'s 8th (ch.)
31. K. to R's 2nd.	31. R. to K. R's 2nd.
32. B. to K. Kt.'s 7th.	

And White wins.

CHAPTER XIV.

SALVIO-COCHRANE GAMBIT.

1. $\frac{\text{P. to K's 4th}}{\text{P. to K's 4th}}$, 2. $\frac{\text{P. to K. B's 4th}}{\text{P. takes P}}$, 3. $\frac{\text{Kt. to K. B's 3rd}}{\text{P. to K. Kt.'s 4th}}$,
4. $\frac{\text{B. to Q. B's 4th}}{\text{P. to K. Kt.'s 5th}}$, 5. $\frac{\text{Kt. to K's 5th}}{\text{Q. to K. R's 5th (ch.)}}$, 6. $\frac{\text{K. to B's sq.}}{\quad}$.

GAME THE FIRST.

6. $\frac{\quad}{\text{Kt. to K. R's 3rd}}$.

GAME THE SECOND.

6. $\frac{\quad}{\text{Kt. to K. B's 3rd}}$.

GAME THE THIRD.

6. $\frac{\quad}{\text{P. to K. B's 6th}}$ (Cochrane's variation).

This opening, of which the earliest example known appears in Salvio's work, 1604, though always called a gambit, is in reality an *offensive defence*, or counter attack to a gambit, like the *Cunningham*. It is a good line of play for the second player, as it transfers the attack into his hands very early in the game. At the same time it is rich in interesting combinations and hair-breadth escapes on both sides.

GAME THE FIRST.

WHITE.	BLACK.
1. P. to K's 4th.	1. P. to K's 4th.
2. P. to K. B's 4th.	2. P. takes P.
3. Kt. to K. B's 3rd.	3. P. to K. Kt.'s 4th.
4. B. to Q. B's 4th.	4. P. to K. Kt.'s 5th.

This advance of the Knight's Pawn, instead of playing out his King's Bishop, is the initial step in the Salvio counter attack.

5. Kt. to K's 5th.

Here, if White leave his Knight to be captured, the *début* resolves itself into the *Muzio Gambit* to be next examined.

5. Q. to K. R's 5th (ch.)

The best way of carrying on the counter movement.

6. K. to B's sq. 6. Kt. to K. R's 3rd.

Salvio also suggests in his treatise the move of 6. $\frac{\qquad}{\text{Kt. to K. B's 3rd}}$, the effect of which shall be shown in Game the Second. Instead of either move, Mr. John Cochrane recommended many years back the advance of Black's Pawn to Bishop's 6th, 6. $\frac{\qquad}{\text{P. to K. B's 6th}}$, and this device appears to fortify the second player's game considerably. (See Game the Third.)

7. P. to Q's 4th. 7. P. to K. B's 6th.

If 7. $\frac{\qquad}{\text{P. to Q's 3rd}}$, 8. $\frac{\text{Kt. to Q's 3rd}}{\text{P. to K. B's 6th}}$, 9. $\frac{\text{P. to K. Kt.'s 3rd}}{\text{Q. to K's 2nd.}}$. (Better than 9. $\frac{\qquad}{\text{Q. to R's 6th (ch.)}}$, &c.) 10. $\frac{\text{Kt. to Q. B's 3rd}}{\qquad}$. (White can also play 10. $\frac{\text{Kt. to K. B's 2nd}}{\qquad}$, as adopted by Steinitz against Anderssen.) 10. $\frac{\qquad}{\text{P. to Q. B's 3rd}}$, 11. $\frac{\text{P. to K. R's 3rd}}{\text{P. takes P.}}$, 12. $\frac{\text{B. takes Kt.}}{\text{B. takes B.}}$, 13. $\frac{\text{Q. takes P.}}{\text{R. to K. Kt.'s sq.}}$, 14. $\frac{\text{Kt. to B's 2nd}}{\text{R. to Kt.'s 3rd}}$, the game is considered to be about equal.

In the above Variation Black might also have played 10. $\frac{\qquad}{\text{B. to K's 3rd}}$, which would possibly have led to 11. $\frac{\text{P. to Q's 5th}}{\text{B. to B's sq.}}$, 12. $\frac{\text{B. to K's 4th}}{\qquad}$, with a fair position.

8. B. to K. B's 4th.

This I am inclined to think is White's most potent reply to 7. $\frac{}{\text{P. to K. B's 6th}}$, but he has the choice of several others which we will briefly dispose of. Firstly, 8. $\frac{\text{Kt. to Q. B's 3rd}}{\text{P. to Q's 3rd}}$, 9. $\frac{\text{Kt. to Q's 3rd}}{\text{P. takes P.}}$, 10. $\frac{\text{K. takes P.}}{\text{B. to K. Kt.'s 2nd}}$, 11. $\frac{\text{Kt. to K. B's 4th}}{\text{Kt. to Q. B's 3rd}}$, 12. $\frac{\text{B. to K's 3rd}}{\text{Castles}}$, 13. $\frac{\text{Q. to Q's 2nd}}{\text{K. to R's sq.}}$, and Black has the better game. Secondly, 8. $\frac{\text{Q. to K's sq.}}{\text{Q. takes Q. (ch.)}}$, 9. $\frac{\text{K. takes Q.}}{\text{P. takes P.}}$, 10. $\frac{\text{R. to K. Kt.'s sq.}}{\text{P. to Q's 3rd}}$, &c. Thirdly, 8. $\frac{\text{P. to K. Kt.'s 3rd}}{\text{Q. to R's 6th (ch.)}}$, 9. $\frac{\text{K. to B's 2nd}}{\text{Q. to Kt.'s 7th (ch.)}}$, 10. $\frac{\text{K. to K's 3rd}}{\text{P. to K. B's 4th}}$, &c. Fourthly, 8. $\frac{\text{P. takes P.}}{\text{P. to Q's 3rd}}$, 9. $\frac{\text{Kt. to Q's 3rd}}{\text{P. takes P.}}$, and the advantage is in each case on Black's side.

8. P. takes P. (ch.)

This is given by the *Handbuch*, but I am inclined to think that 8. $\frac{}{\text{P. to Q's 3rd}}$, as proposed by Mr. Zukertort, is slightly preferable.

9. K. takes P.	9. P. to Q's 3rd.
10. B. takes Kt.	10. B. takes B.
11. Kt. to Q's 3rd.	11. Q. to R's 6th (ch.)
12. K. to B's 2nd.	12. B. to K's 6th (ch.)

With a very superior position.

Game the Second.

WHITE.	BLACK.
1. P. to K's 4th.	1. P. to K's 4th.
2. P. to K. B's 4th.	2. P. takes P.
3. Kt. to K. B's 3rd.	3. P. to K. Kt.'s 4th.
4. B. to Q. B's 4th.	4. P. to K. Kt.'s 5th.
5. Kt. to K's 5th.	5. Q. to K. R's 5th (ch.)
6. K. to B's sq.	6. Kt. to K. B's 3rd.

This is less preferable for Black than 6. $\frac{}{\text{Kt. to K. R's 3rd}}$.

7. Q. to K's sq.

A good move.

He can also play 7. $\frac{\text{Kt. to Q. B's 3rd}}{}$, for which see Variation A; or 7. $\frac{\text{P. to Q's 4th}}{}$, or 7. $\frac{\text{B. takes P. (ch.)}}{}$, which we may as well examine at once.

Suppose, then, in the first case, 7. $\frac{\text{P. to Q's 4th}}{\text{P. to Q's 3rd}}$. (Black may move, too, advantageously here 7. $\frac{}{\text{P. to K. B's 6th}}$, 8. $\frac{\text{P. takes P.}}{\text{P. takes P.}}$, 9. $\frac{\text{Q. takes P.}}{\text{P. to Q's 3rd}}$, 10. $\frac{\text{Kt. takes B's P.}}{\text{B. to K. R's 6th (ch.)}}$, 11. $\frac{\text{K. to Kt.'s sq.}}{\text{R. to K. Kt.'s sq. (ch.)}}$, &c.) 8. $\frac{\text{Kt. to Q's 3rd}}{\text{P. to K. B's 6th}}$, 9. $\frac{\text{Kt. to Q. B's 3rd}}{\text{P. takes P. (ch.)}}$, 10. $\frac{\text{K. takes P.}}{\text{Q. to K. R's 6th (ch.)}}$, I prefer Black's game.

In the second case, 7. $\frac{\text{B. takes P. (ch.)}}{\text{K. to K's 2nd}}$, 8. $\frac{\text{B. to Q. Kt.'s 3rd}}{\text{P. to Q's 3rd}}$, 9. $\frac{\text{Kt. to Q's 3rd}}{\text{Kt. to K. R's 4th}}$, 10. $\frac{\text{Q. to K's sq.}}{\text{P. to K. Kt.'s 6th}}$, 11. $\frac{\text{K. to Kt.'s sq.}}{\text{B. to K. Kt.'s 2nd}}$, 12. $\frac{\text{P. to Q. B's 3rd}}{\text{Q. to K. Kt.'s 4th}}$, 13. $\frac{\text{B. to Q's sq.}}{\text{B. to K. Kt.'s 5th}}$, Black has the advantage in position.

	7. Q. takes Q. (ch.)
8. K. takes Q.	8. P. to Q's 3rd.

If 8. $\frac{}{\text{Kt. takes P.}}$, 9. $\frac{\text{B. takes B's P. (ch.)}}{\text{K. to K's 2nd}}$, 10. $\frac{\text{B. to K. R's 5th}}{\text{P. to Kt.'s 6th}}$, 11. $\frac{\text{P. to K. R's 3rd}}{\text{P. to Q's 3rd}}$, 12. $\frac{\text{Kt. to Q's 3rd}}{\text{B. to K. R's 3rd}}$, 13. $\frac{\text{Kt. to Q. B's 3rd}}{\text{Kt. takes Kt.}}$,

14. $\frac{\text{Q's P. takes Kt.}}{\text{R. to K. B's sq.}}$, 15. $\frac{\text{R. to K. B's sq.}}{}$, White has the superior game.

9. Kt. takes B's P.	9. P. to Q's 4th.
10. B. takes P.	10. Kt. takes B.
11. Kt. takes R.	11. Kt. to K. B's 3rd.
12. P. to Q's 3rd.	12. B. to K. Kt.'s 2nd.
13. P. to Q. B's 3rd.	13. B. takes Kt.
14. B. takes P.	14. P. to Q. B's 3rd.
15. Kt. to Q's 2nd.	

An even game.

Variation A, beginning at White's 7th Move.

7. Kt. to Q. B's 3rd.	7. Kt. to Q. B's 3rd.
8. P. to Q's 4th.	8. Kt. takes Kt.
9. P. takes Kt.	9. Kt. to K. R's 4th.
10. Q. to Q's 5th.	10. Kt. to Kt.'s 6th (ch.)
11. K. to Kt.'s sq.	11. Kt. takes R.
12. Q. takes B's P. (ch.)	12. K. to Q's sq.
13. Q's B. takes P.	13. B. to Q. B's 4th (ch.)
14. K. takes Kt.	14. R. to K. B's sq.
15. B. to K. Kt.'s 3rd.	15. Q. to K. R's 3rd.
16. Q. to Q's 5th.	

An equal game.

Game the Third.

WHITE.	BLACK.
1. P. to K's 4th.	1. P. to K's 4th.
2. P. to K. B's 4th.	2. P. takes P.
3. Kt. to K. B's 3rd.	3. P. to K. Kt.'s 4th.
4. B. to Q. B's 4th.	4. P. to K. Kt.'s 5th.
5. Kt. to K's 5th.	5. Q. to K. R's 5th (ch.)
6. K. to B's sq.	6. P. to K. B's 6th.

BLACK.

WHITE.

Position prior to White's 7th Move.

The above move for Black is, as I have previously remarked, the invention of Mr. Cochrane. It is generally thought to be an improvement on the play of Salvio.

7. P. to Q's 4th.

No better reply than this has yet been found to Mr. Cochrane's variation, though White has a variety of moves at his command. The most feasible beside the move in the text are, first, 7. $\frac{\text{B. takes B's P. (ch.)}}{\quad}$; second, 7. $\frac{\text{Kt. takes B's P.}}{\quad}$; third, 7. $\frac{\text{P. to K. Kt.'s 3rd}}{\quad}$; fourth, 7. $\frac{\text{P. takes P.}}{\quad}$; and fifth, 7. $\frac{\text{Q. to K's sq.}}{\quad}$. These we will presently examine as Variations A, B, C.

	7. P. takes P. (ch.)
8. K. takes P.	8. Q. to K. R's 6th (ch.)
9. K. to Kt.'s sq.	9. Kt. to K. R's 3rd.

If 9. $\frac{\quad}{\text{Kt. to K. B's 3rd}}$, White recovers his lost ground by

10. Kt. takes K. B's P. / P. to Q's 4th (best), 11. B. to K. B's sq. / Q. to K. R's 5th, 12. Kt. takes R. / Kt. takes P.,

13. Q. to K's 2nd / B. to K. Kt.'s 2nd, 14. P. to Q. B's 3rd / P. to Kt.'s 6th, 15. P. takes P. / Q. takes P. (ch.),

16. Q. to K. Kt.'s 2nd / , &c.

10. Q. to Q's 3rd.

If 10. B. to K. B's sq. / Q. to R's 5th, 11. B. takes Kt. / B. takes B., 12. Q. takes P. / Q. takes Q (ch.),

13. Kt. takes Q. / R. to K. Kt.'s sq., 14. B. to K's 2nd / B. to Q. B's 8th, Black should win.

	10. Q. takes Q.
11. P. takes Q.	11. P. to Q's 3rd.
12. B. takes Kt.	12. B. takes B.
13. Kt. takes K. B's P.	13. B. to K's 6th (ch.)
14. K. to Kt.'s 2nd.	14. R. to K. B's sq.
15. R. to K. B's sq.	15. B. takes Q's P.

Black has the advantage.

Variation A, beginning at White's 7th Move.

BLACK.

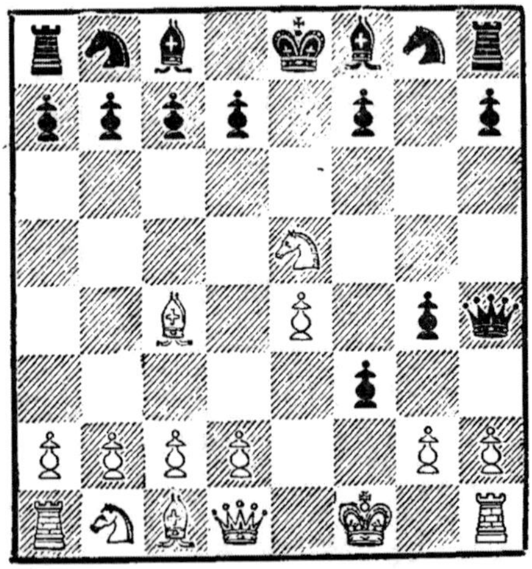

WHITE.

7. B. takes B's P. (ch.)

If 7. $\frac{\text{Kt. takes B's P.}}{\text{Kt. to K. B's 3rd}}$, 8. $\frac{\text{Kt. takes R.}}{\text{Kt. takes P.}}$, 9. $\frac{\text{Q. to K's sq.}}{\text{P. takes P. (ch.)}}$, 10. $\frac{\text{K. takes P.}}{\text{Q. to K. R's 6th (ch.)}}$, 11. $\frac{\text{K. to Kt.'s sq.}}{\text{B. to Q. B's 4th (ch.)}}$, Black has always the better game.

	7. K. to K's 2nd.
8. P. takes P.	

If 8. $\frac{\text{B. takes Kt.}}{\text{R. takes B.}}$, 9. $\frac{\text{P. takes P.}}{\text{P. to Q's 3rd}}$, 10. $\frac{\text{Kt. takes P.}}{\text{R. takes Kt.}}$, 11. $\frac{\text{P. takes R.}}{\text{B. takes P.}}$, 12. $\frac{\text{Q. to K's sq.}}{\text{Q. to K. R's 6th (ch.)}}$, 13. $\frac{\text{K. to Kt.'s sq.}}{\text{B. to Kt.'s 2nd}}$, Black has the advantage. Similarly if 8. $\frac{\text{P. to K. Kt.'s 3rd}}{\text{Q. to K. R's 6th (ch.)}}$, 9. $\frac{\text{K. to B's 2nd}}{\text{Kt. to K. B's 3rd}}$, 10. $\frac{\text{B. to Q. B's 4th}}{\text{P. to Q's 3rd}}$, and whether he advance the attacked Knight to B's 7th, or retreat it to Q's 3rd, Black must secure a better position. If 8. $\frac{\text{Q. to K's sq.}}{\text{P. takes P. (ch.)}}$, 9. $\frac{\text{K. takes P.}}{\text{Q. to K. R's 6th (ch.)}}$, Black should win.

	8. P. to Q's 3rd
9. B. takes Kt.	9. P. takes Kt.
10. B. to Q. B's 4th.	10. P. takes P.
11. Q. takes P.	11. B. to K. R's 6th (ch.)

With an evident superiority.

Variation B, beginning at White's 7th Move.

(See preceding Diagram.)

7. P. to K. Kt.'s 3rd.	7. Q. to K. R's 6th (ch.)
8. K. to B's 2nd.	

If 8. $\frac{\text{K. to K's sq.}}{\text{Q. to Kt.'s 7th}}$, 9. $\frac{\text{R. to K. B's sq.}}{\text{Kt. to K. B's 3rd}}$, and Black has a fine game.

	8. Kt. to K. B's 3rd.
9. P. to Q's 3rd.	

If 9. $\frac{\text{K. to K's 3rd}}{\text{B. to K. R's 3rd (ch.)}}$, 10. $\frac{\text{K. to Q's 3rd}}{\text{P. to Q's 3rd}}$, 11. $\frac{\text{Kt. takes B's P.}}{\text{P. to Q's 4th}}$, 12. $\frac{\text{B. takes P.}}{\text{Kt. takes B.}}$, 13. $\frac{\text{Kt. takes B. (best)}}{\text{Kt. to Q. Kt.'s 5th (ch.)}}$, 14. $\frac{\text{K. to B's 4th}}{\text{Q. takes Kt.}}$, Black has the advantage.

	9. P. to Q's 3rd.
10. Kt. takes B's P.	10. P. to Q's 4th.
11. Kt. takes R.	

If 11. $\frac{\text{B. takes P.}}{\text{Q. to Kt.'s 7th (ch.)}}$, with the better game.

	11. Q. to Kt.'s 7th (ch.)
12. K. to K's 3rd.	12. Kt. to Q. B's 3rd.
13. Kt. to K. B's 7th.	13. K. takes Kt.
14. B. takes P. (ch.)	14. Kt. takes B. (ch.)
15. P. takes Kt.	15. B. to K. R's 3rd (ch.)
16. K. to K's 4th.	16. P. to B's 7th (dis. ch.)

And Black wins.

Variation C, beginning at White's 7th move.

7. P. takes P.

If 7. $\frac{\text{Q. to K's sq.}}{\text{P. takes P. (ch.)}}$, 8. $\frac{\text{K. takes P.}}{\text{Q. to R's 6th (ch.)}}$, &c.

7. Kt. to K. B's 3rd.

Apparently his strongest move.

8. Q. to K's 2nd.

Again White has a variety of moves to choose. None of them, however, seems quite satisfactory. The most feasible are, 8. $\frac{\text{P. to Q's 4th}}{}$, 8. $\frac{\text{B. takes B's P. (ch.)}}{}$, 8. $\frac{\text{Q. to K's sq.}}{}$.

These we can examine before proceeding further. If, then, 8. $\frac{\text{P. to Q's 4th}}{\text{P. to Q's 3rd}}$, 9. $\frac{\text{Kt. takes Kt.'s P.}}{\text{Kt. takes Kt.}}$, 10. $\frac{\text{P. takes Kt.}}{\text{B. takes P.}}$, 11. $\frac{\text{Q. to Q's 3rd}}{\text{B. to K. R's 6th (ch.)}}$, 12. $\frac{\text{K. to K's 2nd}}{\text{B. to Kt.'s 7th.}}$, 13. $\frac{\text{R. to K's sq.}}{\text{B. takes P.}}$,

14. $\frac{\text{Q. to Q. Kt.'s 3rd}}{\text{B. to K's 2nd}}$, Black has the advantage. If 8. $\frac{\text{B. takes B's P. (ch.)}}{\text{K. to K's 2nd}}$, 9. $\frac{\text{B. to Q. B's 4th}}{\text{P. to Q's 3rd}}$, 10. $\frac{\text{Kt. takes P.}}{\quad}$. (If 10 $\frac{\text{Kt. to K. B's 7th}}{\text{P. takes P.}}$, &c.) 10. $\frac{\quad}{\text{Kt. takes Kt.}}$, 11. $\frac{\text{P. takes Kt.}}{\text{B. to K. Kt.'s 2nd}}$, the game is in Black's favour.

If, finally, 8. $\frac{\text{Q. to K's sq.}}{\text{Q. to K. R's 6th (ch.)}}$, 9. $\frac{\text{K. to K's 2nd}}{\text{P. to Q's 3rd}}$, 10. $\frac{\text{Kt. takes Kt.'s P.}}{\text{Kt. takes Kt.}}$, 11. $\frac{\text{P. takes Kt.}}{\text{B. takes P. (ch.)}}$, 12. $\frac{\text{K. to B's 2nd}}{\text{B. to K's 2nd}}$, and Black must win immediately.

	8. P. to Q's 3rd.
9. Kt. takes B's P.	

If 9. $\frac{\text{Kt. takes Kt.'s P.}}{\text{Kt. takes Kt.}}$, 10. $\frac{\text{P. takes Kt.}}{\text{B. takes P.}}$, 11. $\frac{\text{Q. to K's 3rd}}{\text{B. to R's 6th (ch.)}}$, 12. $\frac{\text{K. to K's 2nd}}{\text{R. to K. Kt.'s sq.}}$, the advantage is obviously on Black's side.

	9. P. takes P.
10. Q. to K. B's 2nd.	10. B. to R's 6th (ch.)
11. K. to K's sq.	11. Q. takes P. (ch.)
12. K. to Q's sq.	12. Q. takes B.

And Black must win.

ILLUSTRATIVE GAMES.

Game I.—Between Messrs. Steinitz and Zukertort.

White (Mr S.)	Black (Mr. Z.)
1. P. to K's 4th.	1. P. to K's 4th.
2. P. to K. B's 4th.	2. P. takes P.
3. Kt. to K. B's 3rd.	3. P. to K. Kt.'s 4th.
4. B. to Q. B's 4th.	4. P. to K. Kt.'s 5th.
5. Kt. to K's 5th.	5. Q. to R's 5th (ch.)

6. K. to B's sq.	6. Kt. to K. R's 3rd.
7. P. to Q's 4th.	7. P. to B's 6th.
8. Kt. to Q. B's 3rd.*	8. P. to Q's 3rd.
9. Kt. to Q's 3rd.	9. B. to K. Kt.'s 2nd.†
10. P. to K. Kt.'s 3rd.	10. Q. to Q's sq.
11. Kt. to K. B's 4th.	11. Castles.
12. P. to K. R's 3rd.	12. Kt. to Q. B's 3rd.
13. Kt. to K. R's 5th.	13. P. takes P.
14. Kt. to Q's 5th.	14. Kt. to K. Kt.'s 5th.
15. P. to Q. B's 3rd.	15. Kt. to K's 2nd.
16. Q's Kt. to K. B's 4th.‡	16. Kt. to K. Kt.'s 3rd.
17. Kt. takes P.	17. B. to K's 3rd.
18. B. takes B.	18. P. takes B.
19. Kt. to K. Kt.'s 5th.	19. B. to K. B's 3rd.
20. Q. to Q. Kt.'s 3rd.	20. B. takes Kt.
21. Q. takes K's P. (ch.)	21. R. to B's 2nd.
22. Q. takes K's Kt.	22. B. takes B.
23. R. takes B.	23. Q. to K's sq.
24. P. to Q. B's 4th.	24. P. to Q's 4th.§
25. P. to K's 5th.	25. P. takes P.
26. R. takes P.	26. Q. to Q. Kt.'s 4th.
27. P. to Q. Kt.'s 3rd.	27. Q. to Q. R's 3rd.
28. Kt. to K. B's 6th (ch.)	28. R. takes Kt.
29. P. takes R.	29. Q. takes K. B's P.
30. R. takes P.	30. R. to K's sq.
31. Q. to Q's 7th.	31. Q. to Q. R's 3rd (ch.)
32. R. to Q. B's 4th.	32. R. to K's 2nd.
33. Q. to Q's 5th (ch.)	33. K. to Kt.'s 2nd.
34. R. to K. R's 2nd.	34. P. to Q. Kt.'s 4th.
35. R. to Q. B's 6th.	35. Q. to Q. Kt.'s 2nd.
36. R. takes P. (ch.)‖	36. K. takes R.
37. Q. to R's 5th (ch.)	37. K. to Kt.'s sq.

---

* This is certainly stronger than 8. P. to K. Kt.'s 3rd, but 8. B. to K. B's 4th is also a good move at this point.

† He ought rather to have taken P. with P., checking.

‡ The tempting move of B. to K. Kt.'s 5th would have clearly cost a piece.

§ A bad reply; he ought to have played 24. Q. to Q's 2nd, after which he would have had little inferiority of position.

‖ The terminating moves are very neat.

38. R. takes Kt. (ch.)	38. R. to Kt.'s 2nd.
39. R. to K. R's 6th.	39. K. to B's sq.
40. R. to R's 8th (ch.)	

And wins.

GAME II.—Between Messrs. Hanstein and Der Laza.

WHITE (Mr. H.)	BLACK (Mr. L.)
1. P. to K's 4th.	1. P. to K's 4th.
2. P. to K. B's 4th.	2. P. takes P.
3. Kt. to K. B's 3rd.	3. P. to K. Kt.'s 4th.
4. B. to Q. B's 4th.	4. P. to K. Kt.'s 5th.
5. Kt. to K's 5th.	5. Q. to R's 5th (ch.)
6. K. to B's sq.	6. P. to B's 6th.
7. P. takes P.*	7. P. to Q's 4th.
8. B. takes P.	8. Kt. to K. B's 3rd.
9. B. takes K. B's P. (ch.)	9. K. to K's 2nd.
10. P. to Q's 4th.	10. Kt. to Q. B's 3rd.
11. B. to Q. B's 4th.	11. P. to K. Kt.'s 6th.†
12. K. to K's 2nd.	12. Kt. takes K's P.
13. Kt. to Q. B's 3rd.	13. Kt. to K. B's 7th.
14. R's P. takes P.	14. Q. takes K. Kt.'s P.
15. R. to K. Kt.'s sq.	15. Q. takes Kt. (ch.)
16. P. takes Q.	16. Kt. takes Q.
17. B. to Kt.'s 5th (ch.)‡	17. K. to Q's 2nd.
18. Q's R. takes Kt. (ch.)	18. Resigns.

* The move now generally recommended is 7. P. to Q's 4th.

† Better probably to have taken P. with P., in which case White would have retaken with the Knight.

‡ Very neat and conclusive.

CHAPTER XV.

MUZIO GAMBIT.

$1. \frac{\text{P. to K's 4th}}{\text{P. to K's 4th}}, \quad 2. \frac{\text{P. to K. B's 4th}}{\text{P. takes P.}}, \quad 3. \frac{\text{Kt. to K. B's 3rd}}{\text{P. to K. Kt.'s 4th}},$

$4. \frac{\text{B. to Q. B's 4th}}{\text{P. to K. Kt.'s 5th}}.$

GAME THE FIRST.

$5. \frac{\text{Castles}}{\quad}; \quad 5. \frac{\text{P. to Q's 4th}}{\quad}; \quad 5. \frac{\text{Kt. to Q. B's 3rd}}{\quad};$

$5. \frac{\text{B. takes P. (ch.)}}{\quad}.$

GAME THE SECOND.

$6. \frac{\quad}{\text{B. to K. R's 3rd}}; \quad 6. \frac{\quad}{\text{Kt. to Q. B's 3rd}}; \quad 6. \frac{\quad}{\text{P. to Q's 3rd}}.$

GAME THE THIRD.

$10. \frac{\quad}{\text{P. to Q. B's 3rd}}; \qquad 10. \frac{\quad}{\text{Castles}}.$

The earliest chess writer who treats of this fine variation in the ordinary King's Knight's Gambit is Salvio. He makes no claim to the invention of it. He relates that Don Geronimo Cascio, a chess amateur of remarkable skill, having casually ventured the sacrifice of the Knight when playing with a friend, won the game. Don Cascio told the circumstance to another skilful amateur, Don Muzio, who in turn made it known to Salvio. The origin of the variation was doubtless the difficulty then felt to maintain the King's Gambit attack against Salvio's counter-attack. Whatever its origin, chess players are deeply indebted to Don Cascio for the inspiration which gave birth to one of the most beautiful openings ever known. It is to be regretted that they have shown so little sense of their obligation as to call the *début* by another player's name.

Game the First.

WHITE.	BLACK.
1. P. to K's 4th.	1. P. to K's 4th.
2. P. to K. B's 4th.	2. P. takes P.
3. Kt. to K. B's 3rd.	3. P. to K. Kt.'s 4th.
4. B. to Q. B's 4th.	4. P. to K. Kt.'s 5th.
5. Castles.	

Castling has generally been thought the best move for White; but having resolved to abandon his Knight, he may proceed in his attack by divers courses. The most notable of them is 5. $\frac{\text{P. to Q's 4th}}{}$, which shall be examined in Variation A.

5. P. takes Kt.

At this point Messrs. Kling and Horwitz propose an ingenious diversion for Black, namely to play his Queen to K's 2nd, instead of capturing the Knight at once. The following is an abstract of the analysis :—

5. $\frac{}{\text{Q. to K's 2nd}}$, 6. $\frac{\text{P to Q's 4th}}{}$. (If 6. $\frac{\text{Kt. to K's 5th}}{\text{Q. takes Kt.}}$, 7. $\frac{\text{P. to Q's 4th}}{\text{Q. to K. Kt.'s 2nd}}$, 8. $\frac{\text{R. takes P.}}{\text{Kt. to K. R's 3rd}}$, 9. $\frac{\text{R. to K. B's sq.}}{\text{P. to Q's 3rd}}$, 10. $\frac{\text{B. takes Kt.}}{\text{Q. takes B.}}$, 11. $\frac{\text{B. takes P. (ch.)}}{\text{K. to Q's sq.}}$, 12. $\frac{\text{P. to K's 5th}}{\text{Kt. to Q. B's 3rd}}$, Black wins.) 6. $\frac{}{\text{P. takes Kt}}$, 7. $\frac{\text{Kt. to Q. B's 3rd}}{\text{P. to Q's 3rd}}$. (If 7. $\frac{}{\text{P. takes P.}}$, 8. $\frac{\text{R. takes P.}}{}$, with an overwhelming attack.) 8. $\frac{\text{Kt. to Q's 5th}}{\text{Q. to Q's 2nd}}$, 9. $\frac{\text{Q. takes P.}}{\text{Kt. to Q. B's 3rd}}$, 10. $\frac{\text{Q. takes P.}}{\text{B. to K. Kt.'s 2nd}}$. (If 10. $\frac{}{\text{Kt. takes P.}}$, White may play 11. $\frac{\text{Q. to K. B's 6th}}{\text{Kt. takes Q.}}$,

12. $\frac{\text{Kt. takes Kt. (ch.)}}{}$, even game.) 11. $\frac{\text{Kt. takes P. (ch.)}}{\text{Q. takes Kt.}}$, 12. $\frac{\text{B. takes P. (ch.)}}{\text{K. to B's sq.}}$, 13. $\frac{\text{B. to Q. Kt.'s 3rd (dis. ch.)}}{\text{Kt. to K. B's 3rd}}$, 14. $\frac{\text{Q. to K. R's 4th}}{\text{K. to K's sq.}}$, 15. $\frac{\text{B. to K. Kt.'s 5th}}{\text{R. to K. B's sq.}}$, 16. $\frac{\text{B. takes Kt.}}{\text{B. takes B.}}$, 17. $\frac{\text{R. takes B.}}{\text{R. takes R.}}$, 18. $\frac{\text{Q. takes R.}}{\text{Q. to K's 2nd}}$, 19. $\frac{\text{Q. to K. R's 8th (ch.)}}{\text{K. to Q's 2nd}}$, 20. $\frac{\text{P. to K's 5th}}{}$. I think White has the advantage.

6. Q. takes P. 6. Q. to K. B's 3rd.

Instead of the move in the text, Black may play 6. $\frac{}{\text{Q. to K's 2nd}}$, which Salvio and later authorities, down to the period when Sarratt investigated the opening, looked upon as the best defence. He may also play 6. $\frac{}{\text{B. to K. R's 3rd}}$, 6. $\frac{}{\text{Kt. to Q. B's 3rd}}$, or 6. $\frac{}{\text{P. to Q's 3rd}}$. For the result of these variations see Game the Second.

7. P. to K's 5th.

7. $\frac{\text{P. to Q's 3rd}}{}$, or 7. $\frac{\text{Kt. to Q. B's 3rd}}{}$, is sometimes played, but neither is sufficiently vigorous.

7. Q. takes P.

Seemingly his best move.

If 7. $\frac{}{\text{Q. to K. B's 4th}}$, 8. $\frac{\text{P. to Q's 4th}}{\text{B. to K. R's 3rd}}$, 9. $\frac{\text{Kt. to Q. B's 3rd}}{\text{Kt. to K's 2nd}}$, 10. $\frac{\text{Kt. to K's 4th}}{\text{Castles}}$, 11. $\frac{\text{Kt. to B's 6th (ch.)}}{\text{K. to R's sq.}}$, 12. $\frac{\text{B. to Q's 3rd}}{}$ Black is at a serious disadvantage.

8. P. to Q's 3rd (best). 8. B. to K. R's 3rd.

If 8. $\frac{}{\text{B. to Q. B's 4th (ch.)}}$, 9. $\frac{\text{K. to R's sq.}}{\text{B. to K's 6th}}$, 10. $\frac{\text{B. takes B.}}{\text{Q. takes B.}}$, 11. $\frac{\text{Q. to K. R's 5th}}{\text{Q. to K's 2nd}}$, 12. $\frac{\text{Kt. to Q. B's 3rd}}{}$, White has a fine opening.

9. B. to Q's 2nd.

It appears to be indifferent whether this or 9. $\frac{\text{Kt. to Q. B's 3rd}}{\quad}$ is played first; the other must follow next move, and in either case Black's safest reply is 9. $\frac{\quad}{\text{Kt. to K's 2nd}}$.

	9. Kt. to K's 2nd.
10. Kt. to Q. B's 3rd.	10. Kt. to Q. B's 3rd.

For the result of 10. $\frac{\quad}{\text{P. to Q. B's 3rd}}$, a move by some authorities thought best of all for Black, see Game the Third.

11. Q's. R. to K's sq.	11. Q. to K. B's 4th.

This most important move for the defence is attributed to Mr. Paulsen. I have examined the combinations springing from it with much attention, and I believe it to be a safer line of play for Black than the old course of checking with the Queen at Q. B's 4th. For the result of the latter see Variation B.

BLACK.

WHITE.

Position after Black's 11*th Move.*

In reply to 11. Q. to K. B's 4th, White has the choice of two lines of play open to him, viz., 12. R. to K's 4th, and 12. Kt. to Q's 5th, which we will examine in turn.

In the first place :—

12. R. to K's 4th.

This move, proposed by Mr. Hirschfield, is thought by many preferable to 12. $\frac{\text{Kt. to Q's 5th}}{}$, as played by Mr. Kolisch in his match with Paulsen.

12. Kt. to K's 4th.*

If 12. $\frac{}{\text{P. to Q's 3rd}}$, 13. $\frac{\text{Q's B. takes P.}}{\text{B. takes B.}}$, 14. $\frac{\text{Q's R. takes P.}}{\text{Q. checks.}}$, 15. $\frac{\text{K. to R's sq.}}{\text{Kt. to K's 4th}}$, 16. $\frac{\text{Q. to K. R's 5th}}{}$, White has a fine position.

13. Q. to K's 2nd.	13. P. to Q's 3rd.

If 13. $\frac{}{\text{P. to K. B's 6th}}$, 14. $\frac{\text{B. takes B.}}{\text{P. takes Q.}}$, 15. $\frac{\text{K's R. takes Q.}}{\text{Kt. takes R.}}$, 16. $\frac{\text{R. takes Kt. (ch.)}}{}$, White has the better game by far

So, also, if 13. $\frac{}{\text{Kt. takes B.}}$, 14. $\frac{\text{P. takes Kt.}}{\text{K. to Q's sq.}}$, 15. $\frac{\text{Q's B. takes P.}}{\text{B. takes B.}}$, 16. $\frac{\text{K's R. takes B.}}{\text{Q. checks}}$, 17. $\frac{\text{K. to R's sq.}}{\text{P. to K. B's 4th}}$, 18. $\frac{\text{R. to K's 5th}}{\text{Q. to Q's 3rd}}$

---

* Mr. Zukertort has since pointed out that Black's strongest move is 12. Castles. The following appears to be the correct continuation :—

	12. Castles.
13. Q's B. takes P.	13. B. to Kt's 2nd (best).
14. Q. to K's 2nd.	14. P. to Q's 4th.
15. B. takes Q. B's P.	15. Q. to K. Kt.'s 4th.
16. P. to K. R's 4th.	16. Q. to K. Kt.'s 3rd.
17. Kt. takes P.	17. Kt. takes Kt.
18. B. takes Kt.	18. B. to K. B's 4th.
19. Q's R. to K. B's 4th.	19. B. to K's 3rd.

and Black should win.—[Ed.]

19. $\frac{\text{Kt. to Q. Kt.'s 5th}}{\text{Q. to K. B's 3rd}}$, 20. $\frac{\text{P. to Q. B's 5th}}{\text{P. to Q. R's 3rd}}$, 21. $\frac{\text{Kt. takes B's P.}}{\text{K. takes Kt.}}$,

22. $\frac{\text{R. takes Kt.}}{\text{—}}$, White has the superiority.

14. Q's B. takes P.	14. B. takes B.
15. K's. R. takes B.	15. Q. to K. Kt's 4th.
16. P. to K. R's 4th.	16. Q. to Kt.'s 2nd.
17. R. takes B's P.	

At first it appears that White could gain a winning advantage by now pressing the adverse Knight with his Q's P. I find, however, that Black can effectively turn the tables in that case by playing 17. $\frac{\text{}}{\text{P. to K. B's 4th}}$,

17. Kt. takes R.

Better than 17. $\frac{\text{}}{\text{Q. takes R.}}$, because of 18. $\frac{\text{B. takes Q. (ch.)}}{\text{K. takes B.}}$, 19. $\frac{\text{P. to Q's 4th}}{\text{}}$, &c.

18. R. takes Kt. (ch.)	18. K. to Q's sq.
19. B. takes Kt.	19. B. to Q's 2nd.
20. Kt. to Q's 5th.	20. Q. to Q's 4th (ch.)
21. K. to B's sq.	21. Q. takes K. R's P.
22. R. takes B. (ch.)	22. K. takes R.
23. Q. to K's 6th (ch.)	23. K. to Q's sq.

If 23. $\frac{\text{}}{\text{K. to B's 3rd}}$, 24. $\frac{\text{Kt. to K's 7th (ch.)}}{\text{}}$, and the game must be drawn.

24. Kt. to K. B's 6th	24. Q. to Q. R's 4th.
25. Kt. to Q's 5th.	25. Q. to K. R's 4th.

Drawn game.

In the second place:—

12. Kt. to Q's 5th.	12. K. to Q's sq.
13. B. to Q. B's 3rd.	13. R. to K's sq. (best).

If 13. $\frac{\text{}}{\text{R. to K. Kt.'s sq.}}$, the continuation would be

14. $\frac{\text{R. takes Kt.}}{\text{Kt. takes R.}}$, 15. $\frac{\text{B. to B's 6th}}{\text{R. to K's sq.}}$, 16. $\frac{\text{P. to K. Kt.'s 4th}}{\text{Q. to K. Kt.'s 3rd}}$,*

17. $\frac{\text{Q. to K's 2nd}}{\text{B. to K. B's sq.}}$, and the result, according to the *Handbuch*, should be an even game.

14. Kt. to B's 6th.	14. R. to K. B's sq.
15. P. to K. Kt.'s 4th.	15. Q. to K. Kt.'s 3rd.
16. P. to K. R's 4th.	16. P. to Q's 4th (best)
17. B. takes P.	17. Q's B. takes P.
18. Q. takes B.	

If 18. $\frac{\text{Kt. takes B.}}{\text{R. to K. Kt.'s sq.}}$, 19. $\frac{\text{B. takes Kt.}}{\text{P. takes B.}}$, 20. $\frac{\text{K. to R's 2nd}}{\text{Q. takes Kt.}}$, and wins.

	18. Q. takes Q.
19. Kt. takes Q.	19. R. to K. Kt.'s sq.
20. B. to K. B's 3rd.	20. P. to K. B's 4th.
21. B. to B's 6th.	21. K. to Q's 2nd.
22. P. to Q's 4th.	22. P. takes Kt.

And Black will win.

---

* White may seemingly play with advantage 16. $\frac{\text{R. to K's sq.}}{}$ at this point, and will obtain a winning position if Black reply with 16. $\frac{}{\text{B. to B's sq.}}$, *e.g.* :—

16. R. to K's sq.	16. B. to B's sq.
17. R. to K's 5th.	17. Q. to K. Kt.'s 3rd.
18. Q. to K's 2nd.	18. P. to B's 6th.
19. R. takes Kt.	

And wins.—[ED.]

VARIATION A, BEGINNING AT WHITE'S 5TH MOVE.

BLACK.

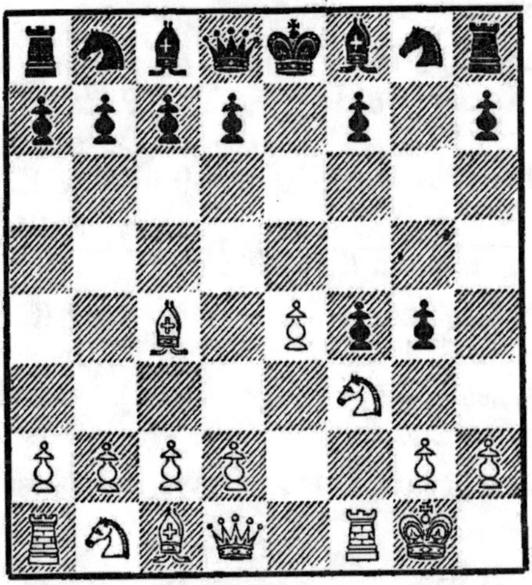

WHITE.

Position prior to White's 5th Move.

5. P. to Q's 4th.

The suggestion of this move, first printed by Koch in his *Elementarbuch*, 1828, was made by an English amateur to Lieutenant-Colonel Donop. It has been exhaustively analyzed by the Indian player Ghulim Kassim, 1829; but although his examination goes far to prove its superiority to the normal move of Castling, it has never been a favourite.

Perhaps now that Mr. Paulsen's move of 11. —— / Q. to K. B's 4th has strengthened the second player's game in the regular opening, the present mode of continuing the attack will come into practice.

5. P. to Q's 4th.

This is thought to be Black's best reply. If 5. —— / P. takes Kt.,

6. Q. takes P. / P. to Q's 4th, 7. B. takes Q's P. / Kt. to K. B's 3rd, 8. Castles / Kt. takes B.,

9. P. takes Kt. / Q. to K. B's 3rd (Mr. Preti recommends 9. —— / B. to K. Kt.'s 2nd),

10. Q's B. takes P. / Q. takes P. (ch.), 11. B. to K's 3rd / Q. to K. R's 5th, 12. Kt. to Q's 2nd / B. to Q's 3rd,

13. $\frac{\text{Q. takes P. (ch.)}}{\text{K. to Q's sq.}}$, 14. $\frac{\text{Kt. to K. B's 3rd}}{\quad}$, White's game is the better one.

6. B. takes Q's P.	6. P. to Q. B's 3rd.
7. B. to Q. Kt.'s 3rd.	7. P. takes Kt.
8. Q. takes P.	8. Q. takes P.
9. Q's B. takes P.	9. Kt. to K. B's 3rd.

If 9. $\frac{\quad}{\text{Q. takes Q. Kt.'s P.}}$, 10. $\frac{\text{Q. to K. R's 5th}}{\quad}$, &c.

10. Kt. to Q's 2nd.	10. B. to K. Kt.'s 5th.
11. Q. to K. Kt.'s 3rd.	11. Kt. takes P.*
12. Kt. takes Kt.	12. Q. takes Kt. (ch.)
13. K. to Q's 2nd.	

White appears to me to have the better game.

Variation B, beginning at Black's 11th Move.

BLACK.

WHITE.

Position prior to Black's 11th Move.

---

* This capture is scarcely so good as 11. $\frac{\quad}{\text{Kt. to Q's 2nd}}$, or 11. $\frac{\quad}{\text{R. to K. Kt.'s sq.}}$, both of which, according to the *Handbuch*, should result in Black's favour.—[Ed.]

11. Q. to Q. B's 4th (ch.)

This was the customary line of play before the introduction of 11. $\frac{\text{}}{\text{Q. to K. B's 4th}}$, which we have just examined.

12. K. to R's sq. — 12. Kt. to Q's 5th.

If 12. $\frac{\text{}}{\text{P. to Q's 3rd}}$, 13. $\frac{\text{Kt. to Q's 5th}}{\text{Kt. to K's 4th}}$, 14. $\frac{\text{R. takes Kt.}}{\text{P. takes R.}}$, 15. $\frac{\text{B. to Kt.'s 4th}}{\text{}}$, the game is in White's favour.

13. R. takes Kt. (ch.)

He may also play with advantage 13. $\frac{\text{Q. to K. R's 3rd}}{\text{}}$, the game then continuing, 13. $\frac{\text{}}{\text{B. to K. Kt.'s 4th}}$, 14. $\frac{\text{Q. to K. R's 5th}}{\text{Q. to K. B's 4th}}$, 15. $\frac{\text{Kt. to K's 4th}}{\text{P. to K. R's 3rd}}$, 16. $\frac{\text{B. to Q. B's 3rd}}{\text{Kt. takes P.}}$, 17. $\frac{\text{Kt. to B's 6th (ch.)}}{\text{K. to Q's sq.}}$, 18. $\frac{\text{Q. takes B's P.}}{\text{Kt takes R.}}$, 19. $\frac{\text{R. takes Kt.}}{\text{Q. to Q. B's 4th}}$, 20. $\frac{\text{P. to Q. Kt.'s 4th}}{\text{Q. to Q's 3rd}}$, 21. $\frac{\text{Kt. to K's 4th}}{\text{}}$, &c.

13. K. takes R.

If 13. $\frac{\text{}}{\text{Q. takes R.}}$, 14. $\frac{\text{Q. to K. R's 5th}}{\text{Kt. to K's 3rd}}$, 15. $\frac{\text{Q. takes B.}}{\text{Q. to K. Kt.'s 4th}}$, 16. $\frac{\text{Q. takes Q.}}{\text{Kt. takes Q.}}$, 17. $\frac{\text{Kt. to Q. Kt.'s 5th}}{\text{K. to Q's sq.}}$, 18. $\frac{\text{B. to Q. B's 3rd}}{\text{}}$, White has still greatly the advantage.

14. Kt. to Q's 5th (ch.) — 14. K. to Q's sq.
15. Q. to K. R's 5th. — 15. Q. to K. B's sq.
16. Q. to K. R's 4th (ch.)

The German *Handbuch* still continues the variation with 16. $\frac{\text{Q's B. takes P.}}{\text{B. takes B.}}$, 17. $\frac{\text{R. takes B.}}{\text{Kt. to K's 3rd}}$, 18. $\frac{\text{Q. to K. R's 4th (ch.)}}{\text{K. to K's sq.}}$ and dismisses it as a drawn battle, although I demonstrated five-and-twenty years ago in the *Chess Player's Handbook* that White must win by the course of play in the text.

	16. P. to K. B's 3rd (best).
17. Q's B. takes P.	17. B. takes B. (best).
18. R. takes B.	18. Kt. to Q. B's 3rd.
19. R. takes K. B's P.	19. Q. to K's sq.
20. R. to K. B's 8th (dis. ch.)	20. Kt. to K's 2nd.
21. Q. takes Kt.	

Mates.

Game the Second.

WHITE	BLACK.
1. P. to K's 4th.	1. P. to K's 4th.
2. P. to K. B's 4th.	2. P. takes P.
3. Kt. to K. B's 3rd.	3. P. to K. Kt.'s 4th.
4. B. to Q. B's 4th.	4. P. to Kt.'s 5th.
5. Castles.	5. P. takes Kt.
6. Q. takes P.	6. Q. to K's 2nd.

As I have remarked before, Black can also play 6. $\frac{}{\text{B. to K. R's 3rd}}$, 6. $\frac{}{\text{Kt. to Q. B's 3rd}}$, and 6. $\frac{}{\text{P. to Q's 3rd}}$, which shall be examined in Variations A and B.

7. Q. takes P.

This is now preferred before 7. $\frac{\text{P. to Q's 4th}}{}$, but it is necessary to show the consequences of that move, and we may as well consider them at once. Suppose, then, if 7. $\frac{\text{P. to Q's 4th}}{\text{Kt. to Q. B's 3rd}}$, 8. $\frac{\text{Q's B. takes P.}}{}$. (If 8. $\frac{\text{Q. takes P.}}{\text{B. to K. R's 3rd}}$, 9. $\frac{\text{B. takes P. (ch.)}}{\text{K. to Q's sq.}}$, 10. $\frac{\text{Q. to K. B's 2nd}}{\text{B. takes B.}}$, 11. $\frac{\text{R. takes B.}}{\text{Kt. to K. R's 3rd}}$, 12. $\frac{\text{B. to Q's 5th}}{\text{R. to K. B's sq.}}$, Black has a better game. So if 8. $\frac{\text{P. to Q. B's 3rd}}{\text{Kt. to K's 4th}}$, 9. $\frac{\text{P. takes Kt.}}{\text{Q. to Q. B's 4th (ch.)}}$, 10. $\frac{\text{K. to R's sq.}}{\text{Q. takes B.}}$,

11. $\frac{\text{B. takes P.}}{\text{P. to Q. Kt.'s 3rd}}$, 12. $\frac{\text{Kt. to Q's 2nd}}{\text{Q. to K's 3rd}}$, 13. $\frac{\text{Kt. to Q. Kt.'s 3rd}}{\text{P. to Q. B's 4th}}$, 14. $\frac{\text{Q's R. to Q's sq.}}{\text{B. to Q. Kt.'s 2nd}}$, 15. $\frac{\text{B. to K. Kt.'s 3rd}}{\text{Kt. to K. R's 3rd}}$, 16. $\frac{\text{P. to K. R's 3rd}}{\text{Castles, Q's side}}$, with a superior game.) 8. $\frac{}{\text{Kt. takes P.}}$, 9. $\frac{\text{Q. to K. R's 5th}}{\text{Kt. to K's 3rd.}}$.

(If 9. $\frac{}{\text{Kt. takes B's P.}}$, 10. $\frac{\text{K. to R's sq.}}{\text{Kt. to K. B's 3rd}}$, 11. $\frac{\text{B. takes P. (ch.)}}{\text{Q. takes B.}}$, 12. $\frac{\text{Q. takes Q. (ch.)}}{\text{K. takes Q.}}$, 13. $\frac{\text{B. to K. Kt.'s 5th}}{\text{B. to Kt.'s 2nd}}$, 14. $\frac{\text{P. to K's 5th}}{\text{Kt. takes Q's R.}}$, 15. $\frac{\text{P. takes Kt.}}{\text{B. to K. B's sq.}}$, Black has the advantage.) 10. $\frac{\text{B. to K's 5th}}{\text{B. to Kt.'s 2nd}}$, 11. $\frac{\text{B. takes Kt.}}{\text{Q. to Q. B's 4th (ch.)}}$, 12. $\frac{\text{K. to R's sq.}}{\text{Q. takes B.}}$, White is at a disadvantage.

7. Kt. to Q. B's 3rd.

If 7. $\frac{}{\text{Q. to Q. B's 4th (ch.)}}$, 8. $\frac{\text{P. to Q's 4th}}{\text{Q. takes P. (ch.)}}$, 9. $\frac{\text{Q's B. to K's 3rd}}{\text{Q. takes K's B.}}$, 10. $\frac{\text{Q. to K's 5th (ch.)}}{}$, White has the better game.

8. B. takes P. (ch.)	8. K. to Q's sq.
9. Kt. to Q. B's 3rd.	9. Q. to K's 4th.
10. Q. takes Q.	10. Kt. takes Q.
11. P. to Q's 4th.	11. Kt. takes B.
12. R. takes Kt.	

White is considered to have about an equivalent for the sacrificed piece.

VARIATION A, BEGINNING AT BLACK'S 6TH MOVE.

BLACK.

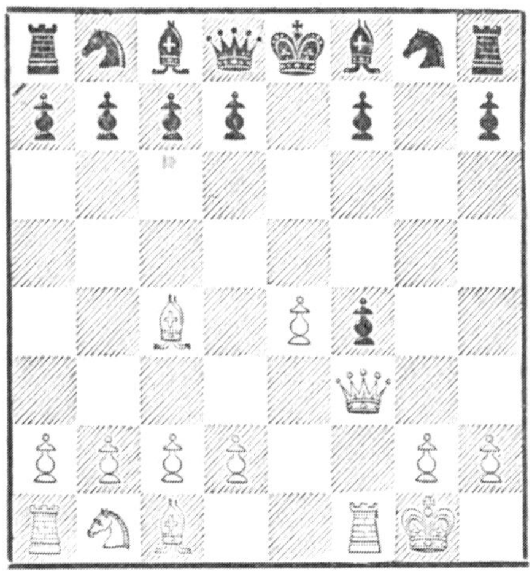

WHITE.

Postion prior to Black's 6th Move.

	6. B. to K. R's 3rd.
7. P. to Q's 4th.	7. Q. to K. B's 3rd.

If 7. ——— / Kt. to Q. B's 3rd, 8. Kt. to Q. B's 3rd / Kt. takes P., 9. Q. to K. R's 5th / Kt. to K's 3rd 10. Q's B. takes P. / B. takes B., 11. R. takes B. / Q. to K's 2nd, 12. B. takes Kt. / Q's P. takes B., 13. Q's R. to K. B's sq. / ———, White has the superiority. If 7. ——— / P. to Q's 3rd, 8. Q's B. takes P. / Q. to K. B's 3rd, 9. Q. to K's 3rd / B. to K's 3rd, 10. P. to Q's 5th / B. to Q's 2nd, 11. Kt. to Q's 2nd / B. takes R., 12. R. takes B. / Q. takes P., 13 Q's R. to K. B's sq. / ———, Black has a bad position. If

7. $\frac{\qquad}{\text{Q. to K's 2nd}}$, 8. $\frac{\text{Q's B. takes P.}}{\text{B. takes B.}}$, 9. $\frac{\text{Q. takes B.}}{\text{Kt. to Q. B's 3rd}}$,
10. $\frac{\text{B. takes B's P. (ch.)}}{\qquad}$, and White has a fine position.

8. P. to K's 5th.	8. Q. to K. B's 4th.
9. Kt. to Q. B's 3rd.	9. Kt. to Q. B's 3rd.
10. Kt. to K's 2nd.	10. K's Kt. to K's 2nd.
11. B. to Q's 3rd.	11. Q. to K's 3rd.
12. P. to Q. B's 3rd.	12. Kt. to K. Kt.'s 3rd.
13. Q. to K. R's 5th.	13. B. to K. Kt.'s 2nd.
14. Q's B. takes P.	14. Castles.
15. Kt. to K. Kt.'s 3rd.	15. Q's Kt. to K's 2nd.
16. Kt. to K's 4th.	16. P. to K. B's 3rd.
17. P. takes P.	17. B. takes P.
18. B. to K's 5th.	

And White's game is decisively superior.

Variation B, beginning at Black's 6th Move.

(*See preceding Diagram.*)

6. Kt. to Q. B's 3rd.

The move of 6. $\frac{\qquad}{\text{P. to Q's 3rd}}$ is very tame and inefficient.
If 6. $\frac{\qquad}{\text{P. to Q's 3rd}}$, 7. $\frac{\text{P. to Q's 4th}}{\text{B. to K. R's 3rd}}$, 8. $\frac{\text{Q's B. takes P.}}{\text{B. takes B.}}$,
9. $\frac{\text{Q. takes B.}}{\text{Q. to K's 2nd}}$, 10. $\frac{\text{B. takes B's P. (ch.)}}{\text{K. to Q's sq.}}$, 11. $\frac{\text{P. to K's 5th}}{\qquad}$, the game is in White's favour.

7. Q. takes P.	7. P. to K. B's 3rd.
8. Kt. to Q. B's 3rd.	8. Q. to K's 2nd (best).
9. B. takes K's Kt.	9. R. takes B.
10. Kt. to Q's 5th.	10. Q. to Q. B's 4th (ch.)
11. K. to R's sq.	11. B. to Q's 3rd.
12. Q. to K. R's 4th.	

White has a fine position.

Game the Third.

WHITE.	BLACK.
1. P. to K's 4th.	1. P. to K's 4th.
2. P. to K. B's 4th.	2. P. takes P.
3. Kt. to K. B's 3rd.	3. P. to K. Kt.'s 4th.
4. B. to Q. B's 4th.	4. P. to K. Kt.'s 5th.
5. Castles.	5. P. takes Kt.
6. Q. takes P.	6. Q. to K. B's 3rd.
7. P. to K's 5th.	7. Q. takes P.
8. P. to Q's 3rd.	8. B. to K. R's 3rd.
9. B. to Q's 2nd.	9. Kt. to K's 2nd.
10. Kt. to Q. B's 3rd.	10. P. to Q. B's 3rd.

In the opinion of many authorities the move of 10. $\frac{}{\text{P. to Q. B's 3rd}}$, was formerly considered preferable to 10. $\frac{}{\text{Kt. to Q. B's 3rd}}$, which we have been examining. How far this opinion may have been modified by Mr. Paulsen's introduction of 11. $\frac{}{\text{Q. to K. B's 4th}}$ in the former case I am not prepared to say.

11. Q's R. to K's sq.

More forcible than 11. $\frac{\text{Kt. to K's 4th}}{}$, a once favourite move.

11. Q. to Q. B's 4th (ch.)

12. K. to R's sq.

White may also play advantageously, I believe, 12. $\frac{\text{R. to K. B's 2nd}}{}$, instead of retiring the King.

12. P. to Q's 4th.

If 12. $\frac{}{\text{Castles}}$, 13. $\frac{\text{Kt. to K's 4th}}{\text{Q. to K. B's 4th}}$, 14. $\frac{\text{P. to K. Kt.'s 4th}}{\text{Q. to K. Kt.'s 3rd}}$, 15. $\frac{\text{P. to K. Kt.'s 5th}}{\text{B. to Kt.'s 2nd}}$, 16. $\frac{\text{Kt. to B's 6th (ch.)}}{\text{K. to R's sq. (best)}}$, 17. $\frac{\text{R. takes Kt.}}{\text{P. to Q's 4th}}$,

18. $\frac{\text{B. to Q. Kt.'s 3rd}}{\text{Q. takes P.}}$, 19. $\frac{\text{R. to K. Kt.'s sq.}}{\text{Q. to K. B's 4th}}$. (If 19. $\frac{}{\text{Q. takes Kt.}}$, 20. $\frac{\text{B. to Q. B's 3rd}}{}$; if 19. $\frac{}{\text{Q. to K. R's 3rd}}$, 20. $\frac{\text{Kt. to K's 8th}}{}$.) 20. $\frac{\text{Q. to K. Kt.'s 2nd}}{\text{B. takes Kt.}}$, 21. $\frac{\text{R. takes K. B's P.}}{\text{R. to K's sq.}}$, 22. $\frac{\text{R. takes B.}}{}$, and White must win.

13. Q. to K. R's 5th. 13. Q. to Q's 3rd.
14. B. takes Q's P.

If 14. $\frac{\text{Kt. to K's 4th}}{\text{P. takes Kt.}}$, 15. $\frac{\text{B. takes P. (ch.)}}{\text{K. to Q's sq.}}$, 16. $\frac{\text{P. takes P.}}{\text{B. to K. Kt.'s 2nd}}$, 17. $\frac{\text{B. to Q. R's 5th (ch.)}}{\text{P. to Kt.'s 3rd}}$, 18. $\frac{\text{R. to Q's sq.}}{\text{Kt. to Q's 4th}}$, 19. $\frac{\text{B. takes Kt.}}{\text{Kt. to Q's 2nd}}$, Black is thought to have the best of the conflict.

14. P. takes B.

If 14. $\frac{}{\text{Q. to K. Kt.'s 3rd}}$, 15. $\frac{\text{R. takes Kt. (ch.)}}{\text{K. takes R.}}$, 16. $\frac{\text{Q. to K's 5th (ch.)}}{}$, White wins. If 14. $\frac{}{\text{Castles}}$, 15. $\frac{\text{R. takes Kt.}}{}$, and again White has the better game.

15. Kt. takes P. 15. K's Kt. to Q. B's 3rd.

If 15. $\frac{}{\text{B. to K. Kt.'s 5th}}$, 16. $\frac{\text{R. takes Kt. (ch.)}}{}$, with the advantage.

16. B. to Q. B's 3rd.

If 16. $\frac{\text{B. to Q. Kt.'s 4th}}{\text{Kt. takes B.}}$, 17. $\frac{\text{R. takes Kt.}}{\text{K. to Q's sq.}}$, Black's game for choice. So too, if 16. $\frac{\text{R. takes Kt. (ch.)}}{\text{Kt. takes R.}}$, 17. $\frac{\text{R. to K's sq.}}{\text{Castles}}$, Black has the better game.

16. B. to Q's 2nd.

He may also play 16. $\frac{}{\text{Q. to K. Kt's 3rd}}$, or 16. $\frac{}{\text{B. to K. Kt.'s 5th}}$, or 16. $\frac{\qquad}{\text{K. to Q's sq.}}$, which we will examine forthwith. In the first place, then, 16. $\frac{\qquad}{\text{Q. to K. Kt.'s 3rd}}$, 17. $\frac{\text{Q. takes Q}}{\text{R's P. takes Q.}}$, 18. $\frac{\text{B. takes R.}}{\text{K. to B's sq.}}$, 19. $\frac{\text{Kt. takes P.}}{\text{B. takes Kt.}}$, 20. $\frac{\text{R. takes B.}}{\text{B. to K. B's 4th}}$, White ought to win. In the second place, 16. $\frac{\qquad}{\text{B. to K. Kt.'s 5th}}$, 17. $\frac{\text{Q. takes B.}}{\text{R. to K. B's sq.}}$, 18. $\frac{\text{R. takes Kt. (ch.)}}{\text{Kt. takes R.}}$, 19. $\frac{\text{R. to K's sq.}}{\text{Q. takes Kt.}}$, 20. $\frac{\text{B. to K. B's 6th}}{\text{Q. to Q's 3rd}}$, 21. $\frac{\text{R. takes Kt. (ch.)}}{\text{Q. takes R.}}$, 22. $\frac{\text{B. takes Q.}}{\text{K. takes B.}}$, 23. $\frac{\text{Q. to K. R's 4th (ch.)}}{\text{K. to Q's 2nd}}$, 24. $\frac{\text{Q. takes B.}}{\text{Q's R. to K's sq.}}$, 25. $\frac{\text{P. to K. R's 4th}}{\qquad}$, White has the superiority. In the third place, 16. $\frac{\qquad}{\text{K. to Q's sq.}}$, 17. $\frac{\text{Kt. takes Kt.}}{\text{R. to K's sq.}}$, 18. $\frac{\text{Kt. takes Kt. (ch.)}}{\text{P. takes Kt.}}$, 19. $\frac{\text{B. to Q. R's 5th (ch.)}}{\text{K. to Q's 2nd}}$, 20. $\frac{\text{R. takes R.}}{\text{K. takes R.}}$, 21. $\frac{\text{R. to K's sq. (ch.)}}{\text{K. to B's sq.}}$, 22. $\frac{\text{B. to Q. Kt's 4th}}{\qquad}$, White must win.

17. B. takes R. (best.)	17. Castles.
18. Kt. takes Kt. (ch.)	18. Kt. takes Kt.
19. Q. takes B's P.	19. R. takes B.
20. R. takes Kt.	20. B. to Q. B's 3rd.

Black may play also 20. $\frac{\qquad}{\text{R. to K. B's sq.}}$, 21. $\frac{\text{Q. takes K. R's P.}}{\text{B. to Q. B's 3rd}}$, 22. $\frac{\text{R. to K. B's 7th}}{\text{Q. to Q's 4th}}$, 23. $\frac{\text{R. takes R. (ch.)}}{\text{B. takes R.}}$, 24. $\frac{\text{Q. to K. R's 3rd (ch.)}}{\qquad}$, White has the superior game.

21. Q. to K's 6th (ch.)	21. Q. takes Q.
22. R. takes Q.	22. B. to K. Kt.'s 4th.
23. P. to K. R's 4th.	23. B. takes R's P.
24. R. takes P.	24. B. to K. Kt.'s 6th.
25. R. to K. Kt.'s 4th.	25. B. to Q's 2nd.
26. R. to Q. B's 4th (ch.)	26. K. to Q's sq.
27. R. to K's 3rd.	27. R. to K. Kt.'s sq.
28. P. to Q's 4th.	

It is difficult to decide which has the advantage.

ILLUSTRATIVE GAMES.

GAME I.—Between Messrs. Wayte and Baucher.

WHITE (Mr. W.)	BLACK (Mr. B.)
1. P. to K's 4th.	1. P. to K's 4th.
2. P. to K. B's 4th.	2. P. takes P.
3. Kt. to K. B's 3rd.	3. P. to K. Kt.'s 4th.
4. B. to B's 4th.	4. P. to Kt.'s 5th.
5. Castles.	5. P. takes Kt.
6. Q. takes P.	6. Q. to K. B's 3rd.
7. P. to K's 5th.	7. Q. takes P.
8. P. to Q's 3rd.	8. B. to K. R's 3rd.
9. B. to Q's 2nd.	9. Kt. to K's 2nd.
10. Kt. to Q. B's 3rd.	10. Q's Kt. to B's 3rd.
11. Q's R. to K's sq.	11. Q. to K. B's 4th.
12. R. to K's 4th.	12. P. to Q's 3rd.*
13. Kt. to Q's 5th.	13. K. to Q's sq.
14. Kt. takes Kt.	14. Kt. takes Kt.
15. Q's B. takes P.	15. B. to K. Kt.'s 2nd.†
16. Q. to K's 2nd.	16. Q. to Q. B's 4th (ch.)
17. B. to K's 3rd.	17. Q. to Q. B's 3rd.
18. B. takes Kt.	18. K. takes R.

And White mates in four moves.

GAME II.—Between Messrs. Kolisch and Paulsen.

WHITE (Mr. K.)	BLACK (Mr. P.)
1. P. to K's 4th.	1. P. to K's 4th.
2. P. to K. B's 4th.	2. P. takes P.
3. Kt. to K. B's 3rd.	3. P. to K. Kt.'s 4th.
4. B. to Q. B's 4th.	4. P. to Kt.'s 5th.
5. Castles.	5. P. takes Kt.

---

* As we have seen from the preceding analysis, Black's correct move at this point is 12. Castles.

† A fatal error. In the vain endeavour to entangle the adverse Queen he only hampers his own.

6. Q takes P.	6. Q. to K. B's 3rd.
7. P. to K's 5th.	7. Q. takes P.
8. P. to Q's 3rd.	8. B. to K. R's 3rd.
9. B. to Q's 2nd.	9. Kt. to K's 2nd.
10. Kt. to Q. B's 3rd.	10. Q's Kt. to B's 3rd.
11. Q's R. to K's sq.	11. Q. to K. B's 4th.*
12. Kt. to Q's 5th.	12. K. to Q's sq.
13. B. to Q. B's 3rd.	13. R. to K. Kt.'s sq.†
14. B. to K. B's 6th.‡	14. B. to K. Kt.'s 4th.§
15. R. takes Kt.	15. B. takes B.
16. R. to K's 4th.	16. B. to K. Kt.'s 4th.
17. P. to K. Kt.'s 4th.	17. Q. to K. Kt.'s 3rd.
18. P. to K. R's 4th.	18. B. takes P.
19. Q. takes B's P.	19. P. to Q's 3rd.
20. Q. takes K. B's P.	20. Q. takes Q.
21. R. takes Q.	21. Kt. to K's 4th.
22. R. takes K. R's P.	22. Kt. takes B.
23. Q's R. takes Kt.	23. P. to Q. B's 3rd.
24. Kt. to Q. B's 7th.	24. R. to Q. Kt.'s sq.
25. Q's R. to K. B's 4th.	25. B. to K's 2nd.
26. Q's R. to B's 7th.	26. K. takes Kt.
27. Q's R. takes B. (ch.)	27. K. to Kt.'s 3rd.
28. K's R. to Kt.'s 7th.	28. R. takes R.
29. R. takes R.	29. B. to K's 3rd.
30. R. to K. Kt.'s 6th.	30. B. takes Q. R's P.
31. R. takes Q's P.	31. R. to K. Kt.'s sq.
32. K. to B's 2nd.	32. R. takes P.

And White resigned.

Game III.—Between Messrs. Sevick and Charleton.

White (Mr. S.)	Black (Mr. C.)
1. P. to K's 4th.	1. P. to K's 4th.
2. P. to K. B's 4th.	2. P. takes P.
3. Kt. to K. B's 3rd.	3. P. to K. Kt.'s 4th.

---

* This defence was, we believe, adopted for the first time in the game under notice.

† Better, as we have seen, to play the Rook to King's square.

‡ Not so good perhaps as R. takes Kt.

§ The correct reply.

4. B. to Q. B's 4th.	4. P. to Kt.'s 5th.
5. Castles.	5. P. takes Kt.
6. Q. takes P.	6. Q. to K's 2nd.*
7. P. to Q's 3rd.	7. Kt. to Q. B's 3rd.
8. Q. takes P.	8. Kt. to K's 4th.
9. Kt. to Q. B's 3rd.†	9. Kt. takes B.
10. Kt. to Q's 5th.	10. Q. to Q. B's 4th (ch.)
11. K. to R's sq.	11. Kt. to Q's 3rd.
12. Q. to K's 5th (ch.)	12. K. to Q's sq.
13. B. to K. Kt.'s 5th (ch.)	13. P. to K. B's 3rd.
14. B. takes P. (ch.)	14. Kt. takes B.

And White mates in four moves.

---

* Not so good as 6. Q. to K. B's 3rd.

† Very well played.

CHAPTER XVI.

ALLGAIER-KIESERITZKY GAMBIT.

1. $\frac{\text{P. to K's 4th}}{\text{P. to K's 4th}}$, 2. $\frac{\text{P. to K. B's 4th}}{\text{P. takes P.}}$, 3. $\frac{\text{Kt. to K. B's 3rd}}{\text{P. to K. Kt.'s 4th}}$.

4. $\frac{\text{P. to K. R's 4th}}{\text{P. to K. Kt.'s 5th}}$, 5. $\frac{\text{Kt. to K. Kt.'s 5th}}{}$.—(Allgaier.)

5. $\frac{\text{Kt. to K's 5th}}{}$.—(Kieseritzky.)

GAME THE FIRST.

5. $\frac{\text{Kt. to K. Kt.'s 5th}}{}$.

GAME THE SECOND.

5. $\frac{\text{Kt. to K's 5th}}{\text{Kt. to K. B's 3rd}}$.

GAME THE THIRD.

5. $\frac{}{\text{B. to K. Kt.'s 2nd}}$.

GAME THE FOURTH.

5. $\frac{}{\text{P. to K. R's 4th}}$.

GAME THE FIFTH.

5. $\frac{}{\text{B. to K's 2nd}}$.

Game the Sixth.

5. $\frac{\quad}{\text{Kt. to Q. B's 3rd}}$.

The present opening differs from the Gambit just examined by White's playing 4. $\frac{\text{P. to K. R's 4th}}{\quad}$, instead of moving 4. $\frac{\text{B. to Q. B's 4th}}{\quad}$, or Castling. This divergence is not of modern origin, as it appears to be from its appellation. It was known to Salvio, to Greco, to Cozio, and Lolli; but Allgaier having given special attention to that branch of it dependent on White moving 5. Kt. to Kt.'s 5th, and Kieseritzky to the more interesting variation 5. Kt. to K's 5th, the *début* has taken their names.

Game the First.

WHITE.	BLACK.
1. P. to K's 4th.	1. P. to K's 4th.
2. P. to K. B's 4th.	2. P. takes P.
3. Kt. to K. B's 3rd.	3. P. to K. Kt.'s 4th.
4. P. to K. R's 4th.	4. P. to K. Kt.'s 5th (best).
5. Kt. to K. Kt.'s 5th.	

It was to the results of this move that Allgaier gave his attention. The variation, analyzed by Kieseritzky, beginning 5. $\frac{\text{Kt. to K's 5th}}{\quad}$, forms the subject of the after games.

5. P. to K. R's 3rd (best).

This is very superior to 5. $\frac{\quad}{\text{P. to K. R's 4th}}$; *e.g.*—

5. $\frac{\quad}{\text{P. to K. R's 4th}}$, 6. $\frac{\text{B. to Q. B's 4th}}{\text{Kt. to K. R's 3rd}}$, 7. $\frac{\text{P. to Q's 4th}}{\text{P. to K. B's 3rd}}$, 8. $\frac{\text{Q's B. takes P.}}{\text{P. takes Kt.}}$, 9. $\frac{\text{P. takes P.}}{\text{Kt. to K. B's 2nd}}$, 10. $\frac{\text{P. to K. Kt.'s 6th}}{\text{Kt. to Q's 3rd.}}$, 11. $\frac{\text{B. takes Kt.}}{\text{P. takes B.}}$, 12. $\frac{\text{B. to K. B's 7th (ch.)}}{\text{K. to K's 2nd}}$, 13. $\frac{\text{Castles}}{\quad}$, and White has the advantage.

6. Kt. takes B's P. — 6. K. takes Kt.
7. B. to Q. B's 4th (ch.)

(For the effect of 7. $\frac{\text{Q. takes P.}}{}$ consult Variation A.)

7. P. to Q's 4th.

8. B. takes P. (ch.)

Black has now the choice of two moves, which we will briefly examine.

In the first place :—

8. K. to Kt.'s 2nd.

9. P. to Q's 4th.

The best reply. If White play 9. $\frac{\text{B. takes Q. Kt.'s P}}{}$, Black must not take Bishop with Bishop, which would admit of his opponent drawing by perpetual check. His best reply is 9. $\frac{}{\text{P. to K. B's 6th}}$, *e.g.* :—9. $\frac{\text{B. takes Kt.'s P.}}{\text{P. to B's 6th}}$, 10. $\frac{\text{B. takes B. (best)}}{\text{Q. takes B.}}$, 11. $\frac{\text{P. takes P.}}{\text{B. to Q's 3rd}}$, 12. $\frac{\text{R. to K. Kt.'s sq.}}{\text{P. to Kt.'s 6th}}$, 13. $\frac{\text{P. to Q's 4th}}{\text{Q. to K. B's 3rd}}$, 14. $\frac{\text{P. to K's 5th}}{}$, or 14. $\frac{\text{Q. to K's 2nd}}{}$; and there is little to choose between the positions.

9. Q. to K. B's 3rd.

The best reply according to the *Handbuch*, but 9. $\frac{}{\text{Kt. to K. B's 3rd}}$, and 9. $\frac{}{\text{P. to K. B's 6th}}$, may also be played.

10. Q. to Q's 3rd. — 10. Kt. to K's 2nd.
11. Kt. to Q. B's 3rd. — 11. Kt. to Q. B's 3rd.
12. P. to K's 5th. — 12. Q. to K. Kt.'s 3rd.
13. B. to K's 4th. — 13. B. to K. B's 5th.

And Black has the superiority.

In the second place :—

8. K. to K's sq.

9. P. to Q's 4th. — 9. Kt. to K's 2nd.

Black may also play 9. $\frac{}{\text{P. to K. B's 6th}}$, 10. $\frac{\text{P. takes P.}}{\text{B. to K's 2nd}}$, 11. $\frac{\text{Castles}}{\text{P. to K. Kt.'s 6th}}$, 12. $\frac{\text{P. to K. B's 4th}}{\text{P. to K. R's 4th}}$, 13. $\frac{\text{B. takes Kt.}}{\text{R. takes B.}}$, 14. $\frac{\text{Q. takes P. (ch.)}}{\text{K. to B's sq.}}$, 15. $\frac{\text{Q. to R's 6th (ch.)}}{\text{R. to Kt.'s 2nd}}$, 16. $\frac{\text{P. to Q. B's 3rd}}{}$, and White appears to be reimbursed for his sacrificed Knight.

10. Kt. to Q. B's 3rd. | 10. B. to K. Kt.'s 2nd.
11. Q's B. takes P. | 11. Q's Kt. to B's 3rd.

If 11. $\frac{}{\text{Kt. takes B.}}$, 12. $\frac{\text{P. takes Kt.}}{}$, with a good game.

If 11. $\frac{}{\text{P. to Q. B's 3rd}}$, 12. $\frac{\text{Q. to Q's 3rd}}{\text{Kt. to Q. R's 3rd}}$. If 12. $\frac{}{\text{P. takes B.}}$, 13. $\frac{\text{Kt. to Kt.'s 5th}}{\text{Kt. to Q. R's 3rd}}$, 14. $\frac{\text{Castles}}{}$, and White has again a good game.

12. B. to K's 3rd.

Followed by 13. Q. to Q's 2nd, with a fine position.

VARIATION A, BEGINNING AT WHITE'S 7TH MOVE.

BLACK.

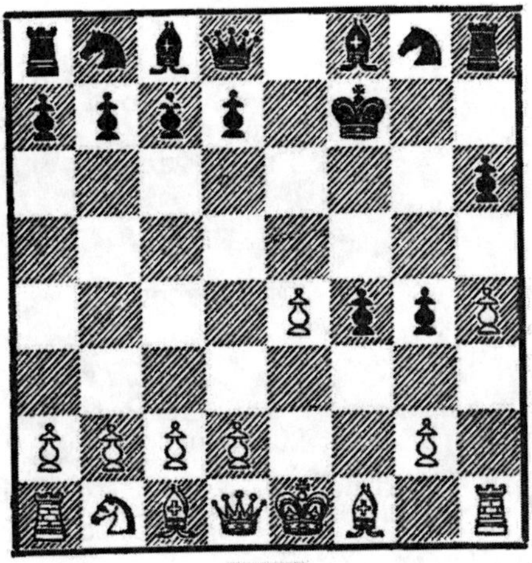

WHITE.

Position prior to White's 7th Move.

7. Q. takes P. — 7. Kt. to K. B's 3rd.

Black may also maintain an advantage by 7. $\frac{\quad}{\text{Q. to K. B's 3rd}}$, 8. $\frac{\text{P. to Q's 4th}}{\text{Q. takes Q's P.}}$, 9. $\frac{\text{Q. takes P. (ch.)}}{\text{Q. to K. B's 3rd}}$, &c.

8. Q. takes B's P. — 8. B. to Q's 3rd.

This embarrassing move was suggested by a German player named Horny. There has not yet been found a satisfactory response to it.

9. B. to Q. B's 4th (ch.)

If 9. $\frac{\text{Q. to K. B's 3rd}}{\text{Kt. to Q. B's 3rd}}$, 10. $\frac{\text{P. to Q. B's 3rd}}{\text{Kt. to K's 4th}}$ 11. $\frac{\text{Q. to K's 2nd}}{\text{Q's Kt. to K. Kt.'s 5th}}$, 12. $\frac{\text{R. to K. R's 3rd}}{\text{Q. to K's 2nd}}$, Black has the better game.

9. K. to Kt.'s 2nd.

10. Q. to K. B's 5th.

It matters nothing whether White play his Queen to B's 2nd, 3rd, or 5th. The game appears equally irretrievable.

10. B. to Kt.'s 6th (ch.)

11. K. to B's sq. — 11. R. to K. B's sq.

Black must win.

Game the Second.

WHITE.	BLACK.
1. P. to K's 4th.	1. P. to K's 4th.
2. P. to K. B's 4th.	2. P. takes P.
3. Kt. to K. B's 3rd.	3. P. to K. Kt.'s 4th.
4. P. to K. R's 4th.	4. P. to K. Kt.'s 5th.
5. Kt. to K's 5th.	

For several years this mode of pursuing the attack was considered greatly superior to that we have been investigating. So many improvements, however, have been discovered in the defence of late, that the discarded form of the opening will probably supersede its supplanter.

5. Kt. to K. B's 3rd.

Opinion is divided between this and the move 5. $\frac{}{\text{B. to K. Kt.'s 2nd}}$, examined in the next game, for Black's best move. He has, however, several feasible lines of defence beside these, the chief of which are 5. $\frac{}{\text{Kt. to Q. B's 3rd}}$, 5. $\frac{}{\text{P. to K. R's 4th}}$, and 5. $\frac{}{\text{B. to K's 2nd}}$, for which see Games IV., V., and VI. If he adopt the old-fashioned course of 5. $\frac{}{\text{P. to Q's 3rd}}$, the result will probably be a drawn battle. *Ex. gr.*, 5. $\frac{}{\text{P. to Q's 3rd}}$, 6. $\frac{\text{Kt. takes Kt.'s P.}}{\text{B. to K's 2nd}}$, 7. $\frac{\text{P. to Q's 4th}}{\text{B. takes P. (ch.)}}$, 8. $\frac{\text{Kt. to B's 2nd}}{\text{Q. to Kt.'s 4th}}$, 9. $\frac{\text{Q. to K. B's 3rd}}{\text{B. to K. Kt.'s 6th}}$, 10. $\frac{\text{Kt. to Q. B's 3rd}}{\text{Kt. to K. B's 3rd}}$, &c. The same result would follow I think from his choosing the novel one of 5. $\frac{}{\text{P. to Q's 4th}}$, 6. $\frac{\text{P. to Q's 4th}}{}$. (If 6. $\frac{\text{Kt. takes Kt.'s P.}}{\text{P. takes P.}}$, the game is equal. If 6. $\frac{\text{P. takes P.}}{\text{B. to K's 2nd}}$, 7. $\frac{\text{Kt. takes Kt.'s P.}}{\text{B. takes P. (ch.)}}$, Black seems to have some slight advantage.) 6. $\frac{}{\text{P. to K. B's 6th}}$, 7. $\frac{\text{Kt.'s P. takes P.}}{\text{B. to K's 2nd}}$, 8. $\frac{\text{B. to K's 3rd}}{\text{B. takes P. (ch.)}}$, 9. $\frac{\text{K. to Q's 2nd}}{\text{B. to K. B's 3rd}}$, and the game ought to be drawn.

6. B. to Q. B's 4th.

If 6. $\frac{\text{Kt. takes Kt.'s P.}}{}$, Black answers with 6. $\frac{}{\text{Kt. takes P. (best)}}$, and soon acquires the superiority.

6. P. to Q's 4th.

Black can also play, perhaps more advantageously,

6. $\frac{\qquad\qquad}{\text{Q. to K's 2nd}}$, 7. $\frac{\text{B. takes P. (ch.)}}{\text{K. to Q's sq.}}$, 8. $\frac{\text{P. to Q's 4th}}{\text{P. to Q's 3rd}}$, 9. $\frac{\text{B. to Q. Kt.'s 3rd}}{\text{P. takes Kt.}}$, 10. $\frac{\text{P. takes P. (dis. ch.)}}{\text{B. to Q's 2nd}}$, 11. $\frac{\text{P. takes Kt.}}{\text{Q. takes P. (ch.)}}$, 12. $\frac{\text{K. to B's sq.}}{\text{B. to Q's 3rd}}$. Black has the better game.

7. P. takes P.	7. B. to Q's 3rd.

The move of B. to K. Kt.'s 2nd deserves consideration here. For example, 7. $\frac{\qquad\qquad}{\text{B. to K. Kt.'s 2nd}}$, 8. $\frac{\text{B. to Q. Kt.'s 5th (ch.)}}{\text{P. to Q. B's 3rd}}$, 9. $\frac{\text{P. takes P.}}{\text{Castles}}$, 10. $\frac{\text{P. to Q. B's 7th}}{\qquad\qquad}$. (Better, I believe, than 10. $\frac{\text{P. takes P.}}{\qquad\qquad}$, because of 10. $\frac{\qquad\qquad}{\text{B. takes Q. Kt.'s P.}}$, 11. $\frac{\text{P. to Q's 4th}}{\text{B. takes P.}}$, 12. $\frac{\text{R. to K. Kt.'s sq.}}{\text{P. to K. B's 6th}}$, &c.) 10. $\frac{\qquad\qquad}{\text{Q. takes B's P.}}$, 11. $\frac{\text{P. to Q's 4th}}{\qquad\qquad}$. Black has the safer game.

8. P. to Q's 4th.	8. Kt. to K. R's 4th.

If 8. $\frac{\qquad\qquad}{\text{Q. to K's 2nd}}$, 9. $\frac{\text{B. takes P.}}{\text{Kt. to K. R's 4th}}$, 10. $\frac{\text{Castles}}{\qquad\qquad}$, and White has the better game.

9. Kt. to Q. B's 3rd.

(For 9. $\frac{\text{Castles}}{\qquad\qquad}$, and 9 $\frac{\text{B. to Q. Kt.'s 5th (ch.)}}{\qquad\qquad}$, consult Variation A.)

9. Q. to K's 2nd.

If 9. $\frac{\qquad\qquad}{\text{Kt. to Kt.'s 6th}}$, 10. $\frac{\text{Q's B. takes P.}}{\text{Kt. takes R.}}$, 11. $\frac{\text{Kt. to K's 4th}}{\text{B. to K. B's 4th}}$, 12. $\frac{\text{B. to K. Kt.'s 5th}}{\text{B. to K's 2nd}}$, 13. $\frac{\text{Kt. takes B's P.}}{\qquad\qquad}$, and should win.

10. B. to Q. Kt.'s 5th (ch.)	10. P. to Q. B's 3rd.

10. $\frac{\qquad\qquad}{\text{K. to B's sq.}}$, is inferior.

11. P. takes P.	11. P. takes P.
12. Kt. to Q's 5th.	12. Q. to K's 3rd (best).
13. Kt. to B's 7th (ch.)	13. B. takes Kt.

14. B. to Q. B's 4th.	14. Q. to K's 2nd.
15. B. takes B's P. (ch.)	15. Q. takes B. (best).
16. Kt. takes Q.	16. K. takes Kt.

And the *Handbuch* decides in favour of Black, but this I think is "not proven."

VARIATION A, BEGINNING AT WHITE'S 9TH MOVE.

BLACK.

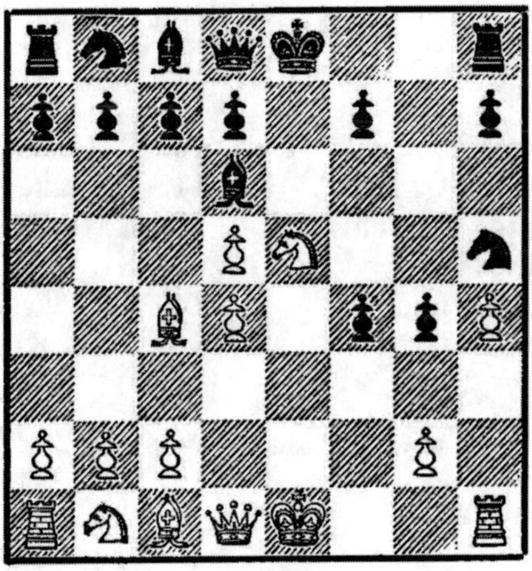

WHITE.

Position prior to White's 9th Move.

In the first place :—

9. Castles.

A favourite move with Anderssen

	9. Q. takes R's P.
10. Q. to K's sq.	10. Q. takes Q.
11. R. takes Q.	11. Castles.
12. Kt. to Q. B's 3rd.	

Some players prefer 12. $\frac{\text{B. to Q's 3rd}}{\quad}$.

	12. B. to K. B's 4th.
13. P. to K. Kt.'s 3rd.	13. P. to K. B's 6th.
14. B. to K. R's 6th.	14. R. to K's sq.
15. Kt. to K. B's 3rd, taking P.	15. Kt. to Q's 2nd.
16. Kt. to K. R's 4th.	16. Kt. takes P.

And Black has the advantage.

In the second place :—

9. B. to Q. Kt.'s 5th (ch.)	9. P. to Q. B's 3rd.

He may also play, without much disadvantage,

9. $\frac{\qquad}{\text{K. to B's sq.}}$

10. P. takes P.	10. P. takes P.
11. Kt. takes Q. B's P.	11. Kt. takes Kt.
12. B. takes Kt. (ch.)	12. K. to B's sq.
13. B. takes R.	13. Kt. to Kt.'s 6th.
14. K. to B's 2nd.	14. Kt. takes R. (ch.)
15. Q. takes Kt.	15. P. to Kt.'s 6th (ch.)

15. $\frac{\qquad}{\text{B. to Q. R's 3rd}}$ is a good move here.*

16. K. to K's sq.

If 16. $\frac{\text{K. to Kt.'s sq.}}{\text{B. to Q. B's 4th}}$. If 16. $\frac{\text{K. to B's 3rd}}{\text{R. to K. Kt.'s sq.}}$,

17. $\frac{\text{Q's B. takes P.}}{\text{Q. to K. B's 3rd}}$, 18. $\frac{\text{Q to Q. B's sq.}}{\text{B. to K. Kt.'s 5th (ch.)}}$, &c.

---

* Anderssen gives 15. B. to K. B's 4th, which the *Schachzeitung* continues as follows :—

	15. B. to K. B's 4th.
16. B. to Q's 5th.	16. K. to Kt.'s 2nd.
17. Kt. to Q. B's 3rd.	17. R. to K's sq.
18. B. to Q. B's 6th.	18. P. to Kt.'s 6th (ch.)
19. K. to B's sq.	19. B. takes Q. B's P.
20. B. takes R.	20. Q. takes B.
21. B. to Q's 2nd.	21. B. to Q's 6th (ch.)
22. K. to Kt.'s sq.	22. Q. to K's 4th.

And Black wins.—Ed.]

	16. Q. to K's 2nd (ch.)
17. K. to Q's sq. (best).	17. B. to Kt.'s 5th (ch.)
18. B. to K. B's 3rd.	18. B. takes B. (ch.)
19. P. takes B.	19. R. to Kt.'s sq.

And Black has much the better game.

Game the Third.

WHITE.	BLACK.
1. P. to K's 4th.	1. P. to K's 4th.
2. P. to K. B's 4th.	2. P. takes P.
3. Kt. to K. B's 3rd.	3. P. to K. Kt.'s 4th.
4. P. to K. R's 4th.	4. P. to K. Kt.'s 5th.
5. Kt. to K's 5th.	5. B. to K. Kt.'s 2nd.

This is an important move. It was first proposed, I believe, by Mr. Paulsen, and it appears to strengthen Black's defence in nearly every variation.

6. P. to Q's 4th.

(For the consequences of 6. $\frac{\text{Kt. takes Kt.'s P.}}{}$, refer to Variation A.)

6. Kt. to K. B's 3rd.

Preferable to taking the Knight.

7. Kt. to Q. B's 3rd.

If 7. $\frac{\text{Q's B. takes P.}}{\text{P. to Q's 3rd.}}$, 8. $\frac{\text{Kt. to Q. B's 4th}}{\text{Kt. takes P.}}$, 9. $\frac{\text{B. to Q's 3rd}}{\text{Q. to K's 2nd}}$, 10. $\frac{\text{Q. to K's 2nd}}{\text{P. to K. B's 4th}}$, Black has a good position. On the other hand, if 7. $\frac{\text{B. to Q. B's 4th}}{\text{Castles}}$. (Black may likewise play 7. $\frac{}{\text{P. to Q's 4th}}$, or 7. $\frac{}{\text{Q. to K's 2nd}}$, with almost equal profit.) 8. $\frac{\text{Q's B. takes P.}}{\text{P. to Q's 3rd}}$, 9. $\frac{\text{Kt. takes K. B's P.}}{\text{R. takes Kt.}}$, 10. $\frac{\text{B. takes R. (ch.)}}{\text{K. takes B.}}$, 11. $\frac{\text{Q. to K's 2nd}}{\text{K. to Kt.'s sq.}}$. Black has the advantage.

	7. P. to Q's 3rd.
8. Kt. to Q's 3rd.	8. Castles.
9. Q's B. takes P.	

If 9. $\frac{\text{Kt. takes P.}}{\text{Kt. takes P.}}$, 10. $\frac{\text{Kt. takes Kt.}}{\text{R. to K's sq.}}$, 11. $\frac{\text{B. to Q's 3rd}}{\text{P. to Q's 4th}}$, with the better game.

	9. Kt. to Q. B's 3rd.
10. Kt. to B's 2nd.	10. Kt. to K. R's 4th.
11. B. to K. Kt.'s 5th.	11. P. to K. B's 3rd.
12. B. to K's 3rd.	12. Kt. to Kt.'s 6th.
13. B. to Q. B's 4th (ch.)	13. K. to R's sq.
14. R. to K. R's 2nd.	14. P. to K. B's 4th.

Black, I think, has an advantage in position.

Variation A, beginning at White's 6th Move.

BLACK.

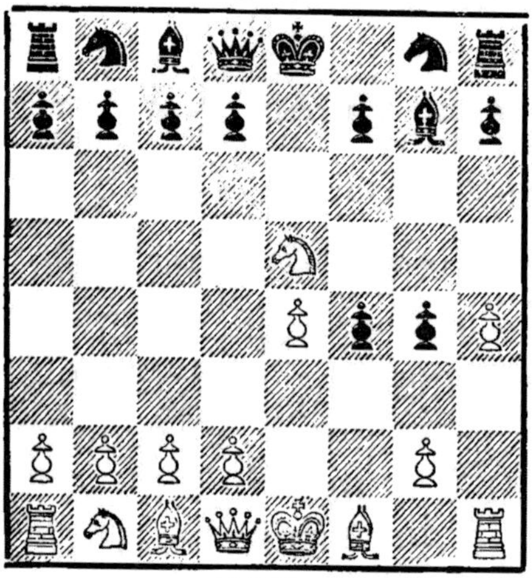

WHITE.

Position prior to White's 6th Move.

6. Kt. takes Kt.'s P.	6. P. to Q's 4th.
7. Kt. to K. B's 2nd.	

If 7. $\frac{\text{Kt. to Q. B's 3rd}}{\text{————}}$, or 7. $\frac{\text{P. to Q's 3rd}}{\text{————}}$, Black can answer

profitably with 7. $\frac{\qquad}{\text{P. takes P.}}$ If 7. $\frac{\text{P. takes P.}}{\text{Q. to K's 2nd (ch.)}}$, 8. $\frac{\text{K. to B's 2nd}}{\text{B. to Q's 5th (ch.)}}$, 9. $\frac{\text{K. to B's 3rd}}{\text{B. takes Kt. (ch.)}}$, 10. $\frac{\text{K. takes B.}}{\text{Kt. to K. B's 3rd (ch.)}}$, with a winning position.

7. Kt. to K's 2nd.

If 7. $\frac{\qquad}{\text{P. takes P.}}$, 8. $\frac{\text{Kt. takes P.}}{\text{Kt. to Q. B's 3rd}}$, 9. $\frac{\text{P. to Q's 3rd}}{\text{Castles}}$, 10. $\frac{\text{Kt. to Q. B's 3rd}}{\text{R. to K's sq.}}$, 11. $\frac{\text{B. to K's 2nd}}{\text{Kt. to Q. B's 3rd}}$, Black has the advantage.

8. P. takes P.

White may also play 8. $\frac{\text{P. to Q's 3rd}}{\qquad}$, but the result should be in favour of his opponent.

	8. Castles.
9. B. to K's 2nd.	9. Kt. to K. B's 4th.
10. Castles.	10. Kt. to Kt.'s 6th.
11. R. to K's sq.	11. B. to Q's 5th.
12. P. to Q. B's 3rd.	12. B. takes Kt. (ch.)
13. K. takes B.	13. Q. takes R's P.

And the position is in Black's favour.

Game the Fourth.

WHITE.	BLACK.
1. P. to K's 4th.	1. P. to K's 4th.
2. P. to K. B's 4th.	2. P. takes P.
3. Kt. to K. B's 3rd.	3. P. to K. Kt.'s 4th.
4. P. to K. R's 4th.	4. P. to K. Kt.'s 5th.
5. Kt. to K's 5th.	5. P. to K. R's 4th.

This move was long considered the best that Black could adopt. It is now in a great measure superseded by 5. $\frac{\qquad}{\text{Kt. to K. B's 3rd}}$, and 5. $\frac{\qquad}{\text{B. to K. Kt.'s 2nd}}$, though it may be played, I think, with perfect security.

6. B. to Q. B's 4th. 6. R. to K. R's 2nd.

He can also play 6. $\frac{\text{Kt. to K. R's 3rd}}{\qquad}$, though not more advantageously. (For example see Variation A.)

7. P. to Q's 4th.

A strong attack may now be got by sacrificing the two minor officers for a Rook and Pawn. *Ex. gr.*, 7. $\frac{\text{Kt. takes B's P.}}{\text{R. takes Kt.}}$, 8. $\frac{\text{B. takes R. (ch.)}}{\text{K. takes R.}}$, 9. $\frac{\text{P. to Q's 4th}}{\text{P. to K. B's 6th}}$, 10. $\frac{\text{P. to K. Kt.'s 3rd}}{\text{P. to Q's 3rd.}}$, 11. $\frac{\text{B. to K. Kt.'s 5th}}{\text{B. to Q's 2nd}}$, but I believe Black can repulse it and have the advantage.

7. P. to Q's 3rd.

8. Kt. to Q's 3rd.

Here again White can give up the Bishop and Knight for Rook and Pawn, and obtain a dashing attack.

8. P. to K. B's 6th.

9. P. takes P.

9. $\frac{\text{P. to K. Kt.'s 3rd}}{\qquad}$ seems equally good.

	9. B. to K's 2nd.
10. B. to K's 3rd.	10. B. takes P. (ch.)
11. K. to Q's 2nd.	11. P. takes P.
12. Q. takes P.	12. B. to K. Kt.'s 5th.
13. Q. to K. B's 4th.	13. Kt. to Q's 2nd.
14. Kt. to Q. B's 3rd.	14. Kt. to Q. Kt.'s 3rd.
15. B. to Q. Kt.'s 3rd.	15. R. to Kt.'s 2nd.
16. P. to K's 5th.	16. B. to Kt.'s 5th.

And there is little advantage on either side.

Variation A, beginning at Black's 6th Move.

BLACK.

WHITE.

Position prior to Black's 6th Move.

	6. Kt. to K. R's 3rd.
7. P. to Q's 4th.	7. P. to Q's 3rd.
8. Kt. to Q's 3rd.	8. P. to K. B's 6th.
9. P. takes P.	

White may also equalise the game by 9. P. to K. Kt.'s 3rd / P. to Q's 4th, 10. P. takes P. / Kt. to K. B's 4th, 11. K. to B's 2nd / B. to K's 2nd, 12. Kt. to K's 5th / —. The game is pretty equal.

	9. B. to K's 2nd.
10. B. to K's 3rd.	

If 10. B. to K. B's 4th / B. takes P. (ch.), 11. K. to Q's 2nd / P. takes P., 12. Q. takes P. / B. to K. Kt.'s 5th, 13. Q. to K's 3rd / —, with a good game.

If 10. $\frac{\text{B. to K. Kt.'s 5th}}{\text{B. takes B.}}$, 11. $\frac{\text{P. takes B.}}{\text{Q. takes P.}}$, 12. $\frac{\text{Q. to Q's 2nd}}{\text{Q. takes Q.}}$,
13. $\frac{\text{Kt. takes Q.}}{\quad}$. Equal game.

	10. B. takes P. (ch.)
11. K. to Q's 2nd.	11. P. takes P.
12. Q. takes P.	12. B. to K. Kt.'s 5th.
13. Q. to K. B's sq.	13. B. to K. Kt.'s 4th.
14. Kt. to K. B's 4th.	

With the better position.

Game the Fifth.

WHITE.	BLACK.
1. P. to K's 4th.	1. P. to K's 4th.
2. P. to K. B's 4th.	2. P. takes P.
3. Kt. to K. B's 3rd.	3. P. to K. Kt.'s 4th.
4. P. to K. R's 4th.	4. P. to K. Kt.'s 5th.
5. Kt. to K's 5th.	5. B. to K's 2nd.

By this step Black gains a momentary advantage, but in the end he is the loser.

6. B. to Q. B's 4th.

Better than taking the King's Knight's Pawn.

	6. B. takes P. (ch.)
7. K. to B's sq.	7. Kt. to K. R's 3rd.

If 7. $\frac{\quad}{\text{P. to Q's 4th}}$, 8. $\frac{\text{B. takes P.}}{\text{Kt. to K. R's 3rd}}$, 9. $\frac{\text{P. to Q's 4th}}{\text{B. to K. Kt.'s 5th}}$,
10. $\frac{\text{P. to K. Kt.'s 3rd}}{\quad}$, White has the superiority.

8. Kt. takes Kt.'s P.	8. Kt. takes Kt.
9. Q. takes Kt.	9. B. to K. Kt.'s 4th.

Preferable to 9. $\frac{\quad}{\text{P. to Q's 4th}}$, because of 10. $\frac{\text{Q. takes P.}}{\text{P. takes B.}}$,
11. $\frac{\text{R. takes B.}}{\quad}$.

10. R. to K. R's 5th.	10. P. to Q's 4th.
11. Q. takes K's B.	11. Q. takes Q.
12. R. takes Q.	12. P. takes B.

White has the better game.

Game the Sixth.

WHITE.	BLACK.
1. P. to K's 4th.	1. P. to K's 4th.
2. P. to K. B's 4th.	2. P. takes P.
3. Kt. to K. B's 3rd.	3. P. to K. Kt.'s 4th.
4. P. to K. R's 4th.	4. P. to K. Kt.'s 5th,
5. Kt. to K's 5th.	5. Kt. to Q. B's 3rd.

A novelty in the defence which is attributed to Mr. Neumann, and which certainly merits regard.

6. P. to Q's 4th.

This is, perhaps, the best rejoinder White can make. He may, however, take the King's Bishop's Pawn with Knight (see Variation A), and make a good fight, I believe. If he exchange Knights the result is unfavourable to him. *Ex.g.*:— 6. $\frac{\text{Kt. takes Kt.}}{\text{Q's P. takes Kt.}}$, 7. $\frac{\text{P. to Q's 4th}}{\text{Kt. to K. B's 3rd}}$, 8. $\frac{\text{Q's B. takes P.}}{\quad}$. (If 8. $\frac{\text{P. to K's 5th}}{\text{Kt. to K. R's 4th}}$, with the better position.) 8. $\frac{\quad}{\text{Kt. takes P.}}$, 9. $\frac{\text{B. to Q's 3rd}}{\text{B. to Q's 3rd}}$. (If 9. $\frac{\quad}{\text{Q. takes Q's P.}}$, 10. $\frac{\text{Q. to K's 2nd}}{\quad}$, and Black must lose something.) 10. $\frac{\text{Q. to Q. B's sq.}}{\quad}$. (If 10. $\frac{\text{B. takes Kt.}}{\text{B. takes B.}}$, Black has the advantage in position. If 10. $\frac{\text{B. takes B.}}{\text{Kt. takes B.}}$, and Black has a Pawn more and the safer situation.) 10. $\frac{\quad}{\text{Kt. to Kt.'s 6th}}$, 11. $\frac{\text{R. to K. R's 2nd}}{\text{Q. to K's 2nd (ch.)}}$, 12. $\frac{\text{K. to Q's sq.}}{\text{B. to K. B's 4th}}$, 13. $\frac{\text{Kt. to Q. B's 3rd}}{\text{Castles, Q's side}}$, with a winning superiority.

	6. Q. to K's 2nd.*
7. Kt. to Q. B's 3rd.	7. Kt. takes Kt.
8. Kt. to Q's 5th.	8. Q. to Q's 3rd.
9. P. takes Kt.	9. Q. takes P.
10. Q's B. takes P.	10. Q. takes K's P. (ch.)
11. Q. to K's 2nd.	11. Q. takes Q. (ch.)
12. B. takes Q.	

And White has a great advantage in situation.

Variation A, beginning at White's 6th Move.

BLACK

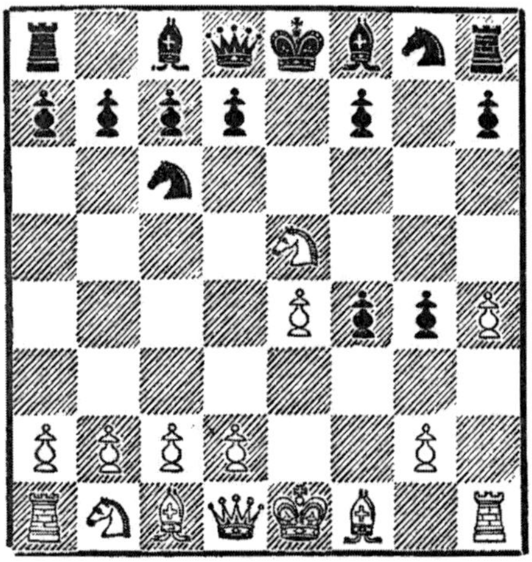

WHITE.

Position prior to White's 6th move.

* This is now acknowledged to be inferior to 6. $\frac{}{\text{Kt. takes Kt.}}$, which the *Handbuch* continues:—6. $\frac{}{\text{Kt. takes Kt.}}$, 7. $\frac{\text{P. takes Kt.}}{\text{P. to Q's 3rd}}$, 8. $\frac{\text{Q's B. takes P.}}{\text{B. to K. Kt.'s 2nd}}$, 9. $\frac{\text{B. to Q. B's 4th}}{\text{Q. to K's 2nd}}$, 10. $\frac{\text{Kt to Q. B's 3rd}}{\text{P. takes P.}}$, and the advantage is with Black. On account of this variation 6. $\frac{\text{Kt. takes Kt.}}{}$ is now generally preferred for White to 6. $\frac{\text{P. to Q's 4th}}{}$, given as best in the text.—[Ed.]

6. Kt. takes K. B's P.	6. K. takes Kt.
7. B. to Q. B's 4th (ch.)	7. P. to Q's 4th.
8. B. takes P. (ch.)	8. K. to K's sq.
9. P. to Q's 3rd.	9. K's Kt. to K's 2nd.

Here again Black can play the move noticed above of 9. $\overline{\text{P. to K. B's 6th}}$ with the same continuation we have just given, but the move in the text seems stronger.

10. B. takes Q's Kt. (ch.)	10. Kt. takes B. (ch.)
11. Q.'s B. takes P.	

And now having *deroquer* the adverse King, and gained two Pawns for his Knight, White has no disadvantage.

ILLUSTRATIVE GAMES.

GAME I.—Between Messrs. G. A. Macdonnell and Bird.

WHITE (Mr. M.)	BLACK (Mr. B.)
1. P. to K's 4th.	1. P. to K's 4th.
2. P. to K. B's 4th.	2. P. takes P.
3. Kt. to K. B's 3rd.	3. P. to K. Kt's 4th.
4. P. to K. R's 4th.	4. P. to Kt.'s 5th.
5. Kt. to K's 5th.	5. P. to K. R's 4th.
6. B. to Q. B's 4th.	6. Kt. to K. R's 3rd.
7. P. to Q's 4th.	7. P. to Q's 3rd.
8. Kt. to Q's 3rd.	8. P. to B's 6th.
9. P. takes P.	9. B. to K's 2nd.
10. B. to K's 3rd.*	10. B. takes R's P. (ch.)
11. K. to Q's 2nd.	11. P. takes P.
12. Q. takes P.	12. B. to K. Kt.'s 5th.
13. Q. to K. B's 4th.	13. Kt. to Q. B's 3rd.
14. Kt. to Q. B's 3rd.	14. Kt. takes Q's P.
15. B. takes Kt.†	15. B. to K. Kt.'s 4th.

* Black may also play B. to K. B's 4th at this point.

† Very well conceived. White obtains a Rook and two minor pieces, with a superior position, in exchange for the Queen.

16. B. takes R.	16. B. takes Q. (ch.)
17. Kt. takes B.	17. Q. to K. Kt.'s 4th.*
18. Kt. to Q's 5th.	18. Kt. to Kt.'s sq.
19. Q's R. to K. Kt.'s sq.	19. Q. to K. R's 3rd.
20. R. takes B.	20. Q. takes B.
21. R. takes Kt. (ch.)	

And Black resigned.

GAME II.—Between Messrs. Steinitz and Deacon.

White (Mr. S.)	Black (Mr. D.)
1. P. to K's 4th.	1. P. to K's 4th.
2. P. to K. B's 4th.	2. P. takes P.
3. Kt. to K. B's 3rd.	3. P. to K. Kt.'s 4th.
4. P. to K. R's 4th.	4. P. to Kt.'s 5th.
5. Kt. to K's 5th.	5. Kt. to K. B's 3rd.
6. B. to Q. B's 4th.	6. P. to Q's 4th.
7. P. takes P.	7. B. to Q's 3rd.†
8. P. to Q's 4th.	8. Kt. to R's 4th.
9. Kt. to Q. B's 3rd.	9. Q. to K's 2nd.
10. B. to Q. Kt.'s 5th (ch.)	10. P. to Q. B's 3rd.
11. P. takes P.	11. P. takes P.
12. Kt. to Q's 5th.	12. Q. to K's 3rd.‡
13. Kt. to B's 7th (ch.)	13. B. takes Kt.
14. B. to Q. B's 4th.	14. Q. to K's 2nd.
15. B. takes K. B's P. (ch.)	15. K. to B's sq.§
16. B. takes Kt.	16. B. takes Kt.
17. P. takes B.	17. Q. takes K's P. (ch.)
18. Q. to K's 2nd.	18. Q. takes B.
19. B. takes K. B's P.	19. B. to K. B's 4th.
20. Castles (K's R.)	20. Kt. to Q's 2nd.
21. B. to K. R's 6th (ch.)	21. K. to B's 2nd.

* He ought to have played P. to Q. B's 3rd. It was all important to prevent the adverse Knight from coming into the game.

† The usual move, but decidedly inferior to B. to K. Kt.'s 2nd.

‡ Possibly 12. Q. to Q's sq. would have been slightly preferable.

§ At this point the German *Handbuch* makes Black play 15. Q. takes B. and dismisses the game in favour of the second player. This, we think, requires a little more demonstration.

22. R. takes B. (ch.)	22. Q. takes R.
23. R. to K. B's sq.	23. Q. takes R. (ch.)
24. Q. takes Q. (ch.)	24. K. to Kt.'s 3rd.
25. B. to K. Kt.'s 5th.	25. P. to K. R's 3rd.
26. Q. to Q's 3rd (ch.)	26. Resigns.

GAME III.—Between Messrs. Blackburne and Zukertort.

White (Mr. B.)	Black (Mr. Z.)
1. P. to K's 4th.	1. P. to K's 4th.
2. P. to K. B's 4th.	2. P. takes P.
3. Kt. to K. B's 3rd.	3. P. to K. Kt.'s 4th.
4. P. to K. R's 4th.	4. P. to Kt.'s 5th.
5. Kt. to K's 5th.	5. B. to Kt.'s 2nd.
6. P. to Q's 4th.	6. Kt. to K. B's 3rd.
7. B. to Q. B's 4th.	7. P. to Q's 4th.*
8. P. takes P.	8. Castles.
9. Kt. to Q. B's 3rd.†	9. P. to Q. B's 4th.
10. P. takes P. (*en pas.*)	10. Q's Kt. takes P.
11. Kt. takes Kt.	11. P. takes Kt.
12. Q's B. takes P.	12. Kt. to K. R's 4th.
13. B. to K's 5th.	13. B. takes B.
14. P. takes B.	14. Q. to Kt.'s 3rd.
15. Q. to Q's 2nd.	15. Q. to Q. B's 4th.
16. Q. to Kt.'s 5th (ch.)	16. Kt. to Kt.'s 2nd.
17. B. to Q's 3rd.	17. R. to K's sq.
18. Castles (Q's R.)	18. R. takes P.
19. Q. to R's 6th.	19. B. to B's 4th.
20. B. takes B.	20. R. takes B.
21. Kt. to K's 4th.	21. Q. to K's 4th.
22. K's R. to K's sq.	22. R. to Kt.'s sq.
23. Kt. to Q. B's 3rd.	23. Q. to B's 2nd.
24. Q. to Q's 6th.	24. Q. to Q. Kt.'s 2nd.
25. P. to Q. Kt.'s 3rd.	25. Kt. to K's 3rd.
26. Kt. to K's 4th.	26. Q. to Q. Kt.'s 5th.
27. R. to B's sq.	27. R. to Q. R's 4th.
28. Kt. to B's 6th (ch.)	28. K. to R's sq.

* Inferior, we think, to Castling at once.

† White might also have played Q's B. takes P., with advantage.

29. Kt. to Q's 7th.	29. Q. takes Q.
30. R. takes Q.	30. R. to Kt.'s 2nd.
31. R. takes K. B's P.	31. Kt. to Q. B's 4th.
32. Q's R. takes B's P.*	32. K. to Kt.'s sq.
33. R. to K's 7th.	33. Kt. takes Kt.
34. R. to B's 8th (ch.)	34. Kt. to B's sq.
35. R. takes R.	35. R. takes P.
36. K. to Q's 2nd.	36. R. to R's 8th.
37. K. to K's 2nd.	37. R. to R's 3rd.
38. K. to K's 3rd.	38. P. to K. R's 4th.
39. K. to K's 4th.	39. R. to K. B's 3rd.

40. R. takes R's P., and wins.

---

* He might also have won by P. to Q. Kt.'s 4th.

CHAPTER XVII.

Cunningham Gambit.

1. $\frac{\text{P. to K's 4th}}{\text{P. to K's 4th}}$, 2. $\frac{\text{P. to K. B's 4th}}{\text{P. takes P.}}$, 3. $\frac{\text{Kt. to K. B's 3rd}}{\text{B. to K's 2nd}}$,

4. $\frac{\text{B. to Q. B's 4th}}{\text{B. to K. R's 5th (ch.)}}$.

Game the First.

5. $\frac{\text{K. to B's sq.}}{}$.

Game the Second.

5. $\frac{\text{P. to K. Kt.'s 3rd}}{}$.

This lively counter attack is found in Cozio, but the credit of bringing it into vogue is due to Mr. Cunningham, a player of considerable eminence towards the end of last century. It is highly ingenious, and productive of many brilliant manœuvres. I cannot, however, recommend it as a trustworthy defence.

Game the First.

WHITE.	BLACK.
1. P. to K's 4th.	1. P. to K's 4th.
2. P. to K. B's 4th.	2. P. takes P.
3. Kt. to K. B's 3rd.	3. B. to K's 2nd.

This move of Black it is which constitutes the novelty of the defence. Instead of maintaining the Gambit Pawn, he endeavours to establish a counter attack, which compels his opponent to look at home.

4. B. to Q. B's 4th.	4. B. to K. R's 5th.
5. K. to B's sq.	

The authorities concur in pronouncing this to be White's best move. He may, however, play, as in the next game, 5. $\frac{\text{P. to K. Kt.'s 3rd}}{\quad}$, if a strong player, without absolute loss, and the variations arising from that course of action are remarkably amusing.

	5. B. to K. B's 3rd.

Black has here three feasible moves, beside the move in the text; namely, 5. $\frac{\quad}{\text{Kt. to K. R's 3rd}}$, 5. $\frac{\quad}{\text{P. to Q's 3rd}}$, and 5. $\frac{\quad}{\text{B. to K. Kt.'s 4th}}$, the result of which may as well be shown at once. In the first place, then, suppose:— 5. $\frac{\quad}{\text{Kt. to K. R's 3rd}}$, 6. $\frac{\text{P. to Q's 4th}}{\text{Kt. to K. Kt.'s 5th}}$, 7. $\frac{\text{Q. to K's 2nd}}{\text{Kt. to K. B's 7th}}$, 8. $\frac{\text{Kt. takes B.}}{\text{Kt. takes R.}}$, 9. $\frac{\text{Kt. to K. B's 3rd}}{\text{Kt. to Kt.'s 6th (ch.)}}$, 10. $\frac{\text{P. takes Kt.}}{\text{P. takes P.}}$, 11. $\frac{\text{B. to K. B's 4th}}{\quad}$. White has the advantage. In the second place, 5. $\frac{\quad}{\text{P. to Q's 3rd}}$, 6. $\frac{\text{P. to Q's 4th}}{\text{Q. to K. B's 3rd}}$, 7. $\frac{\text{P. to K's 5th}}{\text{P. takes P.}}$, 8. $\frac{\text{P. takes P.}}{\text{Q. to K's 2nd}}$, 9. $\frac{\text{Q's B. takes P.}}{\text{B. to K. Kt.'s 5th}}$, 10. $\frac{\text{Kt. to Q. B's 3rd}}{\text{P. to Q. B's 3rd}}$. 11. $\frac{\text{Kt. to K's 4th}}{\quad}$. White has still the better opening. In the third place, 5. $\frac{\quad}{\text{B. to K. Kt.'s 4th}}$, 6. $\frac{\text{P. to Q's 4th}}{\text{P. to Q's 3rd}}$, 7. $\frac{\text{Kt. takes B.}}{\text{Q. takes Kt.}}$, 8. $\frac{\text{Q. to K. B's 3rd}}{\quad}$, with the advantage of position. (For the consequences of 5. $\frac{\quad}{\text{P. to Q's 4th}}$, see Illustrative Game No. II.)

6. P. to K's 5th.	6. B. to K's 2nd.
7. P. to Q's 4th.	7. P. to Q's 4th.
8. B. to K's 2nd.	8. P. to K. Kt.'s 4th.*
9. P. to K. R's 4th.	9. P. to K. Kt.'s 5th.
10. Kt. to K. R's 2nd.	10. P. to K. R's 4th.

If 10. $\frac{\qquad}{\text{P. to K. B's 6th}}$, 11. $\frac{\text{P. takes P.}}{\text{P. to K. Kt.'s 6th}}$, 12. $\frac{\text{Kt. to Kt.'s 4th}}{\text{B. takes P.}}$,

13. $\frac{\text{Kt. to Q. B's 3rd}}{\qquad}$, I prefer the first player's game.

11. Q's B. takes P.	11. B. takes K. R's P.
12. P. to K. Kt.'s 3rd.	12. B. to K. Kt.'s 4th.
13. Kt. takes P.	

White for choice.

Game the Second.

WHITE.	BLACK.
1. P. to K's 4th.	1. P. to K's 4th.
2. P. to K. B's 4th.	2. P. takes P.
3. Kt. to K. B's 3rd.	3. B. to K's 2nd.
4. B. to Q. B's 4th.	4. B. to K. R's 5th (ch.)
5. P. to K. Kt.'s 3rd.	

By this step White lays himself open to the full force of the counter attack. However, I should recommend an inexperienced player to adopt the safer move of 5. $\frac{\text{K. to B's sq.}}{\qquad}$, or even 5. $\frac{\text{K. to K's 2nd}}{\qquad}$, which I have often played successfully.

---

* Nearly all the authorities give this as Black's best move, but 8. $\frac{\qquad}{\text{P. to Q. B's 4th}}$ is unquestionably superior. If White in reply play 9. $\frac{\text{P. to Q. B's 3rd (best)}}{\qquad}$, or 9. $\frac{\text{B. takes P.}}{\qquad}$, Black equally answers with 9. $\frac{\qquad}{\text{Q. to Q. Kt.'s 3rd}}$, and the first player has no very marked superiority.—[Ed.]

	5. P. takes P.
6. Castles.	6. P. takes P. (ch.)
7. K. to R's sq.	7. P. to Q's 4th.

BLACK.

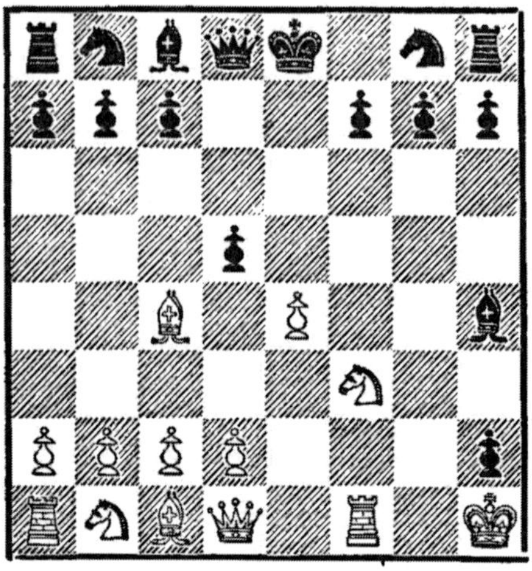

WHITE.

This is a very noticeable position. Black's best move is the move in the text. He may play, however, 7. $\frac{}{\text{B. to K. B's 3rd}}$, for which see Variation A, or 7. $\frac{}{\text{Kt. to K. R's 3rd}}$, or 7. $\frac{}{\text{B. to K's 2nd}}$, or 7. $\frac{}{\text{Q. to K's 2nd}}$, the consequences of which shall be given in Variations B and C.

8. B. takes P.

If 8. $\frac{\text{P. takes P.}}{\text{B. to K. B's 3rd}}$, 9. $\frac{\text{Kt. to K's 5th}}{\text{B. takes Kt.}}$, 10. $\frac{\text{R. to K's sq.}}{\text{Kt. to K's 2nd}}$ 11. $\frac{\text{R. takes B.}}{\text{Castles}}$, Black has the better position.

	8. Kt. to K. B's 3rd.
9. B. takes B's P. (ch.)	

If 9. $\frac{\text{B. to Q. Kt.'s 3rd}}{\text{Kt. takes P.}}$, 10. $\frac{\text{Q. to K's 2nd}}{\text{Q. to K's 2nd}}$, 11. $\frac{\text{B. takes P. (ch.)}}{\text{K. to B's sq.}}$,

12. $\frac{\text{Q. takes P.}}{\text{Kt. to Kt.'s 6th (ch.)}}$, White has an inferior game. So also if 9. $\frac{\text{Kt. takes B.}}{\text{Kt. takes B.}}$, 10. $\frac{\text{P. takes Kt.}}{\text{Q. takes Kt.}}$, 11. $\frac{\text{Q. to K's 2nd (ch.)}}{\text{K. to Q's sq.}}$, Black ought to win.

9. K. takes B.

10. Kt. takes B. — 10. R. to K. B's sq.

11. P. to Q's 3rd.

If 11. $\frac{\text{P. to K's 5th}}{\text{Q. to Q's 4th (ch.)}}$, 12. $\frac{\text{Kt. to K. B's 3rd}}{}$ (taking the Pawn with the King would be very hazardous), 12. $\frac{}{\text{Kt. to K. R's 4th}}$, 13. $\frac{\text{P. to Q. B's 4th}}{\text{Q. to Q. B's 3rd}}$, 14. $\frac{\text{K. takes P.}}{\text{Kt. to K. B's 5th}}$, White has a bad game.

11. P. to K. R's 3rd, or K. to Kt.'s sq.

And Black has a safer game.

Variation A, beginning at Black's 7th Move.

7. B. to K. B's 3rd.

It should be mentioned here that Black will not improve his situation by playing 7. $\frac{}{\text{B. to K. Kt.'s 6th}}$, because of 8. $\frac{\text{Kt. to K's 5th}}{\text{B. takes Kt.}}$, 9. $\frac{\text{Q. to K. R's 5th}}{}$, &c.

8. P. to K's 5th.

White can also play 8. $\frac{\text{Kt. to K's 5th}}{}$, when the probable continuation would be 8. $\frac{}{\text{B. takes Kt.}}$, 9. $\frac{\text{Q. to K. R's 5th}}{\text{Q. to K's 2nd}}$, 10. $\frac{\text{R. takes P.}}{\text{Q. to Q. B's 4th}}$, 11. $\frac{\text{R. to B's 8th (double ch.)}}{\text{K. to K's 2nd}}$,

12. $\frac{\text{P. to Q's 4th}}{\text{Q. takes B.*}}$, 13. $\frac{\text{Q. to K's 8th (ch.)}}{\text{K. to Q's 3rd}}$, 14. $\frac{\text{Q. takes B. (ch.)}}{\text{K. to Q. R's 3rd}}$, 15. $\frac{\text{Kt. to Q. B's 3rd}}{\text{P. to Q's 3rd}}$, 16. $\frac{\text{Kt. takes Q.}}{\text{P. takes Q.}}$, 17. $\frac{\text{Kt. takes P. (ch)}}{}$, followed by 18. $\frac{\text{R. takes B.}}{}$, &c.

	8. P. to Q's 4th.
9. P. takes B.	9. Kt. takes P.
10. B. to Q. Kt.'s 3rd.	10. B. to K's 3rd.
11. P. to Q's 4th.	11. Kt. to K's 5th.
12. B. to K. B's 4th.	12. P. to K. B's 4th.
13. Q's Kt. to Q's 2nd.	

I prefer White's game.

Variation B, beginning at Black's 7th Move.

	7. Kt. to K. R's 3rd.
8. P. to Q's 4th.	8. P. to Q's 4th.

If 8. $\frac{}{\text{Castles}}$, 9. $\frac{\text{B. takes Kt.}}{\text{P. takes B.}}$, 10. $\frac{\text{Kt. to K's 5th}}{\text{P. to Q's 4th}}$, White has the better game.

9. B. takes Kt.	9. Q's P. takes K's B.
10. Kt. to K's 5th.	10. P. takes B.
11. Kt. takes K. B's P.	11. Q. to K's 2nd.
12. Kt. takes R.	12. Q. takes P. (ch.)
13. K. takes P.	13. B. to K. Kt.'s 5th.
14. Kt. to Q. B's 3rd.	14. Q. to K's 3rd.

---

* This is not so good as 12. $\frac{}{\text{Q. takes P.}}$ which would probably be continued as under:—12. $\frac{}{\text{Q. takes P.}}$, 13. $\frac{\text{B. to Kt.'s 5th (ch.)}}{\text{K. to Q's 3rd (best)}}$, 14. $\frac{\text{Kt. to Q's 2nd}}{\text{Kt. to K. B's 3rd}}$, 15. $\frac{\text{Q. to B's 7th}}{\text{Kt. takes K's P.}}$, 16. $\frac{\text{B. to K's 3rd}}{\text{K's Kt. to K's 6th (ch.)}}$, 17. $\frac{\text{K. to Kt.'s 2nd}}{\text{Q. takes B.}}$, and White can draw by perpetual check.

15. Q. to Q's 2nd.	15. B. to K. Kt.'s 4th.
16. Q. to K. B's 2nd.	

With the superior position.

VARIATION C, BEGINNING AT BLACK'S 7TH MOVE.

	7. B. to K's 2nd.

If 7. $\frac{\quad}{\text{Q. to K's 2nd}}$, 8. $\frac{\text{Kt. to Q. B's 3rd}}{\text{P. to Q. B's 3rd}}$, 9. $\frac{\text{P. to Q's 4th}}{\text{P. to Q's 3rd}}$, 10. $\frac{\text{Kt. takes B.}}{\text{Q. takes Kt.}}$, 11. $\frac{\text{B. takes P. (ch.)}}{\text{K. to Q's sq.}}$, 12. $\frac{\text{Q. to K. B's 3rd}}{\text{Kt. to K. B's 3rd}}$, 13. $\frac{\text{P. to K's 5th}}{\quad}$. White's position is more than an equivalent for his deficiency in Pawns.

8. B. takes P. (ch.)	8. K. to B's sq.

If 8. $\frac{\quad}{\text{K. takes B.}}$, 9. $\frac{\text{Kt. to K's 5th (double ch.)}}{\text{K. to K's sq. (best)}}$, 10. $\frac{\text{Q. to K. R's 5th (ch.)}}{\text{P. to K. Kt.'s 3rd}}$, 11. $\frac{\text{Kt. takes P.}}{\text{Kt. to K. B's 3rd}}$, 12. $\frac{\text{R. takes Kt.}}{\text{B. takes R.}}$, 13. $\frac{\text{Kt. to K's 5th (dis. ch.)}}{\text{K. to K's 2nd}}$, 14. $\frac{\text{Q. to B's 7th (ch.)}}{\text{K. to Q's 3rd}}$, 15. $\frac{\text{Kt. to Q. B's 4th (ch.)}}{\quad}$, and White wins.

9. Kt. to K's 5th.	9. Kt. to K. B's 3rd.
10. B. to Q. Kt.'s 3rd.	10. Q. to K's sq.
11. Kt. to B's 7th.	11. R. to K. Kt.'s sq.
12. P. to K's 5th.	12. P. to Q's 4th.
13. P. takes Kt.	13. P. takes P.
14. B. takes Q's P.	

And White has the better game.

ILLUSTRATIVE GAMES.

GAME I.—Between Messrs. Wisker and Bird.

WHITE (Mr. W.)	BLACK (Mr. B.)
1. P. to K's 4th.	1. P. to K's 4th.
2. P. to K. B's 4th.	2. P. takes P.
3. Kt. to K. B's 3rd.	3. B. to K's 2nd.
4. B. to Q. B's 4th.	4. B. to R's 5th (ch.)
5. K. to B's sq.	5. P. to Q's 3rd.*
6. P. to Q's 4th.	6. B. to K. Kt.'s 5th.†
7. Q's B. takes P.‡	7. Q. to K. B's 3rd.
8. B. to K's 3rd.	8. Kt. to Q. B's 3rd.
9. Kt. to Q. B's 3rd.	9. K's Kt. to K's 2nd.
10. B. to K's 2nd.	10. B. takes Kt.
11. P. takes B.	11. Castles (Q's R.)
12. R. to K. Kt.'s sq.	12. P. to Q's 4th.
13. P. to K's 5th.	13. Q. to K's 3rd.
14. K. to Kt.'s 2nd.§	14. Kt. to K. B's 4th.
15. Q. to Q's 2nd.	15. P. to K. B's 3rd.
16. P. to K. B's 4th.	16. P. to K. R's 4th.
17. B. to K. B's 3rd.	17. P. to K. Kt.'s 4th.
18. P. takes Kt.'s P.	18. P. takes Kt.'s P.
19. K. to R's sq.	19. P. to Kt.'s 5th.
20. B. to K. Kt.'s 2nd.	20. B. to K's 2nd.
21. Kt. to K's 2nd.	21. P. to K. R's 5th.
22. P. to Q. Kt.'s 4th.‖	22. Kt. to Kt.'s 6th (ch.)

And White resigned.

---

* The strongest move for the defence in the opinion of the authors of *Théorie und Praxis*.

† The *Handbuch* gives 6. $\frac{\quad}{\text{Q. to K. B's 3rd}}$, and ultimately dismisses the game in favour of the opening player.

‡ This was an error. He ought to have played 7. $\frac{\text{Kt. to Q. B's 3rd}}{\quad}$, which would have left White with a slight advantage.

§ Very well played.

‖ Seemingly a miscalculation. His best move is probably 22. $\frac{\text{Kt. to K. B's 4th}}{\quad}$.

GAME II.—Between Messrs Macdonnell and Bird.

WHITE (Mr. M.)	BLACK (Mr. B.)
1. P. to K's 4th.	1. P. to K's 4th.
2. P. to K. B's 4th.	2. P. takes P.
3. Kt. to K. B's 3rd.	3. B. to K's 2nd.
4. B. to Q. B's 4th.	4. B. to R's 5th (ch.)
5. K. to B's sq.	5. P. to Q's 4th.*
6. B. takes P.	6. Kt. to K. B's 3rd.
7. Kt. to Q. B's 3rd.	7. Castles.
8. Kt. takes B.†	8. Kt. takes B.
9. Kt. takes Kt.	9. Q. takes Kt.
10. Kt. takes Q. B's P.	10. Kt. to Q. B's 3rd.
11. Kt. takes R.	11. Kt. to Q's 5th.
12. P. to Q's 3rd.‡	12. P. to B's 6th.
13. P. to K. Kt.'s 3rd.	13. Q. to R's 6th (ch.)
14. K. to B's 2nd.	14. Q. to Kt.'s 7th (ch.)
15. K. to K's 3rd.	15. Kt. takes B's P. (ch.)
16. K. to B's 4th.	16. P. to K. B's 4th.
17. P. to K's 5th.	17. P. to K. R's 3rd.
18. P. to K. R's 4th.	18. P. to K. Kt.'s 4th (ch.)
19. P. takes P.	19. P. takes P. (ch.)
20. K. takes P.	20. Q. takes P. (ch.)
21. K. to R's 5th.	21. Q. to Kt.'s 5th (ch.)
22. K. to R's 6th.	22. K. to R's 2nd.

And White resigned.

---

* This move, we are inclined to think, is as strong as anything else on the board.

† An error, from the effects of which White never recovers, but the temptation of winning the Rook seemingly blinded him to the consequences. Mr. Macdonnell ought to have played 3. Q. to Q. Kt.'s 3rd.

‡ Had he played 12. P. to Q. B's 3rd, Black would have won at once by B. to K. Kt.'s 5th.

CHAPTER XVIII.

KING'S GAMBIT REFUSED.

$$1.\ \frac{\text{P. to K's 4th}}{\text{P. to K's 4th}},\ 2.\ \frac{\text{P. to K. B's 4th}}{\qquad}.$$

GAME THE FIRST.

$$2.\ \frac{\qquad}{\text{B. to Q. B's 4th}}.$$

GAME THE SECOND.

$$2.\ \frac{\qquad}{\text{P. to Q's 4th}}.$$

GAME THE THIRD.

$$2.\ \frac{\qquad}{\text{P. to Q's 3rd}}.$$

As a rule it is good for the second player to accept the Gambit Pawn. Such games are more entertaining, the combinations being more critical, and they are usually more instructive than the refused Gambits. When, however, the second player has reasons to decline the Pawn, he can do so with perfect safety and, many authorities think, with advantage. The most feasible ways of declining the Gambit are by playing $2.\ \frac{\qquad}{\text{B. to Q. B's 4th}}$, or $2.\ \frac{\qquad}{\text{P. to Q's 4th}}$; but $2.\ \frac{\qquad}{\text{P. to Q's 3rd}}$, $2.\ \frac{\qquad}{\text{Q. to K. B's 3rd}}$, and $2.\ \frac{\qquad}{\text{Q. to K. R's 5th (ch.)}}$, may also be played.

GAME THE FIRST.

WHITE.	BLACK.
1. P. to K's 4th.	1. P. to K's 4th.
2. P. to K. B's 4th.	2. B. to Q. B's 4th.

An embarrassing move for White, because it retards his Castling on the King's side for some time, and thus keeps him in a manner on the defence.

3. Kt. to K. B's 3rd.

This is considered White's best reply.

3. P. to Q's 3rd.

The result of 3. $\frac{}{\text{P. to Q's 4th}}$ shall be shown in Variation A. That of 3. $\frac{}{\text{Kt. to Q. B's 3rd}}$, which is not so beneficial, may be examined at once. Suppose, then, 3. $\frac{}{\text{Kt. to Q. B's 3rd}}$, 4. $\frac{\text{P. takes P.}}{}$ (He may play 4. $\frac{\text{B. to Q. Kt.'s 5th}}{}$ advantageously also.) 4. $\frac{}{\text{Kt. takes P.}}$, 5. $\frac{\text{Kt. takes Kt.}}{\text{Q. to K. R's 5th (ch)}}$, 6. $\frac{\text{P. to K. Kt.'s 3rd}}{\text{Q. takes K's P. (ch.)}}$, 7. $\frac{\text{Q. to K's 2nd}}{\text{Q. takes R.}}$, 8. $\frac{\text{P. to Q's 4th}}{\text{B. to K's 2nd}}$, 9. $\frac{\text{Kt. to K. B's 3rd}}{\text{P. to Q's 3rd}}$, 10. $\frac{\text{B. to K's 3rd}}{\text{B. to K. Kt.'s 5th}}$, 11. $\frac{\text{Q's Kt. to Q's 2nd}}{}$. There can be no doubt that White has the better game.

4. P. to Q. B's 3rd.

For the effect of 4. $\frac{\text{B. to Q. B's 4th}}{}$, and 4. $\frac{\text{P. to Q. Kt.'s 4th}}{}$, see Variation B If 4. $\frac{\text{P. to Q's 4th}}{\text{P. takes P.}}$, 5. $\frac{\text{Kt. takes P.}}{\text{Kt. to K. B's 3rd}}$, 6. $\frac{\text{Kt. to Q. B's 3rd}}{\text{B. to K. Kt.'s 5th}}$, 7. $\frac{\text{B. to K's 2nd}}{\text{B. takes Kt.}}$, 8. $\frac{\text{Q. takes B.}}{\text{B. takes B.}}$, 9. $\frac{\text{Kt. takes B.}}{\text{Q. to K's 2nd}}$, 10. $\frac{\text{Kt. to Q. B's 3rd}}{\text{Kt. to Q. B's 3rd}}$, Black has the superior position.

4. B. to K. Kt.'s 5th.

Better than 4. $\frac{}{\text{Q. to K's 2nd}}$, because of 5. $\frac{\text{P. to Q's 4th}}{\text{K's P. takes Q's P.}}$, 6. $\frac{\text{P. takes P.}}{\text{Q. takes P. (ch.)}}$, 7. $\frac{\text{K. to B's 2nd}}{\text{B. to Q. Kt.'s 5th}}$, 8. $\frac{\text{P. to Q. R's 3rd}}{\text{B. to Q. R's 4th}}$, 9. $\frac{\text{P. to Q. Kt.'s 4th}}{\text{B. to Kt.'s 3rd}}$, 10. $\frac{\text{B. to Q. Kt.'s 5th (ch.)}}{}$, followed by 11. $\frac{\text{R. to K's sq.}}{}$, &c. And also better than 4. $\frac{}{\text{P. to K.B's 4th}}$, because of 5. $\frac{\text{K's P. takes P}}{\text{Q's B. takes P.}}$, 6. $\frac{\text{P. takes P.}}{\text{P. takes P.}}$, 7. $\frac{\text{Q. to K's 2nd}}{\text{P. to K's 5th}}$, 8. $\frac{\text{P. to Q's 4th}}{}$, &c.

According to the *Handbuch*, Black may equalise the game by playing 4. $\frac{}{\text{Kt. to K. B's 3rd}}$. We will consider this in Variation C.

5. B. to K's 2nd.

Better than 5. $\frac{\text{P. to Q's 4th}}{}$, because of 5. $\frac{}{\text{P. takes Q's P.}}$, 6. $\frac{\text{P. takes P.}}{\text{B. takes Kt.}}$, and White has certainly no advantage.

	5. B. takes Kt.
6. B. takes B.	6. Kt. to Q. B's 3rd.
7. P. to Q. Kt.'s 4th.	7. B. to Q. Kt.'s 3rd.
8. P. to Q. Kt.'s 5th.	8. Q's Kt. to K's 2nd.
9. P. to Q's 4th.	9. P. takes Q's P.
10. P. takes P.	10. P. to Q. R's 3rd.
11. P. takes P.	11. R. takes P.
12. B. to K's 2nd.	12. R. to Q. R's 2nd.

White has the freer position.

VARIATION A, BEGINNING AT BLACK'S 3RD MOVE.

BLACK.

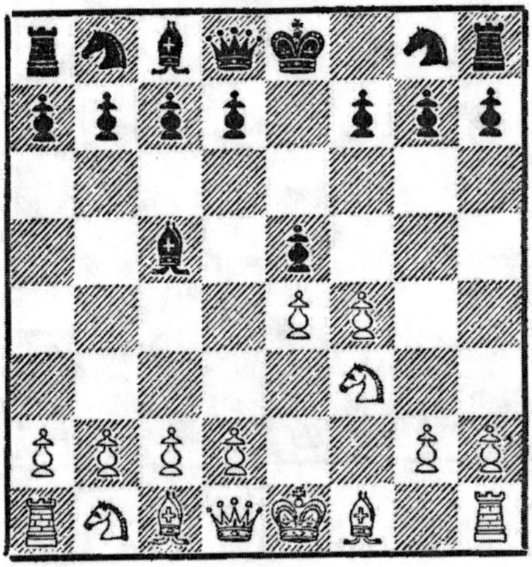

WHITE.

Position prior to Black's 3rd Move.

WHITE.	BLACK.
	3. P. to Q's 4th.
4. K's P. takes P.	4. P. to K's 5th.
5. P. to Q's 4th.	5. P. takes Kt.
6. P. takes B.	6. Q. to K's 2nd (ch.)
7. K. to B's 2nd.	7. P. takes P.
8. B. to Q. Kt.'s 5th (ch.)	8. K. to B's sq.
9. K. takes P.	9. Q. takes P.
10. Kt. to Q. B's 3rd.	10. Kt. to K. B's 3rd.
11. R. to K's sq.	11. B. to K. B's 4th.

The game is about equal.

Variation B, beginning at White's 4th Move.

BLACK.

WHITE.

Position prior to White's 4th Move.

In the first place :—

4. B. to Q. B's 4th.	4. Kt. to K. B's 3rd.

If 4. $\frac{\quad}{\text{B. to K. Kt.'s 5th}}$, 5. $\frac{\text{P. takes P.}}{\text{P. takes P.}}$, 6. $\frac{\text{B. takes P. (ch.)}}{\text{K. takes B.}}$, 7. $\frac{\text{Kt. takes P. (ch.)}}{\quad}$, with an undoubted advantage.

5. P. to Q's 3rd (best).	5. B. to K. Kt.'s 5th.
6. P. to Q. B's 3rd.	6. Kt. to Q. B's 3rd.
7. Q. to K's 2nd.	7. Q. to K's 2nd.
8. B. to K's 3rd.	8. B. takes B.
9. Q. takes B.	9. P. takes P.
10. Q. takes B's P.	10. B. takes Kt.
11. Q. takes B.	

The German *Handbuch* dismisses the game here as equal. But if—

	11. Kt. to K's 4th.
12. Q. to K's 2nd (best).	12. Kt. takes B.
13. P. takes Kt.	13. Q. takes P.

Black has won a Pawn, and his position is superior in strength.

In the second place :—

4. P. to Q. Kt.'s 4th.	4. B. takes P.
5. P. to Q. B's 3rd.	5. B. to Q. B's 4th.
6. B. to Q. B's 4th.	6. Kt. to Q. B's 3rd.
7. P. to Q's 4th.	7. P. takes Q's P.
8. P. takes P.	8. B. to Q. Kt.'s 3rd.
9. Castles.	9. B. to K. Kt.'s 5th.
10. B. to Q. Kt.'s 2nd.	10. B. takes Kt.
11. R. takes B.	11. Kt. to K. B's 3rd.
12. K. to R's sq.	12. Castles.

If 12. $\frac{\quad}{\text{Kt. takes K's P.}}$, 13. $\frac{\text{P. to Q's 5th}}{\quad}$, &c.

13. P. to Q's 5th.	13. Kt. to Q. R's 4th.
14. B. to Q's 3rd.	14. Kt. to K. Kt.'s 5th.
15. Q. to K's sq.	15. P. to K. B's 3rd.
16. Kt. to Q's 2nd.	16. P. to Q. B's 3rd.

White has a showy position, but he is a Pawn minus, and in reality has no advantage in situation over Black.

VARIATION C, BEGINNING AT BLACK'S 4TH MOVE.

	4. Kt. to K. B's 3rd.
5. P. to Q's 4th.	5. P. takes Q's P.
6. P. takes P.	6. B. to Q. Kt.'s 3rd.
7. B. to Q's 3rd.	

If 7. $\frac{\text{Kt. to Q. B's 3rd}}{\text{Castles}}$, 8. $\frac{\text{B. to K's 3rd}}{\text{Kt. to Q. B's 3rd}}$, 9. $\frac{\text{B. to Q's 3rd.}}{\text{Kt. to K. Kt.'s 5th}}$, 10. $\frac{\text{B. to K. Kt.'s sq.}}{\text{P. to K. B's 4th}}$, 11. $\frac{\text{P. to K's 5th}}{\text{P. takes P.}}$, 12. $\frac{\text{B. to Q. B's 4th (ch.)}}{\text{K. to R's sq.}}$, 13. $\frac{\text{Q's P. takes P.}}{\text{Q. takes Q. (ch.)}}$, 14. $\frac{\text{Kt. takes Q.}}{\text{B. takes B.}}$, 15. $\frac{\text{R. takes B.}}{\text{B. to Q's 2nd}}$, there is little difference in the position of the two armies. Of the two, I prefer White's.

	7. Castles.
8. Castles.	8. Kt. to Q. B's 3rd.

9. B. to K's 3rd.	9. Kt. to K. Kt's 5th.
10. Q. to K's 2nd.	10. Q. to K's 2nd.
11. Kt. to Q. B's 3rd.	11. P. to K. B's 4th.
12. P. to K's 5th.	12. P. takes P.
13. Kt. to Q.'s 5th.	13. Q. to Q's 3rd.
14. Kt. takes B.	14. R's P. takes Kt.
15. Q's P. takes P.	15. Q. to K's 2nd.

The game is tolerably equal.

Game the Second.

WHITE.	BLACK.
1. P. to K's 4th.	1. P. to K's 4th.
2. P. to K. B's 4th.	2. P. to Q's 4th.

Opinions are not in accordance as to whether this or 2. $\frac{\quad}{\text{B. to Q. B's 4th}}$, is the most advantageous mode of defence. It is a question difficult to decide. I believe, however, the majority of good judges prefer the latter.

3. P. takes Q's P.	3. P. to K's 5th.

The result of 3. $\frac{\quad}{\text{Q. takes P.}}$ shall be shown in Variation A; that of 3. $\frac{\quad}{\text{P. takes P.}}$ in Variation B.

4. B. to Q. Kt.'s 5th (ch.)	4. P. to Q. B's 3rd.

If 4. $\frac{\quad}{\text{B. to Q's 2nd}}$, 5. $\frac{\text{Q. to K's 2nd}}{\quad}$.

5. P. takes P.	5. P. takes P.

If 5. $\frac{\quad}{\text{Kt. to Q. B's 3rd}}$, 6. $\frac{\text{P. to Q's 4th}}{\text{Kt. to K. B's 3rd}}$, 7. $\frac{\text{P. to Q. B's 3rd}}{\quad}$.

6. B. to Q. B's 4th.	6. Kt. to K. B's 3rd.
7. P. to Q's 4th.	7. Q's Kt. to Q's 2nd.

If 7. $\frac{\quad}{\text{Q. to Q. Kt.'s 3rd}}$, 8. $\frac{\text{Kt. to Q. B's 3rd}}{\text{B. to Q. Kt.'s 5th}}$, 9. $\frac{\text{K's Kt. to K's 2nd}}{\text{B. to K. Kt.'s 5th}}$, 10. $\frac{\text{Castles}}{\quad}$, White has a Pawn plus, and an equal position.

8. Kt. to K's 2nd.	8. Kt. to Q. Kt.'s 3rd.
9. B. to Q. Kt.'s 3rd.	9. B. to Q. R's 3rd.
10. Kt. to Q. B's 3rd.	10. B. to Q. Kt.'s 5th.
11. Castles.	11. B. takes Q's Kt.
12. P. takes B.	12. K's Kt. to Q's 4th.
13. R. to K's sq.	13. Castles.

The game is about even. White has a Pawn more, but his forces are not so well disposed as Black's.

Variation A, beginning at Black's 3rd Move.

Position prior to Black's 3rd Move.

	3. Q. takes P.
4. Kt. to Q. B's 3rd.	4. Q. to K's 3rd.
5. P. takes P.	5. Q. takes P. (ch.)
6. B. to K's 2nd.	6. B. to Q's 3rd.
7. Kt. to K. B's 3rd.	7. Q. to K's 2nd.
8. P. to Q's 4th.	8. B. to K's 3rd.
9. Castles.	

White's position is preferable.

Variation B, beginning at Black's 3rd Move.

(*See preceding Diagram.*)

3. P. takes P.

The *Handbuch* marks this as Black's best reply.

4. B. to Q. Kt.'s 5th (ch.)

White can also play 4. $\frac{\text{Kt. to K. B's 3rd}}{\quad}$; in that case the probable continuation being, 4. $\frac{\quad}{\text{Q. takes P.}}$, 5. $\frac{\text{P. to Q's 4th}}{\text{P. to K. Kt.'s 4th}}$, 6. $\frac{\text{Kt. to Q. B's 3rd}}{\text{B. to Q. Kt.'s 5th}}$, 7. $\frac{\text{K. to B's 2nd}}{\text{B. takes Kt.}}$, 8. $\frac{\text{P. takes B.}}{\text{Kt. to K's 2nd}}$, 9. $\frac{\text{B. to Q's 3rd}}{\quad}$. Equal game.

	4. B. to Q's 2nd.
5. Q. to K's 2nd (ch.)	5. Q. to K's 2nd.
6. Kt. to Q. B's 3rd.	6. Kt. to K. B's 3rd.
7. B. takes B. (ch.)	7. Q's Kt. takes B.
8. P. to Q's 4th.	8. Castles.
9. Q. takes Q.	9. B. takes Q.
10. B. takes P.	10. Kt. to Q. Kt.'s 3rd.

Black must win the doubly attacked Pawn, and he has, I think, a slight advantage in position.

Game the Third.

WHITE.	BLACK.
1. P. to K's 4th.	1. P. to K's 4th.
2. P. to K. B's 4th.	2. P. to Q's 3rd.

This does not look a very promising line of defence, but it may be adopted without seriously compromising Black's game.

3. B. to Q. B's 4th.	3. P. takes P.
4. Kt. to K. B's 3rd.	4. P. to K. Kt.'s 4th (best).
5. P. to K. R's 4th.	5. P. to K. Kt.'s 5th.
6. Kt. to K. Kt.'s 5th.	6. Kt. to K. R's 3rd.
7. P. to Q's 4th.	7. P. to K. B's 3rd.

(For the result of 7. $\frac{\qquad}{\text{Q. to K's 2nd}}$, see Variation A.)

8. Kt. to K's 6th.

White may obtain an attack, which many players would think amply remunerative for the sacrificed Knight, by 8. $\frac{\text{Q's B. takes P.}}{\text{P. takes Kt.}}$, 9. $\frac{\text{P. takes P.}}{\qquad}$, &c.

White	Black
	8. Q. to K's 2nd.
9. P. to Q's 5th.	9. B. takes Kt.
10. P. takes B.	10. Kt. to Q. B's 3rd.
11. Kt. to Q. B's 3rd.	11. Kt. to K's 4th.
12. Kt. to Q's 5th.	12. Q. to K. Kt.'s 2nd
13. B. to Q. Kt.'s 3rd.	13. P. to K. B's 6th.
14. P. to K. Kt.'s 3rd.	14. R. to Q. B's sq.
15. Q. to Q's 4th.	15. P. to Q. B's 3rd.
16. B. takes Kt.	16. Q. takes B.
17. Kt. to K's 3rd.	

White, to my mind, has a great advantage in position; though the *Handbuch* pronounces the game equal.

Variation A, beginning at Black's 7th Move.

BLACK.

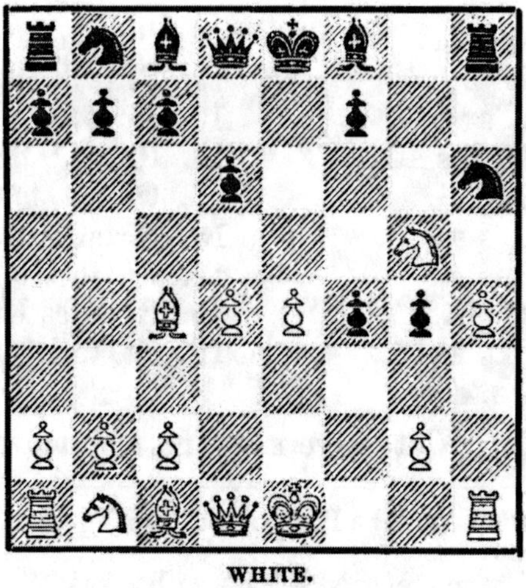

WHITE.

Position prior to Black's 7th Move.

	7. Q. to K's 2nd.
8. Q's B. takes P.	8. P. to K. B's 3rd.
9. Castles.	9. P. takes Kt.
10. B. takes P.	10. Q. to Q's 2nd.
11. Q. to Q's 2nd.	11. Kt. to K. Kt.'s sq.
12. B. to K. B's 7th (ch.)	12. Q. takes B.
13. R. takes Q.	13. K. takes R.
14. Q. to K. B's 4th (ch.)	

White has by far the better game.

ILLUSTRATIVE GAMES.

Game I.—Between Messrs. Schulten and Morphy.

White (Mr. S.)	Black (Mr. M.)
1. P. to K's 4th.	1. P. to K's 4th.
2. P. to K. B's 4th.	2. P. to Q's 4th.
3. P. takes Q's P.	3. P. to K's 5th.
4. Kt. to Q. B's 3rd.	4. Kt. to K. B's 3rd.
5. P. to Q's 3rd.	5. B. to Q. Kt.'s 5th.
6. B. to Q's 2nd.*	6. P. to K's 6th.†
7. B. takes P.	7. Castles.
8. B. to Q's 2nd.‡	8. B. takes Kt.
9. P. takes B.	9. R. to K's sq. (ch.)
10. B. to K's 2nd.	10. B. to K. Kt.'s 5th.
11. P. to Q. B's 4th.	11. P. to Q. B's 3rd.
12. P. takes P.§	12. Q's Kt. takes P.
13. K. to B's sq.	13. R. takes B.
14. Kt. takes R.	14. Kt. to Q's 5th.
15. Q. to Q. Kt.'s sq.	15. B. takes Kt. (ch.)
16. K. to B's 2nd.	16. Kt. to Kt.'s 5th (ch.)
17. K. to Kt.'s sq.	

And White gave mate in seven moves.

---

* Better, perhaps, to take Pawn with Pawn.

† The best reply.

‡ We should have preferred K's Kt. to K's 2nd.

§ A very bad move, which loses the game. He ought to have moved 12. P. to K. R's 3rd.

Game II.—Between Messrs. Steinitz and Blackburne.

White (Mr. S.)	Black (Mr. B.)
1. P. to K's 4th.	1. P. to K's 4th.
2. P. to K. B's 4th.	2. B. to Q. B's 4th.
3. Kt. to K. B's 3rd	3. P. to Q's 3rd.
4. B. to Q. B's 4th.*	4. Kt. to K. B's 3rd.
5. P. to Q's 3rd.	5. Kt. to Q. B's 3rd.
6. P. to Q. B's 3rd.	6. Castles.
7 B. to Q. Kt.'s 3rd.	7. B. to K. Kt.'s 5th.
8. P. to K. B's 5th.	8. P. to Q's 4th.
9. P. to K. R's 3rd.	9. B. takes Kt.
10. Q. takes B.	10. P. takes P.
11. P. takes P.	11. Q. to Q's 3rd.
12. B. to K. Kt.'s 5th.	12. Q's R. to Q's sq.
13. B. to Q. B's 2nd.	13. P. to K. R's 3rd.
14. B. to Q. B's sq.	14. K. to R's 2nd.†
15. P. to K. Kt.'s 4th.	15. K's R. to K's sq.
16. Kt. to Q's 2nd.	16. P. to Q. Kt.'s 4th.
17. Kt. to Q. Kt.'s 3rd.	17. P. to Kt.'s 5th.
18. B. to Q's 2nd.	18. P. takes P.
19. P. takes P.	19. Kt. to Q. R's 4th.
20. Castles (Q's R.)	20. Kt. to Q. B's 5th.
21. K. to Kt.'s sq.	21. Q. to Q. R's 3rd.
22. B. to B's sq.	22. B. to Q. R's 6th.
23. K. to R's sq.	23. B. takes B.
24. R. takes B.	24. Q. to R's 6th.
25. R. to Q. Kt.'s sq.	25. R. to Q's 3rd.
26. R. to R's 2nd.	26. R. to Q. Kt.'s sq.‡
27. B. to Q's 3rd.	27. Kt. to R's 4th.
28. Kt. takes Kt.	28. Q. takes B's P. (ch.)
29. K's R. to Kt.'s 2nd.	29. R. takes R.
30. R. takes R.	30. R. takes B.
31. Q. to K's 2nd.	31. R. to K's 6th.

And White abandoned the game.

---

* We prefer this move to the old-fashioned play of 4. P. to Q. B's 3rd.
† The first step of a very ingenious combination.
‡ All this is admirably managed by Mr. Blackburne.

GAME III.—Between Mr. Thorold and the Rev. W. Wayte.

WHITE (Mr. T.)	BLACK (Mr. W.)
1. P. to K's 4th.	1. P. to K's 4th.
2. P. to K. B's 4th.	2. B. to Q. B's 4th.
3. Kt. to K. B's 3rd.	3. P. to Q's 3rd.
4. P. to Q. B's 3rd.	4. B. to K. Kt.'s 5th.
5. P. to Q's 4th.*	5. P. takes Q's P.
6. P. takes P.	6. B. takes Kt.
7. P. takes B.	7. Q. to R's 5th (ch.)
8. K. to K's 2nd.	8. B. to Q. Kt.'s 3rd.†
9. R. to K. Kt.'s sq.	9. Kt. to Q. B's 3rd.
10. B. to K's 3rd.	10. Kt. to K. B's 3rd.
11. Kt. to Q. B's 3rd.	11. Castles (K's R.)
12. P. to K. B's 5th.	12. K. to R's sq.
13. Q. to Q's 2nd.	13. K's R. to K's sq.
14. Q's R. to K's sq.	14. P. to Q's 4th.‡
15. B. to K. B's 2nd.	15. Q. to K. R's 4th.
16. R. to K. Kt.'s 5th.	16. Q. takes R's P.
17. B. to K. Kt.'s 2nd.	17. P. takes P.
18. R. to K. R's sq.	18. P. takes P. (dble. ch.)
19. K. to Q's sq.	19. Q. to Q's 3rd.
20. B. takes P.	20. Kt. takes P.
21. B. takes P.	21. Q's R. to Q's sq.
22. B. to K. Kt.'s 3rd.	22. Q. to K's 2nd.
23. R. to K's sq.	23. Kt. to Q. Kt.'s 6th.§
24. P. takes Kt.	24. R. takes Q. (ch.)
25. K. takes R.	25. B. to K's 6th (ch.)
26. K. to B's 2nd.	26. Q. to Q. B's 4th.

And Black wins.

---

* The usual move is B. to K's 2nd, but the move in the text has also the authority of the German *Handbuch*.

† At this point the *Handbuch* dismisses the game as even, but most players, we fancy, would take Black's position for choice.

‡ A very judicious move.

§ This is decisive, do what White will.

CHAPTER XIX.

The Queen's Gambit.

(Accepted.)

1. $\frac{\text{P. to Q's 4th}}{\text{P. to Q's 4th}}$, 2. $\frac{\text{P. to Q. B's 4th}}{\text{P. takes P.}}$.

Game the First.

3. $\frac{\text{P. to K's 3rd}}{}$

Game the Second.

3. $\frac{\text{P. to K's 4th}}{}$.

(Declined.)

Game the Third.

2. $\frac{}{\text{P. to K's 3rd}}$; 2. $\frac{}{\text{P. to Q. B's 4th}}$; 2. $\frac{}{\text{P. to Q. B's 3rd}}$.

This is a very early method of opening the game. We find it in the pages of Damiano even. It is perfectly safe, and usually leads to very sound and instructive games. Like other *débuts* on the Queen's side, it is much less in vogue than those on the side of the King, and has never been so exhaustively analysed.

Game the First.

WHITE.	BLACK.
1. P. to Q's 4th.	1. P. to Q's 4th.
2. P. to Q. B's 4th.	2. P. takes P.

The analyses of the Gambits on the King's side tend to prove that as a rule the second player's best course is to take the Gambit Pawn. In the Queen's Gambit, however, from a very early period, it has been considered better for him to decline the Pawn, and play P. to K's 3rd.

3. P. to K's 3rd.

The result of 3. $\frac{\text{P. to K's 4th}}{}$ will be seen in the next game.

3. P. to K's 4th.

If 3. $\frac{}{\text{P. to Q. Kt.'s 4th}}$, 4. $\frac{\text{P. to Q. R's 4th}}{\text{P. to Q. B's 3rd}}$, 5. $\frac{\text{P. takes P.}}{\text{P. takes P.}}$, 6. $\frac{\text{Q. to K. B's 3rd}}{}$, White has a decisive advantage. If 3. $\frac{}{\text{P. to Q. B's 4th}}$, 4. $\frac{\text{P. to Q's 5th}}{}$. (White may also play advantageously 4. $\frac{\text{B. takes P.}}{\text{P. takes P.}}$, 5. $\frac{\text{P. takes P.}}{\text{Kt. to Q. B's 3rd}}$, 6. $\frac{\text{Kt. to K's 2nd}}{\text{P. to K's 4th}}$, 7. $\frac{\text{B. to K's 3rd}}{\text{P. takes P.}}$, 8. $\frac{\text{Kt. takes P.}}{\text{Kt. takes Kt.}}$, 9. $\frac{\text{B. takes Kt.}}{}$, &c.) 4. $\frac{}{\text{P. to K's 3rd}}$, 5. $\frac{\text{P. takes P.}}{\text{P. takes P.}}$, 6. $\frac{\text{B. takes P.}}{\text{B. to Q's 3rd}}$, 7. $\frac{\text{Kt. to K. B's 3rd}}{\text{Kt. to K's 2nd}}$. There is not much to choose between the positions. Perhaps White would play slightly better by 5. $\frac{\text{B. takes P.}}{}$ instead of 5. $\frac{\text{P. takes P.}}{}$.

4. B. takes P.	4. P. takes P.
5. P. takes P.	5. B. to Q's 3rd.
6. Kt. to K. B's 3rd.	6. Kt. to K. B's 3rd.
7. Castles.	7. Castles.

Even game.

Game the Second.

WHITE.	BLACK.
1. P. to Q's 4th.	1. P. to Q's 4th.
2. P. to Q. B's 4th.	2. P. takes P.
3. P. to K's 4th.	3. P. to K's 4th.

Black's best move is that in the text. (For the result of 3. $\frac{\quad}{\text{P. to K. B's 4th}}$, and 3. $\frac{\quad}{\text{P. to Q. B's 4th}}$, see Variation A.)

If 3. $\frac{\quad}{\text{P. to Q. Kt.'s 4th}}$, then follows, as in a previous instance, 4. $\frac{\text{P. to Q. R's 4th}}{\text{P. to Q. B's 3rd}}$, 5. $\frac{\text{P. takes P.}}{\text{P. takes P.}}$, 6. $\frac{\text{Q. to K. B's 3rd}}{\quad}$; or 4. $\frac{\text{P. to Q. R's 4th}}{\text{B. to Q. R's 3rd}}$, 5. $\frac{\text{P. takes P.}}{\text{B. takes P.}}$, 6. $\frac{\text{P. to Q. Kt.'s 3rd}}{\text{P. to K's 3rd}}$, 7. $\frac{\text{P. takes P.}}{\text{B. to Q. R's 3rd}}$, 8. $\frac{\text{R. takes B.}}{\text{Kt. takes R.}}$, 9. $\frac{\text{Q. to Q. R's 4th (ch.)}}{\quad}$, gaining a piece.

4. P. to Q's 5th.	

Taking the K's Pawn with Pawn is manifestly imprudent on account of 4. $\frac{\quad}{\text{Q. takes Q. (ch.)}}$, 5. $\frac{\text{K. takes Q.}}{\text{B. to K's 3rd}}$ or 5. $\frac{\quad}{\text{Kt. to Q. B's 3rd}}$, &c.

	4. P. to K. B's 4th (best).
5. B. takes P.	5. Kt. to K. B's 3rd.

If 5. $\frac{\quad}{\text{P. takes P.}}$, then follows 6. $\frac{\text{Q. to K. R's 5th (ch.)}}{\quad}$, &c.

6. Kt. to K. B's 3rd.	6. B. to Q's 3rd.
7. P. takes P.	7. B. takes P.
8. Castles.	8. Castles.
9. Kt. to Q. B's 3rd.	9. Q's Kt. to Q's 2nd.

The game is considered equal.

VARIATION A, BEGINNING AT BLACK'S 3RD MOVE.

BLACK.

WHITE.

Position prior to Black's 3rd Move.

3. P. to K. B's 4th.

As I have said, Black may also play 3. $\frac{}{\text{P. to Q. B's 4th}}$.

For instance, 3. $\frac{}{\text{P. to Q. B's 4th}}$, 4. $\frac{\text{P. to Q's 5th}}{\text{P. to K's 3rd}}$, 5. $\frac{\text{B. takes P.}}{\text{P. takes P.}}$, 6. $\frac{\text{B. takes P.}}{\text{B. to Q's 3rd}}$, 7. $\frac{\text{Kt. to K. B's 3rd}}{\text{Kt. to K's 2nd}}$. White has a slight advantage.

4. P. to K's 5th.

White can play with equal profit 4. $\frac{\text{B. takes P.}}{\text{P. takes P.}}$, 5. $\frac{\text{Q. to Q. Kt.'s 3rd}}{\text{P. to K's 3rd}}$, 6. $\frac{\text{B. takes P.}}{\text{B. takes B.}}$, 7. $\frac{\text{Q. takes B. (ch.)}}{\text{B. to K's 2nd}}$, 8. $\frac{\text{Q. takes P.}}{}$, &c.

4. B. to K's 3rd.

5. Kt. to Q. R's 3rd. 5. Kt. to Q. B's 3rd.

6. B. to K's 3rd.	6. Kt. to Q. R's 4th.
7. Q. to Q. R's 4th (ch.)	7. P. to Q. B's 3rd.
8. B. to Q's 2nd.	8. Q. takes P.
9. Q. takes Kt.	9. Q. takes Q. Kt.'s P.
10. B. to Q. B's 3rd.	10. Q. to Q. Kt.'s 3rd.
11. Kt. takes P.	

I prefer White's game.

Game the Third.

(Queen's Gambit Declined.)

WHITE.	BLACK.
1. P. to Q's 4th.	1. P. to Q's 4th.
2. P. to Q. B's 4th.	2. P. to K's 3rd.

As I mentioned before, it is considered better for Black to decline the proffered Pawn. Recent examination of the opening, however, disposes me to think that he may make quite as good a defence by accepting the Gambit as by evading it. His best move, when he declines to take the Pawn, appears to be that above. But he can play 2. $\frac{\qquad}{\text{P. to Q. B's 4th}}$, or 2. $\frac{\qquad}{\text{P. to Q. B's 3rd}}$. (See Variations A and B.)

3. Kt. to Q. B's 3rd.	3. P. to Q. B's 4th.

If 3. $\frac{\qquad}{\text{Kt. to K. B's 3rd}}$, 4. $\frac{\text{B. to K. B's 4th}}{\qquad}$. (White may well play also 4. $\frac{\text{B. to K. Kt.'s 5th}}{\text{B. to K's 2nd}}$, 5. $\frac{\text{P. to K's 3rd}}{\text{Castles}}$, &c.) 4. $\frac{\qquad}{\text{P. to Q. B's 4th}}$, 5. $\frac{\text{P. to K's 3rd}}{\text{Kt. to Q. B's 3rd}}$, 6. $\frac{\text{Kt. to K. B's 3rd}}{\text{B. to K's 2nd}}$, White has a well-opened game.

4. P. to K's 3rd.	4. Kt. to K. B's 3rd.
5. Kt. to K. B's 3rd.	5. Kt. to Q. B's 3rd.
6. P. to Q. R's 3rd.	6. P. to Q. R's 3rd.
7. P. to Q. Kt.'s 3rd.	7. P. to Q. Kt.'s 3rd.

8. B. to Q. Kt.'s 2nd.	8. B. to Q. Kt.'s 2nd.
9. P. takes Q's P.	9. K's P. takes P.
10. B. to Q's 3rd.	10. P. takes P.
11. P. takes P.	11. B. to Q's 3rd.
12. Castles.	12. Castles.

Even game.

VARIATION A, BEGINNING AT BLACK'S 2ND MOVE.

	2. P. to Q. B's 4th.
3. P. takes Q's P.	

It strikes me that White obtains at least as good a position by taking the Queen's Bishop's Pawn. For example, 3. $\frac{\text{P. takes Q. B's P.}}{\text{P. to Q's 5th}}$, 4. $\frac{\text{P. to Q. Kt.'s 4th}}{\text{P. to Q. R's 4th}}$. (If 4. $\frac{}{\text{P. to K's 4th}}$, 5. $\frac{\text{Kt. to K. B's 3rd}}{\text{P. to K. B's 3rd}}$, 6. $\frac{\text{P. to K's 3rd}}{\text{P. takes P.}}$, 7. $\frac{\text{Q. takes Q. (ch.)}}{\text{K. takes Q.}}$, 8. $\frac{\text{Q's B. takes P.}}{}$, &c.) 5. $\frac{\text{P. to Q. Kt.'s 5th}}{\text{P. to K's 4th}}$, 6. $\frac{\text{Kt. to K. B's 3rd}}{\text{P. to K. B's 3rd}}$, 7. $\frac{\text{P. to K. R's 3rd}}{}$. (Also 7. $\frac{\text{P. to K's 3rd}}{\text{K's B. takes P.}}$, 8. $\frac{\text{P. takes Q's P.}}{}$, &c., better game.) 7. $\frac{}{\text{Q. to Q. B's 2nd}}$, &c.

	3. Q. takes P.
4. P. to K's 3rd.	4. P. takes P.
5. Kt. to Q. B's 3rd.	5. Q. to Q's sq.
6. P. takes P.	6. P. to K's 3rd.
7. B. to Q. B's 4th.	7. B. to Q's 3rd.

The game is about equal.

VARIATION B, BEGINNING AT BLACK'S 2ND MOVE.

	2. P. to Q. B's 3rd.

Less advantageous than 2. $\frac{}{\text{P. to Q. B's 4th}}$ apparently.

3. Kt. to Q. B's 3rd. | 3. Kt. to K. B's 3rd.

Or 3. $\frac{}{\text{P. takes P.}}$, 4. $\frac{\text{P. to K's 3rd}}{\text{P. to Q. Kt.'s 4th}}$, 5. $\frac{\text{Kt. takes P.}}{\text{P. takes Kt.}}$

6. $\frac{\text{Q. to K. B's 3rd}}{}$, White has the better opening.

4. P. to K's 3rd.	4. B. to K. B's 4th.
5. P. takes P.	5. P. takes P.
6. Q. to Q. Kt.'s 3rd.	6. Q. to Q's 2nd.
7. Kt. to K. B's 3rd.	7. P. to K's 3rd.
8. Kt. to K's 5th.	8. Q. to Q. B's 2nd.
9. B. to Q's 2nd.	

White has a marked superiority in position.

ILLUSTRATIVE GAMES.

Game I.—Between Messrs. Potter and Cousin.

White (Mr. P.)	Black (Mr. C.)
1. P. to Q's 4th.	1. P. to Q's 4th.
2. P. to Q. B's 4th.	2. P. takes P.
3. P. to K's 3rd.	3. P. to K's 4th.
4. B. takes P.	4. P. takes P.
5. P. takes P.	5. Kt. to K. B's 3rd.
6. Kt. to Q. B's 3rd.	6. Kt. to Q. B's 3rd.
7. B. to K's 3rd.	7. B. to Q's 3rd.
8. Kt. to K. B's 3rd.	8. Castles.
9. Castles.	9. P. to Q. R's 3rd.
10. P. to K. R's 3rd.	10. P. to Q. Kt.'s 4th.
11. B. to Q's 3rd.	11. B. to Q. Kt.'s 2nd.
12. R. to Q. B's sq.	12. Q. to Q's 2nd.
13. B. to Q. Kt.'s sq.	13. Kt. to K's sq.
14. Kt. to K's 2nd.	14. P. to K. Kt.'s 3rd.
15. B. to K. R's 6th.	15. Kt. to K. Kt.'s 2nd.
16. Kt. to K. Kt.'s 3rd.	16. B. takes Kt.
17. P. takes B.	17. K's R. to K's sq.

18. P. to K. Kt.'s 4th.	18. R. to K's 2nd.*
19. B. to K. Kt.'s 5th.†	19. K's R. to K's sq.
20. B. to K. B's 6th.	20. Q. to Q's 3rd.
21. Kt. to K. Kt.'s 5th.	21. Kt. to Q's sq.
22. B. to K's 5th.	22. Q. to K's 2nd.
23. Kt. takes K. B's P.	23. Q's Kt. to K's 3rd.‡
24. Kt. to R's 6th (ch.)	24. K. to R's sq.
25. R. to B's 7th.	25. Q. to K. Kt.'s 4th.
26. Q's R. takes P.	26. Q. takes Kt.
27. R. takes B.	27. R. to K. Kt.'s sq.
28. B. to Q. B's 2nd.	28. Q's R. to Q. B's sq.
29. K. to R's 2nd.§	29. Q. to K's 6th.
30. B. to Q. Kt.'s 3rd.	30. Q's R. to K's sq.
31. B. takes Kt.	31. R. takes B.
32. R. takes Kt.	32. R. takes R.
33. R. to Q. Kt.'s 8th (ch.)	

And mates next move.

GAME II.—Between Messrs. Owen and Boden.

WHITE (Mr. O.)	BLACK (Mr. B.)
1. P. to Q's 4th.	1. P. to Q's 4th.
2. P. to Q. B's 4th.	2. P. takes P.
3. P. to K's 4th.	3. P. to K's 4th.
4. P. to Q's 5th.	4. P. to K. B's 4th.
5. B. takes P.	5. Kt. to K. B's 3rd.
6. Kt. to Q. B's 3rd.	6. B. to Q's 3rd.
7. Kt. to K. B's 3rd.	7. P. takes P.
8. Kt. to K. Kt.'s 5th.	8. B. to K. B's 4th.
9. Q. to Q. R's 4th (ch.)	9. Q's Kt. to Q's 2nd.
10. Kt. to K's 6th.	10. Q. to K's 2nd.
11. Castles.	11. P. to Q. R's 3rd.
12. B. to K. Kt.'s 5th.	12. R. to Q. B's sq.

* This strikes us as being a little like lost time.

† Well played. This move gives White a marked advantage.

‡ If 23. Kt. takes Kt., White replies with 24. Q's R. takes P.

§ To avoid the consequences of R. to Q. B's 8th, when the Bishop was played away.

13. P. to K. B's 4th.*	13. P. to K. R's 3rd.
14. B. takes Kt.	14. Q. takes B.
15. P. takes P.	15. B. takes P.
16. R. takes B.	16. Q. takes R.
17. R. to K. B's sq.	17. Q. to K. Kt.'s 5th.
18. B. to K's 2nd.	18. Q. to K. R's 5th.
19. P. to K. Kt.'s 3rd.	19. B. takes P.
20. B. to R's 5th (ch.)	

And wins.

GAME III.—Between Messrs. Anderssen and Szen.

WHITE (Mr. A.)	BLACK (Mr. S.)
1. P. to Q's 4th.	1. P. to Q's 4th.
2. P. to Q. B's 4th.	2. P. to K's 3rd.
3. P. to K's 3rd.	3. Kt. to K. B's 3rd.
4. Kt. to Q. B's 3rd.	4. P. to Q. B's 4th.
5. Kt. to K. B's 3rd.	5. Kt. to Q. B's 3rd.
6. P. to Q. R's 3rd.	6. P. to Q. R's 3rd.
7. P. to Q. Kt.'s 3rd.	7. P. to Q. Kt.'s 3rd.
8. B. to Q. Kt.'s 2nd.	8. B. to Q. Kt.'s 2nd.
9. P. takes Q's P.	9. K's P. takes P.
10. B. to Q's 3rd.	10. P. takes P.
11. P. takes P.	11. B. to Q's 3rd.
12. Castles.	12. Castles.
13. P. to Q. Kt.'s 4th.	13. P. to Q. Kt.'s 4th.
14. R. to Q. B's sq.	14. R. to Q. B's sq.†
15. Q. to Q. Kt.'s 3rd.	15. B. to Q. Kt.'s sq.
16. R. to Q. B's 2nd.	16. R. to K's sq.
17. Kt. to K's 2nd.	17. Kt. to K's 5th.
18. Kt. to K. Kt.'s 3rd.	18. Kt. to K. Kt.'s 4th.
19. Kt. to K's 5th.	19. Kt. to K's 3rd.
20. Kt. to K's 2nd.‡	20. Q's Kt. takes Q's P.
21. R. takes R.	21. Kt. takes Kt. (ch).

* Very ingeniously played.

† It is seldom we see two precisely similar positions at such an advanced period of the game.

‡ An oversight apparently, as it loses a valuable Pawn.

22. B. takes Kt.	22. Q. takes R.
23. R. to Q's sq.	23. Kt. to K. B's 5th.
24. B. to K. Kt.'s 4th.	24. P. to K. B's 4th.
25. P. to Kt.'s 3rd.	25. B. takes Kt.
26. B. takes B.	26. Kt. to K. Kt.'s 3rd.*

White resigns.

---

* The terminating moves are played in Mr. Szen's happiest style.

CHAPTER XX.

THE FRENCH GAME.

$$1. \frac{\text{P. to K's 4th}}{\text{P. to K's 3rd}}.$$

GAME THE FIRST.

$$2. \frac{\text{P. to Q's 4th}}{\text{P. to Q's 4th}}, \quad 3. \frac{\text{P. takes P.}}{}.$$

$$2. \frac{\text{P. to K. B's 4th}}{}.$$

GAME THE SECOND.

$$3. \frac{\text{Kt. to Q. B's 3rd}}{}.$$

The *French Opening*, as it is called, was known as early as Lucena (1497), probably earlier; and at this day one of the most eminent Chess authors who ever lived, M. de Jaenisch, considers Black's first move to be the only satisfactory defence the board presents to $1. \frac{\text{P. to K's 4th.}}{}$

GAME THE FIRST.

WHITE.	BLACK.
1. P. to K's 4th.	1. P. to K's 3rd.
2. P. to Q's 4th.	

Both Jaenisch and the German masters give the preference to this move. The result of 2. $\frac{\text{P. to K. B's 4th}}{}$, which Labourdonnais commended, and 2. $\frac{\text{Kt. to K. B's 3rd}}{}$, will be found in Variation A.

If 2. $\frac{\text{P. to Q. B's 4th}}{\text{P. to Q. B's 4th}}$, 3. $\frac{\text{P. to Q's 4th}}{\text{P. takes P.}}$, 4. $\frac{\text{Q. takes P.}}{\text{Kt. to Q. B's 3rd}}$, 5. $\frac{\text{Q. to Q's sq.}}{\text{B. to Q. B's 4th}}$, 6. $\frac{\text{Kt. to Q. B's 3rd}}{\text{Kt. to K's 2nd}}$, White has certainly no advantage.

2. P. to Q's 4th.

3. P. takes P.

(For 3. $\frac{\text{Kt. to Q. B's 3rd}}{}$ see Game the Second.)

If 3. $\frac{\text{P. to K's 5th}}{\text{P. to Q. B's 4th}}$, 4. $\frac{\text{B. to Q. Kt.'s 5th (ch.)}}{\text{Kt. to Q. B's 3rd}}$, 5. $\frac{\text{P. to Q. B's 3rd}}{\text{Q. to Q. Kt.'s 3rd}}$, 6. $\frac{\text{B. takes Kt. (ch.)}}{\text{P. takes B.}}$, 7. $\frac{\text{Kt. to K. B's 3rd}}{\text{P. takes P.}}$, 8. $\frac{\text{P. takes P.}}{\text{B. to Q. R's 3rd}}$, 9. $\frac{\text{Q's Kt. to Q's 2nd}}{}$, Black has a freer game. So also if 3. $\frac{\text{P. to K's 5th}}{\text{P. to Q. B's 4th}}$, 4. $\frac{\text{P. to Q. B's 3rd}}{\text{Kt. to Q. B's 3rd}}$, 5. $\frac{\text{P. to K. B's 4th}}{\text{Q. to Q. Kt.'s 3rd}}$, 6. $\frac{\text{Kt. to K. B's 3rd}}{\text{B. to Q's 2nd}}$, 7. $\frac{\text{B. to K's 2nd}}{\text{Kt. to K. R's 3rd}}$, Black has the advantage.

3. P. takes P.

4. Kt. to K. B's 3rd.

If 4. $\frac{\text{B. to Q's 3rd}}{\text{Kt. to Q. B's 3rd}}$, 5. $\frac{\text{B. to K's 3rd}}{\text{B. to K's 3rd}}$, 6. $\frac{\text{Kt. to K. B's 3rd}}{\text{Kt. to K. B's 3rd}}$, the game is equal. So if 4. $\frac{\text{P. to Q. B's 4th}}{\text{B. to Q. Kt.'s 5th (ch.)}}$, 5. $\frac{\text{B. to Q's 2nd}}{\text{Q. to K's 2nd (ch.)}}$, 6. $\frac{\text{Q. to K's 2nd}}{\text{B. to K's 3rd}}$, 7. $\frac{\text{P. takes P.}}{\text{B. takes B. (ch.)}}$, 8. $\frac{\text{Kt. takes B.}}{\text{B. takes P.}}$, Black has at least as good a position as his adversary.

4. Kt. to K. B's 3rd.

5. B. to Q's 3rd.

White can also play 5. $\frac{\text{B. to K's 3rd}}{}$, usually followed by 5. $\frac{}{\text{B. to K's 3rd}}$, 6. $\frac{\text{B. to Q's 3rd}}{\text{B. to Q's 3rd}}$, 7. $\frac{\text{Castles}}{\text{Castles}}$, and the game is equal. If 5. $\frac{\text{B. to K. Kt.'s 5th}}{\text{B. to K's 2nd}}$, 6. $\frac{\text{Kt. to Q. B's 3rd}}{\text{Castles}}$, equal game.

5. B. to Q's 3rd.

6. Castles.

6. Castles.

BLACK.

WHITE.

Position prior to White's 7th move.

7. P. to Q. B's 4th.

If 7. $\frac{\text{Kt. to Q. B's 3rd}}{}$, Black can at least equalise the battle by 7. $\frac{}{\text{P. to Q. B's 3rd}}$. If 7. $\frac{\text{B. to K's 3rd}}{\text{B. to K. Kt.'s 5th}}$, 8. $\frac{\text{P. to Q. B's 4th}}{\text{P. takes P.}}$, 9. $\frac{\text{B. takes Q. B's P.}}{\text{P. to Q. B's 3rd}}$, the game is about equal. If 7. $\frac{\text{B. to K. Kt.'s 5th}}{\text{B. to K. Kt.'s 5th}}$, White retains the advantage of the move, but nothing more.

	7. P. takes P. (best).
8. B. takes Q. B's P.	8. B. to K. Kt.'s 5th.
9. B. to K's 3rd (best).	9. P. to Q. B's 3rd.
10. Q's Kt. to Q's 2nd.	10. Q's Kt. to Q's 2nd.
11. Q. to Q. Kt.'s 3rd.	11. Q. to Q. Kt.'s 3rd.
12. Q. to Q. B's 2nd.	12. Q. to Q. B's 2nd.
13. Q's R. to Q. B's sq.	13. Q's R. to Q. B's sq.

In this situation M. de Jaenisch considers the advantage of the first move is reduced to its minimum.

Variation A, beginning at White's Second Move.

In the first place :—

2. P. to K. B's 4th.	2. P. to Q's 4th.
3. P. takes P.	

If 3. $\frac{\text{P. to K's 5th}}{\text{P. to Q. B's 4th}}$, 4. $\frac{\text{P. to Q. B's 3rd}}{\text{Kt. to Q. B's 3rd}}$, 5. $\frac{\text{Kt. to K. B's 3rd}}{\text{P. to K. B's 3rd}}$, 6. $\frac{\text{Kt. to Q. R's 3rd}}{\text{Kt. to K. R's 3rd}}$, 7. $\frac{\text{Kt. to Q. B's 2nd}}{\text{B. to Q's 2nd}}$, 8. $\frac{\text{P. to Q's 4th}}{\text{Q. to Q. Kt.'s 3rd}}$, 9. $\frac{\text{P. to Q. Kt.'s 3rd}}{\text{R. to Q. B's sq.}}$, 10. $\frac{\text{B. to Q's 3rd}}{\text{Kt. to K. B's 2nd}}$, 11. $\frac{\text{B. to K's 3rd}}{\text{P. takes Q's P.}}$, 12. $\frac{\text{Q. B's P. takes P.}}{\text{P. takes P.}}$, 13. $\frac{\text{B's P. takes P.}}{\text{B. to Q. Kt.'s 5th (ch.)}}$, 14. $\frac{\text{B. to Q's 2nd}}{\text{Castles}}$, Black's game is thought to be better than White's.

	3. P. takes P.
4. Kt. to K. B's 3rd.	4. P. to Q. B's 4th.
5. P. to Q's 4th.	5. Kt. to Q. B's 3rd.
6. P. to Q. B's 3rd.	6. Kt. to K. B's 3rd.
7. B. to K's 3rd.	7. Q. to Q. Kt.'s 3rd.
8. P. to Q. Kt.'s 3rd.	8. B. to Q's 2nd.
9. B. to Q's 3rd.	9. R. to Q. B's sq.

Black is considered to have a slight superiority.

In the second place :—

2. Kt. to K. B's 3rd	2. P. to Q's 4th.
3. P. takes P.	3. P. takes P.
4. P. to Q's 4th.	4. Kt. to K. B's 3rd.

The game is quite equal.

Game the Second.

WHITE.	BLACK.
1. P. to K's 4th.	1. P. to K's 3rd.
2. P. to Q's 4th.	2. P. to Q's 4th.
3. Kt. to Q. B's 3rd.	

In the opinion of many of our best players this *sortie* of the Knight is stronger than the customary move of 3. $\frac{\text{P. takes P.}}{}$.

Black has two feasible replies by 3. $\frac{}{\text{Kt. to B's 3rd}}$, and 3. $\frac{}{\text{B. to Q. Kt.'s 5th}}$, which we will briefly dispose of.

In the first place :—

3. Kt. to K. B's 3rd.

This is unquestionably Black's strongest rejoinder to 3. $\frac{\text{Kt. to Q. B's 3rd}}{}$.

4. B. to Q's 3rd.

If 4. $\frac{\text{B. to K. Kt.'s 5th}}{}$, Black replies with 4. $\frac{}{\text{P. takes P.}}$, or 4. $\frac{}{\text{B. to K's 2nd}}$; and if 4. $\frac{\text{P. to K's 5th}}{}$ we have 4. $\frac{}{\text{K's Kt. to Q's 2nd}}$, 5. $\frac{\text{Q's Kt. to K's 2nd}}{\text{P. to Q. B's 4th}}$, 6. $\frac{\text{P. to Q. B's 3rd}}{}$, and I do not think that White has the best of it.

	4. P. to Q. B's 4th (best).
5. P. takes Q's P.	5. Q. B's P. takes P.
6. B. to Kt.'s 5th (ch.)	6. B. to Q's 2nd.
7. B. takes B. (ch.)	

If 7. P. takes K's P. / ——, Black wins a piece by 7. —— / B. takes B.

	7. Q. takes B.
8. Q. takes P.	8. P. takes P.
9. Kt. to K. B's 3rd.	9. Kt. to Q. B's 3rd.

And the positions are about equal.

In the second place :—

	3. B. to Q. Kt.'s 5th.
4. P. takes P.	

This is White's best reply. The move of 4. B. to Q's 3rd / ——, usually given at this point, is certainly inferior, as Black can advantageously reply with 4. —— / P. to Q. B's 4th.

	4. P. takes P.

And White has the better disposed game, owing to the adverse Bishop being disadvantageously posted at Q. Kt.'s 5th. On this variation Mr. Wormald ("Chess Openings," p. 232) remarks:—"Black King's Bishop, instead of being posted at Queen's third square, where he exercises the strongest influence on the adverse game in positions of this class, has been played to a disadvantageous square, and the second player will be ultimately compelled either to lose a move by retiring him, or to exchange him for a comparatively valueless Knight."

ILLUSTRATIVE GAMES.

Game I.—Between Messrs. Morphy and Lowenthal.

White (Mr. M.)	Black (Mr. L.)
1. P. to K's 4th.	1. P. to K's 3rd.
2. P. to Q's 4th.	2. P. to Q's 4th.
3. P. takes P.	3. P. takes P.

4. Kt. to K. B's 3rd.	4. Kt. to K. B's 3rd.
5. B. to Q's 3rd.	5. B. to K's 3rd.
6. Castles.	6. B. to Q's 3rd.
7. Kt. to Q. B's 3rd.	7. P. to Q. B's 3rd.
8. Kt. to K's 5th.	8. Q. to Q. Kt.'s 3rd.
9. B. to K's 3rd.	9. Q's Kt. to Q's 2nd.
10. P. to K. B's 4th.	10. B. takes Kt.
11. B's P. takes B.	11. Kt. to K. Kt.'s 5th.
12. Q. to Q's 2nd.	12. Kt. takes B.
13. Q. takes Kt.	13. Q. takes Q. Kt.'s P.*
14. Kt. to K's 2nd.	14. Q. to R's 6th.
15. Kt. to B's 4th.	15. Q. to K's 2nd.
16. Q's R. to Kt.'s sq.	16. Castles (Q's R.)†
17. B. to K's 2nd.‡	17. Kt. to Q. Kt.'s 3rd.
18. Q. to Q. Kt.'s 3rd.	18. R. to Q's 2nd.
19. Kt. to Q's 3rd.	19. Kt. to Q. B's 5th.
20. Kt. to Q. B's 5th.	20. R. to Q. B's 2nd.
21. Q. to Q. R's 4th.	21. P. to Q. Kt.'s 3rd.
22. B. takes Kt.	22. P. takes Kt.§
23. B. to R's 6th (ch.)	23. K. to Q's 2nd.
24. B. to Q. Kt.'s 7th.	24. R. to Q's sq.
25. B. takes P. (ch.)	

And wins.

GAME II.—Between Messrs. Steinitz and De Vere.

WHITE (Mr. S.)	BLACK (Mr. De V.)
1. P. to K's 4th.	1. P. to K's 3rd.
2. P. to Q's 4th.	2. P. to Q's 4th.
3. Kt. to Q. B's 3rd.	3. B. to Q. Kt.'s 5th.‖
4. P. takes P.	4. P. takes P.

* This capture was not well considered.

† Very hazardous. What was the object of Castling in the face of such a battery as White is now enabled to bring to bear on the hostile King's quarters?

‡ Mr. Morphy, as usual, takes admirable advantage of his opponent's blunder.

§ If P. takes B., White wins at once by R. takes Q. Kt.'s P.

‖ This, as we have pointed out, is inferior to 3. Kt. to K. B's 3rd.

5. Kt. to K. B's 3rd.	5. Kt. to Q. B's 3rd.
6. B. to Q's 3rd.	6. Kt. to K. B's 3rd.
7. Castles.	7. Castles.
8. Kt. to K's 2nd.	8. Kt. to K's 2nd.
9. Kt. to K's 5th.	9. Kt. to K. Kt.'s 3rd.
10. P. to K. B's 4th.	10. Kt. to K's 5th.*
11. P. to Q. B's 3rd.	11. B. to Q. R's 4th.
12. B. takes Kt.	12. P. takes B.
13. Kt. to Kt.'s 3rd.	13. Kt. takes Kt.
14. B's P. takes Kt.	14. B. to Q. Kt.'s 3rd.
15. B. to K's 3rd.	15. P. to K. B's 4th.
16. P. takes P. (*en pas.*)	16. R. takes P.
17. Q. to K. R's 5th.	17. P. to K. Kt.'s 3rd.†
18. Q. to R's 6th.	18. B. to K. B's 4th.
19. B. to K. Kt.'s 5th.	19. Q. to K. B's sq.
20. Q. to K. R's 4th.	20. R. to K's 3rd.
21. R. takes B.‡	21. P. takes R.
22. R. to K. B's sq.	22. P. to K's 6th.
23. R. takes P.	23. Q. to Q's 3rd.
24. R. to K. B's 6th.	Resigns.

---

* A move of very questionable merit.

† It is difficult to find a good reply for Black at this juncture. Perhaps 17. B. to Q's 2nd is less objectionable than any other.

‡ Well played.

CHAPTER XXI.

Sicilian Game.

Game the First.

$$1.\ \frac{\text{P. to K's 4th}}{\text{P. to Q. B's 4th}},\quad 2.\ \frac{\text{P. to Q's 4th}}{\quad}.$$

Game the Second.

$$2.\ \frac{\text{Kt. to K. B's 3rd}}{\quad}.$$

Game the Third.

$$2.\ \frac{\text{B. to Q. B's 4th}}{\quad}.$$

Game the Fourth.

$$2.\ \frac{\text{Kt. to Q. B's 3rd}}{\quad}.$$

Game the Fifth.

$$2.\ \frac{\text{P. to K. B's 4th}}{\quad};\ 2.\ \frac{\text{P. to Q. B's 4th}}{\quad};\ 2.\ \frac{\text{P. to Q. Kt.'s 4th}}{\quad};$$

$$2.\ \frac{\text{P. to Q. Kt.'s 3rd}}{\quad};\ 2.\ \frac{\text{P. to K. Kt.'s 3rd}}{\quad}.$$

The Sicilian Opening has long been a favourite with the leading players. Up to the last twenty years, indeed, it was considered the best, if not the only mode by which the second player could neutralise the advantage which generally accrues to the first from leading off with 1. $\frac{\text{P. to K's 4th}}{\qquad}$. Some variations of the attack, which were introduced by Mr. Szen, in the London Chess Tournament of 1851, have, however, qualified the high opinion of this defence considerably, and many good authorities pronounce it inferior to the French Defence of 1. $\frac{\qquad}{\text{P. to K's 3rd}}$. My own opinion of it is, that although the variation invented by Mr. Szen may have invalidated one particular branch of the defence—though even this I doubt—the Sicilian is still the best opening the second player can adopt against 1. $\frac{\text{P. to K's 4th}}{\qquad}$

Game the First.

WHITE.	BLACK.
1. P. to K's 4th.	1. P. to Q. B's 4th.
2. P. to Q's 4th.	

Jaenisch and other writers of eminence commend this as White's best move. There are many authorities, however, who prefer 2. $\frac{\text{Kt. to K. B's 3rd}}{\qquad}$, and 2. $\frac{\text{Kt. to Q. B's 3rd}}{\qquad}$; for which see the Second and Third Games.

2. P. takes P.

If 2. $\frac{\qquad}{\text{P. to K's 3rd}}$, then follows 3. $\frac{\text{P. to Q's 5th}}{\qquad}$, giving White an advantage.

3. Kt. to K. B's 3rd.

3. $\frac{\text{Q. takes P.}}{\qquad}$ only provokes 3. $\frac{\qquad}{\text{Kt. to Q. B's 3rd}}$, and plays Black's game.

3. P. to K's 3rd.

Instead of this move, Black can play, as in Variation A, 3. $\frac{\qquad}{\text{Kt. to Q. B's 3rd}}$, or, as in Variation B, 3. $\frac{\qquad}{\text{P. to K's 4th}}$.

4. Kt. takes P.	4. Kt. to K. B's 3rd.

The best move according to Anderssen; but I am of opinion that Black may play, with at least equal advantage, 4. $\frac{\quad}{\text{Kt. to Q. B's 3rd}}$, notwithstanding that it exposes him to Szen's attack of 5. $\frac{\text{Kt. to Q. Kt.'s 5th}}{\quad}$, which will be examined in Game the Second.

5. B. to Q's 3rd.

If 5. $\frac{\text{B. to K. Kt.'s 5th}}{\text{Q. to Q. R's 4th (ch.)}}$, 6. $\frac{\text{Q. to Q's 2nd}}{\text{B. to Q. Kt.'s 5th}}$, 7. $\frac{\text{P. to Q. B's 3rd}}{\text{Kt. takes P.}}$, and Black has at least as good a position as White. If 5. $\frac{\text{Kt. to Q. Kt.'s 5th}}{\text{Kt. takes P.}}$, 6. $\frac{\text{B. to K. B's 4th}}{\text{Kt. to Q. R's 3rd}}$, 7. $\frac{\text{P. to K. B's 3rd}}{\text{Q. to Q. R's 4th (ch.)}}$, White has no advantage. If 5. $\frac{\text{Kt. to Q. B's 3rd}}{\text{B. to Q. Kt.'s 5th}}$, 6. $\frac{\text{Kt. to Q. Kt.'s 5th}}{\text{P. to Q's 4th}}$, 7. $\frac{\text{B. to K. Kt.'s 5th}}{\text{P. to Q. R's 3rd}}$, 8. $\frac{\text{B. takes Kt.}}{\text{P. takes B.}}$, 9. $\frac{\text{Kt. to Q's 4th}}{\text{P. takes P.}}$, and Black for choice.

5. Kt. to Q. B's 3rd (best).

Black can also play 5. $\frac{\quad}{\text{B. to Q. B's 4th}}$, 6. $\frac{\text{Kt. to Q. Kt.'s 3rd}}{\text{P. to Q's 4th}}$, 7. $\frac{\text{P. to K's 5th}}{\text{K's Kt. to Q's 2nd}}$, 8. $\frac{\text{Castles}}{\text{B. to Q. Kt.'s 3rd}}$, and equalise the contest.

6. B. to K's 3rd. — 6. B. to K's 2nd.

He may also play 6. $\frac{\quad}{\text{P. to Q's 4th}}$.

7. P. to Q. B's 4th.

If 7. $\frac{\text{Castles}}{\text{Castles}}$, 8. $\frac{\text{P. to K. B's 4th}}{\text{P. to Q's 4th}}$, 9. $\frac{\text{P. to K's 5th}}{\text{Kt. to Q's 2nd}}$, equal game.

7. P. to Q's 4th.

8. Q's B. takes P.	8. P. takes P.
9. P. takes P.	9. Kt. takes P.
10. Kt. takes Kt.	10. P. takes Kt.

Neither party can boast of an advantage.

VARIATION A, BEGINNING AT BLACK'S 3RD MOVE.

BLACK.

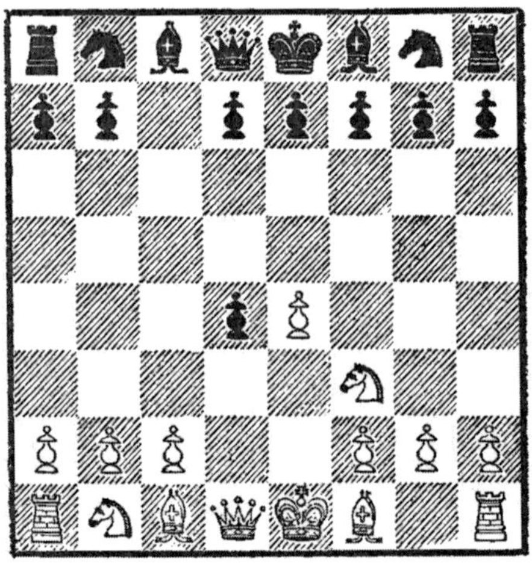

WHITE.

Position prior to Black's 3rd Move.

	3. Kt. to Q. B's 3rd.
4. B. to Q. B's 4th.	

If 4. $\frac{\text{Kt. takes P.}}{\text{P. to K's 3rd}}$, 5. $\frac{\text{B. to K's 3rd}}{\text{Kt. to K. B's 3rd}}$, 6. $\frac{\text{B. to Q's 3rd}}{\text{P. to Q's 4th}}$,

7. $\frac{\text{P. takes P.}}{\text{P. takes P.}}$, the game is equal.

	4. P. to K's 3rd.
5. Kt. takes P.	5. B. to Q. B's 4th.
6. Kt. to Q. Kt.'s 3rd.	6. B. to Q. Kt.'s 3rd.
7. Castles.	7. K's Kt. to K's 2nd.
8. Kt. to Q. B's 3rd.	8. P. to Q. R's 3rd.
9. B. to K. B's 4th.	9. P. to K's 4th.
10. B. to K's 3rd.	10. B. takes B.
11. P. takes B.	11. Castles.

I think White's game is the better one.

VARIATION B, ON BLACK'S 3RD MOVE.

(*See Diagram.*)

	3. P. to K's 4th.
4. B. to Q. B's 4th.	

It is clear that he cannot take the King's Pawn without losing his Knight.

	4. Q. to Q. B's 2nd.
5. Q. to K's 2nd.	5. Kt. to Q. B's 3rd.
6. Castles.	6. B. to K's 2nd.

And Black can apparently maintain the Pawn with some inferiority of position.

GAME THE SECOND.

WHITE.	BLACK.
1. P. to K's 4th.	1. P. to Q. B's 4th.
2. Kt. to K. B's 3rd.	

As I have said, many authorities speak of this move as greatly superior to 2. $\frac{\text{P. to Q's 4th}}{}$. To me the moves appear interchangeable, for if the best after-moves be adopted by both sides, the position becomes the same whether 2. $\frac{\text{Kt. to K. B's 3rd}}{}$ or $\frac{\text{P. to Q's 4th}}{}$ is chosen.

	2. P. to K's 3rd.
3. P. to Q's 4th.	3. P. takes P.

And we have the same position examined in the First Game.

4. Kt. takes P.

Here, if Black is not alarmed at the Szen attack, 5. $\frac{\text{Kt. to Q. Kt.'s 5th}}{}$, the potency of which has been much exaggerated, he will boldly play—

	4. Kt. to Q. B's 3rd.
5. Kt. to Q. Kt.'s 5th.	5. P. to Q. R's 3rd.
6. Kt. to Q's 6th (ch.)	6. B. takes Kt.
7. Q. takes B.	7. Q. to K's 2nd.

If 7. $\frac{\quad}{\text{Kt. to K's 2nd}}$, 8. $\frac{\text{B. to K's 3rd}}{\text{P. to K. B's 4th}}$, 9. $\frac{\text{B. to Q's 3rd}}{\text{Castles}}$, 10. $\frac{\text{Kt. to Q. B's 3rd}}{\text{P. takes P.}}$, 11. $\frac{\text{B. takes P.}}{\text{Kt. to K. B's 4th}}$, 12. $\frac{\text{B. takes Kt.}}{\text{R. takes B.}}$, 13. $\frac{\text{Castles, Q's side}}{\quad}$, with the better game.

8. Q. to K. Kt.'s 3rd.	8. P. to K. B's 4th (best).
9. P. to K's 5th (best).	9. Q. to Q. B's 4th.
10. Q. takes K. Kt.'s P.	

If 10. $\frac{\text{P. to K. B's 4th}}{\text{K. to B's 2nd}}$, with better game. If 10. $\frac{\text{B. to K. B's 4th}}{\text{K's Kt. to K's 2nd}}$, 11. $\frac{\text{Q. takes P.}}{\text{Kt. to K. Kt.'s 3rd}}$, with better game.

	10. Q. takes K's P. (ch.)
11. Q. takes Q.	11. Kt. takes Q.

Equal game.

On the other hand, if Black desire to evade the Szen attack, he can play 4. $\frac{\quad}{\text{Kt. to K. B's 3rd}}$, proceeding as in the First Game.

Game the Third.

WHITE.	BLACK.
1. P. to K's 4th.	1. P. to Q. B's 4th.
2. B. to Q. B's 4th.	

This, though at one time favoured by Anderssen, is not a good response to the Sicilian Defence. (For the consequences of 2. $\frac{\text{Kt. to Q. B's 3rd}}{\quad}$, see Game the Fourth.)

	2. P. to K's 3rd.*
3. Kt. to Q. B's 3rd.	3. Kt. to K's 2nd.
4. Q. to K's 2nd.	

If 4. $\frac{\text{P. to Q's 4th}}{\text{P. takes P.}}$, 5. $\frac{\text{Q. takes P.}}{\text{Kt. to Q. B's 3rd}}$, 6. $\frac{\text{Q. to Q's sq.}}{\text{B. to Q. Kt.'s 5th}}$, and White has an inferior position.

	4. Kt. to Q. B's 3rd.
5. Kt. to K. B's 3rd.	5. P. to Q. R's 3rd.
6. P. to Q's 3rd.	6. Kt. to K. B's 3rd.
7. Castles.	7. B. to K's 2nd.
8. B. to K's 3rd.	8. Castles.

Black has at least as good a game as his adversary has.

Game the Fourth.

WHITE.	BLACK.
1. P. to K's 4th.	1. P. to Q. B's 4th.
2. Kt. to Q. B's 3rd.	

This move has recently come into vogue, and, in the

---

* He may play, perhaps, with more advantage 3. $\frac{\quad}{\text{P. to Q. R's 3rd}}$, *e.g.* :—

	3. P. to Q. R's 3rd.
4. P. to Q. R's 4th.	4. Kt. to Q. B's 3rd.

The *Handbuch* gives 4. $\frac{\quad}{\text{Kt. to K's 2nd}}$, and continues 5. $\frac{\text{P. to Q's 4th}}{\text{P. to Q's 4th}}$, 6. $\frac{\text{P. takes Q's P.}}{\text{K's P. takes P.}}$, 7. $\frac{\text{Q. takes P.}}{\text{Kt. to Q. B's 3rd}}$, &c.

5. P. to Q's 3rd.	5. Kt. to K. B's 3rd.

If 5. $\frac{\quad}{\text{K's Kt. to K's 2nd}}$, White rejoins with 6. $\frac{\text{B. to K. Kt.'s 5th}}{\quad}$, and if 5. $\frac{\quad}{\text{Kt. to Q. Kt.'s 5th}}$, with 6. $\frac{\text{Q. to K's 2nd}}{\quad}$.

6. B. to Q's 2nd.	6. P. to Q's 4th.
7. B. to Q. R's 2nd.	7. B. to K's 2nd (best).

And Black has a slight superiority.—Ed.]

opinion of some of our leading players, it is the best reply White can adopt to 1. $\frac{}{\text{P. to Q. B's 4th}}$.

2. Kt. to Q. B's 3rd (best).

3. Kt. to K. B's 3rd.

This is much superior to 3. $\frac{\text{P. to K. Kt.'s 3rd}}{}$, the correct continuation of which is 3. $\frac{\text{P. to K. Kt.'s 3rd}}{\text{P. to Q's 3rd}}$, 4. $\frac{\text{B. to K. Kt.'s 2nd}}{\text{P. to K's 4th}}$ and Black has the advantage.

3. P. to K's 3rd.

4. P. to Q's 4th.

White may also play 4. $\frac{\text{B. to Q. Kt.'s 5th}}{}$, or 4. $\frac{\text{B. to Q. B's 4th}}{}$, but the latter is inferior.

	4. P. takes P.
5. Kt. takes P.	5. Kt. to K. B's 3rd.
6. P. to Q. R's 3rd.	

If 6. $\frac{\text{B. to Q. Kt.'s 5th}}{}$, or 6. $\frac{\text{K's Kt. to Kt.'s 5th}}{}$, Black equally replies with 6. $\frac{}{\text{B. to Q. Kt.'s 5th}}$.

	6. P. to Q. R's 3rd.
7. B. to Q. B's 4th.	7. P. to Q's 4th.
8. P. takes P.	8. P. takes P.
9. B. to Q. Kt.'s 3rd.	9. B. to Q. B's 4th.

And White has perhaps a slightly freer game.

Game the Fifth.

WHITE.	BLACK.
1. P. to K's 4th.	1. P. to Q. B's 4th.
2. P. to K. B's 4th.	

At one time, up even to within the last thirty years, this was considered the best reply to Black's move. Analysis and practical experience have proved, however, that it is inferior to 2. $\frac{\text{P. to Q's 4th}}{}$, 2. $\frac{\text{Kt. to K. B's 3rd}}{}$, or 2. $\frac{\text{Kt. to Q. B's 3rd}}{}$.

(For the consequences of 2. $\frac{\text{P. to Q. B's 4th}}{}$, 2. $\frac{\text{P. to Q. Kt.'s 4th}}{}$, 2. $\frac{\text{P. to Q. Kt.'s 3rd}}{}$, and 2. $\frac{\text{P. to K. Kt.'s 3rd}}{}$, see Variations A, B, C and D.)

2. P. to K's 3rd.

If 2. $\frac{}{\text{Kt. to Q. B's 3rd}}$, 3. $\frac{\text{Kt. to K. B's 3rd}}{\text{P. to K's 3rd}}$, 4. $\frac{\text{B. to Q. Kt.'s 5th}}{}$, White has some advantage.

3. Kt. to K. B's 3rd.	3. P. to Q's 4th.
4. P. takes P.	4. P. takes P.
5. P. to Q's 4th.	5. Kt. to Q. B's 3rd.

With the better position.

Variation A, beginning at White's 2nd Move.

2. P. to Q. B's 4th.

The objection to this move is that it imprisons White's forces; but it has advantages, and may be played with perfect safety.

2. Kt. to Q. B's 3rd.

If 2. $\frac{}{\text{P. to K's 3rd}}$, 3. $\frac{\text{Kt. to K. B's 3rd}}{\text{Kt. to Q. B's 3rd}}$, 4. $\frac{\text{Kt. to Q. B's 3rd}}{\text{P. to Q. R's 3rd}}$, 5. $\frac{\text{B. to K's 2nd}}{\text{P. to K. Kt.'s 3rd}}$, 6. $\frac{\text{P. to Q's 4th}}{\text{P. takes P.}}$, 7. $\frac{\text{Kt. takes P.}}{\text{B. to K. Kt.'s 2nd}}$, 8. $\frac{\text{Kt. takes Kt.}}{\text{Kt.'s P. takes Kt.}}$, White has a better developed game.

3. Kt. to Q. B's 3rd.	3. P. to Q. R's 3rd.
4. Kt. to K. B's 3rd.	4. P. to K's 3rd.
5. B. to K's 2nd.	5. Kt. to K's 2nd.
6. P. to Q's 4th.	6. P. takes P.
7. Kt. takes P.	7. Kt. to K. Kt.'s 3rd.

And White has no superiority.

Variation B, beginning at White's 2nd Move.

2. P. to Q. Kt.'s 4th.

This constitutes Jaenisch's *Wing Gambit*, and is found in Sarratt. It is ingenious but unprofitable.

2. P. takes P.

Black may also play 2. $\frac{}{\text{P. to Q. Kt.'s 3rd}}$, and have an equal game.

3. P. to Q's 4th.	3. P. to K's 3rd.
4. P. to Q. R's 3rd.	4. P. takes P.
5. Q's B. takes P.	5. B. takes B.
6. R. takes B.	6. Kt. to Q. B's 3rd.

And Black has a Pawn more without any disadvantage in situation. He would, perhaps, even better his game if, at the third move, he played forward his Queen's Pawn, as in the following fragment of a game between Messrs. Heydebrandt and Hanstein:—3. $\frac{}{\text{P. to Q's 4th}}$, 4. $\frac{\text{P. to K's 5th}}{\text{P. to K's 3rd}}$, 5. $\frac{\text{P. to Q. R's 3rd}}{\text{P. takes P.}}$, 6. $\frac{\text{Kt. takes P.}}{\text{B. takes Kt.}}$, 7. $\frac{\text{B. takes B.}}{}$. If Black now give check with his Queen at Queen's Rook's 4th, he will have the better game.

Variation C, on White's 2nd Move.

2. P. to Q. Kt.'s 3rd.

Was advocated by Kieseritzky, who submitted it to the hard test of playing it against Anderssen, not successfully. The *Handbuch* gives the following, which are from one of the games mentioned.

	2. Kt. to Q. B's 3rd.
3. B. to Q. Kt.'s 2nd.	3. P. to Q. R's 3rd.
4. P. to Q. R's 4th.	4. P. to K's 3rd.
5. Kt. to K. B's 3rd.	5. P. to Q's 3rd.
6. Kt. to Q. B's 3rd.	6. Kt. to K. B's 3rd

7. B. to K's 2nd.	7. B. to K's 2nd.
8. Castles.	8. Castles.
9. P. to Q's 4th.	9. P. takes P.
10. Kt. takes P.	10. Q. to Q. Kt.'s 3rd.
11. Kt. takes Kt.	11. P. takes Kt.

It appears to me a move that may be safely played, but which, at the best, gives to White an equal game only.

Variation D, beginning at White's 2nd Move.

2. P. to K. Kt.'s 3rd.

A move which, like 2. $\frac{\text{P. to Q. Kt.'s 3rd}}{\quad}$, may be played without danger and without advantage.

	2. P. to K's 3rd.
3. B. to K. Kt.'s 2nd.	3. P. to K. Kt.'s 3rd.

In a game between Paulsen and Anderssen the moves ran thus:—3. $\frac{\text{Kt. to Q. B's 3rd}}{\text{Kt. to K's 2nd}}$, 4. $\frac{\text{B. to K. Kt.'s 2nd}}{\text{P. to Q's 3rd}}$, 5. $\frac{\text{P. to Q's 3rd}}{\text{Kt. to Q. B's 3rd}}$, 6. $\frac{\text{Kt. to K. R's 3rd}}{\text{P. to Q. R's 3rd}}$, 7. $\frac{\text{Castles}}{\text{B. to Q's 2nd}}$, 8. $\frac{\text{P. to K. B's 4th}}{\text{P. to K. B's 4th}}$. Equal game.

4. P. to Q. B's 3rd.	4. B. to K. Kt.'s 2nd.
5. Kt. to K's 2nd.	5. Kt. to K's 2nd.
6. P. to Q's 3rd.	6. Kt. to Q. B's 3rd.
7. B. to K's 3rd.	7. P. to Q. Kt.'s 3rd.

Equal game.

ILLUSTRATIVE GAMES.

Game I.—Between Messrs. Anderssen and Staunton.

White (Mr. A.)	Black (Mr. S.)
1. P. to K's 4th.	1. P. to Q. B's 4th.
2. P. to Q's 4th.	2. P. takes P.
3. Kt. to K. B's 3rd.	3. P. to K's 3rd.

4. Kt. takes P.	4. B. to Q. B's 4th.
5. Kt. to Q. B's 3rd.	5. P. to Q. R's 3rd.
6. B. to K's 3rd.	6. B. to Q. R's 2nd.
7. B. to Q's 3rd.	7. Kt. to K's 2nd.
8. Castles.	8. Castles.
9. Q. to R's 5th.	9. Kt. to K. Kt.'s 3rd.
10. P. to K's 5th.	10. Q. to Q. B's 2nd.*
11. Q's R. to K's sq.	11. P. to Q. Kt.'s 4th.
12. P. to K. B's 4th.	12. B. to Q. Kt.'s 2nd.
13. Kt. to K's 4th.	13. B. takes Kt.
14. B. takes B.	14. Kt. to Q. B's 3rd.
15. Kt. takes Kt.	15. P. takes Kt.
16. P. to K. Kt.'s 4th.	16. R. to Q's sq.
17. K. to R's sq.	17. P. to Q. B's 4th.
18. R. to K. B's 3rd.	18. Q. to Q. R's 4th.
19. Q's R. to K. B's sq.†	19. Q. to R's 5th.
20. B. to Q's 3rd.	20. Q. takes Q. R's P.
21. R. to K. R's 3rd.	21. P. to K. R's 3rd.
22. P. to K. Kt.'s 5th.	22. R. takes B.
23. P. takes R.	23. Q. to Q's 4th (ch.)
24. Q's R. to K. B's 3rd.	24. Kt. to K's 2nd.
25. P. takes P.	25. P. to K. Kt.'s 3rd.
26. P. to R's 7th (ch.)	26. K. to R's sq.
27. Q. to Kt.'s 5th.	27. Kt. to K. B's 4th.
28. Q. to B's 6th (ch.)	28. Kt. to Kt.'s 2nd.
29. P. to K. B's 5th.‡	29. Q. to Q. Kt.'s 6th.
30. B. to K. R's 6th.	30. Q. to Q's 8th (ch.)
31. K. to Kt.'s 2nd.	31. Q. to K's 7th (ch.)
32. R. to K. B's 2nd.	Resigns.

—GAME II.—Between Messrs. Anderssen and Wyvill.

WHITE (Mr. A.)	BLACK (Mr. W.)
1. P. to K's 4th.	1. P. to Q. B's 4th.
2. B. to Q. B's 4th.	2. P. to K's 3rd.

* An utterly useless move, that augurs ill so early in the game for Black's prospects.

† Very well conceived, and far preferable to the more obvious move of R. to K. Kt.'s sq.

‡ Quite conclusive. The whole game is admirably played by Anderssen, but the defence is altogether unworthy of the second player.

3. Kt. to Q. B's 3rd.	3. P. to Q. R's 3rd.
4. P. to Q. R's 4th.	4. Kt. to Q. B's 3rd.
5. P. to Q's 3rd.	5. P. to K. Kt.'s 3rd.
6. K's Kt. to K's 2nd.	6. B. to K. Kt.'s 2nd.
7. Castles.	7. K's Kt. to K's 2nd.
8. P. to K. B's 4th.	8. Castles.
9. B. to Q's 2nd.	9. P. to Q's 4th.
10. B. to Q. Kt.'s 3rd.	10. Kt. to Q's 5th.
11. Kt. takes Kt.	11. B. takes Kt. (ch.)
12. K. to R's sq.	12. B. to Q's 2nd.
13. P. takes Q's P.	13. B. takes Kt.
14. B. takes B.	14. P. takes P.
15. B. to K. B's 6th.	15. B. to K's 3rd.
16. P. to K. B's 5th.*	16. B. takes P.
17. R. takes B.	17. P. takes R.
18. Q. to K. R's 5th.	18. Q. to Q's 3rd.
19. Q. to K. R's 6th.	19. Q. takes B.
20. Q. takes Q.	Resigns.

---

* The commencement of a beautiful combination, which forces the game.

CHAPTER XXII.

The Centre Counter Gambit.

This defence may be ventured without much danger, but it is not to be commended, as it leaves the first player with a slightly superior game from the outset.

Game the First.

WHITE.	BLACK.
1. P. to K's 4th.	1. P. to Q's 4th.
2. P. takes P. (best).	2. Q. takes P.

(For the consequences of 2. $\frac{\quad}{\text{Kt. to K. B's 3rd}}$ see Game the Second.)

3. Kt. to Q. B's 3rd.	3. Q. to Q. R's 4th.

This, I am inclined to think, is stronger than the old move of 3. $\frac{\quad}{\text{Q. to Q's sq.}}$, to which White can reply with 4. $\frac{\text{P. to Q's 4th}}{\quad}$, with a superior position.

4. P. to Q's 4th.	4. P. to Q. B's 3rd.

Black's best reply. In one of his games with Morphy Anderssen played here 4. $\frac{\quad}{\text{P. to K's 4th}}$, but it is inferior.

5. B. to Q's 2nd.	5. Q. to Q. B's 2nd.

Black has a safe defensive position.

Game the Second.

WHITE.	BLACK.
1. P. to K's 4th.	1. P. to Q's 4th.
2. P. takes P.	2. Kt. to K. B's 3rd.
3. B. to Q. Kt.'s 5th (ch.)	

Seemingly White's only move to preserve the Pawn he has won. He may, however, simplify the position at once at the cost of the Pawn by 3. $\frac{\text{P. to Q's 4th}}{}$.

	3. B. to Q's 2nd.
4. B. to Q. B's 4th.	4. P. to Q. Kt.'s 4th.
5. B. to Q. Kt.'s 3rd.	5. B. to K. Kt.'s 5th.
6. P. to K. B's 3rd (best).	6. B. to K. B's 4th.

He may also play 6. $\frac{}{\text{B. to Q. B's sq.}}$, 7. $\frac{\text{Q. to K's 2nd}}{\text{B. to Q. R's 3rd}}$, &c.

7. Q. to K's 2nd.	7. P. to Q. R's 3rd.
8. P. to Q. B's 4th.	8. P. to Q. B's 3rd.
9. Kt. to Q. B's 3rd.	9. P. to Q. Kt.'s 5th.

And the game is slightly in White's favour. I am inclined to think, however, that he will ultimately have to abandon the Pawn he has won.

ILLUSTRATIVE GAMES.

Game I.—Between Messrs. Morphy and Anderssen.

White (Mr. M.)	Black (Mr. A.)
1. P. to K's 4th.	1. P. to Q's 4th.
2. P. takes P.	2. Q. takes P.
3. Kt. to Q. B's 3rd.	3. Q. to Q. R's 4th.
4. P. to Q's 4th.	4. P. to K's 4th.*

* The correct move, as we have seen, is 4. P. to Q. B's 3rd. The move in the text subjects Black to a restrained position from which he never emancipates himself.

5. P. takes P.	5. Q. takes P. (ch.)
6. B. to K's 2nd.	6. B. to Q. Kt's 5th.
7. Kt. to K. B's 3rd.	7. B. takes Kt. (ch.)
8. P. takes B.	8. Q. takes P. (ch.)
9. B. to Q's 2nd.	9. Q. to Q. B's 4th.
10. R. to Q. Kt.'s sq.	10. Kt. to Q. B's 3rd.
11. Castles.	11. Kt. to B's 3rd.
12. B. to K. B's 4th.	12. Castles.
13. B. takes P.	13. Kt. to Q's 5th.
14. Q. takes Kt.	14. Q. takes B.
15. B. to Q's 3rd.	15. B. to Kt.'s 5th.
16. Kt. to Kt.'s 5th.	16. K's R. to Q's sq.
17. Q. to Q. Kt.'s 4th.	17. B. to B's sq.
18. K's R. to K's sq.	18. P. to Q. R's 4th.
19. Q. to K's 7th.	19. Q. takes Q.
20. R. takes Q.	20. Kt. to Q's 4th.
21. B. takes P. (ch.)	21. K. to R's sq.
22. R. takes B's P.	22. Kt. to B's 6th.
23. Q's R. to K's sq.	23. Kt. takes P.
24. R. to B's 4th.	24. R. to R's 3rd.
25. B. to Q's 3rd.	

And wins.

Game II.—Between Messrs. Steinitz and Mongredien.

White (Mr. S.)	Black. (Mr. M.)
1. P. to K's 4th.	1. P. to Q's 4th.
2. P. takes P.	2. Q. takes P.
3. Kt. to Q. B's 3rd.	3. Q. to Q's sq.
4. P. to Q's 4th.	4. P. to K's 3rd.
5. Kt. to K. B's 3rd.	5. Kt. to K. B's 3rd.
6. B. to Q's 3rd.	6. B. to K's 2nd.
7. Castles.	7. Castles.
8. B. to K's 3rd.	8. P. to Q. Kt.'s 3rd.
9. Kt. to K's 5th.	9. B. to Q. Kt.'s 2nd.
10. P. to K. B's 4th.	10. Q's Kt. to Q's 2nd.
11. Q. to K's 2nd.	11. K's Kt. to Q's 4th.
12. Kt. takes Kt.	12. P. takes Kt.
13. R. to K. B's 3rd.	13. P. to K. B's 4th.
14. R. to K. R's 3rd.	14. P. to K. Kt.'s 3rd.

15. P. to K. Kt.'s 4th.	15. P. takes P.
16. R. takes K. R's P.	16. Kt. takes Kt.
17. B's P. takes Kt.	17. K. takes R.
18. Q. takes P.	18. K's R. to Kt.'s sq.*
19. Q. to R's 5th (ch.)	19. K. to Kt.'s 2nd.
20. Q. to R's 6th (ch.)	20. K. to B's 2nd.
21. Q. to R's 7th (ch.)	21. K. to K's 3rd.
22. Q. to R's 3rd (ch.)†	22. K. to B's 2nd.
23. R. to K. B's sq. (ch.)	23. K. to K's sq.
24. Q. to K's 6th.	24. R. to K. Kt.'s 2nd.
25. B. to K. Kt.'s 5th.	25. Q. to Q's 2nd.
26. B. takes K. Kt.'s P. (ch.)	26. R. takes B.
27. Q. takes R. (ch.)	27. K. to Q's sq.
28. R. to K. B's 8th (ch.)	

And wins.

* It would possibly have been better to play 18. R. to K. B's 4th.

† All this is very pretty.

CHAPTER XXIII.

QUEEN'S BISHOP'S PAWN'S OPENING.

1. $\frac{\text{P. to Q. B's 4th}}{\quad}$.

GAME THE FIRST.

1. $\frac{\quad}{\text{P. to K's 4th}}$.

GAME THE SECOND.

1. $\frac{\quad}{\text{P. to Q. B's 4th}}$.

GAME THE THIRD.

1. $\frac{\quad}{\text{P. to K's 3rd}}$; 1. $\frac{\quad}{\text{P. to K. B's 4th}}$; 1. $\frac{\quad}{\text{P. to Q. Kt.'s 4th}}$.

This manner of beginning the game is found for the first time in Carrera's treatise (1617). As his work is rare, and the analysis he gives of this opening but brief, it may interest modern players to see his moves. "The White beginning," he observes, "with Q. B's Pawn two squares, Black may play K's Pawn, K. B's Pawn, Q's Pawn, or Q. B's Pawn, each two squares; the best of these is the K's Pawn, the worst move is the Q's Pawn.

I.

1. Q. B's P. two squares.	1. K's P. two squares.
2. K's P. one square, or Q's Kt. to Q. B's third square.	2. K. B's P. two squares, or Q. B's P. one square.

II.

1. Q. B's P. two squares.	1. K. B's P. two squares.
2. Q's P. two squares.	2. K's Kt. to K. B's third square.

III.

1. Q. B's P. two squares.	1. Q. B's P. two squares.
2. K. B's P. two squares, or Q's Kt. to Q. B's third square.	2. Q's Kt. to Q. B's third square.

IV.

1. Q. B's P. two squares.	1. Q's P. two squares.
2. P. takes P.	2. Q. takes P.
3. Q's Kt. to Q. B's third square." *	

GAME THE FIRST.

WHITE.	BLACK.
1. P. to Q. B's 4th.	1. P. to K's 4th.

Some authorities prefer 1. $\frac{}{\text{P. to Q. B's 4th}}$, or 1. $\frac{}{\text{P. to K's 3rd}}$, which shall be examined presently, to the move in the text, but there does not appear to be any solid reason for the preference.

2. P. to K's 3rd.

White can likewise play 2. $\frac{\text{Kt. to Q. B's 3rd}}{}$, *ex. gr.*,

2. $\frac{\text{Kt. to Q. B's 3rd}}{\text{Kt. to K. B's 3rd}}$. (Better, I think, than 2. $\frac{}{\text{P. to K. B's 4th}}$.) 3. $\frac{\text{P. to K's 3rd}}{\text{P. to Q's 4th}}$, 4. $\frac{\text{P. takes P.}}{\text{Kt. takes P.}}$, 5. $\frac{\text{P. to Q. R's 3rd}}{\text{B. to K's 3rd}}$, 6. $\frac{\text{Kt. to K. B's 3rd}}{\text{B. to Q's 3rd}}$, 7. $\frac{\text{B. to K's 2nd}}{\text{Castles}}$, 8. $\frac{\text{P. to Q's 4th}}{\text{Kt. takes Kt.}}$,

* Lewis's translation, 1822.

9. $\frac{\text{P. takes Kt.}}{\text{P. to K's 5th}}$, 10. $\frac{\text{Kt. to Q's 2nd}}{\text{P. to K. B's 4th}}$, 11. $\frac{\text{P. to K. B's 4th}}{\text{Q. to K. R's 5th (ch.)}}$, 12. $\frac{\text{P. to K. Kt.'s 3rd}}{\text{Q. to K. R's 6th}}$, 13. $\frac{\text{B. to K. B's sq.}}{\text{Q. to K. R's 3rd}}$. Black has somewhat the better game.

	2. Kt. to K. B's 3rd.
3. Kt. to Q. B's 3rd.	3. P. to Q's 4th.
4. P. to Q's 4th.	

White may also play 4. $\frac{\text{P. takes P.}}{}$, the game continuing 4. $\frac{}{\text{Kt. takes P.}}$, 5. $\frac{\text{Kt. to K. B's 3rd}}{\text{Kt. takes Kt.}}$, 6. $\frac{\text{Q. Kt.'s P. takes Kt.}}{\text{B. to Q's 3rd}}$, 7. $\frac{\text{P. to Q's 4th}}{\text{P. takes P.}}$, 8. $\frac{\text{B's P. takes P.}}{\text{Castles.}}$, 9. $\frac{\text{B. to Q's 3rd}}{\text{Kt. to Q. B's 3rd}}$, 10. $\frac{\text{B. to Q's 2nd}}{}$. The game is about equal.

	4. K's P. takes P.
5. P. takes P.	5. B. to Q. Kt.'s 5th.
6. B. to K. Kt.'s 5th.	6. B. to K's 3rd.
7. Q. to Q. R's 4th (ch.)	7. Kt. to Q. B's 3rd.
8. Kt. to K. B's 3rd.	

And the position is about even.

Game the Second.

WHITE.	BLACK.
1. P. to Q. B's 4th.	1. P. to Q. B's 4th.
2. Kt. to Q. B's 3rd.	

2. $\frac{\text{P. to K's 3rd}}{}$ is also a good move, as shall be shown in Variation A. If 2. $\frac{\text{P. to K. B's 4th}}{\text{P. to K. B's 4th}}$, 3. $\frac{\text{P. to Q's 3rd}}{\text{Kt. to K. B's 3rd}}$, 4. $\frac{\text{Kt. to Q. B's 3rd}}{\text{P. to Q's 3rd}}$, 5. $\frac{\text{P. to K's 4th}}{\text{Kt. to Q. B's 3rd}}$, 6. $\frac{\text{Kt. to K. B's 3rd}}{\text{P. to K's 4th}}$, the game is equal.

	2. P. to K. B's 4th.
3. P. to K's 4th.	3. P. to Q's 3rd.
4. B. to Q's 3rd.	4. P. to K's 3rd.
5. P. takes P.	

White may play advantageously also 5. $\frac{\text{Q. to K's 2nd}}{}$.

	5. P. takes P.
6. Kt. to K. R's 3rd.	6. Kt. to K. B's 3rd.
7. P. to Q. Kt.'s 3rd.	7. Kt. to Q. B's 3rd.
8. Castles.	8. B. to K's 2nd.
9. B. to Q. Kt.'s 2nd.	9. Castles.
10. Kt. to K. B's 4th.	10. Kt. to K. Kt.'s 5th.

White has the freer game.

Variation A, beginning at White's 2nd Move.

2. P. to K's 3rd.	2. P. to K's 4th.

He can, at least as well, play 2. $\frac{}{\text{P. to K's 3rd}}$.

3. Kt. to Q. B's 3rd.	3. Kt. to Q. B's 3rd.
4. K's Kt. to K's 2nd.	4. P. to Q's 3rd.
5. Kt. to K. Kt.'s 3rd.	5. B. to K's 2nd.
6. B. to K's 2nd.	6. Kt. to K. B's 3rd.
7. Castles.	7. Castles.
8. P. to Q. Kt.'s 3rd.	8. P. to Q. R's 3rd.
9. B. to Q. Kt.'s 2nd.	9. B. to K's 3rd.
10. P. to K. B's 4th.	10. P. takes P.
11. R. takes P.	11. P. to Q's 4th.
12. P. takes P.	12. Kt. takes P.
13. Kt. takes Kt.	13. B. takes P.
14. Kt. to K. B's 5th.	

White has the advantage.

Game the Third.

WHITE.	BLACK.
1. P. to Q. B's 4th.	1. P. to K's 3rd.

(For the result of 1. $\frac{\qquad}{\text{P. to K. B's 4th}}$, consult Variation A; of 1. $\frac{\qquad}{\text{P. to Q. Kt.'s 4th}}$, see Variation B.)

2. P. to Q's 4th.	2. P. to Q's 4th.
3. Kt. to Q. B's 3rd.	3. Kt. to K. B's 3rd.

And we have a well-known position of the Queen's Gambit Declined.

Variation A, beginning at Black's 1st Move.

WHITE.	BLACK.
1. P. to Q. B's 4th.	1. P. to K. B's 4th.
2. P. to K's 3rd.	2. P. to K's 3rd.

If 2. $\frac{\qquad}{\text{Kt. to K. B's 3rd}}$, 3. $\frac{\text{P. to Q's 4th}}{\qquad}$.

3. P. to Q's 4th.	

White can play 3. $\frac{\text{P. to Q. R's 3rd}}{\qquad}$, with the probable continuation 3. $\frac{\qquad}{\text{Kt. to K. B's 3rd}}$, 4. $\frac{\text{Kt. to Q. B's 3rd}}{\text{B. to K's 2nd}}$, 5. $\frac{\text{Kt. to K. B's 3rd}}{\text{Castles.}}$, 6. $\frac{\text{P. to Q's 4th}}{\text{P. to Q. Kt.'s 3rd}}$, 7. $\frac{\text{B. to Q's 3rd}}{\qquad}$, and have a good opening.

	3. Kt. to K. B's 3rd.
4. P. to Q. R's 3rd.	4. B. to K's 2nd.
5. Kt. to Q. B's 3rd.	

White has a slightly freer game.

Variation B, beginning at Black's 1st Move.

WHITE.	BLACK.
1. P. to Q. B's 4th.	1. P. to Q. Kt.'s 4th.

This move constitutes what Jaenisch terms the *Counter-*

Wing Gambit. It is not so purposeless as it looks, and if not properly met gives a strong attack to Black.

2. P. to K's 3rd.

And Black will have weakened his position on the Queen's side for nothing.

Jaenisch recommends 2. $\frac{\text{P. to Q. Kt.'s 3rd}}{}$ as the proper move if the Gambit be refused. If it be accepted, he continues the opening thus :—2. $\frac{\text{P. takes P.}}{\text{P. to Q. R's 3rd}}$, 3. $\frac{\text{P. to K's 3rd}}{\text{P. takes P.}}$, 4. $\frac{\text{B. takes P.}}{\text{P. to Q. B's 3rd}}$, 5. $\frac{\text{B. to Q. R's 4th}}{\text{P. to K's 4th}}$, 6. $\frac{\text{Kt. to Q. B's 3rd}}{}$, and declares the opening to be in White's favour. I doubt this ; White has certainly won a Pawn, but his adversary's position more than compensates him for the loss.

ILLUSTRATIVE GAME.

Between Messrs. Barnes and Boden.

White (Mr. Barnes).	Black (Mr. Boden).
1. P. to Q. B's 4th.	1. P. to K's 4th.
2. Kt. to Q. B's 3rd.	2. P. to K. B's 4th.
3. P. to K's 3rd.	3. Kt. to K. B's 3rd.
4. Kt. to K. R's 3rd.	4. P. to Q. B's 4th.
5. P. to Q. Kt.'s 3rd.	5. Kt. to Q. B's 3rd.
6. B. to K's 2nd.	6. K's B. to K's 2nd.
7. Kt. to Q's 5th.	7. P. to K's 5th.
8. P. to K. B's 3rd.	8. P. to Q's 3rd.
9. Kt. takes Kt. (ch.)	9. B. takes Kt.
10. R. to Q. Kt.'s sq.	10. Q. to K's 2nd.
11. P. takes P.	11. P. takes P.
12. Kt. to K. B's 4th.	12. Castles.
13. Castles.	13. P. to Q. Kt.'s 3rd.
14. Kt. to Q's 5th.	14. Q. to Q's sq.
15. Q. to Q. B's 2nd.	15. Q. to K's sq.*
16. Kt. to Q. B's 7th.	16. Q. to K. Kt.'s 3rd.

* The commencement of a capital combination.

17. Kt. takes R.	17. B. to K. R's 6th.
18. R. to K. B's 2nd.	18. Kt. to Q's 5th.*
19. Q. to Q's sq.	19. R. takes Q's Kt.
20. B. to Q. Kt.'s 2nd.	20. B. to K. R's 5th.
21. B. to K. B's sq.	21. B. takes R. (ch.)
22. K. takes B.	22. R. to K. B's sq. (ch.)
23. K. to Kt.'s sq.	23. Kt. to B's 6th (ch.)
24. K. to R's sq.	24. B. to K. Kt.'s 5th.
25. B. to K's 2nd.	25. Kt. takes R's P.
26. K. takes Kt.	26. Q. to K. R's 4th (ch.)
27. K. to Kt.'s 3rd.	27. B. takes B.
28. Q. to K. R's sq.	

Black mated in six moves.

---

* Leading to a pretty finish.

CHAPTER XXIV.

The Inverted Sicilian.

1. $\frac{\text{P. to Q's 4th}}{\text{P. to K. B's 4th}}$.

Game the First.

2. $\frac{\text{P. to K's 4th}}{\quad}$.

Game the Second.

2. $\frac{\text{P. to Q. B's 4th}}{\quad}$.

Game the First.

WHITE.	BLACK.
1. P. to Q's 4th.	1. P. to K. B's 4th.
2. P. to K's 4th.	

I believe this move, which I first suggested, and adopted in a game with Mr. Horwitz (1847), is the strongest answer to 1. $\frac{\quad}{\text{P. to K. B's 4th}}$. White, however, may safely play 2. $\frac{\text{P. to Q. B's 4th}}{\quad}$, as in the next game.

WHITE.	BLACK.
	2. P. takes P.
3. Kt. to Q. B's 3rd.	3. Kt. to K. B's 3rd.

(For the result of 3. $\frac{\quad}{\text{P. to K's 3rd}}$, see Variation A.)

4. B. to K. Kt.'s 5th.	4. P. to Q. B's 3rd.

If 4. $\frac{\quad}{\text{P. to Q's 4th}}$, 5. $\frac{\text{B. takes Kt.}}{\text{K's P. takes B.}}$, 6. $\frac{\text{Q. to K. R's 5th (ch.)}}{\text{P. to K. Kt.'s 3rd}}$, 7. $\frac{\text{Q. takes Q's P.}}{\text{B. to K. R's 3rd}}$, 8. $\frac{\text{Q. takes K's P. (ch.)}}{\quad}$, or 8. $\frac{\text{Kt. takes P.}}{\quad}$, White has an evident superiority.

5. B. takes Kt.	5. K's P. takes B.
6. Kt. takes P.	6. P. to Q's 4th.*
7. Kt. to K. Kt.'s 3rd.	

White can also play advantageously 7. $\frac{\text{Kt. to Q's 2nd}}{\quad}$, with the following continuation :—7. $\frac{\quad}{\text{Q. to K's 2nd (ch.)}}$, 8. $\frac{\text{B. to K's 2nd}}{\text{Q. to Q. Kt.'s 5th}}$, 9. $\frac{\text{K's Kt. to K. B's 3rd}}{\text{Q. takes Q. Kt.'s P.}}$, 10. $\frac{\text{Castles}}{\quad}$, &c.

---

* This is given as best in the German *Handbuch*, but it is inferior to 6. $\frac{\quad}{\text{Q. to Q. Kt.'s 3rd}}$, which first occurred in a game between Messrs. Potter and Steinitz. The correct continuation appears to be—

	6. Q. to Q. Kt.'s 3rd.
7. B. to Q's 3rd.	

Stronger than 7. $\frac{\text{Q. to R's 5th (ch.)}}{\quad}$; *e.g.*, 7. $\frac{\text{Q. to R's 5th (ch.)}}{\text{P. to Kt.'s 3rd}}$, 8. $\frac{\text{Kt. takes P. (ch.)}}{\text{K. to Q's sq. (best)}}$, 9. $\frac{\text{Q. to K. R's 4th}}{\text{B. to K's 2nd}}$, threatening to win a piece by 10. $\frac{\quad}{\text{R. to B's sq.}}$, or 10. $\frac{\quad}{\text{P. to Q. B's 4th}}$.

	7. P. to Q's 4th.
8. Kt. to Q. B's 3rd.	8. Q. takes Kt.'s P.
9. K's Kt. to K's 2nd.	9. B. to Q's 3rd.

If 9. $\frac{\quad}{\text{B. to Q. Kt.'s 5th}}$, White obtains an advantage by 10. $\frac{\text{Castles}}{\text{B. takes Kt.}}$, 11. $\frac{\text{R. to Kt.'s sq.}}{\text{Q. takes R's P.}}$, 12. $\frac{\text{Kt. takes B.}}{\text{Q. to R's 4th}}$, 13. $\frac{\text{Q. to R's 5th (ch.)}}{\quad}$, &c.

10. Castles.	10. Castles.

And Black has won a Pawn. The above were the opening moves of the game previously referred to.—[Ed.]

	7. B. to Q's 3rd.
8. B. to Q's 3rd.	8. Castles.
9. K's Kt. to K's 2nd.	9. P. to K. B's 4th.
10. P. to K. B's 4th.	10. P. to Q. B's 4th.
11. P. to Q. B's 3rd.	11. P. takes P.
12. P. takes P.	

White has a freer position.

Variation A, beginning at Black's 3rd move.

BLACK.

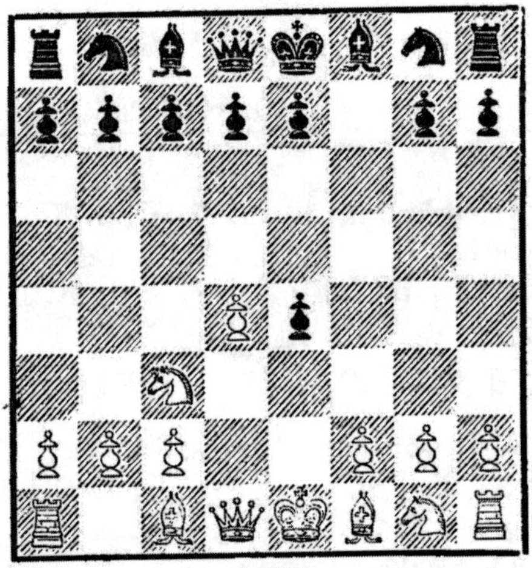

WHITE.

Position prior to Black's 3rd Move.

	3. P. to K's 3rd.
4. Kt. takes P.	

White can also check with the Queen and obtain a slight advantage in position. For example: 4. $\frac{\text{Q. to K. R's 5th (ch.)}}{\text{P. to K. Kt.'s 3rd}}$, 5. $\frac{\text{Q. to K's 5th}}{\text{Kt. to K. B's 3rd}}$, 6. $\frac{\text{Kt. to Q's 5th}}{\text{K. to B's 2nd}}$. (If 6. $\frac{}{\text{B. to K's 2nd}}$, or 6. $\frac{}{\text{B. to K. Kt.'s 2nd}}$, 7. $\frac{\text{Kt. takes P. (ch.)}}{}$, and White has the better game. If 6. $\frac{}{\text{Kt. to Q. B's 3rd}}$, 7. $\frac{\text{Q. takes Kt.}}{}$. If 6. $\frac{}{\text{Kt. takes Kt.}}$, 7. $\frac{\text{Q. takes R.}}{\text{Kt. to K. B's 3rd}}$, 8. $\frac{\text{B. to K. R's 6th}}{}$, and again White has the superiority.) 7. $\frac{\text{Kt. takes Kt.}}{}$. (If 7. $\frac{\text{Q. takes Q. B's P.}}{\text{Kt. takes Kt.}}$, 8. $\frac{\text{Q. takes Q.}}{\text{B. to Q. Kt.'s 5th (ch.)}}$, 9. $\frac{\text{P. to Q. B's 3rd}}{\text{R. takes Q.}}$, 10. $\frac{\text{P. takes B.}}{\text{Kt. takes P.}}$, Black has much the better game.) 7. $\frac{}{\text{Q. takes Kt.}}$, 8. $\frac{\text{Q. to K's 4th, taking P.}}{}$, &c.

4. Kt. to K. B's 3rd.

If 4. $\frac{}{\text{P. to Q's 4th}}$, 5. $\frac{\text{Q. to K. R's 5th (ch.)}}{}$, &c.

5. B. to K. Kt.'s 5th.	5. B. to K's 2nd.
6. B. takes Kt.	6. B. takes B.
7. Q. to K. R's 5th (ch.)	7. P. to K. Kt.'s 3rd.

If 7. $\frac{}{\text{K. to B's sq.}}$, 8. $\frac{\text{Castles}}{}$, having a good game.

8. Q. to Q. B's 5th.	8. Kt. to Q. B's 3rd.
9. Kt. to K. B's 3rd.	9. P. to Q's 3rd.
10. Q. to Q. B's 3rd.	10. Castles.
11. Castles Q's side.	

With a well-opened game.

Game the Second.

WHITE.	BLACK.
1. P. to Q's 4th.	1. P. to K. B's 4th.
2. P. to Q. B's 4th.	2. Kt. to K. B's 3rd.

(For the effect of 2. $\frac{}{\text{P. to K's 3rd}}$, see Variation A.)

3. Kt. to Q. B's 3rd.	3. P. to K's 3rd.

In the *Handbuch* Black plays 3. $\frac{}{\text{P. to Q's 3rd}}$, the game continuing thus:—4. $\frac{\text{B. to K. B's 4th}}{\text{P. to Q. B's 3rd}}$, 5. $\frac{\text{P. to K's 3rd}}{\text{Q. to Q. B's 2nd}}$, 6. $\frac{\text{Kt. to K. B's 3rd}}{\text{Kt. to K. R's 4th}}$, 7. $\frac{\text{B. to K. Kt.'s 5th}}{\text{P. to K. R's 3rd}}$, 8. $\frac{\text{B. to K. R's 4th}}{\text{P. to K. Kt.'s 5th}}$, 9. $\frac{\text{Kt. to Q's 2nd}}{\text{Kt. to K. B's 3rd}}$, 10. $\frac{\text{B. to K. Kt.'s 3rd}}{\text{P. to K's 4th}}$. Equal game.

4. P. to Q. R's 3rd.	4. B. to K's 2nd.
5. Kt. to K. B's 3rd.	5. Castles.
6. P. to K's 3rd.	6. P. to Q's 3rd.
7. B. to Q's 3rd.	7. Kt. to Q. B's 3rd.

White has more command of the field, but the advantage is not important.

Variation A, beginning at Black's 2nd Move.

	2. P. to K's 3rd.
3. Kt. to Q. B's 3rd.	

The *Handbuch* has 3. $\frac{\text{P. to Q. R's 3rd}}{\text{Kt. to K. B's 3rd}}$, 4. $\frac{\text{Kt. to Q. B's 3rd}}{\text{B. to K's 2nd}}$, 5. $\frac{\text{B. to K. B's 4th}}{\text{Castles.}}$, 6. $\frac{\text{P. to K's 3rd}}{\text{P. to Q. Kt.'s 3rd}}$, 7. $\frac{\text{P. to Q's 5th}}{\text{P. to Q's 3rd}}$, 8. $\frac{\text{P. takes P.}}{\text{B. takes P.}}$, &c. Also 3. $\frac{\text{P. to K. B's 4th}}{\text{Kt. to K. B's 3rd}}$, 4. $\frac{\text{Kt. to K. B's 3rd}}{\text{P. to Q. Kt.'s 3rd}}$, 5. $\frac{\text{P. to Q. R's 3rd}}{\text{P. to Q. R's 4th}}$, 6. $\frac{\text{Kt. to Q. B's 3rd}}{\text{B. to Q. Kt.'s 2nd}}$, which is part of a game between Mongredien and Morphy.

	3. Kt. to K. B's 3rd.
4. B. to K. Kt.'s 5th.	4. B. to K's 2nd.
5. P. to K's 3rd.	5. Castles.
6. B. to Q's 3rd.	6. P. to Q. Kt.'s 3rd.
7. K's Kt. to K's 2nd.	7. B. to Q. Kt.'s 2nd.
8. Castles.	

White's position is slightly preferable.

ILLUSTRATIVE GAME.*

—Between Messrs. Schmorl and Max Lange.

WHITE (Mr. S.)	BLACK (Mr. L.)
1. P. to Q's 4th.	1. P. to K. B's 4th.
2. P. to Q. B's 4th.	2. P. to K's 3rd.
3. P. to K's 3rd.	3. Kt. to K. B's 3rd.
4. Kt. to Q. B's 3rd.	4. B. to K's 2nd.
5. Kt. to K. B's 3rd.	5. Castles.
6. B. to Q's 3rd.	6. P. to Q's 3rd.
7. Q. to Q. B's 2nd.	7. Kt. to Q. B's 3rd.
8. P. to Q. R's 3rd.	8. Q. to K's sq.*
9. Castles.	9. Q. to K. R's 4th.
10. Kt. to K's 2nd.	10. P. to K. Kt.'s 4th.†
11. P. to K's 4th.	11. P. to K. B's 5th.
12. Kt. to K's sq.	12. P. to K's 4th.
13. P. to Q's 5th.	13. Kt. to Q's sq.
14. P. to K. B's 3rd.	14. P. to Q. B's 3rd.
15. P. to Q. Kt.'s 4th.	15. B. to Q's 2nd.
16. B. to Q. Kt.'s 2nd.	16. Kt. to K. B's 2nd.
17. P. to K. Kt.'s 4th.‡	17. B. takes Kt.'s P.§
18. P. takes B.	18. Kt. takes P.
19. Kt. to Q. B's 3rd.	19. Kt. to K's 6th.
20. Q. to K's 2nd.	20. P. to K. Kt.'s 5th.
21. B. to Q. B's sq.	21. Kt. takes R.
22. Q. takes Kt.	22. Kt. to Kt.'s 4th.
23. R. to Q. R's 2nd.	23. Kt. to R's 6th (ch.)
24. K. to R's sq.	24. P. to B's 6th.
25. B. to Q. Kt.'s sq.	25. P. to Kt.'s 6th.
26. P. takes P.	26. P. to B's 7th.
27. K. to Kt.'s 2nd.‖	27. P. takes Kt. (becoming a Kt.) (ch.)
28. Q. takes Kt.	28. R. to B's 6th.
29. B. to K's 3rd.	29. Q's R. to K. B's sq.

* A very good move.

† This is also well played.

‡ Well intended, but apparently utterly unconscious of Black's clever reply.

§ A strictly sound sacrifice.

‖ The best reply.

30. B. to Q's 3rd.	30. Kt. to B's 5th (ch.)
31. B. takes Kt.	31. P. takes B.
32. B. to K's 2nd	32. P. takes P.*
33. Q. to K. R's sq.	33. R. to B's 7th (ch.)
34. K. to Kt.'s sq.	34. R. to B's 8th (ch.)
35. B. takes R.	35. R. takes B. (ch.)

And wins.

* The whole of this little game is capitally played by Black.

CHAPTER XXV.

THE HOLLAND GAME AND FIANCHETTO.

$1.\ \dfrac{\text{P. to K. B's 4th}}{}.$

GAME THE FIRST.

$1.\ \dfrac{}{\text{P. to Q's 4th}}.$

GAME THE SECOND.

$1.\ \dfrac{}{\text{P. to K. B's 4th}}.$

GAME THE THIRD.

$1.\ \dfrac{}{\text{P. to K's 4th}}.$

GAME THE FOURTH.

$1.\ \dfrac{\text{P. to K's 4th}}{\text{P. to K. Kt.'s 3rd}}.$

GAME THE FIFTH.

$1.\ \dfrac{\text{P. to K's 4th}}{\text{P. to Q. Kt.'s 3rd}}.$

GAME THE FIRST.

WHITE.	BLACK.
1. P. to K. B's 4th.	1. P. to Q's 4th.
2. P. to K's 3rd.	

If 2. $\frac{\text{Kt. to K. B's 3rd}}{\text{B. to K. Kt.'s 5th}}$, 3. $\frac{\text{Kt. to K's 5th}}{\text{B. to K. B's 4th}}$, 4. $\frac{\text{P. to Q's 3rd}}{\text{}}$.

(If 4. $\frac{\text{P. to K. Kt.'s 4th}}{\text{P. to K's 3rd}}$.) 4. $\frac{\text{}}{\text{P. to K's 3rd}}$, the game is about equal. After 2. $\frac{\text{Kt. to K. B's 3rd}}{\text{}}$, Black can play also 2. $\frac{\text{}}{\text{P. to Q. B's 4th}}$, with the following probable continuation:

3. $\frac{\text{P. to K's 3rd}}{\text{Kt. to Q. B's 3rd}}$, 4. $\frac{\text{B. to Q. Kt.'s 5th}}{\text{P. to Q. R's 3rd}}$, 5. $\frac{\text{B. takes Kt. (ch.)}}{\text{P. takes B.}}$

6. $\frac{\text{Castles}}{\text{P. to K's 3rd}}$, 7. $\frac{\text{P. to Q. B's 4th}}{\text{Kt. to K. R's 3rd}}$, 8. $\frac{\text{Q. to K's 2nd}}{\text{B. to Q's 3rd}}$,

9. $\frac{\text{Kt. to Q. B's 3rd}}{\text{Q. to K's 2nd}}$, 10. $\frac{\text{P. to Q. Kt.'s 3rd}}{\text{P. to K. B's 3rd}}$, 11. $\frac{\text{P. to Q's 3rd}}{\text{Castles}}$,

12. $\frac{\text{P. to K's 4th}}{\text{P. takes K's P.}}$, 13. $\frac{\text{P. takes P.}}{\text{P. to K's 4th}}$, 14. $\frac{\text{P. to K. B's 5th}}{\text{}}$,

but the advantage in this case rests with White.

	2. P. to Q. B's 4th.
3. Kt. to K. B's 3rd.	3. Kt. to Q. B's 3rd.
4. P. to Q's 4th.	4. P. to K's 3rd.
5. P. to Q. B's 4th.	5. Kt. to K. R's 3rd.
6. Kt. to Q. B's 3rd.	6. B. to Q's 3rd.

Black has at least an equal game to his antagonist's.

Game the Second.

BLACK.	WHITE.
1. P. to K. B's 4th.	1. P. to K. B's 4th.
2. Kt. to K. B's 3rd.	

If 2. $\frac{\text{P. to K's 4th}}{\text{P. takes P.}}$, 3. $\frac{\text{Kt. to Q. B's 3rd}}{\text{Kt. to K. B's 3rd}}$, 4. $\frac{\text{P. to Q's 3rd}}{\text{P. takes P.}}$,

5. $\frac{\text{B. takes P.}}{\text{P. to Q's 4th}}$, White has sacrificed a Pawn for no purpose.

	2. Kt. to K. B's 3rd.
3. P. to Q's 4th.	3. P. to Q's 4th.

Equal game.

GAME THE THIRD.

WHITE.	BLACK.
1. P. to K. B's 4th.	1. P. to K's 4th.

A defence proposed by Mr. From, a Danish amateur, by whose name it is generally known.

2. P. takes P.*	2. P. to Q's 3rd.
3. P. takes P. (best).†	3. B. takes P.
4. Kt. to K. B's 3rd.	4. Kt. to K. R's 3rd.
5. P. to K's 3rd.	

White can play 5. $\frac{\text{P. to K's 4th}}{\quad}$, the probable continuation then being 5. $\frac{\quad}{\text{Kt. to K. Kt.'s 5th}}$, 6. $\frac{\text{P. to K. Kt.'s 3rd}}{\text{Kt. takes R's P.}}$, 7. $\frac{\text{R. takes Kt.}}{\text{B. takes P. (ch.)}}$, 8. $\frac{\text{K. to K's 2nd}}{\text{B. takes R.}}$, 9. $\frac{\text{Kt. takes B.}}{\text{P. to K. B's 4th}}$, but in this case he will have a very exposed game. This variation is Mr. From's analysis. I do not see, however, why White should not play as follows:—6. $\frac{\text{Q. to K's 2nd}}{\quad}$. If, then, 6. $\frac{\quad}{\text{Kt. takes R's P.}}$, 7. $\frac{\text{Kt. takes Kt.}}{\text{Q. to K. R's 5th (ch.)}}$, 8. $\frac{\text{K. to Q's sq.}}{\text{B. takes Kt.}}$, 9. $\frac{\text{P. to K. Kt.'s 3rd}}{\quad}$, Black apparently loses a piece without sufficient qualifying advantage.‡

---

* White may also play 2. $\frac{\text{P. to K's 4th}}{\quad}$, and convert the game into a King's Gambit.—[ED.]

† Here again the Opening may be resolved into a form of the King's Gambit Declined by 3. $\frac{\text{Kt. to K. B's 3rd}}{\text{P. takes P.}}$, 4. $\frac{\text{P. to K's 4th}}{\text{B. to Q. B's 4th}}$, 5. $\frac{\text{B. to Q. B's 4th}}{\text{Kt. to Q. B's 3rd}}$, &c.—[ED.]

‡ In addition to 5. $\frac{\text{P. to K's 4th}}{\quad}$ and 5. $\frac{\text{P. to K's 3rd}}{\quad}$, White may also play 5. $\frac{\text{P. to Q's 3rd}}{\quad}$, which would be continued, 5. $\frac{\quad}{\text{Kt. to Kt.'s 5th}}$,

	5. Kt. to K. Kt.'s 5th.
6. Q. to K's 2nd.	

The *Stratégie Raisonnée* pursues the opening thus:—
6. $\frac{\text{B. to K's 2nd}}{\text{Kt. takes R's P.}}$, 7. $\frac{\text{Kt. takes Kt.}}{\text{Q. to K. R's 5th (ch.)}}$, 8. $\frac{\text{K. to B's sq.}}{}$,
and pronounces the game to be in favour of White. But is it so?

	6. Kt. takes R's P.
7. Kt. takes Kt.	7. Q. to K. R's 5th (ch.)
8. K. to Q's sq.	8. B. takes Kt.
9. P. to K. Kt.'s 3rd.	9. Q. takes P.
10. Q. takes B.	

And White appears to me to have a great superiority.

Game the Fourth.

FIANCHETTO DI RE.

1. P. to K's 4th.	1. P. to K. Kt.'s 3rd.

Neither this nor the similar move on the Queen's side is a commendable line of defence. They both subject the player to a very confined game, or compel him to a sacrifice for the purpose of freeing it. Meanwhile they usually afford the adversary time to form a strong central phalanx of pawns and pieces.

2. P. to Q's 4th.

White can likewise play, 2. $\frac{\text{Kt. to Q. B's 3rd}}{}$, *e.g.*:—

---

6. $\frac{\text{B. to K. Kt.'s 5th}}{\text{B. to K's 3rd}}$, 7. $\frac{\text{B. to Q. B's sq.}}{}$, and the first player has the advantage In this last variation White might also play, instead of 6. $\frac{\text{B. to K. Kt.'s 5th}}{}$, 6. $\frac{\text{P. to Q. B's 3rd}}{}$, to which Black's best reply appears to be 6. $\frac{}{\text{Kt. to Q. B's 3rd}}$, as he obviously cannot capture the Rook's Pawn.—[Ed.]

2. $\frac{\text{Kt. to Q. B's 3rd}}{\text{B. to K. Kt.'s 2nd}}$, 3. $\frac{\text{P. to Q's 4th}}{\text{Kt. to Q. B's 3rd}}$, 4. $\frac{\text{B. to K's 3rd}}{\text{P. to K's 3rd}}$, 5. $\frac{\text{P. to K. B's 4th}}{\quad}$, and White has the better situation.

	2. B. to K. Kt.'s 2nd.
3. P. to K. B's 4th.	3. P. to K's 3rd.
4. Kt. to K. B's 3rd.	4. P. to Q. Kt.'s 3rd.
5. P. to Q. B's 4th.	5. B. to Q. Kt.'s 2nd.
6. Kt. to Q. B's 3rd.	6. Kt. to K's 2nd.
7. B. to Q's 3rd.	7. P. to Q's 3rd.
8. Castles.	8. Castles.
9. B. to K's 3rd.	9. Kt. to Q's 2nd.
10. P. to K's 5th.	10. Q. to K's sq.

The advantage is plainly on White's side.

Game the Fifth.

FIANCHETTO DI DONNA.

WHITE.	BLACK.
1. P. to K's 4th.	1. P. to Q. Kt.'s 3rd.

This is less objectionable than the previous opening, but it is not a commendable mode of beginning a game.

2. P. to Q's 4th.

If 2. $\frac{\text{Kt. to Q. B's 3rd}}{\text{B. to Q. Kt.'s 2nd}}$, 3. $\frac{\text{P. to K. Kt.'s 3rd}}{\text{P. to K's 3rd}}$, 4. $\frac{\text{B. to K. Kt.'s 2nd}}{\text{Kt. to K. B's 3rd}}$, 5. $\frac{\text{K's Kt. to K's 2nd}}{\text{P. to Q. B's 4th}}$, 6. $\frac{\text{P. to Q's 3rd}}{\text{B. to K's 2nd}}$, 7. $\frac{\text{Castles}}{\text{P. to Q's 3rd}}$, White has not made so much of the opening as he ought to have done. If 2. $\frac{\text{P. to K. Kt.'s 3rd}}{\text{P. to K's 3rd}}$, 3. $\frac{\text{B. to K. Kt.'s 2nd}}{\text{B. to Q. Kt.'s 2nd}}$, 4. $\frac{\text{Kt. to Q. B's 3rd}}{\text{P. to K. B's 4th}}$, 5. $\frac{\text{K's Kt. to K's 2nd}}{\text{Kt. to K. B's 3rd}}$, 6. $\frac{\text{P. to Q's 3rd}}{\text{B. to Q. Kt.'s 5th}}$, 7. $\frac{\text{Castles}}{\text{B. takes Kt.}}$, 8. $\frac{\text{Kt. takes B.}}{\text{P. takes K's P.}}$, 9. $\frac{\text{Kt. takes P.}}{\text{Kt. takes Kt.}}$, 10. $\frac{\text{Q. to K. R's 5th (ch.)}}{\text{P. to K. Kt.'s 3rd}}$, 11. $\frac{\text{Q. to K's 5th}}{\quad}$, and White has the better position. This last variation forms part of a game between Messrs. Paulsen (White) and Owen.

	2. B. to Q. Kt.'s 2nd.
3. B. to Q's 3rd.	3. P. to K's 3rd (best).
4. Kt. to K. B's 3rd.	4. P. to Q's 4th.

Black sometimes plays 4. $\frac{\qquad}{\text{P. to Q. B's 4th}}$, and in a good game between Messrs. Blackburne and Owen, where this move occurs, the continuation runs,—5. $\frac{\text{P. to Q. B's 3rd}}{\text{Kt. to K. B's 3rd}}$, 6. $\frac{\text{B. to K. Kt.'s 5th}}{\text{P. to K. R's 3rd}}$, 7. $\frac{\text{B. takes Kt.}}{\text{Q. takes B.}}$, 8. $\frac{\text{Castles}}{\text{P. takes P.}}$, 9. $\frac{\text{P. takes P.}}{\text{Kt. to Q. B's 3rd}}$, 10. $\frac{\text{B. to Q. Kt.'s 5th}}{\text{P. to Q. R's 3rd}}$, 11. $\frac{\text{B. takes Kt.}}{\text{B. takes B.}}$, 12. $\frac{\text{Kt. to Q. B's 3rd}}{\text{B. to Q. Kt.'s 4th}}$, 13. $\frac{\text{R. to K's sq.}}{\text{Castles on K's side}}$, 14. $\frac{\text{R. to Q. B's sq.}}{\text{R. to Q. B's sq.}}$, 15. $\frac{\text{R. to K's 2nd}}{\text{P. to Q. Kt.'s 4th}}$, 16. $\frac{\text{Kt. to K's 5th}}{\qquad}$, and although Black has an unusually good game for the opening, it is not equal to White's.

5. P. takes P.	5. P. takes P.
6. Castles.	6. P. to Q. B's 4th.

White has a freer game.

ILLUSTRATIVE GAMES.

Game I.—Between Messrs. Bird and Steinitz.

White (Mr. B.)	Black (Mr. S.)
1. P. to K. B's 4th.	1. P. to K's 4th.
2. P. takes P.	2. P. to Q's 3rd.
3. P. takes P.	3. B. takes P.
4. Kt. to K. B's 3rd.	4. Kt. to K. B's 3rd.
5. P. to Q's 4th.	5. Kt. to Q. B's 3rd.
6. B. to K. Kt.'s 5th.	6. B. to K. Kt.'s 5th.

7. P. to K's 3rd.	7. Q. to Q's 2nd.
8. B. takes Kt.	8. P. takes B.
9. B. to Q. Kt.'s 5th.	9. Castles, Q's R.
10. P. to Q's 5th.	10. Q. to K's 2nd.*
11. B. takes Kt.	11. Q. takes P. (ch).
12. Q. to K's 2nd.	12. Q. to Q. B's 8th (ch.)
13. Q. to Q's sq.	13. Q's R. to K's sq. (ch.)
14. B takes R.	14. R. takes B. (ch).
15. K. to B's 2nd.	15. Q. to K's 6th (ch.)
16. K. to B's sq.	16. B. takes Kt.
17. P takes B.	17. B. to Q. B's 4th.
18. K. to Kt.'s 2nd.	18. R. to K. Kt.'s sq. (ch.)

And wins.

GAME II.—Between Messrs. Macdonnell and Wisker.

WHITE (Mr. M.)	BLACK (Mr. W.)
1. P. to K. B's 4th.	1. P. to Q's 4th.
2. P. to K's 3rd.	2. P. to K. Kt.'s 3rd.
3. Kt. to K. B's 3rd.	3. B. to K. Kt.'s 2nd.
4. B. to K's 2nd.	4. P. to Q. B's 4th.
5. Castles.	5. Kt. to Q. B's 3rd.
6. Q. to K's sq.	6. Q. to Q. Kt.'s 3rd.
7. Kt. to Q. R's 3rd.	7. Kt. to K. R's 3rd.
8. K. to R's sq.	8. P. to Q. R's 3rd.
9. R. to Q. Kt.'s sq.	9. Q. to Q. B's 2nd.
10. P. to Q. Kt.'s 3rd.	10. Castles.
11. B. to Q. Kt.'s 2nd.	11. P. to Q. Kt.'s 4th.
12. B. takes B.	12. K. takes B.
13. R. to Q. B's sq.	13. P. to K. B's 3rd.
14. P. to K. R's 3rd.	14. P. to K's 4th.
15. Kt. to K. R's 2nd.	15. B. to Kt.'s 2nd.
16. P. to Q. B's 3rd.	16. Q's R. to K's sq.†
17. Q. to K. B's 2nd.	17. Kt. to K. B's 4th.
18. P. to K. Kt.'s 4th.	18. Kt. to Q's 3rd.
19. B. to K. B's 3rd.	19. P. takes P.
20. P. takes P.	20. Kt. to K's 5th.

* From this point to the finish the game is very prettily conducted.
† Black has already obtained the better game.

21. B. takes Kt.	21. P. takes B.
22. K. to Kt.'s sq.	22. Kt. to K's 2nd.
23. Kt. to Q. B's 2nd.	23. P. to K. Kt.'s 4th.
24. P. takes P.*	24. P. takes P.
25. Q. to K's 3rd.	25. Kt. to K. Kt.'s 3rd.
26. P. to Q. Kt.'s 4th.	26. R. to K. B's 6th.†
27. R. takes R.	27. P. takes R.
28. Q. to K. B's 2nd.‡	28. R. to K's 7th.
29. Kt. to Q's 4th.	29. P. takes Kt.
30. Q. takes P. (ch.)	30. K. to R's 3rd.
Resigns.	

GAME III.—Between Mr. Thorold and the Rev. W. Wayte.

WHITE (Mr. T.)	BLACK (Mr. W.)
1. P. to K. B's 4th.	1. P. to Q's 4th.
2. Kt. to K. B's 3rd.	2. P. to Q. B's 4th.
3. P. to K's 3rd.	3. P. to K's 3rd.
4. P. to Q. Kt.'s 3rd.	4. Kt. to K. B's 3rd.
5. B. to Q. Kt.'s 2nd.	5. B. to Q's 3rd.
6. Kt. to K's 5th.	6. Castles.
7. P. to Q's 4th.§	7. Kt. to Q. B's 3rd.
8. Kt. to Q. B's 3rd.	8. P. takes P.
9. P. takes P.	9. P. to Q. R's 3rd.
10. B. to K's 2nd.	10. Kt. to K's 5th.
11. Kt. takes Kt.	11. P. takes Kt.
12. Castles.	12. P. to K. B's 4th.
13. P. to Q. B's 4th.	13. Kt. takes Kt.‖
14. K. B's P. takes Kt.	14. B. to K's 2nd.
15. P. to Q's 5th.	15. B. to Q. B's 4th (ch.)
16. K. to R's sq.	16. B. to Q's 2nd.
17. P. to Q. R's 3rd.	17. Q. to K. R's 5th.
18. B. to Q's 4th.	18. B. to K's 2nd.

* A very imprudent capture.

† The winning move.

‡ Had he captured the Rook, Black would have won in a few moves.

§ With the Bishop posted at Q. Kt.'s 2nd, we should have preferred 7. P. to Q's 3rd.

‖ It is worth Black's while to preserve his two Bishops even at the cost of a move.

19. P. to K. Kt.'s 3rd.	19. Q. to K. R's 6th.
20. B. to K's 3rd.	20. Q's R. to B's sq.
21. R. to K. B's 4th.	21. P. to K. Kt.'s 4th.
22. B. to K. B's sq.	22. Q. to K. R's 3rd.
23. R. to K. R's 4th.*	23. Q. to Kt.'s 2nd.
24. R. to R's 5th.	24. B. to K's sq.
25. R. to R's 3rd.	25. Q. takes P.
26. B. to Q's 4th.	26. Q. to Q's 3rd.
27. R. to K. R's 6th.	27. B. to K. Kt.'s 3rd.
28. P. to Q. Kt.'s 4th.	28. P. takes P.
29. B. to Q. B's 5th.	29. Q. to Q's 2nd.
30. B. takes B.	30. Q. takes B.
31. Q. takes P. (ch.)	31. K. to Kt.'s 2nd.
32. R. takes B. (ch.)	32. K. takes R.
33. P. to Q. B's 5th.	33. K's R. to Q's sq.
34. Q. to Q. B's 4th.	34. Q. to K's 4th.
35. R. to K's sq.	35. R. to Q's 5th.

And Black won.

GAME IV.—Between Messrs. Blackburne and Hamel.

WHITE (Mr. B.)	BLACK (Mr. H.)
1. P. to K's 4th.	1. P. to Q. Kt.'s 3rd.
2. P. to Q's 4th.	2. B. to Kt.'s 2nd.
3. P. to K. B's 3rd.	3. P. to K's 3rd.
4. B. to Q's 3rd.	4. P. to Q. B's 4th.
5. P. to Q. B's 3rd.	5. P. takes P.
6. P. takes P.	6. B. to Q. Kt.'s 5th (ch.)
7. Kt. to Q. B's 3rd.	7. Kt. to K's 2nd.
8. Kt. to K's 2nd.	8. Castles.
9. Castles.	9. B. takes Kt.
10. P. takes B.	10. Kt. to K. Kt.'s 3rd.
11. Kt. to K. Kt.'s 3rd.	11. B. to Q. R's 3rd.
12. P. to K. B's 4th.	12. Q. to Q. B's 2nd.
13. P. to K. B's 5th.†	13. Q. takes Q. B's P.‡

* Ingenious; but it turns out unfortunately, owing to the imprisonment of the Rook.

† The advance of this Pawn was evidently the result of profound calculation, and leads presently to positions of singular interest.

‡ This, though dangerous, was compulsory, for the retreat of the

14. B. takes B.	14. Kt. takes B.
15. P. takes Kt.	15. Q. takes R.
16. P. takes R's P. (ch.)	16. K. to R's sq.
17. Kt. to K. R's 5th.	17. P. to K. B's 4th.
18. Kt. to K. B's 4th.	18. K. takes P.
19. Q. to R's 5th (ch.)	19. K. to Kt.'s sq.
20. Kt. to Kt.'s 6th.	20. Q. takes Q's P. (ch.)
21. K. to R's sq.	21. K's R. to K's sq.
22. R. to Q's sq.	22. Q. to Q. B's 6th.
23. P. to K's 5th.*	23. Kt. to Q. B's 4th.
24. B. to K. Kt.'s 5th.	24. Kt. to Q's 6th.†
25. B. to K. B's 6th.	25. Kt. to B's 7th (ch.)
26. K. to Kt.'s sq.	Resigns.

Knight would have been followed by the still farther advance of White's daring Pawn, to the utter ruin of Black's game.

* This and the two succeeding moves of Mr. Blackburne are very fine.

† Unconscious quite of the admirable purpose for which his adversary played his Bishop to Kt.'s 5th.

THE END.